Network Security Principles and Practices

Saadat Malik

Cisco Press

Cisco Press
201 West 103rd Street
Indianapolis, IN 46290 USA

Network Security Principles and Practices

Saadat Malik

Copyright © 2003 Cisco Systems, Inc.

Cisco Press logo is a trademark of Cisco Systems, Inc.

Published by:
Cisco Press
201 West 103rd Street
Indianapolis, IN 46290 USA

Printed in the United States of America 1 2 3 4 5 6 7 8 9 0

First Printing November 2002

Library of Congress Cataloging-in-Publication Number: 2001086635

ISBN: 1-58705-025-0

Warning and Disclaimer

This book is designed to provide information about the fundamental principles and practices associated with network security technologies. Every effort has been made to make this book as complete and accurate as possible, but no warranty or fitness is implied.

The information is provided on an "as is" basis. The author, Cisco Press, and Cisco Systems, Inc. shall have neither liability nor responsibility to any person or entity with respect to any loss or damages arising from the information contained in this book or from the use of the discs or programs that may accompany it.

The opinions expressed in this book belong to the author and are not necessarily those of Cisco Systems, Inc.

Trademark Acknowledgments

All terms mentioned in this book that are known to be trademarks or service marks have been appropriately capitalized. Cisco Press or Cisco Systems, Inc. cannot attest to the accuracy of this information. Use of a term in this book should not be regarded as affecting the validity of any trademark or service mark.

Feedback Information

At Cisco Press, our goal is to create in-depth technical books of the highest quality and value. Each book is crafted with care and precision, undergoing rigorous development that involves the unique expertise of members of the professional technical community.

Reader feedback is a natural continuation of this process. If you have any comments regarding how we could improve the quality of this book, or otherwise alter it to better suit your needs, you can contact us through e-mail at feedback@ciscopress.com. Please be sure to include the book title and ISBN (1-58705-025-0) in your message.

We greatly appreciate your assistance.

Publisher	John Wait
Editor-In-Chief	John Kane
Cisco Systems Program Manager	Anthony Wolfenden
Executive Editor	Brett Bartow
Managing Editor	Patrick Kanouse
Development Editor	Deborah Doorley
Project Editor	Marc Fowler
Copy Editor	Gayle Johnson
Technical Editors	Paul Forbes
	Randy Ivener
	Doug McKillip
Team Coordinator	Tammi Ross
Book Designer	Gina Rexrode
Cover Designer	Louisa Klucznik
Production Team	Octal Publishing, Inc.
Indexer	Tim Wright

CISCO SYSTEMS

Corporate Headquarters
Cisco Systems, Inc.
170 West Tasman Drive
San Jose, CA 95134-1706
USA
http://www.cisco.com
Tel: 408 526-4000
    800 553-NETS (6387)
Fax: 408 526-4100

European Headquarters
Cisco Systems Europe
11 Rue Camille Desmoulins
92782 Issy-les-Moulineaux
Cedex 9
France
http://www-europe.cisco.com
Tel: 33 1 58 04 60 00
Fax: 33 1 58 04 61 00

Americas Headquarters
Cisco Systems, Inc.
170 West Tasman Drive
San Jose, CA 95134-1706
USA
http://www.cisco.com
Tel: 408 526-7660
Fax: 408 527-0883

Asia Pacific Headquarters
Cisco Systems Australia,
Pty., Ltd
Level 17, 99 Walker Street
North Sydney
NSW 2059 Australia
http://www.cisco.com
Tel: +61 2 8448 7100
Fax: +61 2 9957 4350

Cisco Systems has more than 200 offices in the following countries. Addresses, phone numbers, and fax numbers are listed on the Cisco Web site at www.cisco.com/go/offices

Argentina • Australia • Austria • Belgium • Brazil • Bulgaria • Canada • Chile • China • Colombia • Costa Rica • Croatia • Czech Republic • Denmark • Dubai, UAE • Finland • France • Germany • Greece • Hong Kong Hungary • India • Indonesia • Ireland • Israel • Italy • Japan • Korea • Luxembourg • Malaysia • Mexico The Netherlands • New Zealand • Norway • Peru • Philippines • Poland • Portugal • Puerto Rico • Romania Russia • Saudi Arabia • Scotland • Singapore • Slovakia • Slovenia • South Africa • Spain • Sweden Switzerland • Taiwan • Thailand • Turkey • Ukraine • United Kingdom • United States • Venezuela • Vietnam Zimbabwe

About the Author

Saadat Malik, CCIE No. 4955, manages technical support operations for the VPN and Network Security groups at Cisco Systems. As the author of the CCIE Security lab exam and as a member of the team who wrote the CCIE Security qualification exam, he spearheaded the development of the CCIE Network Security certification. He currently serves as a consultant to the CCIE department, helping improve the quality of the CCIE Security lab exam on an ongoing basis. He has years of experience proctoring the CCIE lab exams as well. In the past, Malik taught networking architecture and protocols at the graduate level at San Jose State University. Over the years, 30+ CCIEs (including 9 'double' CCIEs and 2 'triple' CCIEs) have reached these coveted milestones under Saadat's mentoring and technical leadership. He has been a regular speaker for quite a few years at industry events such as Networkers and the IBM Technical Conference, giving talks on advanced topics related to network intrusion detection, troubleshooting VPNs, and advanced IPsec concepts. Saadat holds a master's degree in electrical engineering (MSEE) from Purdue University at West Lafayette.

About the Technical Reviewers

Paul Forbes is a senior network engineer at Trimble Navigation Ltd. He is responsible for the development and operations of Trimble's global VPN, VoIP, and authentication systems. He is also active in intrusion detection and wireless and network management initiatives. He is currently pursuing his CCIE in Security, with the able support and assistance of his wife and erstwhile cat. When he isn't bit plumbing, bicycling and reading take the remainder of his time.

Randy Ivener is a security and VPN specialist with the Cisco Systems, Inc., Advanced Services team. He is a Certified Information Systems Security Professional, Cisco Certified Network Professional, Cisco Security Specialist 1, and ASQ Certified Software Quality Engineer. He has spent several years as a network security consultant, helping companies understand and secure their networks. Ivener has worked with many security products and technologies including firewalls, VPNs, intrusion detection, and authentication systems. Before becoming immersed in security, he spent time in software development and as a training instructor. He graduated from the U.S. Naval Academy and has a master's degree in business administration (MBA).

Doug McKillip, P.E., CCIE No.1851, is an independent consultant specializing in Cisco Certified Training in association with Global Knowledge, a Training Partner of Cisco Systems. He has more than 13 years of experience in computer networking. For the past nine years, he has been actively involved in security and firewalls. McKillip provided both instructional and technical assistance during the initial deployment of the MCNS Version 1.0 training class and has been the lead instructor and course director for Global Knowledge. He holds bachelor's and master's degrees in chemical engineering from MIT and a master's degree in computer science from the University of Delaware. He resides in Wilmington, Delaware.

Dedication

Dedicated,

To my devoted father, Hameed,

Whose unerring faith, astute principles and far-reaching vision built the foundation on which I stand today,

And,

To my loving wife, Alina,

Whose thoughtful encouragement, limitless patience and generous support are building the structure, which will be our life tomorrow.

Acknowledgments

This book would not have been possible without the guidance and work done by a number of individuals who have worked with me over the years at Cisco. Work done by a number of people has helped me put together this book. These folks over the years have toiled tirelessly, trying to find resolutions to customer problems, design new solutions, and come up with the right answers when they are needed most. I have benefited greatly from the work of all these individuals working in various departments, but especially in the Technical Assistance Center (TAC) at Cisco Systems. This indeed is the incubator for the leaders of tomorrow. The list of these individuals is long, but some of the more prominent names are Dianne Dunlap, John Bashinski, Natalie Timms, Wen Zhang, Frederic Detienne, Alok Mittal, Mike Sullenberger, Sujit Ghosh and Qiang Huang. They are some of the people who have done a huge amount of very useful work in the area of Cisco network security design, implementation, and support. These are the folks, among many others, whose work in and understanding of the field of network security have allowed me to produce what is before you today.

These acknowledgments would not be complete without my mentioning Brett Bartow, who was the executive editor for this book. Brett stood by me, encouraging and guiding me from the day I started thinking about writing this book. He was very understanding when I, caught in myriad other responsibilities, some professional and some personal, missed deadlines and fell behind on the book. Yet he was always firm in getting me back on the road. I also want to thank development editor Deborah Doorley, whose encouragement got me through the final stages of the book, and senior development editor Chris Cleveland, who was always there to help me when I needed him.

I think the technical reviewers did a fine job going through this book. But my special thanks to Randy Ivener, who went through the book with a fine-toothed comb and pointed out many places where quality or accuracy were lacking. This book is a lot better for the efforts of Randy, Paul Forbes, and Doug McKillip.

Contents at a Glance

Table of Contents

Foreword

Security incidents and vulnerabilities affecting networks, systems, and information are described frequently in technical journals and the popular press. Since the Morris worm incident in 1988, the number of incidents has more than doubled each year, growing in number as the Internet expands. These incidents include scans of entire networks for the purpose of identifying the network devices and services that are present on the network, directed attacks against vulnerabilities known to exist in these systems and services, and denial of service attacks designed to exhaust bandwidth, CPU, or other resources. The past year saw a number of serious worm attacks, including the well-publicized Code Red and Nimda worms. It is estimated that the impact of the Code Red worm was $2 billion and affected hundreds of thousands of hosts. These worms caused denial of service and also gave the attacker complete control of the victim systems. As it turns out, the vulnerability in Microsoft's Internet Information Service (IIS) was known, and a patch was available at the time of the attacks. Much of the impact of these worms could have been avoided had the vulnerable systems been patched in a timely fashion. More recently, a buffer overflow vulnerability was identified in Apache web servers, affecting nearly 50% of all web servers currently running on the Internet. How long will it take administrators to patch their systems? Will they do so before there is another attack of the magnitude of Code Red? The challenge to contain this trend, and even to reverse it, rests on both the technology vendors and the professionals who are designing, building, and maintaining today's sophisticated networks. Vendors must improve the quality of their products, and professionals responsible for systems and networks must consider security an important and integral component of their network infrastructures.

This book is a valuable asset to network operators and administrators who are tasked with securing these networks. Unlike books that focus on a single security technology, such as firewalls or intrusion detection systems, this book addresses the important task of knowing *when* and *where* to locate specific security technologies within a network. It then provides specific configuration information concerning these technologies. The author has made sure that the configurations are well-explained and tested, and case studies are used to put the theoretical knowledge in perspective. The book's focus provides an in-depth protocol-level understanding of the functioning of various security features. This is important, because it is nearly impossible to provide adequate security throughout your network if you have only a superficial understanding of the features and technologies available. All too often, network security is deployed as a collection of point solutions when what is really needed is a comprehensive, integrated approach. Such an approach is possible only when professionals have an in-depth understanding of how things work.

It's been my pleasure to know the author, Saadat Malik, for years. He is a talented and experienced networking professional who has experience in all the areas covered in the book. Saadat's involvement as the author of the CCIE Security lab exam gives him critical insight into the requirements of the CCIE Network Security certification. This insight and perspective make this book an invaluable asset to those working toward their CCIE Security certification. Furthermore, he has spent a number of years as a senior Technical Assistance Center engineer at Cisco, helping customers troubleshoot problems related to network security. He is the perfect author for this ultimate resource on network security. I highly recommend this book as a must-have for every networking professional working in the area of security.

Barbara Fraser

Co-chair, IP Security (IPsec) working group,The Internet Engineering Task Force (IETF)

Consulting Engineer, Chief Technology Office, Cisco Systems, Inc.

Introduction

This book is focused on providing you with an in-depth understanding of the various network security principles, features, protocols, and implementations in today's networks. Cisco security implementations are used as the basis for the discussions of various topics in this book. The goals of this book are as follows:

- Provide a complete discussion at an advanced level for all topics involved in the implementation of network security in today's networks.

- Provide detailed and in-depth discussion and insight into the workings of the protocols behind network security implementations.

- Discuss the security principles that form the basis of the various network products, features, and implementations.

- Discuss the useful elements of network design aimed at improving the network's security.

- Provide insight into the operational needs and requirements of setting up and then maintaining a secure network.

- Discuss network maintenance and troubleshooting techniques essential to network security.

The book aims to provide an advanced-level discussion of various topics. However, most topics start with the basics to help keep the discussion complete. This helps you read the book more easily if you have a relatively lower level of network security expertise.

This book avoids detailed explanations of how to configure permutations of various commands, assuming that you are familiar with basic network security configurations or that you have the Cisco Command Reference handy. This book explains the workings of various commands by showing their use in real-life case studies rather than discuss them isolated from each other. For the level of audience this book is targeted at, these case studies will result in a more useful study aid than individual command descriptions that can be read in the Command Reference.

Target Audience

This book is targeted toward two main groups of people:

- Non-CCIEs and CCIEs in other disciplines, working toward their CCIE Network Security certification

- Network security professionals who might have already achieved their CCIE in Network Security and who would like to enhance their knowledge of some of the core concepts of network security

The book covers most, if not all, aspects of the CCIE Network Security exam. It prepares the CCIE candidate by providing a mix of detailed discussions into svarious security protocols, network design principles and guidelines as well as documented implementations of the most common design elements. The idea is to give the candidate a flavor of the issues encountered in real-world design challenges and the resulting implementations. That way, when the candidate sees similar challenges on the CCIE laboratory exam, he or she can put them in the proper context and have an in-depth understanding of what is being asked. This is a critical element to the success of anyone who takes the CCIE lab exam.

The book is also targeted at the network security professional who is interested in enhancing his or her knowledge of the various aspects of network security. This book goes into the details of the various principles involved in the design of network security elements such as firewalls and VPNs. It provides a thorough basis and motivation for the functionality of the various products and technologies before discussing the actual implementation of these products and technologies to resolve real-world issues. This book covers advanced features being used in various protocols and how these features allow complicated networking and security issues to be resolved. An in-depth discussion of the workings of various protocols and algorithms is provided.

Features of This Book

The book is a combination of the study of security principles plus protocols and network security implementations. It needs to be both of these things because although CCIE candidates need to understand how the configurations work and how the implementations are done, they also need to have a fair idea of what the underlying principles and protocols are and what protocol issues are being addressed. This is why the book discusses designs and recommendations as well as protocol- and principle-based descriptions of the various elements being covered. This type of analysis is also useful if you want to have a thorough understanding of network security irrespective of your desire to achieve the CCIE Network Security certification.

This book uses the following salient features to help you reach the level of understanding you want as an outcome from this book.

Feature Motivation

This book discusses the motivation for implementing various aspects of network security elements before describing the features and more-detailed aspects. This is important to help you get a solid idea of why the various features and principles are the way they are.

Protocol and Product Implementation Analysis

One of this book's main strengths is the protocol-level discussion it gets into on the protocols that are part of the network security suite. The book also goes into details of how algorithms such as PIX's Adaptive Security Algorithm are implemented. These in-depth studies are necessary for building the in-depth expertise you need.

Line-by-Line Descriptions of All Configurations, Debugs, and show Command Output

One of the important features of this book is line-by-line descriptions of the configurations, debug outputs, and **show** command outputs. This is an important tool to help you understand how the various features just discussed are implemented.

Case Studies

This book makes extensive use of case studies culled from real-life scenarios to further elaborate on the design and product features discussed in the book. The case studies are an integral part of the learning scheme developed by the book. Most of the case studies are adaptations of real scenarios that Cisco's customers have implemented in their networks. As such, they are a useful guide for anyone embarking on a network security design implementation.

Troubleshooting

Troubleshooting is an integral part of any network security implementation. This book has a chapter dedicated to troubleshooting the various implementations covered. Chapter 24 discusses techniques needed and tools available to troubleshoot security implementations. It also offers resolutions to the most commonly seen issues and configuration mistakes.

Review Questions and Answers

Most chapters have a "Review Questions" section at the end that can serve as a useful study aid. The answers appear in Appendix A.

Icons Used in This Book

Throughout this book, you will see a number of icons used to designate Cisco and general networking devices, peripherals, and other items. The following icon legend explains what these icons represent.

Throughout this book, you will see the following icons used for common network devices

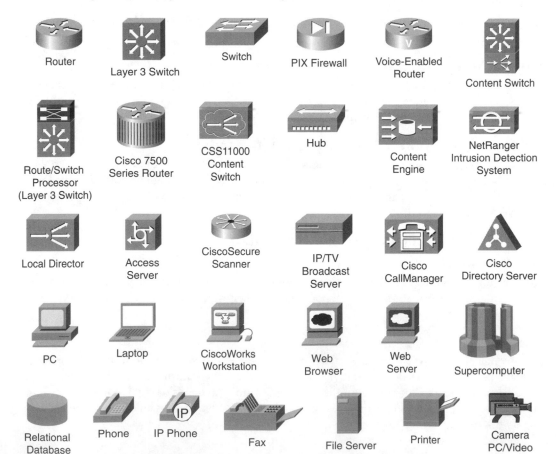

Command Syntax Conventions

The conventions used to present command syntax in this book are the same conventions used in the IOS Command Reference. The Command Reference describes these conventions as follows:

- Vertical bars (|) separate alternative, mutually exclusive elements.

- Square brackets ([ ]) indicate an optional element.

- Braces ({ }) indicate a required choice.

- Braces within brackets ([{ }]) indicate a required choice within an optional element.

- **Bold** indicates commands and keywords that are entered literally as shown. In actual configuration examples and output (not general command syntax), bold indicates commands that are manually input by the user (such as a **show** command).

- *Italic* indicates arguments for which you supply actual values.

Introduction to Network Security

This chapter covers the following key topics:

- **Network Security Goals**—This section discusses the goals of implementing security on a network.

- **Asset Identification**—This section discusses the need to define the assets in a network that need to be protected against network attacks.

- **Threat Assessment**—This section discusses how to recognize the threats unique to a network setup.

- **Risk Assessment**—We discuss what risk means and how it needs to be evaluated for all network assets in order to set up meaningful safeguards.

- **Constructing a Network Security Policy**—We use this section to discuss how to set up a network security policy in light of the definitions established in the previous sections.

- **Elements of a Network Security Policy**—We discuss the pieces that come together to form a network security policy.

- **Implementing a Network Security Policy**—This section discusses technical and nontechnical aspects of implementing a network security policy.

- **Network Security Architecture Implementation**—We discuss how the network policy can be translated into a secure network architecture.

- **Audit and Improvement**—We discuss how audits and continuous improvements are necessary for a successful network security policy implementation.

- **Case Study**—You see how the theories discussed in this chapter can be put into effective use.

## CHAPTER 1

An Introduction to Network Security

This chapter launches the book with a general discussion of developing a motivation for network security. It aims to develop your understanding of some of the common threats against which a network must be protected and discusses at a high level some of the controls that can be put into place to defend against these attacks. A security policy is the foundation of all network security implementations that occur on any given network. It defines the scope and methodology of the security implementations. We will discuss the basic principles of setting up a meaningful security policy and how it can be implemented in a network environment. The later sections of the chapter discuss the value of auditing the security policy implementation and how it needs to be continuously tested and improved.

Network Security Goals

Network security is the process through which a network is secured against internal and external threats of various forms. In order to develop a thorough understanding of what network security is, you must understand the threats against which network security aims to protect a network. It is equally important to develop a high-level understanding of the main mechanisms that can be put into place to thwart these attacks.

Generally, the ultimate goal of implementing security on a network is achieved by following a series of steps, each aimed at clarifying the relationship between the attacks and the measures that protect against them. The following is the generally accepted approach to setting up and implementing security on a site, as suggested by Fites, et al. in *Control and Security of Computer Information Systems* (M. Fites, P. Kratz, and A. Brebner, Computer Science Press, 1989):

Step 1   Identify what you are trying to protect.

Step 2   Determine what you are trying to protect it from.

Step 3   Determine how likely the threats are.

Step 4   Implement measures that protect your assets in a cost-effective manner.

Step 5   Review the process continuously, and make improvements each time you find a weakness.

Asset Identification

Most modern networks have many resources that need to be protected. The reason is that most enterprises today implement network systems to provide information to users across the network in digital format rather than in another form, such as hard copies. Therefore, the number of resources that need to be protected increases significantly. The following list, by no means comprehensive, identifies network resources that need to be protected from various types of attacks:

- Network equipment such as routers, switches, and firewalls
- Network operations information such as routing tables and access list configurations stored on this equipment
- Intangible networking resources such as bandwidth and speed
- Information and the information sources connected to the network, such as databases and information servers
- End hosts connecting to the network to make use of various resources
- Information passing across the network at any given time
- The privacy of the users as identifiable through their usage of the network resources

All these things are considered a network's assets. You need to protect them by formulating and implementing a network security plan.

Threat Assessment

Network attacks are what a network security process aims to protect its network assets against. Network security attacks are attempts, malicious or otherwise, to use or modify the resources available through a network in a way they were not intended to be used. In order to better understand what network attacks are, it is a good idea to look at the types of network attacks. Network attacks in general can be divided into three main categories:

- Unauthorized access to resources or information through the use of a network
- Unauthorized manipulation and alteration of information on a network
- Denial of service

Chapter 14, "What Is Intrusion Detection?", offers a more detailed examination of the various categories of network attacks.

The key word to note in the first two categories of attacks is *unauthorized*. A network security policy defines what is authorized and what is not. However, in general terms, unauthorized access occurs when a user attempts to view or alter information that was not intended for his or her specific use. In some situations it can be fairly difficult to define what was intended for the use of a given user. Therefore, it is imperative to have a security policy in place that is restrictive enough to clearly define a limited number of very specific resources and network elements that a user should be allowed to gain access to.

Information on a network can be either the information contained on end devices connected to the network, such as web servers and databases; information passing through the network; or information relevant to the workings of the networking components, such as the routing tables and access control list configurations. Resources on a network can either be the end devices (network components such as routers and firewalls) or the interconnect mechanisms.

Denial of service is one of the most common types of network attacks. Denial of service occurs when legitimate access to a network resource is blocked or degraded by a malicious act or a mistake.

It is important to note that a network security attack can be intentional or unintentional. The aim of the security mechanisms in a network is not only to protect against planned and coordinated attacks conducted with malicious intent, but also to protect the network and its resources against mistakes made by users. The damages caused by either type of attack can be similar.

Keeping in mind the attacks just outlined, you can start building an outline of the goals of implementing network security on a network. The ultimate goal is to protect the network against the attacks just described. Therefore, a network security implementation should aim to achieve the following goals:

- Ascertain data confidentiality
- Maintain data integrity
- Maintain data availability

Risk Assessment

Having identified the assets and the factors that threaten them, the next step in formulating a network security implementation is to ascertain how likely the threats are in the environment in which the security is being implemented. Realize that although it can be important to protect against all types of attacks, security does not come cheap. Therefore, you must do a proper risk analysis to find out what the most significant sources of attack are and devote the most resources to protecting against them.

Risk assessment can be done in a variety of ways. However, two main factors affect the risk associated with a particular type of threat's materializing:

- The likelihood that that particular attack will be launched against the asset in question
- The cost to the network in terms of damages that a successful attack will incur

The likelihood that an attack will materialize is an important consideration in risk assessment. It is often difficult to have complete information on what types of attacks can be staged against an asset on a network. However, it is important to realize that because a network is being protected to achieve the three goals defined in the preceding section, most risk analysis assessments can be divided into these three categories as well:

- Confidentiality
- Integrity
- Availability

If a network resource's availability is critical and the likelihood of an attack being launched against it is high, this asset's risk level can be considered fairly high. An example of such an asset is a high-visibility web server. Due to its high visibility, it can be a likely target for attackers. Also, it is important for a web server to be available at all times. Therefore, this asset is high-risk in terms of availability. On the other hand, an FTP server that is available only on the internal network and that is invisible to the outside world might require high confidentiality but is not a high-availability risk, because outside attackers do not know of it under normal circumstances. Note that all risk measurements are relative and are conducted keeping in mind the criticality of various assets of the networks vis-á-vis each other.

Risk assessment can be done in quite a few different ways—some quantitative, others qualitative. You must choose a risk assessment technique that can best identify the risks associated with a site.

After you have compiled a list of the risk levels associated with various assets in the network, the next step is to create a policy framework for protecting these resources so that risk can be minimized. Obviously, the policy must prioritize its efforts to mitigate threats against the high-risk assets and then spend the rest of its efforts in attacking the lower-risk assets.

Constructing a Network Security Policy

A network security policy defines a framework to protect the assets connected to a network based on a risk assessment analysis. A network security policy defines the access limitations and rules for accessing various assets connected to a network. It is the source of information for users and administrators as they set up, use, and audit the network.

A network security policy should be general and broad in scope. What this means is that it should provide a high-level view of the principles based on which security-related decisions should be made, but it should not go into the details of how the policy should be implemented. The details can change overnight, but the general principles of what these details are trying to achieve should remain the same.

S. Garfinkel and G. Spafford in *Practical Unix and Internet Security* define the following three roles that a policy should attempt to play:

- Clarify what is being protected and why it is being protected.
- State who is responsible for providing that protection.
- Provide grounds on which to interpret and resolve any later conflicts that might arise.

The first point is an offshoot of the earlier discussion regarding asset identification and risk assessment. Risk assessment in essence is an objective method of outlining why the resources in a network are to be protected. The second point covers who is responsible for ensuring that the security requirements are met. This can be one or more of the following:

- The network's users
- The network's administrators and managers
- The auditors who audit the network's usage
- The managers who have overall ownership of the network and its associated resources

The third point is important because it sets responsibility for issues not covered in the policy on the shoulders of specific individuals rather than leaving them open to arbitrary interpretation.

In order for a security policy to be enforceable, it must be practical to implement given the available technology. A very comprehensive policy that contains elements that are not technically enforceable becomes less than useful.

In terms of ease of use of network resources by the users, there are two types of security policies:

- **Permissive**—Everything not expressly prohibited is allowed.
- **Restrictive**—Everything not expressly permitted is prohibited.

It is generally a better idea from a security perspective to have a restrictive policy and then based on actual usage open it up for legitimate usage. A permissive policy generally has holes no matter how hard you try to plug all the holes.

A security policy needs to balance ease of use, network performance, and security aspects in defining the rules and regulations. This is important, because an overly restrictive security policy can end up costing more than a security policy that is somewhat more lenient but makes up for it in terms of performance gains. Of course, minimum security requirements as identified by risk analysis must be met for a security policy to be practical.

Elements of a Network Security Policy

In order to get a thorough understanding of what a network security policy is, it is instructional to analyze some of the most important elements of a security policy. RFC 2196 lists the following as the elements of a security policy:

1 Computer Technology Purchasing Guidelines which specify required, or referred, security features. These should supplement existing purchasing policies and guidelines.

2 A Privacy Policy which defines reasonable expectations of privacy regarding such issues as monitoring of electronic mail, logging of keystrokes, and access to users' files.

3   An Access Policy which defines access rights and privileges to protect assets from loss or disclosure by specifying acceptable use guidelines for users, operations staff, and management. It should provide guidelines for external connections, data communications, connecting devices to a network, and adding new software to systems. It should also specify any required notification messages (e.g., connect messages should provide warnings about authorized usage and line monitoring, and not simply say "Welcome").

4   An Accountability Policy which defines the responsibilities of users, operations staff, and management. It should specify an audit capability, and provide incident handling guidelines (i.e., what to do and who to contact if a possible intrusion is detected).

5   An Authentication Policy which establishes trust through an effective password policy, and by setting guidelines for remote location authentication and the use of authentication devices (e.g., one-time passwords and the devices that generate them).

6   An Availability statement which sets users' expectations for the availability of resources. It should address redundancy and recovery issues, as well as specify operating hours and maintenance down-time periods. It should also include contact information for reporting system and network failures.

7   An Information Technology System & Network Maintenance Policy which describes how both internal and external maintenance people are allowed to handle and access technology. One important topic to be addressed here is whether remote maintenance is allowed and how such access is controlled. Another area for consideration here is outsourcing and how it is managed.

8   A Violations Reporting Policy that indicates which types of violations (e.g., privacy and security, internal and external) must be reported and to whom the reports are made. A non-threatening atmosphere and the possibility of anonymous reporting will result in a greater probability that a violation will be reported if it is detected.

9   Supporting Information which provides users, staff, and management with contact information for each type of policy violation; guidelines on how to handle outside queries about a security incident, or information which may be considered confidential or proprietary; and cross-references to security procedures and related information, such as company policies and governmental laws and regulations.

Implementing a Network Security Policy

After a security policy has been defined, the next step is implementing it. Implementing a security policy is not a simple matter. It involves technical as well as nontechnical aspects. Although it is challenging enough to find the correct equipment that can work together and implement the security policy in its true spirit, coming up with a design that is workable for all parties concerned is equally challenging.

Here are some points you need to keep in mind before you begin implementing a security policy:

- All stakeholders in the company, including management and end users, must agree or have consensus on the security policy. It is terrifically difficult to maintain a security policy that not everyone is convinced is necessary.

- It's crucial to educate the users and the affected parties, including management, on why security is important. You must make sure that all parties understand the reasons behind the security policy and what is about to be implemented. This education must continue on an ongoing basis such that all newcomers to the company are aware of the network's security aspects.

- Security does not come free. Implementing security is expensive and is often an ongoing expense rather than a one-time cost. It is important to educate the management and the financial people about the cost and risk analysis done in coming up with the security policy.

- You must clearly define the responsibilities of the various people for the various parts of the network and their reporting relationships.

Working on implementing a security policy while keeping these issues in mind can help you implement a security policy both in practice and in spirit.

Network Security Architecture Implementation

As soon as the security policy has been defined, the next step is implementing the policy in the form of a network security design. We will discuss various security principles and design issues throughout this book. The first step to take after a security policy has been created is to translate it into procedures. These procedures are typically laid out as a set of tasks that must be completed to successfully implement the policy. These procedures upon execution result in a network design that can be implemented using various devices and their associated features.

Generally, the following are the elements of a network security design:

- Device security features such as administrative passwords and SSH on the various network components

- Firewalls

- Remote-access VPN concentrators

- Intrusion detection

- Security AAA servers and related AAA services for the rest of the network

- Access-control and access-limiting mechanisms on various network devices, such as ACLs and CAR

All or some of these components come together in a design setup to implement the requirements of the network security policy. We will discuss the various aspects of using these components throughout this book.

Audit and Improvement

As soon as a security policy has been implemented, it is critical to continually analyze, test, and improve it. You can do this through formal audits of the security systems as well as through day-to-day checks based on normal operational measurements. Audits can also take various forms, including automated auditing using various tools such as the Cisco Secure Scanner. These tools look for vulnerabilities that a system on the network might be exposed to.

An important function of audits is keeping network users aware of the security implications of their actions in the network. Audits should be used to identify habits that the users might have formed that can lead to network attacks. It is recommended that audits be scheduled as well as random in nature. A random audit can often catch the organization with its guard down and also reveal penetrability during maintenance, turnaround, and so on.

After various issues have been identified, they can be fixed if their nature is purely techno-logical or they can be transformed into educational programs to educate the users on better network security techniques. Educational programs should focus on the goals of the network security policy and how individuals can help in its implementation. Audit information should be conveyed as points that are simplified for emphasis. Generally, it is preferable not to educate the users on the minute details of things they are doing wrong, but to educate them on the general security policy and use infringements as examples. An audit and education policy that is too hands-on can remove a sense of empowerment from the users, making them think that they can do no wrong until *caught* doing something wrong. This is a dan-gerous behavior to introduce, because no audit policy can check for all incorrect user behaviors.

Case Study

This case study looks at a security policy design and implementation for a typical enterprise network. We will look at the various steps the security policy design goes through and discuss the final outcome as well as the ongoing initiatives in keeping the infrastructure secure.

This case study uses a hypothetical company called Biotech, Inc. Biotech, Inc. is a small to medium-sized enterprise company that has about 5000 users using the corporate network in one site and two remote locations with 250 users in each of these remote locations. In addition, about 250 users telecommute. Most of Biotech, Inc.'s business is pharmaceutical and is not conducted from their public web servers. The public web servers mostly serve to establish a corporate presence. However, an internal web server is used extensively by employees and management to undertake various day-to-day activities as the company tries to be paper-free.

Identification of Assets

In order to create a security policy, it is important to define a list of the assets that are linked to the network.

Biotech, Inc.'s basic infrastructure consists of the following components:

- A total of 5750 users (750 are remote)
- Connection to the ISP
- Company Gateway Router A
- Switch A subdivided into various VLANs for the company's various departments
- LAN connecting the corporate users
- External DNS server
- Internal DNS server
- WINS servers, PDCs and BDCs
- Internal SMTP server
- Routers B and C for internal routing needs
- External web server
- Internal web server
- Back-end databases
- Financial and human resources (HR) records database

Threat Identification

Biotech, Inc.'s network is used mostly by its employees, who are engaged mostly in pharmaceutical research and development (R&D) and marketing and sales programs. The employees use the corporate network not only to exchange information with each other but also to store research and other types of data on database servers. The internal web server houses most of the information the employees want to share with each other. In addition, the HR and financial records for the company and the employees are stored on a database server accessible to select employees (such as managers and HR staff) and financial department staff.

Biotech, Inc.'s management is most concerned about the following threats:

- An outside attacker's gaining access to the back-end databases and the confidential information stored on them
- An outside attacker's defacing the company external website and harming the company's reputation

- An inside or outside attack's bringing down the internal network, resulting in lost employee productivity

- An outside attacker's reading the communications taking place between the employees

- An outside attacker's cutting off the company from the Internet, resulting in lost productivity for employees researching material on the Internet

- An outside attacker's causing the connections between the main company site and the two remote locations and/or the remote telecommuters to be severed, again resulting in productivity loss

- An outside attacker's gaining access to the back-end R&D database

- An outside attacker's gaining access to the financial and HR database and the private records found in it

- An inside attacker's reading communications intended for other company employees and not him or her

- An inside attacker's gaining access to areas on the back-end databases not intended for his or her use

- An inside attacker's bringing down the internal network by starting an attack or making a critical mistake

Of course, there are other threats as well, but the threats listed here are foremost in the minds of the people responsible for the company's assets. Therefore, these are the threats against which the security policy aims to protect the network.

Risk Analysis

The next step in formulating Biotech, Inc.'s network security policy is to do a risk analysis of the threats identified in the preceding section vis-á-vis the assets that are being threatened and come up with a priority list of security policy ingredients.

Because Biotech, Inc. is involved in mostly R&D work, the disruption of a network, although annoying to the employees, is not too threatening as long as it is not prolonged. Research is a time-intensive activity. The company's higher-ups are comfortable that a network that is available most of the time, if not all the time, is something they can live with. They want their corporate presence, meaning the external web server, to be up most of the time. However, the traffic on this server, given the nature of Biotech, Inc.'s business, is not very high at any given time.

Biotech, Inc.'s biggest concern is the confidentiality of their R&D information. Their management is really interested in protecting this information. Data integrity is also high on the list, because loss of data can be a significant problem in terms of lost time. However, confidentiality is at the top of the list for Biotech, Inc.

Based on the priorities set by Biotech, Inc., the following is a very high-level priority list of the goals that the security policy for Biotech Inc. should try to achieve:

- Confidentiality
- Integrity
- Availability

Keeping these three goals in mind, a table is prepared listing the company's most critical assets. Each asset is given a risk rating for each of the three main categories of confidentiality, integrity, and availability, with 5 being very important and 1 being unimportant. Each asset is rated by looking at the threats it is actually exposed to and the degree to which the company is sensitive about threats posed to each asset. An asset that is not exposed to any significant threats but that does contain information the management is sensitive about keeping confidential does not rate very high on the risk chart. On the other hand, an asset that is susceptible to significant threats and that contains confidential information is a high-risk asset. A combination of these factors, the likelihood of an attack on an asset and the cost of such an attack in the mind of the management, determines how high a risk a particular asset is. Table 1-1 shows the critical asset risk rating for Biotech, Inc.

Table 1-1   *Critical Asset Risk Rating for Biotech, Inc.*

Asset	Confidentiality	Integrity	Availability
Back-end database	5	3	2
External web server	2	2	5
Internal LAN	4	2	2
Internet connectivity	2	2	4
Remote access for remote offices and telecommuters	4	2	4
Financial and HR database	4	4	3

As soon as these criteria have been established, the next step is to define a security policy that protects these assets based on the risk assessment done for them. Efforts must be directed to protecting these assets based on the risk rating in each of the three areas of concern outlined in the previous table: confidentiality, integrity and availability.

Definition of a Security Policy

Based on the information collected, the following sections describe what were defined as the basic elements of Biotech Inc.'s security policy.

Scope and Motivation for Defining the Security Policy

Biotech, Inc. makes heavy use of its network resources in its day-to-day workings. In order to ensure that this usage does not result in leakage of confidential data, it is critical for all users of the network to understand and comply with this security policy. This security policy defines the elements that are in place to protect the network's security, including the users and their information.

Accountability Policy

All users of the network are accountable for their behaviors that result in network security concerns. It is the responsibility of every user to be familiar with the guidelines of using the service offered through Biotech, Inc.'s network. It is also the responsibility of every user to report to the system administrator suspected inappropriate use or malicious activity on the network.

Acceptable Usage Policy

Biotech, Inc.'s network is available for use by employees any time of the day or night for the sole purpose of fulfilling the responsibilities that are part of each user's job description. Using network resources for any function over and above that is prohibited.

Computer Technology Purchasing Guidelines

All network-related equipment must be purchased keeping in mind Biotech, Inc.'s requirements for primarily confidentiality and secondly integrity and availability. It is important for the equipment to incorporate mechanisms for secure and confidential administration. All networking equipment must be screened for known major bugs in the code and the vendor's history in fixing such bugs. Security-related equipment should preferably be purchased from vendors that have a proven track record in the area of security.

Access Policy

Access will be strictly restricted. Access will be allowed by assuming that all access is denied unless specifically required.

Access to the back-end databases and the HR and financial databases is given only to employees. These resources must be accessed while an employee is sitting on the local network or from one of the remote sites or by one of the authorized telecommuters (only through company-approved procedures for remote-access users). Access from any other location is prohibited. The decision to allow employees access to various resources will be made by their direct supervisors, along with approval from the Chief Security Officer.

Steps must be taken to stop access to these resources from outside the network. Steps must also be taken to ensure that network intrusions are detected and actions are taken to control the damage and prevent future break-ins.

Access to network resources will be on an as-needed basis. Information assets are protected by giving access to specific groups and denying access to all others. Increasing access privileges for a given asset requires approval from the management.

All remote users must get management approval before they can use the resources to remotely access the corporate network. Users from the remote sites and telecommuters are treated the same as local users who use network resources. Similar access restrictions are placed on these users for accessing the various network resources.

Remote-access users must comply with corporate guidelines and take the following measures to make sure that their PCs are safe to connect to the corporate network:

- Connect only through the VPN concentrators using authentication and encryption.
- Install current corporate-standard antivirus software with the auto-update feature enabled.
- The PC must be password-protected in such a way that a reboot cannot bypass the password process.
- All PCs being used for remote access must have an active personal firewall (approved for remote-access usage) installed.

It is the responsibility of the employees using remote access to ensure that their remote-access equipment is not used by unauthorized individuals to gain access to the resources on the corporate network.

Authentication Policy

All information assets on the network require authentication before someone is given access to them. Access attempts are logged for auditing.

Remote-access users need to go through two layers of authentication—once to authenticate themselves to the access servers connecting them to the network and then to gain access to individual resources on the network.

Authentication is carried out using security servers on the network. Steps must be taken to safeguard the security servers against attacks and intrusions from the outside or inside network.

Authentication should be carried out using one-time passwords. Authentication must be accompanied by authorization and accounting on the security servers. Authorization should be used to restrict user access to resources that are intended for users based on their belonging to a certain group. Accounting should be used to further track authorized user activities. This is a basic safeguard that must be supplemented along with intrusion detection systems.

Availability Statement

The network is available to bona fide users at all times of the day except for outages that occur for various reasons. When a trade-off must be made between confidentiality and network availability, confidentiality is always given priority.

Information Technology Systems and Network Maintenance Policy

All network equipment is managed only by the full-time employees of Biotech, Inc. who have the privileges to do so. Giving an individual permission to work on any network equipment for administrative purposes requires management approval.

Remote access to administer the networking equipment is allowed, but it requires that the access be done using encryption and that authentication for login access take place against the security servers. All management sessions, internal and external, must be encrypted.

Violations and Security Incident Reporting and Handling Policy

Documented processes must be set up to identify when intrusions and network attacks take place. These processes of detection must include manual reporting and automatic reporting tools.

The following processes need to be set up for incident reporting and handling:

- As soon as it has been confirmed that a breach has taken place or an attack is taking place, a process must be invoked to inform all the necessary network administrators of the problem and what their role is in tackling the situation.

- A process needs to be set up to identify all the information that will be recorded to track the attack and for possible prosecution.

- A process must be in place to contain the incident that has occurred or that is occurring. The process must be written keeping in mind that confidentiality is a bigger concern for Biotech Inc. than availability.

- A process must be in place to follow up on attacks that have occurred to make sure that all the vulnerabilities exposed through the attack are corrected and that similar attacks can be avoided in the future.

Supporting Information

All information regarding Biotech, Inc.'s operations must be kept confidential and must never be divulged to sources outside the company. All publicity-related matters should be handled through the Corporate Press Relations office.

Any later conflicts and issues regarding the security policy must be resolved with the intervention of the Chief Security Officer, who bears ultimate responsibility for the security policy.

Table 1-2 shows the contacts and their roles and responsibilities defined in the context of Biotech Inc.'s security policy.

Table 1-2   *Security Policy Contacts and Their Roles*

Title	Role	Responsibilities
Chief Security Officer	Defining and maintaining overall network security policy and its administration	• Main point of contact for changes to be made to the site security policy • Responsible for final approval of new network implementations that might affect network security • Responsible for coordination of cross-departmental communications on security issues • Administrative control over staff directly responsible for network security • Dotted-line control over all company employees in the context of network security
Network administrator	Responsible for day-to-day network operations	• Ensures that the security policy is followed in all network implementations • Main point of contact for network security incidence response
Network architect	Responsible for the ongoing design of the network	• Ensures that the security policy is practical and can be implemented • Creates network designs that are in compliance with the network security policy • Manages ongoing network designs to maintain security • Remains on top of new security threats being introduced to tweak the network's design parameters for better security • Responsible for an ongoing audit of network security implementations to ensure correctness of design

continues

Table 1-2   *Security Policy Contacts and Their Roles (Continued)*

Title	Role	Responsibilities
Network security engineer	Responsible for implementing and configuring network components	• Ensures that network implementations are in accordance with the site security policy and the resulting design • Responsible for correct configurations and verification in order to ensure that the security policy's intent is met • Responsible for ongoing troubleshooting of network-related issues while keeping in mind the security aspects • First point of contact for security incidence response; ensures proper routing and handling of such incidences in cooperation with the other stakeholders • Responsible for an ongoing audit of network security implementations to ensure correctness of configurations

Conclusion

The security policy defined here is used to create a design that can protect the company against the various threats to which it is most vulnerable. The design is created keeping in mind the various features available for various products and bringing them all together to form a cohesive network that implements the rules defined in the network security policy. The rest of this book describes some of the principles, features, and protocols that are available to implement network security policies.

Summary

Network security is a process that starts by defining what your assets are and what you want to protect them from. A network security policy defines the framework used to provide this protection. It is critical for a network security policy to be comprehensive and to be able to cater to the needs of everyone who uses the network. The network security policy is translated into a network design that is implemented using various security products, features, and protocols.

This book is primarily focused on looking at the security principles, features, and protocols that result in the successful implementation of a comprehensive security policy. As we go through the various chapters of this book, you are encouraged to look for the motivation behind why various features are the way they are and the rationale behind the security principles described. This will ultimately result in your gaining a deep level of understanding of network security-related issues. You also will get a broad view of the parameters that bind together a network security architecture.

Review Questions

1 What is the first step when you're starting to think about network security?

2 What are some of a modern network's assets?

3 What is risk assessment?

4 What is the difference between risk assessment and threat assessment?

5 What is the difference between a permissive security policy and a restrictive security policy?

6 What is a privacy policy?

7 What is an access policy?

8 What is an accountability policy?

9 What is an availability statement?

10 What is an information technology system and network maintenance policy?

Building Security into the Network

This chapter covers the following key topics:

- **An Introduction to Security Zones**—This section discusses what security zones are and covers some of the basic concepts concerning how to go about defining security zones in a network.

- **Designing a Demilitarized Zone**—This section defines DMZs and discusses ways to create them.

- **Case Study: Creating Zones Using the PIX Firewall**—This case study describes a zoned network based on the PIX Firewall.

## CHAPTER 2

Defining Security Zones

Security zone definitions play a very important role in setting up a secure network. They not only allow security efforts to be more focused and streamlined but also allow better user access for legitimate users of resources. This chapter looks at what security zones are and how they are part of the network design philosophy. We will then look at what a demilitarized zone (DMZ) is. DMZs are one of the integral components of modern secure network designs. Because firewalls are often used to define the parameters of the security zones on a network, this chapter concludes with a case study that discusses the mechanisms available on the PIX Firewall for creating zones and associated security definitions.

An Introduction to Security Zones

Although the security features available in the various networking devices play an important part in thwarting network attacks, in reality one of the best defenses against network attacks is the network's secure topological design. A network topology designed with security in mind goes a long way in forestalling network attacks and allowing the security features of the various devices to be most effective in their use.

One of the most critical ideas used in modern secure network design is using zones to segregate various areas of the network from each other. Devices placed in the various zones have varying security needs, and the zones provide protection based on these needs. Also, the roles that some devices play (for example, Web servers) leave them especially vulnerable to network attacks and make them more difficult to secure. Therefore, segregating these devices in zones of lesser security dislocated from zones containing more-sensitive and less-attackable devices plays a critical role in the overall network security scheme.

Zoning also allows networks to scale better and consequently leads to more stable networks. Stability is one of the cornerstones of security. A network that is more stable than others is likely also more secure during a stressful attack on its bandwidth resources.

The basic strategy behind setting up zones is as follows:

- The devices with the greatest security needs (the private network) are within the network's most-secure zone. This is generally the zone where little to no access from the public or other networks is allowed. Access is generally controlled using a firewall or other security functions, such as secure remote access (SRA). Strict control of authentication and authorization is often desired in such a zone.

- Servers that need to be accessed only internally are put in a separate private and secure zone. Controlled access to these devices is provided using a firewall. Access to these servers is often closely monitored and logged.

- Servers that need to be accessed from the public network are put in a segregated zone with no access to the network's more-secure zones. This is done to avoid endangering the rest of the network in case one of these servers gets compromised. In addition, if possible, each of these servers is also segregated from the others so that if one of them gets compromised, the others cannot be attacked. Separate zones for each server or each type of server are in order in the securest type of setup. This means that a Web server is segregated from the FTP server by being put in a zone completely separate from the FTP server. This way, if the web server becomes compromised, the chances of the FTP server being accessed and possibly compromised through the privileges gained by the attacker on the Web server are limited. (This type of segregation can also be achieved using the private VLANs available in the 6509 switches from Cisco). These zones are known as DMZs. Access into and out of them is controlled using firewalls.

- Zoning is done in such a way that layered firewalls can be placed in the path to the most sensitive or vulnerable part of the network. This can avoid configuration mistakes in one firewall that allow the private network to be compromised. Many large networks with security needs use different types of firewalls at the network layer to keep the network from becoming compromised due to a bug in the firewall software. Using a PIX Firewall and a proxy server firewall in tandem is one such example. This is also sometimes called the Defense in Depth principle.

Designing a Demilitarized Zone

DMZ is one of the most important zoning term used in network security. A DMZ is the zone in the network that is segregated from the rest of the network due to the nature of the devices contained on it. These devices, often servers that need to be accessed from the public network, do not allow a very stringent security policy to be implemented in the area where they are kept. Therefore, there is a need to separate this zone from the rest of the network.

DMZ is often a subnet that typically resides between the private network and the public network. Connections from the public network terminate on DMZ devices. These servers can oftenalso be accessed relatively securely by private network devices.

There are quite a few ways to create a DMZ. How a DMZ is created depends on the network's security requirements, as well as the budgetary constraints placed on it. Here are some of the most common ways of creating DMZs:

- Using a three-legged firewall to create the DMZ
- Placing the DMZ outside the firewall between the public network and the firewall
- Placing the DMZ outside the firewall but not in the path between the public network and the firewall (also called a "dirty DMZ")
- Creating a DMZ between stacked firewalls

Using a Three-Legged Firewall to Create the DMZ

This is perhaps the most common method of creating a DMZ. This method uses a firewall with three interfaces to create separate zones, each sitting on its own firewall interface. The firewall provides separation between the zones. This mechanism provides a great deal of control over the DMZ's security. This is important because a compromised DMZ can be the first stage of a well-orchestrated attack. Figure 2-1 shows how a DMZ using a three-legged firewall can be set up. Note that a firewall can have many more than three interfaces, allowing a number of DMZs to be created. Each DMZ can have its own special security requirements.

Figure 2-1   *How a DMZ Using a Three-Legged Firewall Can Be Set Up*

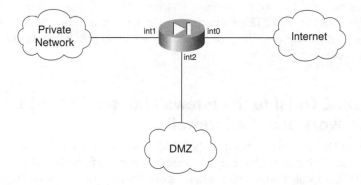

Placing the DMZ Outside the Firewall Between the Public Network and the Firewall

In this setup, the DMZ is exposed to the public side of the firewall. Traffic that needs to pass through the firewall passes through the DMZ first. This setup is not recommended, because you can exercise very little control over the security of the devices sitting on the DMZ.

These devices are practically part of the public domain, with no real protection of their own. Figure 2-2 shows how a DMZ can be created outside a firewall between the public network and the firewall.

Figure 2-2   *A DMZ Can Be Created Outside a Firewall Between the Public Network and the Firewall*

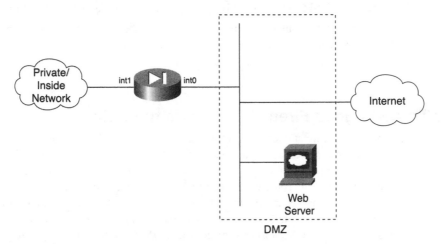

Obviously, this is a fairly insecure way of setting up a DMZ, because the firewall's security capabilities are not used at all in this setup. However, the router on the edge of the network toward the public network can be set up to provide some basic form of security to the machines on the DMZ. This security can be in the form of using access control lists to allow access to the machines sitting on the DMZ for certain port numbers only and denying all other access.

Placing the DMZ Outside the Firewall but not in the Path Between the Public Network and the Firewall

A "dirty DMZ" is very similar to the DMZ described in the preceding section. The only difference is that instead of being located between the firewall and the public network, the DMZ is located off a separate interface of the edge router connecting the firewall to the public network (see Figure 2-3). This type of setup provides very little security to the devices sitting on the DMZ network. However, this setup gives the firewall a little more isolation from the unprotected and vulnerable DMZ network than the setup described in the preceding section. The edge router in this setup can be used to deny all access from the DMZ subnet to the subnet on which the firewall is located. Also, separate VLANs can allow for further Layer 2 isolation between the subnet on which the firewall is located and the DMZ subnet. This is useful in situations where a host on the DMZ subnet becomes compromised and the attacker starts using that host to launch further attacks against the firewall and the network. The added layer of isolation can help slow the advance of the attack toward the firewall in these situations.

Figure 2-3   *A Dirty DMZ*

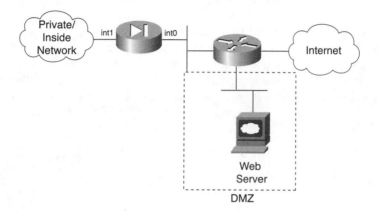

Dirty DMZs are often set up because the firewall is unable to handle the traffic load put on it as it tries to cater to all the traffic that is intended for the internal network as well as the traffic that is intended for the servers on a properly set up DMZ (one created using, for example, the three legged firewall technique). Because the traffic to the servers on the DMZ (which are often public servers) can be considerable, network administrators are forced to locate the servers outside the firewall on a DMZ so that the firewall does not have to process this traffic.

Network administrators often go to significant lengths to make sure that the hosts that are located on the dirty DMZ are particularly strong in the face of most common network attacks. A host that is exposed to a public network and is strengthened to face network attacks is called a *bastion host*. These hosts often have all unnecessary services turned off to prevent an attacker from using these services to gain further access to these hosts. Similarly, any unnecessary ports and communication mechanisms are also removed or disabled to enhance the security of these hosts. An attempt is made to install all necessary patches and hot fixes for the OS that the bastion host is running. Most tools and configuration utilities that can be used to manipulate the host are removed from the host. In addition, the host has extensive logging turned on in order to capture any attempts to compromise it. This can often be an invaluable tool in further improving a host's security. Even after putting all these safeguards in place, an attempt is made to make sure that even if the host becomes compromised, the firewall and the internal network cannot be accessed through the access privileges gained on the bastion host by the attacker. This also often means that the bastion host and the internal private network do not share the same authentication system.

Creating a DMZ Between Stacked Firewalls

In this mechanism of forming DMZs, two firewalls are stacked so that all traffic that needs to go to the private network behind the firewall farthest from the public network must go through both the firewalls. In this scenario, the network between the two firewalls is used as the DMZ. A fair deal of security is available to the DMZ in this case because of the firewall in front of it. However, one drawback is that all traffic going from the private network to the public network must pass through the DMZ network. In this case, a compromised DMZ device can allow an attacker easy access to hijacking or attacking this traffic in various ways. This risk can be mitigated by using private VLANs for the devices between the two firewalls. One of the main drawbacks of this setup is the cost of having two firewalls in place. Figure 2-4 shows how a DMZ stacked between firewalls is set up.

Figure 2-4 *A DMZ Stacked Between Firewalls*

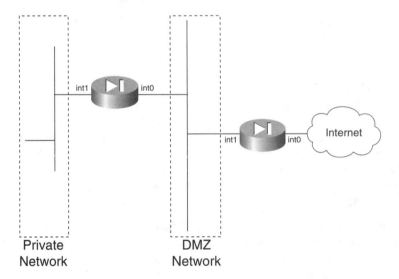

Case Study: Creating Zones Using the PIX Firewall

The PIX Firewall allows up to ten interfaces with varying security levels to be configured (PIX 535 running 6.X can support up to ten interfaces. PIX 525 running 5.3 and above can support up to eight interfaces). One interface needs to be connected to the inside or private network, and one needs to be connected to the public network. The rest of the interfaces can be connected to other networks, each with its own level of security. Thus, the PIX allows up to ten (eight in the case of PIX 525) distinct security zones to be supported on one firewall.

On the PIX Firewall, each interface is configured to have a security level. Essentially, a machine sitting on a low-security interface cannot access a device sitting on a high-security interface unless configuration is specifically done to allow this to occur. However, a device sitting on a high-security interface can access a low-security interface device as long as certain other requirements are met, such as the presence of Network Address Translation for the higher-security network devices. This leads to the obvious conclusion that on the PIX Firewall the DMZ interfaces should be kept at a security level lower than the inside/ private zone interface's security level. This allows the machines on the inside network to access the servers on the DMZ interface. However, the machines on the DMZ interface by default cannot access the hosts on the inside interface.

It should be noted that it is indeed possible to configure the PIX to allow the machines on the DMZ interface to access the inside interface machines, but this requires specific configuration to be done on the PIX, including opening a "hole" in the PIX to allow such traffic through.

PIX Firewall uses a numbering scheme to denote the security level of each interface and its associated zone. The numbering scheme goes from 0 to 100. By default, the inside interface has the number 100 associated with it, which means it has the highest level of security. The outside interface has the number 0 associated with it, which is the lowest level of security. The rest of the interfaces have numbers ranging from 1 to 99. Ideally, all interfaces should have unique security levels. Devices sitting on interfaces that have the same security levels cannot communicate across the PIX even if configured to do so.

The commands described next are used to specify the security levels of the interfaces on the PIX. In this example, Ethernet 0 on the PIX is the outside or public interface, and Ethernet 1 is the inside interface. Ethernet 2 is the DMZ interface. Figure 2-5 shows how a PIX is set up with DMZ and other interfaces in the case study.

The following command defines the name of the Ethernet 0 interface, 'outside', and assigns it a security level of 0:

```
nameif ethernet0 outside security0
```

The following command defines the name of the Ethernet 1 interface, 'inside', and assigns it a security level of 100:

```
nameif ethernet1 inside security100
```

The following command defines the name of the Ethernet 2 interface, 'dmz', and assigns it a security level of 50, which is between the security levels of the outside and inside interfaces.

```
nameif ethernet2 dmz security50
```

Figure 2-5   *How a PIX Is Set Up with DMZ and Other Interfaces in the Case Study*

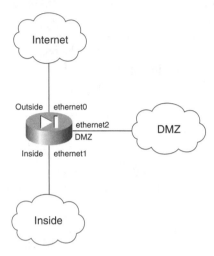

Summary

Zoning is an important concept in security design. Creating zones allows network administrators to set up varying levels of security for various groups of devices found in the
network. With the segregation that a well-designed DMZ offers, even if devices in the less-
secure zones are compromised, there is less risk of devices contained in the other zones
becoming compromised. This chapter discussed what zones are and how they help you
develop a secure network topology. This chapter also detailed DMZs, which form an integral
portion of most network designs nowadays, and various techniques available to set them up.
Finally, a case study focused on the capabilities of the PIX Firewall to set up zones on its
many interfaces. The rest of this book assumes the basic zoning concepts built in this chapter.

Review Questions

  1 What is a DMZ?

  2 What is a dirty DMZ?

  3 What is a bastion host?

  4 Why is logging important on a bastion host?

  5 Why are dirty DMZs often created?

  6 How does the PIX Firewall support zoning?

This chapter covers the following key topics:

- **Physical Security**—This section explores issues related to the physical security of networking equipment.

- **Device Redundancy**—This section deals with many different ways of designing device redundancy to secure a network.

- **Router Security**—This section deals with specific issues related to securing the routers in a network. The emphasis is on techniques available to make attacking the routers themselves a more difficult task.

- **PIX Firewall Security**—This section deals with specific issues related to securing a network's PIX Firewalls. The emphasis is on techniques available to make attacking the PIX Firewalls themselves a more difficult task.

- **Switch Security**—This section deals with specific issues related to securing the switches in a network. The emphasis is on techniques available to make attacking the switches themselves a more difficult task.

## CHAPTER 3

Device Security

To provide security on a network, it is critical that the devices constituting the network be secured against malicious access. This is important because a compromised device can be configured to behave as the attacker wants it to behave. Also, device security is important to help avoid denial of service (DoS) attacks against the device itself.

This chapter discusses some of the most important factors surrounding device security. We will see how physical security is important to a network's overall security and which elements go into building a network's physical security. From this discussion, we will move into a discussion of how to protect devices and consequently networks on a logical level. We will see how redundancy built into the network for various devices can help protect the network in case some of the devices become compromised in a network security attack. Having discussed these aspects of device security, we will discuss examples of the three most important components of most modern networks: routers, switches, and firewalls. We will look at methods of protecting these devices from attacks.

Device security has two main aspects:

- Physical security
- Logical security

Physical security implies placing the device in a location where it is safe from malicious attackers. Also, physical security implies having a redundant system in place such that if the primary system fails, a secondary system in a different physical location can seamlessly replace the function of the primary system.

Logical security implies securing the device against nonphysical attacks, in which the attacker uses data elements rather than physical force to launch an attack. Examples of such attacks are DoS attacks. We will talk about the logical aspects of the security of devices throughout this chapter.

Physical Security

Physical security involves figuring out the potential physical threats to devices and then devising ways to prevent them from affecting network operations. Although it is difficult to provide a comprehensive list of measures to take to ensure this kind of security, the following sections address some important issues to consider when locating a network.

Redundant Locations

Although this might be overkill for some networks, for networks with rigorous security measures, it is often necessary to have a backup or redundant network in a physical location that is completely separate from the primary network. This can also take the shape of splitting up the load on the primary system and routing some of the services to a secondary system that is geographically far away from the primary system. In the case of an outage of the primary system, the secondary system can take over the functioning of the primary system, and vice versa.

Ideally, the physical locations should be separated sufficiently from each other to ensure that natural calamities such as earthquakes and floods affect only one of them at a time rather than hitting both of them at once. However, because distance can also add a certain element of uncertainty in the connection between the two sites, such geographically distant systems need to be extensively tested before deployment and periodically tested afterward to ensure efficient switchover during a failure event.

Network Topographical Design

A network's topographical design can mean a lot to its survival in case of a physical attack on it. It is desirable to have a topology for networks with a redundant core to minimize the effect of an attack carried out on a link between two components of the network. If all the network's components are connected in series to each other, disrupting service between any two means disrupting it between two potentially large segments of the network. Perhaps the most resilient design is that of a fully meshed network in which every network node is directly connected to every other node. However, this type of network can be expensive to build. When set up in this way, a network node can still have connectivity to the rest of the network even if one or more of its direct links goes down. The redundancy built into the network topology ensures a great deal of stability and consequent security. Figure 3-1 shows three main types of network topological designs seen from the perspective of network resilience.

Figure 3-1   *Three Main Types of Network Topological Designs Seen from the Perspective of Network Resilience*

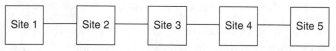

Serialized Topology

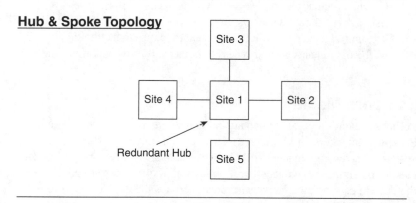

Any One Connection Down Can Bring a Whole Bunch of Sites Down

Hub & Spoke Topology

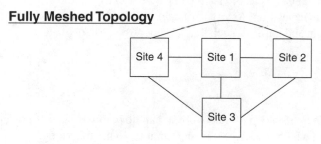

Redundant Hub

Fully Meshed Topology

Secure Location of the Network

There are two main aspects to consider when choosing a secure location to put the main components of a network:

- Finding a location that is sufficiently segregated from the rest of the office infrastructure to make physical intrusions obvious

- A location that is contained within a larger facility so that the security aspects of the larger facility can be used

These two guidelines seem to be at a tangent to each other. However, a good secure location often is a compromise between complete segregation (expensive) and complete integration (security risks).

To secure a location, you can follow these guidelines, among others:

- Restrict access to all networking equipment. Use locks and digital access authorization mechanisms to authenticate people before entering. Log access.

- Use monitoring cameras at entrances as well as in wiring closets of data centers.

- Conduct regular physical security audits to ensure that security breaches are not being risked. Trivial habits such as propping open a door instead of letting it lock can be a substantial security risk. It is important to realize that although a closed door might not be the only means to stop access to devices, it is an important line of defense.

Choosing Secure Media

Perhaps the days are gone when attackers needed physical access to attack a network. Presently, attackers find it much easier to compromise a trusted system and then use that system to eavesdrop on a network. However, physical eavesdropping on a cable can still be used to listen in on privileged communication or as a means to get further access. Among the current cabling mechanisms in place, perhaps the most difficult to eavesdrop on is the optical fiber. Coaxial cables and twisted pairs are easier to wiretap and also radiate energy that can be used to eavesdrop. Any type of cable can be made more secure by enclosing it in a secure medium and wiring it such that it is not possible to damage or access the cabling easily.

Power Supply

Although data is the lifeblood of a network, it can flow only if there is power to run the machines through which it passes. It is important to do the following:

- Properly design the network locations' power supply so that all equipment gets adequate power without overburdening any power systems.

- Have a backup power supply source not only to manage an outage for the whole facility but also to have redundant power supplies for individual devices.

Environmental Factors

It is important to secure a network facility against environmental factors. Attackers can exploit these factors to cause significant disruption to a network. Here are some of the environmental factors you should keep in mind while scrutinizing a network facility for security vulnerabilities:

- Fire
- Earthquakes, storms, and other such natural calamities

Although some of these factors, such as fire, can be guarded against to some extent, the only real solution to protecting the network functionality and data is to have a redundant solution in place, ready to take over form and function in case one of these calamities strikes.

Device Redundancy

Redundancy is an important component of any secure system. Although securing a system can eliminate much vulnerability to an attack, in reality, no number of measures can totally protect a device against all known and to-be-discovered attacks and vulnerabilities. Therefore, it becomes important to have a suitable redundancy mechanism in place. A redundancy mechanism allows a backup device to take over the functionality of a device that has stopped performing its responsibilities due to an attack. Although the backup device might be susceptible to a similar type of attack, it can buy the network administrator valuable time to set up mechanisms to protect against the attack.

There are two primary means of achieving redundancy for a network device:

- Use routing to ensure that an alternative path is chosen in case one or more of the devices on a particular path becomes unavailable.
- Use a redundancy protocol such as Hot Standby Router Protocol (HSRP), Virtual Router Redundancy Protocol (VRRP), or failover between any two devices. This ensures that if one of the two devices goes down, the other device takes over the functionality of the first device. These protocols are especially useful for providing redundancy on the LAN, where the end hosts do not participate in routing protocols. Running a dynamic routing protocol on every end host might be infeasible for a number of reasons, including administrative overhead, processing overhead, security issues, or lack of a routing protocol implementation for some platforms.

The following sections look at the various types of redundancy methods and protocols deployed in networks to ensure security through redundancy.

Routing-Enabled Redundancy

Routing protocols can be set up to allow redundancy between devices. The main philosophy behind this kind of setup is to set up routing in such a way that the routing protocols converge to one set of routes when everything is functioning normally and a different set of routes when some of the devices are out of order.

There are many different ways to achieve routing-based redundancy. We will discuss only two:

- **Statically**—You use static routes with varying weights.

- **Dynamically**—You build a network in a manner that allows a suboptimal path to become an optimal path when a device outage occurs.

Using Static Routes with Varying Weights

Using static routes is the simplest way to set up routing redundancy. Generally, static routes known as floating static routes are used to set up a backup path for the traffic flow if the original path goes down. Example 3-1 shows the configuration needed on a router to set up a floating static router. Figure 3-2 shows the network topology for this example.

Figure 3-2   *Topology for the Router Shown in Example 3-1*

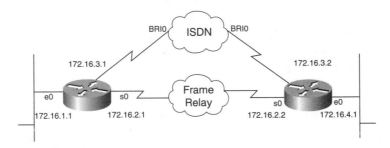

Example 3-1   *Setting Up Floating Static Routes on a Router*

```
interface Ethernet0
 ip address 172.16.1.1 255.255.255.0
!
interface Serial0
 ip address 172.16.2.1 255.255.255.128
 encapsulation frame-relay
 frame-relay map ip 172.16.2.2 102 broadcast
!
interface BRI0
 ip address 172.16.3.1 255.255.255.0
 encapsulation ppp
 dialer map ip 172.16.3.2 name ROUTER2 broadcast 6234020
 dialer load-threshold 5 either
 dialer hold-queue 75
 dialer-group 1
```

Example 3-1 *Setting Up Floating Static Routes on a Router (Continued)*

```
  ppp authentication chap
  ppp multilink
  !
 !The routing protocol is set up to function under normal circumstances when the
 !serial link is up and there is no device failure in the Frame Relay path.

 router eigrp 1
  network 172.16.0.0
  !
 ip classless
 !The static route configured below has an administrative distance of 200
 !configured. Since the default administrative distance of EIGRP routes is less
 !than 200, the routes learned through EIGRP for the 172.16.4.0 network are given
 !precedence under normal circumstances. However, when the Frame Relay link goes
 !down and the EIGRP route disappears, the static route becomes the best available
 !route and is used to bring up the ISDN link.
 ip route 172.16.4.0 255.255.255.0 172.16.3.2 200
 !Access list 101 is set up to define interesting traffic for the ISDN interface.
 !For the ISDN link to stay down when the Frame Relay link is up, any EIGRP routing
 !traffic is stopped from bringing up the ISDN link. Note that when the ISDN link is
 !up due to Frame Relay failure, such traffic still need not pass over the link,
 !because the static route is used to figure out the routing info rather than the
 !EIGRP protocol.
 access-list 101 deny    eigrp any any
 access-list 101 permit ip any any
 !
 dialer-list 1 protocol ip list 101
```

Building Network Redundancy Dynamically

Perhaps the most effective way of guarding against device failures is to design the network in such a way that the routing protocols can find an alternative path to connect any two given parts of the network in case a device fails anywhere on the network.

An example of such a network is a fully meshed network. Variations of the fully meshed network to provide redundancy in the most critical portions of the network can be a suitable alternative to having a completely meshed topology. The idea is for the routing protocol to converge on a different set of available routes when the original set of routes is no longer available due to a device or path failure. Figure 3-3 shows how this works using the RIP routing protocol.

Figure 3-3 *Dynamic Routing Protocols Can Discover a New Route When the Optimal Route Is No Longer Available*

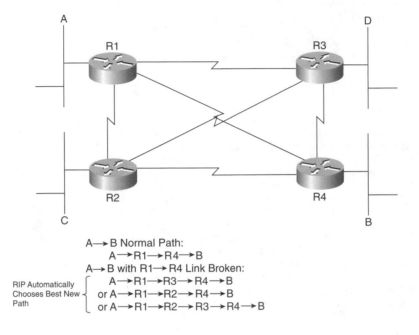

HSRP

HSRP, defined in RFC 2281, is a protocol that is implemented on Cisco routers to allow a failed device to be taken over by another device on a LAN. HSRP allows hosts to view a single router as their default gateway with multiple routers available to take over the functionality of that router in case it fails, without any indication of such a failure to the end hosts. The hosts use a single IP address and MAC address to communicate with their default gateway. However, multiple routers, if they have been set up with HSRP, have the ability to respond to frames sent to this MAC address or to packets destined for this IP address, in case of the failure of what is known as the active router. At any given time, a router known as the *active router* is the one that assumes ownership of this IP address and MAC address. All other routers participating in HSRP are said to be in *standby mode* until the active router fails. At that point, a standby router assumes the ownership of the IP address and the MAC address the hosts consider their default gateway. This allows the hosts to continue sending traffic to their default gateway without any disruption. The IP address and MAC address are often said to belong to a *virtual router* because in effect they do not belong to any physical router but are still used by hosts to communicate with the default gateway.

Process of Determining the Active Router

The active router is one that assumes the identity of the virtual router, meaning that it assumes responsibility for forwarding the packets that hosts send it. All routers that can become active routers are said to form an *HSRP group or a standby group*. When a router is configured to do HSRP, it is configured with the virtual router's virtual IP address. The virtual router MAC address is the MAC address 0x00 0x00 0x0C 0x07 0xAC *XX,* where *XX* represents the HSRP group number. This MAC address does not need to be configured by the router's administrator, but rather should be built into the router's software code.

The router then goes into a state known as *speak* state, in which it sends out HSRP messages called *hellos* containing its priority. All the routers in the HSRP group that are configured with a virtual address send out HSRP messages containing this information. Packets are sent to multicast address 224.0.0.2, which all the routers set up to be part of the HSRP group listen to. When a router does not see a hello message with a priority higher then the one it is set up with, it assumes the role of the active router. It goes into a corresponding state known as *active state*. The router with the second-highest priority becomes the group's *standby router.* At any given time, an HSRP group cannot have more than one active and one standby router.

As soon as a router assumes the responsibility of being the active router, it starts sending out hello messages indicating that it is the active router. The standby router starts sending out corresponding messages. These hellos are sent out periodically. To minimize network traffic, only the active and standby routers send periodic HSRP messages when the protocol has completed the election process. If at some point the standby router receives a message from the active router that has a lower priority than its priority, it can take over the role of the primary router by sending out a hello packet with its priority and containing parameters indicating that it wants to take over as the active router. This is known as a *coup* hello message.

Detecting a Failure

A failure is detected through the exchange of periodic hello message between the active and standby routers. (Because these messages are sent to a multicast address, other routers in the HSRP group also listen to them.) Each hello message from the active router contains a *holdtime*, or a holdtime can be configured on each router in the HSRP group. Upon receiving this message, the standby router starts its *active timer*. The active timer expires after an amount of time equal to the hold time has passed. If the standby router does not receive another hello from the active router before this timer expires, the active router is considered to have failed. If the standby router does not receive another hello message from the active router within this time, it goes into speak state again and starts to announce its priority to all the HSRP routers belonging to the multicast group. If another router in the group also has a virtual IP address configured, it participates in the election process by sending out hello messages with its own priority. The router with the highest priority takes over as the active router, and the next-highest router becomes the standby router.

Similarly, if the standby router fails to send a periodic hello message to the active router within the expiration of the standby timer on the active router, the active router goes into speak state, and the HSRP group goes through an election process to determine the active and standby routers.

HSRP Packet Format

HSRP uses User Datagram Protocol (UDP) port 1985 to send its hello messages. These messages are sent to the multicast address 224.0.0.2 with a TTL of 1 during the transition phases when active and standby routers are being elected. The source address is always the router's actual IP address rather than its virtual IP address.

The packet format as given in RFC 2281 is shown in Figure 3-4.

Figure 3-4   *Packet Format of HSRP Messages*

```
0 1 2 3 4 5 6 7 8 9 0 1 2 3 4 5 6 7 8 9 0 1 2 3 4 5 6 7 8 9 0 1
```

Version	Op Code	State	Hellotime
Holdtime	Priority	Group	Reserved
Authentication Data			
Authentication Data			
Virtual IP Address			

The definitions of the various fields in the packet, as described in RFC 2281, are as follows:

- **Version**—One octet

  The version of the HSRP messages.

- **Op Code**—One octet

  The op code describes the type of message contained in this packet. Possible values are as follows:

  - **0**—Hello
  - **1**—Coup
  - **2**—Resign

  Hello messages are sent to indicate that a router is running and is capable of becoming the active or standby router.

  Coup messages are sent when a router wants to become the active router.

Resign messages are sent when a router no longer wants to be the active router.

- **State**—One octet

  Internally, each router in the standby group implements a state machine. The State field describes the current state of the router sending the message. Possible values are

  - **0**—Initial
  - **1**—Learn
  - **2**—Listen
  - **4**—Speak
  - **8**—Standby
  - **16**—Active

- **Hellotime**—One octet

  This field is meaningful only in hello messages. It contains the approximate amount of time in seconds between hello messages the router sends.

  If the hellotime is not configured on a router, it *may* be learned from the hello message from the active router. The hellotime *should* be learned only if no hellotime is configured and the hello message is authenticated. A router that sends a hello message *must* insert the hellotime that it is using in the Hellotime field in the hello message. If the hellotime is not learned from a hello message from the active router and it is not manually configured, a default value of 3 seconds is recommended.

- **Holdtime**—One octet

  This field is meaningful only in hello messages. It contains the amount of time in seconds that the current hello message should be considered valid.

  If a router sends a hello message, receivers should consider that hello message valid for one holdtime. The holdtime *should* be at least three times the value of the hellotime and *must* be greater than the hellotime. If the holdtime is not configured on a router, it *may* be learned from the hello message from the active router. The holdtime *should* be learned only if the hello message is authenticated. A router that sends a hello message *must* insert the holdtime that it is using in the Holdtime field in the hello message.

  A router that is in active state *must not* learn new values for the hellotime and the holdtime from other routers, although it may continue to use values it learned from the previous active router. It *may* also use the Hellotime and Holdtime values learned through manual configuration. The active router *must not* use one configured time and one learned time. If the holdtime is not learned and it is not manually configured, a default value of 10 seconds is recommended.

- **Priority**—One octet

  This field is used to elect the active and standby routers. When comparing priorities of two different routers, the router with the numerically higher priority wins. In the case of routers with equal priority, the router with the higher IP address wins.

- **Group**—One octet

  This field identifies the standby group. For Token Ring, values between 0 and 2 inclusive are valid. For other media, values between 0 and 255 inclusive are valid.

- **Authentication Data**—Eight octets

  This field contains a clear-text eight-character reused password.

  If no authentication data is configured, the recommended default value is 0x63 0x69 0x73 0x63 0x6F 0x00 0x00 0x00.

- **Virtual IP Address**—Four octets

  The virtual IP address used by this group.

  If the virtual IP address is not configured on a router, it *may* be learned from the hello message from the active router. An address *should* be learned only if no address was configured and the hello message is authenticated.

HSRP Security

HSRP does not provide very strong mechanisms for providing security against attacks using this protocol as a tool. For example, an attacker who has gained access to the internal network can force the routers to choose a nonexistent router as the active router, creating a black hole and causing a resultant DoS attack. The authentication field in the HSRP message is more useful for protecting against misconfigurations rather than against attacks. It contains a password that is sent in clear text in the HSRP messages sent across the network. You will see how VRRP provides a better way of ensuring security in the implementation of a functionality very similar to HSRP.

HSRP Implementations

A typical example of the use of HSRP is illustrated in the following scenario (as documented on Cisco.com). Figure 3-5 shows the network topology for this scenario.

If Router A fails, Router B takes over the functioning on Router A and allows Pat to continue communicating with the Paris network. It is interesting to note that even if the routing converges so that all traffic is routed over a link that is up, the end hosts still might not be able to use the new routes, because they do not participate in any routing. Most hosts use a default gateway configured to point to a router to figure out where to send packets for machines not on the local LAN. Therefore, if Router A goes down, even if the routing protocols figure out another way to get to Router C from the Tokyo network, Pat's machine still sends all packets destined for Marceau's machine to Router A.

Figure 3-5   *Network Topology for the HSRP Implementation*

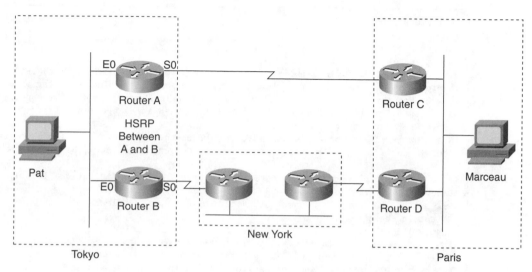

Some end hosts use ARP to figure out where to send their packets. If Pat wants to send a packet to Marceau's machine, Pat's machine ARPs for the IP address of Marceau's machine. Router A replies with its own MAC address to Pat's machine, telling it that it needs to send the packets to Router A. This is known as proxy ARP. In case the link between Router A and Router C goes down, routing might be able to figure out that the way to get the packets from Pat to Marceau is from Router B to Router C. However, Pat's machine does not know about this and continues sending packets to Router A's MAC address.

How HSRP provides redundancy

HSRP gets around the default gateway situation by defining a virtual IP address that is used as the default gateway for all machines instead of the actual address of the primary router, Router A. So when Router B takes over the responsibilities of Router A, the default gateway in all the end hosts does not need to be changed. Rather, Router B simply takes over the responsibility of taking care of packets sent to the virtual IP address.

Similarly, with HSRP configured, the end hosts using proxy ARP send packets to a virtual MAC address rather than the MAC address of the interface of Router A connected toward them. So when Router B takes over from Router A, it assumes the responsibility of taking care of the packets sent to this virtual MAC address.

Example 3-2 shows the configuration needed to set up Router A and Router B for HSRP. The goal is to allow Router B to take over as the active router if either the Ethernet 0 or the Serial 0 interface on Router A goes down.

Example 3-2 *Setting Up HSRP on Router A*

```
hostname RouterA
!
interface ethernet 0
ip address 10.1.1.1 255.255.255.0
!The command below defines the virtual IP address that will be used by the end
!hosts as default gateway. Note that this is the same on the primary router and the
!standby router. The number 1 is used to define the HSRP group to which the primary
!and standby routers will belong. This number is used in each command in the
!configuration that affects group 1.
!Note that at least one router in a standby group needs to have the virtual router
!address configured on it. The rest of the routers can then learn this IP address
!from this router.
!Also note that no virtual MAC address is defined in the configuration. This is
!because upon being turned on, HSRP automatically chooses a MAC address to be the
!virtual MAC address. This does not need to be configured. Please see the
!discussion before this example for details.
standby 1 ip 10.1.1.3
!The command below tells Router A to take over the responsibility of the primary
!router if it is the router with the highest priority in its HSRP group.
!Consequently, if Router A comes back after a failure, it resumes the
!responsibilities of the primary router from the standby Router B and becomes the
!active router. This is because the priority of Router B is left configured at 100,
!which is the default. Priority is determined first by the configured priority value
!and then by the IP address. In each case, a higher value is of greater priority.
!When a higher-priority router preempts a lower-priority router, it sends a coup
!message. When a lower-priority active router receives a coup message or a hello
!message from an active higher-priority router, it changes to speak state and sends
!a resign message.
standby 1 preempt
!The following command sets the priority of Router A to 105. Please note that this
!is the highest in group 1 because Router B's priority is configured to the default
!of 100. The value of 105 was chosen because the serial interface is also being
!tracked in this example. If it goes down, the router's priority decreases to 95,
!causing the standby router to send a coup message and taking over the active
!router status.
standby 1 priority 105
!The authentication string below is used to authenticate the messages being
!exchanged between the active and standby routers to monitor the health of the
!active router. This is an important precaution to preempt any malicious attempts
!to falsely classify a router as down when it is actually up or classify a down
!router as up. However, because the password is sent in clear with hello messages,
!it is at best a very poor method of security. See the discussion before this
!example for more details.

standby 1 authentication test
!The command below sets the time between hello health messages exchanged between
!the active and standby routers to 5 seconds and sets the holdtime before a router
!declares the other as down to 15 seconds.
standby 1 timers 5 15
```

Example 3-2 *Setting Up HSRP on Router A (Continued)*

```
!The standby track command below allows another interface on the router to be
!specified for the HSRP process to monitor to alter the HSRP priority for a given
!group. If the specified interface's line protocol goes down, the HSRP priority is
!reduced. By default, the value is reduced by 10. This means that another HSRP
!router with higher priority can become the active router if it has standby preempt
!enabled.

standby 1 track Serial0
```

Example 3-3 shows the configuration lines for Router B. No value is set up for the standby priority, which defaults to 100.

Example 3-3 *Setting Up HSRP on Router B*

```
hostname RouterB
!
interface ethernet 0
ip address 10.1.1.2 255.255.255.0
standby 1 ip 10.1.1.3
standby 1 preempt
standby 1 authentication test
standby 1 timers 5 15
standby 1 track Serial0
!
```

Failover Protocol

Failover is the protocol that is implemented in Cisco PIX Firewalls to allow the functionality of a failed firewall to be taken over by a standby firewall.

See Chapter 8, "PIX Firewall," for details of how PIX failover works and case studies including the configuration of failover in various manners.

Virtual Router Redundancy Protocol

VRRP is defined in RFC 2338. It is not a very widely deployed protocol on Cisco devices, but it is being adopted by a large number of companies throughout the industry because it is not covered by patents as the HSRP protocol is. Some Cisco devices such as the CVPN3000 concentrators also implement this protocol.

Differences Between HSRP and VRRP

Functionally, VRRP is very similar to HSRP. However, in terms of security, one of its major advantages over HSRP is that it allows authentication to be set up between the devices that are participating in the VRRP group. Also, unlike HSRP, which requires that the virtual router IP address not be the IP address of one of the routers, VRRP allows that to happen. It requires that if the router that "owns" the virtual router address is up and running, it should always be the virtual router master (equivalent to HSRP's active router). However, to ensure that the end hosts do not have to relearn the MAC address in case a failure occurs, it specifies the use of the MAC address 00-00-5E-00-01-*VRID,* where *VRID* is the ID of the virtual router (equivalent to an HSRP group identifier). Another difference is that VRRP does not use the coup or an equivalent message like HSRP does. The state machine for VRRP is simpler than the one used in HSRP. Although HSRP has six states and eight events in its finite state machine, VRRP has only three states and five events.

VRRP Overview

VRRP allows hosts to view a single router as their default gateway, with multiple routers available to take over the functionality of that router in case it fails, without any indication of such a failure to the end hosts. The hosts use a single IP address and MAC address to communicate with their default gateway. However, multiple routers, if they have been set up with VRRP, can, in the event of a failure of the master router, respond to frames sent to this MAC address or packets destined for this IP address. Under normal operations, a router known as the *master router* assumes ownership of this IP address and MAC address. All other routers participating in VRRP are said to be in *backup mode* until the master router fails. At that point, a backup router assumes ownership of the IP address and the MAC address the hosts consider their default gateway. This allows the hosts to continue sending traffic to their default gateway without any disruption. The IP address and MAC address are often said to belong to a *virtual router* because in effect they do not just belong to the master router but are used by hosts to communicate with the default gateway.

Determining the Master Router

The master router has one of its interfaces configured with the virtual router's IP address. This router has the highest priority of 255. All other routers must have a priority lower than this. The router with the second-highest priority assumes the role of the backup router.

Detecting a Failure

A failure is detected through the exchange of periodic advertisement messages sent by the master. Each advertisement from the master router contains an *advertisement interval*, or this interval can be configured on each router in the VRRP group. The standby router calculates a *master_down interval* from this interval as (3 * advertisement_interval) + skew_time. Upon receiving an advertisement from the master, the backup router starts its master_down timer. If the backup router does not receive another advertisement from the master router before this timer expires, the master router is considered to have failed. If the backup router does not receive another advertisement message from the master router within this time, it assumes the role of the master router. It sends an advertisement with its priority value in it. Similarly, all the other routers that were in backup state transition to master state and send out advertisements with their priority in it. All but the router with the highest priority transition back to standby state upon receipt of an advertisement packet with a priority higher than their own.

VRRP Security

The VRRP protocol includes three main authentication methods: no authentication, simple clear-text passwords, and strong authentication using IP authentication with Message Digest 5 (MD5) HMAC.

The strong authentication method uses the IP Authentication Header (AH) protocol. AH is the same protocol used in IPsec. AH provides a method for authenticating the VRRP packet's contents and header. The use of MD5 HMAC implies that a shared secret key is used to generate the hashes. A router sending a VRRP packet generates the MD5 hash and puts it in the advertisement being sent out. Upon receipt, the receiver recalculates the hash on the packet's contents and header, using the same key and MD5. If the result is the same, the message is indeed from a trusted host. If not, it must be discarded. This protects against attackers with access to the LAN sending out advertisements that can affect the election process or disrupt the network in some other way.

In addition, VRRP includes a mechanism (setting TTL = 255 and checking on receipt) that protects against VRRP packets being injected from another remote network. This limits most vulnerabilities to local attacks. HSRP, on the other hand, uses a TTL value of 1 in its messages.

VRRP Packet Format

The IP protocol number assigned by the IANA for VRRP is 112. All VRRP messages are sent to the multicast address 224.0.0.18 with TTL 255.

The IP field's in the VRRP packet are RFCed as follows::

- **Source Address**—The primary IP address of the interface the packet is being sent from.

- **Destination Address**—The IP multicast address as assigned by the IANA for VRRP is 224.0.0.18. This is a link local scope multicast address. Routers *must not* forward a datagram with this destination address, regardless of its TTL.

- **TTL**—The TTL *must* be set to 255. A VRRP router receiving a packet with TTL not equal to 255 *must* discard the packet.

- **Protocol**—The IP protocol number assigned by the IANA for VRRP is 112 (decimal).

The VRRP packet format as given in RFC 2338 is shown in Figure 3-6.

Figure 3-6   *Packet Format of VRRP Messages*

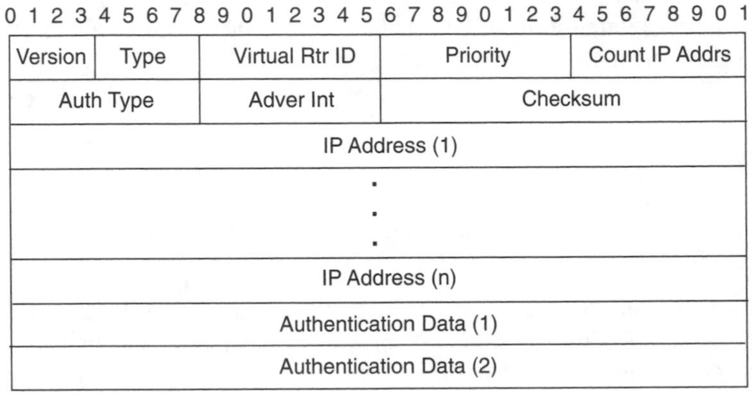

```
0 1 2 3 4 5 6 7 8 9 0 1 2 3 4 5 6 7 8 9 0 1 2 3 4 5 6 7 8 9 0 1
```

Version	Type	Virtual Rtr ID	Priority	Count IP Addrs
Auth Type		Adver Int	Checksum	
IP Address (1)				
.				
.				
.				
IP Address (n)				
Authentication Data (1)				
Authentication Data (2)				

The definitions of the various fields in the packet as described in RFC 2338 are as follows:

- **Version**—Specifies this packet's VRRP protocol version.

- **Type**—Specifies the type of this VRRP packet. The only packet type defined in this version of the protocol is 1, ADVERTISEMENT. A packet with an unknown type *must* be discarded.

- **Virtual Rtr ID (VRID)**—Identifies the virtual router this packet is reporting the status for.

- **Priority**—Specifies the sending VRRP router's priority for the virtual router. Higher values equal higher priority. This field is an 8-bit unsigned integer field.

  The priority value for the VRRP router that owns the IP address(es) associated with the virtual router *must* be 255 (decimal). VRRP routers backing up a virtual router *must* use priority values between 1 and 254 (decimal). The default priority value for VRRP routers backing up a virtual router is 100 (decimal).

  The priority value 0 has special meaning. It indicates that the current master has stopped participating in VRRP. This is used to trigger backup routers to quickly transition to master without having to wait for the current master to time out.

- **Count IP Addrs**—The number of IP addresses contained in this VRRP advertisement.

- **Authentication Type**—Identifies the authentication method being used. Authentication type is unique on a per-interface basis. The authentication Type field is an 8-bit unsigned integer. A packet with an unknown authentication type or that does not match the locally configured authentication method *must* be discarded.

The authentication methods currently defined are

— **0**—No authentication

— **1**—Simple-text password

— **2**—IP authentication header

No authentication—The use of this authentication type means that VRRP protocol exchanges are not authenticated. The contents of the Authentication Data field should be set to 0 on transmission and ignored on receipt.

Simple-text password—The use of this authentication type means that VRRP protocol exchanges are authenticated by a clear-text password. The contents of the Authentication Data field should be set to the locally configured password on transmission. There is no default password.

The receiver *must* check that the authentication data in the packet matches its configured authentication string. Packets that do not match *must* be discarded.

NOTE   There are security implications to using simple-text password authentication.

IP authentication header—The use of this authentication type means that VRRP protocol exchanges are authenticated using the mechanisms defined by the IP authentication header using HMAC-MD5-96. Keys may be configured either manually or via a key distribution protocol.

If a packet is received that does not pass the authentication check due to a missing authentication header or an incorrect message digest, the packet *must* be discarded. The contents of the Authentication Data field should be set to 0 on transmission and ignored on receipt.

- **Advertisement Interval (Adver Int)**—Indicates the time interval (in seconds) between advertisements. The default is 1 second. This field is used to troubleshoot misconfigured routers.

- **Checksum**—Used to detect data corruption in the VRRP message. The checksum is the 16-bit 1's complement of the 1's complement sum of the entire VRRP message, starting with the Version field. To compute the checksum, the Checksum field is set to 0.

- **IP Address(es)**—One or more IP addresses that are associated with the virtual router. The number of addresses included is specified in the Count IP Addrs field. These fields are used to troubleshoot misconfigured routers.

- **Authentication Data**—The authentication string is currently used only for simple-text authentication, similar to the simple-text authentication found in the Open Shortest Path First (OSPF) routing protocol. It has up to eight characters of plain text. If the configured authentication string is shorter than 8 bytes, the remaining space *must* be zero-filled. Any VRRP packet received with an authentication string that does not match the locally configured authentication string *must* be discarded. The authentication string is unique on a per-interface basis. This field has no default value.

Router Security

This section discusses how security can be improved on routers so that any attempts to disable the router, gain unauthorized access, or otherwise impair the functioning of the box can be stopped. It is important to note that these measures in most cases only secure the device itself and do not secure the whole network to which the device is connected. However, a device's security is critical to the network's security. A compromised device can cause the network to be compromised on a larger scale.

The following sections discuss some of the steps you can take to secure a router against attacks aimed at compromising the router itself.

Configuration Management

It is critical to keep copies of the router's configurations in a location other than the router's NVRAM. This is important in the event of an attack that leads to the configuration's being corrupted or changed in some manner. A backed-up configuration can allow the network to come back up very quickly in the manner in which it was supposed to function. This can be achieved by copying the router configurations to an FTP server at regular intervals or whenever the configuration is changed. Cron jobs can also be set up to pull configurations from the routers at regular intervals. Also, many freeware tool sets are available for this functionality, as well as a number of robust commercial packages, such as CiscoWorks2000. This is important in the event of an attack in which a router loses its configuration or has its configuration changed and needs to be restored to its original setting.

You can use the commands described next to copy a router's configuration to an FTP server. Although TFTP can be used as well, FTP is a more secure means of transporting this information.

The **copy** command, shown in Example 3-4, not only defines the IP address of the FTP server to move the file to but also specifies the username (user) and the password (password) to use to log in to the FTP server.

Example 3-4 *Router Configuration Copied to an FTP Server*

```
Router#copy running-config ftp://user:password@10.1.1.1
Address or name of remote host [10.1.1.1]?
Destination filename [Router-config]?
Writing Router-config !!
4500 bytes copied in 5.9 secs (750 bytes/sec)
```

The **ip ftp username** and **ip ftp password** commands can also be used to set up the username and password on the router for FTP.

It is also useful to have a backup of the software images running on a router in case of a network attack that removes the software from the router or corrupts it.

Controlling Access to the Router

It is important to control the accessibility to a router. There are two main mechanisms to gain access to a router for administrative purposes:

- vty ports
- TTY console and auxiliary ports

vty ports are generally used to gain remote interactive access to the router. The most commonly used methods of vty access are Telnet, SSH, and rlogin.

TTY lines in the form of console and auxiliary ports are generally used to gain access when a physical connection is available to the router in the form of a terminal connected to the router or a modem hooked to it. The console port is used to log in to the router by physically connecting a terminal to the router's console port. The aux port can be used to attach to an RS-232 port of a CSU/DSU, a protocol analyzer, or a modem to the router.

vty access to a router using Telnet is by far the most common router administration tool. Console access and access through the aux port using a modem are out-of-band methods often used as a last resort on most networks. However, using a mechanism known as reverse Telnet, it might be possible for remote users to gain access to a router through the auxiliary or console ports. This needs to be protected against as well, as described next.

Controlling vty Access

At a minimum, you can follow these steps to control vty access into a router:

Step 1 Restrict access only via the protocols that will be used by the network administrators.

The commands shown in Example 3-5 set up vty lines 0 through 4 for Telnet and SSH access only. In Cisco IOS Release 11.1, the **none** keyword was added and became the default. Before Cisco IOS Release 11.1, the default keyword was **all**, allowing all types of protocols to connect via the vty lines by default.

Example 3-5 *Setting Up the vty Lines on a Router for Telnet and SSH Access Only*

```
line vty 0 4
 transport input telnet ssh
```

It is important to realize that although Telnet is by far the most popular way of accessing a router for administrative purposes, it is also the most insecure. SSH provides an encrypted mechanism for accessing a router. It is advisable to set up SSH on a router and then disable Telnet access to it.

Step 2 Configure access lists to allow vty access only from a restricted set of addresses.

In Example 3-6, for the vty lines 0 to 3, access list 5 is used. This access list allows access from a restricted set of IP addresses only. However, for the last vty line, line 4, the more-restrictive access list 6 is used. This helps prevent DoS attacks aimed at stopping Telnet access to the router for administrative purposes. Only one session to a vty port can occur at any given time. So an attacker can leave all the ports dangling at the login prompt, denying legitimate use. The restrictive access list on line 4 is an effort to keep at least the last vty line available in such an eventuality. Note that the command **service tcp-keepalives-in** can also be used to track such left-to-idle TCP sessions to the router. This command basically turns on a TCP keepalive mechanism for the router to use for all its TCP connections.

Example 3-6 *Setting Up a Router with Restricted vty Access*

```
service tcp-keepalives-in
service tcp-keepalives-out

line vty 0 3
 access-class 5 in
line vty 4
 access-class 6 in

access-list 5 permit host 10.1.1.43
access-list 5 permit host 10.1.2.19
access-list 5 permit host 10.1.2.23
access-list 5 permit host 10.1.2.67
access-list 5 permit host 10.1.1.49
access-list 5 permit host 10.1.1.101
```

Example 3-6   *Setting Up a Router with Restricted vty Access (Continued)*

```
access-list 5 permit host 10.1.2.67
access-list 5 permit host 10.1.2.109
access-list 5 deny any log

access-list 6 permit 10.1.1.1 0.0.0.0
access-list 6 deny any log
```

It is also a good idea to set up logging for the access lists used to allow Telnet access.

Step 3   Set up short timeouts.

This is an important precaution needed to protect against Telnet DoS attacks, hijacking attacks, and Telnet sessions left unattended, consuming unnecessary resources. The command shown in Example 3-7 sets the timeout value to 5 minutes and 30 seconds. The default is 10 minutes.

Example 3-7   *Setting Up Timeouts for vty Access*

```
line vty 0 4
 exec-timeout 5 30
```

Step 4   Set up authentication for vty access.

It is critical to have user authentication enabled for vty access. This can be done using local or RADIUS/TACACS authentication. Example 3-8 shows local authentication, but RADIUS/TACACS is a more scalable method of setting this up. See Chapters 16 and 19 for more examples of how to use the AAA commands to achieve scalable security.

Example 3-8   *Setting Up Authentication for vty Access*

```
aaa new-model
aaa authentication login for-telnet local

username cisco password 7 <removed>

line vty 0 4
  login authentication for-telnet
```

Controlling TTY Access

A lot of effort spent controlling access through the vty lines can go to waste if the TTY lines are not controlled for access. The TTY lines are harder to use to gain access, because they generally require some sort of physical access to allow access. However, having a number to dial in to the modem hooked to a router's aux port or using reverse Telnet to get into the console port of a router hooked up to a terminal server remotely are both methods still used to gain easy illegitimate access to routers without physical proximity.

Some of the methods that can be used on the vty ports to control access, such as using access lists, cannot be used on TTY lines. However, some other techniques, such as user authentication and disabling protocol access using the **transport** command, are still valid and can be set up in a fashion similar to how vty configurations are done.

If appropriate, the use of TTY lines remotely via reverse Telnet should be disabled. You can do this using the command shown in Example 3-9.

Example 3-9 *Disabling Console Access to a Router*

```
line con0
 transport input none
```

Starting in Cisco IOS version 12.2(2) T, you can access a router's console port using the SSH protocol. This is an important feature, because it gives users much more security. Example 3-10 shows how this is set up. Note that a separate rotary group needs to be defined for each line that will be accessed via SSH. See the next section for the rest of the command needed to allow a router to act as an SSH server and accept connections.

Example 3-10 *Setting Up Only SSH Access to a Router's Console Port*

```
line con0
 login authentication default
 rotary 1
 transport input ssh

ip ssh port 2001 rotary 1
```

Securing Access to the Router

In addition to setting up user authentication on the router, it is also important to use SSH or similar methods to encrypt the communication sessions to the router.

The best way to gain access to a router for administrative purposes is by using an IPsec VPN client. SSH can also be used for this purpose, but the Cisco recommended method of doing this is via IPsec. Going forward, IPsec is the protocol Cisco will promote as the secure router administrative access tool.

Chapter 13, "IPsec," contains a detailed discussion of how to set up IPsec VPNs. Generally, when an IPsec VPN client is set up for accessing a LAN behind a router, two IP addresses are defined on it. One is the IP address of the IPsec gateway (the router) to which it sets up a tunnel. The other IP address is often the subnet behind the router, traffic to which is sent encrypted by the VPN client. In case the VPN client is being used to administer the router, both the gateway IP address and the destination IP address for which the VPN client encrypts traffic are the same. This means that the VPN client encrypts all the traffic it sends to the router gateway, thus establishing secure administrative access.

Setting up SSH on a router is a fairly simple exercise. Note that only SSH version 1.x is supported by Cisco IOS Software. No plans to support version 2 are in the works. Example 3-11 shows how a router can be set up to accept SSH connections.

Example 3-11 *Setting Up a Router to Accept SSH Connections*

```
!The commands below are used to define the router's host name and domain name. This
!is necessary because the RSA keys used for encryption and decryption are named
!using these parameters and also are bound to the router via these parameters.
hostname router1
ip domain-name cisco.com
!The command below is used to generate a default 1024-bit RSA key pair to be used
!for encryption and decryption.
cry key generate rsa
!The following line prevents non-SSH Telnet to the router. Note that all the other
!techniques we looked at in an earlier section on restricting and controlling vty
!access, such as the use of access lists, are also valid here.

line vty 0 4
 transport input ssh
!The following commands when configured in global configuration mode help prevent
!certain types of attacks on the router through SSH. The first command clears out
!SSH connections that have been idle for 60 seconds, whereas the second command
!limits authentication retries to two attempts.
ip ssh time-out 60
ip ssh authentication-retries 2
```

Password Management

The best place for passwords is on an authentication server. But some passwords still might need to be configured on the router itself. It is important to ensure that these passwords are properly encrypted to be secure from prying eyes (people looking over the network administrator's shoulder as he or she works on a configuration). It is important to configure an *enable secret* on the router (rather than a plain password known simply as the *enable password*) to get administrative access to the box. The enable secret uses MD5 to encrypt the password, and the hash is extremely difficult to reverse. Example 3-12 shows its usage.

Cisco IOS version 12.2(8) T introduced the enhanced password security feature. It allows MD5 encryption for username passwords to be configured. Before this feature was introduced, two types of passwords were associated with usernames: type 0, which is a cleartext password visible to any user who has access to privileged mode on the router, and type 7, which has a password with a weak type of encryption. Type 7 passwords can be retrieved from encrypted text by using publicly available tools. Example 3-12 shows how this new feature can be implemented.

It is also important to ensure that the rest of the passwords on the box, such as CHAP passwords, are also encrypted so that a casual view of the configuration does not reveal them. You can do this using the **service password-encryption** command, as shown in Example 3-12. The catch with this command is that it uses type 7 encryption rather than the MD5 hash used by **enable secret** commands. This type of encryption is weaker and easier to crack than MD5 encryption. Password encryption set up using this command is applied to all passwords, including username passwords, authentication key passwords, the privileged command password, console and virtual terminal line access passwords, and Border Gateway Protocol (BGP) neighbor passwords. However, note that with the introduction of the new feature discussed in the preceding section, usernames and their corresponding passwords can now be hidden using MD5 hashing.

Example 3-12 *Setting Up a Router to Encrypt All the Passwords in Its Configuration and Encrypt the Password for Username cisco Using the New MD5 Hashing*

```
Router#(config-t) service password-encryption
Router#(config-t) enable secret x1398y77z998
Router#(config-t) username cisco secret 0 x10y34z009

Router#Write Terminal
<snip>
enable secret 0 $1$53Ew$Dp8.E4JGpg7rKxQa49BF9/
username cisco secret 5 $1$fBYK$rH5/OChyx/
<snip>
line vty 0 4
 password 7 110A1016141D5A5E57
```

Although password encryption can hide passwords from prying eyes, the passwords themselves are still subject to various types of attacks, including dictionary attacks. Therefore, it is still very important to choose strong passwords.

Logging Events on the Router

Logging events on a router is an important part of the security mechanisms on the router. Comprehensive logs with good time stamps can be parsed using various commercially available software to look for relevant information about access to the router or access attempts. It is highly recommended that you use Network Time Protocol (NTP) on routers to allow accurate time stamps to be available. See the following URL for a description of how to set up NTP:

www.cisco.com/univercd/cc/td/doc/product/software/ios121/121cgcr/fun_c/fcprt3/fcd303.htm#xtocid2708216

Example 3-13 demonstrates how to set up logging on the router.

Example 3-13 *Setting Up Logging on a Router*

```
service timestamps debug datetime msec localtime show-timezone
service timestamps log datetime msec localtime show-timezone
!
no logging console
logging buffered 16384
logging trap debugging
logging facility local7
logging 169.223.32.1
logging 169.223.45.8
logging source-interface loopback0
```

Disabling Unnecessary Services

You should disable services such as those listed in Table 3-1 if they are not being actively used on the router. These services can be used as back doors to gain access to the router. Table 3-1 describes the services you should disable if they are inactive and how to do so.

Table 3-1   *Disabling Unnecessary Services*

Service	Legitimate Use of Service	Command(s) Used to Disable Service
TCP small servers	Enables the minor TCP services echo, chargen, discard, and daytime.	**no service tcp-small-serv**
UDP small servers	Enables the minor UDP services echo, chargen, and discard.	**no service udp-small-serv**
Finger server	The Finger protocol allows users throughout the network to get a list of the users currently using a particular routing device. The information displayed includes the processes running on the system, line number, connection name, idle time, and terminal location.	**no ip finger** **no service finger**

continues

Table 3-1 *Disabling Unnecessary Services (Continued)*

Service	Legitimate Use of Service	Command(s) Used to Disable Service
BootP server	BootP uses UDP to formulate a network request to allow a device to obtain and configure its own IP information, such as IP address and subnet mask.	**no ip bootp server**
DHCP	Dynamic Host Configuration Protocol (DHCP) is essentially an extension of BootP. DHCP lets network administrators configure remote hosts from a central configuration server.	**no ip dhcp-server**
Configuration auto-load	The **service config** command is used to let the router automatically configure the system from the file specified by the **boot host** or **boot network** command. If no host or network configuration filenames are specified, the router uses the default configuration files. The default network configuration file is network-confg. The default host configuration file is *host*-confg, where *host* is the router's host name. If the Cisco IOS Software cannot resolve its host name, the default host configuration file is router-confg.	**no boot network** **no service config**
CDP	Cisco Discovery Protocol (CDP) is used primarily to obtain protocol addresses of neighboring devices and to discover those devices' platforms. CDP can also be used to show information about the interfaces your router uses.	**no cdp running** (globally) **no cdp enable** (on an interface)
RCP and RSH	To configure the router to allow remote users to execute commands on it using rsh, use the **ip rcmd rsh-enable** global configuration command. To configure the Cisco IOS Software to allow remote users to copy files to and from the router, use the **ip rcmd rcp-enable** global configuration command.	**no ip rcmd rsh-enable** **no ip rcmd rcp-enable**

Table 3-1   *Disabling Unnecessary Services (Continued)*

Service	Legitimate Use of Service	Command(s) Used to Disable Service
PAD	To enable all packet assembler/disassembler (PAD) commands and connections between PAD devices and access servers, use the **service pad** global configuration command.	**no service pad**
NTP	The Network Time Protocol (NTP) is used to synchronize a router's time to another router or reference time source.	**ntp disable** (on an interface basis)

Using Loopback Interfaces

Loopback interfaces can play an important part in securing a device against attacks. Generally, any router is dependent on a series of services for which it has to access other routers and servers. It is important to make sure that those servers to which the router goes to get certain information accept connections only from a very small block of trusted IP addresses. Considering the entire private addressing scheme as secure can be dangerous as well. Loopbacks can play a vital role in making this happen. A block of IP addresses can be assigned to be used by loopback, and then all routers can be forced to use these loopback IP addresses as source addresses when accessing the servers. The servers can then also be locked down to allow access only from this block of IP addresses.

Some examples of servers to which access can be restricted in this manner are SNMP, TFTP, TACACS, RADIUS, Telnet, and syslog servers. Example 3-14 lists the commands required to force the router to use the IP address on the loopback0 interface as the source address when sending packets to the respective servers.

Example 3-14 *Using Loopback Interfaces' IP address as the Source Address for Packets Being Sent to Various Servers*

```
snmp-server trap-source Loopback0
ip tftp source-interface Loopback0
ip tacacs source-interface Loopback0
ip radius source-interface Loopback0
ip telnet source-interface Loopback0
logging source-interface Loopback0
```

Controlling SNMP as a Management Protocol

Device and network management protocols are important to maintain any network. However, these services can be used as back doors to gain access to routers and/or get information about the devices. The attacker can then use this information to stage an attack.

SNMP is the most commonly used network management protocol. However, it is important to restrict SNMP access to the routers on which it is enabled. On routers on which it is not being used, you should turn it off using the command shown in Example 3-15.

Example 3-15 *Disabling SNMP on a Router*

```
no snmp-server
```

SNMP can be used in read-only, read, and write modes. From a security perspective, it is recommended that you use read-only mode on routers. Although this mode can still give up a lot of information about the router to a hacker, it is safer than read and write modes, which can give you further control over modifying the routers' configurations via SNMP. In either case, it is important to make sure that access into the network via SNMP is blocked at the network's boundary. Example 3-16 shows a pair of access lists on a network edge router to stop SNMP access from outside the network.

Example 3-16 *A Pair of Access Lists on a Network Edge Router Stopping SNMP Access from Outside the Network*

```
access-list 100 deny udp any any eq snmp
access-list 100 deny udp any any eq snmptrap
```

SNMP comes in three flavors: v1, v2, and v3. SNMP v1 and v2 are by their very nature not very secure protocols. The only authentication mechanism available in SNMP v1 and v2 is via community strings. It is important not to use the community strings 'public', 'private', 'cisco', or your company name. These are expected and are commonly used in attacks. You should choose community strings the same way you choose passwords. If the only choice is between v1 and v2, v2 is a somewhat more secure version.

If community strings are also configured for notifications, they must be different from the community strings used for other purposes. This is considered a Best Current Practice with SNMP configuration, and it also avoids unrelated issues with some Cisco IOS Software releases. The SNMP community strings for read-only or read-write access should be protected against unauthorized disclosure occurring from receiving or sniffing a notification message.

Example 3-17 shows you how to configure SNMP in a secure manner on a router.

Example 3-17 *Setting Up SNMP in a Secure Manner on a Router*

```
!The following line defines the community string 5nmc02m as well as the access
!list used to restrict access to the router via SNMP.
snmp-server community 5nmc02m RO 98
!The following line specifies the use of the router's loopback interface as the
!source IP address of the SNMP packets.
snmp-server trap-source Loopback0
```

Example 3-17 *Setting Up SNMP in a Secure Manner on a Router (Continued)*

```
!The following command is used to turn on authentication for traps.
snmp-server trap-authentication
snmp-server enable traps config
!The following command defines the SNMP server to send the traps to.
snmp-server host 215.17.1.1 5nmc02m

access-list 98 permit host 10.1.1.49
```

SNMP v3

SNMP v3 as defined in RFCs 2271 through 2275 provides guidelines for secure implementation of the SNMP protocol. RFC 2271 defines the following as the four major threats against SNMP that SNMP v3 attempts to provide some level of protection against:

- **Modification of information**—The modification threat is the danger that some unauthorized entity might alter in-transit SNMP messages generated on behalf of an authorized user in such a way as to effect unauthorized management operations, including falsifying an object's value.

- **Masquerade**—The masquerade threat is the danger that management operations not authorized for a certain user might be attempted by assuming the identity of a user who has the appropriate authorization.

- **Disclosure**—The disclosure threat is the danger of eavesdropping on exchanges between managed agents and a management station. Protecting against this threat might be required as a matter of local policy.

- **Message stream modification**—The SNMP protocol is typically based on a connectionless transport service that may operate over any subnetwork service. The reordering, delay, or replay of messages can and does occur through the natural operation of many such subnetwork services. The message stream modification threat is the danger that messages might be maliciously reordered, delayed, or replayed to a greater extent than can occur through the natural operation of a subnetwork service to effect unauthorized management operations.

Protection Against Attacks

SNMP v3 aims to protect against these types of attacks by providing the following security elements:

- **Message integrity**—Ensuring that a packet has not been tampered with in transit.

- **Authentication**—Determining that the message is from a valid source.

- **Encryption**—Scrambling a packet's contents to prevent it from being seen by an unauthorized source.

Table 3-2 compares the levels of security provided by each of the SNMP protocols available on networks today.

Table 3-2   *Security in Various Versions of SNMP*

Model	Level	Authentication	Encryption	What Happens
V1	noAuthNoPriv	Community string	No	Uses a community string match for authentication.
V2c	noAuthNoPriv	Community string	No	Uses a community string match for authentication.
V3	noAuthNoPriv	Username	No	Uses a username match for authentication.
V3	authNoPriv	MD5 or SHA	No	Provides authentication based on the HMAC-MD5 or HMAC-SHA algorithms.
V3	authPriv	MD5 or SHA	DES	Provides authentication based on the HMAC-MD5 or HMAC-SHA algorithms. Provides DES 56-bit encryption in addition to authentication based on the CBC-DES (DES-56) standard.

See the following URL for details on how to set up SNMPv3:

http://www.cisco.com/univercd/cc/td/doc/product/software/ios120/120newft/120t/120t3/snmp3.htm

Controlling HTTP as a Management Protocol

If HTTP is not being used to administer the router, it is prudent to turn it off.

The command shown in Example 3-18 ensures that the server is not running.

Example 3-18 *Disabling HTTP Access to a Router*

```
no ip http server
```

If there is a need to configure the HTTP server because web-based configuration of the router is needed, the setup shown in Example 3-19 can be used to keep it secure.

Example 3-19 *Setting Up HTTP Access to the Router in a Secure Manner*

```
!The command below forces the use of a nonstandard port for HTTP
ip http port 8765
!The command below sets up AAA authentication for HTTP
ip http authentication aaa
!The following two lines define an access list to restrict HTTP access to the
!router to only one address, 10.1.1.1
ip http access-class 1
access-list 1 permit ip 10.1.1.1
```

Using CEF as a Switching Mechanism

Quite a few modern SYN floods and distributed denial of service (DDoS) attacks use a large number of random or pseudo-random IP addresses as ultimate targets. Routers using the traditional switching mechanisms need to update routing caches when packets destined for new addresses arrive. An attack aimed at a small number of target hosts does not prove burdensome to the algorithms maintaining these caches, but larger attacks with more end hosts can prove CPU-intensive.

Because CEF replaces the normal routing cache with a data structure that mirrors the entire routing table, CEF does away with the need to update the cache each time a new IP address needs to be routed to. This is a useful feature to have during a large-scale SYN or DDoS attack. Therefore, on routers that have CEF capability, it might be a good idea to use this switching function.

You enable CEF using the command shown in Example 3-20 in global configuration mode.

Example 3-20 *Turning on CEF on a Router*

```
Ip CEF
```

Setting Up the Scheduler from a Security Perspective

When a router is subjected to a large-scale network attack (especially a DDoS attack), it is possible for the router to become so busy responding to the interrupts on its interfaces due to the large number of packets arriving on them that it fails to perform any of the other functions it is configured to perform. Therefore, it is important to configure the router to return to processing process-level tasks besides handling interrupts at a regular interval. This can be achieved by using the **scheduler allocate** or **scheduler interval** command. A typical value to use for these is 500 ms, meaning that the router should return to processing noninterrupt tasks at least every 500 ms. Example 3-21 shows the commands that can be used to manipulate the timer values for these two commands.

Example 3-21 *Configuration Template for the* **scheduler allocate** *and* **scheduler interval** *Commands*

```
!The following command defines the maximum amount of time that can elapse without
!running the lowest-priority system processes.
scheduler interval 500

!The following command, for the Cisco 7200 series and Cisco 7500 series, changes
1the default time that the CPU spends on process tasks and fast switching.
scheduler allocate 30000 2000
```

It is generally recommended that you not change the defaults of the **scheduler allocate** command.

Using NTP

It is important to use NTP to make sure that all the routers on the network are time-synchronized. This is critical from several perspectives:

- It allows logs from security incidents to be interpreted based on time stamps.

- It allows logs to be read and compared across the whole network.

- It allows AAA records to be timed.

Setting up NTP on a router is fairly straightforward. The following link gives details on how to do this:

www.cisco.com/univercd/cc/td/doc/product/software/ios121/121cgcr/fun_c/fcprt3/fc d303.htm#xtocid2708216

It important to set up authentication between devices exchanging NTP information to keep a device from getting incorrect time information from a malicious source. In Example 3-22, Router A is configured as the NTP master. Example 3-23 configures Router B as the NTP slave and how Router B uses it as a source after authenticating it as valid.

Example 3-22 *Setting Up Router A as an NTP Master*

```
Router A: NTP master

!The command below defines the MD5 key to use for authentication. This key !needs
to be the same on all routers doing authentication.
ntp authentication-key 20 md5 04590404 7


ntp trusted-key 20
ntp master 10
```

Example 3-23 *Setting Up Router B as an NTP Slave*

```
Router B:


ntp authentication-key 20 md5 04590404 7
ntp trusted-key 20
!The command below defines the IP address of the NTP master server--Router A in
!this case.
ntp server 144.254.33.100 key 20
```

Login Banners

A login banner is a useful place to put information that can help make the system more secure. Here are some do's and don'ts of what to put in a login banner:

- A login banner should advertise the fact that unauthorized access to the system is prohibited. You can discuss the specific wording with legal counsel.

- A login banner can also advertise the fact that access to the device will be tracked and monitored. This is a legal requirement in certain places. Again, legal counsel can help.

- It is advisable not to include the word "welcome" in a banner.

- It is inappropriate to include information that says anything about the operating system, hardware, or any logical configuration of the device. The least amount of information about the system's ownership and identity should be revealed.

- Other notices to ward off criminal activity may also be included.

When a user connects to the router, the MOTD banner appears before the login prompt. After the user logs in to the router, the EXEC banner or incoming banner is displayed, depending on the type of connection. For a reverse Telnet login, the incoming banner is displayed. For all other connections, the router displays the EXEC banner.

All these banners are configured in global configuration mode as shown in example 3-24.

Example 3-24 *Various Mechanisms Available on Cisco Routers to Set Up Banners*

```
!To define and enable a message-of-the-day (MOTD) banner, use the banner motd
!global configuration command.
banner motd #

!To define and enable a customized banner to be displayed before the username and
!password login prompts, use the banner login global configuration command.
banner login d message d

!To define and enable a banner to be displayed when there is an incoming connection
!to a terminal line from a host on the network, use the banner incoming global
!configuration command.
banner incoming d message d
```

Banners can also be set up using AAA commands, as shown in Example 3-25.

Example 3-25 *Creating Banners to Be Used with AAA*

```
aaa new-model
aaa authentication banner *Text of Banner*
aaa authentication fail-message *Login Failed.*
aaa authentication login default group radius
```

The commands shown in Example 3-25 produce the following output when the user fails to give a correct password:

```
Text of Banner
Username:
Password:
Login Failed.
```

Capturing Core Dumps

One of the consequences of an attack on a router might be the crashing of the router. Because a router often recovers from the crash and continues its business after rebooting, it is important to keep track of the reasons why the router crashed to help fix bugs in the software that were exploited to cause the crash.

Core dumps are a means of collecting such information. When the router crashes, the memory image is stored in a core file, which can be copied to a separate system, such as an FTP server, automatically for future analysis.

Example 3-26 shows how to set up this facility on a router.

Example 3-26 *Setting Up a Router to FTP Core Dumps to an FTP Server*

```
ip ftp username cisco
ip ftp password 7 045802150C2E
!The following command tells the router to use FTP to transfer the core file.
exception protocol ftp
!The following command defines the IP address of the server to transfer the core
file to.
exception dump 169.223.32.1
```

Using service nagle to Improve Telnet Access During High CPU Events

In the event of an attack on a network, excess traffic can seriously impair a router's performance due to high CPU consumption. An attack on the router itself can cause a similar situation. Telnet is often used as a primary mechanism of administering a router. However, when the router load is very high, Telnet can be very slow, and Telnet itself can cause further load on the router CPU. This can delay any work that needs to be done on the router to thwart the attack via Telnet. A service known as *nagle* can be turned on a router to improve telnet performance during such an event. This service can be turned on using the command shown in Example 3-27.

Example 3-27 *Turning on the Nagle Protocol on the Router*

```
service nagle
```

Nagle is an algorithm that can be enabled as a service on a Cisco router. It allows the Cisco router to pace the TCP connection for Telnet in a way that reduces the burden on the CPU and generally improves the performance of the Telnet session. CCO explains the working of this protocol as follows:

> The first character typed after connection establishment is sent in a single packet, but TCP holds any additional characters typed until the receiver acknowledges the previous packet. Then the second, larger packet is sent and additional typed characters are saved until the acknowledgement comes back. The effect is to accumulate characters into larger chunks, and pace them out to the network at a rate matching the round-trip time of the given connection. This method is usually good for all TCP-based traffic. However, do not enable the Nagle slow packet avoidance algorithm if you have XRemote users on X Window sessions.

PIX Firewall Security

The PIX, being a security-specific device, is fairly robust from a security perspective. This section talks about some of the important techniques you can use to make the firewall even more secure from a device perspective. The earlier section "Router Security" talks about the reasons for having most of these safeguards, so I will not repeat them here but rather will concentrate on the actual implementations.

Configuration Management

Managing a configuration away from the PIX box in case of an attack is important. PIX allows configurations to be saved on a TFTP server via the **write net** command. The **write net** command writes the PIX configuration to a TFTP server specified by the **tftp-server** command.

The configuration should be saved regularly and after all changes are made to the PIX setup. It is prudent to save the PIX images to a server as well.

Care needs to be taken with where the TFTP server resides, because the PIX as of version 6.2.1 does not have the concept of a source interface. Therefore, it is possible to misconfigure the PIX and send management-related traffic through a lower-security interface and possibly over an untrusted network.

Controlling Access to the PIX

The PIX Firewall can be accessed in two primary ways:

- vty port
- TTY console

vty access via Telnet ports is the most common way to access a PIX Firewall for administrative purposes. PIX can be accessed from the inside network via plain-text Telnet. However, to access it from the outside interface, an IPsec client needs to be set up to initiate a VPN connection to the PIX using IPsec.

Telnet access needs to be restricted to certain addresses to ensure security. Example 3-28 shows how restricted Telnet access can be set up on a PIX Firewall.

Example 3-28 *Setting Up Restricted Telnet Access on a PIX Firewall*

```
!The following command sets up the PIX to accept Telnet connections from the host
!192.168.1.2 only on the inside interface.
telnet 192.168.1.2 255.255.255.255 inside
!The command below sets up the PIX to accept connections for Telnet on its outside
!interface; however, a VPN needs to be set up to allow this to happen.
telnet 209.165.200.225 255.255.255.224 outside
!The following command can be used to set up a password for Telnet access to the
!PIX. The password defined is saved encrypted in the PIX config.
passwd watag00s1am
```

Telnet access can also be authenticated via a AAA server, as shown in Example 3-29.

Example 3-29 *Setting Up Restricted Telnet Access Using AAA on a PIX Firewall*

```
!The first line below defines the server group, telnetaccess, and the protocol it
!uses, TACACS+.
aaa-server telnetaccess protocol tacacs+
!The line below defines the AAA server IP address that this server group,
!telnetaccess, uses, along with the password to authenticate to this server, cisco.
aaa-server telnetaccess (inside) host 172.18.124.111 cisco timeout 5
!The line below binds the server group configured above to the authentication of
!Telnet access to the PIX.
aaa authentication telnet console telnetaccess
```

Access to the PIX from the TTY ports is harder to control. The best defense is to place PIX in a secure physical location and to ensure that no modems are insecurely connected to the PIX. As soon as an attacker is physically consoled in, it is difficult to stop him or her from undertaking a wide variety of malicious activities. The earlier section "Physical Security" discusses how to ensure that a device such as PIX is protected from physical attacks.

Securing Access to the PIX

You can secure remote access to the PIX using SSH or IPsec. Both methods provide encrypted access to the PIX. We will discuss SSH in this section, leaving VPNs for a later chapter. IPsec is the preferred method for giving administrative access to a PIX.

Example 3-30 illustrates how to use SSH to provide secure and authenticated access to the PIX Firewall. PIX supports SSH version 1.x.

Example 3-30 *Accepting SSH Connections and Authenticating SSH Users Via AAA on a PIX Firewall*

```
!The two commands below are used to define the PIX's host name and domain name.
!This is necessary because the RSA keys used for encryption and decryption are
!named using these parameters and also are bound to the PIX via these parameters.
hostname pix123
domain-name test.com
!The command below is used to generate a 1024-bit RSA public/private key pair to
!be used for encryption and decryption.
ca generate rsa key 1024
!The command below is used to save the keys generated to Flash memory.
ca save all
!The commands below are used to tell the PIX to accept SSH connections on its
!outside interface and to set the idle timeout for SSH sessions to 15 minutes.
ssh 10.1.1.1 255.255.255.255 outside
ssh timeout 7
!Furthermore, the PIX can be set up to do authentication for the SSH users
!connecting to it. The following command defines the AAA server group, ssh123, to
!use for authentication. The AAA server address, 10.1.1.200, and the key to
!authenticate to it, mysecure, are also defined.
aaa-server ssh123 (inside) host 10.1.1.200 mysecure
!The following command binds the AAA server group to the protocol TACACS+.
aaa-server ssh123 protocol tacacs+
!The following command is used to tell the PIX box to do authentication for the
!SSH users using the AAA server group, ssh123, defined above.
aaa authenticate ssh console ssh123
```

Password Management

It is important to set up passwords for gaining privileged access to the PIX. These passwords are by default encrypted to protect against over-the-shoulder-type attacks.

The **enable password** command sets up the PIX to save the password in an encrypted format in the configuration. Example 3-31 shows how to use the **enable password** command on the PIX Firewall.

Example 3-31 *Setting the Enable Password on a PIX Firewall*

```
pixfirewall#enable password test123
```

The use of the keyword encrypted at the end of this configuration line tells the PIX that the password being entered is already encrypted, so it must not encrypt it any further but use it as is. Therefore, the encrypted keyword should be used only when the password has already been encrypted using some other means.

Logging Events on the PIX

Logs are an integral part of the security system that PIX is part of. Whereas PIX Firewall attempts to block intrusion attempts, the logs tell the tale of how the attempt was made. Such information is critical in discovering compromises that have already occurred in the network. This information also gives you clues to misconfigurations of the firewall itself. Example 3-32 shows how this can be set up.

Example 3-32 *Setting Up Logging to a Logging Server on a PIX Firewall*

```
!The following command turns on logging on the PIX.
logging on
!The command below defines the logging server to send the log messages to. You
!must specify the interface on which the server is sitting.
logging host inside 192.168.1.5
!The command below specifies the level up to which logging messages should be sent.
!Generally, level 3 (which is "errors") is sufficient for most production networks.
!However, for troubleshooting purposes, you may choose to log up to the level of
!debugs (level 7). See Chapter 8 for more details on PIX Firewall logging.
logging trap error
!Most UNIX syslog servers expect messages to have the facility set to 20.
logging facility 20
```

PIX log messages have the following format:

```
%PIX-Level-Message_number: Message_text
```

See the following link for a list of PIX messages:

www.cisco.com/univercd/cc/td/doc/product/iaabu/pix/pix_60/syslog/ pixemsgs.htm#11493

Switch Security

For the purpose of our discussion here, I will concentrate on the Catalyst 5500 switches. Similar mechanisms can be used to set up security on other types of switches. Switches perform most of their functions at Layer 2 of the OSI model. They often do not participate in Layer 3 and above operations actively. Consequently, access to switches through various Layer 3 and above functions such as Telnet and rsh is very limited. This provides for switch security as well. This section looks at some of the mechanisms you can put into place to further strengthen switch security.

Configuration Management

It is important in switches, as in any other network device, to back up and save the configurations periodically and/or after you make changes.

On the Catalyst 5500 Supervisor III engines, the commands shown in Example 3-33 are used to copy the configuration file using TFTP. In earlier releases of the engine, the **write network** command works.

Example 3-33 *Process Used on a Switch to TFTP Configuration Files to a TFTP Server*

```
Console> (enable) copy config tftp

IP address or name of remote host []? 172.20.52.3

Name of file to copy to []? cat5000_config.cfg
Upload configuration to tftp:cat5000_config.cfg, (y/n) [n]? y
```

Controlling Access to the Switch

The **ip permit** command lets you restrict access to the switch to specific IP addresses. Example 3-34 shows how the **ip permit** command is used on a Catalyst switch.

Example 3-34 *Setting Up Restricted IP Access to the Switch*

```
Console> (enable) set ip permit enable
!The keyword telnet at the end of the command below ensures that Telnet access to
!the switch is allowed only from the machines in the 172.16.1.0/24 subnet. Access
!to the switch from all other sources is prohibited in all forms.
Console> (enable) set ip permit 172.16.1.0 255.255.255.0 telnet
```

AAA can also be used to control logins to the switch. Example 3-35 shows how AAA can be set up to control login access to a switch.

Example 3-35 *Setting Up AAA to Control Login Access to the Switch*

```
!The following command defines the address of the TACACS server.
Console> (enable) set tacacs server 172.20.52.10
!The command below sets the key to be used for the TACACS server.
Console> (enable) set tacacs key tacacskey197
!The following command configures authentication to take place via TACACS for
!login attempts made to the switch via the "all" mechanism available for doing so.
!The login mechanisms available on a switch are console, HTTP, and Telnet.
Console> (enable) set authentication login tacacs enable all
!The following command sets up authentication to take place via TACACS for
!attempts made to enter privileged mode (enable mode) on the switch via the "all"
!mechanism available for doing so.
Console> (enable) set authentication enable tacacs enable all
```

continues

Example 3-35 *Setting Up AAA to Control Login Access to the Switch (Continued)*

```
!The following two commands disable local authentication because TACACS
!authentication has already been set up for these methods of authentication.
Console> (enable) set authentication login local disable all
Console> (enable) set authentication enable local disable all
```

Securing Access to the Switch

Because Catalyst 5500 switches do not have IPsec support, the best available method of encrypting access is via SSH version 1.x. Example 3-36 shows how SSH is set up on the switch. SSH was introduced on Catalyst switches in version 6.1.

Example 3-36 *Allowing a Switch to Accept SSH Connections*

```
!The command below is used to generate a 1024-bit RSA public/private key pair to
!be used for encryption and decryption.
cat> (enable) set crypto key rsa 1024
!The command below defines the range of IP addresses from where to allow various
!connections, including SSH, to take place.
cat> set ip permit 172.18.124.0 255.255.255.0
!The command below restricts IP access to the switch via SSH only by enabling only
!the SSH permit list. The addresses that belong to the permit list are defined in
!the previous command.
cat> (enable) set ip permit enable ssh
```

Logging Events on the Switch

Comprehensive logs with good time stamps can be parsed using various commercially available software to look for relevant information about access to the router or attempts to get access. It is important to have a setup in place to capture important log messages on a log server. Example 3-37 shows how logging can be set up on a switch.

Example 3-37 *Setting Up Logging to a Logging Server on a Switch*

```
!The first command below defines the IP address of the syslog server to send the
!log messages to.
Console> (enable) set logging server 10.10.10.100
!The line below defines the facility expected by the syslog server in the messages
!sent to it.
Console> (enable) set logging server facility local5
!The command line below sets up all messages with a severity up to 5 to be sent to
!the syslog server.
Console> (enable) set logging server severity 5
!The last command line below turns on the logging based on the parameters above.
Console> (enable) set logging server enable
```

Controlling Management Protocols (SNMP-Based Management)

SNMP should be disabled on the switch if it is not being used. The principles of securing SNMP on the switch are the same as the ones described for the routers. Example 3-38 shows how to set up SNMP in a secure manner on a switch.

Example 3-38 *Allowing Controlled Functioning of the SNMP Protocol on a Switch*

```
!The commands below are used to set up SNMP securely on the switch.
Console> (enable) set snmp community read-only commstr1ing123
Console> (enable) set snmp trap 172.16.10.10 read-only
Console> (enable) set snmp trap enable all
!The following command sets up SNMP access to the switch from the 172.16.10.10
!address only.
console> (enable) set ip permit 172.16.10.10 255.255.255.255 snmp
console> (enable) set ip permit enable snmp
```

Using NTP

NTP plays an important part in getting consistent logs across the network from all devices based on a consistent time line. Although NTP on the Catalyst 5500 series can be set up in client broadcast mode, it is best to define a specific address as the NTP server to synch to and turn on authentication to that server as well. This fends off attacks that use changing time on devices as a component of their overall strategy. Example 3-39 shows how NTP can be set up in a secure manner on a switch.

Example 3-39 *Setting Up NTP in a Secure Manner on a Switch*

```
!The two commands below turn on NTP in client mode (meaning this switch synchs
!itself to a master NTP device) and NTP authentication.
Console> (enable) set ntp authentication enable
Console> (enable) set ntp client enable
!The command below sets up the secret key testmd5key. This key is known to both
!the machines that are synching using NTP. This key is key number 55 in the
!configuration. This is just an identification tag for the key, because more than
!one key can be defined on the switch for various NTP servers to synch to. The key
!is encrypted using MD5 when stored in the configuration for security purposes.
Console> (enable) set ntp key 55 trusted md5 testmd5key
!The switch is set up to use the key 55 defined above for talking to the NTP
!server at 172.20.52.65.
Console> (enable) set ntp server 172.20.52.65 key 55
```

Login Banners

For banners, the same guidelines stated for the routers apply.

The banner is set using the single command shown in Example 3-40.

Example 3-40 *Setting Up Banners on a Switch*

```
Console> (enable) set banner motd #
```

Capturing Core Dumps

Capturing the core dumps from the switch in case of crashes is an important part of post-mortem investigation into security-related attacks. Much of the motivation for setting up core dump captures is the same as the one described for routers. Example 3-41 shows how core dump capture can be set up on a switch.

Example 3-41 *Allowing Core Dumps to Be Captured on a Switch*

```
!The following command sets up the switch to automatically save the core dump file
!upon crashing.
Console> (enable) set system core-dump enable
!The command below defines the filename and the location to which the core dump is
!copied.
Console> (enable) set system core-file slot0:core.hz
```

Summary

Ensuring that the devices that are responsible for regulating traffic in a network are themselves secure is critical to ensuring the security of the overall network infrastructure. This chapter looked at some of the basic physical and logical measures you can take to ensure the security of network devices. Special consideration was given to three main components of a secure network: routers, switches, and PIX Firewalls. Specific features available to protect routers, switches, and firewalls were discussed. The use and abuse of various features available on these devices were also described. Having discussed the features that protect these devices from attacks, this chapter built the foundation for discussing the various security features available on these devices to protect the network of which they are a component. We will look at these features in the rest of Part II and the remainder of this book.

Review Questions

1   What are floating static routes?

2   What is HSRP?

3   Which encryption algorithm is recommended to save passwords on a router?

4   What is a core file?

5 What is the purpose of the nagle protocol service?

6 Which version of SSH is supported on Cisco devices?

7 Is SSH the recommended method of secure administrative access on Cisco routers?

8 What are examples of TTY ports on a router?

9 How does CEF improve router security?

10 What are the methods of accessing a switch?

This chapter covers the following key topics:

- **Building Security into Routing Design**—This section talks about some considerations you should keep in mind when implementing routing protocols in networks.

- **Router and Route Authentication**—This section deals with ways to authenticate routers to each other before accepting routing updates.

- **Directed Broadcast Control**—This section talks about the need to control directed broadcasts on a router.

- **Black Hole Filtering**—This section discusses an alternative technique based on Null interface routing that you can use instead of using access control lists.

- **Unicast Reverse Path Forwarding**—This section talks about how URPF can stop spoofing and certain other types of attacks from occurring.

- **Path Integrity**—This section deals with mechanisms available to subvert normal routing procedures and how to counter them.

- **Case Studies**—The two case studies cover securing the BGP routing protocol and securing the OSPF routing protocol.

## CHAPTER 4

Secure Routing

Routing is perhaps the most critical component in building any network of significant size. In order for a network to operate securely, it is essential that you keep security in mind when building the network's routing infrastructure. This chapter looks at some of the factors you should keep in mind when building a network's routing infrastructure. We will look at some of the most critical considerations when you're designing the routing in a network. We will also look at techniques such as black hole filtering and URPF for augmenting network security. This chapter concludes by talking about the specific security needs and features of the BGP and OSPF routing protocols.

Building Security into Routing Design

In order to have a secure network, it is essential that you build security into how traffic flows in the network. Because routing protocols determine how traffic flows in the network, it is essential to make sure that the routing protocols are chosen and implemented in a manner that is in line with the security requirements of the network. Needless to say, a network with a secure routing architecture is less vulnerable to attacks and oversights than a network with a poorly designed routing structure. A properly designed routing infrastructure can also help reduce the downtime a network suffers during a network attack.

This chapter discusses some of the basic elements that go into some of the most common techniques you can deploy in making routing more secure.

We will start with a generalized discussion of some of the elements you should keep in mind when implementing a routing scheme. After completing this discussion, we will move on to discuss some of the more specific security techniques you can apply to routing implementations on Cisco routers.

Route Filtering

NOTE   For the purpose of this discussion, a private network means a self-contained network connected to the Internet through an ISP. An enterprise network is a good example of such a network.

Proper route filtering is important to any well-implemented network. It is especially important in a private network with routing links to the outside world. It is important in these networks to ensure that route filtering is used to filter out any bogus or undesired routes coming into the private network as well as make sure that only the routes actually contained on the internal network are allowed to be advertised. It is also important to make sure that the only advertised networks are those for which access from outside the private network is desired.

On any private network connected through an ISP to the Internet or a larger public network, the following routes should be filtered from entering the network in most situations (this filtering can also be carried out on the ISP routers):

- **0.0.0.0/0 and 0.0.0.0/8**—Default and network 0 (unique and now historical properties)
- **127.0.0.0/8**—Host loopback
- **192.0.2.0/24**—TEST-NET, generally used for examples in vendor documentation
- **10.0.0.0/8, 172.16.0.0/12, and 192.168.0.0/16**—RFC 1918 private addresses
- **169.254.0.0/16**—End node auto-config for DHCP
- **224.0.0.0/3**—Multicast addresses

The addresses belonging to the address space reserved by IANA can also be blocked. See the following URL for IANA address space allocations: www.iana.org/assignments/ipv4-address-space.

Filters can also be set up to ensure that IP address blocks belonging to a private network are not allowed to be advertised back into the network from outside. This is a necessary precaution to protect the traffic intended for some of the hosts on the inside network from being routed somewhere unintended.

Route filtering can also be used to hide one piece of a network from another. This can be important in organizations that need varying amounts of security in different parts of the network. In addition to having firewalls and other authentication mechanisms in place, route filtering can also rule out the ability of machines in a less-secure network area to reach a more-secure area if they don't have a route to that portion of the network. However, route filtering should not be used as the sole network security measure.

Applying filtering correctly is important as well. It is a good practice to filter both incoming and outgoing routes. Ingress filtering ensures that routes not intended for a network are not flooded into it during an erroneous or malicious activity on another network. Also, if something goes wrong in one part of the network, egress filtering can stop that problem from spreading to the rest of the network.

ISPs can also consider using what is called a *net police filter*, whereby no routes with prefixes more specific than /20 (or perhaps up to /24) are allowed to come in. This is often done to make sure that an attack cannot be staged on a large ISP's router by increasing the size of its routing tables. Routes more specific than /20 are often not needed by large ISPs.

Therefore, an ISP can filter out these routes to keep its routing table from getting out of control in terms of size. How specific a prefix a router should accept should be determined by a network administrator who understands what is necessary for the router to perform its functions properly.

Convergence

Fast convergence is important for having a secure routing infrastructure. A network that is slow to converge takes longer to recover from network-disrupting attacks and thus aggravates problems. On an Internet-wide basis, slow convergence of BGP for interdomain routing can mean a considerable loss of revenue for a large number of people. However, even for a small network, slow convergence can mean loss of productivity for a significant number of people.

A slow-converging network is also liable to be more susceptible to a denial of service (DoS) attack. The loss of one or two nodes at a time, making the network take a long time to converge, could mean that a DoS attack confined to just one node actually spreads to the whole network.

At various points in this chapter, we will touch on convergence and how it can be improved. In general, a network's convergence speed can depend on a lot of factors, including the complexity of the network architecture, the presence of redundancy in the network, the parameters set up for route calculation engines on the various routers, and the presence of loops in the network. The best way to improve convergence speed is for the network administrator to thoroughly understand the workings of the network and then to improve its convergence speed by designing the network around the aspect of faster convergence.

Static Routes

Static routes are a useful means of ensuring security in some circumstances. Static routes might not scale to all situations, but where they do, they can be used to hard code information in the routing tables such that this information is unaffected by a network attack or occurrences on other parts of the network. Static routes are also a useful way to define default route information.

Router and Route Authentication

The reason for having router and route authentication and route integrity arises from the risk of an attacker who configures his or her machine or router to share incorrect routing information with another router that is part of the network being attacked. The attacked router can be tricked into not only sending data to the incorrect destination, but through clever maneuvering can be completely put out of commission as well. Routing changes can also be induced simply to redirect the traffic to a convenient place in the network for the attacker to analyze it. This can result in the attacker's being able to identify patterns of traffic and obtain information not intended for him or her.

An example of such attacks occurs in RIP environments where bogus RIP route advertisements can be sent out on a segment. These updates are conveniently accepted into their routing tables by the routers running RIP unless an authentication mechanism is in place to verify the routes' source.

Another issue that prompts router authentication, especially in BGP, is the fear of an attack wherein a rogue router acting as a BGP speaker and neighbor advertises a lot of specific routes into a core router's routing table, causing the router to stop functioning properly due to the greatly increased size of its routing table.

There are two main ways in which Cisco routers provide security in terms of exchanging routing information between routers:

- Authenticating routers that are sharing routing information among themselves so that they share information only if they can verify, based on a password, that they are talking to a trusted source

- Authenticating the veracity of the information being exchanged and making sure it has not been tampered with in transit

Most major routing protocols support these measures. There are two ways that routers are authenticated to each other when sharing route information:

- By using a clear-text key (password) that is sent along with the route being sent to another router. The receiving router compares this key to its own configured key. If they are the same, it accepts the route. However, this is not a very good method of ensuring security, because the password information is sent in the clear. It is more a method to avoid misconfigurations than anything else. A skilled hacker can easily get around it.

- By using MD5-HMAC, the key is not sent over the wire in plain text. Instead, a keyed hash is calculated using the configured key. The routing update is used as the input text along with the key into the hashing function. This hash is sent along with the route update to the receiving router. The receiving router compares the received hash with a hash it generates on the route update using the preshared key configured on it. If the two hashes are the same, the route is assumed to be from a trusted source. This is a more secure method of authentication than the clear-text password, because the preshared secret is never shared over the wire.

The second method of authentication using MD5-HMAC also allows for checking route integrity. If the route information is tampered with during transit, the receiving router upon calculating the hash on the route information finds the hash to be different from the hash sent by the original router. Even if an attacker intercepts the route information and injects a new hash after changing the route information, the attempt fails, because the attacker does not know the correct key to calculate the hash. That key is known only to the sending and receiving routers. Figure 4-1 shows how route authentication occurs on Cisco routers.

Figure 4-1 *Route Authentication*

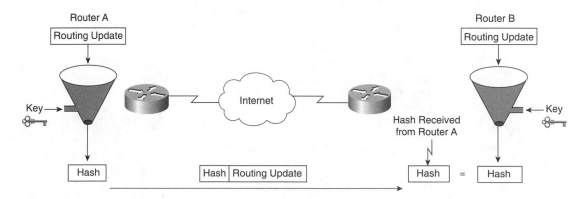

Examples 4-1 through 4-4 show how to set up OSPF, IS-IS, BGP, and RIPv2 (v1 does not support authentication) for route authentication.

Example 4-1 *Setting Up OSPF for MD5 Hash Authentication*

```
interface ethernet1
ip address 10.1.1.1 255.255.255.0
!The command below defines a key-ID, 100, the hashing method to use, md5, and the
!actual key to use in the authentication, cisco. The key-ID must be the same on
!all routers participating in OSPF areas using authentication. The key-ID allows
!the network administrator to change keys one by one on all the routers in an area
!while not breaking the route update process, which continues using the older key
!until all the routers have the new key with the new key-ID.
ip ospf message-digest-key 100 md5 cisco
!
router ospf 1
network 10.1.1.0 0.0.0.255 area 0
!The following command turns on authentication on area0 using MD5 (message digest
!5) hashing.
area 0 authentication message-digest
```

Example 4-2 *Setting Up IS-IS for MD5 Hash Authentication*

```
!The following command defines the name ciscochain to use for the authentication
!key being defined on this router.

key chain ciscochain
```

continues

Example 4-2 *Setting Up IS-IS for MD5 Hash Authentication (Continued)*

```
!The following command defines the key-ID for this particular key. The key-ID
!serves the same purpose as discussed for the OSPF key-ID.
 key 100
!The actual key, cisco123test478, is defined in the command below
 key-string cisco123test478
!
interface Ethernet3
 ip address 10.1.1.1 255.255.255.0
 ip router isis testnetwork
!The command below sets up MD5 authentication for the IS-IS hello packets exchanged
!on this interface. Note that MD5 authentication can be enabled on Level 1 or Level
!2 independently.
 isis authentication mode md5 level-1
!The following command defines which key chain to use for the authentication to
!occur on this interface
 isis authentication key-chain ciscochain level-1
!
router isis testnetwork
 net 49.0001.1720.1600.2002.00
 is-type level-1
!The following command sets up MD5 authentication for IS-IS instance testnetwork.
!This enables authentication to occur for LSP, CSNP, and PSNP packets. Note that
!MD5 authentication can be enabled on Level 1 or Level 2 independently.
 authentication mode md5 level-1
!The following command defines which key chain to use for the authentication to
!occur for this router instance.
 authentication key-chain ciscochain level-1
```

Example 4-3 *Setting Up BGP for MD5 Hash Authentication*

```
router bgp 100
no synchronization
neighbor 166.3.4.89 remote-as 200
neighbor 166.3.4.89 version 4
!The following command turns on MD5 authentication for the neighbor specified using
!the password 'cisco123test556run78'. This forces each segment sent on the TCP
!connection between the two neighbors to be verified using the MD5 methods
!described earlier.
neighbor 166.3.4.89 password cisco123test556run78
```

Example 4-4 *Setting Up RIPv2 for MD5 Hash Authentication*

```
!The following command defines a name 'ciscochain' to use for the authentication
!key being defined on this router.

key chain ciscochain
!The following command defines the key-ID for this particular key. The key-ID
```

Example 4-4   *Setting Up RIPv2 for MD5 Hash Authentication (Continued)*

```
!serves the same purpose as discussed for the OSPF key-ID.
 key 1
!The actual key, cisco123test478, is defined in the command below
 key-string cisco123test478

interface Serial2
  ip address 141.108.0.10 255.255.255.252
!The following command turns on MD5 authentication for RIP on all RIP packets
!exchanged on this interface.
  ip rip authentication mode md5

!The following command defines which key to use for MD5 authentication
  ip rip authentication key-chain ciscochain
```

Note that the preceding examples use only the MD5 method of authentication. The plain-text method of authentication is not shown because it is more of a tool to avoid and detect misconfigurations rather than a method of providing security.

Directed Broadcast Control

Attackers sometimes use directed broadcast capabilities to start attacks such as a smurf attack. (Chapter 21, "Using Access Control Lists Effectively," describes how smurf attacks work.) Directed broadcast allows packets to be broadcast to all the machines on the subnet directly attached to a router. This can be dangerous, because it can lead to packet floods on the network.

To disable this feature on routers, configure the following command on individual interfaces on the router:

```
no ip directed-broadcast
```

Also see Chapter 21 for additional methods of controlling such floods.

Black Hole Filtering

Black hole filtering is an alternative technique you can deploy in place of access control lists to filter out undesired traffic. You create black hole filters by creating specific routes for the traffic that needs to be filtered and then pointing these routes to a null interface. A null interface cannot pass traffic, so it drops the traffic. This has some performance gains over traditional access list filtering. In the case of access lists, the traffic first has to be routed and then subjected to access list processing, which in and of itself can be intensive. However, all that needs to be done in the case of null route filtering, is to route the traffic, saving a resource-intensive step. However, note that null routing is based on the packets' destination IP addresses only, as opposed to access lists, which can work on source address, destination address, and Layer 4 information as well.

ICMP unreachables are disabled on the null interface to avoid generating ICMP unreachable messages for traffic dumped to the null interface. Example 4-5 shows how Null 0 routes can be set up.

Example 4-5 *Configuring Null 0 Routes on a Router*

```
interface Null0
 no icmp unreachables
 !
ip route 127.0.0.0 255.0.0.0 null 0
ip route 171.68.10.0 255.255.255.0 null 0
ip route 224.0.0.0 255.0.0.0 null 0

!Under certain circumstances, a default route to Null 0 in the following form can
!also be implemented as shown below
ip route 0.0.0.0 0.0.0.0 null 0 255
```

The kind of default route shown in Example 4-5 is useful in routing all traffic for which the router does not have a valid route. This can prevent some simple DoS attacks as well as improve performance. However, you should be careful when using this statement. It can easily cause a lot of routing issues if you don't have a good understanding of how the overall routing structure and route redistribution work. Because this route has an administrative distance set to be the maximum possible value of 255, it is applicable only when there is no other default route in the routing table received from a routing protocol, because that route typically has a weight less than 255. If the network administrator defines another default route with an administrative distance of less than 255, that route takes precedence over the Null 0 route, thereby voiding the purpose of having the Null 0 default route.

Unicast Reverse Path Forwarding

Unicast Reverse Path Forwarding (URPF) is a tool implemented on routers to thwart attempts to send packets with spoofed source IP addresses. A spoofed source IP address makes tracking the real source of an attack very difficult. For example, if site A is getting attacked with ICMP floods coming from a source IP address in the range 150.1.1.0/24, the only place for that site to look to stop this kind of attack is the network that contains the 150.1.1.0/24 subnet (site B). However, more than likely, the packets are actually coming from some other network (site C), often compromised too, that does not contain the 150.1.1.0/24 subnet. However, other than tracking the source of the packets one hop at a time, the attacked entity has no way of determining this. In this situation, it would be great if site C's network administrators (and, ideally, the administrators of all the other sites on the Internet) had some sort of mechanism in place on their routers that does not allow packets with source IP addresses not in the range belonging to their respective sites to go out. Although this can be done with an access list, as you will see in Chapter 21, URPF is a much more efficient and effective method.

URPF works by looking for the source IP address of any packet arriving inbound on an interface of a router in its routing table. Logically, if the source IP address belongs to the network behind the router and is not a spoofed address, the routing table contains an entry showing the router a way to get to that address via the interface on which the packet arrived. However, if the address is spoofed, there probably isn't an entry in the routing table, because the address does not lie behind the router, but is stolen from some other network on the Internet (site B in our example). If the router does not find the source IP address when it does the lookup, it drops the packet.

One thing to note here is that URPF needs to have Cisco Express Forwarding (CEF) enabled on the router. URPF looks at the Forwarding Information Base (FIB) that is generated by CEF rather than looking directly at the routing table. This is a more efficient way of doing the lookup. Figure 4-2 demonstrates how URPF works.

Figure 4-2   *URPF*

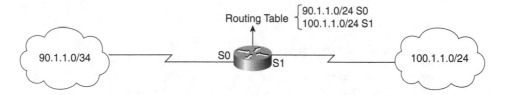

Figure 4-2 shows to two scenarios. In Scenario 1, a packet is allowed to pass through the router after it successfully passes the URPF check. In Scenario 2, a packet is dropped because it fails the URPF check. Let's look at each scenario separately, and in sequence:

Scenario 1:

1 The packet arrives on S0 with a source IP address of 90.1.1.15.

2 URPF does a reverse rate lookup on the source IP address and finds it can be routed back through S0.

3 URPF allows the packet to pass through.

Scenario 2:

1 1.The packet arrives on S1 with a source IP address of 90.1.1.19.

2 URPF does a reverse rate lookup on the source IP address and finds it can be routed back through S0 and not S1.

3 Because the interface on which the packet arrived is not the same one through which it can be routed back, URPF causes the packet to be dropped.

Configuring URPF is fairly simple. However, you should be careful when choosing the right place to configure it. It should not be set up on routers that might have asymmetric routes.

Asymmetric routing is said to occur when the interface through which the router sends return traffic for a packet is not the interface on which the original packet was received. For example, if the original packet is received on interface X, the return traffic for it is sent out via interface Y. Although this might be a perfectly legitimate arrangement for a network, this situation is incompatible with URPF. The reason is that URPF assumes that all routing occurring on a router is symmetric. It drops any traffic received on the router for which the return path is not through the same interface as the one on which the traffic is being received.

Generally, the best place to apply URPF is on the edge of a network. The reason is that this allows URPF's antispoofing capabilities to be available to the entire network rather than just a component of it.

Example 4-6 shows a sample use of the URPF feature.

Example 4-6   *Using the URPF Feature*

```
ip cef
interface Serial 1
  ip unnumbered loopback 1
  ip verify unicast reverse-path
  no ip redirects
  no ip directed-broadcast
  no ip proxy-arp
ip route 10.1.1.0 255.255.255.0 Serial 1
```

In Example 4-6, the Serial 1 interface is connected towards the private network. If the router receives a packet on this interface for which it cannot find a return path through the Serial 1 interface, it drops that packet. Assuming that the static route configured is the only routing information on the router for the internal network, a packet received on the serial 1 interface sourced from a spoofed IP address, such as 10.2.2.1, is dropped, because URPF is unable to find a route back to it through the Serial 1 interface.

Path Integrity

After routing protocols have been set up in a secure fashion, it is important to ensure that all traffic is routed based on the paths calculated as optimum by the routing protocols. However, some features in IP can let changes be made to the routing decisions that routers would make if they were left alone to rely on the routing protocols themselves. Two of the most important features in this regard are ICMP redirects and IP source routing.

ICMP Redirects

ICMP redirects are a way for a router to let another router or host (let's call it A) on its local segment know that the next hop on the same local segment it is using to reach another host (B) is not optimal. In other words, the path should not go through it. Instead, host A should send the traffic directly to the next hop in the optimal path to host B. Although the router forwards the first packet to the optimal next hop, it expects the sending host A to install a route in its routing table to ensure that next time it wants to send a packet to B, it sends it to the optimal next hop. If the router receives a similar packet again, it simply drops it.

Cisco routers send ICMP redirects when all the following conditions are met:

- The interface on which the packet comes into the router is the same interface on which the packet gets routed out.

- The subnet/network of the source IP address is the same subnet/network of the routed packet's next-hop IP address.

- The datagram is not source-routed.

- The router kernel is configured to send redirects.

Although redirects are a useful feature to have, a properly set-up network should not have much use for them. And it is possible for attackers to use redirects to change routing in ways that suit their purposes. So it is generally desirable to turn off ICMP redirects. By default, Cisco routers send ICMP redirects. You can use the interface subcommand **no ip redirects** to disable ICMP redirects.

IP Source Routing

IP source routing is an IP feature that allows a user to set a field in the IP packet specifying the path he or she wants the packet to take. Source routing can be used to subvert the workings of normal routing protocols, giving attackers the upper hand. Although there are a few ways of using source routing, by far the most well-known is loose source record route (LSRR), in which the sender defines one or more hops that the packet must go through to reach a destination.

Unless you have a very specific reason for using source routing, it is often advisable to turn it off:

```
int S0
 no ip source-route
```

One of the ways attackers can use source routing is to reach RFC 1918 private address space (10.x.x.x, 172.16.x.x, or 192.168.x.x networks) from the public network. Under normal circumstances, these networks cannot be reached over the Internet, because Internet routers do not know how to route these IP addresses. However, attackers can use source routing to tell the routers how to deal with these packets. An attacker can specify a router that is attached to both the private and public network as one of the intermediate points in reaching, for example, the 10.1.1.1 address sitting behind that router. Normally, all the routers on the Internet would not know what to do with a packet with a destination set to 10.1.1.1, but in this case they would simply forward the packet to the router specified by the source route option. And because that router has the 10 network directly attached to it, it would forward the packet to the 10.1.1.1 address.

Case Study: Securing the BGP Routing Protocol

This case study looks at how various features available in BGP can be used to strengthen and secure the BGP protocol. It is important to note that although quite a few of the suggestions in this section can be implemented in BGP networks, others might not be suitable for certain networks. You must thoroughly understand how BGP is implemented on a network to be able to suitably apply some of the suggestions culled from this case study.

BGP is the routing protocol that runs most of the interdomain routing on the Internet today. It is also used within large networks. However, for the most part, other interior gateway protocols are used on smaller networks, and then BGP is used to bind these networks together.

The following sections look at a series of features you can use to enhance the security of the BGP protocol.

Note that all the configuration snippets shown here are independent of each other.

BGP Peer Authentication

BGP allows for peer authentication. This is a very useful feature you should use to make BGP networks more secure. See the section "Router and Route Authentication" for a discussion on the usefulness of this feature.

The configuration snippet shown in Example 4-7 sets up authentication for the BGP neighbor 166.3.4.89.

Example 4-7 *Setting Up BGP Authentication*

```
router bgp 100
 neighbor 166.3.4.89 remote-as 200
 neighbor 166.3.4.89 password cisco1234tester678
```

Incoming Route Filtering

It is important to filter all incoming routes to a BGP node. This is especially true for external BGP peerings. However, even for internal peerings, a good filtering scheme controls the spread of problematic or bogus routes.

There are two main mechanisms for doing route filtering based on IP addresses in BGP: access lists and BGP prefix lists. Although access lists are used on a large number of networks today, prefix lists are easier to set up and also are somewhat easier on the CPU than using access control lists. Either one of these techniques can be used to set up filtering.

Please note that the **neighbor prefix-list** command can be used as an alternative to the **neighbor distribute-list** command, but you cannot use both commands in configuring the same BGP peer.

Example 4-8 shows how prefix lists can be used to filter incoming traffic. In this example, the router does not accept any routes with a prefix length greater than /24. This is an example of a net police filter, which we talked about earlier in this chapter.

Example 4-8 *Setting Up BGP Prefix Lists for Incoming Route Filtering*

```
router bgp 100
 network 101.20.20.0
 distribute-list prefix max24 in
!
ip prefix-list max24 seq 5 permit 0.0.0.0/0 ge 8 le 24
```

The prefix list in Example 4-8 is defined by the name max24. The prefix list max24 permits routes with lengths ranging from /8 to /24.

Outgoing Route Filtering

Outgoing route filtering is important in order to make sure that any anomalies found in one network do not spread to another. Also, these filters help ensure that only the routes that actually belong to a network are advertised.

Outgoing filters can be set up in a fashion similar to that of incoming route filters. They can be set up using either ACLs or prefix lists.

BGP Network Advertisement

As we have discussed, stability is an inherent characteristic of a secure system. An unstable system is easier to attack and is liable to get more damage than a stable system. In terms of stability, the best way to advertise a network block to other peers is through the use of the **network** statement. This static method of advertising the network block is more stable than using route redistribution. The configuration snippet shown in Example 4-9 sets up network 131.108.0.0 to be included in the BGP updates.

Example 4-9 *Using the* **network** *Command*

```
router bgp 120
 network 131.108.0.0
```

BGP Multihop

The EBGP multihop feature is used to allow peering between routers not directly connected to each other. In this situation, the two peers need to be given routing information to reach each other to establish the peering. However, this feature should not be enabled unless there is an absolute need for it, because it opens the door for attackers not directly connected to the BGP routers to attempt peering connections to them.

BGP Communications

BGP peers communicate using TCP port 179. It is often a good idea to restrict communication on this port to only the configured peers on any BGP speaking router. This is a deterrent against an attacker's trying to communicate using this port number. You can set up this restriction by configuring the firewalls or using access control lists on routers to achieve the same goal.

Disabling BGP Version Negotiation

BGP negotiates versions during the peering process, which can delay a network's recovery from an attack. It is a good idea to hard-code the BGP version to reduce this delay. In the configuration snippet shown in Example 4-10, BGP version 4 is hard-coded for the neighbor 166.3.4.89.

Example 4-10 *Hard-Coding BGP Version Information*

```
router bgp 100
 no synchronization
 neighbor 166.3.4.89 remote-as 200
 neighbor 166.3.4.89 version 4
```

Maintaining Router Table Depth and Stability

It is conceivable for a malicious attacker to inundate a router's BGP tables with a large number of routes. This can be done by sending a lot of routes to a router such that the router installs these routes in its routing table, increasing the routing table's size. If a large number of such routes are sent to a router, it can lead to a dramatic-enough increase in the size of the router's routing table that its performance degrades dramatically. The routes sent in these types of attacks generally have prefix lengths greater than 24 so that the router does not have more-specific routes already installed in its routing table, forcing it to accept and install the routes sent to it through the attack. This characteristic of these routes is often a means of identifying and controlling such attacks.

Any factor that contributes to the routing table's instability can lead to a decrease in the network's overall security. This instability can be caused by routes in the routing table that keep appearing and disappearing (flapping routes) either because they are injected and removed by an attacker to make a network unstable or because they are a result of bad network design and IP addressing. In either case, it is important to enhance the network's security by either stopping these routes from being installed in the routing table in the first place or by dampening them after they are installed. We will look at some of these methods in the following sections.

Three main methods are generally deployed to control the size of the routing table and the CPU load caused on the router due to more-specific routes that are often not very stable and flapping. Those three main methods are described in detail in the following sections.

Using Police Filters and Null Routes

We discussed the use of net police filters earlier in this chapter. Based on the administrator's comfort level, it might be acceptable to filter out any routes more specific than prefix length /24. Null routes can be used to decrease the load on the CPU caused by the use of access lists for such filtering. See earlier section on 'Black hole filtering' for details on how to implement these types of filters.

Setting Up Route Dampening Values

Generally, on the Internet, the shorter prefix routes are more stable and less liable to changes. It is also true that routes with longer prefixes are often less stable and prone to changes. Having many such longer-prefix routes in the routing table can cause a delay in routing convergence as well as affect the general stability of a heavily loaded router. Therefore, you must make sure that a feature known as *route dampening* is used to suppress the routes that are liable to flapping. Also, it is conceivable that a network attack can be orchestrated wherein routes are made to flap (appear, and then disappear, and so on). If no dampening is set up, this instability can propagate throughout the network as each time the route's condition changes, the BGP peers let each other know about it.

Following is the algorithm used to implement route dampening in BGP (from CCO, www.cisco.com/univercd/cc/td/doc/product/software/ios121/121cgcr/ip_c/ipcprt2/1cdbgp.htm#xtocid62):

> The route dampening feature minimizes the flapping problem as follows. Suppose again that the route to network A flaps. The router in autonomous system 2 (where route dampening is enabled) assigns network A a penalty of 1000 and moves it to history state. The router in autonomous system 2 continues to advertise the status of the route to neighbors. The penalties are cumulative. When the route flaps so often that the penalty exceeds a configurable suppress limit, the router stops advertising the route to network A, regardless of how many times it flaps. Thus, the route is dampened.

> The penalty placed on network A is decayed until the reuse limit is reached, upon which the route is once again advertised. At half of the reuse limit, the dampening information for the route to network A is removed.

In order to maximize the usefulness of route dampening, it is important to selectively dampen some routes more than others. As we have discussed, routes with longer prefixes are generally more unstable, so they need to be strictly regulated using route dampening. However, routes that are traditionally more stable (the ones with shorter prefixes) need to be shown more tolerance. Example 4-11 shows how to achieve this.

Example 4-11 *Using BGP Route Dampening*

```
router bgp 100
!The following command sets up the routes received using the bgp 100 process to be
!subjected to the conditions in the route map strict-and-tolerant.
 bgp dampening route-map strict-and-tolerant
 network 203.250.15.0
 neighbor 192.208.10.5 remote-as 300

route-map strict-and-tolerant permit 10
!This instance of the route map filters out /24 and longer prefix routes for
!dampening.
    match ip address prefix-list slash24andlonger
!The command below sets up dampening for routes that have a /24 and longer prefix
!based on the values defined in this command. The first parameter in the set
!dampening command is the half-life, the second parameter is the reuse limit, the
!third parameter is the suppress limit, and the final parameter is
!max-suppress-time. All these terms were defined earlier except max-suppress-time.
!It is the maximum time (in minutes) a route can be suppressed. The range is from
!1 to 20000; the default is four times the half-life value.
    set dampening 15 750 2000 60
route-map strict-and-tolerant permit 20
    match ip address prefix-list slash212223
!Note the max-suppress-time in the command below. It is less than the one defined
!for slash24andlonger routes because slash212223 routes are considered more stable.
    set dampening 15 750 2000 30
route-map strict-and-tolerant permit 30
!Note the liberal values defined for the very stable slash20andbetter routes
!defined in the command below
    match ip address prefix-list slash20andbetter
    set dampening 5 1500 2000 15


ip prefix-list slash24andlonger seq 10 permit 0.0.0.0/0 ge 24

ip prefix-list slash212223 seq 10 permit 0.0.0.0/0 ge 21 le 23

ip prefix-list slash20andbetter seq 10 permit 0.0.0.0/0 le 20
```

Route dampening is an important feature that enhances the stability of a network's routing architecture and protects it from DoS attacks staged by injecting many unstable routes into a network.

Using the **maximum-prefix** Command

Another technique to control the size of the routing table is to use the **neighbor maximum-prefix** command. This command allows a router to terminate its peering with a neighbor after the number of prefixes received from the neighbor increases beyond a certain limit:

```
router bgp 109
  network 131.108.0.0
  neighbor 129.140.6.6 maximum-prefix 1000
```

This configuration snippet limits the number of prefixes received from the neighbor 129.140.6.6 to 1000. Restricting the size of a routing table is important in environments where there is a risk of an attacker's injecting a lot of very specific routes into the routing table. This can cause a situation in which the routing table becomes very large to maintain and the routing updates become too large and frequent.

Logging Changes in BGP Neighbor Status

BGP allows changes in the status of neighbors of a particular router to be logged. This is an important feature. It lets you detect the neighbor status alternating between up and down and the occurrence of resets. Severely taxed network bandwidth between two neighbors can cause this type of activity. However, this type of activity can also indicate a network DoS attack causing packets to be dropped between peers. This condition requires prompt attention. This condition should be logged, and a system should be set up to regularly monitor the logs.

```
bgp router 100
  neighbor 129.140.5.5
  bgp log-neighbor-changes
```

The command shown in this configuration example sets up the neighbor changes for neighbor 129.140.5.5 to be logged. The logs can be sent to various locations based on the setup of logging on the router.

This case study looked at what is perhaps the most important routing protocol used to connect large networks. Securing BGP and making it stable against network attacks goes a long way toward stopping the spread of attacks. Securing BGP often means securing the communication infrastructures connecting multiple networks. Therefore, the security implemented in BGP is not limited to a single network; it can affect multiple networks.

Case Study: Securing the OSPF Routing Protocol

OSPF is a very commonly used interior gateway protocol. This case study talks about some key ways to improve security in an OSPF implementation. The basic principles motivating these configurations remain the same.

OSPF Router Authentication

OSPF neighbor router authentication works by authenticating the source of any OSPF routes received on the router. Any routes coming from a source that cannot be authenticated are discarded. Example 4-12 shows how authentication is setup in OSPF.

Example 4-12 *Setting Up OSPF for MD5 Hash Authentication*

```
interface ethernet1
ip address 10.1.1.1 255.255.255.0
!The command below defines a key-ID, 100, the hashing method to use, md5, and the
!actual key to use in the authentication, cisco. The key-ID must be the same on all
!routers participating in OSPF areas using authentication. The key-ID allows the
!network administrator to change keys one by one on all the routers in an area
!while not breaking the route update process, which continues using the older key
!until all the routers have the new key with the new key-ID.
ip ospf message-digest-key 100 md5 cisco
!
router ospf 1
network 10.1.1.0 0.0.0.255 area 0
!The following command turns on authentication on area0 using MD5 hashing.
area 0 authentication message-digest
```

OSPF Nonbroadcast Neighbor Configuration

Routers participating in an OSPF network communicate with any devices that are configured correctly to talk to them (with the correct area number, and so on), provided that OSPF is configured to use multicasting to discover neighbors and connect to them. You can further improve security on an OSPF network by configuring the routers explicitly with the IP address of the neighbors with which they are allowed to communicate and form neighbor relationships. Example 4-13 shows how OSPF can be set up in a nonbroadcast manner with specified neighbors.

Example 4-13 *Setting Up OSPF in a Nonbroadcast Manner*

```
interface Serial0
 ip address 10.0.1.1 255.255.255.0
 !The command below sets up OSPF to use nonbroadcast mechanisms to establish
 !neighborhood relationships with its peers.
 ip ospf network point-to-multipoint non-broadcast

 encapsulation frame-relay
 no keepalive
 frame-relay local-dlci 200
 frame-relay map ip 10.0.1.3 202
 frame-relay map ip 10.0.1.4 203
```

Example 4-13 *Setting Up OSPF in a Nonbroadcast Manner (Continued)*

```
 frame-relay map ip 10.0.1.5 204
 no shut
 !
router ospf 1
 network 10.0.1.0 0.0.0.255 area 0
!The commands below give the specific IP addresses of the OSPF neighbors for this
!router.
 neighbor 10.0.1.3 cost 5
 neighbor 10.0.1.4 cost 10
 neighbor 10.0.1.5 cost 15
```

Using Stub Areas

Stub areas are OSPF areas into which information on external routes cannot be sent. The routers in the stub area rely on a default route generated by the area border router (ABR) for destinations outside the stub area. Using stub areas can be good for security because the whole area is forced to have only a single point of exit through an ABR. This can reduce the security risk because the network administrator knows the single point to screen for malicious activity. Another advantage of stub areas is that they reduce the load on the routers because they have to work with only a single default route rather than a whole bunch of routes. The decreased router load should result in increased stability, which is synonymous with security during a network attack. Example 4-14 shows how to set up stub areas in an OSPF network. Figure 4-3 illustrates the topology used in Example 4-14.

Figure 4-3 *Topology Used in Example 4-15*

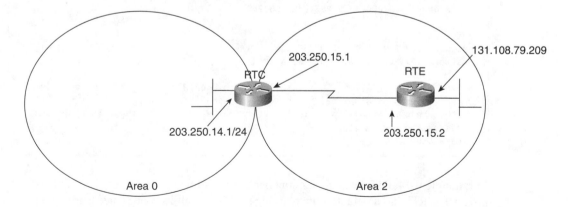

Example 4-14 *Setting Up an OSPF Stub Area*

```
RTC#
interface Ethernet 0
  ip address 203.250.14.1 255.255.255.0

 interface Serial1
  ip address 203.250.15.1 255.255.255.252

 router ospf 10
  network 203.250.15.0 0.0.0.3 area 2
  network 203.250.14.0 0.0.0.255 area 0



!The following command sets area 2 as a stub area. The keyword no-summary at the
!end of the command ensures that not only E2 and E1 routes but also interarea
!routes are suppressed from entering the stub area. Instead, a default route is
!injected into the area to serve as the routing info. (See the CCO documentation
!for more information on the various types of OSPF routes.)

  area 2 stub no-summary
  area 2 default cost 10


RTE#

 interface Ethernet1
  ip address 131.108.79.209 255.255.255.240

 interface Serial1
  ip address 203.250.15.2 255.255.255.252

router ospf 10
  network 203.250.15.0 0.0.0.255 area 2
  network 131.108.0.0 0.0.255.255 area 2

!The command below allows the other router in area 2 to know that the area is
!being set up as a stub area. Unless this is done, the router will not establish
!neighborhood relationships with the rest of the routers in the area configured to
!consider the area a stub.
  area 2 stub
```

In Example 4-14, RTE is the router contained in the stub area. Based on the stub area's properties, RTE has a default route pointing to RTC for all its routing needs to the rest of the OSPF areas.

Using Loopback Interfaces as the Router IDs

Using loopbacks as the router ID is an important technique to ensure stability and consequently security in an OSPF network. Whenever a loopback is configured with an IP address
on a router, OSPF uses that loopback as the router ID in its OSPF processes, even if it is not
the highest address on the router. If a normal interface is used as the router ID, if that interface goes down (for example, during a network attack), the router has to recalculate all the
routing information and transmit it to its peers. This can entail a significant amount of CPU
overhead on all the routers sending and receiving the information, and it is bandwidth-
consumptive. The use of a loopback interface gets around this situation.

Tweaking SPF Timers

Based on a network's size and general stability, it might be appropriate to tweak the SPF
timers so that the effects of a few routers going down momentarily or general route
instability can be held to a bare minimum:

```
Router OSPF 100
 timers spf 10 20
```

The two parameters in the **timers SPF** command are *spf-delay* and *spf-holdtime*. *spf-delay*
is the delay time, in seconds, between when OSPF receives a topology change and when
it starts an SPF calculation. *spf-holdtime* is the minimum time, in seconds, between two
consecutive SPF calculations. The SPF timer values can be increased to increase the amount
of time before a router, upon receiving a topology change, starts its OSPF shortest-path
recalculation. Although this can increase the stability of a network under attack that has a
number of routes flapping due to a network attack, it also increases the time a router takes
to adapt to a necessary change in network topology. This can result in the redundant design
of an OSPF network taking longer to kick in than normal. A network administrator must
look closely at his or her network design to decide whether to adjust this parameter.

Route Filtering

As in any other routing protocol setup, it is desirable to control the routes that are allowed
in an OSPF area. The principle of what types of traffic to filter is the same, as we have
discussed previously.

There are two main methods of doing route filtering for OSPF routing information
exchanged between OSPF-speaking routers:

- Area filters
- Neighbor database filter

The area filter is generally set up on an ABR. Its purpose is to filter out type 3 LSAs from
being propagated to any of the areas covered by the ABR. This ensures that only type 3
LSAs are allowed that the network administrator expects to be in the ABR's routing tables,

ruling out any maliciously injected routes. Example 4-15 gives a general example of how to filter routes in OSPF networks. The administrator sets up the actual routes that should be filtered based on his or her knowledge of the network topology. The neighbor database filter is used to filter outgoing LSAs to a neighboring OSPF router.

Example 4-15 *Setting UP OSPF Area Filters*

```
router ospf 10
    network 203.250.15.0 0.0.0.3 area 2
    network 203.250.14.0 0.0.0.255 area 0
    area 2 filter-list prefix-list AREA_2 in

ip prefix-list AREA_2  deny  128.213.63.0/24
```

Similar to the area filter shown in this example, neighbor database filters can be used to filter outgoing LSAs to a specific neighbor. This is a preferred method of route filtering because it stops the LSAs from being sent out in the first place rather than filtering them after they have been received. However, the technique shown in Example 4-15 is more effective from a security point of view where the network administrator might not have control over the types of LSAs and routes a rogue device produces.

Summary

This chapter discussed in detail how to secure the routing protocols that run any network. Aspects of secure routing were discussed, including router authentication. Techniques that can be used to enhance the security of routing protocols, such as route filtering and route advertisements, were also discussed. In addition, specific details for making BGP and OSPF routing architectures more secure were delved into. This chapter concluded with case studies involving BGP and OSPF routing protocols. This chapter lays the groundwork for other chapters and discussions. Specifically, this chapter supplements the discussions on security as implemented at the service provider level, as discussed in Part VII, "Service Provider Security," of this book.

Review Questions

1   What is a net police filter?

2   Why is fast convergence important for security?

3   What is a null interface?

4   What is prefix filtering?

5   Which algorithm is used for BGP peer authentication?

6 Turning off directed broadcasts can protect against what types of attacks?

7 Why is it important to set up good route dampening values in BGP?

8 What is the danger of having BGP multihop enabled?

9 What is an advantage of using loopback interfaces as the router ID in OSPF?

10 What is IP source routing?

This chapter covers the following key topics:

- **General Switch and Layer 2 Security**—This section discusses some of the basic steps you can take to make Layer 2 environments and switches more secure.

- **Port Security**—This section discusses how to restrict access on a port basis.

- **IP Permit Lists**—This section talks about using IP permit lists to restrict access to the switch for administrative purposes.

- **Protocol Filtering and Controlling LAN Floods**—This section talks about controlling floods on LANs.

- **Private VLANs on Catalyst 6000**—This section deals with setting up private VLANs on Catalyst 6000 switches to provide Layer 2 isolation to connected devices.

- **Port Authentication and Access Control Using the IEEE 802.1x Standard**—This section talks about how the 802.1x protocol can be used to improve security in a switched environment by providing access control on devices attaching to various ports.

## CHAPTER 5

Secure LAN Switching

In order to provide comprehensive security on a network, it is important take the concept of security to the last step and ensure that the Layer 2 devices such as the switches that manage the LANs are also operating in a secure manner.

This chapter focuses on the Cisco Catalyst 5000/5500 series switches. We will discuss private VLANs in the context of the 6000 series switches. Generally, similar concepts can be implemented in other types of switches (such as the 1900, 2900, 3000, and 4000 series switches) as well.

Security on the LAN is important because some security threats can be initiated on Layer 2 rather than at Layer 3 and above. An example of one such attack is one in which a compromised server on a DMZ LAN is used to connect to another server on the same segment despite access control lists on the firewall connected on the DMZ. Because the connection occurs at Layer 2, without suitable measures to restrict traffic on this layer, this type of access attempt cannot be blocked.

General Switch and Layer 2 Security

Some of the basic rules to keep in mind when setting up a secure Layer 2 switching environment are as follows:

- VLANs should be set up in ways that clearly separate the network's various logical components from each other. VLANs lend themselves to providing segregation between logical workgroups. This is a first step toward segregating portions of the network needing more security from portions needing lesser security. It is important to have a good understanding of what VLANs are. VLANs are a logical grouping of devices that might or might not be physically located close to each other.

- If some ports are not being used, it is prudent to turn them off as well as place them in a special VLAN used to collect unused ports. This VLAN should have no Layer 3 access.

- Although devices on a particular VLAN cannot access devices on another VLAN unless specific mechanisms for doing so (such as trunking or a device routing between the VLANs) are set up, VLANs should not be used as the sole mechanism for providing security to a particular group of devices on a VLAN. VLAN protocols are not constructed with security as the primary motivator behind them. The protocols that are used to establish VLANs can be compromised rather easily from a security perspective and allow loopholes into the network. As such, other mechanisms such as those discussed next should be used to secure them.

- Because VLANs are not a security feature, devices at different security levels should be isolated on separate Layer 2 devices. For example, having the same switch chassis on both the inside and outside of a firewall is not recommended. Two separate switches should be used for the secure and insecure sides of the firewall.

- Unless it is critical, Layer 3 connectivity such as Telnets and HTTP connections to a Layer 2 switch should be restricted and very limited.

- It is important to make sure that trunking does not become a security risk in the switching environment. Trunks should not use port numbers that belong to a VLAN that is in use anywhere on the switched network. This can erroneously allow packets from the trunk port to reach other ports located in the same VLAN. Ports that do not require trunking should have trunking disabled. An attacker can use trunking to hop from one VLAN to another. The attacker can do this by pretending to be another switch with ISL or 802.1q signaling along with Dynamic Trunking Protocol (DTP). This allows the attacker's machine to become a part of all the VLANs on the switch being attacked. It is generally a good idea to set DTP on all ports not being used for trunking. It's also a good idea to use dedicated VLAN IDs for all trunks rather than using VLAN IDs that are also being used for nontrunking ports. This can allow an attacker to make itself part of a trunking VLAN rather easily and then use trunking to hop onto other VLANs as well.

Generally, it is difficult to protect against attacks launched from hosts sitting on a LAN. These hosts are often considered trusted entities. As such, if one of these hosts is used to launch an attack, it becomes difficult to stop it. Therefore, it is important to make sure that access to the LAN is secured and is provided only to trusted people.

Some of the features we will discuss in the upcoming sections show you ways to further secure the switching environment.

The discussion in this chapter revolves around the use of Catalyst 5*xxx* and 6*xxx* switches. The same principles can be applied to setting up security on other types of switches.

Port Security

Port security is a mechanism available on the Catalyst switches to restrict the MAC addresses that can connect via a particular port of the switch. This feature allows a specific MAC address or a range of MAC addresses to be defined and specified for a particular port. A port set up for port security only allows machines with a MAC address belonging to the range configured on it to connect to the LAN. The port compares the MAC address of any frame arriving on it with the MAC addresses configured in its allowed list. If the address matches, it allows the packet to go through, assuming that all other requirements are met. However, if the MAC address does not belong to the configured list, the port can either simply drop the packet (restrictive mode) or shut itself down for a configurable amount of time. This feature also lets you specify the number of MAC addresses that can connect to a certain port.

MAC Address Floods and Port Security

Port security is especially useful in the face of MAC address flooding attacks. In these attacks, an attacker tries to fill up a switch's CAM tables by sending a large number of frames to it with source MAC addresses that the switch is unaware of at that time. The switch learns about these MAC addresses and puts them in its CAM table, thinking that these MAC addresses actually exist on the port on which it is receiving them. In reality, this port is under the attacker's control and a machine connected to this port is being used to send frames with spoofed MAC addresses to the switch. If the attacker keeps sending these frames in a large-enough quantity, and the switch continues to learn of them, eventually the switch's CAM table becomes filled with entries for these bogus MAC addresses mapped to the compromised port.

Under normal operations, when a machine receiving a frame responds to it, the switch learns that the MAC address associated with that machine sits on the port on which it has received the response frame. It puts this mapping in its CAM table, allowing it to send any future frames destined for this MAC address directly to this port rather than flood all the ports on the VLAN. However, in a situation where the CAM table is filled up, the switch is unable to create this CAM entry. At this point, when the switch receives a legitimate frame for which it does not know which port to forward the frame to, the switch floods all the connected ports belonging to the VLAN on which it has received the frame. The switch continues to flood the frames with destination addresses that do not have an entry in the CAM tables to all the ports on the VLAN associated with the port it is receiving the frame on. This causes two main problems:

- Network traffic increases significantly due to the flooding done by the switch. This can result in a denial of service (DoS) for legitimate users of the switched network.
- The attacker can receive frames that are being flooded by the switch and use the information contained in them for various types of attacks.

Figure 5-1 shows how MAC address flooding can cause CAM overflow and subsequent DoS and traffic analysis attacks.

Figure 5-1   *MAC Address Flooding Causing CAM Overflow and Subsequent DoS and Traffic Analysis Attacks*

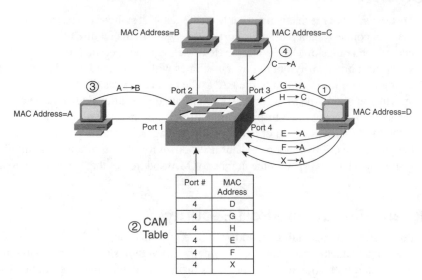

Figure 5-1 shows a series of steps that take place to orchestrate a MAC address flooding attack. Given below is the list of steps that takes place as shown in the Figure 5-1:

Step 1   A compromised machine is attached to port 4. Frames sourced from fictitious MAC address denoted by G, H, E and F etc. are sent on the port 4. The actual MAC address of the compromised machine is denoted by D.

Step 2   Due to the flooding of frames on port 4, the CAM table of the switch fills up and it is unable to 'learn' any more MAC address and port mappings.

Step 3   A host situated on port 1 with a MAC address denoted by A, sends a frame sourced from the MAC address A to MAC address B. The switch is unable to learn and associate port 1 with the MAC address A since its CAM table is full.

Step 4   Host on port 3 with a MAC address denoted by C sends a frame to MAC address A. Since the switch does not have an entry in its CAM table for A, it floods the frame to all its ports in that VLAN. This results in flooding causing DOS as well as an opportunity for traffic analysis by the attacker who receives the flooded frames on port 4 as well.

The danger of attacking a switch by flooding the CAM table can be avoided either by hard-coding the MAC addresses that are allowed to connect on a port or by limiting the number of hosts that are allowed to connect on a port. Both these features are part of the port security feature set on Cisco switches.

The switch configuration shown in Example 5-1 enables port security on port 1 of module 2. The MAC address 00-90-2b-03-34-08 is configured as the only MAC that is allowed to access the LAN using this port. In case of a violation, meaning another MAC address trying to use this port, the port shuts down for 600 minutes, or 10 hours.

Example 5-1   *Port Security Using Various Parameters Enabled on a Switch*

```
Console> (enable) set port security 2/1 enable
Console> (enable) set port security 2/1 enable 00-90-2b-03-34-08
Console> (enable) set port security 2/1 shutdown 600
```

Example 5-2 shows how you can restrict the number of MAC addresses a switch learns on a port.

Example 5-2   *Restricting the Number of MAC Addresses a Switch Learns on a Port*

```
Console> (enable) set port security 3/2 maximum 20
```

In Example 5-2, the number of MAC addresses that the switch can learn on the port is restricted to a maximum of 20. By setting this threshold to 1, the first MAC address that the switch learns on a port can be made the only address it allows on that particular port.

As you can see, setting up port security, especially to allow only certain MAC addresses to connect to the various ports, can be very administratively resource-consumptive. However, it is still a useful safeguard against the type of attack discussed in this section.

IP Permit Lists

IP permit lists are used to restrict Telnet, SSH, HTTP, and SNMP traffic from entering the switch. This feature allows IP addresses to be specified that are allowed to send these kinds of traffic to the switch.

The configuration shown in Example 5-3 on a switch enables the **ip permit list** feature and then restricts Telnet access to the switch from the 172.16.0.0/16 subnet and SNMP access from 172.20.52.2 only. The host, 172.20.52.3, is allowed to have both types of access to the switch.

Example 5-3   *Setting Up IP Permit Lists on a Switch to Control Various Types of Access*

```
Console> (enable) set ip permit enable
Console> (enable) set ip permit 172.16.0.0 255.255.0.0 telnet
Console> (enable) set ip permit 172.20.52.2 255.255.255.255 snmp
Console> (enable) set ip permit 172.20.52.3 all
```

IP permit lists are an essential feature to configure on a switch in situations where Layer 3 access to the switch is needed. As stated earlier, Layer 3 access to a switch should remain fairly limited and controlled.

Protocol Filtering and Controlling LAN Floods

Attackers can cause broadcast floods to disrupt communications over the LAN. You saw an example of this in the section "MAC Address Floods and Port Security." Therefore, it is important to control flooding on the switches. There are two main ways to do this:

- Set up threshold limits for broadcast/multicast traffic on ports
- Use protocol filtering to limit broadcasts/multicasts for certain protocols

Catalyst switches allow thresholds for broadcast traffic to be set up on a per-port basis. These thresholds can be set up either in terms of bandwidth consumed by broadcasts on a port or in terms of the number of broadcast packets being sent across a port. It is best to use the first method in most cases, because it is done in hardware and also because variable-length packets can render the second method meaningless.

The following command sets the threshold for broadcast and multicast packets on ports 1 to 6 of module 2 at 75%. This implies that as soon as 75% bandwidth of the port on a per-second basis is consumed by broadcast/multicast traffic, all additional broadcast/multicast traffic for that 1-second period is dropped.

```
Console> (enable) set port broadcast 2/1-6 75%
```

Protocol filtering provides another very useful mechanism for isolating and controlling environments that are susceptible to flooding attacks. Using the protocol-filtering feature on Catalyst switches, you can define protocol groups. Each group has certain protocols associated with it. It also has a set of ports that belong to it. Only the broadcast or multicast traffic for the protocols associated with a group is allowed to be sent to the ports that belong to that group. You should realize that although VLANs also create broadcast domains for the ports associated with them, protocol-filtering groups allow these domains to be created based on various protocols as well. Using protocol filtering, ports that have hosts on them that do not need to participate in the broadcast traffic for a certain protocol can be made part of a group that does not allow broadcast traffic for that protocol.

With the Catalyst 5000 family of switches, packets are classified into the following protocol groups:

- IP (ip)
- IPX (ipx)
- AppleTalk, DECnet, and Banyan VINES (group)
- Packets not belonging to any of these protocols

A port can be configured to belong to one or more of these four groups and be in any one of the following states for that group:

- On
- Off
- Auto

If the configuration is set to on, the port receives all the flood (broadcast/multicast traffic) traffic for that protocol. If the configuration is set to off, the port does not receive any flood traffic for that protocol. If the configuration is set to auto, a port becomes a member of the protocol group only after the device connected to the port transmits packets of the specific protocol group. The switch detects the traffic, adds the port to the protocol group, and begins forwarding flood traffic for that protocol group to that port. Autoconfigured ports are removed from the protocol group if the attached device does not transmit packets for that protocol within 60 minutes. Ports are also removed from the protocol group when the supervisor engine detects that the link on the port is down. Example 5-4 shows how port filtering can be configured on a switch.

Example 5-4 *Port Filtering Configured on a Switch*

```
Console> (enable) set port protocol 2/1-6 ip on
Console> (enable) set port protocol 2/1-6 ipx off
Console> (enable) set port protocol 2/1-6 group auto
```

The configuration shown in Example 5-4 sets up ports 1 to 6 on module 2 for protocol filtering. Ports 1 to 6 have only the IP group set to on and IPX is turned off. Therefore, these ports do not receive any broadcast traffic for IPX. However, ports 1 to 6 are also set up to be in group "group" in the auto state. This means that if the switch detects a host on any of these ports sending out AppleTalk, DECnet, and Banyan VINES traffic, it enables these ports for broadcast traffic for these protocols as well.

Port filtering can be used in conjunction with the bandwidth or packet threshold-based flood control discussed earlier in this section.

Private VLANs on the Catalyst 6000

The Catalyst 6000 product line has introduced some enhancements to the switching arena for security purposes. We will discuss some of these in this section and see how they can be a useful security element in Layer 2 design.

A normal VLAN does not allow devices connected to it to be segregated from each other on Layer 2. This means that if a device on a VLAN becomes compromised, other devices on the same VLAN can also be attacked from that compromised device.

Private VLANs allow restrictions to be placed on the Layer 2 traffic on a VLAN.

There are three types of private VLAN ports:

- **Promiscuous ports**—Communicates with all other private VLAN ports. This is generally the port used to communicate with the router/gateway on a segment.

- **Isolated ports**—Has complete Layer 2 isolation from other ports within the same private VLAN, with the exception of the promiscuous port.

- **Community ports**—Communicate among themselves and with their promiscuous ports. These ports are isolated at Layer 2 from all other ports in other communities or isolated ports within their private VLAN.

In essence, isolating a port stops any other machine on the same logical or physical segment as the machines on the isolated portfrom sending any traffic to this port.

When a port is isolated, all machines connected to the network using this port are provided complete isolation from traffic in all other ports, except for the promiscuous port. This means that no machines located on any of the other ports on the switch can send any traffic to the machines located on the isolated VLAN port. It is similar to placing two ports in two separate VLANs. The isolated ports communicate with the rest of the world through the promiscuous VLAN port, which can send traffic to and receive traffic from the isolated VLAN ports. Figure 5-2 gives a graphical view of which ports can communicate with which other ports in a private VLAN setup.

Figure 5-2   *Private VLANs*

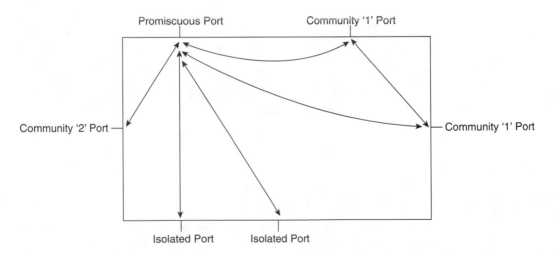

In order to set up private VLANs, a primary VLAN is created that contains the promiscuous ports, and then the secondary VLANs are created that contain the isolated or community ports. These two components are then bound together. Example 5-5 shows how a private VLAN is set up on a Catalyst 6000 switch.

Example 5-5   *A Private VLAN Set Up on a Catalyst 6000 Switch*

```
!The configuration line below creates the primary VLAN and gives it the name 7.
6500 (enable) set vlan 7 pvlan-type primary
!The line below defines the secondary VLAN, 42, and configures it to be an isolated
!VLAN.
6500 (enable) set vlan 42 pvlan-type isolated
!The line below binds the primary and secondary VLANs (7 and 42, respectively) and
!defines the ports that belong to the isolated VLAN 42.
6500 (enable) set pvlan 7 42 3/9-10
!The line below defines the first port (3/31) that is used as the promiscuous port
!in this setup.
6500 (enable) set pvlan mapping 7 42 3/31
!The line below defines the second port (3/32) that is used as a promiscuous port.
6500 (enable) set pvlan mapping 7 42 3/32
```

Example 5-5 shows how to create a private VLAN and set it up so that ports 3/31 and 3/32 are the promiscuous ports and ports 3/9 and 3/10 are the isolated ports. Note that the isolated ports can communicate with the promiscuous ports and vice versa, but they cannot communicate with each other.

ARP Spoofing, Sticky ARP, and Private VLANs

A security problem that private VLANs resolve is that of ARP spoofing. Network devices often send out what is known as a *gratuitous ARP* or *courtesy ARP* to let other machines on their broadcast domain known their IP address and the corresponding MAC address. This generally happens at bootup, but it can also occur at regular intervals after that. An attacker who has gained access to a compromised machine on the LAN can force the compromised machine to send out gratuitous ARPs for IP addresses that do not belong to it. This results in the rest of the machines sending their frames intended for those IP addresses to the compromised machine. This type of attack can have two consequences:

- It can result in a DoS attack if the attacker spoofs the IP address/MAC address of the network's default gateway in its gratuitous ARPs. This causes all the machines on the broadcast domain to send the traffic destined for the default gateway to the compromised host, which in turn can simply drop this traffic, resulting in a DoS.

- The attacker can analyze the traffic being sent to it and use the information found therein for various malicious activities.

Private VLANs offer protection from this type of attack by providing isolation between various ports on a VLAN. This stops an attacker from receiving traffic from the machines, sitting on all the other ports on a switch, on a port that has a compromised machine sitting on it.

Another feature, known as *sticky ARP*, which is available in conjunction with private VLANs, can also help mitigate these types of attacks. The sticky ARP feature makes sure that the ARP entries that are learned by the switch on the private VLANs do not age out and cannot be changed. Suppose an attacker somehow compromises and takes control of a machine on a private VLAN. He tries to do ARP spoofing by sending out gratuitous ARPs, announcing the machine as the owner of a certain MAC address/IP address mapping that it does not own. The switch ignores these ARPs and doesn't update its CAM tables to reflect these mappings. If there is a genuine need to change a port's MAC address, the administrator must do so manually.

Port Authentication and Access Control Using the IEEE 802.1x Standard

802.1x is the standard developed by IEEE to provide a mechanism for authentication to occur for devices that connect to various Layer 2 devices such as switches using IEEE 802 LAN infrastructures (such as Token Ring and Ethernet).

The primary idea behind the standard is devices that need to access the LAN need to be authenticated and authorized before they can connect to the physical or logical port of the switch that is responsible for creating the LAN environment. In the case of Ethernet and Token Ring, the ports are physical entities that a device plugs into. However, in the case of setups such as the IEEE 802.11b wireless setup, the ports are logical entities known as *associations*. In either case, the standard's primary goal is to allow for controlled access to the LAN environment.

802.1x Entities

The 802.1x standard defines the following three main entities that take part in the access control method set up in this standard:

- **Supplicant**—This device needs to access the LAN. An example is a laptop that needs to connect to a LAN.

- **Authenticator**—This device is responsible for initiating the authentication process and then acting as a relay between the actual authentication server and the supplicant. This device is generally also the device that is responsible for the overall workings of the LAN. An example of this type of device is a Catalyst 6000 switch to which various supplicants can connect and be authenticated and authorized via the 802.1x standard before being allowed to use the ports on the switch for data traffic.

- **Authentication server**—This device is responsible for doing the actual authentication and authorization on behalf of the authenticator. This device contains profile information for all the users of the network in a database format. It can use that information to authenticate and authorize users to connect to the ports on the authenticator. An example of an authentication server is the Cisco Secure ACS.

Figure 5-3 shows these three entities in a graphical format.

Figure 5-3 *The Three Entities Defined in the 802.1x Standard*

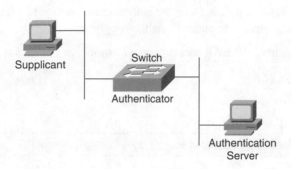

In addition to these three main entities, the 802.1 defines some other entities as well. One of these is the Port Access Entity (PAE). The PAE is essentially responsible for maintaining the functionality of the 802.1x standard on the authenticator or the supplicant or both. It can be viewed as the daemon that is responsible for the functioning of the 802.1x standard. For our purposes, we will assume that this entity is transparent to the network administrator as we talk about various aspects of this standard.

NOTE   The authenticator and the authentication server can be colocated on the same system.

802.1x Communications

In order for the 802.1x standard to function, communication needs to occur between the three entities just defined. 802.1x protocol uses an RFC standard known as Extensible Authentication Protocol (EAP) to facilitate this communication. The authentication data between the three entities is exchanged using EAP packets that are carried either in EAPOL frames (between the supplicant and the authenticator, as discussed later) or in TACACS+, RADIUS, or some other such protocol's packets (between the authenticator and the authenticating server). The following sections look at each of these pieces and discuss how they come together to form the 802.1x communication infrastructure.

EAP

EAP is a fairly flexible protocol. It was originally designed to carry only PPP authentication parameters, but it also can be used by other protocols such as 802.1x for their authentication needs.

EAP can carry authentication data between two entities that want to set up authenticated communications between themselves. It supports a variety of authentication mechanisms, including one-time password, MD5 hashed username and password, and transport layer security (discussed later). EAP, using the packets described in the next section, allows the authenticator, the supplicant, and the authentication server to exchange the information they need to exchange to authenticate the supplicant.

RFC 2284 defines the EAP packet format as shown in Figure 5-4.

Figure 5-4   *EAP Packet Format*

```
0                   1                   2                   3
0 1 2 3 4 5 6 7 8 9 0 1 2 3 4 5 6 7 8 9 0 1 2 3 4 5 6 7 8 9 0 1
+-----------------+-----------------+-----------------------------+
|      Code       |    Identifier   |            Length           |
+-----------------+-----------------+-----------------------------+
|     Data . . .                                                  |
+----------------------------------+
```

RFC 2284 defines the various fields in this packet as follows:

- **Code**—The Code field is one octet. It identifies the type of EAP packet. EAP codes are assigned as follows:
    - **1**—Request
    - **2**—Response
    - **3**—Success
    - **4**—Failure
- **Identifier**—The Identifier field is one octet. It aids in matching responses with requests.
- **Length**—The Length field is two octets. It indicates the length of the EAP packet, including the Code, Identifier, Length, and Data fields. Octets outside the range of the Length field should be treated as data link layer padding and should be ignored on receipt.
- **Data**—The Data field is zero or more octets. The format of the Data field is determined by the Code field.

EAP makes use of four types of messages:

- Request
- Response
- Success
- Failure

The request and response messages are used for the bulk of the messaging used in EAP. These messages can be further classified into the following six most important types of messages (note that more message types are being defined all the time for various purposes):

- Identity
- Notification
- NAK
- MD5-Challenge
- One-time password
- Transport-Level Security (TLS)

The *identity message* is generally sent by the authenticator in the 802.1x scheme of things to the supplicant. The purpose of this message is to ask the supplicant to send its identity information (such as the username) to the authenticator. The supplicant responds with an EAP-Response message of the same type containing the requested information.

The *notification message* is used to display a message on the supplicant machines that the user can see. This message is sent by the authenticator. This message could be a notification that a password is about to expire or some other notification of this type.

The *NAK message* is generally sent by the supplicant to the authenticator when the authentication mechanism offered by the authenticator is unacceptable to the supplicant.

The *MD-5 challenge messages* are sent in the form of EAP Request and Response messages to allow the supplicant to authenticate itself using a method of authentication that is analogous to PPP CHAP protocol using MD5 hashing. The Request contains a "challenge" message to the peer. A Response *must* be sent in reply to the Request. The Response may be either Type 4 (MD5-Challenge) or Type 3 (NAK). The NAK reply indicates the peer's desired authentication mechanism type.

One-time password messages implement a one-time password authentication system as defined in RFC 1938. The Request message contains an OTP challenge. It is responded to in the form of a Response message of the same one-time password type or the NAK type message. If NAK is used to respond to the challenge, the NAK reply indicates the peer's desired authentication mechanism type.

Transport-Layer Security (TLS) messages allow a supplicant to authenticate itself with the authentication server after doing a key exchange and integrity-protected ciphersuite negotiation. The workings of EAP-TLS are described in RFC 2716. EAP-TLS allows the supplicant and the authentication server to use digital certificates to authenticate each other. This is a more scalable mechanism for doing authentication than using a database of usernames and passwords. Also, EAP-TLS is a mutual authentication method, which means that both the client and the server prove their identities.

The next section covers how these messages are used to perform the 802.1x functionality.

Using EAP as the Underlying Communications Mechanism in 802.1x

As stated earlier, the 802.1x standard uses EAP as the underlying mechanism for carrying authentication information back and forth between the three entities—the supplicant, the authenticator, and the authenticating server. In general, the authenticator sends the first EAP-Request message of the identity type to the supplicant to ask for the supplicant's identity. (The supplicant can also start this process if it so desires.) The supplicant returns an EAP-Response message containing its identity, such as its username. The authenticator receives this message and forwards it to the authentication server. From this point onward, the authenticator becomes a pass-through device. It forwards the EAP messages received from the authentication server to the supplicant and the EAP messages received from the supplicant to the authentication server. However, the authenticator remains knowledgeable of the exchange and waits for the success or failure of the exchange to enable the port to which the supplicant wants to connect (in case authentication success occurs). The authentication server, in response to the EAP-Response message containing the supplicant's identity, sends the supplicant an EAP message corresponding to the type of authentication it wants to do with this particular supplicant. The supplicant responds to the authentication server (via the authenticator). It either sends an EAP Response frame of the same type that the authentication server has indicated with a response to what the authentication server has asked for (for example, a one-time password generated on the supplicant) or sends back an EAP-NAK if it does not want to use this particular method of authentication. If NAK is used, the NAK reply indicates the peer's desired authentication mechanism type. EAP messages are sent back and forth until the authentication server sends either an EAP-Success or EAP-Failure message to the supplicant. At this point, the authenticator, upon seeing this message (EAP-Success), opens the port, on which the supplicant has been sending EAP traffic, for normal data activity as well. Figure 5-5 shows an example of EAP exchange involving a successful OTP authentication.

Figure 5-5 *EAP Exchange Involving Successful OTP Authentication*

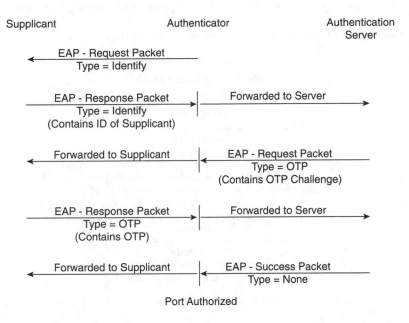

EAPOL

We have looked at EAP, which is the underlying 802.1x protocol. But we have not looked at how EAP messages are actually framed and transported from the supplicant to the authenticator. The 802.1x defines an encapsulating/framing standard to allow communication between the supplicant and the authenticator to take place. This encapsulation mechanism is known as *EAP Over LANs (EAPOL)*. EAPOL encapsulation is defined separately for both the Token Ring and Ethernet environments. EAPOL allows the EAP messages to be encapsulated using the EAPOL frames for transport between the supplicant and the authenticator. As soon as these frames reach the authenticator, it strips off the EAPOL headers, puts the EAP packet in a RADIUS or TACACS+ (or some other similar protocol) packet, and sends it to the authenticating server. Figure 5-6 shows the relationship between the supplicant and the authenticator using EAPOL.

Figure 5-6 *Relationship Between the Supplicant and the Authenticator Using EAPOL*

Supplicant ◄——— EAP Over EAPOL ———► Authenticator

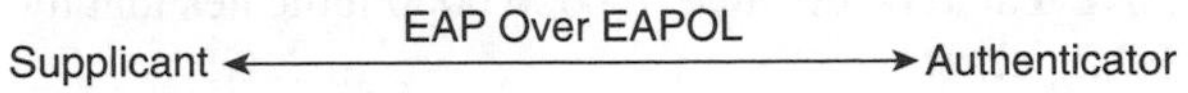

EAPOL uses the same basic frame format as the Ethernet of the Token Ring frames. Figure 5-7 shows the frame format for EAPOL using Ethernet 802.3 (Ethernet).

Figure 5-7   *Frame Format for EAPOL Using Ethernet 802.3*

PAE Ethernet Type = 88-8E
Protocol Version = 0000 0001
Packet Type EAP Packet or EAP-OL Start or EAPOL - Logoff or EAPOL-Key or EAPOL-Encapsulated-ASF-Alert
Packet Body Length = Length of Body Field in Octets
Packet Body (Only present if EAP-Packet, EAPOL-key or EAPOL-Encapsulated- ASF-Alert)

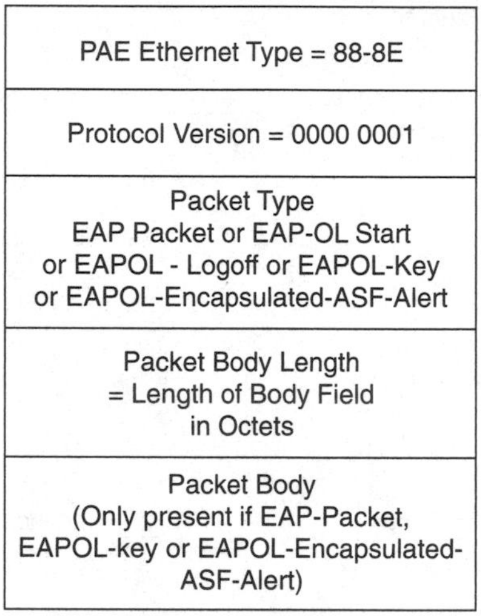

In summary, communications between the supplicant and the authenticator occur using EAP packets encapsulated using EAPOL. The authenticator then encapsulates the EAP frames in TACACS+ or RADIUS packets and sends them to the authentication server.

The various fields in the EAPOL are defined in the 802.1x standard as follows:

- **PAE Ethernet Type**—This field is two octets in length. It contains the Ethernet Type value assigned for use by the PAE.

- **Protocol Version**—This field is one octet in length, taken to represent an unsigned binary number. Its value identifies the version of EAPOL protocol supported by the sender of the EAPOL frame. An implementation conforming to this specification uses the value 0000 0001 in this field.

- **Packet Type**—This field is one octet in length, taken to represent an unsigned binary number. Its value determines the type of packet being transmitted. The following types are defined:

  — **EAP-Packet**—A value of 0000 0000 indicates that the frame carries an EAP packet.

  — **EAPOL-Start**—A value of 0000 0001 indicates that the frame is an EAPOL-Start frame.

- **EAPOL-Logoff**—A value of 0000 0010 indicates that the frame is an explicit EAPOL-Logoff request frame.

- **EAPOL-Key**—A value of 0000 0011 indicates that the frame is an EAPOL-Key frame.

- **EAPOL-Encapsulated-ASF-Alert**—A value of 0000 0100 indicates that the frame carries an EAPOL-Encapsulated-ASF-Alert.

All other possible values of this field are unused, because they are reserved for use in potential future extensions to this protocol.

The EAPOL-Encapsulated-ASF-Alert packet type is provided for use by the Alerting Standards Forum (ASF) as a means of allowing alerts (that is, specific SNMP traps) to be forwarded through a port that is in the Unauthorized state. All EAPOL frames with this packet type that are received on the uncontrolled port are passed to the protocol entity responsible for handling ASF alerts for validation and further processing in accordance with the relevant ASF protocol specifications.

- **Packet Body Length**—This field is two octets in length, taken to represent an unsigned binary number. The value of this field defines the length in octets of the Packet Body field. A value of 0 indicates that there is no Packet Body field.

- **Packet Body**—The Packet Body field is present if the Packet Type contains the value EAP-Packet, EAPOL-Key, or EAPOL-Encapsulated-ASF-Alert. For all other values of Packet Type, this field is not present.

In a frame carrying a Packet Type of EAP-Packet, this field contains an EAP packet. Exactly one EAP packet is encapsulated.

In a frame carrying a Packet Type of EAPOL-Key, this field contains a key descriptor. Exactly one key descriptor is encapsulated.

In a frame carrying a Packet Type of EAPOL-Encapsulated-ASF-Alert, this field contains an ASF alert. Exactly one ASF alert frame is encapsulated.

The Role of RADIUS, TACACS+, and Other Authentication Protocols in 802.1x

The communication between the authenticator and the authentication server takes place via a protocol such as RADIUS or TACACS+. The normal functionality of these protocols is evoked so that communication between these two entities can take place. The EAP packets that are sent to the authenticator using EAPOL encapsulation are decapsulated from EAPOL and are then put into TACACS+ or RADIUS packets and are sent to the authentication server. RADIUS is generally the preferred back-end protocol, because it has EAP encapsulation extensions built into it. Figure 5-8 shows the use of TACACS+/RADIUS protocols in the 802.1x setup.

Figure 5-8 *TACACS+/RADIUS Protocols in the 802.1x Setup*

802.1x Functionality

This section puts together all the pieces of the 802.1x protocol discussed in the preceding sections and summarizes how 802.1x provides port authentication to supplicants.

The 802.1x functionality is based on a series of exchanges between the supplicant, authenticator, and authentication server. The authenticator plays an important role in these exchanges because it not only acts as a go-between for the supplicant and the authenticating server but also is responsible for enabling the port to which the supplicant is trying to connect for normal data traffic if the authentication is indeed successful.

The authentication process starts with the supplicant trying to connect to one of the ports on the authenticator. At this point, the port is open only for EAPOL traffic. The authenticator sees the port's operational state change to enable due to the supplicant's connecting to it and requests authentication from the supplicant. This is done by sending an EAP-Request/ Identity frame to the supplicant. This message is sent encapsulated in an EAPOL frame. The supplicant responds by sending back an EAP-Response/Identity frame containing information about its identity, such as username/password. This message is also sent encapsulated in an EAPOL frame. The authenticator decapsulates the EAP message from the EAPOL frame and repackages this EAP frame in a RADIUS or TACACS+ packet and forwards it to the authentication server. The authentication server, upon receiving this packet, responds with an EAP-Response message that is based on the authentication method that the authentication server wants to use for this particular supplicant. This message is encapsulated in a TACACS+ or RADIUS packet. Upon receiving this message, the authenticator strips off the TACACS+/RADIUS header, encapsulates the EAP message in an EAPOL frame, and forwards it to the supplicant. This back-and-forth EAP exchange between the supplicant and the authentication server via the authenticator continues until the authentication either succeeds or fails, as indicated by an EAP-Success or EAP-Failure message sent by the authentication server to the supplicant. Upon seeing an EAP-Success message, the authenticator enables the port on which the supplicant is connected for normal data traffic. In addition to enabling the port for this type of traffic, the authenticator can place the port in a specific VLAN based on the information it receives from the authentication server. Figure 5-9 shows the overall 802.1x architecture and flow using EAP over EAPOL and EAP over TACACS+/RADIUS.

Figure 5-9   *Overall 802.1x Architecture and Flow Using EAP Over EAPOL and EAP Over TACACS+/RADIUS*

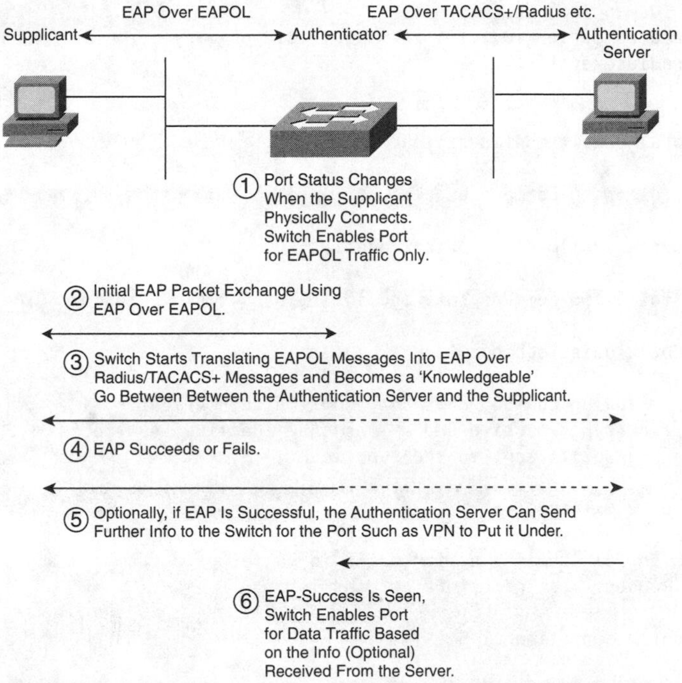

Setting Up Catalyst 6000 to Do Port Authentication Using 802.1x

Most of the newer versions of the Cisco switches support 802.1x port authentication. The Catalyst 6000 supports 802.1x starting in version 6.2. Refer to the documentation for the other types of switches for support information.

Example 5-6 shows how a Catalyst 6000 can be set up to do 802.1x authentication for devices connecting to its ports. RADIUS is used in this example as the authentication protocol. TACACS+ or Kerberos can also be used on the Catalyst to perform this role. However, RADIUS is generally the recommended protocol because it has built-in extensions that support EAP frames.

Example 5-6 *Setting Up a Catalyst 6000 to do 802.1x Authentication for Devices Connecting to Its Ports*

```
# RADIUS configuration
set radius server 10.1.1.1 auth-port 1812 primary
set radius key test


# Global 802.1x configuration

!The following command enables 802.1x globally on the Catalyst 6000

set dot1x system-auth-control enable

!The following command sets the idle time between authentication attempts.

set dot1x quiet-period 60

!The following command sets how long the authenticator waits before retransmitting
!if it does not receive an EAP-Response/Identity type to the EAP-Request/Identity
!type message it sent to the supplicant.

set dot1x tx-period 5

!This is how long the switch waits for a response from the supplicant to any
!EAP-Request message before retransmitting

set dot1x supp-timeout 5

!Below is a timeout similar to the one before this. The only difference is that in
!this case this timeout is for the switch waiting on the authentication server
!rather than the supplicant to respond to its EAP messages.

set dot1x server-timeout 10

!The command below defines the maximum number of times the authenticator sends an
!EAP-Request to the supplicant before stopping

set dot1x max-req 3

!The time shown below is the time after which the switch reauthenticates the
!supplicants connected to its various authorized ports.

set dot1x re-authperiod 3600

# Port Level 802.1x configuration

!The command below enables 802.1x on port 5/1. Note that having done this line of
!configuration, you must initialize the port by issuing the command set port dot1x
!mod/port initialize

set port dot1x 5/1 port-control auto
```

Example 5-6   *Setting Up a Catalyst 6000 to do 802.1x Authentication for Devices Connecting to Its Ports*

```
!The command below forces the state of port 5/3 to force-authorized permanently
!until this command is changed for this port. This is equivalent to disabling
!802.1x on this port. This command forces the port to become authorized for any
!and all hosts connecting to it. The network administrator wants to have no
!security enabled in port 5/3 in this example.

set port dot1x 5/3 port-control force-authorized

!The command below forces port 5/48 into the force-unauthorized state permanently
!until this command is changed for this port. This ensures that no one can
!authenticate and use this port. The network administrator in this example does
!not want anyone to use port 5/48.

set port dot1x 5/48 port-control force-unauthorized

!The command below sets up the port to allow multiple hosts to connect to it after
!the first host connecting to it has passed through the normal 802.1x
!authentication process. Note the security risk involved in using this feature.

set port dot1x 5/1 multiple-host enable

!The command below ensures that for the ports specified only a single host is
!allowed to connect to a port after authentication. Hosts are identified using
!their MAC addresses.

set port dot1x 5/2,5/4-47 multiple-host disable

!The command below ensures that the supplicants connected to the specified ports
!are prompted for reauthentication after the globally defined re-authperiod
!expires.

set port dot1x 5/2,5/4-47 re-authentication enable

!Automatic reauthentication has been disabled using the command below. Manual
!reauthentication can still be initiated by the network administrator.

set port dot1x 5/1 re-authentication disable
```

Please note that in Example 5-6 the RADIUS server also returns the following RFC 2868 attributes to the Catalyst 6000:

- **[64]**—Tunnel-Type = VLAN
- **[65]**—Tunnel-Medium-Type = 802
- **[81]**—Tunnel-Private-Group-Id = VLAN NAME

Attribute [64] must contain the value VLAN (type 13). Attribute [65] must contain the value 802 (type 6). Attribute [81] specifies the VLAN name in which the successfully authenticated 802.1x supplicant should be put.

Summary

This chapter talked about issues related to security on Layer 2 networks. General recommendations to secure a LAN environment were discussed, as were various features available on the Catalyst switches to make the switching environment more secure. We looked at how some of the more well-known attacks can be orchestrated at Layer 2 of the OSI model. We also looked at ways to control these attacks using various features available in the Catalyst line of switches. We looked at methods of securing the ports on a switch, including the emerging 802.1x standard. Although the discussion focused on the high-end Catalyst switches—namely, the 5500 and 6500 switches—the concepts are generic and can be carried over to other switches as well with the appropriate commands and configurations. The discussion in this chapter is an important building block for your understanding of the overall security infrastructure in place in modern networks.

Review Questions

1   Why is it imprudent to rely on VLANs to provide isolation and security?

2   What does port security do?

3   Which protocols are covered under IP permit lists?

4   What is an isolated VLAN port?

5   What is a promiscuous VLAN port?

6   What is the purpose of the 802.1x standard?

7   What is EAP?

8   What is the purpose of the EAPOL standard?

9   What is the purpose of EAP-Request Identity type messages?

10   What is the EAP-Response NAK message used for?

This chapter covers the following key topics:

- **Security Benefits of Network Address Translation**—This section discusses the security benefits that result from setting up Network Address Translation.

- **Disadvantages of Relying on NAT for Security**—This section discusses the consequences of depending on Network Address Translation for site security.

## CHAPTER 6

Network Address Translation and Security

Network address translation (NAT) is the mechanism by which a packet's IP addresses are modified to be something other than what they originally were. This is a requirement for networks that use the RFC 1918 addressing scheme. These IP addresses cannot be routed on the Internet and therefore need to be converted to routable IP addresses at the edge of the network before they are passed to a public network, such as the Internet. Because NAT can hide a network's IP addresses, this offers some amount of security to the network that has NAT the setup. However, you can't depend solely on NAT for security. This chapter discusses the security benefits of having NAT running on the network's periphery. It then discusses how depending solely on NAT for protection can be a dangerous choice.

While there are a few reasons for using NAT, the primary reason that networks use RFC 1918 addressing is to reduce IP address consumption. Routable IP addresses are expensive and limited in number. A specific form of NAT called Overload NAT provides a useful solution to this problem. Overload NAT, also known as Port Address Translation (PAT), works differently from normal one-to-one NAT, whereby each RFC 1918 address is converted to its own unique routable IP address. In Overload NAT, the RFC 1918 addresses are translated to a small number of routable IP addresses (often just one routable IP address, frequently that of the router's external interface).

The device doing PAT distinguishes between the traffic destined for the various RFC 1918 addresses by tracking the source TCP or UDP ports used when the connection is initiated. Figure 6-1 shows how PAT works.

NAT is sometimes confused with *proxy servers*. However, these are two completely different entities. NAT is a Layer 3 occurrence that uses Layer 4 information when doing PAT. On the other hand, proxy servers usually work on Layer 4 or higher of the OSI model. The most significant difference between the two mechanisms is the way they work. Although NAT is completely transparent to the source and destination devices, proxy servers require the source machine to be configured to make requests to the proxy server, which then facilitates the connection on behalf of the source machine. This is completely different from NAT, in which neither the source nor the destination machines need to know about the device doing the NAT.

Figure 6-1 *Port Address Translation*

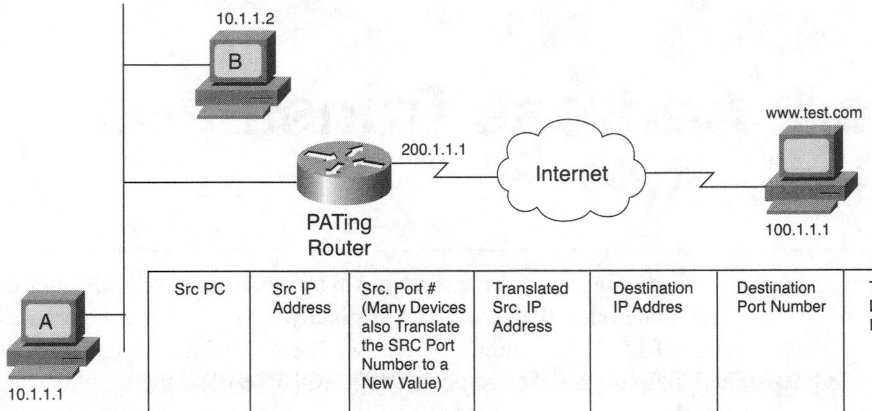

Src PC	Src IP Address	Src. Port # (Many Devices also Translate the SRC Port Number to a New Value)	Translated Src. IP Address	Destination IP Addres	Destination Port Number	Translated Destination IP Address
A	10.1.1.1	3759	200.1.1.1	100.1.1.1	80	100.1.1.1
B	10.1.1.2	2119	200.1.1.1	100.1.1.1	80	100.1.1.1

Security Benefits of Network Address Translation

NAT used in PAT mode can be a source of security for the network that is using PAT to translate its private addresses.

To understand this, assume that the device doing the NAT is a router that is sitting on the edge of the network, with one interface connected to the RFC 1918 private network and another interface connected to the Internet. When a device sitting behind the router wants to go out to the Internet, it sends packets to the router. The router then translates the source address into a globally routable address and puts the source IP address and source TCP or UDP port number in its NAT tables.

When the reply packets are delivered to the router, destined for the globally routable IP address, the router looks at the destination port number (remember, the source and destination port numbers are flipped in the return packet). Based on a lookup of its NAT table, the router determines which RFC 1918 address to send the packet to. It changes the destination address to the private address found in its NAT table and forwards the packet appropriately. The important point to realize in this operation is that the router can change back the IP address only if it has an entry for the destination port number in its NAT table. If for some reason that entry got cleared out and the router received a packet destined for the globally routable address, it would simply discard it, because it would not know where to send the packet. This property is at the crux of PAT's secure nature. Unless a NAT (PAT) entry is created on the router in its NAT table that contains the port number and private to global address mapping, the router does not forward any packets to the RFC 1918 network. Therefore, any connections not initiated from the inside are not allowed through the PAT device. This is a significant measure of security. However, you will see in the next section why this is not the type of security you can really rely on.

Disadvantages of Relying on NAT for Security

Although NAT provides some level of protection to the networks sitting behind it, it is important to understand that it is by no means a comprehensive security solution.

The following sections outline some of the most obvious reasons why NAT should not be considered a security mechanism, despite the illusion of security it provides.

No Tracking of Protocol Information Other Than the Port Number Information

The NAT table, created on the NAT device that is used to track the outgoing and incoming connections, does not track any of the other information contained in the packets. Information such as the packet sequence numbers, the TCP handshake, and UDP progress-based timers are some of the pieces of information that most firewalls track in order to prevent the usage of the connections established through the firewall by attackers spoofing IP addresses. NAT does not track any of this information, because it does not need to for the purposes of creating and maintaining NAT translations. Chapter 8, "PIX Firewall," contains a detailed discussion of the algorithm that PIX Firewall uses to provide security.

No Restriction on the Type of Content Flowing Based on PAT Tables

NAT also does not concern itself with protecting the hosts from malicious data being sent on the NAT connections established by the hosts themselves. You can only protect your network from such malicious content by having a firewall and an intrusion detection system in place.

Limited Control on Initial Connections

NAT does not have any real control over who can initiate connections from the inside network to the outside network. Although an access list is configured to define which hosts can initiate NAT connections, this is a rudimentary measure at best.

By using route maps and extended access control lists, you can put further restraints on what traffic can be NATed. However, this is not the ideal way to restrict traffic. It is difficult to implement with the same granularity as standard access control mechanisms, and it can be resource-intensive for the router.

In light of this, NAT is a useful mechanism for increasing the available IP address space. It can also be a convenient tool for some other network design aspects. However, it should not be relied on to provide security. When used on a security device such as a firewall in conjunction with other security features, NAT provides definite enhancements to the security provided by the firewall. However, it should not be used in isolation as a security mechanism. It does provide some measure of security. However, this always needs to be enhanced with additional tools and products designed specifically with security in mind, such as firewalls and intrusion detection systems.

Summary

NAT and PAT, which is a special form of NAT, are useful features for getting around the issue of limited IP address space. However, because PAT restricts connections to being initiated from the public side to the private side of a PAT device, it is sometimes considered a good-enough security mechanism in and of itself. This chapter discussed why this incorrect impression can lead to a false sense of security, which is more dangerous than knowing that you don't have any security. We discussed some of the main reasons why PAT cannot be relied on to provide network security. However, in conjunction with the security features available on a security device such as a firewall, PAT can augment a network's security.

Review Questions

1 What is port address translation?

2 What is the primary difference between NAT and proxy?

3 What is PAT's security advantage?

4 What is the difference between connection table maintenance for PAT and that of a firewall?

Firewalls

This chapter covers the following key topics:

- **Firewalls**—This section defines firewalls and lays the groundwork for discussing firewall products.

- **Types of Firewalls**—This section talks about the different kinds of firewalls in place in the industry today.

- **Positioning of Firewalls**—This section describes the important concept of positioning a firewall in a network.

## CHAPTER 7

What Are Firewalls?

Firewalls are an integral part of any secure network. As we continue the discussion of the various security features and designs, it is important to take an in-depth look at how firewalls protect a network.

This chapter is the first in a series of three chapters on firewalls. This chapter lays the foundation for an understanding of what firewalls in general are. We will discuss some of the most common features of firewalls and how these features are used to make a network secure. The next two chapters use the technical foundation built in this chapter to analyze the PIX and IOS firewalls.

Firewalls

The term *firewall* has many definitions in the industry. The definition depends on how and to what extent a firewall is used in a network. Generally, a firewall is a network device that, based on a defined network policy, implements access control for a network.

Apart from doing this basic job, firewalls are often used as network address translating devices, because they often tend to sit on the edge of a network and serve as entry points into the network. Figure 7-1 shows the basic philosophy of a firewall setup.

Some important characteristics distinguish a serious, industrial-strength firewall from other devices that go only halfway toward providing a true security solution are:

- Logging and notification ability
- High-volume packet inspection
- Ease of configuration
- Device security and redundancy

Figure 7-1   *Basic Firewall Philosophy*

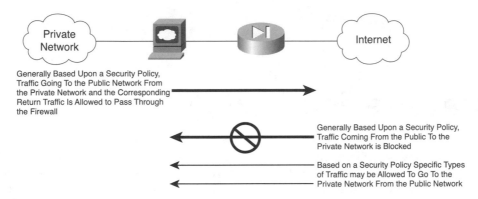

Generally Based Upon a Security Policy,
Traffic Going To the Public Network From
the Private Network and the Corresponding
Return Traffic Is Allowed to Pass Through
the Firewall

Generally Based Upon a Security Policy,
Traffic Coming From the Public To the
Private Network is Blocked

Based on a Security Policy Specific Types
of Traffic may be Allowed To Go To the
Private Network From the Public Network

Logging and Notification Ability

A firewall is not much good unless it has a good logging facility. Good logging not only allows network administrators to detect if attacks are being orchestrated against their networks, but it also lets them detect if what is considered normal traffic originating from trusted users is being used for ungainly purposes. Good logging allows network administrators to filter much information based on traffic tagging and get to the stuff that really matters very quickly. Obviously, good logging is different from logging everything that happens.

"Good logging" also refers to notification ability. Not only do you want the firewall to log the message, but you also want it to notify the administrator when alarm conditions are detected. Notification is often done by software that sorts through the log messages generated by the firewall device. Based on the criticality of the messages, the software generates notifications in the form of pages, e-mails, or other such means to notify a network administrator. The purpose of the notification is to let the administrator make a timely modification to either the configuration or the software image of the firewall itself to decrease the threat and impact of an attack or potential attack.

High-Volume Packet Inspection

One test of a firewall is its ability to inspect a large amount of network traffic against a configured set of rules without significantly degrading network performance. How much a firewall should be able to handle varies from network to network, but with today's demanding networks, a firewall should not become a bottleneck for the network it is sitting on. It is important to keep a firewall from becoming a bottleneck in a network because of its placement in the network. Firewalls are generally placed at the periphery of a network and are the only entry point into the network. Consequently, a slowdown at this critical place in the network can slow down the entire network.

Various factors can affect the speed at which a firewall processes the data passing through it. Most of the limitations are in hardware processor speed and in the optimization of software code that keeps track of the connections being established through the firewall. Another limiting factor is the availability of the various types of interface cards on the firewall. A firewall that can support Gigabit Ethernet in a Gigabit Ethernet environment is obviously more useful than one that can only do Fast Ethernet in a faster network such as Gigabit Ethernet.

One thing that often helps a firewall process traffic quickly is to offload some of the work to other software. This work includes notifications, URL filter-based access control, processing of firewall logs for filtering important information, and other such functions. These often-resource-intensive functions can take up a lot of the firewall's capacity and can slow it down.

Ease of Configuration

Ease of configuration includes the ability to set up the firewall quickly and to easily see configuration errors. Ease of configuration is very important in a firewall. The reason is that many network breaches that occur in spite of a firewall's being in place are not due to a bug in the firewall software or the underlying OS on which the firewall sits. They are due to an error in the firewall's configuration! Some of the "credit" for this goes to the person who configures the firewall. However, an easy-to-configure firewall mitigates many errors that might be produced in setting it up.

It is important for a firewall to have a configuration utility that allows easy translation of the site security policy into the configuration. It is very useful to have a graphical representation of the network architecture as part of the configuration utility to avoid common configuration errors. Similarly, the terminology used in the configuration utility needs to be in synch with normally accepted security site topological nomenclature, such as DMZ zones, high-security zones, and low-security zones. Use of ambiguous terminology in the configuration utility can cause human error to creep in.

Centralized administrative tools that allow for the simultaneous management of multiple security devices, including firewalls, are very useful for maintaining uniformly error-free configurations.

Device Security and Redundancy

The security of the firewall device itself is a critical component of the overall security that a firewall can provide to a network. A firewall that is insecure itself can easily allow intruders to break in and modify the configuration to allow further access into the network. There are two main areas where a firewall needs to have strength in order to avoid issues surrounding its own security:

- **The security of the underlying operating system**—If the firewall software runs on a separate operating system, the vulnerabilities of that operating system have the potential to become the vulnerabilities of the firewall itself. It is important to install the firewall software on an operating system known to be robust against network security threats and to keep patching the system regularly to fill any gaps that become known.

- **Secure access to the firewall for administrative purposes**—It is important for a firewall to have secure mechanisms available for allowing administrative access to it. Such methods can include encryption coupled with proper authentication mechanisms. Weakness in the implementation of such access mechanisms can allow the firewall to become an easy target for intrusions of various kinds.

An issue related to device security is the firewall's ability to have a redundant presence with another firewall in the network. Such redundancy allows the backup device to take up the operations of a faulty primary device. In the case of an attack on the primary device that leaves it nonoperational, redundancy also allows for continued operation of the network.

Types of Firewalls

In order to gain a thorough understanding of firewall technology, it is important to understand the various types of firewalls. These various types of firewalls provide more or less the same functions that were outlined earlier. However, their methods of doing so provide differentiation in terms of performance and level of security offered.

The firewalls discussed in this section are divided into five categories based on the mechanism that each uses to provide firewall functionality:

- Circuit-level firewalls
- Proxy server firewalls
- Nonstateful packet filters
- Stateful packet filters
- Personal firewalls

These various types of firewalls gather different types of information from the data flowing through them to keep track of legitimate and illegitimate traffic and to protect against unauthorized access. The type of information they use often also determines the level of security they provide.

Circuit-Level Firewalls

These firewalls act as relays for TCP connections. They intercept TCP connections being made to a host behind them and complete the handshake on behalf of that host. Only after the connection is established is the traffic allowed to flow to the client. Also, the firewall makes sure that as soon as the connection is established, only data packets belonging to the connection are allowed to go through.

Circuit-level firewalls do not validate the payload or any other information in the packet, so they are fairly fast. These firewalls essentially are interested only in making sure that the TCP handshake is properly completed before a connection is allowed. Consequently, these firewalls do not allow access restrictions to be placed on protocols other than TCP and do not allow the use of payload information in the higher-layer protocols to restrict access.

Proxy Server Firewalls

Proxy server firewalls work by examining packets at the application layer. Essentially a proxy server intercepts the requests being made by the applications sitting behind it and performs the requested functions on behalf of the requesting application. It then forwards the results to the application. In this way it can provide a fairly high level of security to the applications, which do not have to interact directly with outside applications and servers.

Proxy servers are advantageous in the sense that they are aware of application-level protocols and they can restrict or allow access based on these protocols. They also can look into the data portions of the packets and use that information to restrict access. However, this very capability of processing the packets at a higher layer of the stack can contribute to the slowness of proxy servers. Also, because the inbound traffic has to be processed by the proxy server as well as the end-user application, further degradation in speed can occur. Proxy servers often are not transparent to end users who have to make modifications to their applications in order to use the proxy server. For each new application that must go through a proxy firewall, modifications need to be made to the firewall's protocol stack to handle that type of application.

Nonstateful Packet Filters

Nonstateful packet filters are fairly simple devices that sit on the periphery of a network and, based on a set of rules, allow some packets through while blocking others. The decisions are made based on the addressing information contained in network layer protocols such as IP and, in some cases, information contained in transport layer protocols such as TCP or UDP headers as well.

Nonstateful packet filters are fairly simple devices, but to function properly they require a thorough understanding of the usage of services required by a network to be protected. Although these filters can be fast because they do not proxy any traffic but only inspect it as it passes through, they do not have any knowledge of the application-level protocols or the data elements in the packet. Consequently, their usefulness is limited. These filters also do not retain any knowledge of the sessions established through them. Instead, they just keep tabs on what is immediately passing through.. The use of simple and extended access lists (without the **established** keyword) on routers are examples of such firewalls.

Stateful Packet Filters

Stateful packet filters are more intelligent than simple packet filters in that they can block pretty much all incoming traffic and still can allow return traffic for the traffic generated by machines sitting behind them. They do so by keeping a record of the transport layer connections that are established through them by the hosts behind them.

Stateful packet filters are the mechanism for implementing firewalls in most modern networks. Stateful packet filters can keep track of a variety of information regarding the packets that are traversing them, including the following:

- Source and destination TCP and UDP port numbers
- TCP sequence numbering
- TCP flags
- TCP session state based on the RFCed TCP state machine
- UDP traffic tracking based on timers

Stateful firewalls often have built-in advanced IP layer handling features such as fragment reassembly and clearing or rejecting of IP options.

Many modern stateful packet filters are aware of application layer protocols such as FTP and HTTP and can perform access-control functions based on these protocols' specific needs.

Personal Firewalls

Personal firewalls are firewalls installed on personal computers. They are designed to protect against network attacks. These firewalls are generally aware of the applications running on the machine and allow only connections established by these applications to operate on the machine.

A personal firewall is a useful addition to any PC because it increases the level of security already offered by a network firewall. However, because many of the attacks on today's networks originate from inside the protected network, a PC firewall is an even more useful tool, because network firewalls cannot protect against these attacks. Personal firewalls come in a variety of flavors. Most are implemented to be aware of the applications running on the PC. However, they are designed to not require any changes from the user applications running on the PC, as is required in the case of proxy servers.

Positioning of Firewalls

Positioning a firewall is as important as using the right type of firewall and configuring it correctly. Positioning a firewall determines which traffic will be screened and whether there are any back doors into the protected network. Some of the basic guidelines for positioning a firewall are as follows:

- **Topological location of the firewall**—It is often a good idea to place a firewall on the periphery of a private network, as close to the final exit and initial entry point into the network as possible. The network includes any remote-access devices and VPN concentrators sitting on the its periphery. This allows the greatest number of devices on the private network to be protected by the firewall and also helps keep the boundary of the private and public network very clear. A network in which there is ambiguity as to what is public and what is private is a network waiting to be attacked.

  Certain situations might also warrant placing a firewall within a private network in addition to placing a firewall at the entry point. An example of such a situation is when a critical segment of the network, such as the segment housing the financial or HR servers, needs to be protected from the rest of the users on the private network.

  Also, in most cases firewalls should not be placed in parallel to other network devices such as routers. This can cause the firewall to be bypassed. You should also avoid any other additions to the network topology that can result in the firewall's getting bypassed.

- **Accessibility and security zones**—If there are servers that need to be accessed from the public network, such as Web servers, it is often a good idea to put them in a demilitarized zone (DMZ) built on the firewall rather than keep them inside the private network. The reason for this is that if these servers are on the internal network and the firewall has been asked to allow some level of access to these servers from the public network, this access opens a door for attackers. They can use this access to gain control of the servers or to stage attacks on the private network using the access holes created in the firewall. A DMZ allows publicly accessible servers to be placed in an area that is physically separate from the private network, forcing the attackers who have somehow gained control over these servers to go through the firewall again to gain access to the private network.

- **Asymmetric routing**—Most modern firewalls work on the concept of keeping state information for the connections made through them from the private network to the public network. This information is used to allow only the packets belonging to the legitimate connections back into the private network. Consequently, it is important that the exit and entry points of all traffic to and from the private network be through the same firewall. If this is not the case, a firewall may drop packets belonging to legitimate connections started from the internal network for which it has no state information. This scenario is known as asymmetric routing.

- **Layering firewalls**—In networks where a high degree of security is desired, often two or more firewalls can be deployed in series. If the first firewall fails, the second one can continue to function. This technique is often used as a safeguard against network attacks that exploit bugs in a firewall's software. If one firewall's software is vulnerable to an attack, hopefully the software of the second firewall sitting behind it will not be. Firewalls from different vendors are often used in these setups to ensure that one incorrect or compromised implementation can be backed up by the other vendor's implementation.

Positioning a firewall can be a complicated issue in a large network with multiple subsegments and entry points. Often a network that has not used a firewall in the past needs to be restructured to allow a firewall to be placed properly to protect it. This is necessary to create a single point of entry and exit and to remove the issue of asymmetric routing.

Summary

Firewalls are a critical component of any secure network. Firewalls in one form or another provide restricted access to a network based on a defined security policy. In order to make the best use of a firewall's capabilities, however, it is critical to position it in the network where it can provide the most security coverage possible.

This chapter is the building block for the more-specific discussions to follow in the next two chapters. We will discuss how the PIX and IOS firewalls (which are examples of stateful packet filters) are implemented and positioned, keeping in mind the principles discussed in this chapter.

This chapter covers the following key topics:

- **Adaptive Security Algorithm**—This section discusses ASA, the algorithm used to construct the PIX Firewall.

- **Basic Features of the PIX Firewall**—This section talks about basic features available in the PIX Firewall. It builds the basis for a discussion of some of the firewall's advanced features.

- **Advanced Features of the PIX Firewall**—This section details of some of the advanced security features incorporated into the PIX Firewall.

- **Case Studies**—This section contains case studies involving PIX Firewall implementations.

## CHAPTER 8

PIX Firewall

PIX Firewall is an example of a stateful packet filter. PIX also can work on higher layers of the protocol stack for various protocols such as FTP, RealAudio, and others that need the firewall to be aware of them at the application layer. PIX Firewall is a standalone firewall that runs on its own operating system rather than run as an application on top of another OS. This chapter discusses the functioning of the PIX Firewall and some of its advanced features that are important in using it as a firewall in today's complex networks.

Adaptive Security Algorithm

Adaptive Security Algorithm (ASA) is the foundation on which the PIX Firewall is built. It defines how PIX examines traffic passing through it and applies various rules to it. The basic concept behind ASA is to keep track of the various connections being formed from the networks behind the PIX to the public network. Based on the information collected about these connections, ASA allows packets to come back into the private network through the firewall. All other traffic destined for the private network and coming to the firewall is blocked.

ASA also defines the information PIX saves for any given connection made through it (this is called state information in the case where TCP is being used as the transport protocol). It can include a variety of information from the IP and the transport headers. The ASA algorithm also defines how the state and other information is used to track the sessions passing through the PIX. To achieve this behavior, PIX keeps track of the following information:

- IP packet source and destination information
- TCP sequence numbers and additional TCP flags
- UDP packet flow and timers

The following sections discuss how ASA deals with the TCP and UDP traffic passing through the PIX Firewall.

TCP

TCP is relatively easy to inspect, because it is connection-oriented. All the firewall has to do is keep track of each session being formed, utilized, and terminated. ASA only allows for the packets conforming to the state, in which the firewall believes the connection should be in, to go through the firewall. All other packets are dropped. However, TCP has a couple of inherent weaknesses that require ASA to perform a few modifications on the TCP packets passing through it to ensure security:

- The Initial Sequence Number (ISN) generated by TCP for its connections is not random. This can result in TCP session hijacking (see case study in Chapter 14, "What Is Intrusion Detection?," for an example of how this can be done). The ASA algorithm takes care of this problem by calculating a more random sequence number, inputting this number as the sequence number in the outgoing packets and storing the difference between the two random numbers. When return traffic for that particular packet is received, it replaces the changed sequence number with the correct one before forwarding the packet to the host on the inside private network.

- SYN flooding is a reality in TCP environments. To somewhat mitigate the problem of SYN floods occurring for servers sitting behind the firewall, ASA keeps track of the synchronization requests coming in through the firewall. If the synchronization does not result in a full-blown session in a given amount of time and/or the number of such half-open sessions increases beyond a certain limit (both are configurable), the firewall starts closing such connections.

A recent enhancement to the PIX ASA implementation (in version 5.2 and later) causes the PIX to proxy for connection attempts to servers or other resources sitting behind it (SYNs) after the number of incomplete connections through the PIX reaches a configurable limit (a limit on embryonic connections). The PIX responds to SYN requests with SYN ACKs and continues proxying the connection until the three-way TCP handshake is complete. After that, it allows the connection through to the server or resource sitting behind it on the private or DMZ network. This way, only legitimate connections are allowed to be made through the PIX, and the rest are dropped based on configurable timeouts on the PIX. This is an important feature, because it limits the exposure of the servers sitting behind the PIX to SYN floods.

Figures 8-1 and 8-2 are a step-by-step overview of how a TCP connection through the PIX is handled. Figure 8-1 illustrates the TCP transmission (initialization) process and Figure 8-2 illustrates the TCP termination process.

Figure 8-1 shows the sequence of events that take place as a host sitting behind the PIX initiates a TCP connection to the outside world. The SYN packet from the host is used to create the connection entry in the PIX because this is the first packet for the connection that this host is initiating. The PIX creates the entry after examining the rules set up for such an entry to be created. The PIX performs the necessary address translation on the packet and forwards it after saving the packet's state information—the IP addresses, the port information, the TCP flags, and the sequence number. The PIX also further randomizes the sequence number before forwarding it. PIX keeps track of the delta in the original and the new sequence number so that it can restore it in the return packet.

Figure 8-1 *TCP Initiation and Transmission*

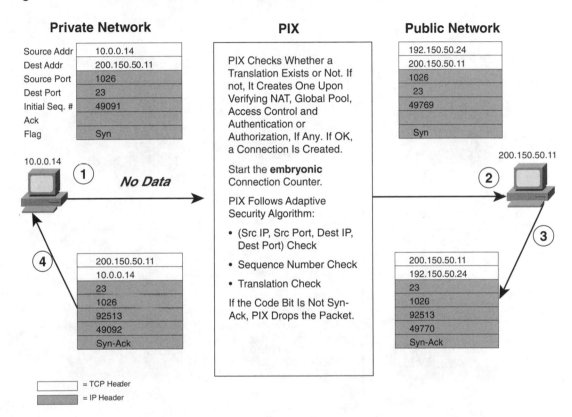

The return traffic sent to the host arrives at the PIX with the TCP flag set to SYN-ACK and the sequence number incremented by 1. PIX ASA looks through its state information tables and verifies that the information provided by this packet is what it would have expected from a return packet to the one that was originally sent. Because this is indeed the case, PIX changes the sequence number to take out the change it had made while randomizing the sequence number of the initial packet that was sent out, modifies the IP addresses and port information in accordance with its NAT tables, and forwards the packet on to the host that originated the first packet.

After the TCP initial three way handshake is complete, PIX tracks the packet flow for the TCP connection established through it, allowing only legitimate packets belonging to the flow to come back.

Figure 8-2 shows how the PIX ASA processes a TCP termination. After the host has completed exchanging information and wants to terminate the TCP connection, it sends a TCP packet with the flag set to FIN. This signals the end of the connection to the remote host to which it was connected. ASA sees the FIN packet passing through and waits for the FIN-ACK to arrive. After this happens, it closes the connection.

Figure 8-2   *TCP Termination*

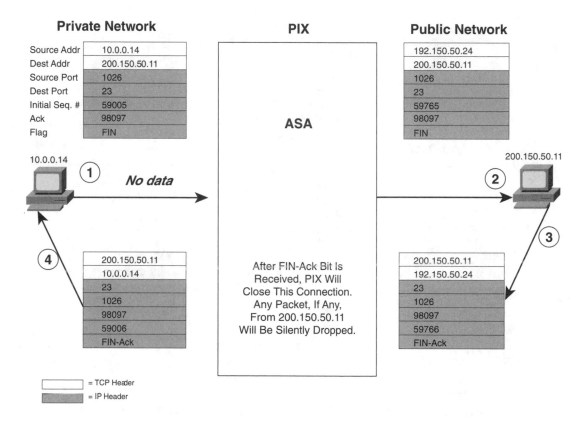

UDP

UDP is more difficult to track through a firewall. It is connectionless, and no state machine is involved that would allow the ASA to determine the initiator of a connection or the current state. ASA consequently tracks UDP sessions based on a timer. Whenever a UDP session is generated through the PIX, ASA creates a connection slot based on the source and destination IP addresses and port numbers in the packet and starts a timer. All return traffic for that particular connection slot is allowed to go through until the timer expires.

This timer, which is an idle timer, expires when no UDP traffic flows through the PIX in a certain UDP session for a configurable amount of time. Although this allows some amount of security, the control is not as rigid as in TCP processing.

Figure 8-3 is a step-by-step overview of how a UDP session is processed by the ASA through a PIX Firewall.

Figure 8-3   *UDP Transmission*

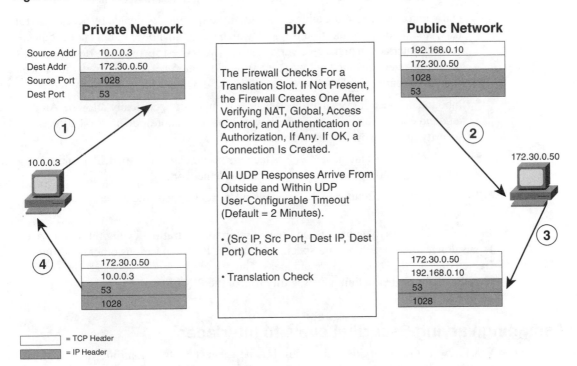

Basic Features of the PIX Firewall

This section discusses some of the basic features of the PIX Firewall. These features are the fundamental building blocks of the PIX Firewall. After we have established how the PIX achieves basic firewalling, we will go into a more detailed discussion of some of the PIX's advanced features. As you will see in the following discussion, a firewall with just the basic features can cater to most of a simple network's needs. However, to increase the firewall's utility when you're faced with some of the more complicated application layer protocol connection setups and to increase the firewall's usefulness when you're faced with unique network topologies, some of the advanced features come in handy.

Stateful Inspection of Traffic Using the ASA

We have discussed in detail how the ASA works. This section looks at some of the basic rules the PIX Firewall uses to control access into a network. These rules also set up the basis for all other traffic flowing through the PIX.

PIX Firewall uses the following basic set of rules to determine how traffic flows through it:

- No packets can traverse the PIX Firewall without a translation, connection, and state.

- Outbound connections are allowed, except those specifically denied by access control lists. An outbound connection is one in which the originator or client is on a higher security interface than the receiver or server. The highest security interface is always the inside interface, and the lowest is the outside interface. Any perimeter interface can have security levels between the inside and outside values.

- Inbound connections or states are denied, except those specifically allowed. An inbound connection or state is one in which the originator or client is on a lower security interface or network than the receiver or server.

- All ICMP packets are denied unless they are specifically permitted. This includes echo replies to pings originated from the inside network.

- All attempts to circumvent the previous rules are dropped, and a message is sent to syslog.

PIX uses these rules to define a basic firewall setup for the traffic flowing through it. After this is done, you can set up more-specific constraints based on various other conditions to tighten or relax the security in certain areas. The rest of this section looks at some of the techniques for further defining the security role of the PIX Firewall.

Assigning Varying Security Levels to Interfaces

PIX Firewall allows varying security levels to be assigned to its various interfaces. This key technique allows for the implementation of a security policy calling for varying levels of security control in a network's different segments. These segments are usually called *security zones*.

A PIX Firewall can have from two to ten interfaces. Each interface can be assigned a level from 0 to 100. A lower level number means that an interface belongs to a relatively less-secure part of the network as compared to an interface that has a higher level number. Typically, the interface connected to the public network has a 0 level assigned to it. This describes a very low level of security. The interface sitting on the private network has a security level of 100, meaning that it is the most secure. DMZ interfaces have security levels between 0 and 100. By default, traffic can flow freely from a high security level interface to a low security level interface, provided that a network address translation (xlate) is built for the traffic's source IP addresses. PIX keeps track of the connections for this traffic and allows the return traffic through. However, for traffic to flow from a low security level to a high security level, rules need to be explicitly defined on the PIX Firewall, allowing this traffic to go through. This is done using access control lists or conduit statements. These rules are in addition to the creation of static xlates for this type of traffic when going from a lower to a higher security level. You will see examples of how to implement these in the case studies at the end of this chapter.

Access Control Lists

Access control lists (ACLs) open holes in the PIX Firewall to allow traffic from a public or less-secure portion of the network to go to a private or more-secure portion of the network. The connection is initiated from the public or less-secure network. For a machine on a DMZ network to access the private network behind the PIX, an access list must be created, specifying that this type of traffic needs to be allowed. This access list is needed because the DMZ is a less-secure network than the private network. Access lists are needed in addition to a static Network Address Translation (NAT) entry to allow this to happen. A static translation is needed because traffic going from a less-secure network to a higher-security network does not have the luxury of using the NAT setup for traffic moving from a more-secure network to a less-secure network. A permanent translation in the opposite direction is needed to accommodate this type of traffic.

Often access lists are used to allow connections to be made to web or mail servers sitting on the DMZ network of the PIX from the public network. Access lists control these connections based on a combination of source address, destination address, protocol numbers, and port numbers. ICMP packets can also be controlled using ACLs. Be careful when using them. Opening the PIX for more than what is required can lead to network intrusions. The site's security policy plays a critical role in defining the ACLs on a PIX Firewall.

Extensive Logging Capabilities

PIX allows extensive logging to take place for traffic flowing through it. **show** commands and packet dumps can also be used to obtain extensive information on the traffic flowing through the PIX. However, for normal circumstances, system logs sent to a syslog server are often sufficient for tracking malicious activity on a network. In addition to giving an insight into any malicious activity, the syslog messages are also a source of debugging information for troubleshooting PIX configuration issues. A PIX Firewall records the following types of syslog messages:

- Connection events (for example, connections denied by the PIX Firewall configuration or address translation errors)
- AAA (authentication, authorization, and accounting) events
- Failover events reported by one or both units of a failover pair

- FTP/URL events (for example, successful file transfers or blocked Java applets)
- Mail Guard/SNMP events
- PIX Firewall management events (for example, configuration events or Telnet connections to the PIX Firewall console port)
- Routing errors

The syslog messages can be sent to the PIX console, a Telnet session, or a logging server. The amount of information displayed when the messages are sent to the console is limited as compared to the information sent to the logging server. A general strategy is to use the syslog messages appearing on the console for basic debugging needs and to use the syslog server if more-detailed information on individual messages is needed.

PIX conforms to the standard syslog logging levels:

- **0**—Emergency. System unusable message.
- **1**—Alert. Take immediate action.
- **2**—Critical condition.
- **3**—Error message.
- **4**—Warning message.
- **5**—Notification. Normal but significant condition.
- **6**—Informational message.
- **7**—Debug message, log FTP command, or WWW URL.

Enabling logging at any level enables logging for all levels up to that level.

Individual messages within a specific logging level can be disabled so that routine messages don't inundate the syslog file. PIX logs can be sent to any standard syslog server, including the PIX Firewall syslog server, the PIX Firewall manager, and Cisco Security Manager. Some commercially available software, such as Private Eye, also allow extensive reporting to be done on the syslog messages generated by the PIX Firewall.

PIX Firewall also can act as an Inline Intrusion Detection System (IDS) and send logging messages related to this functionality. See Chapter 15, "Cisco Secure Intrusion Detection," for information on how PIX performs this role.

Basic Routing Capability, Including Support for RIP

PIX supports some basic routing. This includes the use of default routes, static routes, and Routing Information Protocol (RIP). However, routing functionality in a PIX Firewall is minimal. PIX also is unable to reroute packets received on one of its interfaces to another machine located on the same interface. RIP support is limited to PIX's being able to accept route information on its various interfaces. PIX can broadcast a default route only if it is configured to do so via RIP. In addition, PIX cannot propagate the RIP information learned from a network attached to one of its interfaces to a network attached to another of its interfaces. PIX does however support RIPv2's security features.

Network Address Translation

PIX can perform NAT for packets traversing any two of its interfaces. PIX's default behavior is to require NAT. This means that NAT must be set up for a connection state to be created, regardless of the level of the interface from which the packet originates. PIX allows NAT rules to be set up separately for various sets of interfaces. This allows flexibility in how NAT is deployed on the PIX. One method of NAT may be used for one pair of interfaces, and another may be used for another pair of interfaces. The most common use of NAT is when the private network behind the PIX uses an RFC 1918 space. PIX can convert the source addresses of the packets leaving this network into a globally routable address configured on it. PIX then maintains state information for this translation so that it can route the return traffic to the correct host on the internal network. NAT can also be used between two interfaces on the PIX, neither of which is on the public network, so they do not use a globally routable address space. In this case, NAT occurs from an RFC 1918 space to an RFC 1918 space. While the practical need for having this type of translation may be limited, PIX requires NAT to be setup in order to pass traffic between any two interfaces. PIX can do both one-to-one and one-to-many NAT. For a more detailed discussion of NAT's security aspects, see Chapter 6, "Network Address Translation and Security."

The PIX Firewall also provides static Port Address Translation (PAT). This capability can be used to send multiple inbound TCP or UDP services to different internal hosts through a single global address. The global address can be a unique address or a shared outbound PAT address or it can be shared with the external interface.

The PIX Firewall (in version 6.2 and later) also can do address translation for the source IP addresses of packets going from a low-security interface to a high-security interface. This functionality does not remove the need to have a static translation to be able to access the machines sitting on a higher security level from a lower security level.

Failover and Redundancy

Failover in PIX allows a standby system to take over the functionality of the primary system as soon as it fails. This changeover can be set up to be stateful, meaning that the connection information stored on the failing PIX is transferred to the PIX taking over. Before getting into a discussion of how failover takes place on the PIX Firewall, it is useful to define some of the terminology that the PIX uses for the failover functionality.

Active Unit Versus Standby Unit

The active unit actively performs normal network functions. The standby unit only monitors, ready to take control should the active unit fail to perform.

Primary Unit Versus Secondary Unit

The failover cable has two ends, primary and secondary. The primary unit is determined by the unit that has the end of the failover cable marked "primary." The secondary unit is connected to the end of the failover cable marked "secondary."

System IP Address Versus Failover IP Address

The system IP address is the IP address of the primary unit (upon bootup). The failover IP address is the IP address of the secondary unit.

State information for stateful failover is communicated to the PIX taking over through an Ethernet cable joining the two PIXes. However, the actual detection of whether a unit has failed takes place via keepalives passed over a serial cable connected between the two PIXes (see note later on in the section on enhancements made in ver 6.2 of PIX). Both units in a failover pair communicate through the failover cable, which is a modified RS-232 serial link cable that transfers data at 117,760 baud (115 KB). The data provides the unit identification of primary or secondary, indicates the other unit's power status, and serves as a communication link for various failover communications between the two units. For the failover to work correctly, the hardware, software, and configurations on the two PIXes need to be identical. It is simple enough to use commands on the PIX to synch the configurations of the two PIXes, but the hardware and software must be matched up manually. The two units send special failover hello packets to each other over all network interfaces and the failover cable every 15 seconds. The failover feature in PIX Firewall monitors failover communication, the other unit's power status, and hello packets received at each interface. If two consecutive hello packets are not received within a time determined by the failover feature, failover starts testing the interfaces to determine which unit has failed, and it transfers active control to the standby unit. If a failure is due to a condition other than a loss of power on the other unit, the failover begins a series of tests to determine which unit failed. These tests are as follows:

- **Link up/down test**—This is a test of the network interface card. If an interface card is not plugged into an operational network, it is considered failed (for example, a switch failed due to a faulty port, or a cable is unplugged).

- **Network activity test**—This is a received network activity test. The unit counts all received packets for up to 5 seconds. If any packets are received during this interval, the interface is considered operational, and testing stops. If no traffic is received, the ARP test begins.

- **ARP test**—The ARP test consists of reading the unit's ARP cache for the ten most recently acquired entries. One at a time, the unit sends ARP requests to these machines, attempting to stimulate network traffic. After each request, the unit counts all received traffic for up to 5 seconds. If traffic is received, the interface is considered operational. If no traffic is received, an ARP request is sent to the next machine. If at the end of the list no traffic has been received, the ping test begins.

- **Broadcast ping test**—The ping test consists of sending out a broadcast ping request. The unit then counts all received packets for up to 5 seconds. If any packets are received during this interval, the interface is considered operational, and testing stops. If no traffic is received, the testing starts again with the ARP test.

The purpose of these tests is to generate network traffic to determine which (if either) unit has failed. At the start of each test, each unit clears its received packet count for its interfaces. At the conclusion of each test, each unit looks to see if it has received any traffic. If it has, the interface is considered operational. If one unit receives traffic for a test and the other unit does not, the unit that received no traffic is considered failed. If neither unit has received traffic, go to the next test.

The PIX taking over assumes the IP addresses as well as the MAC addresses of the failed PIX, allowing for transparency for the hosts attached to the interfaces of the failed PIX. The unit that activates assumes the IP and MAC addresses of the previously active unit and begins accepting traffic. The new standby unit assumes the failover IP and MAC addresses of the unit that was previously the active unit. Because network devices see no change in these addresses, no ARP entries change or time out anywhere on the network.

In general, the following events can often cause a PIX Firewall to fail over to a backup:

- Running out of memory. PIX looks for out-of-memory errors for 15 consecutive minutes before it fails over.

- Power outage on the primary PIX, or a reboot.

- An interface's going down for more than 30 seconds.

You can also force a failover manually by issuing the **failover active** command on the secondary PIX Firewall.

In case of a stateful failover, the following information is replicated from the primary PIX to the secondary PIX:

- The configuration
- TCP connection table, including timeout information for each connection
- Translation (xlate) table
- System up time; that is, the system clock is synchronized on both PIX Firewall units

The rules for the replication of the configuration are as follows:

- When the standby unit completes its initial bootup, the active unit replicates its entire configuration to the standby unit.

- The commands are sent via the failover cable.

- The **write standby** command can be used on the active unit to force the entire configuration to the standby unit.

- The configuration replication only replicates configurations from memory to memory. After replication, a **write mem** is needed to write the configuration into Flash memory.

Some of the significant information that is not replicated is as follows:

- User authentication (uauth) table

- ISAKMP and IPsec SA table

- ARP table

- Routing information

The secondary PIX must rebuild this information to perform the functions of the primary PIX, which has failed.

Version 6.2 of the PIX Firewall adds more functionality to the PIX failover feature set. From this version on, the failover communication can take place over the Ethernet cable used to copy state information from the primary PIX to the secondary PIX. This gets rid of the need to use a separate serial failover cable, thus overcoming distance limitations created by its use. A dedicated LAN interface and a dedicated switch/hub (or VLAN) are required to implement LAN-based failover. A crossover Ethernet cable cannot be used to connect the two PIX Firewalls. PIX LAN failover uses IP protocol 105 for communication between the two PIXes.

Authentication for Traffic Passing Through the PIX

PIX allows for what is known as cut-through proxy authentication for various services being accessed through the PIX. PIX allows the data flow to be established through it and entered into the ASA as a valid state only if the authentication occurring during the establishment of that connection succeeds. This also means that as soon as the connection is established after authentication, PIX lets the rest of the packets belonging to that connection go through without having to check them for authentication again. The parameters for this authentication are provided through an initial HTTP, Telnet, or FTP session. Authentication can take place on both inbound and outbound traffic, to and fro from a private network on the PIX.

TACACS+ and Radius are the AAA servers supported by the PIX.

The basic PIX features just discussed form the framework of most common PIX operations. The case studies later in this chapter cover the use of these features. Each case study uses some or all of the features. It is important for the you to refer back and forth between the case studies and the sections describing the various features to get a thorough understanding of how PIX works.

Advanced Features of the PIX Firewall

Apart from the basic features covered in the preceding sections, PIX also supports some fairly advanced features, complementing its capability to provide basic packet filtering based on the ASA. These features serve various purposes in the PIX Firewall. Most of them, such as the alias and some of the **sysopt** commands, are used to provide additional flexibility to the PIX Firewall to fit into a networking environment without changing the existing setup. Others, such as the various guards, are used to provide additional security to the networks protected by the PIX Firewall.

The following sections discuss these features, how they work, and the problems they are used to solve.

Alias

The PIX's alias feature is used to set up a mechanism whereby the destination IP addresses contained in packets going from one interface to another are NATed (translated). This is necessary in various situations, especially where an external DNS server is used to resolve the names for servers on the inside or DMZ networks, where an IP address is being illegally used in the private network behind the PIX, or where two enterprise networks are merged to form one network across a PIX Firewall. The **alias** command not only translates the destination IP addresses, but can also doctor the DNS responses passing through the PIX to comply with the translation taking place on the destination IP addresses.

The following sections discuss in detail how the alias feature works. PIX aliasing allows either of the following objectives to be achieved:

- NAT on the destination IP addresses
- "DNS doctoring" by the alias feature

NAT on the Destination IP Addresses

Normally PIX does NAT on the source IP addresses for packets going from the high security level to the low security level. However, the **alias** command allows NAT to occur on the destination IP addresses as well. This means that if a host on the inside network sends a packet to destination IP address A, PIX redirects that packet to destination address B after changing the destination IP address in the packet to B.

An example of using the **alias** command in this manner occurs when hosts located on the inside network use an external DNS server to resolve the name of a server sitting on the PIX Firewall's DMZ interface. The server is physically configured with an RFC 1918 address that is statically translated into a globally routable address on the PIX to allow access from the outside world. If a client on the private network tries to access the server and send a DNS request to the DNS server, the DNS server replies with the server's globally routable address, not its RFC 1918 address. The PIX is set up to do aliasing such that when the client on the internal network sends a packet to the globally routable IP address of the server on the DMZ, the PIX translates the destination IP address to that of the server's RFC 1918 address and forwards the packet to its DMZ interface. Another way to resolve this problem is to have separate internal and external DNS servers, but this is not always possible.

Figure 8-4 depicts how the alias feature can be used to deal with this scenario.

Figure 8-4   *How the Alias Feature Does NAT on the Destination IP Addresses*

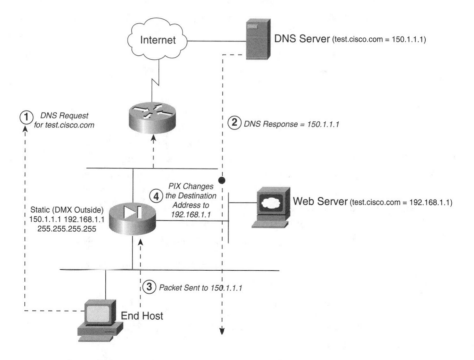

"DNS Doctoring" by the Alias Feature

The PIX's alias feature can also doctor or modify the responses, passing through the PIX Firewall, sent to a client by a DNS server. This is a very useful feature when an external DNS server is the only DNS server available to the clients sitting on the PIX's inside network.

An example of the use of this feature occurs when an RFC 1918 address server is on the PIX Firewall's inside interface. This server is accessible to the outside world via a static translation created on the PIX Firewall for the RFC 1918 address to a globally routable address. If a client tries to access this server using its name, the DNS server responds by sending back the server's globally routable address to the client. This is obviously not the desired result. Therefore, the PIX using the alias feature doctors the DNS response from the DNS server and changes the resolved address to the server's RFC 1918 address on the inside network. This way, the client can access the server using its private address. Of course, another way around this problem is to use external and internal DNS servers. However, that is not always an available option.

Figure 8-5 depicts how the alias feature can be used to deal with this scenario.

Figure 8-5   *How the Alias Feature Does DNS Doctoring*

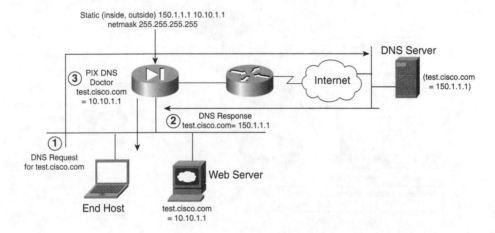

Another problem network administrators can run into is when they use an IP address (for one of their machines on the inside or a DMZ network) that is legally being used by a server somewhere on the Internet. This works fine as long as this machine's source address gets NATed to something else while going to the Internet. However, if one of the other machines on the private network tries to reach that Internet server using its name, the address returned by the DNS server is actually the address of the machine sitting on the local network with the duplicate address. Consequently, the machine trying to reach the Internet server sends the packet to the local machine instead of the Internet server. The **alias** command can be used to correct this behavior. The **alias** command allows the PIX Firewall the change (doctor) the address returned in the DNS response from the DNS server into a unique address not found on the local network. When the machine trying to reach the Internet server sends its packets to this new address, the PIX changes the destination address back to the Internet server's correct address and sends the packet on to the public Internet.

Figure 8-6 depicts how the alias feature deals with this scenario.

Figure 8-6 *How the Alias Feature Circumvents Overlapping IP Addresses*

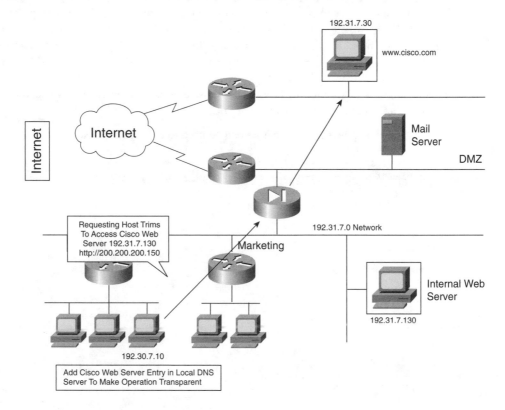

The PIX Firewall can get the same functionality described here by using the outside address NAT functionality (bidirectional NAT) in the PIX Firewall (version 6.2 and later). This allows for DNS doctoring (with the use of the DNS keyword), as well as doing NAT on the source addresses for traffic going from a low-security interface to a high-security interface. The details of the actual functionality achieved, however, are the same.

x Guards

The various guards on the PIX are designed to protect against specific types of network attacks. These guards act as an additional layer of defense to protect the network on top of the basic PIX Firewall features already enabled on the firewall.

Basically, four special features called guards are available in PIX:

- Flood
- Frag
- Mail
- DNS

Flood Guard

This feature is used to mitigate the danger of a denial of service (DoS) attack using AAA login attempts. This feature limits the number of failed AAA authentication attempts to make such attacks more difficult to stage. This feature is on by default.

Frag Guard

This feature allows control over the PIX's tolerance and treatment of fragmented packets. PIX restricts the number of fragments that are headed for a host protected by the PIX to 100 full fragments per second. Also, by default the PIX code does not allow an IP packet to be fragmented into more than 24 fragments. In addition, PIX restricts fragments that arrive without a proper header from being forwarded to hosts behind it. These measures allow fragmentation attacks in which the attacker sends a large number of fragments to an end host to be avoided. These attacks are very resource-consumptive, because the end host has to allocate a significant amount of resources to reassembling the packets, especially if they are out of sequence.

IP fragments also do not contain the TCP or UDP port information that PIX needs to perform its various PAT functions. Consequently, PIX has no way to switch a fragmented packet through it, because it does not know which xlate to use to switch it. Also, PIX cannot create an xlate for packets going from high-security to low-security interfaces, because there is no port information to work from.

An obvious solution is to reassemble all pertinent IP fragments into an IP packet and then switch it. However, full reassembly is expensive in term of buffer space reservation, which needs to be done to put the fragments together. Buffer space needs to be allocated to re-create the original packet after all the fragments have arrived and are ready to be coalesced. This buffer space is in addition to the buffer space needed to simply store the fragments as they arrive. The firewall has to wait for the last fragment to arrive.

To minimize buffer preallocation, a reassembly mechanism known as **virtual reassembly** is used. With virtual reassembly, fragments are not combined, so no buffer preallocation is needed. However, to provide the benefits of full reassembly, each fragment set is verified for integrity, such as the header information and various fragment attacks, and is tagged with the transport header information. In this manner, without allocating any significant buffer resources, the fragments are switched through the PIX port address translation mechanism based on the tagged information. It is not a requirement for the first fragment containing the port information to arrive first on the PIX Firewall. However, the PIX Firewall does not forward the packet to the next-hop box until all the packet's fragments have arrived at it and have been verified and tagged with the transport information contained in the initial fragment.

NOTE   ICMP packets are still reassembled in full rather than being virtually reassembled.

PIX also allows the use of the **fragment** command to allow various parameters for fragmentation to be configured. This is especially useful in environments where fragmentation for legitimate reasons is very likely. An example of such an environment is an NFS environment. See the PIX command reference for the 6.1 code for details on this command.

PIX Firewall versions before 5.1.4 required that the fragments be received in sequence, with the fragment containing the header arriving first. In Linux-based environments, this behavior can be catastrophic. Therefore, it should be disabled pending a review of the operating conditions of the servers and applications. The Linux OS, if it must fragment packets, has a habit of delivering them in reverse order. This is perfectly acceptable in TCP/IP, but the PIX with frag guard enabled used to drop any fragmented packets that arrived out of order, effectively dropping all fragmented traffic in a Linux environment. Similar problems occurred if PIX Firewall was used as a tunnel for FDDI packets between routers. Consequently, this requirement was removed from 5.1.4 code onward.

Mail Guard

The mail guard feature is used to make sure that only a minimal set of seven SMTP commands can be sent to a mail server sitting behind the PIX Firewall. This helps prevent attacks on the mail server. The seven commands from RFC 821 are HELO, MAIL, RCPT, DATA, RSET, NOOP, and QUIT. The PIX Firewall intercepts the rest of the commands, such as KILL and WIZ, and responds with an OK. This lulls an attacker using these commands into believing that the mail server is receiving these commands and acknowledging them. You enable this feature using the **fixup protocol smtp 25** command in the newer PIX versions. The use of this command also alleviates the need for having a mail relay on the edge of the network.

Although this PIX feature is very useful in stopping certain types of SMTP attacks launched using a set of commands other than the seven just listed, this behavior can be very disruptive for certain mail server environments such as ones that use Microsoft Exchange, which uses ESMTP. Therefore, you should use this PIX feature with care and turn it off if absolutely necessary.

DNS Guard

DNS guard is a feature used in the PIX to stop DNS-based DoS attacks. DNS DoS attacks occur when an attacker poses as a DNS server to which a DNS resolution request has been sent and then floods the user requesting the DNS resolution with DNS responses. PIX mitigates these types of attacks by doing the following:

- PIX does not allow more than one DNS response from any DNS server.
- If a client queries more than one DNS server, as soon as PIX sees one of them respond to a DNS request, it closes the hole it opened (the access list hole plus the xlate) to allow responses from the other DNS servers.

Advanced Filtering

PIX Firewall has built-in traffic filtering features that can block certain types of traffic based on its content. ActiveX and Java applets are two kinds of traffic that can be stopped from reaching the private network via the PIX. Also, using software from Websense, PIX allows for more sophisticated filtering of content based on the types of websites being visited.

Websense runs separately from the PIX Firewall. It contains an extensive database of URLs arranged in various categories. PIX uses the Websense protocol to interact with the Websense server to find out if the URLs contained in the HTTP GET requests passing through it are allowed or not. The Websense server makes this decision based on the policy set on it by the administrator based on the site security policy. Using the Websense server provides the following three elements to the PIX Firewall setup:

- URL filtering allows the PIX Firewall to check outgoing URL requests against the policy defined on the Websense server.
- Username logging tracks the username, group, and domain name on the Websense server.
- Username lookup lets the PIX Firewall use the user authentication table to map the host's IP address to the username.

Using the Websense server to filter malicious URL requests can be resource-intensive on a heavily loaded PIX. Although most of the heavy processing is carried out on the Websense server, the communication still needs to take place from within the PIX Firewall software. PIX gets around some of this slowness by building within itself a cache of URLs and the responses generated for them by the Websense server. This lets faster checks be carried out on the most frequently accessed URLs without needing to consult the Websense server. The size of this cache can be configured on the PIX Firewall. However, using the cache feature does bypass one useful feature of the Websense server: URL logging. URL logging allows the Websense server to log various types of information about the URL and the user associated with it. With caching enabled, this feature is no longer in use.

PIX deals with the Java applets being downloaded within an HTML page by going into the page's HTML code and commenting out the Java applet source code. This way, the end user still receives the web page but does not get the Java applet that is embedded in it.

Multimedia Support

Multimedia support through a firewall is tricky for two main reasons.

The first is that a firewall often does NAT for the RFC 1918 addresses sitting on the private network behind it. Because many multimedia applications embed IP addresses in some of their payload packets, the firewall has to dig into the packet and change these IP addresses as well in accordance with the NAT rules set up on it.

The second reason why supporting multimedia traffic is often difficult is that many multimedia applications, instead of using fixed and predetermined port numbers, actually negotiate the port numbers that are to be used for the data to be transferred. This creates problems because the firewall must create address translation entries for these ports. It also causes problems because the firewall often must take into account the fact that as soon as the multimedia client sitting behind it has initiated a connection to a multimedia server, the server might try to establish an independent connection back to the client on the negotiated port. The firewall must open a hole for that connection to take place based on the negotiation that took place between the client and the server.

Figure 8-7 illustrates the two problems just discussed.

A good example of one such implementation where PIX has to take care of a complicated transaction between a client and a server is the implementation of VoIP using H.323 with GK (Gate Keeper) or a proxy server with SIP. VoIP deployments usually involve many endpoints, and customers often have limited IP addresses for each of these endpoints, resulting in a need to do PAT. Adding support for PAT with H.323 and SIP allows customers to expand their network address space using a single global address.

To support PAT with the H.323 or SIP fixup, first the correct PAT for the embedded IP/port in the H.323/SIP message needs to be found and the embedded IP address must be changed in the payload. Then the correct media connections based on the ports that were negotiated during the signaling need to be opened. If a PAT does not exist, one needs to be created. A PAT does not exist if there has been no outbound traffic from that particular host on a particular port. Or perhaps a PAT did exist but was torn down because it expired or was removed by the user. This leads to another problem where the clients register with either the proxy server (for SIP) or the GK (for H.323). The registrations tell the proxy server or GK that the client can be reached at a certain IP address/port. These registrations last for a specific timeout value determined by both client and server. This means that PIX must sniff this timeout value from the negotiation between the client and the server and modify the dynamic PAT timeout value on itself to match this VOIP timeout value.

Figure 8-7   *PIX Multimedia Support: Two Main Issues and Their Resolutions*

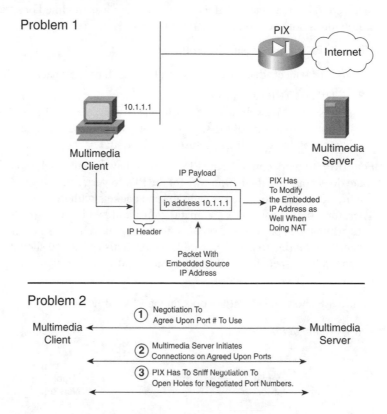

Apart from H.323 and SIP, PIX also supports RTSP, RAS v2, RealAudio Streamworks, CU-SeeMe, Internet Phone, IRC, Vxtreme, and VDO Live.

Spoof Detection or Unicast RPF

Unicast Reverse Path Forwarding (URPF) forces the PIX to examine all packets received as input on an interface to make sure that:

- The source address and source interface appear in the routing table.

- The return path for the source IP address is through the same interface on which the packet was received.

URPF checks to see if any packet received at the PIX's interface arrives on the best return path (return route) to the packet's source. If the packet was received on an interface which happens to be the interface in the best reverse-path route, the packet is forwarded as normal. If there is no reverse-path route on the same interface from which the packet was received, this might mean that the source address was modified or spoofed. Also if URPF simply does not find a reverse path for the packet, the packet is dropped.

URPF in PIX is implemented as follows:

- ICMP packets that have no session have each of their packets checked by URPF.
- UDP and TCP have sessions, so the initial packet requires a reverse-route lookup. Subsequent packets arriving during the session are checked using an existing state maintained as part of the session. Noninitial packets are checked to ensure that they arrive on the same interface used by the initial packet.

For URPF to work correctly, the PIX needs to have a route to the source IP address. If that route does not exist, there is no way for the PIX to verify that the packet was received from a source that does not have the right to send packets with that specific source IP address. Therefore, before using this command, you should add a static **route** command for every network that can be accessed on the interfaces you want to protect or you should set up proper RIP routing to gather this information. This command should be enabled only if routing is fully specified. PIX Firewall stops traffic on the interface specified if routing is not in place.

Figure 8-8 shows how URPF works on the PIX Firewall.

Figure 8-8   *URPF Feature in PIX*

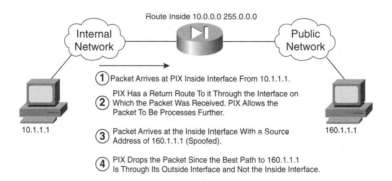

Protocol Fixup

PIX uses protocol fixup to deal with special behaviors, exhibited by certain protocols, that cannot be dealt with by the ASA in its normal mode of operation. You saw an example of this in the section "Multimedia Support". Another example of such protocol behavior is exhibited by FTP. Active FTP requires that after the client has initiated a connection to the server (a command session), the server should connect to the client (a data session) using a different port number combination than the one the client used to initiate the connection.

The server initiates this connection on its own rather than respond back to the initial connection the client has opened. Assuming that the client is sitting behind a PIX firewall, this requires the PIX to find out the new port number on which the server would connect to the client. PIX finds out this port by listening to the initial conversation between the client and the server taking place on the command session connection initiated by the client. Then the PIX sets up a translation if one is required and opens a hole in the firewall for the packets to go through to the client sitting on the inside. This requires special handling and is called 'ftp protocol fixup'. The **fixup protocol** command allows the PIX administrator to change the port number that the PIX looks for to start this special handling procedures. For example, using the **fixup protocol ftp 2021** command, PIX can be forced to monitor port 2021 to tell it to start using the special ftp fixup procedures. Please note that Passive FTP requires the client to initiate the command connection as well as the subsequent data connection. This eliminates the need for the firewall to be aware of the ftp negotiations taking place and the subsequent special handling.

Other protocols supported by the PIX fixup are HTTP, SMTP, RSH, SQLNET, and H.323.

Miscellaneous sysopt Commands

sysopt commands are used to turn on some system features that are used for some very specific network behaviors. These commands allow the PIX to modify its behavior to respond to a unique set of circumstances, such as issues on the network with the path MTU or devices that do not follow the normal protocol sequences.

Examples of some of the most commonly used **sysopt** commands are provided in the following sections.

sysopt connection timewait Command

The **sysopt connection timewait** command is necessary to cater to end host applications whose default TCP terminating sequence is a simultaneous close instead of the normal shutdown sequence (see RFC 793). In a simultaneous close, both ends of the transaction initiate the closing sequence, as opposed to the normal sequence in which one end closes and the other end acknowledges before initiating its own closing sequence.

The default behavior of the PIX Firewall is to track the normal shutdown sequence and release the connection after two FINs and the acknowledgment of the last FIN segment. This quick release heuristic lets the PIX Firewall sustain a high connection rate.

When simultaneous close occurs two FINs are sent across the PIX, one from each end of the connection. In order to close the connections on both ends of the TCP connection using simultaneous close, both ends must receive acknowledgements of the FINs they have sent out. However, the PIX thinks that the closing sequence is a normal TCP close sequence rather than a simultaneous close sequence. So after seeing the two FINs and then the acknowledgement from one end, it closes out the connection on the firewall as it would if it were a normal close sequence. However, in this case, one end of the TCP connection is left waiting, in the CLOSING state, for a response to the FIN it has sent out. Many sockets in the CLOSING state can degrade an end host's performance. For instance, some WinSock mainframe clients are known to exhibit this behavior and degrade the performance of the mainframe server. Old versions of HP/UX are also susceptible to this behavior. Enabling the **sysopt connection timewait** command creates a quiet-time window for the abnormal close-down sequence to complete. What this means is that after the PIX has seen what is considers to be the close of a connection, it waits 15 seconds before it closes out the connections. This wait time allows simultaneously closing connections to close on both ends properly since hopefully the final ACK gets transmitted during the 15 seconds of grace period. Please note however, that the PIX waits 15 seconds for all connection closes once this feature has been turned on, irrespective of whether they are normal closes or simultaneous closes. This can result in significant degradation of performance in environments where there are a lot of new connections being created and a lot of old connections being terminated in large quantities. This is the reason this feature is turned off by default.

sysopt noproxyarp Command

The **sysopt noproxyarp** command allows you to disable proxy ARPs on a PIX Firewall interface.

Proxy ARP in PIX is used mainly when the PIX wants to receive packets destined for a certain IP address on one of its interfaces and forward them to another interface connected to it. An example of this is the PIX proxy ARPing for the addresses contained in PIX's global pool of NAT addresses for the hosts sitting on the inside private network behind the PIX, provided that an xlate has been created by traffic originating from the inside network. Upon receiving the packets destined for these addresses, the PIX forwards them to the inside network after performing the normal checks and translations.

In general, while Proxy ARPing a perfectly legitimate feature of networking, Proxy ARP should be best thought of as a temporary transition mechanism. Its use should not be encouraged as part of a stable solution. A number of potential problems are associated with its use, including hosts' inability to fall back to alternative routes if a network component fails, and the possibility of race conditions and bizarre traffic patterns if the bridged and routed network segments are not clearly delineated.

Using specific routes and default gateway routes eliminates the need for end hosts to use proxy ARPing as a mechanism for routing packets.

The **sysopt noproxyarp** command is generally used in situations where it is inappropriate for the PIX to respond with proxy ARPing due to network misconfigurations or bugs. An example of such a situation is shown in Figure 8-9.

Figure 8-9   **sysopt nonproxyarp** *Feature Usage*

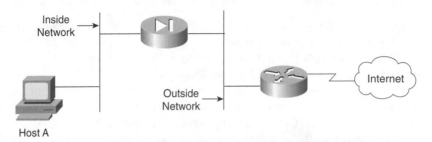

The PIX in this scenario is set up with a **nat (inside) 0 0 0** command, which implies that PIX will not translate any of the IP addresses on the inside network. Due to how the **nat 0** command is designed, the PIX starts to proxy ARP on the outside interface for any and all addresses upon being configured in this manner. Consequently, if host A wants to access the Internet and sends an ARP and the PIX proxy ARPs before the router can respond, host A would be sending traffic destined for the Internet to the PIX, which is incorrect routing. The way around this scenario is to turn off proxy ARP on the PIX. However, after you do this, the PIX stops ARPing for all addresses, even the ones for which it should ARP. Now the router needs to be set up with routes for the inside network behind the PIX so that it does not have to rely on the PIX proxy ARPing for that network. This situation would never have arisen if the **nat 0** command were set up with specific IP address ranges contained on the inside network. The **noproxyarp** command allows the system administrator to get over this mix of misconfiguration and product shortcoming.

sysopt connection tcpmss Command

The **sysopt connection tcpmss** command forces proxy TCP connections to have a maximum segment size no greater than a configurable number of bytes. This command requests that each side of a TCP connection not send a packet of a size greater than *x* bytes. The negotiation for mss is done during the initial TCP connection establishment.

The number of bytes can be a minimum of 28 and any maximum number. You can disable this feature by setting this value to 0. By default, the PIX Firewall sets 1380 bytes as the **sysopt connection tcpmss** even though this command does not appear in the default configuration. The calculation for setting the TCP maximum segment size to 1380 bytes is as follows:

$$1380 \text{ data} + 20 \text{ TCP} + 20 \text{ IP} + 24 \text{ AH} + 24 \text{ ESP\_CIPHER}$$
$$+ 12 \text{ ESP\_AUTH} + 20 \text{ IP} = 1500 \text{ bytes}$$

1500 bytes is the MTU for Ethernet connections. It is recommended that the default value of 1380 bytes be used for Ethernet and mixed Ethernet and Token Ring environments. If the PIX Firewall has all Token Ring interfaces, the MTU can be set to 4056. However, if even one link along the path through the network is not a Token Ring, setting the number of bytes to such a high value might cause poor throughput. In its 1380-byte default value, this command increases throughput of the **sysopt security fragguard** command.

Because the TCP maximum segment size is the maximum size that an end host can inject into the network at one time (see RFC 793 for more information on the TCP protocol), the **tcpmss** command allows for improved performance in network environments where the path MTU discovery is not taking place properly because an end host is not responding to requests to lower its MTU or a firewall is sitting next to the end host dropping the ICMP packets being sent to the end host to request a reduction in its MTU. The **tcpmss** command forces the size of the TCP segments to a small value during TCP's initialization sequence, thereby eliminating the need for ICMP type 3 code 4 messages to be used to try and reduce the MTU. Also, most end hosts, even the ones that do not respond to ICMP messages requesting a decrease in packet size, do respond to **tcpmss** negotiation favorably.

Multicast Support

PIX Firewall allows multicast traffic to be passed through it (in version 6.2 and later). PIX Firewall allows statically configurable multicast routes or the use of an IGMP helper address for forwarding IGMP reports and leave announcements. PIX also allows filtering to be done on the multicast traffic passing through the PIX.

Figure 8-10 shows how the PIX Firewall acting as a proxy agent forwards IGMP report and leave messages to a multicast-enabled router, which updates PIM based on these messages. The result is that the end hosts on the internal network can receive the multicast video traffic from the server on the Internet.

Figure 8-11 shows another scenario in which the multicast server is sitting behind the PIX Firewall. In this case, the PIX Firewall's role is to forward the multicast traffic received from the server sitting behind it to a multicast router. The router then uses PIM-based mechanisms to forward the traffic for distribution to end hosts listening for this traffic.

The following summarizes the PIX Firewall's multicast support:

- Access list filters can be applied to multicast traffic to permit or deny specific protocols and ports.

- NAT and PAT can be performed on the multicast packet source addresses only.

- Multicast data packets with destination addresses in the 224.0.0.0/24 address range are not forwarded. However, everything else in the 224.0.0.0/8 address range *is* forwarded.

- IGMP packets for address groups within the 224.0.0.0 to 224.0.0.255 range are not forwarded, because these addresses are reserved for protocol use.

- NAT is not performed on IGMP packets. When IGMP forwarding is configured, the PIX Firewall forwards the IGMP packets (report and leave) with the IP address of the helper interface as the source IP address.

Figure 8-10 *PIX Firewall Multicast Support: Multicast Clients Behind the PIX*

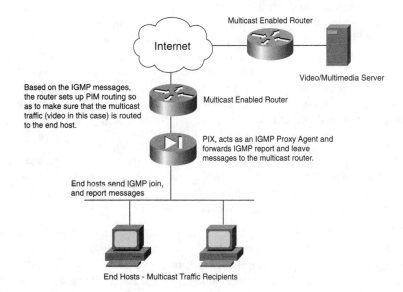

Multicast Routing
(Multicast Receivers Behind the PIX)

Figure 8-11 *PIX Firewall Multicast Support: Multimedia Server Behind the PIX*

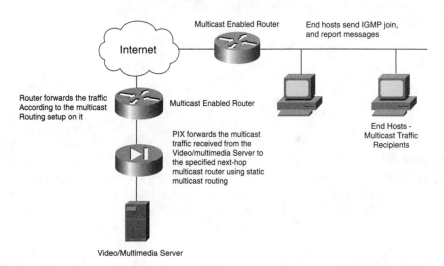

Multicast Routing
(Multicast Server Behind the PIX)

Fragment Handling

Fragment handling in PIX for traffic passing through the PIX is done in line with most accepted practices of how to deal with fragments in the networking community. However, with the advent of virtual reassembly PIX can do more than what most internet devices can do in this regard. In general, for most internet devices, the access control mechanisms on the networking device are applied to the first initial fragment of a stream of fragments (FO=0). The rest of the fragments are allowed to pass through without being subjected to additional checks as long as they pass the Layer 3 access control parameters. However, since the PIX does virtual reassembly of packets (please see section on 'Frag Guard' for more details of how virtual reassembly works), it is able to look for further information in the fragments it collects for reassembly. Since the flow information is tagged with each fragment during virtual re-assembly, atleast the layer 4 information is looked at while processing fragments in PIX.

PIX also provides additional protection against certain DOS fragment attacks by using the state information it stores for each connection to validate whether a fragment is to be allowed through. Fragments received for hosts without xlates built for them are discarded. Matching is performed using IP source and destination address and protocol type.

PIX collects all the fragments reaching it, whether it is doing complete reassembly or virtual reassembly on the fragments. It collects fragments until it has verified the fragments' integrity, has checked for common fragment attack patterns (see the following discussion of two such attacks), and has ascertained from the initial fragment that the packet does indeed deserve to be allowed through the PIX based on the stored state information. This allows for a fair amount of security for the hosts sitting behind the firewall. They are protected from the burden of allocating resources for the reassembly of the fragments part of a fragment DoS attack reaching them. PIX does not forward any fragments to the end host if it suspects a fragment attack based on the information in the fragments, if it does not receive all the packet's fragments, or if it does not have a state built for the packet of which the fragments are a part to go through the PIX.

Two types of fragment attacks described in RFC 1858 can be significant threats to a network:

- Tiny fragment attack
- Overlapping fragment attack

Tiny Fragment Attack

The tiny fragment attack is staged by sending an IP packet with the first fragment so small that it contains only the source and destination port information for TCP, not the TCP flags. These are sent in the next fragment. If the access lists were set up to drop or allow packets based on the TCP flags, such as SYN=0 or 1 or ACK=0 or 1, they cannot test the first fragment for this information. Also, since most network devices do not do reassembly of packets passing through them, they do not check the rest of the fragments and let them pass through. This way, an attacker can get an illegitimate packet through to an end host sitting behind these devices.

Newer versions of PIX protect against this type of an attack through the use of virtual re-assembly. Virtual re-assembly insures that the flag information whether it is in the first fragment or other fragments is looked at before the packet is forwarded.

Older versions of PIX, protects against this type of attack by using the following algorithm to test packets:

IF FO=1 and PROTOCOL=TCP THEN
drop packet

FO=1 refers to the second fragment of the tiny fragment attack packet. FO is 1 only if the first fragment (the initial fragment) is so small that the second fragment has an offset of only eight octets, or FO=1. This forces the PIX to drop this fragment, thereby stopping any reassembly at the end host because now one of the IP packet fragments is missing. The "interesting" fields (meaning the fields containing the port information and the flags of the common transport protocols, except TCP) lie in the first eight octets of the transport header, so it isn't possible to push them into a nonzero offset fragment. So the threat of this attack does not exist for these protocols.

Overlapping Fragment Attack

The overlapping fragment attack makes use of the conditions set out in RFC 791 for reassembly of IP fragments for end hosts. It describes a reassembly algorithm that results in new fragments overwriting any overlapped portions of previously received fragments. This behavior allows an attacker to send the TCP flags in two fragments of the IP packet. The first fragment contains flags that are allowed to pass through the configured access list (SYN=0). However, the same flags are repeated in the second fragment and this time are set to a different value (SYN=1). The access list allows the first fragment to go through because it matches the requirements. The access list does not run any tests on the remaining fragments. Therefore, when an end host receives the two fragments, it overwrites the first fragment's flags with the ones in the second fragment, defeating the purpose of the access list. This type of attack can be stopped using the same algorithm used for the tiny fragment attack. For all the relevant TCP header information to be contained in the first fragment and to not overlap with another fragment, the second fragment's minimum offset must be 2 (meaning that the first fragment contains at least 16 octets). Therefore, dropping fragments with FO=1, PIX eliminates the possibility of this type of attack as well.

Case Studies

This section covers some case studies that highlight how the PIX can be used in real-world scenarios. The purpose of these case studies is twofold. The primary purpose is to put into a more practical and implementation-oriented light all the material that has been discussed in this chapter. The secondary purpose is to review how to set up PIX in real-world scenarios with a suitable juxtaposition of commands.

PIX with Three Interfaces, Running a Web Server on the DMZ

A PIX with three interfaces is one of the most commonly used PIX hardware configurations in use in most enterprise networks today. The three interfaces are the inside, the outside, and a DMZ interface. As discussed earlier, the DMZ interface is used to house the servers that are to be accessed from the public network. In this case study, the server is a web server sitting on the DMZ interface. Example 8-1 shows the configuration for a PIX Firewall with three interfaces with a web server residing on the DMZ interface.

This case study also gives a detailed description of all the commands that go into setting up a PIX. In the case studies after this, only the commands that have not been explained in this case study are described.

Figure 8-12 shows the network topology for this case study.

Figure 8-12 *Network Topology for This Case Study*

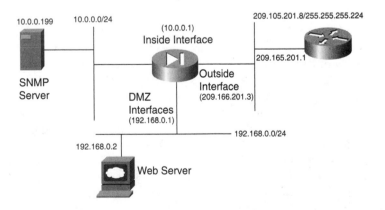

Example 8-1 *PIX Firewall with Three Interfaces Residing on the DMZ Interface*

```
Pixfirewall#wr t
!The nameif commands are used to name the interfaces of the PIX and assign them a
!security level.

nameif ethernet0 outside security0
```

Example 8-1 *PIX Firewall with Three Interfaces Residing on the DMZ Interface (Continued)*

```
nameif ethernet1 inside security100
nameif ethernet2 dmz security50

!The interface commands that follow define the physical medium to which the
!interfaces are connected

interface ethernet0 10baset
interface ethernet1 10baset
interface ethernet0 100basetx
```

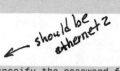 *should be ethernet2*

```
!The command below is used to specify the password for getting into the privileged
!or enable mode of the PIX firewall.
enable password <removed>  encrypted
!The command below specifies the password used to specify the password for Telnet
!access to the PIX firewall.
passwd <removed>  encrypted
!The IP address commands that follow are used to give IP addresses to the PIX
!interfaces using the names defined above

ip address outside 209.165.201.3 255.255.255.224
ip address inside 10.0.0.1 255.255.255.0
ip address dmz 192.168.0.1 255.255.255.0

!The hostname command defines the name of the PIX

hostname pixfirewall

!The fixup commands that follow turn on the fixup functionality for the PIX box,
!as discussed in the preceding sections

fixup protocol ftp 21
fixup protocol http 80
fixup protocol smtp 25
fixup protocol h323 1720
fixup protocol rsh 514
fixup protocol sqlnet 1521

!The arp command defines the time after which the ARP entries in the ARP cache
!maintained by the PIX are flushed out

arp timeout 14400

!The no failover command below suggests that this is a standalone PIX

no failover

!The names command that follows turns on the use of the name command. The name
!command is used here to allow you to use the word 'webserver' in the
!configuration instead of typing its whole IP address, 192.168.0.2

names
```

continues

Example 8-1 *PIX Firewall with Three Interfaces Residing on the DMZ Interface (Continued)*

```
name 192.168.0.2 webserver

!The pager command that follows is used to specify the number of lines in a
!page of output that are displayed before the 'more' prompt appears

pager lines 24

!The logging command defines what kind of messages are to be logged and to where.
!In this case, debugging messages are being logged to the PIX buffer

logging buffered debugging

!The nat command that follows states that if a packet arrives on the inside
!interface with a source address in subnet 10.0.0.0/24, it should be NATed using
!the global command defined by 'global (<interface name>) 1', where 'interface
!name' is the name of the interface to which the packet is routed based on the
!destination IP address. Please note that the number '1' is used to tie a pair of
!NAT and global commands together. Any number would do as long as both the NAT and
!global commands use it.
!The nat/global command is used only for traffic originating from a higher
!security level interface destined for a lower security level interface. It does
!not impact traffic originated from a lower security level interface destined for a
!higher security level interface. Also note that the tag number '0' cannot be used
!in a nat command unless the intent is not to translate the addresses on the higher
!security interface into any other range of addresses. A typical example is where
!the network on the inside has a globally routable address space with no need to do
!address translation. This is typically known as NAT 0.
nat (inside) 1 10.0.0.0 255.255.255.0

!The nat command that follows is being deployed in similar fashion as described
!in the previous comment. The only difference is that the traffic is assumed to be
!arriving at the DMZ interface rather than the inside interface. Please note that
!more than one nat command can be tied to the same 'global' command, as is
!happening here.

nat (dmz) 1 192.168.0.0 255.255.255.0

!The two global commands that follow are tied to the two nat commands defined
!above. The first global command defines the range of IP addresses to be used to
!translate the private IP address of packets arriving on the inside or DMZ
!interfaces and destined for the outside interface. This command is used for a
!one-to-one NAT translation, meaning that once the 21 IP addresses (209.165.201.10-
!209.165.201.30) defined herein are finished, this command cannot do any more
!translations. That is where the second global command kicks in. This command, with
!only one address specified, is used to do PAT on the packets, exactly how the first
!command did one-to-one NAT on the packets. This way it can translate numerous
!private IP addresses to this one globally routable address and still be able to
!distinguish between them based on the port number used.
global (outside) 1 209.165.201.10-209.165.201.30

global (outside) 1 209.165.201.5
```

Example 8-1 *PIX Firewall with Three Interfaces Residing on the DMZ Interface (Continued)*

```
!The global command that follows is used to translate the private IP addresses of
!the packets arriving on the inside interface destined for the DMZ interface.
!Please note that this is a one-to-one NAT only, meaning that only 11 hosts on the
!inside network can access the DMZ network at a time. Also, please note that the
!IP addresses defined in this command are private. This is OK because the packets
!are not going out on a public network, just the DMZ network.
global (dmz) 1 199.168.0.10-199.168.0.20

!The command that follows is used to create a static NAT translation through the
!PIX firewall. This is needed because you have a web server on the DMZ network
!that needs to be accessed from the public network using the IP address
!209.165.201.6 instead of its private address, 192.168.0.2. Please note that we
!are taking advantage of the 'name' command here to avoid typing in the IP address.
!Also note that the server will still be accessible from the inside network using
!its 192 address because you are not creating any static translation between the
!inside interface and the DMZ interface. None is needed because the inside network
!is on a higher security level than the DMZ interface and can access it without
!needing static translations or access list permissions.

static (dmz,outside) 209.165.201.6 webserver

!The access list below is being created to allow the world sitting on the public
!network to access the web server using its globally routable address on port 80
!only. The access group command applies the access list to the outside interface
!in the incoming direction, or the direction from which the traffic coming from the
!public network is entering the public interface. Please note that PIX access lists
!can be applied only in the "in" direction. As always, there is an implicit deny
!statement at the bottom of the access list.

access-list acl_out permit tcp any host 209.165.201.6 eq http

access-group acl_out in interface outside
!The rip passive command below turns on RIP on the outside interface such that the
!PIX listens for RIP updates on this interface and updates its routing tables.
!Also note that RIP v2 authentication has been turned on. The number at the end is
!the key ID, which must be the same on the router and the PIX sharing updates.

rip outside passive version 2 authentication md5 keyforsaadat 2

!The rip default command forces the PIX to send a default RIP route to other RIP
!devices sitting on the outside interface

rip outside default version 2 authentication md5 keyforsaadat 2

!The rip passive command below is similar to the previous command, but in this case
!RIP v1 is being used, which does not support authentication

rip inside passive version 1

!The rip passive command below is similar to the commands above, but in this case
!although RIP v2 is being used, no authentication has been turned on because the
```

continues

Example 8-1 *PIX Firewall with Three Interfaces Residing on the DMZ Interface (Continued)*

```
!DMZ network is considered somewhat safe

rip dmz passive version 2


!The route outside command below is a default route. If the PIX is unable to
!determine the interface to which it must forward a packet using its ARP table, it
!must use the route table to find out what to do. The interface name in the route
!commands specifies the interface on which the PIX must send an ARP request for
!the IP address listed as the default gateway if it does not already have it in its
!ARP cache. Once the PIX has the MAC address of the IP address specified in the
!route command, it forwards the packet on the interface specified in the route
!command using this MAC address as the destination. The number 1 at the end
!specifies the metric for the route. A metric is used to choose the better route if
!more than one route is configured for the same destination.

route outside 0.0.0.0 0.0.0.0 209.165.201.1 1

!The timeout command below is used to define the time it will take a NAT
!translation created through the PIX to be removed after it has not been used for
!the time specified in this command. The value configured is 1 hour

timeout xlate 1:00:00

!The timeout command below defines how long the PIX will allow a connection to
!remain idle before it removes the entry. Please note that although the TCP
!protocol itself does not have a timeout built into it, the PIX firewall does
!implement its own timeout for such connections. The value configured here is 1
!hour. The half-closed time is used to specify how long PIX will allow a half-
!closed connection to linger. This is an important timer to take care of
!applications that get killed without getting the chance to close their TCP
!connections entirely. The UDP timer is for UDP connections through the PIX, as
!discussed in the ASA section on UDP

timeout conn 1:00:00 half-closed 0:10:00
udp 0:02:00 rpc 0:10:00 h323 0:05:00
sip 0:30:00 sip_media 0:02:00

!The timer that follows defines how long the PIX caches a user's
!authentication and authorization credentials. The absolute keyword runs the
!times continuously, irrespective of whether the user is idle

timeout uauth 0:05:00 absolute

!The sysopt commands below turn on some of the security features that are
!desirable for specific network environments. Please see the discussion in the
!sections on sysopt commands and the x guard features for more details

sysopt connection timewait
sysopt connection tcpmss
sysopt security fragguard
```

Example 8-1   *PIX Firewall with Three Interfaces Residing on the DMZ Interface (Continued)*

```
!The commands that follow are used to specify SNMP information on the PIX. The
!SNMP community string is a shared secret among the SNMP management station and
!the network nodes being managed. PIX Firewall uses the key to determine if the
!incoming SNMP request is valid. The SNMP server host is the IP address of the SNMP
!management station to which traps should be sent and/or from which the SNMP
!requests come.

snmp-server community saadatmalik123456789

snmp-server location Building 42, Sector 54

snmp-server contact Saadat Malik

snmp-server host inside 10.0.0.199

!The commands that follow are used to define the MTU of the interface connected
!to the PIX. PIX fragments any IP datagrams larger than 1500 bytes

mtu outside 1500
mtu inside 1500
mtu dmz 1500

!The telnet commands below specify the IP address 10.0.0.93 on the inside network
!from which telnetting to the PIX is allowed. Also specified is the timeout in
!minutes for idle Telnet sessions to the PIX itself (not to devices behind the PIX
!or elsewhere)
telnet 10.0.0.93 inside
telnet timeout 5

!The terminal width command specifies the number of characters displayed on one
!line when looking at output on the PIX

terminal width 80
```

This case study not only gave you an overview of one of the most commonly used PIX configurations but also reviewed the most common commands in the PIX setup. Larger PIX setups, meaning ones involving more than just the three interfaces, are done using configurations similar to the configuration in Example 8-1.

PIX Set up for Failover to a Secondary Device

PIX failover, as discussed in this and the preceding chapters, is one of the most important characteristics a firewall can have. Failover capabilities allow a network to maintain high availability faced with device failures. For failover to work smoothly, it is important to have the two PIXes sharing the responsibilities of the primary and secondary failover configured correctly before the failure occurs.

This case study shows how a primary PIX Firewall is configured to fail over to a secondary unit. Because at any time, depending on whether a PIX has failed, either the primary or the secondary PIX might be passing traffic, the terms *active* and *standby* are used to designate which PIX is passing the traffic.

Here are some things to keep in mind when setting up PIX Firewall failover:

- **Hardware/software**—Both the PIXes must have the same hardware and software.

- **Interface connections**—All the interfaces of the two PIXes must be connected to each other in some fashion, even if they are not in use and are in a shutdown state.

- **Standby PIX**—The standby PIX must not be configured independently. It must be write-erased and configured using the **write standby** command on the primary PIX.

- **Stateful failure**—If stateful failover is desired, one interface on each of the two PIXes must be sacrificed and used to connect the two PIXes via an Ethernet cable for this functionality to take place. This cable is in addition to the normal serial cable used to carry the heartbeat between the two devices (see the preceding failover discussion for a more detailed analysis of how this works). If a crossover cable is used to connect the stateful failover interfaces, a failure of the failover interface does not force a failover of the PIX, because the failover interfaces on both boxes go down.

- **show failover**—This command can be used to check the status of the primary or secondary device. This command provides information on which PIX is in active mode and which is in standby mode.

Figure 8-13 shows the network topology for this case study.

Figure 8-13 *Network Topology for This Case Study*

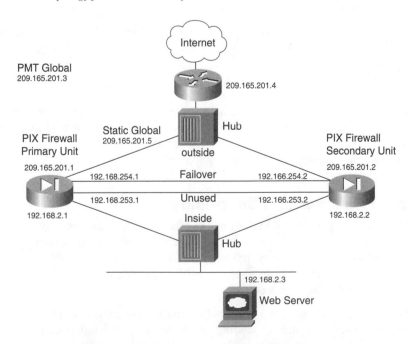

In the configuration of the primary PIX device shown in Example 8-2, the commands related to failover are described in detail. The preceding case study describes the rest of the commands.

Example 8-2 *Configuration of the Primary PIX Device*

```
pixfirewall#wr t
nameif ethernet0 outside security0
nameif ethernet1 inside security100
nameif ethernet2 failover security10
nameif ethernet3 unused security20
enable password xxx encrypted
passwd xxx encrypted
hostname pixfirewall
fixup protocol ftp 21
fixup protocol http 80
fixup protocol smtp 25
fixup protocol h323 1720
fixup protocol rsh 514
fixup protocol sqlnet 1521
names
pager lines 20
no logging timestamp
no logging standby
logging console errors
no logging monitor
no logging buffered
no logging trap
logging facility 20
logging queue 512
interface ethernet0 10baset
interface ethernet1 10baset
interface ethernet2 100full
interface ethernet3 10baset
mtu outside 1500
mtu inside 1500
mtu failover 1500
mtu unused 1500
ip address outside 209.165.201.1  255.255.255.224
ip address inside 192.168.2.1 255.255.255.0
ip address failover 192.168.254.1 255.255.255.0
ip address unused 192.168.253.1  255.255.255.252

!The failover command turns on failover functionality

failover
!The failover IP address commands below are used to define the IP addresses for the
!interfaces on the secondary unit so that when the write standby command is
!executed, these addresses get assigned to the interfaces on the secondary PIX.

failover ip address outside 209.165.201.2
failover ip address inside 192.168.2.2
```

continues

Example 8-2 *Configuration of the Primary PIX Device (Continued)*

```
failover ip address failover 192.168.254.2
failover ip address unused 192.168.253.2

!The failover link command specifies which interface will be used to carry the
!state information to the standby PIX in case of a failover

failover link failover
failover poll 15

arp timeout 14400
global (outside) 1 209.165.201.3 netmask 255.255.255.224
nat (inside) 1 0.0.0.0 0.0.0.0 0 0
static (inside,outside) 209.165.201.5 192.168.2.5 netmask 255.255.255.255 0 0
access-list acl_out permit tcp any 209.165.201.5 eq 80
access-list acl_out permit icmp any any
access-group acl_out in interface outside


no rip outside passive
no rip outside default
no rip inside passive
no rip inside default
no rip failover passive
no rip failover default
route outside 0.0.0.0 0.0.0.0 209.165.201.4 1
timeout xlate 1:00:00
timeout conn 1:00:00 half-closed 0:10:00

udp 0:02:00 rpc 0:10:00 h323 0:05:00

sip 0:30:00 sip_media 0:02:00
telnet timeout 5
terminal width 80
```

PIX Set up to Use the alias Command for a Server Sitting on the DMZ

This case study shows a way of using the **alias** command. This command is set up so that it can deliver the results discussed in the section "NAT on the Destination IP Addresses." Example 8-3 provides a complete configuration for setting up the PIX Firewall to use the alias feature to achieve this result.

Consider a web server. If the web server and the client trying to access it are on the same PIX interface, the normal way of configuring the **alias** command (**alias** *<Name of interface on which the server and client are located> <RFC 1918 address of the server> <Statically translated address of the server>*) works fine. The **alias** command doctors the DNS server response for the name of the web server such that the client trying to connect to the server uses its private IP address to connect to it.

However, problems arise when the web server is sitting on a subnet connected to a different interface of the PIX than the client. In that case, the normal way of configuring the **alias** command does not work. The reason for this is that when the client sends a packet to the web server's private IP address provided to it by the doctoring PIX, the PIX translates it back into the web server's public or globally routable address and routes it out the public or outside interface. Of course, this is incorrect because the web server is not located on the public network but rather on a DMZ segment.

The way to fix this problem is to reverse the IP addresses configured in the **alias** command, as demonstrated in Example 8-3. Due to the reversal, the PIX no longer doctors the DNS response to another address, because it does not match the **alias** command setup. However, when the client sends a packet to the web server's globally routable address, the PIX dutifully changes the destination address to the web server's private address and then sends it to the interface on which the web server is located.

Figure 8-14 shows the network topology for this case study.

Figure 8-14 *Network Topology for This Case Study*

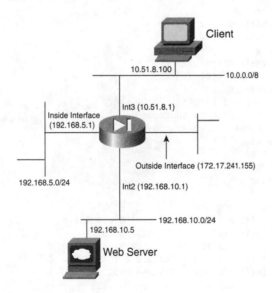

Example 8-3 *Configuring the PIX Firewall to Use the Alias Feature*

```
pixfirewall#wr t
PIX Version 5.2(5)
nameif ethernet0 outside security0
nameif ethernet1 inside security100
nameif ethernet2 intf2 security10
```

continues

Example 8-3 *Configuring the PIX Firewall to Use the Alias Feature (Continued)*

```
nameif ethernet3 intf3 security15
nameif ethernet4 intf4 security20
nameif ethernet5 intf5 security25
enable password 8Ry2YjIyt7RRXU24 encrypted
passwd 2KFQnbNIdI.2KYOU encrypted
hostname pixfirewall
 names
!The access list that follows is used to allow access to the web server

access-list 101 permit tcp any host 172.17.241.250 eq www
access-list 101 permit icmp any any

no pager
logging on
no logging timestamp
no logging standby
logging console emergencies
no logging monitor
no logging buffered
no logging trap
no logging history
logging facility 20
logging queue 512
interface ethernet0 10full
interface ethernet1 10full
interface ethernet2 10full
interface ethernet3 10full
interface ethernet4 auto shutdown
interface ethernet5 auto shutdown
mtu outside 1500
mtu inside 1500
mtu intf2 1500
mtu intf3 1500
mtu intf4 1500
mtu intf5 1500
ip address outside 172.17.241.155 255.255.255.0
ip address inside 192.168.5.1 255.255.255.0
ip address intf2 192.168.10.1 255.255.255.0
ip address intf3 10.51.8.1 255.0.0.0
ip address intf4 127.0.0.1 255.255.255.255
ip address intf5 127.0.0.1 255.255.255.255

arp timeout 14400
!The command below sets up a global pool of one address for doing port address
!translation. The IP address used is the IP address of the outside interface
!itself. This is another way of defining a global pool of addresses.
global (outside) 1 interface

global (intf2) 1 192.168.5.101-192.168.5.200
nat (inside) 1 192.168.5.0 255.255.255.0 0 0
nat (intf3) 1 10.51.8.1 255.255.255.0 0 0
```

Example 8-3 *Configuring the PIX Firewall to Use the Alias Feature (Continued)*

```
!This static command is used to allow users on the public network to access the
!web server using its globally routable address

static (intf2,outside) 172.17.241.250 192.168.10.5 netmask 255.255.255.25 5 0 0

!Please note how the alias command is configured. The normal way of configuring
!the alias command is as follows:
! alias (inside) 192.168.10.5 172.17.241.250 255.255.255.255
!Generic syntax:
! alias (interface) dnat_ip foreign_ip mask
!As you can see, the addresses have been swapped due to reasons explained above

alias (inside) 172.17.241.250 192.168.10.5 255.255.255.255

access-group 101 in interface outside
timeout xlate 3:00:00
timeout conn 1:00:00 half-closed 0:10:00 udp 0:02:00 rpc 0:10:00 h323 0:05:00 si
p 0:30:00 sip_media 0:02:00
timeout uauth 0:05:00 absolute
route outside 0.0.0.0 0.0.0.0 172.17.241.200 1
aaa-server TACACS+ protocol tacacs+
aaa-server RADIUS protocol radius
no snmp-server location
no snmp-server contact
snmp-server community public
no snmp-server enable traps
floodguard enable
no sysopt route dnat
isakmp identity hostname
telnet timeout 5
ssh timeout 5
terminal width 80
: end
```

Here is an explanation of the flow of events in Example 8-3:

Step 1   The client on the inside sends a DNS query to a DNS server.

Step 2   The DNS server responds with the IP address 172.17.241.250 to the PIX.

Step 3   The inside client tries to access 172.17.241.250 and sends a packet with
this IP address as the destination to the PIX Firewall. However, because
of the presence of the **alias** command, PIX does destination address
translation and sends the packet to 192.168.10.5, which is the web server.

If the **alias** command were configured in the normal fashion:

```
alias (inside) 192.168.10.5 172.17.241.250 255.255.255.255
```

the following would have been the sequence of events:

Step 1   The client on the inside sends a DNS query to a DNS server.

Step 2   The DNS server responds with the IP address 172.17.241.250 to the PIX, which alters this response to 192.168.10.5 because of the presence of the **alias** command.

Step 3   The inside client tries to access 192.168.10.5 and sends a packet with this IP address as the destination to the PIX Firewall. However, because of the presence of the **alias** command, PIX does not simply forward the packet to intf2. It performs destination address translation on the packet and sends it to 172.17.241.250 via the outside interface.

Step 4   The connection fails, because this IP address is in the same segment as the PIX outside interface and is left for a host that is supposedly directly connected.

PIX Set up for Cut-Through Proxy Authentication and Authorization

As discussed earlier, PIX can perform authentication for connections established through it. It also can perform authorization for the connections using an AAA server. Cut-through proxy refers to the fact that as soon as a user has been authenticated through the PIX Firewall, the PIX keeps a record of that user's authentication credentials and switches the rest of the packets from that user based on these credentials without going through the authentication phase again.

This case study shows how to set up authentication and authorization for users trying to access a server located at 99.99.99.99 via FTP, Telnet, or HTTP. The authorization parameters (not shown here) are fairly simple, restricting certain users to only a subset of the three services offered by this server (only HTTP and FTP).

Example 8-4 shows how a PIX is set up to do authorization and authentication. Figure 8-15 shows the network topology for this case study.

Figure 8-15   *Network Topology for This Case Study*

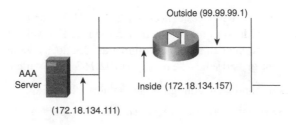

Example 8-4 *How PIX Is Set up to Do Authorization and Authentication*

```
pixfirewall#wr t
PIX Version 5.2
nameif ethernet0 outside security0
nameif ethernet1 inside security100
enable password 8Ry2YjIyt7RRXU24 encrypted
passwd OnTrBUG1Tp0edmkr encrypted
hostname pixfirewall
fixup protocol ftp 21
fixup protocol http 80
fixup protocol h323 1720
fixup protocol rsh 514
fixup protocol smtp 25
fixup protocol sqlnet 1521
fixup protocol sip 5060
names
!
!The access list that follows is used later in the configuration to define the
!traffic that will be subjected to AAA services

access-list 101 permit tcp any any eq telnet
access-list 101 permit tcp any any eq ftp
access-list 101 permit tcp any any eq www
!
!The access list below is used to allow access to the host located at 99.99.99.99
!via WWW, FTP, or Telnet.

access-list 110 permit tcp any 99.99.99.99 eq www
access-list 110 permit tcp any 99.99.99.99 eq ftp
access-list 110 permit tcp any 99.99.99.99 eq telnet
access-group 110 in interface outside
!
pager lines 24
logging on
no logging timestamp
no logging standby
no logging console debugging
no logging monitor
no logging buffered
no logging trap debugging
no logging history
no logging facility 20
logging queue 512
interface ethernet0 auto
interface ethernet1 10baset
mtu outside 1500
mtu inside 1500
ip address outside 99.99.99.1 255.255.255.0
ip address inside 172.18.124.157 255.255.255.0
ip audit info action alarm
ip audit attack action alarm
```

continues

Example 8-4 *How PIX Is Set up to Do Authorization and Authentication (Continued)*

```
no failover
failover timeout 0:00:00
failover poll 15
failover ip address outside 0.0.0.0
failover ip address inside 0.0.0.0
arp timeout 14400
global (outside) 1 99.99.99.10-99.99.99.20 netmask 255.255.255.0
nat (inside) 1 172.18.124.0 255.255.255.0 0 0
static (inside,outside) 99.99.99.99 172.18.124.114 netmask 255.255.255.255 0 0

access-list 110 permit tcp any 99.99.99.99 eq www
access-list 110 permit tcp any 99.99.99.99 eq ftp
access-list 110 permit tcp any 99.99.99.99 eq telnet
route inside 0.0.0.0 0.0.0.0 172.18.124.1 1

timeout xlate 3:00:00
timeout conn 1:00:00 half-closed 0:10:00 udp 0:02:00 rpc 0:10:00 h323 0:05:00
si p 0:30:00 sip_media 0:02:00
timeout uauth 0:05:00 absolute
!
!The commands that follow are used to define  server groups. The server group is
!identified by the group tag, in this case AuthInbound and AuthOutbound. This
!group tag is used to bind authentication and authorization commands to an AAA
!server. Please note that we are not using the two server groups defined by
!default in PIX, TACACS+, and RADIUS, but instead are defining our own, called
!AuthInbound and AuthOutbound.

aaa-server TACACS+ protocol tacacs+
aaa-server RADIUS protocol radius

!The name of the first server group is defined in the command that follows

aaa-server AuthInbound protocol tacacs+

!The server group name is bound to the actual IP address of the AAA server in the
!command below. The server key, cisco, is also defined

aaa-server AuthInbound (inside) host 172.18.124.111 cisco timeout 5

!Another server group is defined in the lines that follow because the intent is to
!authenticate outbound connections using RADIUS rather than TACACS+

aaa-server AuthOutbound protocol radius
aaa-server AuthOutbound (inside) host 172.18.124.111 cisco timeout 5
!
!The first two commands that follow define what traffic is subject to
!authentication via the server groups defined above. The AAA authorization command
!turns on authorization for the traffic matching access list 101. Please note that
!a user needs to be authenticated before authorization can take place. From
!version 6.2, PIX allows per-user access lists to be downloaded from a RADIUS
!server. Please see the chapter on AAA authorization for more details on how to
!set up a user profile for this to happen.
```

Example 8-4 *How PIX Is Set up to Do Authorization and Authentication (Continued)*

```
aaa authentication match 101 outside AuthInbound
aaa authentication match 101 inside AuthOutbound
aaa authorization match 101 outside AuthInbound

no snmp-server location
no snmp-server contact
snmp-server community public
no snmp-server enable traps
floodguard enable
no sysopt route dnat
isakmp identity hostname
telnet timeout 5
ssh timeout 5
terminal width 80

: end
```

The PIX saves the credentials of an authenticated user in a data structure known as *uauth*. The user can access resources through the PIX until either the idle timer or the absolute timer of uauth expires. After that, the user has to authenticate again to access the resources sitting behind the PIX.

Scaling PIX Configurations Using Object Groups and Turbo ACLs

Object groups (introduced in PIX 6.2) are a very useful mechanism for controlling the size of the PIX configurations and avoiding inputting redundant information in the PIX. Object grouping provides a way to reduce the number of access rules required to describe complex security policies. Object groups allow two main things to happen:

- Group several hosts that have similar access requirements such that a single access rule can be applied to all of them, rather than creating a separate rule for each host. This also helps make the configuration more meaningful and easily comparable to the network access policy.

- Group several services or protocols so that they can be applied to a range of hosts at the same time. This again avoids the need to create a separate rule for each host that needs to use these services.

TurboACL is a feature introduced with PIX Firewall version 6.2 that improves the average search time for access control lists containing a large number of entries. The TurboACL feature causes the PIX Firewall to compile tables for ACLs; this improves searching of long ACLs. If an ACL contains more than 19 entries and is set up for turbo access list compilation, PIX compiles the access list for faster processing. This is a useful feature to have in environments that require a large number of access lists to be set up.

Example 8-5 describes how object groups and Turbo ACLs are used. The implementation of LAN failover, meaning stateful failover using LAN instead of the serial cable, is also discussed. This feature allows the distance limitations between the primary and secondary PIX to be overcome among other things.

Figure 8-16 shows the network setup via the configuration.

Figure 8-16 *Network Topology for This Case Study*

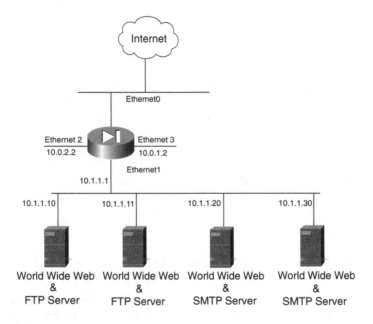

Example 8-5 *How Object Groups and Turbo ACLs Are Used*

```
pixfirewall#wr t
Building configuration...
: Saved
:
PIX Version 6.2(1)
nameif ethernet0 outside security0
nameif ethernet1 inside security100
nameif ethernet2 failstate security20
nameif ethernet3 LANfail security30
enable password <removed> encrypted
passwd <removed> encrypted
hostname pixfirewall
domain-name sjpki.com
fixup protocol ftp 21
fixup protocol http 80
fixup protocol h323 h225 1720
```

Example 8-5   *How Object Groups and Turbo ACLs Are Used (Continued)*

```
fixup protocol h323 ras 1718-1719
fixup protocol ils 389
fixup protocol rsh 514
fixup protocol rtsp 554
fixup protocol smtp 25
fixup protocol sqlnet 1521
fixup protocol sip 5060
fixup protocol skinny 2000
names
!The following command defines an object group called host_group_1. This object
!group groups two hosts' IP addresses, 100.1.1.10 and 100.1.1.11. These are called
!network objects. Both these addresses are the statically translated IP addresses
!of the 10.1.1.10 and 10.1.1.11 hosts, which are two of the servers on the inside
!network. The purpose of grouping these two servers' IP addresses is to apply
!similar access rules to them using access lists.

object-group network host_group_1
  network-object host 100.1.1.10
  network-object host 100.1.1.11

!Similarly, host_group_2 defines another set of two hosts, 100.1.1.20 and
!100.1.1.30, again two servers.

object-group network host_group_2
  network-object host 100.1.1.20
  network-object host 100.1.1.30

!all_groups defines a third set of group objects. However, this time, instead of
!having individual hosts as group objects, the entire host_group_1 and host_group
!2 are the two group objects. This group is used where there is a need to apply a
!policy to all four servers rather than just two.

object-group network all_groups
  group-object host_group_1
  group-object host_group_2

!The outbound_services object defines a different type of object group than the
!ones defined above. Instead of defining host IP addresses, this group defines two
!services, tcp port 80 (www) and smtp (25). These two services are grouped so that
!they can be applied together to hosts on the inside networks wanting to access the
!public network.

object-group service outbound_services tcp
  port-object eq www
  port-object eq smtp

!The three access lists below use the network object groups defined above to apply
!the rules to the entire object groups in one instance rather than multiple
!instances.
```

continues

Example 8-5 *How Object Groups and Turbo ACLs Are Used (Continued)*

```
access-list grp_2 permit tcp any object-group host_group_2 eq smtp

!The command below turns on the turbo access list feature for the access list
!grp_2.

access-list grp_2 compiled
access-list grp_1 permit tcp any object-group host_group_1 eq ftp
access-list grp_1 compiled
access-list all permit tcp any object-group all_groups eq www
access-list all compiled

!The access list below is used to restrict outbound access from internal hosts.
!All hosts except the servers are allowed only WWW and SMTP access outbound. The
!services object group is used to define the services allowed for these hosts.

access-list outbound_services_acl permit ip host 10.1.1.10 any
access-list outbound_services_acl permit ip host 10.1.1.11 any
access-list outbound_services_acl permit ip host 10.1.1.20 any
access-list outbound_services_acl permit ip host 10.1.1.30 any
access-list outbound_services_acl permit tcp 10.1.1.0 255.255.255.0 any
  object-group outbound_services
access-list outbound_services_acl compiled
pager lines 24
no logging console debugging
no logging monitor debugging
interface ethernet0 100full
interface ethernet1 100full
interface ethenret3 100full
interface ethernet4 100full
ip address outside 100.1.1.1 255.0.0.0
ip address inside 10.1.1.1 255.255.255.0
ip address failstate 10.0.1.2 255.255.255.0
ip address LANfail 10.0.2.2 255.255.255.0

!The failover IP address commands below are used to define the IP addresses that
!will be used by the primary PIX to talk to the secondary PIX.

failover ip address outside 100.1.1.100
failover ip address inside 10.1.1.100
failover ip address failstate 10.0.1.100
failover ip address LANfail  10.0.2.100
!The first two failover commands are the same as the ones described in the earlier
!failover example. However, please note that four new failover lan commands have
!been introduced that define the interface that will be used for the LAN failover
!communications to occur. Also a key used to authenticate and encrypt messages
!between the two PIXes.

failover
failover poll 15
failover lan unit primary
failover lan interface LANfail
failover lan key L6nfa1lk4y
```

Example 8-5 *How Object Groups and Turbo ACLs Are Used (Continued)*

```
failover lan enable
pdm history enable
arp timeout 14400
static (inside,outside) 100.1.1.10 10.1.1.10 netmask 255.255.255.255 0 0
static (inside,outside) 100.1.1.11 10.1.1.11 netmask 255.255.255.255 0 0
static (inside,outside) 100.1.1.20 10.1.1.20 netmask 255.255.255.255 0 0
static (inside,outside) 100.1.1.30 10.1.1.30 netmask 255.255.255.255 0 0
access-group grp_2 in interface outside
access-group outbound_services_acl in interface inside
route outside 0.0.0.0 0.0.0.0 100.1.1.2 1
timeout xlate 3:00:00
timeout conn 1:00:00 half-closed 0:10:00 udp 0:02:00 rpc 0:10:00 h323 0:05:00
timeout uauth 0:05:00 absolute
aaa-server TACACS+ protocol tacacs+
aaa-server RADIUS protocol radius
aaa-server LOCAL protocol local
aaa-server AuthOutbound protocol radius
no snmp-server location
no snmp-server contact
snmp-server community public
no snmp-server enable traps
floodguard enable
sysopt connection permit-ipsec
no sysopt route dnat
isakmp identity address
telnet 10.1.1.0 255.255.255.0 inside
telnet timeout 5
ssh 171.69.89.139 255.255.255.255 outside

ssh timeout 30
terminal width 80
Cryptochecksum:76c0494bcaa4aa2563cd11cb922375a4
: end
[OK]
```

Although the object groups reduce the complexity of the configuration, the **show access-list** command can still be used to view the ACL configuration in its entirety with all the object groups expanded into individual elements.

Summary

PIX Firewall has a comprehensive suite of features that allow it to perform basic firewall functions with speed. It also has an array of advanced features that can be used to take care of specific network situations and various types of attacks. This chapter built on the basic discussion of firewalls from the preceding chapter and constructed the framework under which the PIX Firewall works. It is interesting to note that most of the more complicated implementations of the PIX seen in the field are various permutations of the use of some of the advanced features found in the PIX. Because the PIX Firewall forms the basis of any secure Cisco network security architecture, a thorough understanding of the topics in this chapter is crucial to understanding the various other techniques discussed in the other chapters.

Review Questions

1   How does ASA keep track of UDP connections?

2   What does ASA do to the TCP sequence number of packets passing through it?

3   What does the PIX's mail guard feature do?

4   What is the purpose of the ARP test in PIX's failover mechanism?

5   What is the purpose of the **sysopt connection tcpmss** command?

6   What is the purpose of PIX's **telnet** command?

7   What is the purpose of the **alias** command?

8   What is the purpose of the failover Ethernet cable?

9   How is the PAT address specified in the PIX configuration?

This chapter covers the following key topics:

- **Context-Based Access Control**—This section discusses CBAC, the mechanism behind the firewall implementation on IOS running routers.

- **Features of IOS Firewall**—This section talks about features available in the IOS Firewall.

- **Case Study**: **CBAC on a Router Configured with NAT**—This section contains a comprehensive case study involving an IOS Firewall implementation.

IOS Firewall

IOS Firewall, part of the CiscoSecure Integrated Software, is a stateful packet-filter firewall that runs on a router, providing firewall capabilities in addition to the router's normal routing functionality. This chapter discusses how the IOS Firewall operates and some of the important characteristics that define its role in the network. We will start by discussing the Context-Based Access Control (CBAC) mechanism that is at the core of the IOS Firewall functionality and then discuss more specific features embedded in the IOS Firewall software.

Context-Based Access Control

CBAC is similar to the Adaptive Security Algorithm (ASA) discussed in the preceding chapter. It too is a mechanism that allows the router to look at the packets flowing through it and, based on the connections that have been established through the router, decide which traffic to allow through and which to stop. Three pieces of the puzzle come together to create the CBAC technology as we know it in the Cisco IOS Software today:

- Dynamic modification of the extended access lists by CBAC to allow passage to the appropriate response protocols/ports for applications initiated from the inside
- Inspection of the application level and transport level protocols
- Control of the number and length of sessions based on the information collected by inspecting packets

These three elements form the IOS Firewall functionality. As a part of the IOS Firewall setup, extended access lists are in place on the router. They block all traffic headed for the networks protected by the IOS Firewall unless entries are configured in them to allow access to specific hosts, such as Web servers or FTP servers on the protected networks. CBAC dynamically modifies these access lists to open holes to allow responses to the traffic originated from the protected networks. In addition to doing this basic firewall work, the IOS Firewall can also accommodate the special needs of certain application protocols, such as FTP and RealAudio. The IOS Firewall recognizes the content contained in the data portion of the traffic for these protocols and modifies the IOS Firewall's behavior to accommodate these protocols. Chapter 8, "PIX Firewall," discussed the requirements for some of these protocols, such as the multimedia protocols. IOS Firewall also maintains the connections that are established through it. It tracks half-open connections, the total number of connections through it, and other parameters for these connections. A more detailed discussion of this maintenance behavior appears later in this chapter.

CBAC Functionality

We will go through how the various pieces discussed in the last section play a part in making a router act as a firewall.

Assume that the router you are working with is on the edge of a network. It has a private network behind it and a public network such as the Internet on its other side. The first thing that is done in setting up the IOS Firewall is to configure an access list and apply it to the incoming interface(s) of the router connected to the Internet. If the internal network has machines that need to be accessed from the Internet, holes are opened in the access control list to allow that to occur. These holes are static entries that need to be created in the inbound access list to allow port- or protocol-specific connections to servers that need to be accessible from the Internet.

Next, the router is set up to inspect packets that are leaving the router and going to the Internet. These packets originate on the private network behind the router. Inspection allows the router to keep track of the sessions that are established by the machines behind the router accessing machines on the Internet. By keeping track of these sessions, the router can allow the return traffic to come back to the machines that originated the traffic. It does so by opening holes dynamically in the access list configured on the router's incoming interface. These holes allow only the traffic specific to the session that was established from the private network behind the router.

The following is a description of how the states are maintained within a router. This discussion is similar to the one in Chapter 8 that describes how the ASA creates and maintains information for TCP and UDP sessions on a PIX. This list summarizes what the IOS Firewall does to perform its work as a stateful packet filter:

- Transport and application state and context need to be maintained for the protocol that needs inspection. This is done with a state information structure (SIS). A SIS is created for each logical session. For TCP, a connection initiation sequence causes a SIS to be created. For UDP, a session is created as soon as a UDP packet for a particular combination of addresses and ports is seen. TCP and UDP payloads are inspected only if they carry the application-level protocol you want to inspect (the port number is checked). At a minimum, the SIS uniquely identifies a connection (addresses and ports). In addition, other information, such as TCP connection state, TCP sequence number, and an inactivity timer, is maintained as appropriate.

- A SIS is deleted when the session or connection is terminated.

- The inactivity timer is used to deallocate the SISs of TCP connections if you do not see the complete TCP termination sequence.

- For UDP sessions, the inactivity timer is used to deallocate the associated structure.

- Out-of-sequence TCP packets are dropped. Duplicated data is not presented to the application inspection modules.

- TCP packets with invalid sequence numbers are dropped. TCP packets with sequence numbers outside the window are considered invalid.

- The reassembly of IP packets is not supported. It's assumed that the TCP implementation employs MTU discovery to keep fragmentation at the IP layer from happening. See the section "Fragment Handling in IOS Firewall" for more details on this topic.

- CBAC does not inspect packets originated by the IOS Firewall router.

- ICMP packets are not inspected because they do not contain state information like TCP or UDP packets. ICMPs must be managed manually using static entries in the access control lists.

- CBAC ignores ICMP unreachable packets.

The third piece of the implementation occurs when the sessions passing through the router are controlled using the information collected with the inspection mechanism. This is done in part to protect against a flooding attack or unusual consumption of memory due to a large number of SISs. To review, a SIS is created for a new TCP connection or for the first UDP packet containing address and port information not seen before. If the number of control blocks (SISs) in the half-open state reaches a threshold, half-open SISs are deleted to accommodate a new session.

The inspection engine also monitors the rate of new TCP connection requests. If this is higher than a maximum value, half-open SISs are deleted for every new connection request.

The values for these thresholds can be configured.

Because the main purpose of a router is routing, care should be taken in evaluating when CBAC is enabled on a router. CBAC uses approximately 600 bytes of memory per connection (350 for SIS and 250 for the dynamic entry in the ACL). However, this can be considerable load if the traffic to be evaluated is heavy and the router has a lot of additional routing load to process. CBAC evaluates access lists using an accelerated method (CBAC hashes access lists and evaluates the hash) that improves performance. However, in larger implementations, you should follow the guidelines for maximizing the performance of access control lists given in Chapter 21, "Using Access Control Lists Effectively."

Features of IOS Firewall

IOS Firewall comes with an array of features that make it suitable for deployment in today's complex network environments. Not only does CBAC offer basic features such as TCP session tracking and UDP session timing, but it also allows application-level protocols to be handled well by the router running the CBAC feature set. In addition, CBAC has extensive

DOS prevention features that are critical to any network. This section discusses the main features that the IOS Firewall offers a network.

Transport Layer Inspection

At the transport layer, IOS Firewall can inspect for the two primary transport protocols, TCP and UDP. The firewall can inspect all packets that are sent across the firewall router using these protocols. Consequently, it can keep track of the corresponding sessions for opening holes in the access list as well as protecting against denial of service (DoS) attacks.

This kind of generic inspection lets you use CBAC for application-layer protocols whose data streams the router doesn't know how to parse. With generic TCP inspection, for example, you can permit Telnet traffic, even though no inspection is specific to Telnet. Generic TCP inspection works only for protocols that use a single TCP connection, initiated from the client side. It creates a single channel in response to the TCP SYN packet that opens the TCP connection and destroys the channel in response to the TCP finish (FIN) packets that close the conversation. Generic UDP inspection works only for protocols that use a single client host/port pair and a single server host/port pair. It creates a channel in response to the first packet the client sends to the server and leaves that channel open until there's been no activity for a specified period of time.

Application Layer Inspection

Apart from inspecting all the TCP or UDP packets by enabling inspection at the transport layer, the IOS Firewall also allows inspection to take place at the application layer for the various protocols passing through the IOS Firewall. This is important for protocols that use more than one TCP or UDP connection to pass data or control information between two machines. One good example of such a protocol is FTP. In addition to opening a data port for the data traffic for FTP to flow, CBAC also ensures that no data port connection is allowed if FTP authentication fails in the control session. Another application-level protocol that CBAC can manage is H323.

We discussed the behavior of these protocols in the preceding chapter. In order to deal with this behavior, the IOS Firewall requires that inspection be enabled specifically for these application level protocols. As soon as that is done, the firewall looks out for the initiation of traffic related to these protocols and then deals with them appropriately. Simply doing generic TCP or UDP inspection does not allow these special protocols to work correctly.

Table 9-1 lists the application-level protocols that are supported through the IOS Firewall.

Table 9-1   *IOS Firewall Application-Level Protocols*

Application Protocol	Protocol Keyword
CU-SeeMe	**cuseeme**
FTP	**ftp**

Table 9-1   *IOS Firewall Application-Level Protocols (Continued)*

Application Protocol	Protocol Keyword
H.323	**h323**
Microsoft NetShow	**netshow**
UNIX r commands (**rlogin**, **rexec**, **rsh**)	**rcmd**
RealAudio	**realaudio**
SMTP	**smtp**
SQL*Net	**sqlnet**
StreamWorks	**streamworks**
TFTP	**tftp**
VDOLive	**vdolive**

Filtering for Invalid Commands

IOS Firewall can screen for protocol abuses that might occur. One of its important capabilities is rejecting commands in the SMTP protocol flow that are not defined in the SMTP RFC. However, this behavior is not turned on by default when inspection for TCP is turned on. You need to turn it on by specifically inspecting for the SMTP protocol. Another protocol abuse the IOS Firewall can avoid is for FTP. The firewall does not allow third-party hacks of the FTP protocol (three-way FTP transfers) to go through the firewall.

Java Blocking

IOS Firewall can detect Java applets in packets and block them from reaching hosts behind it. You configure this functionality on the IOS Firewall by specifying an access list containing the address of the hosts from which malicious code might be expected. Then you use this access list to be aware of Java scripts for packets coming from these hosts. Of course, you can configure the access list so that the traffic from all IP addresses except a few is considered to contain malicious Java content and thereby is stopped from going through when a Java applet is detected in such traffic. Applets that are transmitted as embedded archives are not recognized and therefore cannot be blocked. When a Java applet is blocked, a reset is sent to the server sending the packet.

Note that Java blocking is different from Java filtering. With Java blocking, the HTTP traffic with the Java signature is blocked. With Java filtering, the Java .exe is filtered but the accompanying HTML is allowed to pass.

Safeguarding Against Denial of Service Attacks

CBAC uses a variety of mechanisms to protect against various types of DoS attacks. These defense mechanisms are based primarily on the state information kept on the IOS Firewall for the various types of messages.

CBAC's Thresholds and Timeouts

CBAC uses timeout and threshold values to manage session state information, helping to determine when to drop sessions that do not become fully established. Setting timeout values for network sessions helps prevent DoS attacks by freeing up system resources, dropping sessions after a specified amount of time. Setting threshold values for network sessions helps prevent DoS attacks by controlling the number of half-open sessions, which limits the amount of system resources applied to half-open sessions. When a session is dropped, CBAC sends a reset message to the devices at both of the session's endpoints (source and destination). When the system under DoS attack receives a reset command, it releases, or frees up, processes and resources related to that incomplete session.

CBAC provides three thresholds against DoS attacks:

- The total number of half-open TCP or UDP sessions
- The number of half-open sessions based on time
- The number of half-open TCP-only sessions per host

If a threshold is exceeded, CBAC has two options:

- Send a reset message to the endpoints of the oldest half-open session, making resources available to service newly arriving SYN packets.

- In the case of half-open TCP-only sessions, CBAC blocks all SYN packets temporarily for the duration configured by the threshold value. When the router blocks a SYN packet, the TCP three-way handshake is never initiated, which prevents the router from using memory and processing resources needed for valid connections.

DoS detection and prevention require that a CBAC inspection rule be created and applied on an interface. The inspection rule must include the protocols that need to be monitored against DoS attacks. For example, if TCP inspection is enabled on the inspection rule, CBAC can track all TCP connections to watch for DoS attacks. If the inspection rule includes FTP protocol inspection but not TCP inspection, CBAC tracks only FTP connections for DoS attacks.

An unusually high number of half-open sessions (either absolute or measured as the arrival rate) could indicate that a DOS attack is occurring. *For TCP, "half-open" means that the session has not reached the established state—the TCP three-way handshake has not yet been completed. For UDP, "half-open" means that the firewall has detected no return traffic.*

CBAC measures both the total number of existing half-open sessions and the rate of session establishment attempts. Both TCP and UDP half-open sessions are counted in the total number of sessions and also in terms of various rate measurements. Rate measurements are made several times per minute.

When the number of existing half-open sessions rises above a threshold (the max-incomplete high number), the software deletes half-open sessions as required to accommodate new connection requests. The software continues deleting half-open requests as necessary until the number of existing half-open sessions drops below another threshold (the max-incomplete low number).

When the rate of new connection attempts rises above a threshold (the one-minute high number), the software deletes half-open sessions as required to accommodate new connection attempts. The software continues deleting half-open sessions as necessary until the rate of new connection attempts drops below another threshold (the one-minute low number). The rate thresholds are measured as the number of new session connection attempts detected in the last 1-minute sample period.

"Calm" and "Aggressive" States

When the number of half-open sessions or the calculated half-open rate exceeds their respective high threshold values, the code attempts to remove a half-open session for each new session. When such a condition happens, a syslog message is displayed. Here is an example of one such message:

```
%FW-4-ALERT_ON: getting aggressive, count (1100/1100)
current 1-min rate: 39
```

This message contains the actual number of half-open sessions and the configured high threshold (1100/1100), as well as the calculated 1-minute half-open session rate (39). As shown in the message, the IOS Firewall is in "aggressive mode" at this point.

When the number of half-open sessions or the calculated half-open rate crosses its respective low threshold value, the code stops removing a half-open session for each new session. When such a condition happens, a syslog message is emitted. Here is an example of such a message:

```
%FW-4-ALERT_OFF: calming down, count (900/900) current 1-
min rate: 9
```

This message contains the actual number of half-open sessions and the configured low threshold (900/900), as well as the calculated 1-minute half-open session rate (9). As shown in the message, the IOS Firewall is in "calm mode" at this point.

Per-Host DoS Prevention Technique

CBAC's DoS parameters can be set up on a per-host basis too. The protected host is one that resides on a protected network behind the IOS Firewall. Host-specific DoS parameters are established using the max-incomplete host threshold and a block-time timeout parameters. Whenever the max-incomplete host threshold is exceeded, the software drops half-open sessions differently, depending on whether the block-time timeout is zero or a positive nonzero number. If the block-time timeout is zero, the software deletes the oldest existing half-open session for the host for every new connection request to the host and lets the SYN packet through. If the block-time timeout is greater than zero, the software deletes all existing half-open sessions for the host and then blocks all new connection requests to the host. The software continues blocking all new connection requests until the block-time expires.

An Example of DoS Prevention Using the IOS Firewall

An example of a DoS attack that the IOS Firewall protects against is the TCP SYN flood. A TCP SYN attack occurs when an attacking source host generates TCP SYN packets with random unused source IP addresses and sends them in rapid succession to a victim host. The victim destination host sends a SYN ACK back to the source address and adds an entry to the connection queue. Because the SYN ACK is destined for an incorrect or nonexistent host, the acknowledgment is never completed, and the entry remains in the connection queue for the victim until a timer expires. The connection queue fills up, and legitimate users cannot use TCP services. However, with CBAC, TCP packets flow from the outside only in response to traffic sent from the inside. The attacking host can't get its packets through, and the attack does not succeed. In addition (even if static entries in the ACL have been created to allow traffic to reach hosts acting as web and ftp servers), by inspecting inbound on the external interface, CBAC can account for half-open connections through the firewall and can begin closing those half-open connections in an aggressive mode. The firewall calms down as soon as the number of half-open connections settles down to a user-defined value.

Fragment Handling in IOS Firewall

IOS Firewall, unlike the PIX Firewall, does not do reassembly, either full or virtual. The IOS Firewall has two ways in which it deals with fragments arriving at the router doing CBAC:

- Allow noninitial fragments to pass through the CBAC modified access lists. This is the default behavior in IOS Firewalls. Indeed, it is the only behavior available in up through all 11.2- and 11.3-based versions, including 11.2P and 11.3T, and up through 12.0-based versions through 12.0(1) and 12.0(2)T.

  The noninitial fragments are inspected only for IP-layer information. If that information matches one of the entries (dynamic or otherwise) in the incoming access control list, IOS Firewall allows the fragments to go through. No further checks based on transport layer information or verification of the fragments against various fragment attacks are performed. The initial fragment is the only fragment subjected to transport layer information checks, because it contains the information for those checks to take place.

- Maintain interfragment state and verify fragments against fragment attacks. IOS Firewall can be set up or configured to maintain state information for the fragments passing through it. When this is set up, the firewall keeps track of the fragments arriving at the firewall and allows only those noninitial fragments to go through for which the initial fragment was allowed to go through based on the CBAC checks.

Fragments arriving out of sequence, including the ones that arrive before the initial fragment, are dropped. This can have a significant impact on networks that have a lot of fragmentation and have fragments arriving out of sequence at the firewall.

The amount of memory dedicated to maintaining fragmentation state is limited in order to reduce the chance of DoS attacks against the firewall router itself. Fragmentation state is created only in response to initial fragments and is kept until either all fragments of the datagram in question have been processed or a timeout expires. Initial fragments received when fragmentation state resources are exhausted are discarded. Unfragmented traffic is never discarded because of lack of fragment state memory. Even when the system is under heavy attack with fragmented packets, legitimate fragmented traffic, if any, still gets some fraction of the firewall's fragment state resources, and legitimate unfragmented traffic flows unimpeded.

Fragment lengths are also checked for legality. Fragment offsets are checked to avoid port-number overwrite attacks, such as the ones discussed in the preceding chapter. This offset check duplicates the check already applied by extended access lists for unusual configurations in which CBAC is being used without access lists. You set up and turn on fragment inspection using the following command:

```
ip inspect name inspection-name fragment [max number timeout number]
```

See the appropriate command reference for more details on how to configure this command.

Case Study: CBAC on a Router Configured with NAT

This section covers a case study showing how CBAC is implemented in a real-world situation. This case study is used to further delineate some of the ideas explored in this chapter.

CBAC on a router configured with NAT is one of the most common CBAC setups. One of the important issues to realize in a NAT setup is that for traffic entering the router's public interface, such as coming from the Internet, the packets are first processed through the access list applied to the interface, and then denatting occurs. This is why the incoming access list is opened for the PAT pool addresses of the machines sitting on the private network behind the router. Table 9-2 outlines the general order of operation for traffic traversing a router interface. Note that inside-to-outside means that the traffic goes from the protected network behind the IOS Firewall to the IOS Firewall and then is passed to the public or less-secure network (outside).

In Example 9-1, note that the incoming access list (112) has been opened for two kinds of traffic permanently or statically. This means that these kinds of traffic are allowed to pass through the firewall irrespective of whether dynamic holes have been created in the firewall's access list by traffic originating from the private network going to the public network. The first kind of such traffic is Telnet traffic originating from the next-hop router going to the outside interface of the firewall router. This hole has been opened for administrative purposes. However, the second kind of traffic is perhaps more significant. These are the various types of ICMP messages passing through the firewall.

Table 9-2   *Order of Operations for Traffic Traversing a Router*

Inside-to-Outside	Outside-to-Inside
If IPsec, check input access list	If IPsec, check input access list
Decryption,for Cisco Encryption Technology (CET) or IPsec	Decryption,for CET or IPsec
	Check the input access list
Check the input access list	Check input rate limits
Check input rate limits	Input accounting
Input accounting	Inspect
Inspect	NAT outside to inside (global-to-local translation)
Policy routing	
Routing	Policy routing
Redirect to the Web cache	Routing
NAT inside to outside (local-to-global translation)	Redirect to the Web cache
	Crypto (check the map and mark it for encryption)
Crypto (check the map and mark it for encryption)	Check the output access list
Check the output access list	Inspect
Inspect	TCP intercept
TCP intercept	Encryption
Encryption	

There are two main reasons why holes need to be opened in the firewall statically for ICMP traffic. The first reason is that CBAC does not work for ICMP traffic. If ICMP traffic originates from the inside private network, no inspection of such packets and subsequent opening of dynamic holes in the access lists configured on the firewall takes place. The second reason is to allow some of the important types of ICMP packets, such as the ICMP Packet Too Big packet, to come through the firewall. These are important informational messages that allow the router as well as the Internet on the whole to function in a healthy fashion.

In Example 9-1, inspection occurs on the interface connected to the router's private network. Inspection is carried out for the traffic going *into* the private interface. This is correct intuitively as well, because you want to inspect traffic going into the private interface on its way to the public interface and out to the public network so that dynamic holes in the firewall's incoming access list can be created for the return traffic. You can also apply the inspection on the outside interface rather than on the inside interface and inspect traffic going out rather than coming in. This is often the best way to set things up, especially when multiple private interfaces are involved and it is a hassle to configure each of them with the inspection command. Figure 9-1 shows the network topology used in this case study.

Figure 9-1   *Network Topology for the Case Study: CBAC on a Router Configured with NAT*

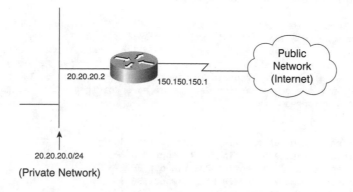

Example 9-1   *Configuration to Setup a Router to Act as a Firewall*

```
Router#write terminal
Current configuration:
!
version 12.0
service timestamps debug uptime
service timestamps log uptime
no service password-encryption
!
hostname router
!
enable secret 5 <removed>
enable password <removed>
!
ip subnet-zero
!
```

continues

Example 9-1 *Configuration to Setup a Router to Act as a Firewall (Continued)*

```
!Following, some of the parameters used to control DoS flooding are defined.
!The max-incomplete high command defines the number of half-open
!connections that cause the software to start deleting half-open
!connections. The max-incomplete low command defines the number of
!connections at which the firewall stops deleting the half-open
!connections. The one-minute high and low commands perform a similar
!function as the previous two commands, but they are used to define the
!limits under which the firewall operates when monitoring the half-open
!connections being opened on a per-minute basis. Note that for TCP,
!half-open connections are the ones for which the connection has not
!reached the established state, whereas for UDP, half-open means a
!connection for which no return traffic has been detected.

ip inspect max-incomplete high 800
ip inspect max-incomplete low 600
ip inspect one-minute high 800
ip inspect one-minute low 600

!Following, the firewall's basic configuration is set up. Apart from
!configuring which protocols will be inspected, the timeouts for
!the dynamic holes created in the firewall's access list are also
!defined. Note that the timeouts specified for the specific
!protocols take precedence over the timeouts specified for TCP or
!UDP, which are used as the default if no specific protocol timeouts
!are configured.


ip inspect name ethernetin cuseeme timeout 3600
ip inspect name ethernetin ftp timeout 3600
ip inspect name ethernetin h323 timeout 3600
ip inspect name ethernetin http timeout 3600
ip inspect name ethernetin rcmd timeout 3600
ip inspect name ethernetin realaudio timeout 3600
ip inspect name ethernetin smtp timeout 3600
ip inspect name ethernetin sqlnet timeout 3600
ip inspect name ethernetin streamworks timeout 3600
ip inspect name ethernetin tcp timeout 3600
ip inspect name ethernetin tftp timeout 30
ip inspect name ethernetin udp timeout 15
ip inspect name ethernetin vdolive timeout 3600

!The inspect command below is used to turn on Java applet blocking, as
!defined by access list 3.

ip inspect name ethernetin http java-list 3

 !
 interface Ethernet0
 ip address 20.20.20.2 255.255.255.0

!The access list below is used to allow only the hosts on the inside
!private network to send packets to the router on their way to the
```

Example 9-1 *Configuration to Setup a Router to Act as a Firewall (Continued)*

```
!public network.

 ip access-group 101 in
 no ip directed-broadcast
 ip nat inside

!This is the inspection command we discussed above

 ip inspect ethernetin in
 !
 !
 interface Serial0
 ip address 150.150.150.1 255.255.255.0

!The access list applied below is used to control access from the public side
!of the router.
!This is also the access list in which holes are opened dynamically to allow
!return traffic through.

 ip access-group 112 in
 no ip directed-broadcast
 ip nat outside

 !
 !
 ip nat pool serialzero 150.150.150.3 150.150.150.254 netmask 255.255.255.0

 ip nat inside source list 1 pool serialzero
 ip classless
 ip route 0.0.0.0 0.0.0.0 150.150.150.2
 ip route 20.30.30.0 255.255.255.0 20.20.20.1
 !
 access-list 1 permit 20.0.0.0 0.255.255.255

!The access list below is the one used to permit Java applets from the IP
!address 216.157.100.247. The implicit deny at the end of the access list
!prohibits Java applets from being accepted from any other IP address

 access-list 3 permit 216.157.100.247
 access-list 101 permit tcp 20.0.0.0 0.255.255.255 any
 access-list 101 permit udp 20.0.0.0 0.255.255.255 any
 access-list 101 permit icmp 20.0.0.0 0.255.255.255 any

!Access list 112 below is opened for ICMP traffic as well as some
!Telnet traffic. See the detailed discussion above for why this is done

 access-list 112 permit icmp any 150.150.150.0 0.0.0.255 unreachable
 access-list 112 permit icmp any 150.150.150.0 0.0.0.255 echo-reply
 access-list 112 permit icmp any 150.150.150.0 0.0.0.255 packet-too-big
 access-list 112 permit icmp any 150.150.150.0 0.0.0.255 time-exceeded
```

continues

Example 9-1 *Configuration to Setup a Router to Act as a Firewall (Continued)*

```
access-list 112 permit icmp any 150.150.150.0 0.0.0.255 traceroute
access-list 112 permit icmp any 150.150.150.0 0.0.0.255 administratively-prohibited
access-list 112 permit icmp any 150.150.150.0 0.0.0.255 echo
access-list 112 permit tcp host 150.150.150.2 host 150.150.150.1 eq 22
access-list 112 deny   ip 127.0.0.0 0.255.255.255 any
access-list 112 deny   ip any 192.168.0.0 0.0.255.255
access-list 112 deny   ip any 10.0.0.0 0.255.255.255
access-list 112 deny   ip any 172.16.0.0 0.15.255.255
access-list 112 deny   ip any any log
!
line con 0
 transport input none
line aux 0
line vty 0 4
 password <removed>
 login
!
end
```

Example 9-1 is a good example of how to use CBAC in a real-life scenario. Because access control lists play an important part in the firewall's functioning, it is important to keep in mind some of the rules discussed in Chapter 21 for setting up access control lists.

Summary

IOS Firewall is a useful tool to have on a router from a security point of view. Although the IOS Firewall provides a fairly adequate amount of firewall security, you should keep in mind the load on the router while implementing this feature on a router. Not only does IOS Firewall's feature set provide basic stateful packet filtering functionality, but it also has a fair number of add-on features, such as application-level protocol awareness and DoS attack detection and prevention.

This chapter concludes our discussion of firewalls. However, later we will revisit some of the access control list techniques and deal with service provider security features. That discussion will complete the discussion of the use of firewalls and filtering techniques to protect networks against various types of attacks.

Review Questions

1 What is meant by Java blocking in the IOS Firewall world?

2 How does the IOS Firewall protect against TCP SYN floods?

3 How does FTP work through the IOS Firewall?

4 How does IOS Firewall keep track of UDP sessions?

5 Are TCP and UDP payload inspected if you are inspecting only for TCP and UDP on the IOS Firewall?

PART IV

Virtual Private Networks

- **VPNs Defined**—This section gives a basic definition of VPNs and describes the various types of VPNs.

- **VPN Types**—This section discusses the different types of VPNs, based on how they are constructed and used.

CHAPTER **10**

The Concept of VPNs

Virtual Private Networks (VPNs) are an integral part of the modern-day's expanding
networks. They allow a network's security to stay intact while the network is expanded to
incorporate additional elements. This chapter introduces VPNs and how they function. We
will discuss the various types of VPNs in order to get a firm grip on how and where you will
encounter VPN setups. This chapter lays the foundation for a more-specific discussion of
some of the important VPN protocols in the chapters to follow.

VPNs Defined

In order to understand the various types of VPNs, you must first have a clear understanding
of what they are.

A *VPN* is a means of carrying private traffic over a public network. It is often a means of
connecting two private networks across a public network such as the Internet. A private network is essentially a network that is not freely accessible to the public. This means that a
set of rules governs who can be part of the private network and who can use it as a transit
medium. A VPN is called virtual because to the users on either end, the two private networks seem to be seamlessly connected to each other. In other words, they are *virtually* part
of one private network comprised of the two networks combined. However, this is only
virtual. In reality, a public network is in between the two private networks.

VPNs are often constructed by connecting two or more private networks using an encrypted
tunnel. This way, the traffic in transit across the public network is hidden from the people
who are not part of the private networks. The next section discusses various types of VPNs
based on how they are constructed and the functions they perform.

VPN Types Based on Encryption Versus No-Encryption

VPNs can be divided into various types based on how they are constructed or the goals they
are constructed to achieve. This section looks at the various types of VPNs used in the
industry today.

Based on the use of encryption or lack thereof, VPNs can be divided into two main
categories: encrypted and nonencrypted.

Encrypted VPNs

Encrypted VPNs utilize various types of encryption mechanisms to secure the traffic flowing across the public network. This is generally done to allow the VPN traffic to traverse a publicly accessible network such as the Internet. A good example of such VPNs are those constructed using IPsec. IPsec sets up a VPN that encrypts traffic using an encryption algorithm for passage across a public network such as the Internet.

Nonencrypted VPNs

Nonencrypted VPNs are constructed to connect two or more private networks so that users on both networks can seamlessly access resources sitting on either network. However, the security of the traffic that flows from one private network to another is either not ensured at all or is ensured using means other than encryption. These means include route segregation, in which only the traffic flowing between the two private networks can be routed to either of them (MPLS VPNs). In cases where security is not ensured by the primary mechanism providing the VPN functionality, such as with GRE-based VPNs, often higher-layer encryption (such as SSL) is used to provide data confidentiality.

Both types of VPNs just described can provide the necessary amount of security based on a security policy. However, encrypted VPNs usually are considered the primary means of creating a secure VPN. Other types of VPNs, such as MPLS VPNs, depend on a trust of the ISP and the security and integrity of the routing functionality. Although a trustworthy ISP can provide this, more often than not, VPN design tends to tilt in the direction of encrypted VPNs. Also, nonencrypted types of VPNs often are complemented by some form of encryption.

VPN Types Based on OSI Model Layer

VPNs can also be classified based on the OSI model layer at which they are constructed. This is an important distinction to make. For example, in the case of encrypted VPNs, the layer at which encryption occurs can determine how much traffic gets encrypted, as well as the level of transparency for the VPN's end users.

Based on the OSI model layers, VPNs can be divided into the following three main categories:

- Data link layer VPNs
- Network layer VPNs
- Application layer VPNs

Data Link Layer VPNs

With data link layer VPNs, two private networks are connected on Layer 2 of the OSI model using a protocol such as Frame Relay or ATM. Although these mechanisms provide a suitable way of creating VPNs, they are often expensive, because they require dedicated Layer 2 pathways to be created. Frame Relay and ATM protocols inherently do not provide encryption mechanisms. They only allow traffic to be segregated based on which Layer 2 connection it belongs to. Therefore, if you need further security, it is important to have some sort of encryption mechanism in place.

Network Layer VPNs

Network layer VPNs are created using Layer 3 tunneling and/or encryption techniques. An example is the use of the IPsec tunneling and encryption protocol to create VPNs. Other examples are GRE and L2TP protocols. It is interesting to note that although L2TP tunnels Layer 2 traffic, it uses Layer 3, the IP layer, to do this. Therefore, it is classified as a network layer VPN.

The following chapters focus on network layer VPNs. Network layers provide a very suitable place to do encryption. The network layer is low enough in the stack to provide seamless connectivity to all applications running on top of it and is high enough to allow suitable granularity for the traffic that needs to be part of the VPN based on the extensive IP Addressing architecture in place. Due to its natural positioning in the IP market, Cisco focuses on network layer encryption as the main mechanism for creating VPNs.

Application Layer VPNs

Application layer VPNs are created to work specifically with certain applications. One very good example of such VPNs are SSL-based VPNs. SSL provides encryption between Web browsers and servers running SSL. Another good example is SSH. SSH is pushed as a mechanism for encrypted and secure login sessions to various network devices. SSH can encrypt and thus create VPNs for other application layer protocols, such as FTP and HTTP.

One of the main drawbacks of application layer VPNs is that often they are not seamless. The user must perform an action to enable the end devices for creating the VPN for each of the various applications. As new services and corresponding applications are added, support for them must be developed as well. This is unlike network layer and link layer VPNs, which provide seamless VPN connectivity for all applications after the basic VPN has been set up.

Figure 10-1 shows VPNs at the various OSI model layers.

Figure 10-1 *The Three Main Types of VPNs Based on the OSI Model Layers*

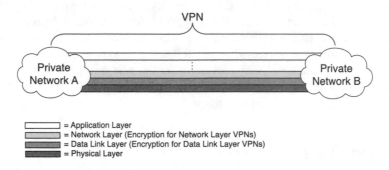

VPN Types Based on Business Functionality

VPNs are set up to achieve some business goals. These business goals can be used to classify VPNs into two further categories:

- Intranet VPNs
- Extranet VPNs

Intranet VPNs

Intranet VPNs are created to connect two or more private networks within the same organization. These often come into existence when a remote office needs to be connected to headquarters or when a company is acquired and needs to have its network integrated into the acquirer's main network.

Extranet VPNs

Extranet VPNs are used to connect private networks belonging to more than one organizational unit. These are often used in B-2-B scenarios in which two companies want to conduct business together. A company's partners can also be allowed to use the company's resources by giving them access through a VPN across the Internet.

Figure 10-2 shows how intranet and extranet VPNs fit into the overall VPN picture.

Figure 10-2 *Intranet and Extranet VPNs*

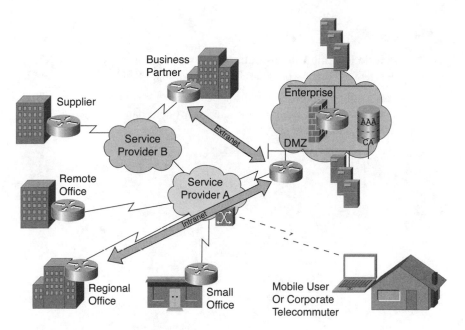

Summary

VPNs are one of the most critical network security tool. The reason for their widespread use is the rapid expansion in reliance on the networking resources available within corporate networks. The need for these resources to be accessible to remote users, home users, remote offices, partners, and others has fueled the growth of VPNs. Although VPNs can be set up in quite a few different ways, the primary goals are the same: seamless connectivity and maintenance of the security of the networks participating in the VPN.

This chapter defined VPNs and listed the various types of VPNs. Different types based on functionality, construction, and business goals were discussed. The goal of this chapter was to lay a foundation for the specific VPN protocols that will be discussed in the following chapters. Later chapters call on the concepts discussed in this chapter to augment more-specific discussions.

This chapter covers the following topics:

- **Generic Routing Encapsulation**—This section discusses what GRE is and gives an overview of how it works based on the two main RFCs that describe GRE.

- **Case Studies**—This section discusses three case studies involving real-life GRE implementations. Configurations and **show** commands are included to help you understand each case study.

## CHAPTER 11

GRE

Generic Routing Encapsulation (GRE) is a protocol often used in networks to tunnel traffic from one private network to another. Although GRE does not offer encryption services, it does provide low overhead tunneling. This chapter looks at the implementations of GRE through the RFCs that were written for it and compares the differences among them. We will analyze the various fields available in the GRE header. Based on this foundation, we will discuss case studies involving the deployment of GRE. We will look at some of the more common uses of GRE, such as using GRE to seamlessly combine routing protocols running on the networks being connected through GRE and using GRE to tunnel non-IP traffic.

GRE

GRE is used to encapsulate an arbitrary layer protocol over another arbitrary layer protocol. In general, GRE allows a tunnel to be created using a certain protocol, which then hides the contents of another protocol carried within the tunnel.

We will mostly discuss the use of IPv4 as the carrying mechanism for GRE with any arbitrary protocol nested inside.

Figure 11-1 shows the general format for encapsulated packets using GRE.

The delivery header can be the IPv4 header. The payload packet can also be an IPv4 header, or it can be another protocol. GRE allows non-IP protocols to be carried in the payload. GRE packets using IPv4 headers are classified as IP protocol type 47. This is an important piece of information when you create filters for GRE. If the packet encapsulated within GRE is also IPv4, the GRE header's Protocol Type field is set to 0x800.

Figure 11-1 *GRE Packet Format*

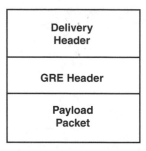

Two main implementations of GRE exist in the field—one based on RFC 1701, and one based on the newer RFC 2784, which is also a proposed standard. RFC 2784 implementations interoperate with RFC 1701 implementations to some extent, but some of the features offered in RFC 1701 have been deprecated in RFC 2784. We will talk about the interoperability after discussing the RFC 1784 implementation. A new RFC, 2890, will also be discussed because it introduces some modifications to the RFC 2784 behavior.

Figure 11-2 shows the format of the GRE header based on RFC 1701.

Figure 11-2 *GRE Header Format Based on RFC 1701*

```
0 1 2 3 4 5 6 7 8 9 0 1 2 3 4 5 6 7 8 9 0 1 2 3 4 5 6 7 8 9 0 1
```

C	R	K	S	s	Recur	Flags	Ver	Protocol Type

Checksum (Optional)	Offset (Optional)

Key (Optional)

Sequence Number (Optional)

Routing (Optional)

The interesting fields in this header are as follows:

- **Flags**—The following descriptions are taken from RFC 1701 with comments added for clarification:

  - **Checksum Present (bit 0)**—If the Checksum Present bit is set to 1, the checksum field is present and contains valid information. If either the Checksum Present bit or the Routing Present bit is set, *both* the Checksum and Offset fields are present in the GRE packet.

— **Routing Present (bit 1)**—If the Routing Present bit is set to 1, the Offset and Routing fields are present and contain valid information. If either the Checksum Present bit or the RoutingPresent bit is set, *both* the Checksum and Offset fields are present in the GRE packet.

— **Key Present (bit 2)**—If the Key Present bit is set to 1, the Key field is present in the GRE header. Otherwise, the Key field is not present in the GRE header.

— **Sequence Number Present (bit 3)**—If the Sequence Number Present bit is set to 1, the Sequence Number field is present. Otherwise, the Sequence Number field is not present in the GRE header.

— **Strict Source Route (bit 4)**—It is recommended that this bit be set to 1 only if all the routing information consists of strict source routes.

— **Recursion Control (bits 5–7)**—Recursion control contains a 3-bit unsigned integer that contains the number of additional encapsulations that are permissible. This *should* default to 0.

— **Version Number (bits 13–15)**—The Version Number field *must* contain the value 0.

- **Protocol Type**—The Protocol Type field contains the protocol type of the packet in the payload of the GRE packet. For example, when IP is the protocol being carried inside the GRE packet, this field is set to 0x800.

- **Checksum**—This field is used to ensure the integrity of the GRE header and the payload packet. It contains an IP checksum of the GRE header and the payload packet.

- **Key**—The Key field contains a number that is used to authenticate the GRE packet's encapsulator. This is a very weak form of security offered by GRE. In essence, the key prevents misconfiguration or injection of packets from a foreign source. The two tunnel endpoints accept GRE packets only with the correct key in the header. The key needs to be manually configured on both the endpoints. This is obviously not a feature to be relied on for security, because as soon as an attacker figures out the key simply by looking at a GRE packet, he or she can generate as authentic a GRE packet as the original encapsulator.

  Another use of the key is to identify individual traffic flow within a tunnel. For example, packets might need to be routed based on context information not present in the encapsulated data. The Key field provides this context and defines a logical traffic flow between encapsulator and decapsulator. An example of this is the not very widely-deployed multipoint GRE tunnels. These tunnels require that a key be defined in order for the traffic to be distinguished. For the sake of this chapter, we will focus on the more common point-to-point GRE tunnels.

- **Sequence Number**—The two endpoints can use the sequence number to track the sequence in which packets are being received and optionally drop packets that arrive out of sequence. This is useful when carrying passenger protocols that function poorly when they receive packets out of order (such as LLC2-based protocols).

- **Routing**—The Routing field lists Source Route Entries (SREs). This field is not very commonly used. It is used when there is a need to do source routing on GRE packets.

Having discussed the RFC 1701 implementation of GRE, let's look at the RFC 2784 implementation. RFC 2784 deprecates three of the optional fields in GRE (sequence number, key, and routing) and gets rid of the flags that are used in the 1701 RFC with the exception of the checksum flag. In the place of these flags, 0s are inserted. This ensures interoperability between the 1701 and 2784 implementations if the packets are being sent by a 2784 sender to a 1701 receiver. The 1701 implementation treats the 0s as an indication that the sequence number, key, and routing options are simply not being used. However, if the sender is a 1701 implementation and sets one of the dropped-in-2784 flags to a 1, the packets must be dropped by the 2784 implementation.

Figure 11-3 shows the format of the GRE header based on RFC 2784.

Figure 11-3 *GRE Header Format Based on RFC 2784*

0 1 2 3 4 5 6 7 8 9 0 1 2 3 4 5 6 7 8 9 0 1 2 3 4 5 6 7 8 9 0 1			
C	Reserved0	Ver	Protocol Type
Checksum (Optional)		Reserved1 (Optional)	

All the fields in the 2784 header have already been explained in the preceding section on RFC 1701 implementation.

A new RFC, RFC 2890, reintroduces two of the flags and two of the optional fields to be used with the specifications of RFC 2784. These flags and fields are for the Key and Sequence Number options.

The latest version of the 12.2T code of the Cisco IOS Software implements RFC 2784 with the enhancements of RFC 2890.

Figure 11-4 shows the format of the GRE header based on RFC 2784 combined with the RFC 2890 enhancements.

Figure 11-4 *GRE Header Format Based on RFC 2784 and the RFC 2890 Enhancements*

0 1 2 3 4 5 6 7 8 9 0 1 2 3 4 5 6 7 8 9 0 1 2 3 4 5 6 7 8 9 0 1					
C	K	S	Reserved0	Ver	Protocol Type
Checksum (Optional)				Reserved1 (Optional)	
Key (Optional)					
Sequence Number (Optional)					

GRE is often used in conjunction with another encryption protocol to provide security. The VPNs set up using GRE are insecure because GRE does not provide a means of securely encrypting its payload. Means of providing this encryption often reside on the application layer, allowing GRE to create the tunnel needed to connect the private networks while the application layer encryption protocol secures the data. In such situations, GRE mainly acts as a transport medium for carrying the traffic from one private network to another.

In Cisco devices, GRE also is sometimes used together with a network layer encryption protocol such as IPsec. Most often the reason for doing so is to use some of the features of the GRE protocol or to overcome some of the shortcomings of the network layer encryption protocol's implementation. One example is using the GRE protocol to encapsulate non-IP traffic and then encrypting the GRE packet using the IPsec protocol. This is done because of the IPsec protocol's inability to encrypt non-IP traffic. Encapsulating non-IP traffic such as AppleTalk within GRE lets private networks running these protocols to be securely connected using IPsec. This chapter has an example of one such implementation. Also, routing protocols such as EIGRP that use multicast traffic for their routing updates can be encapsulated in GRE and then tunneled using IPsec for security. IPsec does not allow encapsulation of multicast traffic.

Case Studies

This section discusses some of the most commonly used GRE implementations. We will look at some of the GRE features we have already discussed and see how they can be implemented using Cisco IOS Software. PIX does not support GRE, but it can be set up to allow GRE traffic to pass through it.

A Simple GRE Tunnel Connecting Two Private Networks

The most basic GRE implementation you can do is a GRE tunnel between two peer routers, GRE-1 and GRE-2. In this case study, the two routers are connected through a serial link, and then a GRE tunnel is built on top of that link. In order to push traffic into the GRE tunnel, rather than having it go without encapsulation over the plain serial link, a static route statement is added on both the routers. This static route basically states that in order to get to the private network behind the other router, the most suitable path is through the tunnel interface. One more thing to note in these configurations is that the naming of the tunnel interfaces is completely local to the router on which the tunnel is being configured. It has no bearing on the other router connecting to it. The other router is concerned with the configuration under the tunnel interface rather than its name.

The **tunnel source** and **tunnel destination** commands basically establish what the IP addresses will be on the outer header tagged by the GRE protocol. Obviously, these addresses need to be globally routable if you will be sending the GRE packets over the

Internet. However, the packets encapsulated within the GRE packet need not have globally routable addresses, because these addresses are hidden from the Internet by the GRE encapsulation.

Starting in version 12.2, the Cisco IOS Software supports GRE keepalives. This allows GRE to detect if the path between the source and destination of the GRE tunnel has become unusable, in which case it brings down the line protocol for the GRE tunnel.

Other options can be enabled under the tunnel interface. They are discussed in the description of RFC 1701 earlier in this chapter.

The scenario used in this case study is typical in which two offices are linked using a GRE tunnel. The purpose of such a GRE tunnel is often to give users in both offices the ability to see each other's private networks as if they were all one homogenous network. Although GRE allows the two networks to come together, GRE offers no security such as encryption of the traffic. Other means must be utilized on the application or network layer to provide this type of security. When you use GRE with IPsec, the GRE keepalives are encrypted like any other traffic. As with user data packets, if the IKE and IPsec security associations are not already active on the GRE tunnel, the first GRE keepalive packet triggers IKE/IPsec initialization. Figure 11-5 represents the GRE implementation discussed in this case study, and Example 11-1 shows the configurations of the two routers.

Figure 11-5 *GRE Implementation for This Case Study*

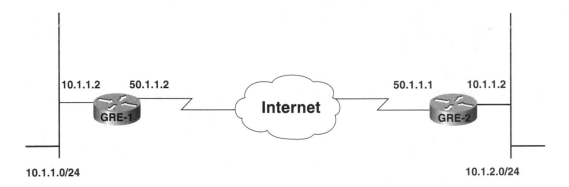

Example 11-1 *Configurations of the Two Routers Used in This Case Study*

```
GRE-1#
!
version 12.2
service timestamps debug uptime
service timestamps log uptime
no service password-encryption
!
hostname GRE-1
```

Example 11-1 *Configurations of the Two Routers Used in This Case Study (Continued)*

```
!The tunnel interface is set up using the interface tunnel command. It is a
!logical interface.

interface Tunnel0
 ip unnumbered Serial1

!The command below sets up the keepalive feature for GRE tunnels. Based on the
!parameters entered into this command, GRE keepalive packets are sent every 5
!seconds. 4 is the number of times this router continues sending keepalive
!packets without response before bringing the tunnel interface protocol down.
 keepalive 5 4
!Tunnel source and destination specify the IP addresses that will be used as the
!source address and the destination address in the GRE header
 tunnel source Serial1
 tunnel destination 50.1.1.2
!
interface Ethernet0
 ip address 10.1.1.2 255.255.255.0
!
!
interface Serial1
 ip address 50.1.1.1 255.255.255.0
 encapsulation ppp
!
ip classless

!The static route below is used to push traffic destined for the network behind the
!other router, into the GRE tunnel
ip route 10.1.2.0 255.255.255.0 Tunnel0
!

line con 0
line aux 0
line vty 0 4
 login
!
end

GRE-1#

GRE-2#
!
version 12.2
service timestamps debug uptime
service timestamps log uptime
no service password-encryption
!
hostname GRE-2
ip subnet-zero
!The command below defines the tunnel interface on this router. Please note that
!the numbering of the tunnels has only local significance.
```

continues

Example 11-1 *Configurations of the Two Routers Used in This Case Study (Continued)*

```
interface Tunnel0
 ip unnumbered Serial0
 keepalive 5 4
 tunnel source Serial0
 tunnel destination 50.1.1.1
!
interface Ethernet0
 ip address 10.1.2.1 255.255.255.0
!

!
interface Serial0
 ip address 50.1.1.2 255.255.255.0
 encapsulation ppp
 no fair-queue
 clockrate 9600

!
ip classless
!The static route below is used to push traffic destined for the network behind
!the other router, into the GRE tunnel
ip route 10.1.1.0 255.255.255.0 Tunnel0
no ip http server
!
!
line con 0
 transport input none
line aux 0
line vty 0 4
!
end

GRE-2#
```

The configuration shown here is a very simple implementation of GRE using static routes. GRE also can be set up using routing protocols. The functionality of GRE interfaces in that case is exactly the same as any physical interface.

GRE Between Multiple Sites

This case study represents a scenario in which multiple sites are connected via separate GRE tunnels. The thing to remember in this setup is that GRE tunnels are point-to-point, meaning that for each set of two routers to talk to each other, there must be a dedicated GRE tunnel between them. For example, three routers cannot share the same tunnel. Consequently, in order to connect the router named Router3 to the other two routers, you must configure two GRE tunnel interfaces on it. The other two routers cannot communicate with each other directly in this setup. They have to go through Router3 to reach one another. This example doesn't show this, but it is possible to set up one more tunnel interface on each spoke router and have them communicate directly with each other. I will leave that as an exercise for you to try. Also note that Example 11-2 uses OSPF to distribute routing information between the routers rather than using static routes. Understandably, this is a more scalable solution than using static routes.

In this setup, the loopback interface is used as the source of the tunnel interface. Although it isn't very useful when there is a single egress interface, this setup can be very useful when redundant egress interfaces are available. In that case, if one of the egress interfaces goes down, the GRE tunnel can continue working by finding a path to the GRE tunnel destination through one of the other egress interfaces. However, if the tunnel interface is tied to the egress interface and the egress interface goes down, the GRE tunnel goes down with it. A loopback interface has the added facility of always staying up, meaning that it gives the tunnel interface the maximum chance of finding an alternative route if the primary route becomes unavailable because an interface goes down.

Figure 11-6 shows the scenario used in this case study. Example 11-2 shows the configurations of the three routers.

Figure 11-6 *Scenario Used in This Case Study*

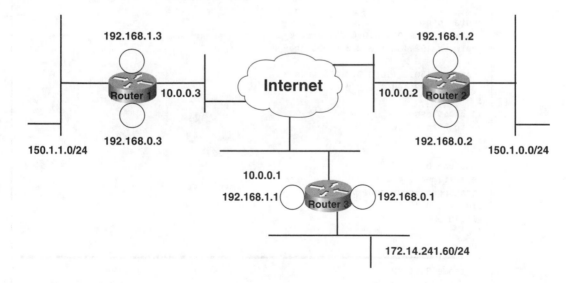

Example 11-2 *Configurations of the Three Routers Used in This Case Study*

```
hostname Router 1
!
ip subnet-zero
!
```

continues

Example 11-2 *Configurations of the Three Routers Used in This Case Study (Continued)*

```
interface Loopback0
 ip address 192.168.1.3 255.255.255.0
!
interface Loopback1
 ip address 192.168.0.3 255.255.255.0
!
!Tunnel 0 is the GRE tunnel to Router2.

interface Tunnel0
!The IP address of the tunnel interface is tied to the IP address of the loopback
!interface
 ip unnumbered Loopback1
 tunnel source Loopback0
 tunnel destination 192.168.1.1

!
interface Ethernet0
 ip address 10.0.0.3 255.255.255.0
!
interface Ethernet1
ip address 150.1.1.1 255.255.255.0
!
!
router ospf 1
 network 10.0.0.0 0.0.0.255 area 0
 network 192.168.1.0 0.0.0.255 area 2

 network 150.1.1.0 0.0.0.255 area 3
 network 192.168.0.0 0.0.0.255 area 1
!
ip classless
no ip http server
!
!
line con 0
 exec-timeout 0 0
 transport input none
line vty 0 4
 login
!
end
```
```
hostname Router2
!
!
ip subnet-zero
!
isdn switch-type basic-net3
isdn voice-call-failure 0
!
```

Example 11-2 *Configurations of the Three Routers Used in This Case Study (Continued)*

```
!
interface Loopback0
 ip address 192.168.1.2 255.255.255.0
interface Loopback1
 ip address 192.168.0.2 255.255.255.255
 !
interface Tunnel0
 ip unnumbered Loopback1
 tunnel source Loopback0
 tunnel destination 192.168.1.1

 !
interface Ethernet0
 ip address 10.0.0.2 255.255.255.0
 !
interface Ethernet1
 ip address 150.1.0.1 255.255.255.0
 no ip route-cache
 no ip mroute-cache
 !
 !
router ospf 1
 network 10.0.0.0 0.0.0.255 area 0
 network 192.168.1.0 0.0.0.255 area 2

network 150.1.0.0 0.0.0.255 area 4
network 192.168.0.0 0.0.0.255 area 1
 !
ip classless
no ip http server
 !
 !
line con 0
 exec-timeout 0 0
 transport input none
line vty 0 4
 login
 !
end
```

```
hostname Router3
!
ip subnet-zero
!
cns event-service server
!
controller ISA 5/1
!
interface Loopback0
 ip address 192.168.1.1 255.255.255.0
```

continues

Example 11-2 *Configurations of the Three Routers Used in This Case Study (Continued)*

```
!
interface Loopback1
 ip address 192.168.0.1 255.255.255.255
!
interface Tunnel0
 ip unnumbered Loopback1
 tunnel source Loopback0
 tunnel destination 192.168.1.2
!
interface Tunnel1
 ip unnumbered Loopback1
 tunnel source Loopback0
 tunnel destination 192.168.1.3
!
interface FastEthernet0/0
 ip address 172.17.241.60 255.255.255.0
 no ip route-cache
 no ip mroute-cache
 duplex auto
 speed auto
!
interface FastEthernet0/1
 ip address 10.0.0.1 255.255.255.0
 no ip mroute-cache
 duplex auto
 speed auto
!

!

!
router ospf 1
 network 10.0.0.0 0.0.0.255 area 0
 network 192.168.1.0 0.0.0.255 area 2

 network 172.17.241.0 0.0.0.255 area 5
 network 192.168.0.0 0.0.0.255 area 1
!
ip classless
!
line con 0
 exec-timeout 0 0
 transport input none
line aux 0
line vty 0 15
!
end
```

You can use GRE to seamlessly connect multiple sites in a fully or partially meshed scenario. In addition to carrying all the routing traffic in such a mesh, GRE tunnels can encapsulate and carry privately addressed networks over a public network such as the Internet.

On of the most common problems you encounter while setting up a GRE tunnel using routing protocols is when the tunnel flaps (goes up and down continuously). The most common reason for this is that the router gets routing information that says that in order to get the GRE packet to the other end of the tunnel, it needs to route the packet to the tunnel interface rather than to the physical interface. However, to get the packet through the tunnel, the router needs to figure out how to get to the other end of the tunnel. The way to get to the other end of the tunnel (according to the router's information) is through the tunnel interface, and so on. Consequently, the router goes into a loop, and you see the tunnel going down because the router is unable to determine how to get to the other end of the tunnel.

The message you get on the router is something like this:

> "Tunnel0 temporarily disabled due to recursive routing"

There are two ways to get around this problem:

- Use a static route for the endpoint of the GRE tunnel interfaces. This way, you can specify that the best way to get to the GRE tunnel's other endpoint is through the physical interface, not the tunnel interface.

- Use route filtering to make sure that the router does not learn about the networks to which the GRE tunnel interface belongs through the tunnel interface.

GRE Between Two Sites Running IPX

This case study shows one of the major advantages that GRE tunnels offer network administrators. GRE tunnels can encapsulate IP as well as non-IP traffic. This lets protocols such as IPX be carried across the GRE tunnel. This is a major limitation in the design of the IPsec protocol suite, which cannot handle non-IP or multicast traffic.

Figure 11-7 shows the setup of the IPX networks AA and BB, which are connected using the GRE tunnel. Example 11-3 shows the configurations of the two routers used in this case study.

Figure 11-7 *Graphical Example for This Case Study*

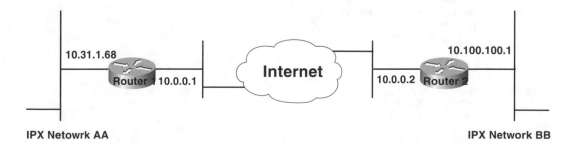

IPX Netowrk AA   IPX Network BB

Example 11-3 *Configurations of the Two Routers and Outputs for the* **show** *Commands and pings Used in the Case Study 'GRE Between Two Sites Running IPX'*

```
router1#write terminal
Building configuration...
Current configuration:!
version 12.0
service timestamps debug uptime
service timestamps log uptime
no service password-encryption
!
hostname router1
!
enable password <removed>
!
ip subnet-zero
no ip domain-lookup
!
ipx routing 00e0.b06a.40fc
!
!

interface Loopback0
 ip address 100.1.1.1 255.255.255.0
 no ip directed-broadcast
!
interface Tunnel0
 ip unnumbered Ethernet0
 no ip directed-broadcast
 no ip route-cache
 no ip mroute-cache
 ipx network CC
 tunnel source Ethernet0
 tunnel destination 10.0.0.2
 !
interface Ethernet0
 ip address 10.0.0.1 255.255.255.0
 no ip directed-broadcast
 no ip route-cache
 no ip mroute-cache
 !
interface Ethernet1
 ip address 10.31.1.68 255.255.255.0
 no ip directed-broadcast
 no keepalive
 ipx network AA
!

!
router rip
 network 10.0.0.0
 network 100.0.0.0
 !
```

Example 11-3 *Configurations of the Two Routers and Outputs for the* **show** *Commands and pings Used in the Case Study 'GRE Between Two Sites Running IPX' (Continued)*

```
ip classless
ip route 171.68.120.103 255.255.255.255 10.31.1.1
no ip http server
!
!
line con 0
 exec-timeout 0 0
 transport input none
line aux 0
line vty 0 4
 login
!
end
```

```
router1#show ipx route
Codes: C - Connected primary network,    c - Connected secondary network
       S - Static, F - Floating static, L - Local (internal), W - IPXWAN
       R - RIP, E - EIGRP, N - NLSP, X - External, A - Aggregate
       s - seconds, u - uses, U - Per-user static

3 Total IPX routes. Up to 1 parallel paths and 16 hops allowed.

No default route known.

C          AA (NOVELL-ETHER),   Et1
C          CC (TUNNEL),         Tu0
R          BB [151/01] via      CC.00e0.b06a.4114,    0s, Tu0

router1#
router1#ping ipx BB.00e0.b06a.4115

Type escape sequence to abort.
Sending 5, 100-byte IPXcisco Echoes to BB.00e0.b06a.4115, timeout is 2 seconds:
!!!!!
Success rate is 100 percent (5/5), round-trip min/avg/max = 44/44/44 ms
router1#
```

```
router2#write terminal
Building configuration...

Current configuration:
!
version 12.0
no service password-encryption
!
hostname router2
```

continues

Example 11-3 *Configurations of the Two Routers and Outputs for the* **show** *Commands and pings Used in the Case Study 'GRE Between Two Sites Running IPX' (Continued)*

```
!
ip subnet-zero
no ip domain-lookup
!
ipx routing 00e0.b06a.4114
!
!
interface Loopback0
 ip address 200.1.1.1 255.255.255.0
 no ip directed-broadcast
!
interface Tunnel0
 ip unnumbered Ethernet0
 no ip directed-broadcast
 no ip route-cache
 no ip mroute-cache
 ipx network CC
 tunnel source Ethernet0
 tunnel destination 10.0.0.1
 !
interface Ethernet0
 ip address 10.0.0.2 255.255.255.0
 no ip directed-broadcast
 no ip route-cache
 no ip mroute-cache
 !
interface Ethernet1
 ip address 10.100.100.1 255.255.255.0
 no ip directed-broadcast
 no keepalive
 ipx network BB


!
router rip
 network 10.0.0.0
 network 200.1.1.0
!
ip classless
no ip http server
!
line con 0
 exec-timeout 0 0
 transport input none
line aux 0
line vty 0 4
 login
!
end
```

Example 11-3 *Configurations of the Two Routers and Outputs for the* **show** *Commands and pings Used in the Case Study 'GRE Between Two Sites Running IPX' (Continued)*

```
router2#show ipx route
Codes: C - Connected primary network,    c - Connected secondary network
       S - Static, F - Floating static, L - Local (internal), W - IPXWAN
       R - RIP, E - EIGRP, N - NLSP, X - External, A - Aggregate
       s - seconds, u - uses, U - Per-user static

3 Total IPX routes. Up to 1 parallel paths and 16 hops allowed.

No default route known.

C          BB (NOVELL-ETHER),   Et1
C          CC (TUNNEL),         Tu0
R          AA [151/01] via        CC.00e0.b06a.40fc,   13s, Tu0
router2#
router2#ping ipx AA.00e0.b06a.40fd

Type escape sequence to abort.
Sending 5, 100-byte IPXcisco Echoes to AA.00e0.b06a.40fd, timeout is 2 seconds:
!!!!!
Success rate is 100 percent (5/5), round-trip min/avg/max = 44/44/44 ms
```

Tunneling IPX and AppleTalk traffic is one of the important uses of GRE tunneling. GRE also allows routing updates for these protocols to be exchanged, allowing full connectivity between the networks. The fact that GRE has an interface dedicated to it in the Cisco IOS Software CLI is very useful for simplifying the configurations for these types of setups.

Summary

This chapter discussed the GRE protocol in detail. The GRE protocol is a useful mechanism for carrying traffic across IP networks that normally could not be carried across the networks in its native form. Although GRE itself is not a secure means of carrying traffic across an IP network, it does facilitate the implementation of various schemes that aid security. One such example is the use of GRE in conjunction with IPsec to carry non-IP traffic. Another example is the use of GRE to connect two private networks that use private non-routable addresses. GRE encapsulation is often used in conjunction with other means of securing traffic, such as IPsec. In such topologies, some of the useful features of GRE complement the security offered by IPsec. Chapter 13, "IPsec," contains examples of how GRE is used in conjunction with IPsec to form VPNs.

Review Questions

1 What does GRE stand for?

2 Is it possible to use a private IP address as the "tunnel destination" IP address when using GRE to carry traffic over the public Internet?

3 How many pairs of routers can one GRE tunnel connect?

4 What is the most common reason for using loopback interfaces as the source of a GRE tunnel?

5 How do you identify a GRE packet on a sniffer trace?

6 What does recursive routing mean in the context of a GRE tunnel?

This chapter covers the following topics:

- **Overview of Layer 2 Tunneling Protocol**—This section defines L2TP, discusses different types of L2TP tunnels, and covers the benefits of using this method of setting up VPNs.

- **Functional Details of L2TP**—Because L2TP is fairly involved, this section gives details on how an L2TP session gets established.

- **Case Studies**—This section covers case studies involving L2TP implementations aimed at solidifying your understanding of L2TP.

## CHAPTER 12

L2TP

This chapter talks about the Layer 2 Tunneling Protocol (L2TP). L2TP uses IP to create a tunnel in which Layer 2 frames are encapsulated. We will look at the types of L2TP tunnels as you try to gain an understanding of L2TP. We will look at the messages that are exchanged in the L2TP setup and also look at the overall flow of events leading to an L2TP tunnel's being set up. Toward the end of the chapter, we will go into two case studies of how Cisco routers can be set up to serve as LAC and LNS.

Overview of Layer 2 Tunneling Protocol

L2TP is a protocol that is used to tunnel PPP over a public network using IP. This protocol allows for the encapsulation of any Layer 3 protocol in its packets because of the fact that the tunneling occurs on Layer 2, thereby making things transparent to Layer 3 and above. Like GRE, L2TP does not provide encryption mechanisms for the traffic it tunnels. Instead, it relies on another protocol such as IPsec or an application layer encryption mechanism to provide that type of security.

The functioning of L2TP is fairly simple, as shown in Figure 12-1. The end device, often a user PC or laptop, establishes a PPP connection to a server known as the LAC (L2TP Access Concentrator) using dialup POTS, DSL, and so on. The LAC then initiates an L2TP tunneling session, using normal IP, to the remote device with which the originating device wants to set up a session. This remote device is called the LNS (L2TP Network Server). Typically the authentication, authorization, and accounting (AAA) of the end user is done on the LNS itself using a local database or AAA server.

In running L2TP over an IP backbone, UDP is used as the carrier of all L2TP traffic, including the control traffic used to set up the tunnel between the LNS and the LAC. Of course, the LNS and the LAC need to have IP connectivity between them to be able to set up the tunnel between themselves. The initiator of the tunnel uses UDP port 1701 to send its packets. Figure 12-2 shows how the three layers involved in L2TP—IP, PPP, and L2TP—are stacked.

Figure 12-1 *L2TP Setup*

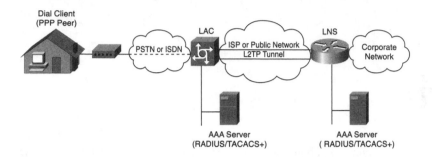

Figure 12-2 *L2TP Tunnel Layers*

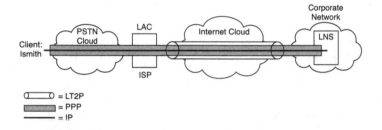

The cost advantage of having L2TP is that the client does not need to establish a Layer 2 connection to the LNS. This could result in long-distance phone call charges, such as in cases in which the client and the LNS are not in the same geographic location. Instead, the IP network is used to carry the Layer 2 data between the LAC and the LNS, in effect bypassing the PSTN network.

One important case of setting up an L2TP session is one in which the end user uses a machine that acts as a LAC, thereby eliminating the need for a separate LAC. In this case, the client needs to have an IP session already set up to communicate on the IP layer with the LNS. The client then creates a "virtual PPP" connection to the LNS and tunnels the subsequent PPP packets inside an L2TP tunnel terminating on the LNS.

Types of L2TP Tunnels

Based on the discussion in the preceding section, you can see that L2TP tunnels can be divided into two categories.

The type of L2TP tunnel in which the client is completely unaware of the presence of an L2TP connection is called *compulsory tunneling*. Figure 12-3 shows how an LAC and LNS communicate to set up compulsory L2TP tunneling.

Figure 12-3 *Compulsory L2TP Tunneling*

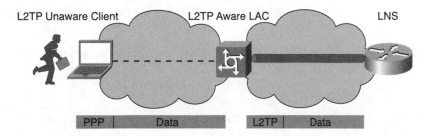

The other type of L2TP tunnel, *voluntary tunneling*, is where the client is aware of L2TP. After establishing a PPP link with the LAC, the client sends L2TP traffic encapsulated in the PPP traffic to the LNS through the LAC. In a way, the client plays the role that the LAC plays in compulsory tunneling. Figure 12-4 shows how this type of tunneling is set up.

Figure 12-4 *Voluntary L2TP Tunneling*

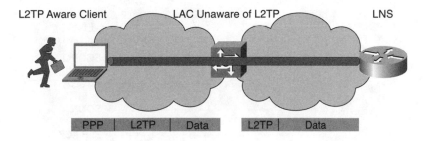

Functional Details of L2TP

This section discusses the process through which L2TP is set up. Assuming the scenario in which the LAC and the client are separated from each other (compulsory tunneling), the L2TP setup starts with the client's initiating a PPP connection to the LAC. Upon receiving the connection request, the LAC does LCP negotiation with the client and challenges the client for authentication credentials. The client supplies these credentials such as a username, domain name, and password. The LAC uses the domain name to ascertain which LNS it needs to contact because it might be set up to work with multiple domains or different companies, each of which might have a separate LNS. This lookup can be done locally on the LAC or through an AAA security server. In either case, the LAC finds the LNS it needs to communicate with and begins establishing an L2TP tunnel with the LNS.

The L2TP tunnel setup is negotiated in two stages:

Stage 1: A control session is set up between the LAC and the LNS.

Stage 2: The actual L2TP tunnel for passing the data is created (this is also called creating a session).

Multiple sessions may exist across a single tunnel, and multiple tunnels may exist between the same LAC and LNS.

Control Connection Establishment

The control connection is the initial connection that must be achieved between an LAC and LNS before sessions may be brought up. Establishing the control connection includes securing the peer's identity, as well as identifying the peer's L2TP version, framing, and bearer capabilities.

A three-message exchange is used to set up the control connection. Figure 12-5 illustrates a typical message exchange.

Figure 12-5   *Control Connection Establishment*

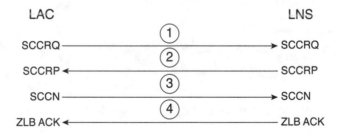

Control Connection management Message Types Shown Here:

1 (SCCRQ) Start-Control-Connection-Request
2 (SCCRP) Start-Control-Connection-Reply
3 (SCCN) Start-Control-Connection-Connected

The ZLB ACK is sent if no further messages are waiting in queue for that peer.

Session Establishment

After successful control connection establishment, individual sessions may be created. Each session corresponds to a single PPP stream between the LAC and LNS. Unlike control connection establishment, session establishment is directional with respect to the LAC and LNS. The LAC asks the LNS to accept a session for an incoming call, and the LNS asks the LAC to accept a session for placing an outgoing call.

Incoming Call Establishment

A three-message exchange is employed to set up the session. Figure 12-6 illustrates a typical sequence of events.

Figure 12-6 *Incoming Call Establishment*

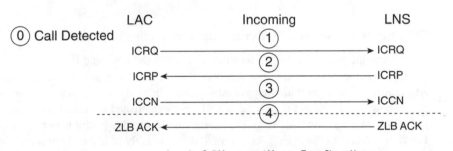

```
        LAC              Incoming            LNS
  (0) Call Detected                  (1)
      ICRQ ——————————————————————————————▶ ICRQ
                                     (2)
      ICRP ◀—————————————————————————————— ICRP
                                     (3)
      ICCN ——————————————————————————————▶ ICCN
  - - - - - - - - - - - - - - - - - (4)- - - - - - - - - - - - - - - -
      ZLB ACK ◀————————————————————————————— ZLB ACK
```

Incoming Call Management Message Types Shown Here:

10 (ICRQ) Incoming-Call-Request
11 (ICRP) Incoming-Call-Reply
12 (ICCN) Incoming-Call-Connected

The ZLB ACK is sent if no further messages are waiting in queue for that peer.

Outgoing Call Establishment

A three-message exchange is employed to set up the session. Figure 12-7 illustrates a typical sequence of events.

Figure 12-7 *Outgoing Call Establishment*

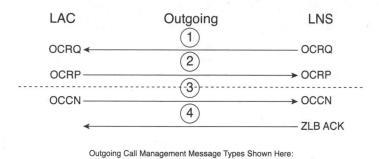

Outgoing Call Management Message Types Shown Here:

7 (OCRQ) Outgoing-Call-Request
8 (OCRP) Outgoing-Call-Reply
9 (OCCN) Outgoing-Call-Connected

The ZLB ACK is sent if no further messages are waiting in queue for that peer.

As soon as the tunnel has been established between the LAC and the LNS, the LAC forwards the authentication response it received from the client, along with any other PPP negotiation parameters it has negotiated with the client to the LNS. The LNS then provides the response to the client through the tunnel it has established with the LAC. Upon receiving the L2TP message, the LAC strips the header and forwards the PPP negotiation message to the client. As far as the client is concerned, this is exactly as if the client were directly connected to the LNS and doing PPP negotiation with it. It is oblivious to how the PPP packets are brought to it. As soon as the authentication phase of PPP successfully completes, the client continues sending PPP frames to the LAC which tunnels them through to the LNS. The LNS strips the L2TP header from the packets and treats them from then on as if it were a PPP session from a directly connected client. The return traffic is similarly encapsulated in L2TP and sent to the LAC. The LAC strips it from the L2TP headers and forwards the PPP frame to the client.

Figure 12-8 shows the complete set of transactions that occur between the client, LAC, and LNS when L2TP-based connectivity is established.

Header Format

L2TP control channel and data channel packets share the same format.

Figure 12-9 shows the header format for the L2TP packets.

Figure 12-8 *Transaction Flow for L2TP Establishment*

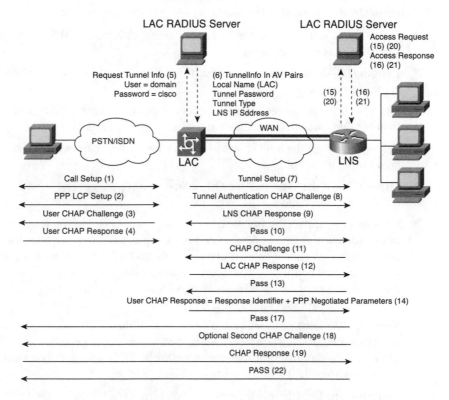

Figure 12-9 *Header Format for the L2TP Packets*

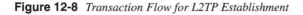

0		1		2		3	
0 1 2 3 4 5 6 7 8 9	0 1 2 3 4 5 6	7 8 9 0 1 2 3 4 5	6 7 8 9 0 1			

| T | L | x | x | S | x | O | P | x | x | x | x | Ver | Length (Optional) |

Tunnel ID	Session ID
Ns (Optional)	Nr (Optional)
Offset Size (Optional)	Offset Pad... (Optional)

The header contains a number of fields that are used to identify the contents of the data or the control channel messages. The following list defines and describes these:

- **Type (T)** — The T bit indicates the type of message. It is set to 0 for a data message and to 1 for a control message.

- **Length (L)** — If the L bit is 1, the Length field is present. This bit *must* be set to 1 for control messages.

- **x bits** — The x bits are reserved for future extensions. All reserved bits *must* be set to 0 on outgoing messages and ignored on incoming messages.

- **Sequence (S)** — If the S bit is set to 1, the Ns and Nr fields are present. The S bit *must* be set to 1 for control messages.

- **Offset (O)** — If the O bit is 1, the Offset Size field is present. The O bit *must* be set to 0 for control messages.

- **Priority (P)** — If the P bit is 1, this data message should receive preferential treatment in its local queuing and transmission. For example, LCP echo requests used as keep-alives for the link should generally be sent with this bit set to 1. Without it, a temporary interval of local congestion could result in interference with keepalive messages and unnecessary loss of the link. This feature is for use only with data messages. The P bit *must* be set to 0 for all control messages.

- **Version** — Ver *must* be 2, indicating the version of the L2TP data message header described RFC 2661. The value 1 is reserved to permit the detection of L2F (RFC 2341) packets should they arrive intermixed with L2TP packets. Packets received with an unknown Ver field *must* be discarded.

- **Length** — The Length field indicates the total length of the message in octets.

- **Tunnel ID** — Tunnel ID indicates the identifier for the control connection. L2TP tunnels are named by identifiers that have local significance only. That is, the same tunnel is given different tunnel IDs by each end of the tunnel. The tunnel ID in each message is that of the intended recipient, not the sender. Tunnel IDs are selected and exchanged as Assigned Tunnel ID AVPs during the creation of a tunnel.

- **Session ID** — Session ID indicates the identifier for a session within a tunnel. L2TP sessions are named by identifiers that have local significance only. That is, the same session is given different session IDs by each end of the session. The session ID in each message is that of the intended recipient, not the sender. Session IDs are selected and exchanged as Assigned Session ID AVPs during the creation of a session.

- **Ns** — Ns indicates the sequence number for this data or control message, beginning at 0 and incrementing by 1 (modulo 2**16) for each message sent.

- **Nr** — Nr indicates the sequence number expected in the next control message to be received. Thus, Nr is set to the Ns of the last in-order message received plus 1 (modulo 2**16). In data messages, Nr is reserved. If it is present (as indicated by the S bit), it *must* be ignored upon receipt.

- **Offset**—The Offset Size field, if present, specifies the number of octets past the L2TP header at which the payload data is expected to start. Actual data within the offset padding is undefined. If the Offset field is present, the L2TP header ends after the last octet of the offset padding.

It is interesting to note that because PPP is the protocol being tunneled, the client can use any and all Layer 3 protocols, such as IP, IPX, and AppleTalk, to communicate with the LNS. There are no restrictions on the type of traffic that may be sent across the tunnel, as is the case with the IPsec VPNs, which cannot handle non-IP or multicast traffic.

Case Studies

In the case studies that follow we will look into how L2TP can be setup in a couple of commonly utilized real life scenarios. While the first case study is a plain vanilla L2TP setup, the second one is more involved in that it uses IPsec to protect L2TP connections. This is a setup which has recently come into vogue for L2TP setups because of the need for a well managed encryption mechanism in L2TP. IPsec seems to fill these shoes well.

Setting up Compulsory L2TP Tunneling

This case study shows a compulsory tunneling L2TP setup. In this scenario, the LAC is aware of L2TP and sets up a tunnel with the LNS. The client is unaware of the presence of L2TP and simply dials up to the LAC using PPP. Then it is tunneled over to the LNS.

In Cisco IOS Software configurations, the term Virtual Private Dialup Networking (VPDN) is used to classify the types of setups that L2TP belongs to. This is why much of the configuration uses the term VPDN.

Figure 12-10 shows the setup of the network used in this case study.

Figure 12-10 *Network Setup for This Case Study*

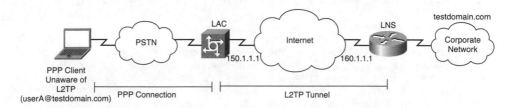

Example 12-1 shows the configuration on the LAC.

Example 12-1 *Configuration on the LAC*

```
LAC#write terminal

version 12.1
service timestamps debug datetime msec localtime show-timezone
service timestamps log datetime msec localtime show-timezone
hostname LAC
!AAA setup on the LAC. Local authentication and authorization is being used.
!See Part 6 of the book for examples on how to use AAA servers to set up L2TP.
aaa new-model
aaa authentication ppp default local
aaa authorization network default local

enable password cisco
!
username jane-admin password 0 cisco
!
ip subnet-zero
!
!The command below is used to toggle VPDN on. VPDN is a generic term that
!includes L2TP.
vpdn enable
!Instructs the LAC to first attempt to tunnel VPDN calls based on the user domain
!name, and to then attempt to tunnel based on the DNIS number if the user does not
!have a domain name.
vpdn search-order domain dnis
!
!This is the VPDN group for the service provider.
vpdn-group 1

!Configures a request dial-in VPDN subgroup.
 request-dialin

!Configures L2TP as the tunnel protocol.
  protocol l2tp

!Specifies that users with the domain name testdomain.com will be tunneled by this
!VPDN group.
  domain testdomain.com

!Specifies the IP address of the service provider LNS. The priority keyword is
!necessary only if the service provider had multiple LNSs. To equally share the
!load of calls between all the LNSs, each IP address would be given the same
!priority number. To specify an LNS as a backup, it would be given a higher-
!priority number.
 initiate-to ip 160.1.1.1 priority 1

!Configures the local name that the ISP will use to identify itself for L2TP
!tunnel authentication with the service provider LNS. If the ISP expands to a
!stacked-LAC environment, it needs to use the same local name on all the LACs.
 local name LAC
```

Example 12-1 *Configuration on the LAC (Continued)*

```
!Configures the L2TP tunnel password that is used to authenticate L2TP tunnels
!with LNS. Both tunnel endpoints must have the same L2TP tunnel password
!configured.
 l2tp tunnel password 7 s4cr4t
 !
!Configures the IP addresses of DNS servers that translate host names to IP
!addresses.
async-bootp dns-server 150.1.1.70 150.1.1.140

isdn switch-type primary-5ess
cns event-service server
mta receive maximum-recipients 0

controller T1 0

!Configures the T1 framing type as super frame (ESF).
 framing esf

!Configures the LAC to get its primary clocking from T1 controller 0.
 clock source line primary

!Configures the T1 line code type as B8ZS.
 linecode b8zs

 pri-group timeslots 1-24

controller T1 1
 framing esf
 clock source line secondary 1
 linecode b8zs
 pri-group timeslots 1-24
 !
controller T1 2
 framing esf
 clock source line secondary 2
 linecode b8zs
 pri-group timeslots 1-24
 !
controller T1 3
 framing esf
 clock source line secondary 3
 linecode b8zs
 pri-group timeslots 1-24

interface Serial0:23
 no ip address
 encapsulation ppp
 ip mroute-cache
 dialer-group 1
```

continues

Example 12-1 *Configuration on the LAC (Continued)*

```
 isdn switch-type primary-5ess

 ppp authentication chap pap
 ppp multilink
!
!The same configuration on serial interface 0:23 is applied to the other three D
!channels (serial interfaces 1:23, 2:23, and 3:23).
interface Serial1:23
 no ip address
 encapsulation ppp
 ip mroute-cache
 dialer-group 1
 isdn switch-type primary-5ess
 isdn incoming-voice modem
 fair-queue 64 256 0
 ppp authentication chap pap
 ppp multilink
!
interface Serial2:23
 no ip address
 encapsulation ppp
 ip mroute-cache
 dialer-group 1
 isdn switch-type primary-5ess
 isdn incoming-voice modem
 fair-queue 64 256 0
 ppp authentication chap pap
 ppp multilink
!
interface Serial3:23
 no ip address
 encapsulation ppp
 ip mroute-cache
 dialer-group 1
 isdn switch-type primary-5ess
 isdn incoming-voice modem
 fair-queue 64 256 0
 ppp authentication chap pap
 ppp multilink
!
!The interface below is the LACs connecting interface toward the LNS.
interface FastEthernet0
 ip address 150.1.1.1 255.255.255.0
 duplex full
 speed 100
!
!Configures the group-asynchronous interface that controls the configuration of
!all asynchronous interfaces on the LAC.
interface Group-Async1
 ip unnumbered FastEthernet0
 encapsulation ppp
```

Example 12-1 *Configuration on the LAC (Continued)*

```
!Configures interactive mode on the asynchronous interfaces. Interactive mode
!allows for dial-in clients to either receive a router prompt or establish a PPP
!session, as opposed to dedicated mode, which allows dial-in clients to only
!establish PPP sessions.
 async mode interactive
!Specifies the range of asynchronous interfaces that are included in the group.
 group-range 1 60
 !
ip default-gateway 150.1.1.100
ip classless
ip route 0.0.0.0 0.0.0.0 150.1.1.100
no ip http server
!
line con 0
 transport input none
!Specifies the range of modems.
line 1 60
!The following two autoselect commands relate to the interactive mode on the
!asynchronous interfaces.
!Displays the username:password prompt as the modems connect.
 autoselect during-login
!Enables PPP dial-in clients to bypass the EXEC prompt and automatically start PPP.
 autoselect ppp
!Enables support for both incoming and outgoing modem calls.
 modem InOut
!Specifies which protocols can be used for outgoing connections from these lines.
!transport output pad telnet rlogin udptn v120 lapb-ta
line aux 0
line vty 0 4
 password cisco
end
```

Example 12-2 shows the configuration on the LNS for this case study.

Example 12-2 *Configuration on the LNS*

```
LNS#write terminal

version 12.1

service timestamps debug datetime msec localtime show-timezone
service timestamps log datetime msec localtime show-timezone

hostname LNS
!
!Similar to the AAA configuration done on the LAC
aaa new-model
aaa authentication login default local
aaa authentication ppp default local
aaa authorization network default local
```

continues

Example 12-2 *Configuration on the LNS (Continued)*

```
enable password <removed>
!
username <removed> password 7 <removed>

!Configures the username and password for the VPDN user.
username UserA@testdomain.com password <removed>

ip subnet-zero

ip name-server 150.1.1.70

vpdn enable
!
!Creates the VPDN group for the LNS.
vpdn-group 1

!Creates an accept dial-in VPDN subgroup.
 accept-dialin

!Specifies L2TP as the tunneling protocol.
  protocol l2tp

!Instructs the LNS to clone virtual access interfaces for VPDN sessions from
!virtual template 1.
  virtual-template 1

!Specifies that this VPDN group will negotiate L2TP tunnels with LACs that identify
!themselves with the local name LAC.
 terminate-from hostname LAC

!Configures the L2TP tunnel password that is used to authenticate L2TP tunnels with
!LAC. Both tunnel endpoints must have the same L2TP tunnel password configured.
 l2tp tunnel password 7 s4cr4t

!Instructs the LNS to use the IP address of Fast Ethernet interface 0/0 for all
!traffic for this VPDN group. This command should be used when the LNS has more
!than one IP address configured on it.
 source-ip 160.1.1.1
 !
!Configures the IP addresses of DNS servers that translate host names to IP
!addresses.
async-bootp dns-server 165.1.1.10 165.2.2.10

!Configures the IP addresses of WINS servers that provide dynamic NetBIOS names
!that Windows devices use to communicate without IP addresses.
async-bootp nbns-server 165.1.1.11 165.2.2.11
 !
 !
cns event-service server
```

Example 12-2 *Configuration on the LNS (Continued)*

```
!Configures the IP address of FastEthernet 0/0, through which all VPDN traffic
!passes.
interface FastEthernet0/0

 ip address 160.1.1.1 255.255.255.0
 media-type MII
 full-duplex
 !
interface Serial2/0
 ip unnumbered FastEthernet0/0
 !
!Creates virtual template 1, which is used to clone virtual access interfaces for
!incoming VPDN sessions.
interface Virtual-Template1
 ip unnumbered FastEthernet0/0

!Instructs the LNS to assign an IP address to VPDN sessions from the default pool.
 peer default ip address pool default

!Enables CHAP authentication using the local username database.
 ppp authentication chap
 encapsulation ppp
 !
!Creates a pool of IP addresses that are assigned to incoming VPDN sessions.
ip local pool default 162.1.1.1 162.1.1.150

ip classless
ip route 0.0.0.0 0.0.0.0 Serial2/0
no ip http server
!
line con 0
 transport input none

line aux 0
line vty 0 4
 password 7 cisco

end
```

Example 12-3 shows the debugs on the LAC for this case study. Note that all lines not preceded by timestamps are comments.

Example 12-3 *Debugs on the LAC*

```
The call is received:

*August 17 1:09:22.659: ISDN Se0:23: RX <-  SETUP pd = 8  callref = 0x17

Bearer capability 0x8090A2 indicates that it is an analog call:
```

continues

Example 12-3 *Debugs on the LAC (Continued)*

```
*August 17 1:09:22.659:          Bearer Capability i = 0x8090A2
*August 17 1:09:22.659:          Channel ID i = 0xA98393
*August 17 1:09:22.659:          Called Party Number i = 0x80, '1123', Plan:Unknown
*August 17 1:09:22.659: VDEV_ALLOCATE: 1/7 is allocated
*August 17 1:09:22.663: ISDN Se0:23: TX -> CALL_PROC pd = 8  callref = 0x8017
*August 17 1:09:22.663:          Channel ID i = 0xA98393
*August 17 1:09:22.663: EVENT_FROM_ISDN::dchan_idb=0x62171A04, call_id=0x1F, ces=1
  bchan=0x12, event=0x1, cause=0x0
*August 17 1:09:22.663: EVENT_FROM_ISDN:(001F): DEV_INCALL at slot 1 and port 7
*August 17 1:09:22.663: CSM_PROC_IDLE: CSM_EVENT_ISDN_CALL at slot 1, port 7
```

These MICA technologies modem debug lines indicate that the call is sent to MICA
   modem 1/7:

```
*August 17 1:09:22.663: Mica Modem(1/7): Configure(0x1 = 0x0)
*August 17 1:09:22.663: Mica Modem(1/7): Configure(0x23 = 0x0)
*August 17 1:09:22.663: Mica Modem(1/7): Call Setup
*August 17 1:09:22.663:  Enter csm_connect_pri_vdev function
*August 17 1:09:22.663: csm_connect_pri_vdev:tdm_allocate_bp_ts() call. BP TS all0
*August 17 1:09:22.663: ISDN Se0:23: TX -> ALERTING pd = 8  callref = 0x8017
*August 17 1:09:22.763: Mica Modem(1/7): State Transition to Call Setup
*August 17 1:09:22.763: Mica Modem(1/7): Went offhook
*August 17 1:09:22.763: CSM_PROC_IC2_RING: CSM_EVENT_MODEM_OFFHOOK at slot 1,
  port 7
*August 17 1:09:22.763: ISDN Se0:23: TX -> CONNECT pd = 8  callref = 0x8017
*August 17 1:09:22.819: ISDN Se0:23: RX <- CONNECT_ACK pd = 8  callref = 0x17
*August 17 1:09:22.823: ISDN Se0:23: CALL_PROGRESS: CALL_CONNECTED call id 0x1F, 0
*August 17 1:09:22.823: EVENT_FROM_ISDN::dchan_idb=0x62171A04, call_id=0x1F, ces=1
  bchan=0x12, event=0x4, cause=0x0
*August 17 1:09:22.823: EVENT_FROM_ISDN:(001F): DEV_CONNECTED at slot 1 and port 7
*August 17 1:09:22.823: CSM_PROC_IC6_WAIT_FOR_CONNECT: CSM_EVENT_ISDN_CONNECTED at
  slot 1 and port 7
*August 17 1:09:22.823: Mica Modem(1/7): Link Initiate
*August 17 1:09:26.903: Mica Modem(1/7): State Transition to Connect
*August 17 1:09:31.407: Mica Modem(1/7): State Transition to Link
*August 17 1:09:42.815: Mica Modem(1/7): State Transition to Trainup
*August 17 1:09:46.775: Mica Modem(1/7): State Transition to EC Negotiating
*August 17 1:09:47.375: Mica Modem(1/7): State Transition to Steady State
```

LAC and the client have successfully negotiated, and asynchronous interface 8 is
   assigned to the call and brought up:

```
*August 17 1:09:52.595: %LINK-3-UPDOWN: Interface Async8, changed state to up
```

PPP negotiation begins on asynchronous interface 8 with Link Control Protocol
   (LCP) negotiation:

```
*August 17 1:09:52.595: As8 PPP: Treating connection as a dedicated line
*August 17 1:09:52.595: As8 PPP: Phase is ESTABLISHING, Active Open
```

Example 12-3 *Debugs on the LAC (Continued)*

```
*August 17 1:09:52.595: As8 LCP: O CONFREQ [Closed] id 1 len 25
*August 17 1:09:52.595: As8 LCP:    ACCM 0x000A0000 (0x0206000A0000)
```

LAC requires that the client authenticate with CHAP:

```
*August 17 1:09:52.595: As8 LCP:    AuthProto CHAP (0x0305C22305)
*August 17 1:09:52.595: As8 LCP:    MagicNumber 0x28C9DAF1 (0x050628C9DAF1)
*August 17 1:09:52.595: As8 LCP:    PFC (0x0702)
*August 17 1:09:52.595: As8 LCP:    ACFC (0x0802)
*August 17 1:09:53.471: As8 LCP: I CONFREQ [REQsent] id 3 len 23
*August 17 1:09:53.471: As8 LCP:    ACCM 0x000A0000 (0x0206000A0000)
*August 17 1:09:53.471: As8 LCP:    MagicNumber 0x3D675D0F (0x05063D675D0F)
*August 17 1:09:53.471: As8 LCP:    PFC (0x0702)
*August 17 1:09:53.471: As8 LCP:    ACFC (0x0802)
*August 17 1:09:53.471: As8 LCP:    Callback 6  (0x0D0306)
```

LAC rejects the client request for callback service, and the client then resends
 its request without the rejected callback option:

```
*August 17 1:09:53.475: As8 LCP: O CONFREJ [REQsent] id 3 len 7
*August 17 1:09:53.475: As8 LCP:    Callback 6  (0x0D0306)
*August 17 1:09:54.595: As8 LCP: TIMEout: State REQsent
*August 17 1:09:54.595: As8 LCP: O CONFREQ [REQsent] id 2 len 25
*August 17 1:09:54.595: As8 LCP:    ACCM 0x000A0000 (0x0206000A0000)
*August 17 1:09:54.595: As8 LCP:    AuthProto CHAP (0x0305C22305)
*August 17 1:09:54.595: As8 LCP:    MagicNumber 0x28C9DAF1 (0x050628C9DAF1)
*August 17 1:09:54.595: As8 LCP:    PFC (0x0702)
*August 17 1:09:54.595: As8 LCP:    ACFC (0x0802)
*August 17 1:09:54.703: As8 LCP: I CONFACK [REQsent] id 2 len 25
*August 17 1:09:54.703: As8 LCP:    ACCM 0x000A0000 (0x0206000A0000)
*August 17 1:09:54.703: As8 LCP:    AuthProto CHAP (0x0305C22305)
*August 17 1:09:54.707: As8 LCP:    MagicNumber 0x28C9DAF1 (0x050628C9DAF1)
*August 17 1:09:54.707: As8 LCP:    PFC (0x0702)
*August 17 1:09:54.707: As8 LCP:    ACFC (0x0802)
*August 17 1:09:56.483: As8 LCP: I CONFREQ [ACKrcvd] id 4 len 23
*August 17 1:09:56.483: As8 LCP:    ACCM 0x000A0000 (0x0206000A0000)
*August 17 1:09:56.483: As8 LCP:    MagicNumber 0x3D675D0F (0x05063D675D0F)
*August 17 1:09:56.483: As8 LCP:    PFC (0x0702)
*August 17 1:09:56.483: As8 LCP:    ACFC (0x0802)
*August 17 1:09:56.483: As8 LCP:    Callback 6  (0x0D0306)
*August 17 1:09:56.483: As8 LCP: O CONFREJ [ACKrcvd] id 4 len 7
*August 17 1:09:56.483: As8 LCP:    Callback 6  (0x0D0306)
*August 17 1:09:56.579: As8 LCP: I CONFREQ [ACKrcvd] id 5 len 20
*August 17 1:09:56.579: As8 LCP:    ACCM 0x000A0000 (0x0206000A0000)
*August 17 1:09:56.579: As8 LCP:    MagicNumber 0x3D675D0F (0x05063D675D0F)
*August 17 1:09:56.579: As8 LCP:    PFC (0x0702)
*August 17 1:09:56.579: As8 LCP:    ACFC (0x0802)
*August 17 1:09:56.579: As8 LCP: O CONFACK [ACKrcvd] id 5 len 20
*August 17 1:09:56.579: As8 LCP:    ACCM 0x000A0000 (0x0206000A0000)
*August 17 1:09:56.579: As8 LCP:    MagicNumber 0x3D675D0F (0x05063D675D0F)
```

continues

Example 12-3 *Debugs on the LAC (Continued)*

```
*August 17 1:09:56.579: As8 LCP:    PFC (0x0702)
*August 17 1:09:56.579: As8 LCP:    ACFC (0x0802)
```

LCP negotiation is complete:

```
*August 17 1:09:56.579: As8 LCP: State is Open
*August 17 1:09:56.579: As8 PPP: Phase is AUTHENTICATING, by this end
```

LAC sends a CHAP challenge, and the client replies with a CHAP response:

```
*August 17 1:09:56.579: As8 CHAP: O CHALLENGE id 1 len 30 from "LAC"
*August 17 1:09:56.707: As8 CHAP: I RESPONSE id 1 len 40 from "UserA@testdomain.com"
*August 17 1:09:56.707: As8 PPP: Phase is FORWARDING
*August 17 1:09:56.707: As8 VPDN: Got DNIS string 1123
```

VPDN determines the domain name of the username and searches the VPDN groups for a
   matching domain name:

```
*August 17 1:09:56.707: As8 VPDN: Looking for tunnel -- testdomain.com --
*August 17 1:09:56.707: As8 VPDN/LAC/1: Got tunnel info for testdomain.com
*August 17 1:09:56.707: As8 VPDN/LAC/1:    LAC LAC
*August 17 1:09:56.707: As8 VPDN/LAC/1:    l2tp-busy-disconnect yes
```

LAC sends the L2TP tunnel password to LNS at IP address 160.1.1.1:

```
*August 17 1:09:56.707: As8 VPDN/LAC/1:    l2tp-tunnel-password xxxxxx
*August 17 1:09:56.707: As8 VPDN/LAC/1:    IP 160.1.1.1
*August 17 1:09:56.711: As8 VPDN/1: curlvl 1 Address 0: 160.1.1.1, priority 1
*August 17 1:09:56.711: As8 VPDN/1: Select non-active address 160.1.1.1, priority 1
```

LAC assigns the tunnel the local tunnel ID 8173:

```
*August 17 1:09:56.711: Tnl 8173 L2TP: SM State idle
```

LAC sends a Start-Control-Connection-Request (SCCRQ) message to LNS to begin L2TP
   tunnel negotiation:

```
*August 17 1:09:56.711: Tnl 8173 L2TP: O SCCRQ
*August 17 1:09:56.711: Tnl 8173 L2TP: Tunnel state change from idle to
  wait-ctl-reply
*August 17 1:09:56.711: Tnl 8173 L2TP: SM State wait-ctl-reply
*August 17 1:09:56.711: As8 VPDN: Find LNS process created
*August 17 1:09:56.711: As8 VPDN: Forward to address 160.1.1.1
*August 17 1:09:56.711: As8 VPDN: Pending
*August 17 1:09:56.711: As8 VPDN: Process created
```

LAC receives a Start-Control-Connection-Reply (SCCRP) message from LNS, which
   indicates that LNS received the SCCRQ message:

```
*August 17 1:09:56.715: Tnl 8173 L2TP: I SCCRP from LNS
```

Example 12-3 *Debugs on the LAC (Continued)*

```
LAC and LNS successfully authenticate their L2TP tunnel passwords, and LAC changes
   the tunnel state to established:

*August 17 1:09:56.715: Tnl 8173 L2TP: Got a challenge from remote peer, LNS
*August 17 1:09:56.715: Tnl 8173 L2TP: Got a response from remote peer, LNS
*August 17 1:09:56.715: Tnl 8173 L2TP: Tunnel Authentication success
*August 17 1:09:56.715: Tnl 8173 L2TP: Tunnel state change from wait-ctl-reply to
   established

LAC sends a Start-Control-Connection-Connected (SCCN) message to LNS, which
   completes L2TP tunnel negotiation. This debug line also contains tunnel ID 15991
   from LNS for this tunnel:

*August 17 1:09:56.715: Tnl 8173 L2TP: O SCCCN  to LNS tnlid 15991
*August 17 1:09:56.715: Tnl 8173 L2TP: SM State established
*August 17 1:09:56.719: As8 VPDN: Forwarding...
*August 17 1:09:56.719: As8 VPDN: Bind interface direction=1
*August 17 1:09:56.719: Tnl/Cl 8173/6 L2TP: Session FS enabled
*August 17 1:09:56.719: Tnl/Cl 8173/6 L2TP: Session state change from idle to
   wait-for-tunnel
*August 17 1:09:56.719: As8 Tnl/Cl 8173/6 L2TP: Create session
*August 17 1:09:56.719: Tnl 8173 L2TP: SM State established

LAC sends an Incoming-Call-Request (ICRQ) message to L2TP tunnel 15991 on LNS,
   which begins L2TP session negotiation. LAC assigns local session ID 6 to this
   session:

*August 17 1:09:56.719: As8 Tnl/Cl 8173/6 L2TP: O ICRQ to LNS 15991/0
*August 17 1:09:56.719: As8 Tnl/Cl 8173/6 L2TP: Session state change from
   wait-for-tunnel to wait-reply

LAC has received an Incoming-Call-Reply (ICRP) message from LNS (not shown in the
   debug output), which indicates that it has accepted the ICRQ message:

*August 17 1:09:56.719: As8 VPDN: UserA@testdomain.com is forwarded

LAC sends an Incoming-Call-Connected (ICCN) message to LNS, which completes the
   L2TP session negotiation. LNS has assigned the local session ID 4 to this
   session:

*August 17 1:09:56.723: As8 Tnl/Cl 8173/6 L2TP: O ICCN to LNS 15991/4

The L2TP session is now established, and the line protocol on asynchronous
   interface 8 is brought up.

*August 17 1:09:56.723: As8 Tnl/Cl 8173/6 L2TP: Session state change from
   wait-reply to established
*August 17 1:09:57.719: %LINEPROTO-5-UPDOWN: Line protocol on Interface Async8,
   changed state to up
*August 17 1:09:57.823: Mica Modem(1/7): State Transition to Steady State Speedshg
*August 17 1:09:59.083: Mica Modem(1/7): State Transition to Steady State
LAC#
```

Example 12-4 shows the debugs on the LNS for this case study. Note that all lines not preceded by timestamps are comments.

Example 12-4 *Debugs on the LNS*

LNS receives an SCCRQ message from LAC, which identifies the tunnel with ID 8173.
  LNS considers ID 8173 to be the remote ID, and LAC considers it to be the local
  ID:

```
*August 17 1:09:02.313: L2TP: I SCCRQ from LAC tnl 8173
```

LNS identifies this tunnel with the local ID 15991:

```
*August 17 1:09:02.313: Tnl 15991 L2TP: Got a challenge in SCCRQ, LAC
*August 17 1:09:02.313: Tnl 15991 L2TP: New tunnel created for remote LAC, address
  150.1.1.1
```

LNS replies to LAC with an SCCRP message:

```
*August 17 1:09:02.313: Tnl 15991 L2TP: O SCCRP  to LAC tnlid 8173
*August 17 1:09:02.313: Tnl 15991 L2TP: Tunnel state change from idle to
  wait-ctl-reply
```

LNS receives an SCCN message from LAC containing its L2TP tunnel password. LNS
  successfully authenticates the tunnel and changes the tunnel state to
  established:

```
*August 17 1:09:02.317: Tnl 15991 L2TP: I SCCCN from LAC tnl 8173
*August 17 1:09:02.317: Tnl 15991 L2TP: Got a Challenge Response in SCCCN from LAC
*August 17 1:09:02.321: Tnl 15991 L2TP: Tunnel Authentication success
*August 17 1:09:02.321: Tnl 15991 L2TP: Tunnel state change from wait-ctl-reply to
  established

*August 17 1:09:02.321: Tnl 15991 L2TP: SM State established

LNS receives an ICRQ message from LAC. LNS assigns local session ID 4 to this
  session:

*August 17 1:09:02.321: Tnl 15991 L2TP: I ICRQ from LAC tnl 8173
*August 17 1:09:02.321: Tnl/Cl 15991/4 L2TP: Session FS enabled
*August 17 1:09:02.321: Tnl/Cl 15991/4 L2TP: Session state change from idle to
  wait-for-tunnel
*August 17 1:09:02.321: Tnl/Cl 15991/4 L2TP: New session created
```

LNS replies with an ICRP message to LAC and then receives an ICCN message
  confirming the session establishment:

```
*August 17 1:09:02.321: Tnl/Cl 15991/4 L2TP: O ICRP to LAC 8173/6
*August 17 1:09:02.325: Tnl/Cl 15991/4 L2TP: I ICCN from LAC tnl 8173, cl 6
*August 17 1:09:02.325: Tnl/Cl 15991/4 L2TP: Session state change from wait-connect
  to established
*August 17 1:09:02.325: UserA@testdomain.com Tnl/Cl 15991/4 L2TP: Session
  sequencing
```

Example 12-4 *Debugs on the LNS (Continued)*

```
LNS now creates a virtual access interface for the L2TP session. Virtual access
  interface 1 is reused:

*August 17 1:09:02.325: Vt1 VTEMPLATE: Unable to create and clone vaccess
*August 17 1:09:02.325: Vi1 VTEMPLATE: Reuse Vi1, recycle queue size 0

Virtual access interface 1 is assigned the MAC address 0090.ab09.c000:

*August 17 1:09:02.325: Vi1 VTEMPLATE: Hardware address 0090.ab09.c000

VPDN acknowledges the creation of the virtual access interface for
  UserA@testdomain.com. LNS designates virtual access interface 1 as an
  asynchronous interface and clones the configuration from virtual template 1:

*August 17 1:09:02.325: Vi1 VPDN: Virtual interface created for
  UserA@testdomain.com
*August 17 1:09:02.325: Vi1 VPDN: Set to Async interface
*August 17 1:09:02.325: Vi1 PPP: Phase is DOWN, Setup
*August 17 1:09:02.325: Vi1 VPDN: Clone from Vtemplate 1 filterPPP=0 blocking
*August 17 1:09:02.325: Vi1 VTEMPLATE: Has a new cloneblk vtemplate, now it has
  vtemplate
*August 17 1:09:02.325: Vi1 VTEMPLATE: ************* CLONE VACCESS1 **************
*August 17 1:09:02.329: Vi1 VTEMPLATE: Clone from Virtual-Template1
interface Virtual-Access1
default ip address
no ip address
encap ppp
ip unnumbered Serial2/0
peer default ip address pool default
ppp authentication chap
ip unnum fas 0/0
peer default ip address pool default
end

The following message indicates that LNS first erroneously attempted to configure
  the IP unnumbered serial 2/0 command, which is not allowed, because serial
  interface 2/0 is also unnumbered. Instead, the virtual access interface is
  configured with the IP unnumbered fastethernet 0/0 command:

*August 17 1:09:02.385: Vi1 VTEMPLATE: Messages from (un)cloning ...
Cannot use an unnumbered interface: Serial2/0
Virtual access interface 1 is brought up:
3w0d: %LINK-3-UPDOWN: Interface Virtual-Access1, changed state to up
*August 17 1:09:02.385: Vi1 PPP: Treating connection as a dedicated line
*August 17 1:09:02.385: Vi1 PPP: Phase is ESTABLISHING, Active Open
*August 17 1:09:02.385: Vi1 LCP: O CONFREQ [Closed] id 1 len 25
*August 17 1:09:02.385: Vi1 LCP:    ACCM 0x000A0000 (0x0206000A0000)
*August 17 1:09:02.385: Vi1 LCP:    AuthProto CHAP (0x0305C22305)
*August 17 1:09:02.385: Vi1 LCP:    MagicNumber 0xFD07FFBB (0x0506FD07FFBB)
```

continues

Example 12-4 *Debugs on the LNS (Continued)*

```
*August 17 1:09:02.385: Vi1 LCP:    PFC (0x0702)
*August 17 1:09:02.385: Vi1 LCP:    ACFC (0x0802)
*August 17 1:09:02.385: Vi1 VPDN: Bind interface direction=2
*August 17 1:09:02.389: Vi1 PPP: Treating connection as a dedicated line
```

LAC has forwarded information from the LCP negotiation with the client, and LNS
then forces this information onto virtual access interface 1:

```
*August 17 1:09:02.389: Vi1 LCP: I FORCED CONFREQ len 21
*August 17 1:09:02.389: Vi1 LCP:    ACCM 0x000A0000 (0x0206000A0000)
*August 17 1:09:02.389: Vi1 LCP:    AuthProto CHAP (0x0305C22305)
*August 17 1:09:02.389: Vi1 LCP:    MagicNumber 0x28C9DAF1 (0x050628C9DAF1)
*August 17 1:09:02.389: Vi1 LCP:    PFC (0x0702)
*August 17 1:09:02.389: Vi1 LCP:    ACFC (0x0802)
*August 17 1:09:02.389: Vi1 VPDN: PPP LCP accepted rcv CONFACK
*August 17 1:09:02.389: Vi1 VPDN: PPP LCP accepted sent CONFACK
*August 17 1:09:02.389: Vi1 PPP: Phase is AUTHENTICATING, by this end
```

LNS sends a CHAP challenge to UserA@testdomain.com that replies with a CHAP
response. LNS then authenticates the CHAP response and sends a CHAP success:

```
*August 17 1:09:02.389: Vi1 CHAP: O CHALLENGE id 2 len 30 from "LNS"
*August 17 1:09:02.389: Vi1 CHAP: I RESPONSE id 1 len 40 from
  "UserA@testdomain.com"
*August 17 1:09:02.389: Vi1 CHAP: O SUCCESS id 1 len 4
*August 17 1:09:02.389: Vi1 PPP: Phase is UP
*August 17 1:09:02.389: Vi1 IPCP: O CONFREQ [Closed] id 1 len 10
*August 17 1:09:02.389: Vi1 IPCP:    Address 160.1.1.1 (0x0306C0A83001)
*August 17 1:09:02.501: Vi1 IPCP: I CONFREQ [REQsent] id 1 len 40
*August 17 1:09:02.501: Vi1 IPCP:    CompressType VJ 15 slots CompressSlotID (0x02)
*August 17 1:09:02.501: Vi1 IPCP:    Address 0.0.0.0 (0x030600000000)
*August 17 1:09:02.501: Vi1 IPCP:    PrimaryDNS 0.0.0.0 (0x810600000000)
*August 17 1:09:02.501: Vi1 IPCP:    PrimaryWINS 0.0.0.0 (0x820600000000)
*August 17 1:09:02.501: Vi1 IPCP:    SecondaryDNS 0.0.0.0 (0x830600000000)
*August 17 1:09:02.501: Vi1 IPCP:    SecondaryWINS 0.0.0.0 (0x840600000000)
*August 17 1:09:02.501: Vi1 AAA/AUTHOR/IPCP: Start.  Her address 0.0.0.0, we want
  0.0.0.0
*August 17 1:09:02.501: Vi1 AAA/AUTHOR/IPCP: Done.  Her address 0.0.0.0, we want
  0.0.0.0
```

LNS assigns the IP address 162.1.1.1 to the client from the default IP address
pool:

```
*August 17 1:09:02.501: Vi1 IPCP: Pool returned 162.1.1.1
*August 17 1:09:02.501: Vi1 IPCP: O CONFREJ [REQsent] id 1 len 10
*August 17 1:09:02.501: Vi1 IPCP:    CompressType VJ 15 slots CompressSlotID (0x02)
*August 17 1:09:02.501: Vi1 CCP: I CONFREQ [Not negotiated] id 1 len 15
*August 17 1:09:02.501: Vi1 CCP:    MS-PPC supported bits 0x00000001 (0x1206000000)
*August 17 1:09:02.501: Vi1 CCP:    Stacker history 1 check mode EXTENDED (0x11050)
*August 17 1:09:02.501: Vi1 LCP: O PROTREJ [Open] id 2 len 21 protocol CCP
*August 17 1:09:02.501: Vi1 LCP:    (0x80FD0101000F1206000000000111050001)
```

Example 12-4 *Debugs on the LNS (Continued)*

```
*August 17 1:09:02.501: Vi1 LCP:  (0x04)
*August 17 1:09:02.517: Vi1 IPCP: I CONFACK [REQsent] id 1 len 10
*August 17 1:09:02.517: Vi1 IPCP:    Address 160.1.1.1 (0x0306C0A83001)
```

```
The line protocol on virtual access interface 1 is brought up:
```

```
3w0d: %LINEPROTO-5-UPDOWN: Line protocol on Interface Virtual-Access1, changed
  state to up
```

```
*August 17 1:09:04.385: Vi1 LCP: TIMEout: State Open
*August 17 1:09:04.389: Vi1 IPCP: TIMEout: State ACKrcvd
*August 17 1:09:04.389: Vi1 IPCP: O CONFREQ [ACKrcvd] id 2 len 10
*August 17 1:09:04.389: Vi1 IPCP:    Address 160.1.1.1 (0x0306C0A83001)
*August 17 1:09:04.821: Vi1 IPCP: I CONFACK [REQsent] id 2 len 10
*August 17 1:09:04.821: Vi1 IPCP:    Address 160.1.1.1 (0x0306C0A83001)
```

```
The client requests IP addresses for DNS and WINS servers:
```

```
*August 17 1:09:05.477: Vi1 IPCP: I CONFREQ [ACKrcvd] id 2 len 34
*August 17 1:09:05.477: Vi1 IPCP:    Address 0.0.0.0 (0x030600000000)
*August 17 1:09:05.477: Vi1 IPCP:    PrimaryDNS 0.0.0.0 (0x810600000000)
*August 17 1:09:05.477: Vi1 IPCP:    PrimaryWINS 0.0.0.0 (0x820600000000)
*August 17 1:09:05.477: Vi1 IPCP:    SecondaryDNS 0.0.0.0 (0x830600000000)
*August 17 1:09:05.477: Vi1 IPCP:    SecondaryWINS 0.0.0.0 (0x840600000000)
*August 17 1:09:05.477: Vi1 AAA/AUTHOR/IPCP: Start.  Her address 0.0.0.0, we want
  162.1.1.1
*August 17 1:09:05.477: Vi1 AAA/AUTHOR/IPCP: Done.  Her address 0.0.0.0, we want
  162.1.1.1
```

```
LNS replies with the IP addresses of the DNS and WINS servers:
```

```
*August 17 1:09:05.477: Vi1 IPCP: O CONFNAK [ACKrcvd] id 2 len 34
*August 17 1:09:05.477: Vi1 IPCP:    Address 162.1.1.1 (0x0306C0A83101)
*August 17 1:09:05.477: Vi1 IPCP:    PrimaryDNS 165.1.1.10 (0x8106AC17010A)
*August 17 1:09:05.477: Vi1 IPCP:    PrimaryWINS 165.1.1.11 (0x8206AC17010B)
*August 17 1:09:05.477: Vi1 IPCP:    SecondaryDNS 165.2.2.10 (0x8306AC17020A)
*August 17 1:09:05.481: Vi1 IPCP:    SecondaryWINS 165.2.2.11 (0x8406AC17020B)
*August 17 1:09:05.589: Vi1 IPCP: I CONFREQ [ACKrcvd] id 3 len 34
*August 17 1:09:05.589: Vi1 IPCP:    Address 162.1.1.1 (0x0306C0A83101)
*August 17 1:09:05.589: Vi1 IPCP:    PrimaryDNS 165.1.1.10 (0x8106AC17010A)
*August 17 1:09:05.589: Vi1 IPCP:    PrimaryWINS 165.1.1.11 (0x8206AC17010B)
*August 17 1:09:05.589: Vi1 IPCP:    SecondaryDNS 165.2.2.10 (0x8306AC17020A)
*August 17 1:09:05.589: Vi1 IPCP:    SecondaryWINS 165.2.2.11 (0x8406AC17020B)
*August 17 1:09:05.589: Vi1 AAA/AUTHOR/IPCP: Start.  Her address 162.1.1.1, we
  want 162.1.1.1
*August 17 1:09:05.589: Vi1 AAA/AUTHOR/IPCP: Reject 162.1.1.1, using 162.1.1.1
*August 17 1:09:05.589: Vi1 AAA/AUTHOR/IPCP: Done.  Her address 162.1.1.1, we want
  162.1.1.1
```

continues

Example 12-4 *Debugs on the LNS (Continued)*

```
LNS receives positive acknowledgment that the client received the IP addresses for
  the DNS and WINS servers:

*August 17 1:09:05.593: Vi1 IPCP: O CONFACK [ACKrcvd] id 3 len 34
*August 17 1:09:05.593: Vi1 IPCP:    Address 162.1.1.1 (0x0306C0A83101)
*August 17 1:09:05.593: Vi1 IPCP:    PrimaryDNS 165.1.1.10 (0x8106AC17010A)
*August 17 1:09:05.593: Vi1 IPCP:    PrimaryWINS 165.1.1.11 (0x8206AC17010B)
*August 17 1:09:05.593: Vi1 IPCP:    SecondaryDNS 165.2.2.10 (0x8306AC17020A)
*August 17 1:09:05.593: Vi1 IPCP:    SecondaryWINS 165.2.2.11 (0x8406AC17020B)
*August 17 1:09:05.593: Vi1 IPCP: State is Open

LNS installs the route to 162.1.1.1, the IP address of the client:

*August 17 1:09:05.593: Vi1 IPCP: Install route to 162.1.1.1
LNS#
```

Please note that the following debug commands need to be turned on to generate the above output:

```
debug isdn q931
debug modem csm
debug ppp authentication
debug ppp negotiation
debug vpdn event
debug vpdn l2x-events
```

Protecting L2TP Traffic Using IPsec in a Compulsory Tunneling Setup

As mentioned earlier, L2TP by default does not provide encryption services. Although it does have mechanisms to authenticate the LNS and LAC to each other, there is often a need for encryption to further secure the L2TP traffic. PPP can provide an encryption mechanism too. However, it is very rudimentary and does not provide the level of authentication, integrity, replay protection, and key management that is needed in a proper encryption, integrity, and authentication suite. In addition, the authentication provided is on a per-session basis rather than per-packet basis. Therefore, L2TP often relies on other protocols such as IPsec to provide encryption services for it.

RFC 3193 outlines the following as the main security threats that an L2TP setup can face:

1　An adversary may try to discover user identities by snooping data packets.

2　An adversary may try to modify packets (both control and data).

3　An adversary may try to hijack the L2TP tunnel or the PPP connection inside the tunnel.

4 An adversary can launch denial of service attacks by terminating PPP connections, or L2TP tunnels.

5 An adversary may attempt to disrupt the PPP ECP negotiation in order to weaken or remove confidentiality protection.

Alternatively, an adversary may wish to disrupt the PPP LCP authentication negotiation so as to weaken the PPP authentication process or gain access to user passwords.

Because it provides a comprehensive suite of protocols addressing most of the threats just outlined, IPsec is often used in conjunction with L2TP to provide encryption, integrity, and authentication services between the LAC and the LNS. L2TP uses UDP 1701 packets for communication between the LNS and the LAC. This communication includes both control and data messages. The use of the UDP 1701 port allows IPsec to recognize the L2TP traffic easily and provide it with the security features built into the IPsec suite.

IPsec can be set up on the same routers that act as the LAC and the LNS. This can be done because L2TP encapsulation occurs before IPsec processing. So by the time the packet hits the IPsec processes, it is ready with the L2TP header and the UDP header and can be encrypted using IPsec.

Chapter 13, "IPsec," has more details on IPsec commands and configurations.

Figure 12-11 shows the setup of the network used in this case study.

Figure 12-11 *Network Setup for This Case Study*

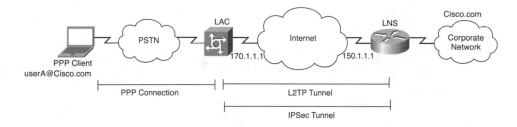

Example 12-5 shows the configuration on the LAC for this case study.

Example 12-5 *Configuration on the LAC*

```
LAC#write terminal

Current configuration:
!
version 12.0
!
hostname LAC
!
enable password <removed>
!
username LAC password <removed>
ip subnet-zero
```

continues

Example 12-5 *Configuration on the LAC (Continued)*

```
vpdn enable
!
vpdn search-order domain

!VPDN group 1 is set up to create connections to the LNS.

vpdn-group 1
 request dialin l2tp ip 150.1.1.1 domain cisco.com
 local name LAC
 l2tp tunnel password 7 s4cr4t

crypto isakmp policy 1
 authentication pre-share
 group 2
 lifetime 3600
 crypto isakmp key cisco address 150.1.1.1
 crypto ipsec transform-set transform esp-des

crypto map L2TP 10 ipsec-isakmp
 set peer 150.1.1.1
 set transform-set transform
 match address 101
!
interface Ethernet0
 ip address 10.1.1.1 255.255.255.0
 no ip directed-broadcast
!
!Since this is the interface from which the L2TP traffic will originate, the
!crypto map for IPsec is being applied to this interface.

interface Serial0
 ip address 170.1.1.1 255.255.255.0
 no ip directed-broadcast
 crypto map L2TP
!
interface Async1
 ip unnumbered Ethernet0
 no ip directed-broadcast
 encapsulation ppp
 async mode dedicated
 peer default ip address pool mypool
 ppp authentication chap
!
!The pool defined below is used to assign addresses to the clients.
ip local pool mypool 10.1.1.100 10.1.1.110
ip classless
ip route 0.0.0.0 0.0.0.0 170.1.1.100
!The access list below is used to identify the L2TP traffic for IPsec. It is
!interesting to note that UDP source and destination ports 1701 are used to
!identify L2TP traffic. Although RFC 2661 does not mandate the use of a source
```

Example 12-5 *Configuration on the LAC (Continued)*

```
!1701 for the originator of an L2TP connection, Cisco LAC uses this port as the
!source.
access-list 101 permit udp host 170.1.1.1 eq 1701 host 150.1.1.1 eq 1701
!
line con 0
exec-timeout 0 0
transport input none
line 1
 autoselect during-login
 autoselect ppp
 modem InOut
 transport input all
 speed 38400
 flowcontrol hardware
line aux 0
line vty 0 4
```

Example 12-6 shows the configuration on the LNS for this case study.

Example 12-6 *Configuration on the LNS*

```
LNS#write terminal

Current configuration:
!
version 12.0
service timestamps debug datetime msec localtime show-timezone
service timestamps log datetime msec localtime show-timezone
service password-encryption
!
hostname LNS
!
enable password
!
username LNS password <removed>
ip subnet-zero
!
!Configures the username and password for the VPDN user.
username UserA@cisco.com password <removed>
!
vpdn enable
!
!VPDN group 1 is set up to accept connections from the LAC. Virtual Template 1 is
!being used to clone virtual access interfaces.
vpdn-group 1
 accept dialin l2tp virtual-template 1 remote LAC
 local name LNS
 l2tp tunnel password 7 s4cr4t
```

continues

Example 12-6 *Configuration on the LNS (Continued)*

```
crypto isakmp policy 1
 authentication pre-share
 group 2
 lifetime 3600
crypto isakmp key cisco address 170.1.1.1

crypto ipsec transform-set transform esp-des

crypto map L2TP 10 ipsec-isakmp
 set peer 170.1.1.1
 set transform-set transform
 match address 101
!
interface Ethernet0
 ip address 100.1.1.150 255.255.255.0
 no ip directed-broadcast
 no keepalive
!
!Below is the configuration of the virtual template that will be used to clone the
!virtual access interfaces for the clients connecting through the LAC. A pool is
!defined as well to allocate addresses to the incoming clients.
interface Virtual-Template1
 ip unnumbered Ethernet0
 no ip directed-broadcast
 peer default ip address pool mypool
 ppp authentication chap
!
!Since this is the interface from which the L2TP traffic will originate, the
!crypto map for IPsec is applied to this interface.
interface Serial0
 ip address 150.1.1.1 255.255.255.0
 crypto map L2TP
!
!The pool defined below is used to assign addresses to the clients.

ip local pool mypool 100.1.1.1 100.1.1.100
ip classless
!
ip route 0.0.0.0 0.0.0.0 150.1.1.53

!The access list below is used to identify the L2TP traffic for IPsec.

access-list 101 permit udp host 150.1.1.1 eq 1701 host 170.1.1.1 eq 1701
!
line con 0
exec-timeout 0 0
transport input none
line aux 0
line vty 0 4
password
login
!
end
```

Example 12-6 shows how compulsory L2TP tunneling can be protected using IPsec. Note that voluntary tunneling can also be protected using IPsec. You will see an example of that in one of the case studies in Chapter 13.

Summary

This chapter discussed L2TP as one of the protocols used to create VPNs. L2TP is a useful protocol in some situations, because it allows a simulated PPP connection to the LNS device to be set up. This is a suitable means of creating a VPN, provided that a means of encryption is used to protect the L2TP tunnel. Because it operates at Layer 2, L2TP can carry almost any Layer 3 protocol. This is unlike Layer 3 VPN protocols such as IPsec. However, L2TP has major shortcomings in that it does not provide encryption, integrity, and authentication mechanisms on a per-packet basis. This shortcoming is often overcome by combining L2TP with another protocol, such as IPsec. L2TP was discussed in this chapter using local authentication and authorization on the LACs and LNSs. Obviously, this is not a very scalable method of setting up L2TP. Part VI of this book looks at how to set up L2TP using an AAA server.

Review Questions

1   What do LAC and LNS stand for?

2   What is the purpose of the ZLB ACK message?

3   What is the purpose of tunnel authentication in the router configuration?

4   Which port number does L2TP use?

5   How can L2TP reduce dial setup costs?

This chapter covers the following topics:

- **Types of IPsec VPNs**—This section lays out the two main types of IPsec VPNs.

- **Composition of IPsec**—This section introduces the protocols that are combined to create the IPsec protocol suite.

- **Introduction to IKE**—This section discusses some of the basic information about IKE and how it works in the context of the IPsec protocol.

- **IPsec Negotiation Using the IKE Protocol**—This section talks about how IKE is used to negotiate IPsec tunnels between two peers. Packet-by-packet details of all transactions are given for main mode, aggressive mode, and quick mode negotiations.

- **IKE Authentication Methods**—This section discusses the IKE authentication methods while focusing on the most important means of authentication available in IKE– Digital Certificates.

- **Encryption and Integrity Checking Mechanisms in IPsec**—This section covers the details of the various hashing and encryption mechanisms used in IPsec.

- **Packet Encapsulation in IPsec**—This section talks about how packets are encapsulated in IPsec using ESP or AH in tunnel or transport mode.

- **IKE Enhancements for Remote-Access Client IPsec**—This section talks about the mode config, x-auth, and NAT transparency features implemented to facilitate remote-access client IPsec.

- **IPsec Dead Peer Discovery Mechanism**—This section talks about the keepalive mechanism implemented in IPsec.

- **Case Studies**—This section discusses case studies involving real-life IPsec implementations. Configurations and debugs are included to aid in your understanding of each case study.

IPsec

IPsec (IP Security) is a suite of protocols used to create virtual private networks (VPNs). According to the IETF, it is defined as follows:

> A security protocol in the network layer will be developed to provide cryptographic security services that will flexibly support combinations of authentication, integrity, access control, and confidentiality.

In the most commonly used scenario, IPsec allows an encrypted tunnel to be created between two private networks. It also allows for authenticating the two ends of the tunnel. However, the IPsec protocol allows only for the encapsulation and encryption of IP data (unlike GRE, which can tunnel but not encrypt non-IP traffic), so to create a tunnel for non-IP-based traffic, IPsec must be used in conjunction with a protocol such as GRE, which allows for the tunneling of non-IP protocols.

IPsec is becoming the de facto standard for creating VPNs in the industry. It has been implemented by a large number of vendors, and interoperability between multivendor devices makes IPsec a very good option for building VPNs. Due to IPsec's growing acceptance and importance in the VPN world, we will discuss it in detail in this chapter.

We will start this chapter by discussing the types of setups IPsec is used to implement. We will then take that basic knowledge and go into a very detailed discussion of the three main protocols in IPsec—IKE, ESP, and AH. We will do a packet-by-packet analysis of how IKE and its component protocols are used to negotiate IPsec tunnels. We will discuss IKE in its various forms, as well as the different authentication methods. This will lead us into a more detailed and separate discussion of the authentication mechanisms available to IPsec. We will look at the advantages and disadvantages of preshared keys, digital signatures, and encrypted nonces. We will then go into a detailed discussion of how encryption and integrity checking (two of the cornerstones of IPsec) are built into IPsec. We will conclude our discussion of IPsec by talking about special enhancements made to IPsec to take care of remote-access VPN client environments.

Types of IPsec VPNs

There are a number of ways to categorize IPsec VPNs. However, it is instructive to look at IPsec in light of the two main VPN design issues it tries to resolve:

- The seamless connection of two private networks to form one combined virtual private network

- The extension of a private network to allow remote-access users (also known as *road warriors*) to become part of the trusted network

Based on these two designs, IPsec VPNs can be divided into two main categories:

- LAN-to-LAN IPsec implementations (also known as *site-to-site VPNs*)

- Remote-access client IPsec implementations

LAN-to-LAN IPsec Implementations

LAN-to-LAN IPsec is a term often used to describe an IPsec tunnel created between two LANs. These are also called *site to site* IPsec VPNs. LAN-to-LAN VPNs are created when two private networks are merged across a public network such that the users on either of these networks can access resources on the other network as if they were on their own private network.

IPsec provides a means of negotiating and establishing an encrypted tunnel between two sites. Generally, tunneling is important, because the two private networks often use RFC 1918 addressing, which needs to be tunneled to traverse the public network. IPsec lets you define what traffic is to be encrypted and how it is to be encrypted. We will look at the details of how IPsec achieves this in the next few sections. Some examples of LAN-to-LAN and site-to-site IPsec setups are shown in Figure 13-1.

Figure 13-1 *Types of IPsec VPNs: LAN-to-LAN and Site-to-Site IPsec*

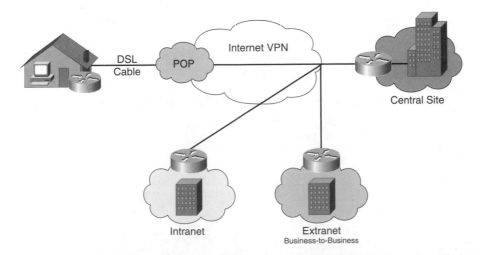

Remote-Access Client IPsec Implementations

Remote-access client IPsec VPNs are created when a remote user connects to an IPsec router or access server using an IPsec client installed on the remote user's machine. Generally, these remote-access machines connect to the public network or the Internet using dialup or some other similar means of connectivity. As soon as basic connectivity to the Internet is established, the IPsec client can set up an encrypted tunnel across the pubic network or the Internet to an IPsec termination device located at the edge of the private network to which the client wants to connect and be a part of. These IPsec termination devices are also known as IPsec remote-access *concentrators*.

Remote-access implementation of IPsec comes with its own unique set of challenges. In the site-to-site scenario, the number of IPsec peers, meaning the devices that terminate IPsec tunnels, may be limited. However, in the case of remote-access IPsec VPNs, the number of peers can be substantial, even running into the tens of thousands for larger implementations. These scenarios require special scalable mechanisms for authentication key management because maintaining all the keys for all the users might become an impossible task. Later in this chapter we will look at some of the important features that have been added to IPsec to handle remote-access clients setups. Some examples of remote-access IPsec setups are shown in Figure 13-2.

Figure 13-2 *Types of IPsec VPNs: Remote-Access IPsec*

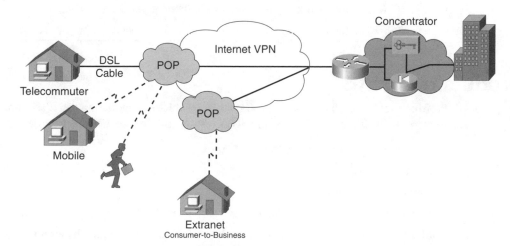

Composition of IPsec

IPsec combines three main protocols to form a cohesive security framework:

- Internet Key Exchange (IKE) protocol

- Encapsulating Security Payload (ESP) protocol
- Authentication Header (AH) protocol

Of these three protocols, IKE and ESP are the ones that are mostly deployed together. Although AH is also an important component of the IPsec protocol suite, not that many deployments of IPsec have this protocol turned on for use. In general, much of AH's functionality is embedded in ESP. Therefore, in our discussions in the rest of this chapter, we will focus our attention on ESP, and much of the discussion will assume that we are talking about ESP unless otherwise stated. For example, while discussing quick-mode exchanges in the following sections, we will assume that the goal is to do ESP.

IKE is used to negotiate the parameters between two IPsec peers for setting up a tunnel between them. We will look in detail at the workings of IKE in the next section. ESP provides the encapsulation mechanism for IPsec traffic. We will go into a more detailed discussion of ESP later in this chapter as well.

Table 13-1 describes the three main components of the IPsec protocol suite.

Table 13-1   *Psec Combines Three Main Protocols to Form a Cohesive Security Framework*

Protocol	Description
IKE	Provides a framework for negotiating security parameters and establishing authenticated keys.
ESP	Provides a framework for encrypting, authenticating, and securing data.
AH	Provides a framework for authenticating and securing data.

Introduction to IKE

IKE or Internet key exchange is the protocol responsible for negotiating the IPsec tunnel characteristics between two IPsec peers. IKE's responsibilities in the IPsec protocol include

- Negotiating protocol parameters
- Exchanging public keys
- Authenticating both sides
- Managing keys after the exchange

IKE solves the problems of manual and unscalable IPsec implementation by automating the entire key-exchange process. This is one of IPsec's critical requirements.

IKE, like IPsec, is also a combination of three different protocols:

- **SKEME**—Provides a mechanism for using public key encryption for authentication purposes.

- **Oakley**—Provides a mode-based mechanism for arriving at an encryption key between two IPsec peers.
- **ISAKMP**—Defines the architecture for message exchange, including packet formats and state transitions between two IPsec peers.

IKE combines these three protocols in one framework to provide IPsec the facilities just discussed. Figure 13-3 shows these three main components of IKE.

Figure 13-3 *Composition of the IKE Protocol*

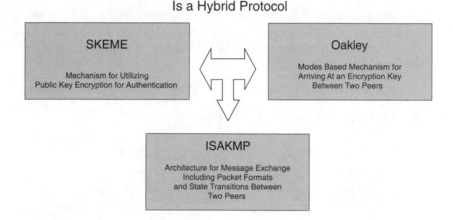

IKE is defined as a standard in RFC 2409. Although IKE does provide a great deal of functionality to the IPsec protocol, some shortcomings in the protocol structure make it difficult to implement in code and scale to new challenges. Work is under way to improve the workings of the IKE protocol and its restandardization in an improved format. This is called the "son-of-IKE" or IKE v2 initiative. See the IETF website for more information on this initiative.

IKE is a two phase protocol. An IPsec tunnel is set up between two peers through the following sequence of events:

Step 1 Interesting traffic is received or generated by one of the IPsec peers on an interface that has been configured to initiate an IPsec session for this traffic.

Step 2 Main mode or aggressive mode negotiation using IKE results in the creation of an IKE Security Association (SA) between the two IPsec peers.

Step 3 Quick mode negotiation using IKE results in the creation of two IPsec SAs between the two IPsec peers.

Step 4 Data starts passing over an encrypted tunnel using the ESP or AH encapsulation techniques (or both).

Based on Steps 2 and 3, you can see that IKE is a two-phase protocol. Phase 1 is accomplished using main mode or aggressive mode exchanges between the peers, and Phase 2 is accomplished using quick mode exchanges.

This list shows how IKE behaves in a two-phase mechanism:

Step 1 In a Phase 1 exchange, peers negotiate a secure, authenticated channel with which to communicate. Main mode or aggressive mode accomplishes a Phase I exchange.

Step 2 In a Phase 2 exchange, security associations are negotiated on behalf of IPsec services. Quick mode accomplishes a Phase II exchange.

Main-mode exchange takes place through the exchange of a total of six messages between the two IPsec peers. If aggressive mode is used, only three messages complete Phase 1 of the exchange. Quick-mode exchange is done using an additional three messages exchanged between the two IPsec peers.

Figure 13-4 shows main mode, aggressive mode, and quick mode in IKE.

Figure 13-4 *IKE Main Mode, Aggressive Mode, and Quick Mode*

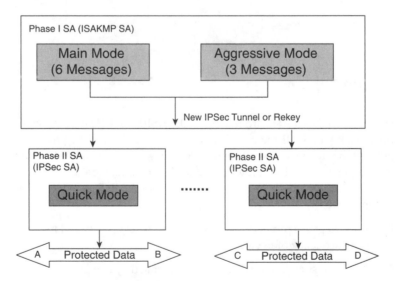

Goals of Main Mode (or Aggressive Mode)

The primary goals of main mode (or aggressive mode) are

- Agreeing on a set of parameters that are to be used to authenticate the two peers and to encrypt a portion of the main mode and all of the quick mode exchange. None of the aggressive mode is encrypted if it is used as the method for negotiation.

- Authenticate the two peers to each other.

- Generate keys that can be used to generate keying material for actual encryption of data as soon as the negotiations have been completed.

All the information negotiated in main mode or aggressive mode, including the keys that are later used to generate the keys to encrypt the data, is stored as what is known as IKE or ISAKMP security association (SA). Any two IPsec peers have only one ISAKMP security association between them.

Goals of Quick Mode

The primary role of quick mode is allow the two peers to agree on a set of attributes for creating the IPsec security associations that will be used to encrypt (in the case of ESP) the data between the two hosts. Also, in the case of PFS (Perfect Forward Secrecy, which you'll read about later), quick mode is responsible for redoing the Diffie-Hellman (DH) exchange so that new keying material is available before the IPsec data encryption keys are generated.

The next section analyzes how IKE is used to negotiate the IPsec parameters between IPsec peers using main (or aggressive) and quick mode.

IPsec Negotiation Using the IKE Protocol

IKE negotiates IPsec tunnels between two IPsec peers. This negotiation can be done using a combination of main-mode and quick-mode exchanges or a combination of aggressive-mode and quick-mode exchanges. This section looks at the various packets and message types that are used in these exchanges to do the negotiation. We will look at three types of negotiations that IKE carries out:

- Main mode using preshared key authentication followed by quick-mode negotiation

- Main mode using digital signature authentication followed by quick-mode negotiation

- Aggressive mode using preshared key authentication followed by quick-mode negotiation

In addition to these types, the following types of negotiations can also take place:

- Main mode using encrypted nonces authentication followed by quick-mode negotiation

- Aggressive mode using digital signature authentication followed by quick-mode negotiation

However, we will not go into the details of the last two types because the first three are by far the most common permutations used. We will focus on the most commonly used types of negotiations to aid your understanding.

Main Mode Using Preshared Key Authentication Followed by Quick Mode Negotiation

As stated earlier, this negotiation takes place with the exchange of a total of six messages between the two IPsec peers in main mode followed by three messages exchanged during quick mode.

In the following sections we will walk through the preparation for, as well as the actual exchange of, each message involved in this negotiation.

IKE Phase 1 (Main Mode): Preparation for Sending Messages 1 and 2

The first two messages in the IKE main mode negotiation are used to negotiate the various values, hash mechanisms, and encryption mechanisms to use for the later half of the IKE negotiations. In addition, information is exchanged that will be used to generate keying material for the two peers.

However, before the first two messages can be exchanged, the negotiation's initiator and responder must calculate what are known as *cookies*. These cookies are used as unique identifiers of a negotiation exchange.

The two peers generate a pseudo-random number that is used for anticlogging purposes. These cookies are based on a unique identifier for each peer (src and destination IP addresses) and therefore protect against replay attacks. The ISAKMP RFC states that the method of creating the cookie is implementation-dependent but suggests performing a hash of the IP source and destination address, the UDP source and destination ports, a locally generated random value, time, and date. The cookie becomes a unique identifier for the rest of the messages that are exchanged in IKE negotiation.

The following list shows how each peer generates its cookie:

- **Generation of the initiator cookie**—An 8-byte pseudo-random number used for anti-clogging

  CKY-I = md5{(src_ip, dest_ip), random number, time, and date}

- **Generation of the responder cookie**—An 8-byte pseudo-random number used for anti-clogging

  CKY-R = md5{(src_ip, dest_ip), random number, time, and date}

IKE uses payloads and packet formats defined in the ISAKMP protocol to do the actual exchange of information. The packets exchanged consist of the ISAKMP header and a series of *payloads* that are used to carry the information needed to carry out the negotiation.

IKE Phase 1 (Main Mode): Sending Message 1

Let's look at the first message sent across by the IPsec initiator to the respondent and look at the various fields in this message.

Figure 13-5 shows the first IKE message being sent.

Figure 13-5 *Sending IKE Main Mode Message 1*

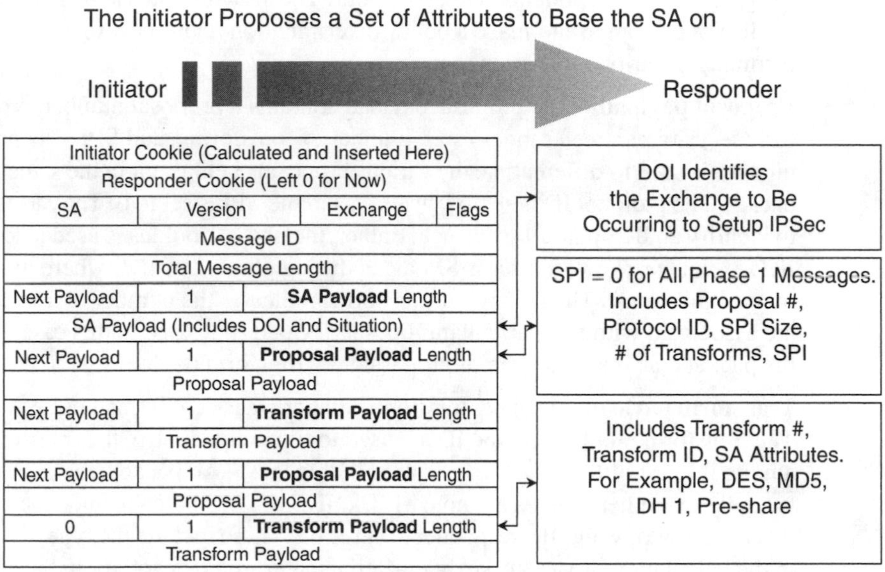

The Initiator Proposes a Set of Attributes to Base the SA on

Initiator ➤ Responder

Initiator Cookie (Calculated and Inserted Here)			
Responder Cookie (Left 0 for Now)			
SA	Version	Exchange	Flags
Message ID			
Total Message Length			
Next Payload	1	**SA Payload** Length	
SA Payload (Includes DOI and Situation)			
Next Payload	1	**Proposal Payload** Length	
Proposal Payload			
Next Payload	1	**Transform Payload** Length	
Transform Payload			
Next Payload	1	**Proposal Payload** Length	
Proposal Payload			
0	1	**Transform Payload** Length	
Transform Payload			

DOI Identifies the Exchange to Be Occurring to Setup IPSec

SPI = 0 for All Phase 1 Messages. Includes Proposal #, Protocol ID, SPI Size, # of Transforms, SPI

Includes Transform #, Transform ID, SA Attributes. For Example, DES, MD5, DH 1, Pre-share

Figure 13-5 shows the ISAKMP header and five payloads. There is one SA payload and two pairs of proposal and transform payloads.

NOTE   All payloads have a field that defines the length of that particular payload. In all the figures in this chapter depicting packet formats, the name of the payload in this field is highlighted to clearly distinguish between the various payloads.

Let's look at each of these in turn:

- **ISAKMP header**—The ISAKMP header contains the initiator's cookie, and the responder's cookie is left at 0 for the responder to calculate and fill in. The next payload field contains a value signifying that the next payload is the SA payload.

- **SA payload**—The SA payload contains two important pieces of information. Because ISAKMP is a generic protocol with packet and message formats that can be used to negotiate any number of protocols, it is important to specify that this particular ISAKMP exchange is taking place for IPsec negotiation. Therefore, the SA payload contains a Domain of Interpretation (DOI), which says that this message exchange is for IPsec. The other important piece of information is the situation. The situation definition is a 32-bit bitmask that represents the environment under which the IPsec SA proposal and negotiation are carried out. The situation provides information that the responder can use to make a policy determination about how to process the incoming security association request.

- **Proposal payload**—The proposal payload contains a proposal number, protocol ID, SPI (security parameter index) size, number of transforms, and SPI. The proposal number is used to differentiate the various proposals being sent in the same ISAKMP packet. The protocol ID is set to ISAKMP, and the SPI is set to 0. The SPI is not used to identify an IKE phase 1 exchange. Rather, the pair of cookies is used to identify the IKE exchange. We will discuss SPI again during phase 2 of IKE where its use is of more significance. The number of transforms indicates the number of transforms that are associated with this particular proposal payload (only one in this case). Note that the packet contains two pairs of proposal and transform payloads.

- **Transform payload**—Includes transform number, transform ID, and IKE SA attributes. The transform number and the ID are used to uniquely identify the transform from among the rest of the transforms offered in this ISAKMP packet (this sample packet has only one other transform, though). The IKE SA attributes include the attributes that the initiator wants the responder to agree on. These include the type of hash to use in the calculation of various keying materials later in the negotiation, the encryption mechanism to use to encrypt IKE negotiation messages as soon as a shared secret has been established, the Diffie-Hellman exchange mechanism to use, the method of authentication to use, and the timeout values of the IKE SAs negotiated. In this example, assume that the method of authentication being offered is preshared, meaning that a preshared key has been defined on the initiator and responder out of band.

For the sake of this example, assume that the initiator offered the responder the following transform attributes in the first payload. Don't worry about what it offered in the second payload, because we will assume that the responder agrees to what is offered in the first pair of transform and proposal payloads and does not have to worry about the second pair:

- **Encryption mechanism**—DES
- **Hashing mechanism**—MD5-HMAC
- **Diffie-Hellman group**—1
- **Authentication mechanism**—Preshared

All ISAKMP messages are carried in a UDP packet with destination port 500.

IKE Phase 1 (Main Mode): Sending Message 2

Message 2 is the response from the responder to the packet that was sent by the initiator. Most of the fields are the same as in the packet sent by the initiator, so we will discuss the differences only. Note that only one proposal and transform payload is included in the response because the responder agrees to only one proposal/transform pair and returns that as the agreed-on pair.

Figure 13-6 shows the second IKE message being sent.

Figure 13-6 *Sending IKE Main Mode Message 2*

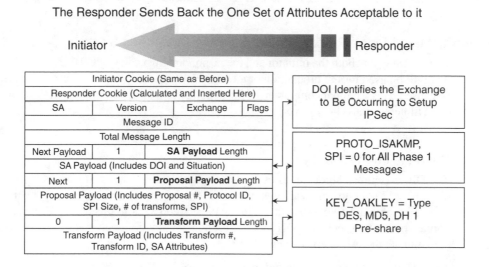

Here are the payloads included in this message:

- **ISAKMP header**—You can see that the ISAKMP header now has both cookie fields set to their respective values.

- **SA payload**—The SA payload contains pretty much the same material that was sent by the initiator.

- **Proposal payload**—The proposal payload contains the information for the proposal that the responder has decided to accept.

- **Transform payload**—The transform payload contains the elements of the transform that the responder has decided to accept.

For the sake of our example, assume that the responder accepted the first proposal described in the preceding section:

- **Encryption mechanism**—DES

- **Hashing mechanism**—MD5-HMAC

- **Diffie-Hellman group** — 1
- **Authentication mechanism** — Preshared

NOTE   IKE SA timeouts are also negotiated using the transform payloads. The acceptable transform payload must not only have all the other IKE attributes contained in it that are agreeable to the responder, but it also must have an IKE SA timeout value that is equal to or less than the responder that it is set up to accept. If no such transform is included, the negotiation fails.

IKE Phase 1 (Main Mode): Preparation for Sending Messages 3 and 4

The next step that both the initiator and the responder must carry out is to generate material that will be used for the production of a Diffie-Hellman shared secret between the two. Because DH is a critical component of the negotiation taking place between the two peers, we will here discuss how it works.

Diffie-Hellman Algorithm

The Diffie-Hellman algorithm is used in IKE negotiations to allow the two peers to agree on a shared secret, to generate keying material for subsequent use, without knowing any secrets beforehand. (Note that although the preshared secret in this example is already defined on the two peers, the DH secret is used in conjunction with that preshared secret to authenticate the two peers to each other.)

The DH algorithm relies on the following property:

There exists a DH public value = X_a

such that

$X_a = g^a \bmod p$

where

g is the generator

p is a large prime number

a is a private secret known only to the initiator

And there exists another DH public value = X_b

such that

$X_b = g^b \bmod p$

where

g is the generator

p is a large prime number

b is a private secret known only to the responder

Then the initiator and the responder can generate a shared secret known only to the two of them by simply exchanging the values X_a and X_b with each other. This is true because

initiator secret $= (X_b)^a \bmod p = (X_a)^b \bmod p =$ responder secret

This value is the shared secret between the two parties and is also equal to g^{ab}.

Coming back to IKE, in order to calculate the DH secret between the two peers, the two peers calculate the DH public values and send them to each other. In addition, a value known as a *nonce* is also generated and exchanged. A nonce is a very large random number generated using certain mathematical techniques. It is used in later calculations of the keying material. The following lists describe the preparation for sending message 3 of the IKE.

First, the two peers independently generate a DH public value:

- Generation of the DH public value by the initiator

  DH public value $= X_a$

  $X_a = g^a \bmod p$

  where

  g is the generator

  p is a large prime number

  a is a private secret known only to the initiator

- Generation of the DH public value by the responder

  DH public value $= X_b$

  $X_b = g^b \bmod p$

  where

  g is the generator

  p is a large prime number

  b is a private secret known only to the responder

As soon as the DH public values have been calculated, the two peers also independently calculate the nonces:

- Generation of a nonce by the initiator

  initiator nonce $= N_i$

- Generation of a nonce by the responder

  responder nonce = N_r

IKE Phase 1 (Main Mode): Sending Message 3

The third message is sent from the initiator to the responder. The ISAKMP header is similar to the one contained in the earlier messages, complete with cookies. However, two new payloads are introduced in this message—the key exchange payload and the nonce payload.

- **Key exchange (KE) payload**—The KE payload is used to carry the DH public value X_a generated for doing DH.
- **Nonce payload**—The nonce payload contains the nonce generated in accordance with the preceding discussion.

Figure 13-7 shows message 3 of IKE being sent.

Figure 13-7 *Sending Message 3 of IKE*

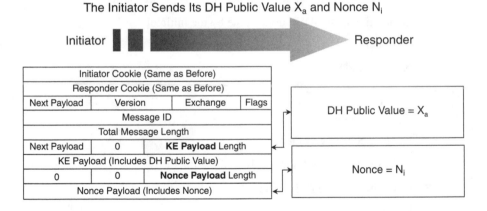

IKE Phase 1 (Main Mode): Sending Message 4

The fourth message is sent from the responder to the initiator. It is very similar to message 3 in that it contains the corresponding DH public value and the nonce for the responder.

Figure 13-8 shows message 4 of IKE being sent.

Figure 13-8 *Sending Message 4 of IKE*

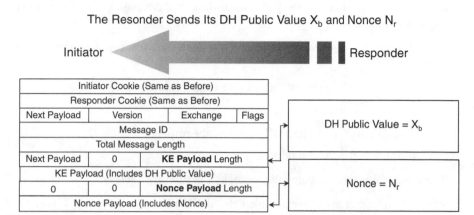

IKE Phase 1 (Main Mode): Preparation for Sending Messages 5 and 6

Before messages 5 and 6 can be sent, the two peers must calculate the DH shared secret. In addition, based on the exchanged nonce, the DH secret calculated, and the preshared keys stored on the two peers, three sets of keys must be generated that will be used to authenticate the two peers to each other as well as to encrypt subsequent IKE exchanges.

Three keys are generated by each peer. These keys come out to be the same on both ends due to the nature of the DH exchange and the rest of the elements used to generate the keys. These keys are called session keys (SKEYs). The three keys being generated are as follows:

- **SKEYID_d**—This key is used to calculate subsequent IPsec keying material.

- **SKEYID_a**—This key is used to provide data integrity and authentication to subsequent IKE messages.

- **SKEYID_e**—This key is used to encrypt subsequent IKE messages.

Now that both ends have the keying material generated, the rest of the IKE exchange can occur confidentially using encryption done using **SKEYID_e**.

Note that for the keys to be generated correctly, each peer must find the corresponding preshared key for its peer. A number of preshared keys might be configured on both the peers for each of the many peers they communicate with. However, the ID payload identifying the peer's IP address or the host name does not arrive until the next message is exchanged. Therefore, each peer must find the preshared key for its peer by using the source IP address from which it is receiving the ISAKMP packets. The reason for sending the ID payload later is to hide it by using encryption afforded by the keys that have been generated in this step. We will look at the problems this method can pose in the discussion of aggressive mode.

For the two peers to generate their SKEYIDs, they must first calculate their shared DH secret:

- Calculation of the shared DH secret by the initiator

  shared secret = $(X_b)^a \bmod p$

- Calculation of the shared DH secret by the responder

  shared secret = $(X_a)^b \bmod p$

These two values end up being the same, g^{ab}, as discussed earlier.

After the DH secret has been calculated, the SKEYIDs can be generated. Figure 13-9 shows the session keys being generated by the initiator, and Figure 13-10 shows the session keys being generated by the responder.

Figure 13-9 *Session Keys Being Generated by the Initiator*

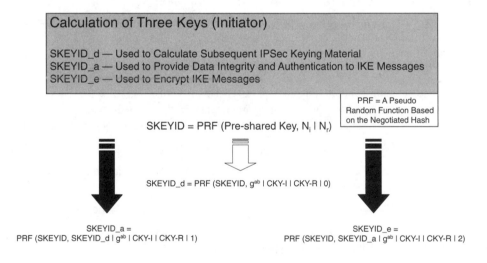

Figure 13-10 *Session Keys Being Generated by the Responder*

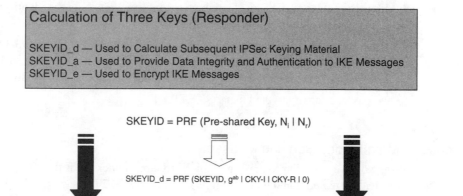

Calculation of Three Keys (Responder)

SKEYID_d — Used to Calculate Subsequent IPSec Keying Material
SKEYID_a — Used to Provide Data Integrity and Authentication to IKE Messages
SKEYID_e — Used to Encrypt IKE Messages

$$\text{SKEYID} = \text{PRF (Pre-shared Key, } N_i \mid N_r)$$

$$\text{SKEYID\_d} = \text{PRF (SKEYID, } g^{ab} \mid \text{CKY-I} \mid \text{CKY-R} \mid 0)$$

SKEYID_a =
PRF (SKEYID, SKEYID_d l g^{ab} l CKY-I l CKY-R l 1)

SKEYID_e =
PRF (SKEYID, SKEYID_a l g^{ab} l CKY-I l CKY-R l 2)

IKE Phase 1 (Main Mode): Sending Message 5

Message 5 is sent with the usual ISAKMP header, but it contains two new payloads—the identity payload and the hash payload. Figure 13-11 shows message 5 of IKE being sent.

Figure 13-11 *Sending Message 5 of IKE*

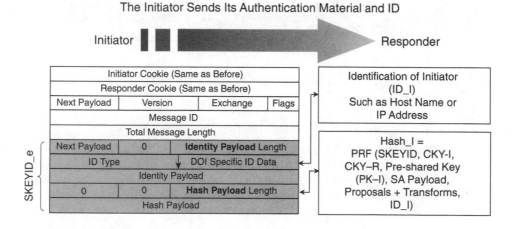

The Initiator Sends Its Authentication Material and ID

Initiator → Responder

Initiator Cookie (Same as Before)			
Responder Cookie (Same as Before)			
Next Payload	Version	Exchange	Flags
Message ID			
Total Message Length			
Next Payload	0	**Identity Payload** Length	
ID Type		DOI Specific ID Data	
Identity Payload			
0	0	**Hash Payload** Length	
Hash Payload			

SKEYID_e

Identification of Initiator
(ID_I)
Such as Host Name or
IP Address

Hash_I =
PRF (SKEYID, CKY-I,
CKY–R, Pre-shared Key
(PK–I), SA Payload,
Proposals + Transforms,
ID_I)

Here are the various payloads included in the message:

- **Identity payload**—This payload contains information about the identity of the initiator. This is in the form of the initiator's IP address or host name.

- **Hash payload**—The hash payload is calculated as shown in Figure 13-11. The hash is used for authentication purposes. The responder calculates the same hash on its end. If the two hashes come out to be the same, authentication is said to have taken place.

The two payloads are encrypted using SKEYID_E.

IKE Phase 1 (Main Mode): Sending Message 6

Message 6 is very similar to message 5 in that the responder sends the corresponding authentication material and its ID. Figure 13-12 shows IKE message 6 being sent.

Figure 13-12 *Sending Message 6 of IKE*

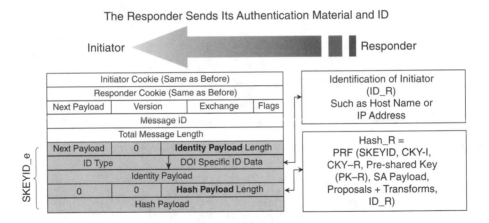

The contents of the packets are encrypted using SKEYID_E.

Completion of IKE Phase 1 (Main Mode) Using Preshared Keys

The main mode of IKE is completed using the material received in the last two messages of IKE exchange. The two sides authenticate each other by recalculating the hash and comparing it to the one they received in the hash payload. If the two values are the same, the two sides are considered to have successfully authenticated.

The following list shows how the two peers use the authentication hashes received from each other to verify each other's authenticity:

- Initiator authenticates the responder

  Step 1   Decrypt the message using SKEYID_E.

  Step 2   Find the configured PK-R (pre-shared key or responder) using ID_R.

  Step 3   Calculate Hash_R on its own.

  Step 4   If received Hash_R = self-generated Hash_R, authentication is successful!

- Responder authenticates the initiator

  Step 1   Decrypt the message using SKEYID_E.

  Step 2   Find the configured PK-I (pre-shared key or initiator) using ID_I.

  Step 3   Calculate Hash_I on its own.

  Step 4   If received Hash_I = self-generated Hash_I, authentication is successful!

At this point, the IKE SA is established, and main mode using preshared key authentication is complete. The next step, quick mode, is discussed in the next section.

IKE Phase 2 (Quick Mode): Preparation for Sending Messages 1 and 2

Just as the main mode was used to agree upon parameters for the IKE SA, quick mode is used to negotiate some of the parameters of IPsec security association. In our example, we will assume that the initiator has decided to use a property known as Perfect Forward Secrecy (PFS).

PFS

PFS is a property that the initiator of an IKE negotiation can "suggest" to the responder. This suggestion is made by sending a key exchange attribute payload during the first message of quick mode. If the responder agrees to do PFS, it continues the quick mode exchange. Otherwise, it returns "Attributes Not Supported," and the initiator can continue without PFS if it is so configured.

PFS is a property that forces the peers (if they agree to it) to generate a new DH secret during the quick mode exchange. This allows the encryption keys used to encrypt data to be generated using a new DH secret. This ensures added secrecy. If the original DH secret were to somehow get compromised, this new secret can ensure privacy for the data. Also, because the negotiations for the new DH are carried out using encrypted traffic, this new DH secret has an added element of secrecy.

Note that it is not possible to negotiate the DH group the way it was offered and accepted in main mode, because quick mode has only one exchange in which the DH exchange must take place. Therefore, the PFS DH group configured on both ends must match.

To ensure PFS, the two peers generate the numbers needed to perform DH exchange once again. This is done in exactly the same manner as was done in phase 1 of IKE. The following list describes how this is done by the two peers. The apostrophe on top of the various values is used to signify the fact that these values are different from the DH values calculated in phase 1 of IKE:

- Execution of DH by the initiator again to ensure PFS:

  New nonce generated: N_i'

  New DH public value = X_a'

  $X_a' = g^a \bmod p$

  where

  g is the generator

  p is a large prime number

  a is a private secret known only to the initiator

- Execution of DH by the responder again to ensure PFS:

  New Nonce Generated: N_r'

  New DH public value = X_b'

  $X_b' = g^b \bmod p$

  where

  g is the generator

  p is a large prime number

  b is a private secret known only to the responder

IKE Phase 2 (Quick Mode): Sending Message 1

Message 1 from the initiator to the responder contains payloads you have already seen in the main mode negotiation. The contents of the payloads are, of course, different. Note the presence of the key exchange payload for requesting PFS. In addition, the new nonce is also sent across.

The hash payload contains a hash calculated on some of the elements that were agreed on in phase 1, as well as some of the payloads contained in this message itself. The purpose of the hash is to authenticate the peer again.

In addition, the message contains proposals and transform pairs for the IPsec SAs to be formed. The proposal payload includes the type of encapsulation to use, AH or ESP, and an SPI. The SPI is an interesting element. It is a 32-bit number that is chosen by the initiator to uniquely identify the outgoing IPsec SA that is generated as a result of this negotiation in its database of security associations (it might be talking to a lot more than one peer at a time). The responder, upon seeing the SPI, makes sure that it is not the same as one of the SPIs it is using and starts using it for its incoming IPsec SA. It also proposes an SPI for its outgoing (and the initiator's incoming) SA, which the initiator agrees to after checking.

The associated transform payload includes parameters such as tunnel or transport mode, SHA or MD5 for integrity checking in ESP or AH, and lifetimes for the IPsec security association.

A new payload type introduced in this message is the ID payload. The ID payload contains the proxy identities on whose behalf the initiator does the negotiation. These are generally IP address subnets, but they can have more fields, such as port, too. In the case of a site-to-site IPsec set up with two gateways doing IPsec negotiations with each other, the proxy IDs are based on rules defined on the gateways that define what type of traffic is supposed to be encrypted by the peers.

Note that most of the message is still encrypted using one of the keys generated in phase 1.

For the sake of our example, assume that the initiator offers the following transform attributes for the IPsec SA in one of the transform and proposal payload sets:

- **Encapsulation**—ESP
- **Integrity checking**—SHA-HMAC
- **DH group**—2
- **Mode**—Tunnel

Figure 13-13 shows the first message of IKE quick mode being sent.

NOTE   Unlike IKE timeout negotiation, which is very strict, timeout negotiation in quick mode for the IPsec SA is more lenient. If the initiator proposes a transform that, all other things being acceptable, contains a timeout value that is higher than the timeout configured on the responder, the responder does not fail the negotiation. Instead, it simply returns the transform payload with the timeout modified to the lower value configured on it. The initiator then sets up the IPsec with this lower value.

Note that this behavior is different from the behavior shown in the negotiation of the IKE lifetime. A transform with a timeout higher than the one configured on the responder is unacceptable. If none of the transforms carry acceptable attributes, including an equal or lower timeout, the negotiation simply fails.

The difference in the behaviors is due to the fact that the IPsec SA timeout negotiation is done after authentication has taken place, whereas the IKE timeout negotiation is done between unauthenticated peers with no trust established.

Figure 13-13 *Sending the First Message of IKE Quick Mode*

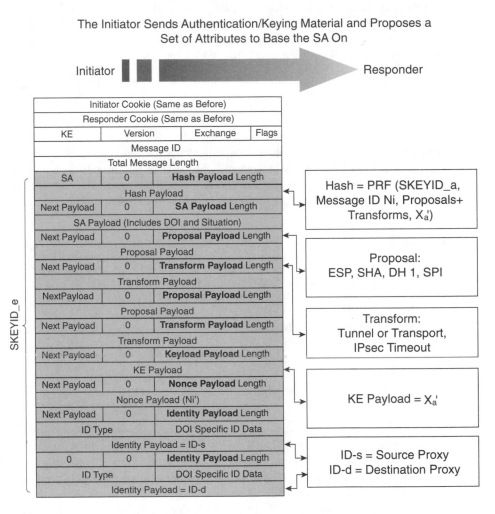

Figure 13-14 shows how the lifetimes are negotiated between two peers.

Figure 13-14 *IKE and IPsec Lifetime Negotiation*

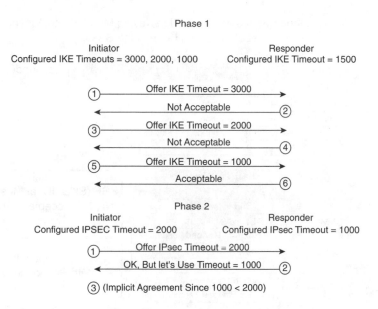

IKE Phase 2 (Quick Mode): Sending Message 2

The second message is sent by the responder in response to the initiator's first message. The fields are pretty much the same, with a few changes. Most notably, only the proposal and the transform payloads that were acceptable are returned to the initiator.

The proposal payload contains the SPI of the outgoing SA for the responder rather than the SPI that was sent by the initiator.

The hash payload contains the hash of only the payloads that are contained in this message. This hash acts as proof of the responder's liveness because it contains a hash of the two latest nonces as well the message ID, proving to the initiator that the responder has indeed received its initial packet and is ready to receive its encrypted messages.

The responder looks at the IDs offered by the initiator in the ID payloads and compares them to the proxy IDs defined on itself. If its policy permits the IDs that are being offered by the initiator, the negotiation continues. Otherwise, a failure occurs.

Figure 13-15 shows message 2 of quick mode being sent.

Figure 13-15 *Sending Message 2 of Quick Mode*

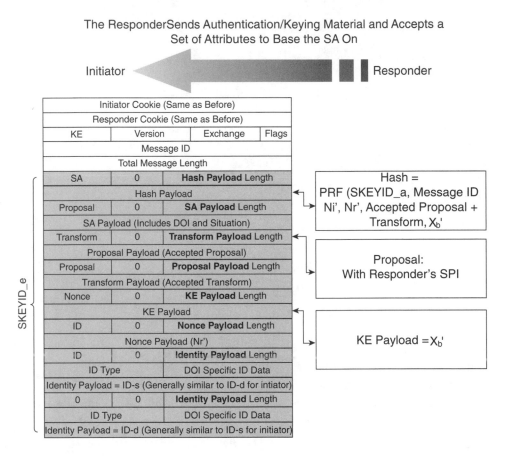

IKE Phase 2 (Quick Mode): Preparation for Sending Message 3

Before the last message can be sent for quick mode, the two ends must use the information sent relative to DH to generate a new DH secret and use this secret in conjunction with SKEYID_d and some of the other parameters to generate the IPsec encryption/decryption keys. The following are the steps taken by the two peers to generate the keys:

- Initiator generates IPsec keying material

  Step 1   Generate new DH shared secret = $(X_b')^a \bmod p$

  Step 2   IPsec session key for incoming IPsec SA = PRF (SKEYID_d, protocol (ISAKMP), new DH shared secret, SPI_r, N_i', N_r')

  Step 3   IPsec session key for outgoing IPsec SA = PRF (SKEYID_d, protocol (ISAKMP), new DH shared secret, SPI_i, N_i', N_r')

- Responder generates IPsec keying material

    Step 1   Generate new DH shared secret = $(X_a')^b$ mod p

    Step 2   IPsec session key for incoming IPsec SA = PRF (SKEYID_d, protocol (ISAKMP), new DH shared secret, SPI_i, N_i', N_r')

    Step 3   IPsec session key for outgoing IPsec SA = PRF (SKEYID_d, protocol (ISAKMP), new DH shared secret, SPI_r, N_i', N_r')

As soon as the IPsec key is generated, the tunnel is pretty much ready to become operational. Only one additional messageis sent which concludes the quick mode negotiation.

Please note that two keys are generated on the initiator and the responder: one for the outgoing SA (which matches the key for the incoming SA key on the peer) and one for the incoming SA (which matches the key for the outgoing SA key on the peer).

IKE Phase 2 (Quick Mode): Sending Message 3

The last message of the IKE exchange is sent to verify the liveness of the responder. This is necessary for two reasons. The first reason is that the responder needs some way to know that the initiator received its first and only message of quick mode and correctly processed it. The second reason is to avoid a limited denial of service attack orchestrated by an attacker by replaying a first message of the quick mode exchange from the initiator to the receiver. By sending another message with the correct message ID and latest nonces hashed, the initiator proves to the responder that it has not only received its nonces but also is a live and current peer. Figure 13-16 shows how the final message is sent to the responder.

Figure 13-16 *Sending Message 3 of Quick Mode*

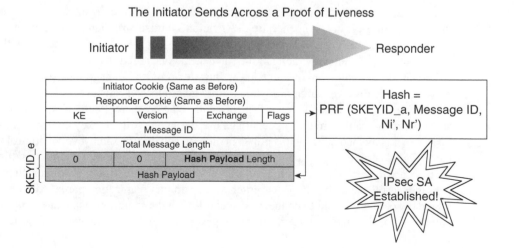

After message 3 has been received by the receiver, IPsec's quick mode is concluded. All the goals of IKE—authentication, negotiation of the encryption algorithm, and other attributes needed to generate the encrypted packets—have been negotiated. Now the agreed-on IPsec SAs can be used to exchange encrypted traffic.

NOTE   Note that while it is not a requirement per the RFC, the responder can also send the initiator a message similar to the message 3 discussed above to verify its liveliness.

Main Mode Using Digital Signature Authentication Followed by Quick Mode Negotiation

Another important method of authentication used in IKE is digital signatures. We will discuss the use and workings of digital signatures in a later section. Here the changes in main mode of IKE negotiation are described. You might want to read the section on digital signatures (PKI) first and then come back to this section.

The only difference in the preshared and digital signatures method of authentication occurs in the fifth and sixth IKE messages that are sent. The first four messages of main mode and all the quick mode messages remain the same as in preshared key-based IKE negotiation.

Let's look at the preparation and sending of messages 5 and 6 for digital signatures to appreciate the difference.

IKE Phase 1 (Main Mode): Preparation for Sending Messages 5 and 6 Using Digital Signatures

The first difference that is quite evident is the way the SKEYs are generated when using digital signatures. Instead of generating PRF outputs with the preshared secret as one of the components, the PRF output is generated using the DH secret g^{ab} instead, along with the rest of the parameters, which are the same as the ones used in the preshared method. Obviously, at this point, anyone who knows how to do IPsec can negotiate (using a hit-and-miss method to discover configured transforms and proposals) and have the keys generated, which would be valid on both ends. The effect that the preshared secret has, of limiting successful negotiations to those peers that have the same preshared key configured, is not visible in this method up until this point. In order to achieve the same level of control when using digital certificates, a successful negotiation is restricted by either manually setting up each peer with the public key of the peers to which it is allowed to connect or enrolling each peer in a certificate authority (CA) server with a certain organization name. All peers to which the peer is allowed to connect must enroll with the same certificate authority server and belong to the same organization. Messages 5 and 6 of the exchange contain the certificates of the two peers. These certificates contain the identity of the two peers, including the organization ID.

Figure 13-17 shows the mechanism through which the keys are generated on the initiator in the digital signatures method of conducting main mode negotiation.

Figure 13-17 *How Keys Are Generated on the Initiator in the Digital Signatures Method of Main Mode Negotiation*

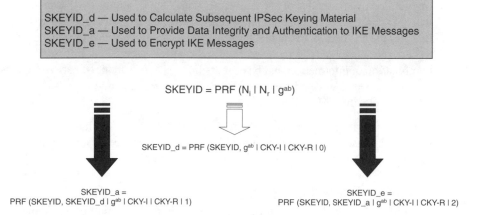

Figure 13-18 shows the mechanism through which the keys are generated on the responder in the digital signatures method of conducting main mode negotiation.

Figure 13-18 *How Keys Are Generated on the Responder in the Digital Signatures Method of Main Mode Negotiation*

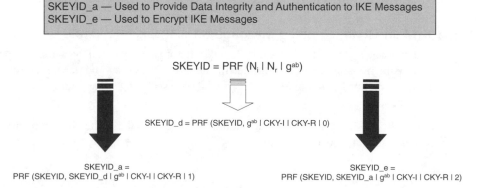

IKE Phase 1 (Main Mode): Sending Message 5 Using Digital Signatures

The message 5 sent by the initiator contains two new payloads in addition to the ones we have already looked at—signature and certificate.

Signature Payload

This payload contains the initiator's signature. In general, a signature is a known value encrypted with an individual's private key. A signature provides nonrepudiation, meaning that because data encrypted using a private key can only be decrypted using its corresponding public key, the sender of the data cannot back out of admitting that he or she sent the data. No one else but that person possesses the private key (corresponding to the public key) that was used to decrypt the data. Obviously, the assumption is that the data is known a priori to both the sender and the receiver. In the case of message 5, this information is indeed a combination of information that has either already been exchanged between the two parties or that has been generated based on exchanged information and is the same on both sides (for example, the SKEYID).

The hash that is encrypted using the private key is generated by hashing the accepted proposal and transform payloads along with certain other values, as shown in Figure 13-19.

Certificate Payload

We will discuss the format of a certificate in detail in the section on IKE authentication methods. For now, it is sufficient to say that the certificate contained in the certificate payload is tied to a unique host name (or some other similar attribute) that is the sender's host name. The certificate also contains the sender's public key, which is used to decrypt the signature sent in the same message. The certificate is issued for a certain organization ID. Both the IPsec peers must belong to the same organization, and both must trust the CA issuing the certificate for the certificate to be acceptable to both of them.

Figure 13-19 shows the initiator sending message 5 in the digital signatures method of conducting main mode negotiation.

IKE Phase 1 (Main Mode): Sending Message 6 Using Digital Signatures

The message 6 sent by the responder to the initiator is pretty much the same as the message sent by the initiator. It contains the certificate of the responder and the signature generated using the private key of the responder and the corresponding values stored on it through the IKE exchanges so far.

Figure 13-20 shows the responder sending message 6 in the digital signatures method of conducting main mode negotiation.

Figure 13-19 *Initiator Sending Message 5 in the Digital Signatures Method of Main Mode Negotiation*

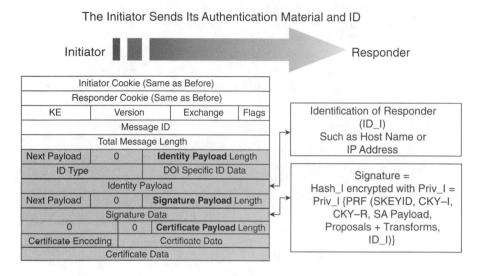

Figure 13-20 *Responder Sending Message 6 in the Digital Signatures Method of Main Mode Negotiation*

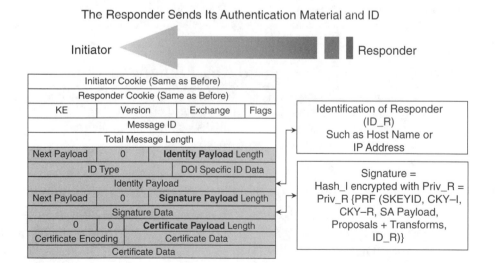

IKE Phase 1 (Main Mode): Completion of Authentication Using Digital Signatures

As soon as both the initiator and responder have compared the ID of the peer with the ID set up in its configuration by the system administrator as the ID to which it is allowed to establish a peering relationship, the authentication process using digital signatures is completed by both the initiator and the responder. This is done by decrypting the encrypted Hash_I using the public key of the other side received through its certificate. The hashes are then compared in a manner similar to the method used in preshared authentication to verify that they are the same. If they are, the two sides are assumed to be authenticated.

- Initiator authenticates the responder

  Step 1 Decrypt the message using SKEYID_E.

  Step 2 Decrypt Hash_R using Pub_R.

  Step 3 Calculate Hash_R on its own.

  Step 4 If received Hash_R = self-generated Hash_R, authentication is successful!

- Responder authenticates the initiator

  Step 1 Decrypt the message using SKEYID_E.

  Step 2 Decrypt Hash_I using Pub_I.

  Step 3 Calculate Hash_I on its own.

  Step 4 If received Hash_I = self-generated Hash_I, authentication is successful!

As soon as main mode has been completed as just described, quick mode goes through exactly the same steps as in the preshared authentication method.

Aggressive Mode Using Preshared Key Authentication

This section discusses aggressive mode, an alternative for main mode functions. Aggressive mode is completed using only three messages instead of the six used in main mode. However, the speed comes at a cost. We will discuss the shortcomings at the end of this section, after you have seen how aggressive mode works.

IKE Phase 1 (Aggressive Mode): Preparation for Sending Messages 1 and 2

The preparation for sending messages 1 and 2 in aggressive mode is the same as the combination of the preparations done in main mode prior to sending messages 1, 2, 3, and 4.

Essentially, all the information needed to generate the DH secret is exchanged in the first two messages exchanged between the two peers. No opportunity is given to negotiate the DH group by offering a series of DH group values by the initiator to the receiver. Instead, both have to agree on a DH group immediately or fail negotiation.

In addition, if the preshared secret method of authentication is being used in aggressive mode, the identity of the peer that is also exchanged in the first two packets is sent in the clear. This is unlike main mode negotiation. However, the advantage of this is that the ID can now be used to search for the pre-shared key belonging to the peer. As mentioned in the discussion of main mode, this ID does not arrive until after the pre-shared key has been found by using the source IP address of the negotiation IP packets.

IKE Phase 1 (Aggressive Mode): Sending Message 1

The first message sent by the initiator contains all the material needed for the responder to generate a DH secret. This means that the initiator sends the key exchange payload and the nonce payload with the appropriate values generated in them. In addition, an ID payload is sent. The message also includes one or more pairs of proposal and transform payloads for the responder to chose from.

Figure 13-21 shows the first message of IKE aggressive mode being sent from the initiator to the responder.

Figure 13-21 *Sending the First Message of IKE Aggressive Mode from the Initiator to the Responder*

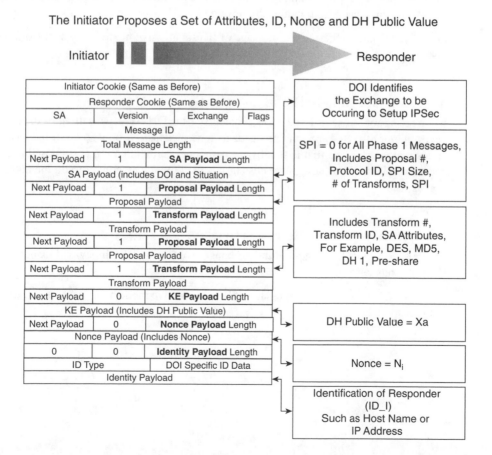

All the payloads sent in message 1 were described in detail in the section on main mode.

IKE Phase 1 (Aggressive Mode): Preparation for Sending Message 2

Upon the receipt of the first packet, the responder has all the material it needs to generate the DH secret. It goes ahead and generates the DH secret. If the preshared secret is being used, the responder finds the preshared secret by using the ID from the ID payload it received in the previous message. It then uses the DH secret and the preshared secret along with other attributes to calculate the three keys, just as is done in main mode. Having created the keys, it uses the SKEYID to generate Hash_R for authentication purposes.

IKE Phase 1 (Aggressive Mode): Sending Message 2

Message 2, sent by the responder to the initiator, contains the proposal and transform pair to which the responder has agreed, as well as the hash for authentication purposes generated by the responder. It also contains all the material the initiator needs to generate its DH secret. The message also contains the responder's ID.

Figure 13-22 shows the second message of IKE aggressive mode being sent from the responder to the initiator.

IKE Phase 1 (Aggressive Mode): Preparation for Sending Message 3

Upon receipt of message 2, the initiator calculates the DH secret as well, finds the preshared key, generates the SKEYS, and proceeds to generate Hash_R on its own. If the hash it generates matches the one that is sent by the responder, authentication is supposed to have occurred. The initiator now generates Hash_I to allow the responder to do the authentication as well.

IKE Phase 1 (Aggressive Mode): Sending Message 3

The initiator sends message 3 of the exchange, containing a hash payload loaded with the Hash_I it has generated.

Figure 13-23 shows the third message of IKE aggressive mode being sent from the initiator to the responder.

Figure 13-22 *Sending the Second Message of IKE Aggressive Mode from the Responder to the Initiator*

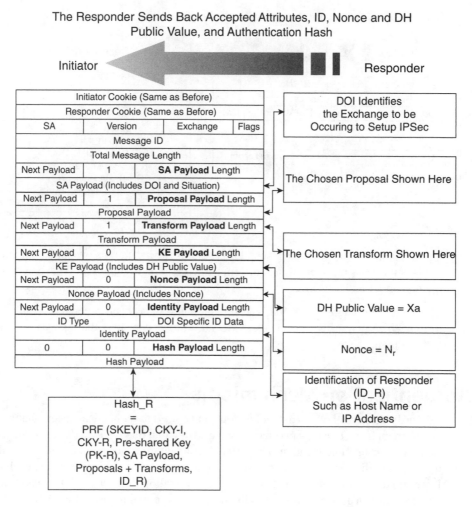

Figure 13-23 *Sending the Third Message of IKE Aggressive Mode from the Initiator to the Responder*

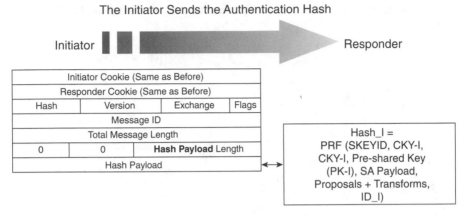

Upon receipt of this hash, the responder generates the hash on its own and compares it to the Hash_I it has received. If they match, authentication is supposed to have occurred on the responder end as well.

This concludes aggressive mode. The keying material has been generated, and the peers have been authenticated. The quick mode that follows is exactly the same as the one that follows main mode.

IKE Authentication Mechanisms

Primarily three methods of authentication can be used to authenticate peers that want to establish an IPsec tunnel between themselves. Note that this is called *device authentication* rather than user authentication. The difference is that in device authentication, the devices that are actually doing IPsec communication on behalf of a user authenticate each other. User authentication (also called extended authentication in IPsec) is done in addition to device authentication and is for specific users who are making use of the IPsec services offered by the IPsec-enabled devices. We will talk about extended authentication in a later section of this chapter.

The three main mechanisms of device authentication are

- Preshared keys
- Digital signatures
- Encrypted nonces

Preshared Keys

Preshared keys can be used to authenticate peers by defining the same key on both the IPsec peers. This method of authentication is obviously very simple to set up. However, this is not a very scalable method. For example, if an IPsec device has 100 peers, 100 preshared keys need to be set up manually—one for each. This process has to be repeated on each of the 101 devices.

Also, this method does not scale when the remote clients are trying to authenticate to an IPsec gateway using main mode authentication. These clients are assigned IP addresses from their ISPs unknown to the IPsec gateway. Because in main mode authentication the peer's IP address is used to find its key to do the authentication, it is not possible to define a key on the gateway that can be used to authenticate these clients. One way around this problem is to use aggressive mode, which exchanges the ID of the IPsec peers in the first message exchanged. This allows the ID, if it is sent as the name of the remote client, to be used to find the preshared key for it. However, this is not a very secure method, because the ID is sent in the clear. We will discuss an enhancement to this method using extended authentication in a later section.

What Are Public and Private Keys?

Both of the methods that we will discuss next use the concept of a public/private key pair. Public/private key pairs are an important concept in security. Basically, the public/private key pair provides the following important properties:

- Data encrypted using the public key can be decrypted only using the corresponding private key.

- Data encrypted using the private key can be decrypted only using the corresponding public key.

The first property is used for confidentiality purposes. The private key of a public/private pair is known only to the owner of the peer and no one else. On the other hand, the public key can be known to as many individuals or devices that need to send data confidentially to the owner. So, data sent to the owner of the pair encrypted using the public key can be decrypted only by the owner, because no one else but the owner possesses the private key to decrypt the data. This makes the data confidential.

The second property is used for authentication purposes. To authenticate himself to someone, the owner can send data encrypted using his private key to the other party. He also sends the original data along with the encrypted data. If the receiver can decrypt the data using the sender's public key, it knows the sender is who he says he is, because no one else could have correctly encrypted the data.

You will see the use of these properties in the methods discussed next.

Digital Signatures

Digital signatures, one of the methods you saw used in the earlier description of IKE, is a method that lends itself to being scalable when used in conjunction with a certificate authority. The authentication relies on the use of public/private key pairs being generated on both the IPsec peers. The public keys are exchanged either out of band the way preshared keys are exchanged, by the system administrators of the two IPsec peers, or during the IKE negotiation (using digital certificates). When the keys are exchanged during the IKE negotiation, they are contained in a certificate payload. The certificate, in addition to holding the public key, has information about the sender, such as the sender's name and the organization he belongs to.

Figure 13-24 shows the contents of a digital certificate.

Figure 13-24 *Contents of a Digital Certificate*

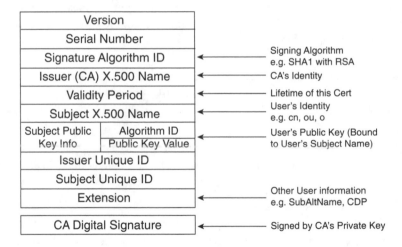

For the certificate to be acceptable to the receiver, it must be issued by a certificate authority server that is trusted by both the sender and the receiver. Also, the sender and the receiver must belong to the same organizational unit. This ensures that only the IPsec peers who are administratively allowed to speak to each other can do so.

Another important benefit that digital signatures provide is that of nonrepudiation. Nonrepudiation means that the sender cannot back out of the claim that he or she initiated an authentication exchange. This happens because the digital signature sent during the IKE negotiation is encrypted using the sender's private key. It can be decrypted only using the sender's public key. Because the contents of the signature or the clear-text info (Hash_I or Hash_R) is known to both peers, the peer can say for sure that the sender sent the signature, because it could only have been encrypted using the sender's public key.

The process of using digital certificates starts with each of the IPsec peers sending a request for the CA certificate (containing the CA's public key) to the CA. The CA responds with the certificate. The peer then sends a certificate request encrypted using the CA's public key to the CA. The request contains the peer's public key. The CA sends back a certificate containing information about the peer, such the peer's name, IP address, and the organization it belongs to. The certificate also contains the peer's public key and a signature generated by encrypting the public key and the rest of the information in the certificate using the CA's private key.

When a certificate is offered by a peer to another peer, the receiving party can decrypt the signature using the CA's public key and thus verify that the public key contained in the certificate was actually issued to the sender by the CA.

Figure 13-25 shows the process of using digital certificates.

Figure 13-25 *Using Digital Certificates*

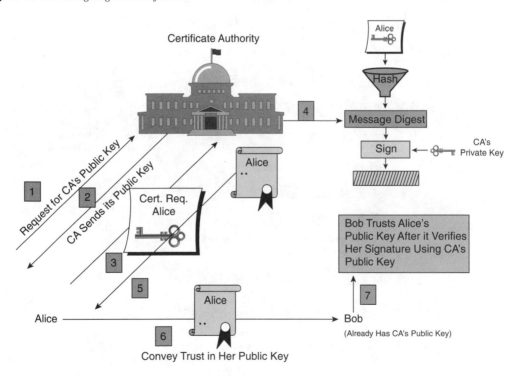

Encrypted Nonces

Another authentication method that can be used in IKE is encrypted nonces. As the name suggests, this method involves encrypting the nonces that are sent during the DH information exchange. Nonces, as you might recall, are pseudo-random numbers exchanged between the peers and used in the generation of the SKEYs. Because encrypting the nonces can protect against some man-in-the-middle attacks that can be staged against the DH algorithm, this is a useful technique to employ. The nonces are encrypted by the initiator using the receiver's public keys. The public keys need to be exchanged between the peers before the IKE negotiation begins. This is necessary because the third and fourth packets of the exchange, which carry the nonces, need to have the nonces encrypted via the peer's public key, and there is no mechanism for certificate exchange before the third message of the exchange. When encrypted nonces are used, the peers also send their IDs encrypted with their respective public keys.

Figure 13-26 shows IKE main mode negotiation using encrypted nonces.

Figure 13-26 *IKE Main Mode Negotiation Using Encrypted Nonces*

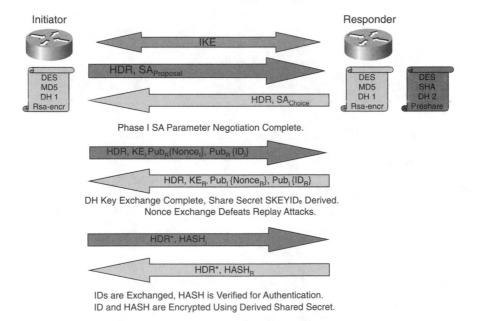

Encryption and Integrity-Checking Mechanisms in IPsec

As soon as the IPsec SAs are established, the next step is to start performing the encryption using DES or 3DES encryption if ESP was set up as the encapsulation mechanism. In addition to encryption, both ESP and AH require that integrity checking hashes be included in the packets. This section discusses how encryption and integrity checking work.

Encryption

Encryption is performed using a symmetric key algorithm known as Data Encryption Standard (DES) or its stronger cousin, Triple DES (3DES). *Symmetric key algorithm* means that a single key is used to encrypt as well as decrypt data. Although the keys for the incoming and outgoing IPsec SAs on a given peer are different, the key used by the sender to encrypt the data and the key used by the receiver to decrypt the data are the same. This key is the one that is established during IKE's quick mode.

DES is used in its Cipher Block Chaining (CBC) mode of operation. Cipher blocking chaining connects a series of cipher blocks to encrypt the clear text. A cipher block is basically the DES encryption algorithm that converts a fixed-length block of clear text into a block of cipher text of the same length using a key that is known to the encryptor as well as the decryptor. Decryption is done applying the same algorithm in reverse using the same key. The fixed length of the clear text is called the *block size*. The block size for DES is 64 bits. The key used is 56 bits in length.

To encrypt a clear-text message that might be longer than the 64-bit block size, the individual algorithm blocks are chained. CBC is the most commonly deployed method of chaining. In CBC mode, each clear-text block is XORed with the encrypted output from the operation done on the previous block of clear text. An initialization vector (IV) is used as the "seed" for providing the input for the first block of data. This ensures that the same information fed into the CBC chain does not repeatedly produce the same output.

Figure 13-27 shows the workings of the DES CBC mode.

The initialization vector for any given packet is different from the initialization vector used for any other packet. The IV is a random sequence of bits. It is sent to the receiver of the encrypted packet in the packet's ESP header. The IV is encrypted to further protect the data's confidentiality. Because it is only 64 bits in length, it can be encrypted using a single cipher block, allowing it to be decrypted on the packet's receipt and then used in the chaining to decrypt the rest of the packet.

3DES encryption is done by chaining the CBC blocks, as shown in Figure 13-28. 3DES encryption is achieved by first encrypting a 64-bit block of data using a 56-bit key and a CBC DES block. The encrypted data is then decrypted using a different 56-bit key. The result is then encrypted using another 56-bit key. The resultant total key length is 56 * 3 = 168 bits.

Figure 13-27 *DES CBC Mode*

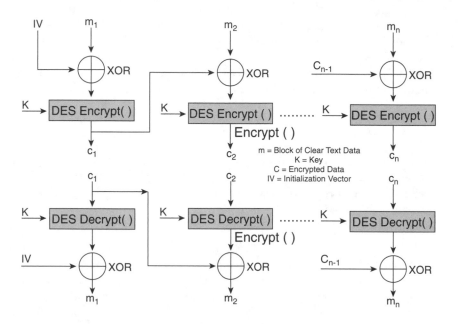

Figure 13-28 *3DES Encryption*

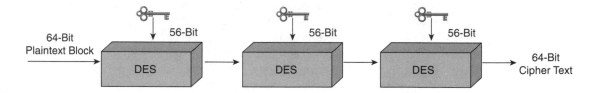

Integrity Checking

The integrity checking in ESP and AH is done using HMAC (Message Authentication Codes using Hashing), a mechanism for message authentication using cryptographic hash functions. HMAC can be used with any iterative cryptographic hash function in combination with a shared secret key. IPsec uses the MD5 or SHA-1 hashing algorithm. Hashing (as opposed to encryption) is a nonreversible function, meaning that as soon as a hash has been created from clear text, it is impossible or extremely difficult to retrieve the clear text from the cipher text. The hashes in ESP and AH work by calculating a hash on the packet whose integrity is to be ensured and attaching this hash to the end of the packet. When the receiver gets the packet, it again calculates the hash on the packet and finds out if the hash it received and the one it calculated, match. If they do, the data was not tampered with in transit.

Figure 13-29 shows integrity checking using hashes.

Figure 13-29 *Integrity Checking Using Hashes*

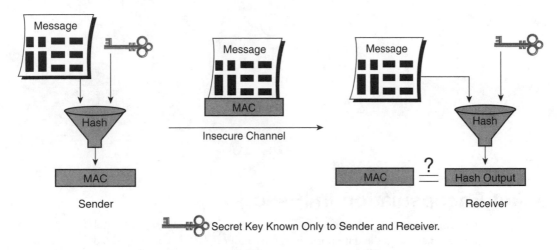

Integrity checking is done on the entire original packet in ESP, including the ESP header. In AH, not only the original packet and the AH header are included in the integrity check, but the new IP header attached to the packet is included as well. Although this can be useful against some types of attacks involving modification of packet headers in transit, it can be very troublesome in environments where NAT occurs on the packets. Because NAT modifies the IP header, AH considers the integrity checking to have failed for that reason. ESP does not have this problem, because its integrity check does not include the new IP header.

MD5 provides 128 bits of output, and SH provides 160 bits of output. However, both of these outputs are concatenated at the 96th bit, and only the first 96 bits are included as the integrity hash in the packets being sent. SHA, although computationally slower than MD5, is considered the stronger of the two hashes.

Figure 13-30 shows how hashes are used in ESP and AH for integrity checking.

The next section contains more details on how ESP and AH encapsulation occur in IPsec.

Figure 13-30 *Use of Hashes in ESP and AH*

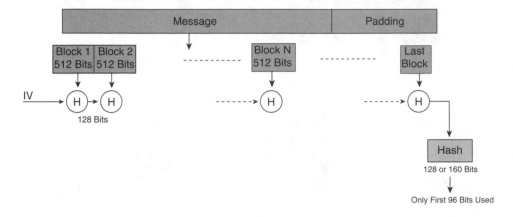

Packet Encapsulation in IPsec

Packet encapsulation is handled by ESP or AH or both for an IPsec tunnel. Encapsulation includes encrypting the data portion of the header if ESP is being used, adding the appropriate header to provide the IPsec peer with information on how to decrypt the data (for ESP), and generating hashes to be used by the peer for verifying that the data (and the IP header in the case of AH) was not tampered with in transit.

Encapsulation can occur in two main ways:

- Transport mode
- Tunnel mode

Transport Mode

In transport mode, the original IP header of the packet that is being encrypted is used to transport the packet. An additional header for ESP or AH (or both) is inserted between the packet's IP header and its IP payload. This mode of operation requires that the original IP header contain addresses that can be routed over the public network.

Tunnel Mode

In tunnel mode, the original IP header is not used to transport the packet. Instead, a new IP header is tagged in front of the ESP or AH (or both) header. This IP header contains the IP addresses of the two IPsec peers as the source and destination IP addresses rather than the IP addresses of the originating host and the destination host. This mode allows end hosts with RFC 1918 IP addressing to participate in a virtual private network set up across the Internet, because the IP addresses of the IPsec gateways are used to transport and route the packets rather than the IP addresses of the end hosts. Tunnel mode is by far the most widely used mode in IPsec deployments.

Figure 13-31 shows the format of the packet that is created using tunnel and transport modes using AH.

Figure 13-31 *Packet Format Using AH in Tunnel and Transport Modes*

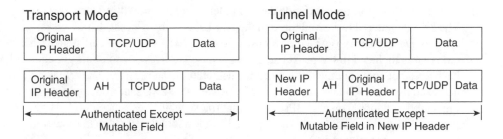

Figure 13-32 shows the format of the packet that is created using tunnel and transport modes using ESP.

Figure 13-32 *Packet Format Using ESP in Tunnel and Transport Modes*

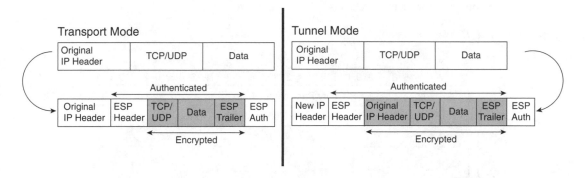

Note the difference in the amount of the packet that AH and ESP provide authentication or integrity checking for. Although ESP provides integrity checking for all of the packet expect the IP header, AH provides integrity checking for the IP header as well. This means that, for example, if the IP header is modified during transit due to NAT, the hash checking fails at the receiving IPsec peer. This can be a source of problems in environments that do static NAT translation in the path of the IPsec tunnel.

Also note that AH and ESP can be used together as well. In that case, the AH header is tagged on, and the associated processing is done first, followed by the ESP processing. Obviously, the order is reversed at the receiving IPsec peer.

ESP (Encapsulating Security Payload)

Encapsulating Security Payload (ESP) is the protocol that defines how the IPsec protocol encapsulates the original IP packet and how it provides encryption and authentication for the data therein. ESP also protects against anti-replay attacks.

ESP uses DES or 3DES to provide data confidentiality by encrypting the packet's contents. The keying material is derived through the IKE negotiation process discussed earlier in this chapter. Data integrity is provided by using MD5 or SHA hashes to calculate hashes on the data that is included in the packet such that in case the packet's contents are changed, the hash does not come out the same when recalculated by the receiver. The replay detection is achieved by using sequence numbers in the packets that ESP sends out and then implementing a sliding window on each IPsec peer that tracks which sequence numbers have been received. The RFC recommends a 32-packet window, but the PIX and the router implement a 32- and 64-packet window, respectively.

ESP is classified as IP protocol 50, and its format is defined in RFC 2406.

Figure 13-33 shows the format of the ESP header. Most of this header is sent in the clear to the IPsec peer because it contains information needed to decrypt the packet for the peer. However, a portion of the header containing the initialization vector is sent encrypted to the remote peer for security reasons.

Figure 13-33 *ESP Header Format*

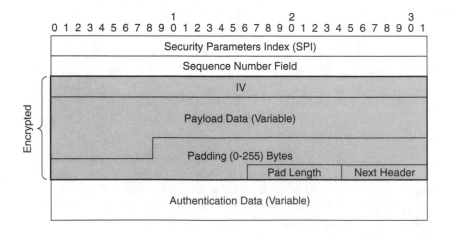

AH (Authentication Header)

AH is the protocol used within the IPsec suite that authenticates the data as well as the IP header. It is a form of encapsulation not used very often in IPsec deployments. AH provides no mechanisms for encrypting the data. All it provides is a hash that allows a check to be made on the data and the packet's IP header to ensure that the data was not tampered with in transit. Checking the IP header for integrity sets AH apart from ESP, which checks only the packet's data portion, not its IP header. However, as discussed earlier, this property of AH can cause problems in a NAT environment. AH, like ESP, also allows for anti-replay protection by using sequence numbers and sliding windows to keep track of packets received and packets that are yet to be sent. Replay detection works with each IPsec peer by keeping track of the sequence numbers of the packets it has received and advancing a window as it receives newer sequence numbers. It drops any packets that arrive outside this window or that are repeated.

AH is classified as IP protocol 51 and is defined in RFC 2402.

Figure 13-34 shows the format of the AH header.

Figure 13-34 *AH Header Format*

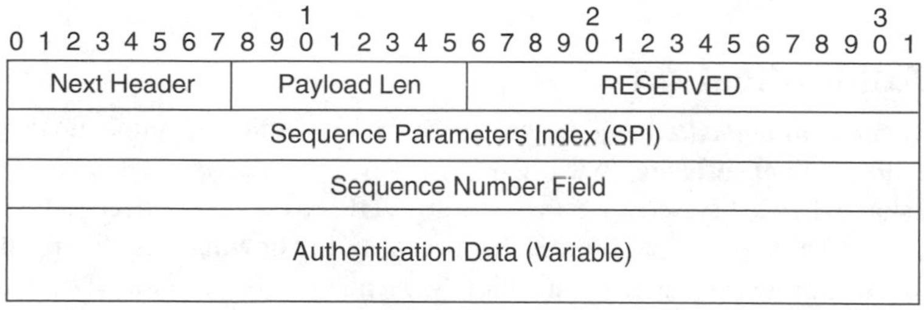

Next Header	Payload Len	RESERVED
Sequence Parameters Index (SPI)		
Sequence Number Field		
Authentication Data (Variable)		

IKE Enhancements for Remote-Access Client IPsec

Remote Access IPsec provided through VPN clients connecting to IPsec gateways is a very important IPsec scenario. However, remote-access clients provide some particularly difficult challenges for IKE. We will list these challenges first and then talk about how IKE has been extended to meet these challenges:

- IPsec clients use unknown-to-gateway IP addresses to connect to the gateway, making it impossible to define unique address-based preshared keys. These are the IP addresses that have been assigned to these clients by their ISPs.

- For the IPsec clients to be treated as part of the private network to which they are connected, they must enter the private network with known IP addresses and not the IP addresses assigned to them by the ISP.

- The IPsec clients must use the DNS server, DHCP server, and other such servers provided on the private network as the primary sources of information rather than use the ISP's server, which does not have information regarding the internal resources.

- IPsec clients often connect from behind Port Address Translation (PAT) devices (such as DSL or cable routers doing PAT). Because ESP encrypts all the port information in the TCP or UDP header, PAT can no longer function as normal.

These four challenges have resulted in some extensions being implemented in the IKE protocol that allow the IPsec client implementations to overcome these challenges and provide maximum benefit to the users while ensuring security.

NOTE   Currently, most of these techniques are still in the Internet draft stage at IETF and have not been converted into full-fledged RFCs.

Next we will discuss the four most important features that have been added to IKE to get around the issues just outlined.

Extended Authentication

Extended authentication allows the user of the IPsec client to authenticate itself, rather than the IPsec client software, to the IPsec gateway. This allows what is known as a *wildcard* preshared key to be used for authenticating all IPsec clients connecting to the IPsec gateway using the same preshared secret. The insecurity in allowing this to happen is overcome by doing one more stage of authentication—extended authentication. Extended authentication is done on a per-user basis, generally by the IPsec gateway in collaboration with a TACACS+ or RADIUS server.

Extended authentication (also called x-auth) occurs after IKE's phase 1 (the authentication phase) has been completed. This is why it is also said to occur in phase 1.5 of IKE.

Figure 13-35 shows the placement of x-auth and mode config in IKE negotiation.

X-auth takes place with the gateway sending the client an *attributes payload*. The attributes payload contains zero-length attributes for the attributes that the gateway wants the client to provide. An example is username(), password(). On receiving this message, the client either responds with a fail if it does not know how to provide these, which fails the negotiation, or responds by putting values into the attribute payload. An example is username(john), password(D04). After receiving the attributes, the gateway checks the credentials' validity and notifies the client of the success or failure. The client responds with an attributes payload of type config_ack. Quick mode is started at this point if the authentication was successful.

Figure 13-35 *Placement of X-Auth and Mode Config in IKE Negotiation*

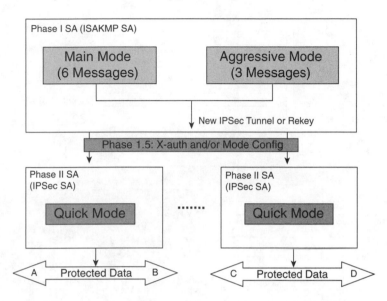

Figure 13-36 shows the negotiation of x-auth during IKE negotiation. Figures 13-37 and 13-38 show how attribute request and reply payloads are exchanged between the peers to complete x-auth.

Figure 13-36 *Negotiation of X-Auth During IKE Negotiation*

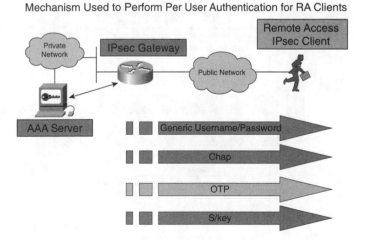

Figure 13-37 *Start of Extended Authentication with the Exchange of Attribute Payloads Using ISAKMP Messages*

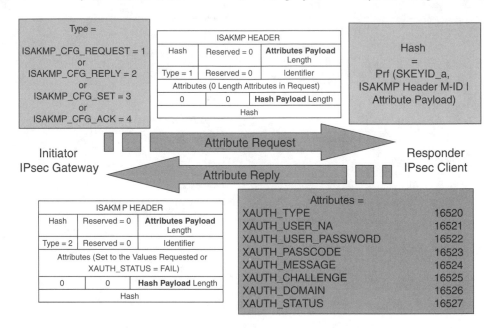

Figure 13-38 *Completion of Extended Authentication with the Exchange of Attribute Payloads Using ISAKMP Messages*

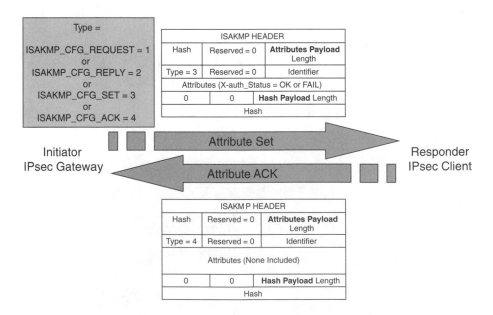

Mode Configuration

Mode configuration is a method employed to take care of the second and third challenges listed at the start of this section. It allows an IP address to be assigned to the client as well as DNS and other server IP addresses to be pushed to the client.

The IP address pushed to the client is called the *Internal IP address*. When this feature is not turned on, the IP header of the packet that is encrypted and encapsulated in the ESP payload contains the same source IP address as the outside IP header: the address assigned to the client by the ISP. However, with this feature turned on, the source address in the encapsulated packet is changed to this Internal IP address in all packets that are sent using ESP. This way, when the gateway decapsulates and decrypts the ESP packet, the packet that comes out has a predictable Internal IP address assigned to it.

In addition to the internal IP address, mode configuration pushes the other parameters, such as the DNS server IP address, the DHCP server IP address, and the NetBIOS name server IP address, to the client as well. The client installs these servers as its primary DNS and also installs other types of servers. This allows the client to resolve the names of the machines on the private network, among other things.

Mode config works using the same type of payload that x-auth uses. It occurs after x-auth has occurred, still in phase 1.5. However, unlike x-auth, in this case it is the client that requests the attributes from the gateway. (In some older versions of IOS, this was not necessarily the case, meaning that the client did not ask for the attributes but simply waited for them to be pushed.) The client may ask for whatever attributes it wants, and the gateway can reply with whatever attributes it deems appropriate to push and ignore others. In addition, the gateway can also push attributes the client didn't request.

Figure 13-39 shows the negotiation of mode configuration during IKE negotiation. Figure 13-40 shows the packet format of the attributes payload exchanged between the two peers for completing mode config.

NAT Transparency

NAT transparency is a mechanism introduced in IPsec to get around the problem of the encryption of TCP/UDP ports in ESP from stopping PAT from occurring. This problem is overcome by encapsulating the ESP packet in a UDP header with the necessary port information in it to allow the PAT to work correctly. Upon receiving these packets, the gateway strips the UDP header and processes the rest of the packet normally. IKE negotiation, which occurs using UDP port 500, does not have this problem; only ESP has this issue.

Figure 13-41 shows the tagging of a UDP header on top of the original ESP header.

Figure 13-39 *Negotiation of Mode Configuration During IKE Negotiation*

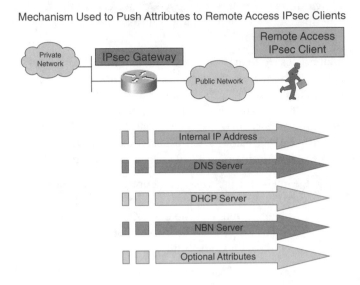

Figure 13-40 *Mode Config Is Completed by Exchanging Attribute Payloads Between the Gateway and the IPsec Client*

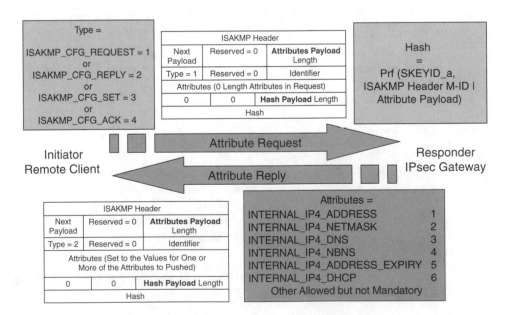

Figure 13-41 *Tagging on a UDP Header to Traverse PAT*

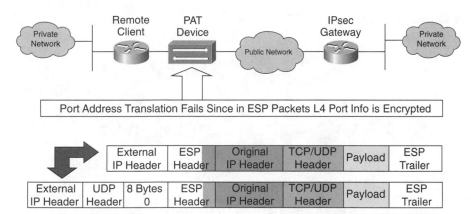

The UDP header is created based on a port number that is pushed from the gateway to the client upon being requested in the mode config request by the client. Currently, the PAT "detection" must be done by the person who is using the IPsec client. In other words, the person has to configure the client to let it know that it needs to ask the gateway for UDP header information. Various Internet drafts currently under consideration at IETF allow for automatic detection of PAT in the IPsec path using methods that depend on the same lines of reasoning due to which AH breaks in the presence of NAT—meaning using a hash to see if the packet's IP header gets modified in transit.

Current implementations of IOS and PIX IPsec do not support PAT traversal. However, support for this feature is expected soon.

IPsec Dead Peer Discovery Mechanism

IPsec provides a mechanism for a peer to send a delete notification payload via IKE to its peers when it is disconnecting an IPsec SA. However, in many cases this notification payload never gets sent, either because the peer gets disconnected too abruptly (a system crash) or due to network issues (someone pulls a laptop's Ethernet cable). In these cases, it is important to have a dead peer discovery mechanism that can allow for the discovery of such peers so that data loss does not occur when a peer sends packets to a peer that is no longer alive. (In effect, an IPsec peer can keep sending traffic to a dead peer for extended periods of time.) This mechanism is implemented using a technique called Dead Peer Discovery (DPD).

DPD works through the use of a notify payload, which is sent to the peer before new data is about to be sent after a period of inactivity longer than a configured "worry metric" has elapsed. Passage of IPsec traffic is considered proof of liveness. If it is alive, the peer acknowledges the notify payload by sending back one of it own.

Figure 13-42 shows the basic elements of the DPD protocol.

Figure 13-42 *Basic Functionality of the DPD Protocol*

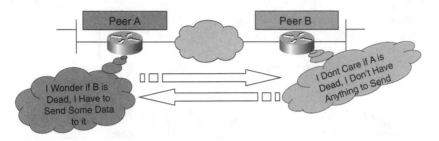

Figure 13-43 shows how the DPD protocol is used to gather information regarding a peer's liveness.

Figure 13-43 *DPD Protocol Operation*

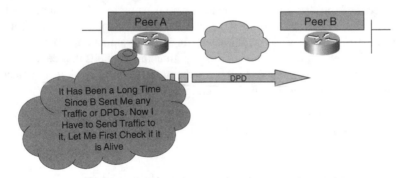

For this mechanism to work, a vendor ID payload must be exchanged in the IKE main mode exchange, signifying that the two hosts support this type of mechanism. The worry metric is defined locally. This type of need-only-based mechanism greatly reduces the load on the peer by *not* using periodic keepalives which might or might not be needed. Also, the DPD mechanism allows the sending of R-U-THERE messages when a gateway wants to clean up its resources after a while and wants to know if some of the idle clients are still alive.

Figure 13-44 shows how the DPD notifications just discussed are exchanged.

Figure 13-44 *Exchange of DPD Notifications*

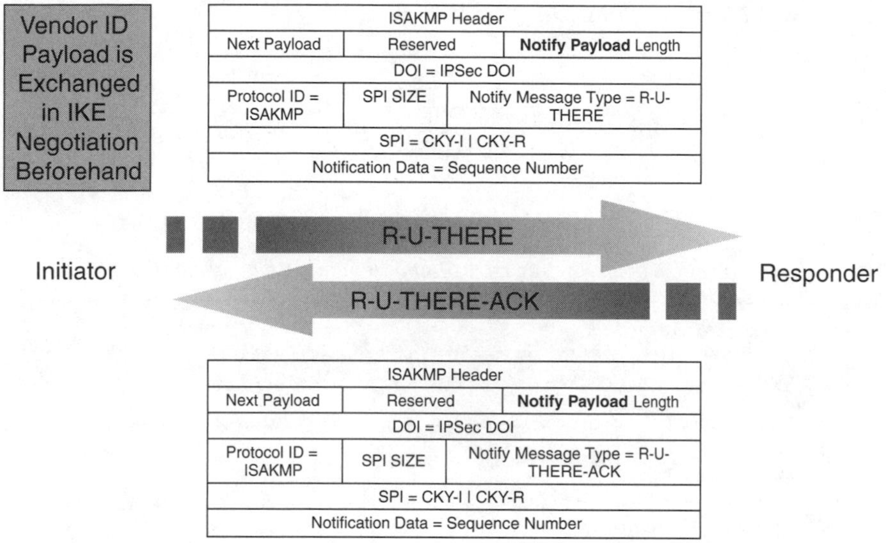

Case Studies

This section discusses a number of case studies showing the implementation of the concepts discussed in this chapter. Configurations, debugs, and **show** command output are included to help you understand the contents better.

It would be very educational for you to compare the debug output with the earlier step-by-step explanation of IKE to try to understand where each IKE negotiation step takes place.

Router-to-Router IPsec Using Preshared Keys as the Authentication Mechanism

This is the most basic and common type of IPsec VPN. This VPN falls under the category of LAN-to-LAN VPNs. The authentication method used here is preshared keys. The following case studies have examples of more-secure authentication methods.

We will use this case study to do a detailed analysis of a basic configuration. Then, based on this analysis, we will talk about add-ons and changes in the rest of the case studies.

Examples 13-1 and 13-2 show configurations of routers acting as initiators and responders of IPsec negotiations respectively. Examples 13-3 and 13-4 show the **debug** output for these two routers. Examples 13-5 and 13-6 are used to discuss the output of the **show** commands for these two routers.

Figure 13-45 shows the network diagram for this case study.

Figure 13-45 *Network Diagram for This Case Study*

Example 13-1 *Configuration of the Router Acting as the Initiator of the IPsec Negotiation*

```
hostname Initiator
!The ISAKMP policy defines the attributes which will be negotiated with peers for
!the IKE SA.
crypto isakmp policy 1
!The encryption method defined below is used for encrypting the IKE negotiation
!packets using SKEYID_e
 encr 3des
!The hash algorithm defined below is used to generate the hashes which are used for
!IKE authetnication purposes.
 hash sha
!The line below defines the authentication method as pre-shared key authentication
 authentication pre-share
!
!
!The line below defines the pre-shared key for the peer at the IP address
!172.16.172.20. Please note that the initiator will search through its config for
!this key using the source IP address of the IKE negotiation packets it is receiving.
crypto isakmp key jw4ep9846804ijl address 172.16.172.20
!The following line defines the transform set for use with IPsec. This transform set
!specifies the name of the transform set as 'myset'. The encapsulation method defined
!is ESP and the encryption algorithm to use is 3DES (triple DES). The last part of
!this command specifies MD5 as the ESP integrity checking hash.
crypto ipsec transform-set myset esp-3des esp-md5-hmac
!
!
!The following configuration is for the crypto map named 'vpn'. Crypto maps
!essentially bind the entire IPsec configuration together. Various elements of IPsec
!defined in various places in the configuration are tied together using the crypto
!map. 10 is the instance number for the map here. Instance numbers are used to
!specify the order in which multiple crypto maps are parsed in a config. The key
!word 'ipsec-isakmp' is used to specify that this particular crypto map is to be
!used for IPsec rather than CET.
crypto map vpn 10 ipsec-isakmp
!The command line below defines the IP address of the IPsec peer.
 set peer 172.16.172.20
!The line below defines the transform set to use for this crypto map.
 set transform-set myset
!The line below specifies the access list which will be define traffic which will
!either trigger IKE negotiation or be used to verify that the proxy Ids being offered
!during an IKE negotiation are valid.
 match address 101
```

Example 13-1 *Configuration of the Router Acting as the Initiator of the IPsec Negotiation (Continued)*

```
!
!
interface Ethernet0/0
 ip address 10.1.1.1 255.255.255.0
!

interface Ethernet1/0
 ip address 172.16.172.10 255.255.255.0
!The line below is used as a toggle switch to turn on IPsec functionality as defined
!by the crypto map vpn.
 crypto map vpn
!
!
!The access list define below is used to specify interesting traffic for IPsec.
access-list 101 permit ip 10.1.1.0 0.0.0.255 10.1.2.0 0.0.0.255
!
```

Example 13-2 *Configuration of the Router Acting as the Responder of the IPsec Negotiation*

```
hostname Responder

crypto isakmp policy 1
 encr 3des
 hash sha
 authentication pre-share
crypto isakmp key jw4ep9846804ijl address 172.16.172.10
!
crypto ipsec transform-set myset esp-3des esp-md5-hmac
!
crypto map vpn 10 ipsec-isakmp
 set peer 172.16.172.10
 set transform-set myset
 match address 101

interface Ethernet0/0
 ip address 10.1.2.1 255.255.255.0
!

interface Ethernet1/0
 ip address 172.16.172.20 255.255.255.0
 crypto map vpn
!
access-list 101 permit ip 10.1.2.0 0.0.0.255 10.1.1.0 0.0.0.255
```

NOTE   In Example 13-3, the explanation of the debug is followed by the actual debugs for that explanation.

Example 13-3 *Debugs of the Router Acting as the Initiator of the IPsec Negotiation*

```
Initiator#show debug
Cryptographic Subsystem:
  Crypto ISAKMP debugging is on
  Crypto Engine debugging is on
  Crypto IPSEC debugging is on

A#ping
Protocol [ip]:
Target IP address: 10.1.2.1
Repeat count [5]:
Datagram size [100]:
Timeout in seconds [2]:
Extended commands [n]: y
Source address or interface: 10.1.1.1
Type of service [0]:
Set DF bit in IP header? [no]:
Validate reply data? [no]:
Data pattern [0xABCD]:
Loose, Strict, Record, Timestamp, Verbose[none]:
Sweep range of sizes [n]:
Type escape sequence to abort.
Sending 5, 100-byte ICMP Echos to 10.1.2.1, timeout is 2 seconds:

!The ping source and destination addresses matched the match address access list
!for the crypto map VPN. 'local' is the local tunnel endpoint, and 'remote' is the
!remote crypto endpoint as configured in the map. src proxy is the src interesting
!traffic as defined by the match address access list. dst proxy is the destination
!interesting traffic as defined by the match address access list.

00:04:10: IPSEC(sa_request): ,
  (key eng. msg.) OUTBOUND local= 172.16.172.10, remote= 172.16.172.20,
    local_proxy= 10.1.1.0/255.255.255.0/0/0 (type=4),
    remote_proxy= 10.1.2.0/255.255.255.0/0/0 (type=4),

!The protocol and the transforms are specified by the crypto map that has been
!hit, as are the lifetimes

    protocol= ESP, transform= esp-3des esp-md5-hmac ,
    lifedur= 3600s and 4608000kb,
    spi= 0x8EAB0B22(2393574178), conn_id= 0, keysize= 0, flags= 0x400C

!Begins main mode exchange. The first two packets negotiate phase I SA parameters.
00:04:10: ISAKMP: received ke message (1/1)
00:04:10: ISAKMP: local port 500, remote port 500
00:04:10: ISAKMP (0:1): Input = IKE_MESG_FROM_IPSEC, IKE_SA_REQ_MM
```

Example 13-3 *Debugs of the Router Acting as the Initiator of the IPsec Negotiation (Continued)*

```
!MM stands for main mode, and QM stands for quick mode. The IKE debugs show which
!stage of IKE the negotiation is in, such as MM1. As you saw in the discussion of
!IKE, main mode is divided into six portions or messages, and quick mode into
!three.
Old State = IKE_READY  New State = IKE_I_MM1

00:04:10: ISAKMP (0:1): beginning Main Mode exchange
00:04:10: ISAKMP (0:1): sending packet to 172.16.172.20 (I) MM_NO_STATE
00:04:10: ISAKMP (0:1): received packet from 172.16.172.20 (I) MM_NO_STATE
00:04:10: ISAKMP (0:1): Input = IKE_MESG_FROM_PEER, IKE_MM_EXCH
Old State = IKE_I_MM1  New State = IKE_I_MM2

00:04:10: ISAKMP (0:1): processing SA payload. message ID = 0

!The preshared key is searched for and found based on the source IP address of IKE
!negotiation packets.

00:04:10: ISAKMP (0:1): found peer pre-shared key matching 172.16.172.20
00:04:10: ISAKMP (0:1): Checking ISAKMP transform 1 against priority 1 policy

!These are the parameters offered by the other side. Policy 1 is the policy set up
!on this router.

00:04:10: ISAKMP:        encryption 3DES-CBC
00:04:10: ISAKMP:        hash SHA
00:04:10: ISAKMP:        default group 1
00:04:10: ISAKMP:        auth pre-share
00:04:10: ISAKMP:        life type in seconds
00:04:10: ISAKMP:        life duration (VPI) of  0x0 0x1 0x51 0x80

!The policy 1 on this router and the attributes offered by the other side matched.

00:04:10: ISAKMP (0:1): atts are acceptable. Next payload is 0
00:04:10: ISAKMP (0:1): Input = IKE_MESG_INTERNAL, IKE_PROCESS_MAIN_MODE
Old State = IKE_I_MM2  New State = IKE_I_MM2

!The third and fourth packets complete Diffie-Hellman exchange.

00:04:10: ISAKMP (0:1): sending packet to 172.16.172.20 (I) MM_SA_SETUP
00:04:10: ISAKMP (0:1): Input = IKE_MESG_INTERNAL, IKE_PROCESS_COMPLETE
Old State = IKE_I_MM2  New State = IKE_I_MM3
00:04:10: ISAKMP (0:1): received packet from 172.16.172.20 (I) MM_SA_SETUP
00:04:10: ISAKMP (0:1): Input = IKE_MESG_FROM_PEER, IKE_MM_EXCH
Old State = IKE_I_MM3  New State = IKE_I_MM4
00:04:10: ISAKMP (0:1): processing KE payload. message ID = 0
00:04:10: ISAKMP (0:1): processing NONCE payload. message ID = 0
00:04:10: ISAKMP (0:1): found peer pre-shared key matching 172.16.172.20
00:04:10: ISAKMP (0:1): SKEYID state generated
00:04:10: ISAKMP (0:1): processing vendor id payload
```

continues

Example 13-3 *Debugs of the Router Acting as the Initiator of the IPsec Negotiation (Continued)*

```
!Note below that some vendor ID payloads are being exchanged. These are necessary
!to gauge the peer's ability to do the things described in the vendor payload. For
!example, below, VID payloads for Unity Protocol Support (a new protocol
!introduced by Cisco for its newer version of VPN clients) and dead peer discovery
!are received.
00:04:10: ISAKMP (0:1): vendor ID is Unity
00:04:10: ISAKMP (0:1): processing vendor id payload
00:04:10: ISAKMP (0:1): vendor ID is DPD
00:04:10: ISAKMP (0:1): processing vendor id payload
00:04:10: ISAKMP (0:1): speaking to another IOS box!
00:04:10: ISAKMP (0:1): processing vendor id payload
00:04:10: ISAKMP (0:1): Input = IKE_MESG_INTERNAL, IKE_PROCESS_MAIN_MODE
Old State = IKE_I_MM4  New State = IKE_I_MM4


!The fifth and sixth packets complete IKE authentication. Phase I SA is
!established.

00:04:10: ISAKMP (0:1): SA is doing pre-shared key authentication using id type
ID_IPV4_ADDR
00:04:10: ISAKMP (1): ID payload
        next-payload : 8
        type         : 1
        protocol     : 17
        port         : 500
        length       : 8
00:04:10: ISAKMP (1): Total payload length: 12
00:04:10: ISAKMP (0:1): sending packet to 172.16.172.20 (I) MM_KEY_EXCH
00:04:10: ISAKMP (0:1): Input = IKE_MESG_INTERNAL, IKE_PROCESS_COMPLETE
Old State = IKE_I_MM4  New State = IKE_I_MM5

00:04:10: ISAKMP (0:1): received packet from 172.16.172.20 (I) MM_KEY_EXCH
00:04:10: ISAKMP (0:1): Input = IKE_MESG_FROM_PEER, IKE_MM_EXCH
Old State = IKE_I_MM5  New State = IKE_I_MM6

00:04:10: ISAKMP (0:1): processing ID payload. message ID = 0
00:04:10: ISAKMP (0:1): processing HASH payload. message ID = 0
00:04:10: ISAKMP (0:1): SA has been authenticated with 172.16.172.20
00:04:10: ISAKMP (0:1): Input = IKE_MESG_INTERNAL, IKE_PROCESS_MAIN_MODE
Old State = IKE_I_MM6  New State = IKE_I_MM6

00:04:10: ISAKMP (0:1): Input = IKE_MESG_INTERNAL, IKE_PROCESS_COMPLETE
Old State = IKE_I_MM6  New State = IKE_P1_COMPLETE

!Begin quick mode exchange. IPsec SA will be negotiated in quick mode.

00:04:10: ISAKMP (0:1): beginning Quick Mode exchange, M-ID of 965273472
00:04:10: ISAKMP (0:1): sending packet to 172.16.172.20 (I) QM_IDLE
00:04:10: ISAKMP (0:1): Node 965273472, Input = IKE_MESG_INTERNAL, IKE_INIT_QM
Old State = IKE_QM_READY  New State = IKE_QM_I_QM1

00:04:10: ISAKMP (0:1): Input = IKE_MESG_INTERNAL, IKE_PHASE1_COMPLETE
```

Example 13-3 *Debugs of the Router Acting as the Initiator of the IPsec Negotiation (Continued)*

```
Old State = IKE_P1_COMPLETE  New State = IKE_P1_COMPLETE

00:04:10: ISAKMP (0:1): received packet from 172.16.172.20 (I) QM_IDLE

!The IPsec SA proposal offered by the far end is checked against the local crypto
!map configuration


00:04:10: ISAKMP (0:1): processing HASH payload. message ID = 965273472
00:04:10: ISAKMP (0:1): processing SA payload. message ID = 965273472
00:04:10: ISAKMP (0:1): Checking IPsec proposal 1
00:04:10: ISAKMP: transform 1, ESP_3DES
00:04:10: ISAKMP:    attributes in transform:
00:04:10: ISAKMP:        encaps is 1
00:04:10: ISAKMP:        SA life type in seconds
00:04:10: ISAKMP:        SA life duration (basic) of 3600
00:04:10: ISAKMP:        SA life type in kilobytes
00:04:10: ISAKMP:        SA life duration (VPI) of  0x0 0x46 0x50 0x0
00:04:10: ISAKMP:        authenticator is HMAC-MD5

!The proposal 1 and transform 1 offered by the other end are found to be
!acceptable.

00:04:10: ISAKMP (0:1): atts are acceptable.
00:04:10: IPSEC(validate_proposal_request): proposal part #1,
  (key eng. msg.) INBOUND local= 172.16.172.10, remote= 172.16.172.20,
    local_proxy= 10.1.1.0/255.255.255.0/0/0 (type=4),
    remote_proxy= 10.1.2.0/255.255.255.0/0/0 (type=4),
    protocol= ESP, transform= esp-3des esp-md5-hmac ,
    lifedur= 0s and 0kb,
    spi= 0x0(0), conn_id= 0, keysize= 0, flags= 0x4
00:04:10: ISAKMP (0:1): processing NONCE payload. message ID = 965273472
00:04:10: ISAKMP (0:1): processing ID payload. message ID = 965273472
00:04:10: ISAKMP (0:1): processing ID payload. message ID = 965273472

!Two IPsec SAs have been negotiated--an incoming SA with the SPI generated by the
!local machine, and an outbound SA with the SPIs proposed by the remote end.


00:04:10: ISAKMP (0:1): Creating IPsec SAs
00:04:10:         inbound SA from 172.16.172.20 to 172.16.172.10
        (proxy 10.1.2.0 to 10.1.1.0)
00:04:10:         has spi 0x8EAB0B22 and conn_id 2029 and flags 4
00:04:10:         lifetime of 3600 seconds
00:04:10:         lifetime of 4608000 kilobytes
00:04:10:         outbound SA from 172.16.172.10   to 172.16.172.20
        (proxy 10.1.1.0       to 10.1.2.0      )
00:04:10:         has spi -343614331 and conn_id 2030 and flags C
00:04:10:         lifetime of 3600 seconds
00:04:10:         lifetime of 4608000 kilobytes
```

continues

Example 13-3 *Debugs of the Router Acting as the Initiator of the IPsec Negotiation (Continued)*

```
!The IPsec SA info negotiated by IKE is populated into the router's SADB.


00:04:10: IPSEC(key_engine): got a queue event...
00:04:10: IPSEC(initialize_sas): ,
  (key eng. msg.) INBOUND local= 172.16.172.10, remote= 172.16.172.20,
    local_proxy= 10.1.1.0/255.255.255.0/0/0 (type=4),
    remote_proxy= 10.1.2.0/255.255.255.0/0/0 (type=4),
    protocol= ESP, transform= esp-3des esp-md5-hmac ,
    lifedur= 3600s and 4608000kb,
    spi= 0x8EAB0B22(2393574178), conn_id= 2029, keysize= 0, flags= 0x4
00:04:10: IPSEC(initialize_sas): ,
  (key eng. msg.) OUTBOUND local= 172.16.172.10, remote= 172.16.172.20,
    local_proxy= 10.1.1.0/255.255.255.0/0/0 (type=4),
    remote_proxy= 10.1.2.0/255.255.255.0/0/0 (type=4),
    protocol= ESP, transform= esp-3des esp-md5-hmac ,
    lifedur= 3600s and 4608000kb,
    spi= 0xEB84DC85(3951352965), conn_id= 2030, keysize= 0, flags= 0xC

!IPsec SA created in SADB, sent out last packet with commit bit set. IPsec tunnel
!established.



00:04:10: IPSEC(create_sa): sa created,
  (sa) sa_dest= 172.16.172.10, sa_prot= 50,
    sa_spi= 0x8EAB0B22(2393574178),
    sa_trans= esp-3des esp-md5-hmac , sa_conn_id= 2029
00:04:10: IPSEC(create_sa): sa created,
  (sa) sa_dest= 172.16.172.20, sa_prot= 50,
    sa_spi= 0xEB84DC85(3951352965),
    sa_trans= esp-3des esp-md5-hmac , sa_conn_id= 2030
00:04:10: ISAKMP (0:1): sending packet to 172.16.172.20 (I) QM_IDLE
00:04:10: ISAKMP (0:1): deleting node 965273472 error FALSE reason ""
00:04:10: ISAKMP (0:1): Node 965273472, Input = IKE_MESG_FROM_PEER, IKE_QM_EXCH
Old State = IKE_QM_I_QM1  New State = IKE_QM_PHASE2_COMPLETE
```

Example 13-4 *Output of **show** Commands on the Router Acting as the Initiator of the IPsec Negotiation*

```
!The command below shows the state of the crypto ISAKMP SA. It is shown here in
!QM IDLE, meaning that quick mode has completed successfully.
Initiator#show crypto isakmp sa
dst              src              state         conn-id    slot
172.16.172.20    172.16.172.10    QM_IDLE             1      0

!The command below gives details on both the incoming and outgoing IPsec SAs. It
!gives information on the attributes negotiated during the exchange as well as
!statistics for how many packets have been exchanged via each of these SAs.
Initiator#show crypto ipsec sa
```

Example 13-4 *Output of* **show** *Commands on the Router Acting as the Initiator of the IPsec Negotiation (Continued)*

```
interface: Ethernet1/0
    Crypto map tag: vpn, local addr. 172.16.172.10

   local  ident (addr/mask/prot/port): (10.1.1.0/255.255.255.0/0/0)
   remote ident (addr/mask/prot/port): (10.1.2.0/255.255.255.0/0/0)
   current_peer: 172.16.172.20
    PERMIT, flags={origin_is_acl,}
    #pkts encaps: 4, #pkts encrypt: 4, #pkts digest 4
    #pkts decaps: 4, #pkts decrypt: 4, #pkts verify 4
    #pkts compressed: 0, #pkts decompressed: 0
    #pkts not compressed: 0, #pkts compr. failed: 0, #pkts decompress failed: 0
    #send errors 6, #recv errors 0

     local crypto endpt.: 172.16.172.10, remote crypto endpt.: 172.16.172.20
     path mtu 1500, media mtu 1500
     current outbound spi: EB84DC85

     inbound esp sas:
      spi: 0x8EAB0B22(2393574178)
        transform: esp-3des esp-md5-hmac ,
        in use settings ={Tunnel, }
        slot: 0, conn id: 2029, flow_id: 1, crypto map: vpn
        sa timing: remaining key lifetime (k/sec): (4607998/3347)
        IV size: 8 bytes
        replay detection support: Y

     inbound ah sas:

     inbound pcp sas:

     outbound esp sas:
      spi: 0xEB84DC85(3951352965)
        transform: esp-3des esp-md5-hmac ,
        in use settings ={Tunnel, }
        slot: 0, conn id: 2030, flow_id: 2, crypto map: vpn
        sa timing: remaining key lifetime (k/sec): (4607999/3347)
        IV size: 8 bytes
        replay detection support: Y

     outbound ah sas:

     outbound pcp sas:
```

```
!The command below basically prints the configuration of the crypto map on the
!router
```

```
Initiator#show crypto map
Crypto Map "vpn" 10 ipsec-isakmp
        Peer = 172.16.172.20
```

continues

Example 13-4 *Output of* **show** *Commands on the Router Acting as the Initiator of the IPsec Negotiation (Continued)*

```
        Extended IP access list 101
            access-list 101 permit ip 10.1.1.0 0.0.0.255 10.1.2.0 0.0.0.255
        Current peer: 172.16.172.20
        Security association lifetime: 4608000 kilobytes/3600 seconds
        PFS (Y/N): N
        Transform sets={ myset, }
        Interfaces using crypto map vpn:
                Ethernet1/0
```

Example 13-5 *Debugs of the Router Acting as the Responder of the IPsec Negotiation*

```
Responder#show debug
Cryptographic Subsystem:
  Crypto ISAKMP debugging is on
  Crypto Engine debugging is on
  Crypto IPSEC debugging is on

1w1d: ISAKMP (0:0): received packet from 172.16.172.10 (N) NEW SA
1w1d: ISAKMP: local port 500, remote port 500
1w1d: ISAKMP (0:1): Input = IKE_MESG_FROM_PEER, IKE_MM_EXCH
Old State = IKE_READY  New State = IKE_R_MM1

1w1d: ISAKMP (0:1): processing SA payload. message ID = 0
1w1d: ISAKMP (0:1): found peer pre-shared key matching 172.16.172.10
1w1d: ISAKMP (0:1): Checking ISAKMP transform 1 against priority 1 policy
1w1d: ISAKMP:        encryption 3DES-CBC
1w1d: ISAKMP:        hash SHA
1w1d: ISAKMP:        default group 1
1w1d: ISAKMP:        auth pre-share
1w1d: ISAKMP:        life type in seconds
1w1d: ISAKMP:        life duration (VPI) of  0x0 0x1 0x51 0x80
1w1d: ISAKMP (0:1): atts are acceptable. Next payload is 0
1w1d: ISAKMP (0:1): Input = IKE_MESG_INTERNAL, IKE_PROCESS_MAIN_MODE
Old State = IKE_R_MM1  New State = IKE_R_MM1

1w1d: ISAKMP (0:1): sending packet to 172.16.172.10 (R) MM_SA_SETUP
1w1d: ISAKMP (0:1): Input = IKE_MESG_INTERNAL, IKE_PROCESS_COMPLETE
Old State = IKE_R_MM1  New State = IKE_R_MM2

1w1d: ISAKMP (0:1): received packet from 172.16.172.10 (R) MM_SA_SETUP
1w1d: ISAKMP (0:1): Input = IKE_MESG_FROM_PEER, IKE_MM_EXCH
Old State = IKE_R_MM2  New State = IKE_R_MM3

1w1d: ISAKMP (0:1): processing KE payload. message ID = 0
1w1d: ISAKMP (0:1): processing NONCE payload. message ID = 0
1w1d: ISAKMP (0:1): found peer pre-shared key matching 172.16.172.10
1w1d: ISAKMP (0:1): SKEYID state generated
1w1d: ISAKMP (0:1): processing vendor id payload
1w1d: ISAKMP (0:1): vendor ID is Unity
1w1d: ISAKMP (0:1): processing vendor id payload
```

Example 13-5 *Debugs of the Router Acting as the Responder of the IPsec Negotiation (Continued)*

```
1w1d: ISAKMP (0:1): vendor ID is DPD
1w1d: ISAKMP (0:1): processing vendor id payload
1w1d: ISAKMP (0:1): speaking to another IOS box!
1w1d: ISAKMP (0:1): processing vendor id payload
1w1d: ISAKMP (0:1): Input = IKE_MESG_INTERNAL, IKE_PROCESS_MAIN_MODE
Old State = IKE_R_MM3  New State = IKE_R_MM3

1w1d: ISAKMP (0:1): sending packet to 172.16.172.10 (R) MM_KEY_EXCH
1w1d: ISAKMP (0:1): Input = IKE_MESG_INTERNAL, IKE_PROCESS_COMPLETE
Old State = IKE_R_MM3  New State = IKE_R_MM4

1w1d: ISAKMP (0:1): received packet from 172.16.172.10 (R) MM_KEY_EXCH
1w1d: ISAKMP (0:1): Input = IKE_MESG_FROM_PEER, IKE_MM_EXCH
Old State = IKE_R_MM4  New State = IKE_R_MM5

1w1d: ISAKMP (0:1): processing ID payload. message ID = 0
1w1d: ISAKMP (0:1): processing HASH payload. message ID = 0
1w1d: ISAKMP (0:1): SA has been authenticated with 172.16.172.10
1w1d: ISAKMP (0:1): Input = IKE_MESG_INTERNAL, IKE_PROCESS_MAIN_MODE
Old State = IKE_R_MM5  New State = IKE_R_MM5

1w1d: ISAKMP (0:1): SA is doing pre-shared key authentication using id type ID
  _IPV4_ADDR
1w1d: ISAKMP (1): ID payload
        next-payload : 8
        type         : 1
        protocol     : 17
        port         : 500
        length       : 8
1w1d: ISAKMP (1): Total payload length: 12
1w1d: ISAKMP (0:1): sending packet to 172.16.172.10 (R) QM_IDLE
1w1d: ISAKMP (0:1): Input = IKE_MESG_INTERNAL, IKE_PROCESS_COMPLETE
Old State = IKE_R_MM5  New State = IKE_P1_COMPLETE

1w1d: ISAKMP (0:1): Input = IKE_MESG_INTERNAL, IKE_PHASE1_COMPLETE
Old State = IKE_P1_COMPLETE  New State = IKE_P1_COMPLETE

1w1d: ISAKMP (0:1): received packet from 172.16.172.10 (R) QM_IDLE
1w1d: ISAKMP (0:1): processing HASH payload. message ID = 965273472
1w1d: ISAKMP (0:1): processing SA payload. message ID = 965273472
1w1d: ISAKMP (0:1): Checking IPsec proposal 1
1w1d: ISAKMP: transform 1, ESP_3DES
1w1d: ISAKMP:    attributes in transform:
1w1d: ISAKMP:        encaps is 1
1w1d: ISAKMP:        SA life type in seconds
1w1d: ISAKMP:        SA life duration (basic) of 3600
1w1d: ISAKMP:        SA life type in kilobytes
1w1d: ISAKMP:        SA life duration (VPI) of  0x0 0x46 0x50 0x0
1w1d: ISAKMP:        authenticator is HMAC-MD5
1w1d: ISAKMP (0:1): atts are acceptable.
```

continues

Example 13-5 *Debugs of the Router Acting as the Responder of the IPsec Negotiation (Continued)*

```
1w1d: IPSEC(validate_proposal_request): proposal part #1,
  (key eng. msg.) INBOUND local= 172.16.172.20, remote= 172.16.172.10,
    local_proxy= 10.1.2.0/255.255.255.0/0/0 (type=4),
    remote_proxy= 10.1.1.0/255.255.255.0/0/0 (type=4),
    protocol= ESP, transform= esp-3des esp-md5-hmac ,
    lifedur= 0s and 0kb,
    spi= 0x0(0), conn_id= 0, keysize= 0, flags= 0x4
1w1d: ISAKMP (0:1): processing NONCE payload. message ID = 965273472
1w1d: ISAKMP (0:1): processing ID payload. message ID = 965273472
1w1d: ISAKMP (0:1): processing ID payload. message ID = 965273472
1w1d: ISAKMP (0:1): asking for 1 spis from ipsec
1w1d: ISAKMP (0:1): Node 965273472, Input = IKE_MESG_FROM_PEER, IKE_QM_EXCH
Old State = IKE_QM_READY  New State = IKE_QM_SPI_STARVE

1w1d: IPSEC(key_engine): got a queue event...
1w1d: IPSEC(spi_response): getting spi 3951352965 for SA
        from 172.16.172.20   to 172.16.172.10   for prot 3
1w1d: ISAKMP: received ke message (2/1)
1w1d: ISAKMP (0:1): sending packet to 172.16.172.10 (R) QM_IDLE
1w1d: ISAKMP (0:1): Node 965273472, Input = IKE_MESG_FROM_IPSEC, IKE_SPI_REPLY
Old State = IKE_QM_SPI_STARVE  New State = IKE_QM_R_QM2

1w1d: ISAKMP (0:1): received packet from 172.16.172.10 (R) QM_IDLE
1w1d: ISAKMP (0:1): Creating IPsec SAs
1w1d:         inbound SA from 172.16.172.10 to 172.16.172.20
        (proxy 10.1.1.0 to 10.1.2.0)
1w1d:         has spi 0xEB84DC85 and conn_id 2029 and flags 4
1w1d:         lifetime of 3600 seconds
1w1d:         lifetime of 4608000 kilobytes
1w1d:       outbound SA from 172.16.172.20   to 172.16.172.10   (proxy 10.1.2.0
to 10.1.1.0        )
1w1d:         has spi -1901393118 and conn_id 2030 and flags C
1w1d:         lifetime of 3600 seconds
1w1d:         lifetime of 4608000 kilobytes
1w1d: ISAKMP (0:1): deleting node 965273472 error FALSE reason "quick mode done
  (await()"
1w1d: ISAKMP (0:1): Node 965273472, Input = IKE_MESG_FROM_PEER, IKE_QM_EXCH
Old State = IKE_QM_R_QM2  New State = IKE_QM_PHASE2_COMPLETE

1w1d: IPSEC(key_engine): got a queue event...
1w1d: IPSEC(initialize_sas): ,
  (key eng. msg.) INBOUND local= 172.16.172.20, remote= 172.16.172.10,
    local_proxy= 10.1.2.0/255.255.255.0/0/0 (type=4),
    remote_proxy= 10.1.1.0/255.255.255.0/0/0 (type=4),
    protocol= ESP, transform= esp-3des esp-md5-hmac ,
    lifedur= 3600s and 4608000kb,
    spi= 0xEB84DC85(3951352965), conn_id= 2029, keysize= 0, flags= 0x4
1w1d: IPSEC(initialize_sas): ,
  (key eng. msg.) OUTBOUND local= 172.16.172.20, remote= 172.16.172.10,
    local_proxy= 10.1.2.0/255.255.255.0/0/0 (type=4),
    remote_proxy= 10.1.1.0/255.255.255.0/0/0 (type=4),
    protocol= ESP, transform= esp-3des esp-md5-hmac ,
```

Example 13-5 *Debugs of the Router Acting as the Responder of the IPsec Negotiation (Continued)*

```
        lifedur= 3600s and 4608000kb,
        spi= 0x8EAB0B22(2393574178), conn_id= 2030, keysize= 0, flags= 0xC
1w1d: IPSEC(create_sa): sa created,
  (sa) sa_dest= 172.16.172.20, sa_prot= 50,
    sa_spi= 0xEB84DC85(3951352965),
    sa_trans= esp-3des esp-md5-hmac , sa_conn_id= 2029
1w1d: IPSEC(create_sa): sa created,
  (sa) sa_dest= 172.16.172.10, sa_prot= 50,
    sa_spi= 0x8EAB0B22(2393574178),
    sa_trans= esp-3des esp-md5-hmac , sa_conn_id= 2030
1w1d: ISAKMP (0:1): purging node 965273472
```

Example 13-6 *Output of* **show** *Commands on the Router Acting as the Responder of the IPsec Negotiation*

```
Responder#show cry isa sa
dst             src             state           conn-id    slot
172.16.172.10   172.16.172.20   QM_IDLE               1       0

Responder#show crypto ipsec sa

interface: Ethernet1/0
    Crypto map tag: vpn, local addr. 172.16.172.20

   local  ident (addr/mask/prot/port): (10.1.2.0/255.255.255.0/0/0)
   remote ident (addr/mask/prot/port): (10.1.1.0/255.255.255.0/0/0)
   current_peer: 172.16.172.10
     PERMIT, flags={origin_is_acl,}
    #pkts encaps: 4, #pkts encrypt: 4, #pkts digest 4
    #pkts decaps: 4, #pkts decrypt: 4, #pkts verify 4
    #pkts compressed: 0, #pkts decompressed: 0
    #pkts not compressed: 0, #pkts compr. failed: 0, #pkts decompress failed: 0
    #send errors 0, #recv errors 0

    local crypto endpt.: 172.16.172.20, remote crypto endpt.: 172.16.172.10
    path mtu 1500, media mtu 1500
    current outbound spi: 8EAB0B22

    inbound esp sas:
     spi: 0xEB84DC85(3951352965)
       transform: esp-3des esp-md5-hmac ,
       in use settings ={Tunnel, }
       slot: 0, conn id: 2029, flow_id: 1, crypto map: vpn
       sa timing: remaining key lifetime (k/sec): (4607998/3326)
       IV size: 8 bytes
       replay detection support: Y

    inbound ah sas:

    inbound pcp sas:
```

continues

Example 13-6 *Output of* **show** *Commands on the Router Acting as the Responder of the IPsec Negotiation*

```
        outbound esp sas:
         spi: 0x8EAB0B22(2393574178)
           transform: esp-3des esp-md5-hmac ,
           in use settings ={Tunnel, }
           slot: 0, conn id: 2030, flow_id: 2, crypto map: vpn
           sa timing: remaining key lifetime (k/sec): (4607999/3326)
           IV size: 8 bytes
           replay detection support: Y

        outbound ah sas:

        outbound pcp sas:

Initiator#show cry map
Crypto Map "vpn" 10 ipsec-isakmp
        Peer = 172.16.172.10
        Extended IP access list 101
            access-list 101 permit ip 10.1.2.0 0.0.0.255 10.1.1.0 0.0.0.255
        Current peer: 172.16.172.10
        Security association lifetime: 4608000 kilobytes/3600 seconds
        PFS (Y/N): N
        Transform sets={ myset, }
        Interfaces using crypto map vpn:
                Ethernet1/0
```

Router-to-Router IPsec Using Digital Signatures with Digital Certificates

This case study uses digital signatures instead of preshared keys, making it a more secure and scalable VPN setup. Various CA servers work with Cisco routers. Among them are CA servers from vendors, Microsoft, VeriSign, and Baltimore.

A router administrator needs to go through the following steps to obtain a certificate for the router:

Step 1 Generate a public/private key pair.

(a) Generate a general-purpose key pair.

This pair is generated using this command:

crypto key generate rsa

In this case, the pair of public and private keys is used for both the signature mode of authentication and the encrypted nonce form of authentication.

(b) Generate special-purpose key pairs.

This pair is generated using this command:

crypto key generate rsa usage-keys

In this case, two pairs of public and private keys are generated—one to be used for encrypted nonce authentication (if used), and one for the signature mode of authentication (if configured). Generating two pairs of keys reduces the keys' exposure during negotiation, thus reducing the risk of their compromise.

Step 2   Enroll with a certificate authority server.

To properly authenticate each other, both IPsec peers must enroll to obtain digital certificates. Both the IPsec peers must obtain certificates from the same CA server (or different CA servers belonging to the same root CA). They must also belong to the same organization. Often this organization name is specified as a domain name that both routers agree on.

Upon enrollment, each router gets one certificate for each of its public keys. If a single general-purpose key was generated, only one certificate is issued. If usage keys are configured, two certificates are obtained—one for each public key.

In addition to the certificates for the router's public key, a certificate for the CA itself is also downloaded to the router.

If a registration authority (RA) is used, two additional RA certificates are downloaded on the router.

NOTE   The CA server administrator must ensure that a certificate is issued only to routers and devices that genuinely belong to an organization or domain. As discussed earlier, this ensures that only devices that are meant to administratively talk to each other can do so. Routers reject certificates that do not belong to the domain or organization they are allowed to interoperate with.

Cisco routers have an automatic mechanism for enrolling themselves in CA servers—Simple Certificate Enrollment Protocol (SCEP). SCEP allows the router to be enrolled in a CA using the following simple commands:

```
test1-isdn(config)#crypto ca identity testCA
test1-isdn(ca-identity)#enrollment url http://cisco-CA
```

```
test1-isdn(ca-identity)#exit
test1-isdn(config)#crypto ca authenticate testCA
test1-isdn(config)#crypto ca enroll testCA
```

The **crypto ca identity** command defines a tag to be used to define the CA server configuration on the router. **enrollment url** specifies the CA server's URL that is accessed using SCEP to obtain the certificate. The command **crypto ca authenticate** is used to obtain the CA server's certificate, and the command **crypto ca enroll** is used to obtain certificates for each public key on the router.

Some CAs have an RA as part of their implementation. An RA is essentially a server that acts as a proxy for the CA so that CA functions can continue when the CA is offline. In this case, the CA signs all the certificates, and a separate RA acts as the PKI server for the enrollment transactions.

If an RA is in use, an additional command is configured in crypto ca-identity CLI mode:

```
test1-isdn(ca-identity)#enrollment mode ra
```

CA servers can also export the certificates to an LDAP server for distribution. If that is the case, the URL for the LDAP server must also be specified using the following command:

```
test1-isdn(ca-identity)#query url ldap://server-ldap
```

Another important thing to note is that when certificates are used during negotiation, the certificate's distinguished name is used as the identity rather than the router's configured ISAKMP identity.

In the following configuration examples, it is interesting to note that no ISAKMP policy is configured. In this situation, the router uses the default ISAKMP policy set up in its internal code. The default ISAKMP policy, which is numbered 65535, is as follows:

> **Encryption algorithm**—DES
> **Hash algorithm**—Secure Hash Algorithm (SHA)
> **Authentication method**—Rivest Shamir Adleman (RSA) signature
> **Diffie-Hellman group**—#1 (768-bit)
> **Lifetime**—86400 seconds, no volume limit

Figure 13-46 shows the network diagram for this case study. Examples 13-7 and 13-8 show the configuration on the two routers used in this case study while Example 13-9 shows the debug output on the lab-isdn router.

Figure 13-46 *Network Diagram for This Case Study*

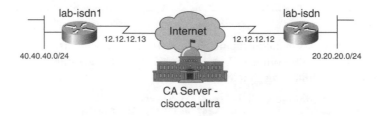

Example 13-7 *Configuration of the Router lab-isdn1*

```
lab-isdn1#wr t
Building configuration...

Current configuration:
!
version 11.3
service timestamps debug datetime msec
!
hostname lab-isdn1
!
enable secret 5 <removed>
!
username lab-isdn password 0 cisco
ip host ciscoca-ultra 171.69.54.46
ip host lab-isdn 12.12.12.12
ip domain-name cisco.com
ip name-server 171.68.10.70
ip name-server 171.68.122.99
isdn switch-type basic-ni1
!
crypto ipsec transform-set mypolicy ah-sha-hmac esp-des esp-sha-hmac
!
crypto map test 10 ipsec-isakmp
 set peer 12.12.12.12
 set transform-set mypolicy
 match address 144
!
!The configuration below defines the CA server to be used by the router. The
!configuration also contains the certificates downloaded by the router from the CA
!server.

crypto ca identity bubba
 enrollment url http://ciscoca-ultra

crypto ca certificate chain bubba
!Below is the router's certificate for the signature public key.
 certificate 3E1ED472BDA2CE0163FB6B0B004E5EEE
  308201BC 30820166 A0030201 0202103E 1ED472BD A2CE0163 FB6B0B00 4E5EEE30
  0D06092A 864886F7 0D010104 05003042 31163014 06035504 0A130D43 6973636F
  20537973 74656D73 3110300E 06035504 0B130744 65767465 73743116 30140603
  55040313 0D434953 434F4341 2D554C54 5241301E 170D3938 30343038 30303030
  30305A17 0D393930 34303832 33353935 395A303B 31273025 06092A86 4886F70D
  01090216 18737461 6E6E6F75 732D6973 646E312E 63697363 6F2E636F 6D311030
  0E060355 04051307 35363739 39383730 5C300D06 092A8648 86F70D01 01010500
  034B0030 48024100 D2D125FF BBFC6E56 93CB4385 5473C165 BC7CCAF6 45C35BED
  554BAA0B 119AFA6F 0853F574 5E0B8492 2E39B5FA 84C4DD05 C19AA625 8184395C
  6CBC7FA4 614F6177 02030100 01A33F30 3D300B06 03551D0F 04040302 05203023
  0603551D 11041C30 1A821873 74616E6E 6F75732D 6973646E 312E6369 73636F2E
  636F6D30 09060355 1D130402 3000300D 06092A86 4886F70D 01010405 00034100
  04AF83B8 FE95F5D9 9C07C105 F1E88F1A 9320CE7D 0FA540CF 44C77829 FC85C94B
```

continues

Example 13-7 *Configuration of the Router lab-isdn1 (Continued)*

```
    8CB4CA32 85FF9655 8E47AC9A B9D6BF1A 0C4846DE 5CB07C8E A32038EC 8AFD161A
    quit
!Below is the CA's certificate for the CA server's public key
 certificate ca 3051DF7169BEE31B821DFE4B3A338E5F
    30820182 3082012C A0030201 02021030 51DF7169 BEE31B82 1DFE4B3A 338E5F30
    0D06092A 864886F7 0D010104 05003042 31163014 06035504 0A130D43 6973636F
    20537973 74656D73 3110300E 06035504 0B130744 65767465 73743116 30140603
    55040313 0D434953 434F4341 2D554C54 5241301E 170D3937 31323032 30313036
    32385A17 0D393831 32303230 31303632 385A3042 31163014 06035504 0A130D43
    6973636F 20537973 74656D73 3110300E 06035504 0B130744 65767465 73743116
    30140603 55040313 0D434953 434F4341 2D554C54 5241305C 300D0609 2A864886
    F70D0101 01050003 4B003048 024100C1 B69D7BF6 34E4EE28 A84E0DC6 FCA4DEA8
    04D89E50 C5EBE862 39D51890 D0D4B732 678BDBF2 80801430 E5E56E7C C126E2DD
    DBE9695A DF8E5BA7 E67BAE87 29375302 03010001 300D0609 2A864886 F70D0101
    04050003 410035AA 82B5A406 32489413 A7FF9A9A E349E5B4 74615E05 058BA3CE
    7C5F00B4 019552A5 E892D2A3 86763A1F 2852297F C68EECE1 F41E9A7B 2F38D02A
    B1D2F817 3F7B
    Quit
!Below is the router's certificate for the encryption public key.
 certificate 503968D890F7D409475B7280162754D2
    308201BC 30820166 A0030201 02021050 3968D890 F7D40947 5B728016 2754D230
    0D06092A 864886F7 0D010104 05003042 31163014 06035504 0A130D43 6973636F
    20537973 74656D73 3110300E 06035504 0B130744 65767465 73743116 30140603
    55040313 0D434953 434F4341 2D554C54 5241301E 170D3938 30343038 30303030
    30305A17 0D393930 34303832 33353935 395A303B 31273025 06092A86 4886F70D
    01090216 18737461 6E6E6F75 732D6973 646E312E 63697363 6F2E636F 6D311030
    0E060355 04051307 35363739 39383730 5C300D06 092A8648 86F70D01 01010500
    034B0030 48024100 BECE2D8C B32E6B09 0ADE0D46 AF8D4A1F 37850034 35D0C729
    3BF91518 0C9E4CF8 1A6A43AE E4F04687 B8E2859D 33D5CE04 2E5DDEA6 3DA54A31
    2AD4255A 756014CB 02030100 01A33F30 3D300B06 03551D0F 04040302 07803023
    0603551D 11041C30 1A821873 74616E6E 6F75732D 6973646E 312E6369 73636F2E
    636F6D30 09060355 1D130402 3000300D 06092A86 4886F70D 01010405 00034100
    B3AF6E71 CBD9AEDD A4711B71 6897F2CE D669A23A EE47B92B B2BE942A 422DF4A5
    7ACB9433 BD17EC7A BB3721EC E7D1175F 5C62BC58 C409F805 19691FBD FD925138
    quit
!
interface Ethernet0
 ip address 40.40.40.40 255.255.255.0
 no ip mroute-cache
!
interface BRI0
 ip address 12.12.12.13 255.255.255.0
 encapsulation ppp
 no ip mroute-cache
 dialer idle-timeout 99999
 dialer map ip 12.12.12.12 name lab-isdn 4724171
 dialer hold-queue 40
 dialer-group 1
 isdn spid1 919472411800 4724118
 isdn spid2 919472411901 4724119
 ppp authentication chap
 crypto map test
```

Example 13-7 *Configuration of the Router lab-isdn1 (Continued)*

```
!
ip classless
ip route 0.0.0.0 0.0.0.0 12.12.12.12
access-list 144 permit ip 40.40.40.0 0.0.0.255 20.20.20.0 0.0.0.255
dialer-list 1 protocol ip permit
!
line con 0
 exec-timeout 0 0
line vty 0 4
 password ww
 login
!
end
```

Example 13-8 *Configuration of the Router lab-isdn*

```
lab-isdn#write terminal
Building configuration...

Current configuration:
!
version 11.3
service timestamps debug datetime msec

!
hostname lab-isdn
!
enable secret 5 <removed>
!
username lab-isdn1 password 0 cisco
ip host ciscoca-ultra 171.69.54.46
ip host lab-isdn1 12.12.12.13
ip domain-name cisco.com
ip name-server 171.68.10.70
ip name-server 171.68.122.99
isdn switch-type basic-ni1
!
crypto ipsec transform-set mypolicy ah-sha-hmac esp-des esp-sha-hmac
!
crypto map test 10 ipsec-isakmp
 set peer 12.12.12.13
 set transform-set mypolicy
 match address 133
!
crypto ca identity lab
 enrollment url http://ciscoca-ultra

crypto ca certificate chain lab
```

continues

Example 13-8 *Configuration of the Router lab-isdn (Continued)*

```
!Below is the router's certificate for the signature public key.
 certificate 44FC6C531FC3446927E4EE307A806B20

  308201E0 3082018A A0030201 02021044 FC6C531F C3446927 E4EE307A 806B2030
  0D06092A 864886F7 0D010104 05003042 31163014 06035504 0A130D43 6973636F
  20537973 74656D73 3110300E 06035504 0B130744 65767465 73743116 30140603
  55040313 0D434953 434F4341 2D554C54 5241301E 170D3938 30343038 30303030
  30305A17 0D393930 34303832 33353935 395A305A 31263024 06092A86 4886F70D
  01090216 17737461 6E6E6F75 732D6973 646E2E63 6973636F 2E636F6D 311E301C
  060A2B06 0104012A 020B0201 130E3137 312E3638 2E313137 2E313839 3110300E
  06035504 05130735 36373939 3139305C 300D0609 2A864886 F70D0101 01050003
  4B003048 024100B8 F4A17A70 FAB5C2E3 39186513 486779C7 61EF0AC1 3B6CFF83
  810E6D28 B3E4C034 CD803CFF 5158C270 28FEBCDE CB6EF2D4 83BDD9B3 EAF915DB
  78266E96 500CD702 03010001 A3443042 300B0603 551D0F04 04030205 20302806
  03551D11 0421301F 82177374 616E6E6F 75732D69 73646E2E 63697363 6F2E636F
  6D8704AB 4475BD30 09060355 1D130402 3000300D 06092A86 4886F70D 01010405
  00034100 BF65B931 0F960195 ABDD41D5 622743D9 C12B5499 B3A8EB30 5005E6CC
  7FDF7C5B 51D13EB8 D46187E5 A1E7F711 AEB7B33B AA4C6728 7A4BA692 00A44A05 C5CF973F
 quit
!Below is the CA's certificate for the CA server's public key
 certificate ca 3051DF7169BEE31B821DFE4B3A338E5F
  30820182 3082012C A0030201 02021030 51DF7169 BEE31B82 1DFE4B3A 338E5F30
  0D06092A 864886F7 0D010104 05003042 31163014 06035504 0A130D43 6973636F
  20537973 74656D73 3110300E 06035504 0B130744 65767465 73743116 30140603
  55040313 0D434953 434F4341 2D554C54 5241301E 170D3937 31323032 30313036
  32385A17 0D393831 32303230 31303632 385A3042 31163014 06035504 0A130D43
  6973636F 20537973 74656D73 3110300E 06035504 0B130744 65767465 73743116
  30140603 55040313 0D434953 434F4341 2D554C54 5241305C 300D0609 2A864886
  F70D0101 01050003 4B003048 024100C1 B69D7BF6 34E4EE28 A84E0DC6 FCA4DEA8
  04D89E50 C5EBE862 39D51890 D0D4B732 678DBBF2 80801430 E5E56E7C C126E2DD
  DBE9695A DF8E5BA7 E67BAE87 29375302 03010001 300D0609 2A864886 F70D0101
  04050003 410035AA 82B5A406 32489413 A7FF9A9A E349E5B4 74615E05 058BA3CE
  7C5F00B4 019552A5 E892D2A3 86763A1F 2852297F C68EECE1 F41E9A7B 2F38D02A
  B1D2F817 3F7B
 Quit
!Below is the router's certificate for the encryption public key.
 certificate 52A46D5D10B18A6F51E6BC735A36508C
  308201E0 3082018A A0030201 02021052 A46D5D10 B18A6F51 E6BC735A 36508C30
  0D06092A 864886F7 0D010104 05003042 31163014 06035504 0A130D43 6973636F
  20537973 74656D73 3110300E 06035504 0B130744 65767465 73743116 30140603
  55040313 0D434953 434F4341 2D554C54 5241301E 170D3938 30343038 30303030
  30305A17 0D393930 34303832 33353935 395A305A 31263024 06092A86 4886F70D
  01090216 17737461 6E6E6F75 732D6973 646E2E63 6973636F 2E636F6D 311E301C
  060A2B06 0104012A 020B0201 130E3137 312E3638 2E313137 2E313839 3110300E
  06035504 05130735 36373939 3139305C 300D0609 2A864886 F70D0101 01050003
  4B003048 024100D7 71AD5672 B487A019 5ECD1954 6F919A3A 6270102E 5A9FF4DC
  7A608480 FB27A181 715335F4 399D3E57 7F72B323 BF0620AB 60C371CF 4389BA4F
  C60EE6EA 21E06302 03010001 A3443042 300B0603 551D0F04 04030207 80302806
  03551D11 0421301F 82177374 616E6E6F 75732D69 73646E2E 63697363 6F2E636F
  6D8704AB 4475BD30 09060355 1D130402 3000300D 06092A86 4886F70D 01010405
  00034100 8AD45375 54803CF3 013829A8 8DB225A8 25342160 94546F3C 4094BBA3
```

Example 13-8 *Configuration of the Router lab-isdn (Continued)*

```
    F2F5A378 97E2F06F DCFFC509 A07B930A FBE6C3CA E1FC7FD9 1E69B872 C402E62A A8814C09
     quit
    !
    interface Ethernet0
     ip address 20.20.20.20 255.255.255.0
    !
    interface BRI0
     description bri to rtp
     ip address 12.12.12.12 255.255.255.0
     no ip proxy-arp
     encapsulation ppp
     no ip mroute-cache
     bandwidth 128
     load-interval 30
     dialer idle-timeout 99999
     dialer hold-queue 40
     dialer-group 1
     isdn spid1 919472417100 4724171
     isdn spid2 919472417201 4724172
     ppp authentication chap
     crypto map test
    !
    ip classless
    ip route 0.0.0.0 0.0.0.0 12.12.12.13
    access-list 133 permit ip 20.20.20.0 0.0.0.255 40.40.40.0 0.0.0.255
    dialer-list 1 protocol ip permit
    !
    line con 0
     exec-timeout 0 0
    line vty 0 4
     password ww
     login
    !
    end
```

Example 13-9 *Debugs on the Router lab-isdn*

```
lab-isdn#show debug
Cryptographic Subsystem:
  Crypto ISAKMP debugging is on
  Crypto Engine debugging is on
  Crypto IPSEC debugging is on
lab-isdn#

lab-isdn#
*Mar 21 20:16:50.871: ISAKMP (4): processing SA payload. message ID = 0
*Mar 21 20:16:50.871: ISAKMP (4): Checking ISAKMP transform 1 against priority
  65535
        policy
```

continues

Example 13-9 *Debugs on the Router lab-isdn (Continued)*

```
*Mar 21 20:16:50.875: ISAKMP:        encryption DES-CBC
*Mar 21 20:16:50.875: ISAKMP:        hash SHA
*Mar 21 20:16:50.875: ISAKMP:        default group 1
!The authentication method shown below is RSA sig. This is the authentication
!method being offered by the other side.
*Mar 21 20:16:50.875: ISAKMP:        auth RSA sig
*Mar 21 20:16:50.879: ISAKMP (4): atts are acceptable. Next payload is 0
*Mar 21 20:16:50.879: Crypto engine 0: generate alg param

*Mar 21 20:16:54.070: CRYPTO_ENGINE: Dh phase 1 status: 0
!The RSA signature authentication process starts here
*Mar 21 20:16:54.090: ISAKMP (4): SA is doing RSA signature authentication
*Mar 21 20:16:57.343: ISAKMP (4): processing KE payload. message ID = 0
*Mar 21 20:16:57.347: Crypto engine 0: generate alg param

*Mar 21 20:17:01.168: ISAKMP (4): processing NONCE payload. message ID = 0
*Mar 21 20:17:01.176: Crypto engine 0: create ISAKMP SKEYID for conn id 4
*Mar 21 20:17:01.188: ISAKMP (4): SKEYID state generated
*Mar 21 20:17:07.331: ISAKMP (4): processing ID payload. message ID = 0
!The cert payload contains the certificate of the other side
*Mar 21 20:17:07.331: ISAKMP (4): processing CERT payload. message ID = 0
*Mar 21 20:17:07.497: ISAKMP (4): cert approved with warning
!The signature payload contains a hash encrypted with the sender's private key
*Mar 21 20:17:07.600: ISAKMP (4): processing SIG payload. message ID = 0
!The encrypted hash is decrypted using the public key in the certificate, bringing
!the hash out for use in the authentication process.
*Mar 21 20:17:07.608: Crypto engine 0: RSA decrypt with public key
*Mar 21 20:17:07.759: generate hmac context for conn id 4
!Based on comparing hashes, the authentication is found to be successful.
*Mar 21 20:17:07.767: ISAKMP (4): SA has been authenticated
*Mar 21 20:17:07.775: generate hmac context for conn id 4
!This router is now encrypting Hash_I with its private key to send to the receiver
!as its signature. This allows the receiver to authenticate it, just as it has
!authenticated the receiver.
*Mar 21 20:17:07.783: Crypto engine 0: RSA encrypt with private key
*Mar 21 20:17:08.672: CRYPTO_ENGINE: key process suspended and continued
*Mar 21 20:17:08.878: CRYPTO_ENGINE: key process suspended and continued
*Mar 21 20:17:09.088: CRYPTO_ENGINE: key process suspended and continued
*Mar 21 20:17:09.291: CRYPTO_ENGINE: key process suspended and continued
*Mar 21 20:17:09.493: CRYPTO_ENGINE: key process suspended and continued
*Mar 21 20:17:09.795: CRYPTO_ENGINE: key process suspended and continued
*Mar 21 20:17:10.973: generate hmac context for conn id 4
*Mar 21 20:17:10.981: ISAKMP (4): processing SA payload. message ID =
  -538880964*Mar 21 20:17:10.981: ISAKMP (4): Checking IPsec proposal 1
*Mar 21 20:17:10.981: ISAKMP: transform 1, AH_SHA_HMAC
*Mar 21 20:17:10.985: ISAKMP:    attributes in transform:
*Mar 21 20:17:10.985: ISAKMP:       encaps is 1
*Mar 21 20:17:10.985: ISAKMP:       SA life type in seconds
*Mar 21 20:17:10.985: ISAKMP:       SA life duration (basic) of 3600
*Mar 21 20:17:10.989: ISAKMP:       SA life type in kilobytes
*Mar 21 20:17:10.989: ISAKMP:       SA life duration (VPI) of
  0x0 0x46 0x50 0x0
```

Example 13-9 *Debugs on the Router lab-isdn (Continued)*

```
*Mar 21 20:17:10.993: ISAKMP (4): atts are acceptable.
*Mar 21 20:17:10.993: ISAKMP (4): Checking IPsec proposal 1
*Mar 21 20:17:10.993: ISAKMP: transform 1, ESP_DES
*Mar 21 20:17:10.997: ISAKMP:    attributes in transform:
*Mar 21 20:17:10.997: ISAKMP:       encaps is 1
*Mar 21 20:17:10.997: ISAKMP:       SA life type in seconds
*Mar 21 20:17:10.997: ISAKMP:       SA life duration (basic) of 3600
*Mar 21 20:17:11.001: ISAKMP:       SA life type in kilobytes
*Mar 21 20:17:11.001: ISAKMP:       SA life duration (VPI) of
  0x0 0x46 0x50 0x0
*Mar 21 20:17:11.001: ISAKMP:       HMAC algorithm is SHA
*Mar 21 20:17:11.005: ISAKMP (4): atts are acceptable.
*Mar 21 20:17:11.005: IPSEC(validate_proposal_request): proposal part #1,
  (key eng. msg.) dest= 12.12.12.12, SRC= 12.12.12.13,
    dest_proxy= 20.20.20.0/0.0.0.0/0/0,
    src_proxy= 40.40.40.0/0.0.0.16/0/0,
    protocol= AH, transform= ah-sha-hmac ,
    lifedur= 0s and 0kb,
    spi= 0x0(0), conn_id= 0, keysize= 0, flags= 0x4
*Mar 21 20:17:11.013: IPSEC(validate_proposal_request): proposal part #2,
  (key eng. msg.) dest= 12.12.12.12, SRC= 12.12.12.13,
    dest_proxy= 20.20.20.0/0.0.0.0/0/0,
    src_proxy= 40.40.40.0/0.0.0.16/0/0,
    protocol= ESP, transform= esp-des esp-sha-hmac ,
    lifedur= 0s and 0kb,
    spi= 0x0(0), conn_id= 0, keysize= 0, flags= 0x4
*Mar 21 20:17:11.021: ISAKMP (4): processing NONCE payload. message ID = -538880964
*Mar 21 20:17:11.021: ISAKMP (4): processing ID payload. message ID = -538880964
*Mar 21 20:17:11.021: ISAKMP (4): processing ID payload. message ID = -538880964
*Mar 21 20:17:11.025: IPSEC(key_engine): got a queue event...
*Mar 21 20:17:11.029: IPSEC(spi_response): getting spi 112207019 for SA
        from 12.12.12.13      to 12.12.12.12      for prot 2
*Mar 21 20:17:11.033: IPSEC(spi_response): getting spi 425268832 for SA
        from 12.12.12.13      to 12.12.12.12      for prot 3
*Mar 21 20:17:11.279: generate hmac context for conn id 4
*Mar 21 20:17:11.612: generate hmac context for conn id 4
*Mar 21 20:17:11.644: ISAKMP (4): Creating IPsec SAs
*Mar 21 20:17:11.644:         inbound SA from 12.12.12.13      to 12.12.12.12
        (proxy 40.40.40.0     to 20.20.20.0      )
*Mar 21 20:17:11.648:         has spi 112207019 and conn_id 5 and flags 4
*Mar 21 20:17:11.648:         lifetime of 3600 seconds
*Mar 21 20:17:11.648:         lifetime of 4608000 kilobytes
*Mar 21 20:17:11.652:         outbound SA from 12.12.12.12      to 12.12.12.13
        (proxy 20.20.20.0     to 40.40.40.0      )
*Mar 21 20:17:11.652:         has spi 83231845 and conn_id 6 and flags 4
*Mar 21 20:17:11.656:         lifetime of 3600 seconds
*Mar 21 20:17:11.656:         lifetime of 4608000 kilobytes
*Mar 21 20:17:11.656: ISAKMP (4): Creating IPsec SAs
*Mar 21 20:17:11.656:         inbound SA from 12.12.12.13      to 12.12.12.12
        (proxy 40.40.40.0     to 20.20.20.0      )
```

continues

Example 13-9 *Debugs on the Router lab-isdn (Continued)*

```
*Mar 21 20:17:11.660:            has spi 425268832 and conn_id 7 and flags 4
*Mar 21 20:17:11.660:            lifetime of 3600 seconds
*Mar 21 20:17:11.664:            lifetime of 4608000 kilobytes
*Mar 21 20:17:11.664:            outbound SA from 12.12.12.12     to 12.12.12.13
        (proxy 20.20.20.0     to 40.40.40.0     )
*Mar 21 20:17:11.668:            has spi 556010247 and conn_id 8 and flags 4
*Mar 21 20:17:11.668:            lifetime of 3600 seconds
*Mar 21 20:17:11.668:            lifetime of 4608000 kilobytes
*Mar 21 20:17:11.676: IPSEC(key_engine): got a queue event...
*Mar 21 20:17:11.676: IPSEC(initialize_sas): ,
  (key eng. msg.) dest= 12.12.12.12, SRC= 12.12.12.13,
    dest_proxy= 20.20.20.0/255.255.255.0/0/0,
    src_proxy= 40.40.40.0/255.255.255.0/0/0,
    protocol= AH, transform= ah-sha-hmac ,
    lifedur= 3600s and 4608000kb,
    spi= 0x6B024AB(112207019), conn_id= 5, keysize= 0, flags= 0x4
*Mar 21 20:17:11.680: IPSEC(initialize_sas): ,
  (key eng. msg.) SRC= 12.12.12.12, dest= 12.12.12.13,
    src_proxy= 20.20.20.0/255.255.255.0/0/0,
    dest_proxy= 40.40.40.0/255.255.255.0/0/0,
    protocol= AH, transform= ah-sha-hmac ,
    lifedur= 3600s and 4608000kb,
    spi= 0x4F60465(83231845), conn_id= 6, keysize= 0, flags= 0x4
*Mar 21 20:17:11.687: IPSEC(initialize_sas): ,
  (key eng. msg.) dest= 12.12.12.12, SRC= 12.12.12.13,
    dest_proxy= 20.20.20.0/255.255.255.0/0/0,
    src_proxy= 40.40.40.0/255.255.255.0/0/0,
    protocol= ESP, transform= esp-des esp-sha-hmac ,
    lifedur= 3600s and 4608000kb,
    spi= 0x19591660(425268832), conn_id= 7, keysize= 0, flags= 0x4
*Mar 21 20:17:11.691: IPSEC(initialize_sas): ,
  (key eng. msg.) SRC= 12.12.12.12, dest= 12.12.12.13,
    src_proxy= 20.20.20.0/255.255.255.0/0/0,
    dest_proxy= 40.40.40.0/255.255.255.0/0/0,
    protocol= ESP, transform= esp-des esp-sha-hmac ,
    lifedur= 3600s and 4608000kb,
    spi= 0x21240B07(556010247), conn_id= 8, keysize= 0, flags= 0x4
*Mar 21 20:17:11.699: IPSEC(create_sa): sa created,
  (sa) sa_dest= 12.12.12.12, sa_prot= 51,
    sa_spi= 0x6B024AB(112207019),
    sa_trans= ah-sha-hmac , sa_conn_id= 5
*Mar 21 20:17:11.703: IPSEC(create_sa): sa created,
  (sa) sa_dest= 12.12.12.13, sa_prot= 51,
    sa_spi= 0x4F60465(83231845),
    sa_trans= ah-sha-hmac , sa_conn_id= 6
*Mar 21 20:17:11.707: IPSEC(create_sa): sa created,
  (sa) sa_dest= 12.12.12.12, sa_prot= 50,
    sa_spi= 0x19591660(425268832),
    sa_trans= esp-des esp-sha-hmac , sa_conn_id= 7
*Mar 21 20:17:11.707: IPSEC(create_sa): sa created,
  (sa) sa_dest= 12.12.12.13, sa_prot= 50,
```

Example 13-9 *Debugs on the Router lab-isdn (Continued)*

```
     sa_spi= 0x21240B07(556010247),
     sa_trans= esp-des esp-sha-hmac , sa_conn_id= 8
*Mar 21 20:18:06.767: ISADB: reaper checking SA, conn_id = 4
lab-isdn#
```

Using digital certificates allows IPsec implementations to scale very well. However, using digital certificates requires that a proper CA server system be set up to distribute the certificates. This can be somewhat intensive at the beginning, but after it is done, the rewards are security and scalability.

Router-to-Router IPsec Using RSA Encrypted Nonces

The RSA encrypted keys method is another way to authenticate two end devices using IPsec. This method involves generating RSA keys, as done when using certificates. However, one of the issues with using RSA encrypted nonces is that this method requires the public key of the two peers to be available on the two peers before the third message of the IKE exchange is sent. This is because the third and fourth messages of IKE exchange include nonces, which this method of authentication needs to protect by encrypting them with the receiver's public key. Because the first two messages do not allow a certificate payload to be exchanged, the certificates containing the public keys must be exchanged out of band between the two peers before the IKE process can begin.

The RSA public keys can be exchanged by first generating them and then copying and pasting them into the peer's configuration.

In the following example, the public key for the 2516 router is being copied manually to the 2511 router:

```
wan2511(config)#crypto key pubkey-chain rsa
wan2511(config-pubkey-chain)#named-key wan2516.cisco.com
wan2511(config-pubkey-key)#key-string
Enter a public key as a hexidecimal number ....

wan2511(config-pubkey)#$86F70D 01010105 00034B00 30480241 00DC3DDC 59885F14
wan2511(config-pubkey)#$D918DE FC7ADB76 B0B9DD1A ABAF4884 009E758C 4064C699
wan2511(config-pubkey)#$220CB9 31E267F8 0259C640 F8DE4169 1F020301 0001
wan2511(config-pubkey)#quit
wan2511(config-pubkey-key)#^Z
wan2511#
```

Another interesting thing to note is the way the ID is encrypted during the IKE authentication process. The identity might be too large for all of it to be encrypted in the peer's public key. So the order in which the ID is used in this method of authentication is distinguished name, FQDN, IP address.

Examples 13-10 and 13-11 show the configuration on the two routers used in this case study while example 13-12 shows the debug output on the 'wan2511' router. Figure 13-47 shows the network diagram for this case study.

Figure 13-47 *Network Diagram for This Case Study*

Example 13-10 *Configuration of the Router wan2511*

```
wan2511#show run
Building configuration...

Current configuration:
!
version 11.3
service timestamps debug datetime msec
!
hostname wan2511
!
enable password <removed>
!
no ip domain-lookup
!The command below is used to define the name resolution for the peer to which
!this router will be talking IPsec
ip host wan2516.cisco.com 20.20.20.20
ip domain-name cisco.com
!
crypto isakmp policy 1
!The command below sets up RSA encrypted nonces as the method of authentication.
 authentication rsa-encr
 group 2

crypto isakmp identity hostname
!
crypto ipsec transform-set auth2 ah-sha-hmac esp-des esp-sha-hmac
!
crypto map test 10 ipsec-isakmp
 set peer 20.20.20.20
 set transform-set auth2
 match address 133
!
!Below is the public key for the peer router, wan2516. This key was received by
!this router via a key-exchange mechanism. However, this can be done manually as
!well (cut and paste).

crypto key pubkey-chain rsa
 named-key wan2516.cisco.com
```

Example 13-10 *Configuration of the Router wan2511 (Continued)*

```
  key-string
   305C300D 06092A86 4886F70D 01010105 00034B00 30480241 00DC3DDC 59885F14
   1AB30DCB 794AB5C7 82D918DE FC7ADB76 B0B9DD1A ABAF4884 009E758C 4064C699
   3BC9D17E C47581DC 50220CB9 31E267F8 0259C640 F8DE4169 1F020301 0001
  quit
!
interface Ethernet0
 ip address 50.50.50.50 255.255.255.0
!
interface Serial0
 ip address 20.20.20.21 255.255.255.0
 encapsulation ppp
 no ip mroute-cache
 crypto map test
!
interface Serial1
 no ip address
 shutdown
!
ip classless

ip route 60.0.0.0 255.0.0.0 20.20.20.20
access-list 133 permit ip 50.50.50.0 0.0.0.255 60.60.60.0 0.0.0.255
!
line con 0
 exec-timeout 0 0
 password ww
 login

line vty 0 4
 password ww
 login
!
end
```

Example 13-11 *Configuration of the Router wan2516*

```
wan2516#write terminal

Building configuration...

Current configuration:
!
version 11.3
no service pad
service timestamps debug datetime msec
!
hostname wan2516
```

continues

Example 13-11 *Configuration of the Router wan2516 (Continued)*

```
!
enable password ww
!
no ip domain-lookup

ip host wan2511.cisco.com 20.20.20.21
ip domain-name cisco.com
!
crypto isakmp policy 1authentication rsa-encr
 group 2

crypto isakmp identity hostname
!
crypto ipsec transform-set auth2 ah-sha-hmac esp-des esp-sha-hmac
!
crypto map test 10 ipsec-isakmp
 set peer 20.20.20.21
 set transform-set auth2
 match address 144
!
!The key below is the public key of the peer
crypto key pubkey-chain rsa
 named-key wan2511.cisco.com
  key-string
    305C300D 06092A86 4886F70D 01010105 00034B00 30480241 00E9007B E5CD7DC8
    6E1C0423 92044254 92C972AD 0CCE9796 86797EAA B6C4EFF0 0F0A5378 6AFAE43B
    3A2BD92F 98039DAC 08741E82 5D9053C4 D9CFABC1 AB54E0E2 BB020301 0001
  quit
!
!
interface Ethernet0
 ip address 60.60.60.60 255.255.255.0
!
interface Serial0
 ip address 20.20.20.20 255.255.255.0
 encapsulation ppp
 clockrate 2000000
 crypto map test
!
ip default-gateway 20.20.20.21
ip classless
ip route 0.0.0.0 0.0.0.0 20.20.20.21
access-list 144 permit ip 60.60.60.0 0.0.0.255 50.50.50.0 0.0.0.255
!
line con 0
 exec-timeout 0 0
 password ww
 login
line aux 0
 password ww
 login
```

Example 13-11 *Configuration of the Router wan2516 (Continued)*

```
line vty 0 4
 password ww
 login
!
end
```

Example 13-12 *Debugs on the Router wan2511*

```
wan2511#show debug
Cryptographic Subsystem:
  Crypto ISAKMP debugging is on

wan2511#
*Mar  1 00:27:23.279: ISAKMP (6): processing SA payload. message ID = 0
*Mar  1 00:27:23.279: ISAKMP (6): Checking ISAKMP transform 1 against priority 1
  policy
*Mar  1 00:27:23.283: ISAKMP:      encryption DES-CBC
*Mar  1 00:27:23.283: ISAKMP:      hash SHA
*Mar  1 00:27:23.283: ISAKMP:      default group 2
!The authentication method offered by the peer is RSA encrypted nonces
*Mar  1 00:27:23.287: ISAKMP:      auth RSA encr
*Mar  1 00:27:23.287: ISAKMP:      life type in seconds
*Mar  1 00:27:23.287: ISAKMP:      life duration (basic) of 240
*Mar  1 00:27:23.291: ISAKMP (6): atts are acceptable. Next payload is 0
*Mar  1 00:27:32.055: ISAKMP (6): Unable to get router cert to find DN!
!RSA encrypted nonce authentication has started
*Mar  1 00:27:32.055: ISAKMP (6): SA is doing RSA encryption authentication
*Mar  1 00:27:41.183: ISAKMP (6): processing KE payload. message ID = 0
!Both the ID payload and the nonce payload are encrypted using the peer's public
!key
*Mar  1 00:27:51.779: ISAKMP (6): processing ID payload. message ID = 0
*Mar  1 00:27:54.507: ISAKMP (6): processing NONCE payload. message ID = 0
*Mar  1 00:27:57.239: ISAKMP (6): SKEYID state generated
*Mar  1 00:27:57.627: ISAKMP (6): processing KE payload. message ID = 0
*Mar  1 00:27:57.631: ISAKMP (6): processing ID payload. message ID = 0
*Mar  1 00:28:00.371: ISAKMP (6): processing NONCE payload. message ID = 0
*Mar  1 00:28:13.587: ISAKMP (6): processing HASH payload. message ID = 0
!Authentication has succeeded at this point
*Mar  1 00:28:13.599: ISAKMP (6): SA has been authenticated
*Mar  1 00:28:13.939: ISAKMP (6): processing SA payload. message ID = -161552401
*Mar  1 00:28:13.943: ISAKMP (6): Checking IPsec proposal 1
*Mar  1 00:28:13.943: ISAKMP: transform 1, AH_SHA_HMAC
*Mar  1 00:28:13.943: ISAKMP:    attributes in transform:
*Mar  1 00:28:13.947: ISAKMP:      encaps is 1
*Mar  1 00:28:13.947: ISAKMP:      SA life type in seconds
*Mar  1 00:28:13.947: ISAKMP:      SA life duration (basic) of 3600
*Mar  1 00:28:13.951: ISAKMP:      SA life type in kilobytes
*Mar  1 00:28:13.951: ISAKMP:      SA life duration (VPI) of
  0x0 0x46 0x50 0x0
```

continues

Example 13-12 *Debugs on the Router wan2511 (Continued)*

```
*Mar  1 00:28:13.955: ISAKMP (6): atts are acceptable.
*Mar  1 00:28:13.959: ISAKMP (6): Checking IPsec proposal 1
*Mar  1 00:28:13.959: ISAKMP: transform 1, ESP_DES
*Mar  1 00:28:13.959: ISAKMP:    attributes in transform:
*Mar  1 00:28:13.963: ISAKMP:       encaps is 1
*Mar  1 00:28:13.963: ISAKMP:       SA life type in seconds
*Mar  1 00:28:13.963: ISAKMP:       SA life duration (basic) of 3600
*Mar  1 00:28:13.967: ISAKMP:       SA life type in kilobytes
*Mar  1 00:28:13.967: ISAKMP:       SA life duration (VPI) of
 0x0 0x46 0x50 0x0
*Mar  1 00:28:13.971: ISAKMP:       HMAC algorithm is SHA
*Mar  1 00:28:13.971: ISAKMP (6): atts are acceptable.
*Mar  1 00:28:13.975: ISAKMP (6): processing NONCE payload. message ID = -161552401
*Mar  1 00:28:13.979: ISAKMP (6): processing ID payload. message ID = -161552401
*Mar  1 00:28:13.979: ISAKMP (6): processing ID payload. message ID = -161552401
*Mar  1 00:28:14.391: ISAKMP (6): Creating IPsec SAs
*Mar  1 00:28:14.391:         inbound SA from 20.20.20.20     to 20.20.20.21
          (proxy 60.60.60.0     to 50.50.50.0     )
*Mar  1 00:28:14.395:         has spi 437593758 and conn_id 7 and flags 4
*Mar  1 00:28:14.399:         lifetime of 3600 seconds
*Mar  1 00:28:14.399:         lifetime of 4608000 kilobytes
*Mar  1 00:28:14.403:         outbound SA from 20.20.20.21     to 20.20.20.20
          (proxy 50.50.50.0     to 60.60.60.0     )
*Mar  1 00:28:14.403:         has spi 411835612 and conn_id 8 and flags 4
*Mar  1 00:28:14.407:         lifetime of 3600 seconds
*Mar  1 00:28:14.407:         lifetime of 4608000 kilobytes
*Mar  1 00:28:14.411: ISAKMP (6): Creating IPsec SAs
*Mar  1 00:28:14.411:         inbound SA from 20.20.20.20     to 20.20.20.21
          (proxy 60.60.60.0     to 50.50.50.0     )
*Mar  1 00:28:14.415:         has spi 216990519 and conn_id 9 and flags 4
*Mar  1 00:28:14.415:         lifetime of 3600 seconds
*Mar  1 00:28:14.419:         lifetime of 4608000 kilobytes
*Mar  1 00:28:14.419:         outbound SA from 20.20.20.21     to 20.20.20.20
          (proxy 50.50.50.0     to 60.60.60.0     )
*Mar  1 00:28:14.423:         has spi 108733569 and conn_id 10 and flags 4
*Mar  1 00:28:14.423:         lifetime of 3600 seconds
*Mar  1 00:28:14.427:         lifetime of 4608000 kilobytes
wan2511#
```

The encrypted nonce IKE authentication method does not scale as well as the digital
signatures method of authentication using digital certificates. This is because the peers'
public keys have to be manually exchanged. However, if scalability is not a concern, and if
the other device can be trusted to provide the correct public key, this method can provide a
level of security comparable to digital certificates. In fact, there is additional security,
because the nonces are exchanged encrypted rather than in the clear, providing an added
level of security against some DH attacks.

One-to-Many Router IPsec

This is a common scenario often used when a company has multiple offices connecting to each other. The setup in this case study is fully meshed, meaning that each site can talk to every other site directly rather than having to go through a hub in the middle. While you can apply only one crypto map to an interface, a crypto map can have multiple instances, each instance being used for a unique site.

Examples 13-13, 13-14 and 13-15 show the configurations on each of the three routers used in this case study. Figure 13-48 shows the network diagram for this case study.

Figure 13-48 *Network Diagram for This Case Study*

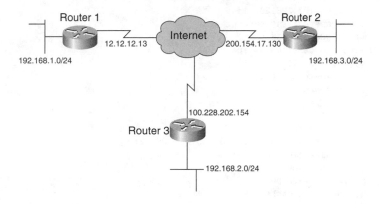

Example 13-13 *Configuration of Router1*

```
router1#write terminal
Building configuration...
Current configuration:
!
version 12.0
service timestamps debug uptime
service timestamps log uptime
!
hostname router1
!
logging buffered 4096 debugging
enable password
!
clock timezone est 8
ip subnet-zero
!
crypto isakmp policy 4
  authentication pre-share
crypto isakmp key xxxxxx1234 address 100.228.202.154
```

continues

Example 13-13 *Configuration of Router1 (Continued)*

```
crypto isakmp key xxxxxx5678 address 200.154.17.130
!
!
crypto ipsec transform-set encrypt-des esp-des esp-sha-hmac
!
!
crypto map combined local-address Serial0

!Instance 20 of the crypto map below is used for the first peer, and instance 30
!is for the second peer. The router uses whichever instance of the crypto map has
!the access list matching the traffic coming through.
crypto map combined 20 ipsec-isakmp
  set peer 100.228.202.154
  set transform-set encrypt-des
  match address 106
crypto map combined 30 ipsec-isakmp
  set peer 200.154.17.130
  set transform-set encrypt-des
  match address 105
!
!
interface Serial0
  ip address 100.232.202.210 255.255.255.252
  no ip directed-broadcast
  ip nat outside
  no ip route-cache
  no ip mroute-cache
  no fair-queue
  no cdp enable
  crypto map combined
!
interface FastEthernet0
  ip address 192.168.1.1 255.255.255.0
  no ip directed-broadcast
  ip nat inside
  no cdp enable
!
!
ip nat inside source route-map nonat interface Serial0 overload
ip classless
ip route 0.0.0.0 0.0.0.0 100.232.202.209
ip route 192.168.2.0 255.255.255.0 100.232.202.209
ip route 192.168.3.0 255.255.255.0 100.232.202.209
no ip http server
!
access-list 105 permit ip 192.168.1.0 0.0.0.255 192.168.3.0 0.0.0.255
access-list 106 permit ip 192.168.1.0 0.0.0.255 192.168.2.0 0.0.0.255
access-list 150 deny ip 192.168.1.0 0.0.0.255 192.168.2.0 0.0.0.255
access-list 150 deny ip 192.168.1.0 0.0.0.255 192.168.3.0 0.0.0.255
access-list 150 permit ip 192.168.1.0 0.0.0.255 any
no cdp run
```

Example 13-13 *Configuration of Router1 (Continued)*

```
route-map nonat permit 10
  match ip address 150
!
!
line con 0
  transport input none
  line aux 0
  password 7 aaaaaaa
  login local
  modem InOut
  transport input all
  speed 38400
  flowcontrol hardware
line vty 0 4
  exec-timeout 30 0
  password aaaaaa
login
!
end
```

Example 13-14 *Configuration of Router2*

```
router2#write terminal
Current configuration:
!
version 12.0
service timestamps debug uptime
service timestamps log uptime
service password-encryption
!
hostname router2
!
enable secret 5 <removed>
enable password 7 <removed>
!
clock timezone EST 8
ip subnet-zero
!
crypto isakmp policy 4
  authentication pre-share
crypto isakmp key xxxxxx101112 address 100.228.202.154
crypto isakmp key xxxxxx5678 address 100.232.202.210
!
!
crypto ipsec transform-set 1600_box esp-des esp-sha-hmac
!
!
crypto map combined local-address Ethernet1
```

continues

Example 13-14 *Configuration of Router2 (Continued)*

```
crypto map combined 7 ipsec-isakmp
  set peer 100.232.202.210
  set transform-set 1600_box
  match address 105
crypto map combined 8 ipsec-isakmp
  set peer 100.228.202.154
  set transform-set 1600_box
  match address 106
!
!
!
interface Ethernet0
  ip address 192.168.3.1 255.255.255.0
  no ip directed-broadcast
  ip nat inside
!
interface Ethernet1
  ip address 200.154.17.130 255.255.255.224
  no ip directed-broadcast
  ip nat outside
  crypto map combined
!
ip nat inside source route-map nonat interface Ethernet1 overload
ip classless
ip route 0.0.0.0 0.0.0.0 200.154.17.129

no ip http server
!

access-list 105 permit ip 192.168.3.0 0.0.0.255 192.168.1.0 0.0.0.255
access-list 106 permit ip 192.168.3.0 0.0.0.255 192.168.2.0 0.0.0.255
access-list 150 deny ip 192.168.3.0 0.0.0.255 192.168.1.0 0.0.0.255
access-list 150 deny ip 192.168.3.0 0.0.0.255 192.168.2.0 0.0.0.255
access-list 150 permit ip any any
route-map nonat permit 10
  match ip address 150
!

line con 0
  password 7 aaaaa
  transport input none
line vty 0 4
  exec-timeout 0 0
  password 7 aaaaaa
login
!
end
```

Example 13-15 *Configuration of Router3*

```
router3#write terminal
Current configuration:
!
version 12.0
service timestamps debug uptime
service timestamps log uptime

!
hostname router3
!
logging buffered 4096 debugging
enable secret 5 <removed>
enable password <removed>
!
clock timezone est 8
ip subnet-zero
!
!
crypto isakmp policy 4
  authentication pre-share
crypto isakmp key xxxxxx1234 address 100.232.202.210
crypto isakmp key xxxxxx101112 address 200.154.17.130
!
crypto map combined local-address Serial0
crypto map combined 7 ipsec-isakmp
  set peer 100.232.202.210
  set transform-set encrypt-des
  match address 106
crypto map combined 8 ipsec-isakmp
  set peer 200.154.17.130
  set transform-set 1600_box
  match address 105
!
!
interface Serial0
  ip address 100.228.202.154 255.255.255.252
  no ip directed-broadcast
  ip nat outside
  crypto map combined
!
interface FastEthernet0
  ip address 192.168.2.1 255.255.255.0
  no ip directed-broadcast
  ip nat inside
  no cdp enable
!
!
ip nat inside source route-map nonat interface Serial0 overload
ip classless
ip route 0.0.0.0 0.0.0.0 100.228.202.153
```

continues

Example 13-15 *Configuration of Router3 (Continued)*

```
no ip http server
!
access-list 105 permit ip 192.168.2.0 0.0.0.255 192.168.3.0 0.0.0.255
access-list 106 permit ip 192.168.2.0 0.0.0.255 192.168.1.0 0.0.0.255
access-list 150 deny   ip 192.168.2.0 0.0.0.255 192.168.3.0 0.0.0.255
access-list 150 deny   ip 192.168.2.0 0.0.0.255 192.168.1.0 0.0.0.255
access-list 150 permit ip 192.168.2.0 0.0.0.255 any
no cdp run
route-map nonat permit 10
  match ip address 150
!
!
line con 0
  transport input none
line aux 0
  password aaaa
  login local
  modem InOut
  transport input all
  speed 115200
  flowcontrol hardware
line vty 0 4
  exec-timeout 30 0
  password aaaaa
login
!
no scheduler allocate
end
```

Although the configurations shown here are for a setup in which a fully meshed environment is desirable, a partially meshed setup can be arranged as well. The accessibility of peers is determined by the crypto maps set up on the peers.

In addition to the mesh setup seen in this case study, another type of setup is a hub-and-spoke setup. In this type of setup, a hub site routes all the encrypted traffic to the peers.

High-Availability-IPsec-Over-GRE Setup

IPsec over GRE is a popular implementation mechanism often used in conjunction with IPsec. It is especially useful in some cases in which IPsec alone cannot fulfill the setup's requirements, such as when multicast traffic needs to be tunneled. This list summarizes the cases in which IPsec over GRE is often used:

- To send multicast or broadcast traffic over the VPN link.
- To send non-IP protocol-based traffic over the VPN link.

- To have high availability. By participating in routing protocols, GRE tunnels can allow IPsec tunnels to stay up even when a primary path goes down. This happens when the routing protocol allows a peer to realize that its peer cannot be reached via a given path and then converges on a different path to access the peer.

- To scale an IPsec implementation. GRE allows a single IPsec access control element (ACE) to specify the traffic that needs to be encrypted. This is done with the use of a "GRE any any" ACE defining IPsec interesting traffic.

  Note that although "any any" in an ACE is not recommended to be used to define IPsec interesting traffic, it is acceptable to use such an ACE in conjunction with using GRE with IPsec. The reason the use of an ACE with plain IPsec is discouraged is that it results in *all* traffic to and from the router being encrypted, which is often an undesirable outcome. However, with GRE, the amount of traffic that is to be encrypted is not all the traffic, just the traffic that has already been GRE-encapsulated, thereby reducing the all-encompassing behavior of the "any any" ACE.

Using GRE with IPsec to encapsulate and encrypt multicast traffic is very useful in setups in which there is a need to route routing protocols such as EIGRP over the tunnel. Using GRE allows two networks to be seamlessly connected in terms of routing.

IPsec is often used in transport mode with GRE because GRE can provide the tunneling that IPsec tunnel mode provides. Therefore, not using IPsec tunnel mode saves some amount of packet overhead.

GRE can carry this kind of traffic, but it does not have the IPsec protocol's encryption-handling capabilities. Therefore, a combination of the two works well. The overhead to the packet added by GRE is often insignificant as compared to IPsec. The sequence of events that takes place in this setup is as follows: The plain-text packet is first encapsulated using the GRE protocol. After this is done, IPsec takes over and encrypts the GRE packet. The crypto map needs to be applied to the physical interface and the tunnel interface. This statement is true for any logical interface you might be using in an IPsec setup (such as BVI interfaces). In this case study we see IPX traffic sent encrypted across the VPN link.

Examples 13-16, 13-17 and 13-18 show the configurations on each of the three routers used in this case study. Figure 13-49 shows the network diagram for this case study.

Figure 13-49 *Network Diagram for This Case Study*

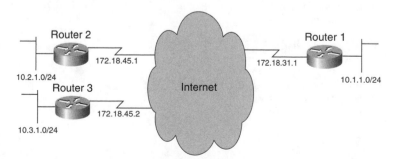

Example 13-16 *Configuration of Router1*

```
router1#write terminal
Current configuration:
!
version 12.0
service timestamps debug uptime
service timestamps log uptime
!
hostname router1
!
logging buffered 4096 debugging
enable secret 5 <removed>
enable password <removed>
!
clock timezone est 8
ip subnet-zero
!

crypto isakmp policy 10
 authentication pre-share
crypto isakmp key cisco123 address 172.18.45.1
crypto isakmp key cisco345 address 172.18.45.2
!
crypto ipsec transform-set one esp-des esp-md5-hmac
mode transport
!
!Crypto map for router 2
crypto map gre 10 ipsec-isakmp
 set peer 172.18.45.1
 set transform-set one
 match address gre1
!Crypto map for router 3
crypto map gre 20 ipsec-isakmp
 set peer 172.18.45.2
 set transform-set one
 match address gre2
!
!Tunnel to router 1
interface Tunnel0
 ip address 10.4.1.1 255.255.255.0
 tunnel source 172.18.31.1
 tunnel destination 172.18.45.1
 crypto map gre
!
!Tunnel to router 2
interface Tunnel1
 ip address 10.4.2.1 255.255.255.0
 tunnel source 172.18.31.1
 tunnel destination 172.18.45.2
 crypto map gre
!
```

Example 13-16 *Configuration of Router1 (Continued)*

```
!
interface Ethernet0
 ip address 10.1.1.1 255.255.255.0
!
interface Serial0
 ip address 172.18.31.1 255.255.255.0
 crypto map gre
!
!
ip classless
ip route 172.18.0.0 255.255.0.0 serial0
!Below is the configuration for GRE used to do the routing over the GRE tunnels
ip eigrp 100
 network 10.0.0.0
!
!
!To reduce the number of access lists, in case a large number of peers are set up,
!a simple GRE any any access list can be used to define the interesting traffic.
!Only one such access list is needed.

ip access-list extended gre1
 permit gre host 172.18.31.1 host 172.18.45.1
!
ip access-list extended gre2
 permit gre host 172.18.31.1 host 172.18.45.2
```

Example 13-17 *Configuration of Router2*

```
router2#write terminal
Current configuration:
!
version 12.0
service timestamps debug uptime
service timestamps log uptime
!
hostname router2
!
logging buffered 4096 debugging
enable secret 5 <removed>
enable password <removed>
!
clock timezone est 8
ip subnet-zero
!

crypto isakmp policy 10
 authentication pre-share
crypto isakmp key cisco123 address 172.18.31.1
```

continues

Example 13-17 *Configuration of Router2 (Continued)*

```
!
crypto ipsec transform-set one esp-des esp-md5-hmac
 mode transport
!
crypto map gre 10 ipsec-isakmp
 set peer 172.18.31.1
 set transform-set one
 match address gre1
!
!
interface Tunnel0
 ip address 10.10.1.1 255.255.255.0
 tunnel source 172.18.45.1
 tunnel destination 172.18.31.1
 crypto map gre
!
!
interface Ethernet0
 ip address 10.2.1.1 255.255.255.0
!
interface Serial0
 ip address 172.18.45.1 255.255.255.0
 crypto map gre
!
!
ip classless
ip route 172.18.0.0 255.255.0.0 serial0

ip eigrp 100
 network 10.0.0.0
!
!
ip access-list extended gre1
 permit gre host 172.18.45.1 host 172.18.31.1
!
```

Example 13-18 *Configuration of Router3*

```
router3#write terminal
Current configuration:
!
version 12.0
service timestamps debug uptime
service timestamps log uptime
!
hostname router3
!
logging buffered 4096 debugging
enable secret 5 <removed>
enable password <removed>
```

Example 13-18 *Configuration of Router3 (Continued)*

```
!
clock timezone est 8
ip subnet-zero
!

crypto isakmp policy 10
 authentication pre-share
crypto isakmp key cisco345 address 172.18.31.1

!
crypto ipsec transform-set one esp-des esp-md5-hmac
 mode transport
!
crypto map gre 10 ipsec-isakmp
 set peer 172.18.31.1
 set transform-set one
 match address gre1
!
!
interface Tunnel0
 ip address 10.5.1.1 255.255.255.0
 tunnel source 172.18.45.2
 tunnel destination 172.18.31.1
 crypto map gre
!
!

interface Ethernet0
 ip address 10.3.1.1 255.255.255.0
!
interface Serial0
 ip address 172.18.45.2 255.255.255.0
 crypto map gre
!
!
ip classless
ip route 172.18.0.0 255.255.0.0 serial0

ip eigrp 100
 network 10.0.0.0
!
!
ip access-list extended gre1
 permit gre host 172.18.45.2 host 172.18.31.1
!
```

Remote-Access IPsec Using X-Auth, Dynamic Crypto Maps, Mode Config, and Preshared Keys

This case study is essentially a compilation of a number of features that can be used with remote-access IPsec VPNs.

- As discussed earlier, x-auth (extended authentication) is the method used to allow users to authenticate themselves on a per-user basis rather than use only a wildcard preshared secret shared by all the users.

- Dynamic crypto maps allow the router to accept connections from VPN clients whose IP addresses it does not know.

- Mode configs allow the router to assign IP addresses to the VPN clients after they have connected to it. This address, known as the internal IP address, is different from the IP address assigned to the clients when they connect to the ISP. The ISP address is used to carry the IPsec packet over the Internet. The internal IP address, often a private address, is embedded in the IPsec packet and is used to communicate with the private network behind the router.

The configuration in this case study is based on Cisco Secure VPN Client 1.1. The router configuration is included in Example 13-19 while the configuration for the VPN client is shown in Example 13-20. Figure 13-50 shows the network diagram for this case study.

Figure 13-50 *Network Diagram for This Case Study*

Example 13-19 *Configuration of the Router Called Concentrator*

```
Concentrator#show running-config
Building configuration...

Current configuration:
!
version 12.0
service timestamps debug uptime
service timestamps log uptime
!
hostname Concentrator
!
enable secret 5 <removed>
enable password ww
!
aaa new-model
```

Example 13-19 *Configuration of the Router Called Concentrator (Continued)*

```
!The command below defines the mechanism to use for extended authentication

aaa authentication login xauth local
!The user defined below will be used to authenticate the x-auth clients
username ciscouser password 0 cisco1234

!
ip subnet-zero
!
crypto isakmp policy 10
 hash md5
 authentication pre-share

!The wildcard preshared key is configured because the client's IP address is
!unknown

crypto isakmp key cisco123 address 0.0.0.0

!Here we identify the pool to use to assign addresses to the VPN clients

crypto isakmp client configuration address-pool local mypool

!Binding the extended authentication list to the crypto map being used

crypto map REMOTEACCESS client authentication list xauth
!


crypto ipsec transform-set RTP-TRANSFORM esp-des esp-md5-hmac
!
crypto dynamic-map vpn 1
 set transform-set RTP-TRANSFORM
!
!The following commands request that IP addresses be assigned to the VPN clients

crypto map REMOTEACCESS client configuration address initiate
crypto map REMOTEACCESS client configuration address respond

!Below is the static crypto map that points to a dynamic crypto map. This is
!applied to the router's outside interface. Note that a dynamic crypto map cannot
!be applied directly to an interface.

crypto map REMOTEACCESS 1 ipsec-isakmp dynamic vpn
!
interface Ethernet0/0
ip address 150.1.1.1 255.255.255.0
crypto map REMOTEACCESS
!
```

continues

Example 13-19 *Configuration of the Router Called Concentrator (Continued)*

```
!
interface Ethernet0/1
ip address 11.10.1.1 255.255.255.0
no ip directed-broadcast
!
!This is the pool from which we assign addresses to the clients

ip local pool mypool 10.1.10.0 10.1.10.254
ip nat translation timeout never
ip nat translation tcp-timeout never
ip nat translation udp-timeout never
ip nat translation finrst-timeout never
ip nat translation syn-timeout never
ip nat translation dns-timeout never
ip nat translation icmp-timeout never
ip classless
ip route 0.0.0.0 0.0.0.0 10.103.1.1
no ip http server
!
dialer-list 1 protocol ip permit
dialer-list 1 protocol ipx permit
!
line con 0
transport input none
line aux 0
line vty 0 4
password <removed>
login
!
end
```

Example 13-20 *Configuration of a VPN Client Connecting to the Router Called Concentrator*

```
VPN CLIENT CONFIGURATION

VPNClient - Pre-shared, Wild-card, Mode-config
Name of connection:
Remote party address = IP_Subnet = 10.1.1.0, Mask 255.255.255.0
Connect using Secure Gateway Tunnel to 150.1.1.1
My Identity:
Select certificate = None
ID_Type = ip address (171.68.118.143), pre-shared key and fill in key ('cisco123')
Security policy = defaults
Proposal 1 (Authen) = DES, MD5
Proposal 2 (Key Exchange) = DES, MD5, Tunnel
```

PIX IPsec Combining LAN-to-LAN and Remote-Access Setups

The PIX Firewall can also terminate IPsec tunnels. This case study shows a setup in which the PIX terminates a LAN-to-LAN and remote-access IPsec tunnel. The same crypto map is used for both the VPN clients and the LAN-to-LAN connection. Different instance numbers are applied to distinguish between the crypto maps used for the two types of tunnels. The VPN-relevant configuration is shown in bold.

Example 13-21 shows the configuration on the PIX firewall for this case study. Example 13-22 shows the setup of the router connecting to the PIX using IPsec. Figure 13-51 shows the network diagram for this case study.

Figure 13-51 *Network Diagram for This Case Study*

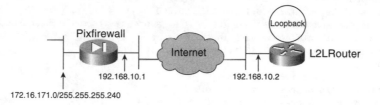

Example 13-21 *Configuration of the PIX Called Pixfirewall*

```
pixfirewall#write terminal
PIX Version 5.2
nameif ethernet0 outside security0
nameif ethernet1 inside security100
nameif ethernet2 dmz security50
access-list bypassingnat permit ip 172.16.0.0 255.255.0.0 10.1.100.0 255.255.255.0
access-list bypassingnat permit ip 172.16.0.0 255.255.0.0 10.1.1.0 255.255.255.0
access-list bypassingnat permit ip host 20.1.1.1 host 10.1.1.1
access-list inboundtraffic permit icmp any any
access-list inboundtraffic permit tcp any host 192.168.10.100 eq telnet
access-list 101 permit ip host 20.1.1.1 host 10.1.1.1
enable password <removed> encrypted
passwd <removed> encrypted
hostname pixfirewall
fixup protocol ftp 21
fixup protocol http 80
fixup protocol smtp 25
fixup protocol h323 1720
fixup protocol rsh 514
fixup protocol sqlnet 1521
names
pager lines 24
no logging timestamp
no logging standby
no logging console debugging
```

continues

Example 13-21 *Configuration of the PIX Called Pixfirewall (Continued)*

```
no logging monitor
no logging buffered
no logging trap
no logging history
logging facility 20
logging queue 512
interface ethernet0 auto
interface ethernet1 auto
interface ethernet2 auto
mtu outside 1500
mtu inside 1500
mtu dmz 1500
ip address outside 192.168.10.1 255.255.255.0
ip address inside 172.16.171.5 255.255.255.240
ip address dmz 127.0.0.1 255.255.255.255
!The command below defines the pool of addresses from which addresses get assigned
!to the clients connecting to the PIX via mode config
ip local pool vpnpool 10.1.100.240-10.1.100.250
no failover
failover timeout 0:00:00
failover ip address outside 0.0.0.0
failover ip address inside 0.0.0.0
failover ip address dmz 0.0.0.0
arp timeout 14400
global (outside) 1 192.168.10.20-192.168.10.30 netmask 255.255.255.0
global (outside) 1 192.168.10.19 netmask 255.255.255.0
!The NAT command configured below stops NAT from occurring for IP addresses pairs
!that the PIX considers IPsec interesting traffic. This includes packets destined
!for the remote LAN as well as pool addresses assigned to the VPN clients. See the
!access list bypassingnat above to see which addresses are defined to bypass NAT.
nat (inside) 0 access-list bypassingnat
nat (inside) 1 172.16.0.0 255.255.0.0 0 0
static (inside,outside) 192.168.10.100 172.16.171.13 netmask 255.255.255.255 0 0
static (inside,outside) 20.1.1.1 20.1.1.1 netmask 255.255.255.255 0 0
access-group inboundtraffic in interface outside
route outside 0.0.0.0 0.0.0.0 192.168.10.2 1
route inside 20.0.0.0 255.0.0.0 172.16.171.13 1
route inside 171.68.0.0 255.255.0.0 172.16.171.1 1
route inside 172.16.0.0 255.255.0.0 172.16.171.1 1
timeout xlate 3:00:00 conn 1:00:00 half-closed 0:10:00 udp 0:02:00
timeout rpc 0:10:00 h323 0:05:00
timeout uauth 0:05:00 absolute
aaa-server TACACS+ protocol tacacs+
aaa-server RADIUS protocol radius
aaa-server myserver protocol tacacs+
aaa-server myserver (inside) host 171.68.178.124 cisco timeout 5
no snmp-server location
no snmp-server contact
snmp-server community public
no snmp-server enable traps
floodguard enable
```

Example 13-21 *Configuration of the PIX Called Pixfirewall (Continued)*

```
!The sysopt command below allows IPsec traffic to bypass the security checks
!performed by the PIX on incoming traffic from a low- to a high-security
!interface. The assumption is that IPsec takes care of nongenuine packets and
!drops them.
sysopt connection permit-ipsec
!The command below defines the transform set to use for IPsec.
crypto ipsec transform-set mysetdes esp-des esp-md5-hmac
!The command below defines the dynamic crypto map used to accept VPN client
!traffic.
crypto dynamic-map mydynmap 10 set transform-set mysetdes
!The crypto map below is used for the LAN-to-LAN tunnels that will be established
!by the PIX.
crypto map newmap 20 ipsec-isakmp
crypto map newmap 20 match address 101
crypto map newmap 20 set peer 192.168.10.2
crypto map newmap 20 set transform-set mysetdes
!The crypto map below is used to tie to the dynamic crypto map defined above.
!Note that this is simply another instance of the crypto map configured for the
!LAN-to-LAN tunnel, because only one crypto map can be applied to a PIX interface.
This !crypto map points to the dynamic crypto map defined above.
crypto map newmap 30 ipsec-isakmp dynamic mydynmap
!The two commands below set up the PIX to do mode configuration for the remote-
!access clients, allowing it to initiate as well as accept requests for mode
!configuration
crypto map newmap client configuration address initiate
crypto map newmap client configuration address respond
!The command below ties the authentication to be done for extended authentication
!to the server defined as 'myserver'
crypto map newmap client authentication myserver
!The command below applies the crypto map to the outside interface
crypto map newmap interface outside
!The isakmp enable command in PIX is an additional command needed for ISAKMP
!configs
!isakmp enable outside
!The preshared secret defined below is the wildcard key for the remote-access
!clients.
isakmp key mysecretkey address 0.0.0.0 netmask 0.0.0.0
!The command below defines the preshared secret for the router. It also has the
!keywords 'no-xauth' and 'no-config-mode' at the end, which specify that x-auth and
!config mode are not to be done with this peer
isakmp key myotherkey address 192.168.10.2 netmask 255.255.255.255 no-xauth no-
config-mode
isakmp identity address
!The command below is used to define the pool that will be used to assign
!addresses via mode config to the VPN clients
isakmp client configuration address-pool local vpnpool outside
!The commands below define the parameters of the ISAKMP policy on the PIX
isakmp policy 10 authentication pre-share
isakmp policy 10 encryption des
isakmp policy 10 hash md5
isakmp policy 10 group 1
```

continues

Example 13-21 *Configuration of the PIX Called Pixfirewall (Continued)*

```
telnet timeout 5
terminal width 80

: end
```

Example 13-22 *Configuration of the Router L2LRouter*

```
L2LRouter#write terminal
Router Configuration
Current configuration:
!
version 12.0
service timestamps debug uptime
service timestamps log uptime

!
hostname L2LRouter
!
aaa new-model
!
ip subnet-zero
!
!
crypto isakmp policy 10
 hash md5
 authentication pre-share
 lifetime 1000
crypto isakmp key myotherkey address 192.168.10.1
!
crypto ipsec transform-set strong esp-des esp-md5-hmac
!
crypto map topix 10 ipsec-isakmp
 set peer 192.168.10.1
 set transform-set strong
 match address 101
!
interface Loopback0
 ip address 10.1.1.1 255.255.255.255
 no ip directed-broadcast
!
interface Ethernet0/0
 ip address 192.168.10.2 255.255.255.0
 no ip directed-broadcast
 crypto map topix

!
ip classless
ip route 0.0.0.0 0.0.0.0 192.168.10.1
no ip http server
```

Example 13-22 *Configuration of the Router L2LRouter (Continued)*

```
!
access-list 101 permit ip host 10.1.1.1 host 20.1.1.1
!
line con 0
 transport input none
line aux 0
line vty 0 4
!
end
```

IPsec Over L2TP Using Voluntary Tunneling

This case study describes the use of the Windows 2000 built-in L2TP and IPsec client to connect to a router. The L2TP tunnel is encrypted using IPsec. In the preceding chapter we looked at an example of compulsory tunneling in which the LAC did the tunneling on behalf of the client. In this case study, L2TP is done by the client itself. This type of scenario is known as *voluntary tunneling*. In addition, IPsec is also run between the client and the IPsec gateway, ensuring that L2TP is protected via the security features offered by IPsec.

Figure 13-52 shows the network diagram for this case study.

Figure 13-52 *Network Diagram for This Case Study*

Setting Up IPsec on the Windows 2000 Host

A description of how to setup Windows 2000 to connect to a router follows. However, the reader is advised to read the following detailed documents on the Microsoft website for more detailed information on how to setup Windows 2000 to do L2TP/IPsec:

"How to Configure a L2TP/IPsec Connection Using Pre-shared Key Authentication" (Q240262)

Although IPsec is part of the Windows 2000 installation, you must enable it via the Microsoft Management Console (MMC) to configure the IPsec service:

Enabling IPsec Service

Step 1   Select **Start > Run** and type **mmc**.

Step 2   The window Console1 opens. From here, select **Add/Remove Snap-in**.

Step 3   Click the **Add** button. A list of snap-ins appears.

Step 4   Go down the list and select **IP Security Policy Management**, and then click **Add**.

Step 5   Close the Add window and return to the console.

Defining an IPsec Policy and associated rules

Three default policies are available by default on the console:

- **Client Respond Only**—Allows unsecured communications but negotiates security if requested by the server.
- **Secure Server**—For all IP traffic, always require security using Kerberos.
- **Server (Request Security)**—For all IP traffic, always request security using Kerberos.

Note that these are defaults only. You can change the information. For example, you can use IKE authentication methods other than Kerberos, but the best thing to do is create your own policy.

To create a customized policy, follow this procedure:

Step 1   Right-click the IP Security Policies icon and select Create IP Security Policy.

Step 2   Use the wizard to create your first policy. Select the defaults until you are asked about the authentication method for IKE. Select either Digital certificates or Pre-Shared key. If you select certificates, you must have access to the certificate authority you want to use, you must have already retrieved the CA's certificate, and you must have enrolled your client with the CA. If you have not done these things, you cannot browse for a CA. You can select something else and then come back later and change it. For this case study assume that pre-shared key was chosen.

Step 3   After creating the policy, you can right-click it and select **properties** to edit it. The default rule is already applied to the policy. You can edit this rule shown as '<dynamic>', or, for simplicity, create a new one.

Step 4   Click **Add**, and go to the **New Rule Properties** window. A number of tabs will be present on this window. In the following steps we will go through each of these tabs to setup the rules needed to configure IPsec to occur for the L2TP traffic.

Step 5   Select **IP Filter List**, click **Add**, name the list, and either use the wizard or add the parameters manually. For L2TP you must configure three lists. The concept is that all traffic in the L2TP tunnel is protected by your IPsec policy. All three lists will be for UDP traffic. The first one will specify traffic going from UDP source port 1701 to UDP destination port 1701. The second one will specify traffic going from UDP source port 1701 to any UDP destination port and the last list will be for traffic coming from any UDP source port and going to the UDP destination port 1701. When adding the filters, remember that you are specifying what traffic you are applying your IPsec policy to. In this case, the policy is applied to the L2TP tunnel, so you are setting up a transport mode IPsec connection between the client and the gateway. Your tunnel endpoints are usually the client's IP address and the gateway's IP address. Follow these steps:

Step 6   Apply the filter list, and move on to filter action.

Step 7   The **Filter action** tab is where you specify your IPsec policy. You can use the wizard or create it manually. You may add more than one combination of algorithms (this is analogous to creating multiple transform sets in Cisco IOS). All combinations are proposed to the gateway.

Step 8   You use the **Authentication Methods** tab to edit the authentication method used during IKE main mode peer authentication. You can define multiple authentication methods. In our example we have defined the preshared key 'ciscosys' on this screen.

Step 9   The **Tunnel Setting** tab is used to define IPsec's transport and tunnel modes. For L2TP, you are setting up a transport mode IPsec connection, so you must select **This rule does not specify an IPsec Tunnel**.

Step 10   The **Connection Type** tab allows you to apply this policy to individual adapters or to all adapters in your PC. You are now finished defining your rule. Make sure you select it from the list and apply it.

Step 11   The actual IKE parameters are accessed via the **General** tab, next to the **Rules** tab. You can change the IKE lifetime. If you click **Advanced**, you may edit the attributes in the IKE proposals.

Step 12   After you have finished defining your customized policy, return to the Console screen. Right-click the new policy and select **assign**. By doing this, you assign this policy to any adapter or connection you specified during the creation of the policy rules. For example, if you applied this

rule to all remote-access connections, when you assign the policy, that
rule is assigned to any L2TP connections initiated by this PC.

Configuring the Windows 2000 Client for L2TP

To complete the setup for L2TP over IPsec, you must set up L2TP on the Windows 2000
client. You must define and configure your L2TP connection by doing the following:

Step 1   Select either **Start > Settings > Control Panel > Network > Dial-up
Connections** or **Start > Settings > Network > Dial-up Connections >
Make New Connection**.

Step 2   Use the wizard to create a connection called L2TP. This connection
connects to a private network through the Internet. You also need to
specify the L2TP tunnel gateway's IP address or name (10.0.0.7 in this
example).

Step 3   The new connection appears in the Network and Dial-up Connections
window in Control Panel. Right-click it to edit its properties.

Step 4   Under the **Networking** tab, make sure that the 'Type of Server I am
calling' is set to L2TP. If you plan on allocating a dynamic internal
address to this client from the gateway, via either a local pool or DHCP,
select TCP/IP protocol, thenmake sure that the client is configured to
obtain an IP address automatically. You may also issue DNS information
automatically. The **Advanced** button lets you define static WINS and
DNS information, and the **Options** tab lets you turn off IPsec or assign a
different policy to the connection.

Step 5   Under the **Security** tab, you can define the user authentication
parameters, such as PAP, CHAP, MS-CHAP, or Windows domain logon.

Step 6   As soon as the connection is configured, double-click it to pop up the
login screen, and then select **connect**.

During the connection lifetime, statistics are available via the VPN connection icon in the
bottom-right corner of the toolbar. IPsec status is available through Ipsecmon.

Example 13-23 outlines the commands required for L2TP and IPsec on the router.

Example 13-23 *Configuration of the Router LNS*

```
LNS#write terminal
version 12.0
service timestamps debug uptime
service timestamps log uptime
!
hostname LNS
```

Example 13-23 *Configuration of the Router LNS (Continued)*

```
!
boot system flash c4500-is56-mz

!Enable AAA services here
aaa new-model
aaa authentication ppp default radius local
enable secret 5 <removed>
enable password cisco
!
username munchkin password 7 <removed>
ip subnet-zero
ip domain-name cisco.com
ip name-server 10.0.0.4
!
!Enable VPN/VPDN services and define groups and their particular variables
vpdn enable
!
vpdn-group 1
!Default L2TP VPDN group
!Allow the router to accept incoming requests.
 accept dialin l2tp virtual-template 1
!Tunnel authentication is used in the LNS to LAC, aka NAS-initiated L2TP tunnel.
!Users are authenticated at the NAS or LNS before the tunnel is established.
!So it is not required for client-initiated tunnels.
 no l2tp tunnel authentication
!

!These are the IKE policies the router will accept
crypto isakmp policy 4
!
crypto isakmp policy 5
 hash md5
!
crypto isakmp policy 6
 hash md5
 group 2
!
!Use this for IKE and wildcard preshared keys
crypto isakmp key ciscosys address 0.0.0.0
!
!
!Define the IPsec policies the router will accept/propose. For L2TP connections,
!the mode should be transport
crypto IPsec transform-set desmd5tr esp-des esp-md5-hmac
 mode transport
crypto IPsec transform-set ahshatr ah-sha-hmac
 mode transport
crypto IPsec transform-set ahmd5tr ah-md5-hmac
 mode transport
!
```

continues

Example 13-23 *Configuration of the Router LNS (Continued)*

```
!Set up a dynamic crypto map template
crypto dynamic-map dyna 1

set transform-set ahmd5tr
 match address 110
 !
!If you are using RSA signatures, include your CA identity. This identity is
!configured to use the Microsoft CA with SCEP support.
 !
crypto ca identity cisco.com
 enrollment retry count 100
 enrollment mode ra
 enrollment url http://cisco-b0tpppy88:80/certsrv/mscep/mscep.dll
 crl optional
 !
!Certs removed for keeping the configs short
 !
crypto ca certificate chain cisco.com
 certificate 615D1CBC000000000006
 certificate ra-sign 710685AF000000000004
 certificate 615D299B000000000007
 certificate ca 578242EB5428E68A4D02516EF449B266
 certificate ra-encrypt 71068B79000000000005
 !
!Apply the dynamic crypto map template to an actual crypto map
crypto map iosmsdyn 1 IPsec-isakmp dynamic dyna
 !
 !
interface Ethernet0
 ip address 10.0.0.7 255.255.255.0
 no ip redirects
 no ip directed-broadcast
 crypto map iosmsdyn
 !
 !
interface Virtual-Template1
 ip unnumbered Ethernet0
 no ip directed-broadcast
 peer default ip address pool vpdn
 ppp authentication ms-chap
 !
router rip
 redistribute connected
 redistribute static
network 192.168.0.0
 !
!Define your local address pool and any other dynamically assigned information
ip local pool vpdn 192.168.2.10 192.168.2.15
no ip classless
ip route 0.0.0.0 0.0.0.0 192.168.0.100
no ip http server
```

Example 13-23 *Configuration of the Router LNS (Continued)*

```
!
access-list 110 permit udp host 192.168.0.7 any eq 1701
access-list 110 permit udp any eq 1701 host 192.168.0.7
access-list 110 permit udp host 192.168.0.7 eq 1701 any
!
!
radius-server host 192.168.0.4 auth-port 1645 acct-port 1646
radius-server key kitchen
!
line con 0
 transport input none
line aux 0
line vty 0 4
 password cisco
!
end
```

Tunnel Endpoint Discovery (TED) with IPsec

This case study covers a special feature available in Cisco router implementations. TED allows a router to dynamically configure its IPsec peer address without your having to configure it manually in the router configs. This is a useful scalability feature that lets you set up a large number of peers simply by defining an access list for their interesting traffic and then allowing TED to find out who the peers are. The catch is that the interesting traffic must be defined using globally routable addresses if the VPN is being set up over the Internet. This is necessary because TED uses normal routing to figure out where the IPsec peers are.

TED works by using a probe packet that is sent with the destination address set to the IP address defined as the destination IP in the packet received on the router from a network behind the router. This probe is intercepted by the IPsec router sitting in front of the destination IP address. This router gleans the necessary information about the proxy IDs that prompted the first router to send out a probe. Then it sends back a probe reply with proxy IDs that are either the same as the ones that were sent by the initiator or are a subset of the those. These proxy IDs are the ones that are used by the initiator to negotiate the IPsec tunnel.

Figure 13-53 shows the process through which a router discovers its IPsec peer after being configured with only an access list specifying the interesting traffic for IPsec.

Figure 13-54 shows the format of the TED probe that a router sends to try and discover its peer and the probe response that is sent in response by the discovered peer. The ID payloads contain the source addresses configured on the router as interesting traffic (source proxy ID) and the ID of the initiator coded as its IP address. This allows the peer intercepting the probe to know which address it is supposed to send the probe reply to. Examples 13-24 and 13-25 show how to set up routers to do TED discovery. Examples 13-26 through 13-29 show various debugs and **show** commands for the successful setup. Figure 13-55 shows the network diagram for this case study.

Figure 13-53 *TED Discovery Process*

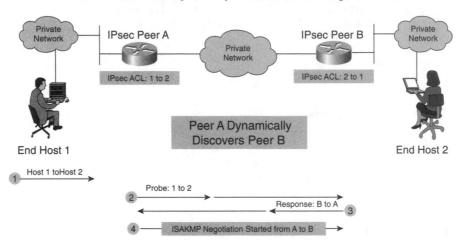

Mechanism Used to Dynamically Discover Peer and Negotiate Proxies

Figure 13-54 *TED Probe and TED Probe Response Packet Structure*

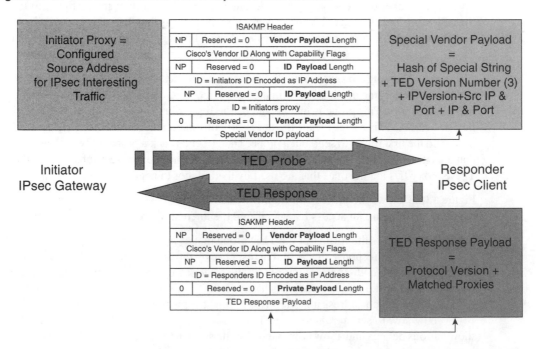

Figure 13-55 *Network Diagram for This Case Study*

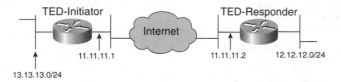

Example 13-24 *Configuration of the Router TED-Initiator*

```
TED-Initiator#show running-config
Building configuration...

Current configuration:
!
version 12.0
service timestamps debug uptime
service timestamps log uptime

!
hostname TED-Initiator
!
enable secret 5 <removed>
enable password <removed>
!
ip subnet-zero
!
crypto isakmp policy 10
 authentication pre-share
!One of the issues with using a preshared key with TED is the need to use a
!wildcard preshared key because the peer's address is not known beforehand. A
!resolution to this is to use digital certificate-based digital signatures as the
!authentication method.
crypto isakmp key abc123 address 0.0.0.0
 !
crypto ipsec transform-set ted-transforms esp-des esp-md5-hmac
!Note that no peer address has been configured in the crypto map below.
crypto dynamic-map ted-map 10
 set transform-set ted-transforms
 match address 101
 !
!The keyword discover in the crypto map below triggers the use of TED

crypto map tedtag 10 ipsec-isakmp dynamic ted-map discover
 !
interface Ethernet0/0
 ip address 13.13.13.13 255.255.255.0
 no ip directed-broadcast
 no mop enabled
```

continues

Example 13-24 *Configuration of the Router TED-Initiator (Continued)*

```
!
interface Ethernet0/1
 ip address 11.11.11.1 255.255.255.0
 crypto map tedtag
!
ip classless
ip route 0.0.0.0 0.0.0.0 11.11.11.2
no ip http server
!
access-list 101 permit ip 13.13.13.0 0.0.0.255 12.12.12.0 0.0.0.255
access-list 101 permit icmp 13.13.13.0 0.0.0.255 12.12.12.0 0.0.0.255
!
line con 0
 transport input none
line aux 0
line vty 0 4
 password ww
 login
!
end
```

Example 13-25 *Configuration of the Router TED-Responder*

```
TED-Responder#show running-config
Building configuration...

Current configuration:
!
version 12.0
service timestamps debug uptime
service timestamps log uptime

!
hostname TED-Responder
!
enable secret 5 <removed>
enable password <removed>
!


!
crypto isakmp policy 10
 authentication pre-share
crypto isakmp key abc123 address 0.0.0.0
!
crypto ipsec transform-set ted-transforms esp-des esp-md5-hmac
!
crypto dynamic-map ted-map 10
 set transform-set ted-transforms
 match address 101
```

Example 13-25 *Configuration of the Router TED-Responder (Continued)*

```
!
crypto map tedtag 10 ipsec-isakmp dynamic ted-map discover
!
interface Ethernet0/0
 ip address 12.12.12.12 255.255.255.0
 no ip directed-broadcast
 no mop enabled
!
interface Ethernet0/1
 ip address 11.11.11.2 255.255.255.0
 crypto map tedtag
!
ip classless
ip route 0.0.0.0 0.0.0.0 11.11.11.1
no ip http server
!
access-list 101 permit ip 12.12.12.0 0.0.0.255 13.13.13.0 0.0.0.255
access-list 101 permit icmp 12.12.12.0 0.0.0.255 13.13.13.0 0.0.0.255

!
line con 0
 transport input none
line aux 0
line vty 0 4
 password ww
 login
!
no scheduler allocate
end
```

Example 13-26 *Debugs on the Router TED-Initiator*

```
TED-Initiator#show debug
Cryptographic Subsystem:
  Crypto ISAKMP debugging is on
  Crypto Engine debugging is on
  Crypto IPSEC debugging is on
TED-Initiator#
!The TED process has started. The proxy IDs are shown in the message below.
01:33:56: IPSEC(tunnel discover request): ,
  (key eng. msg.) src= 13.13.13.14, dest= 12.12.12.13,
    src_proxy= 13.13.13.0/255.255.255.0/0/0 (type=4),
    dest_proxy= 11.11.11.1/255.255.255.255/0/0 (type=1),
    protocol= ESP, transform= esp-des esp-md5-hmac ,
    lifedur= 3600s and 4608000kb,
    spi= 0x0(0), conn_id= 0, keysize= 0, flags= 0x4044
01:33:56: GOT A PEER DISCOVERY MESSAGE FROM THE SA MANAGER!!!
01:33:56: src = 13.13.13.14 to 12.12.12.13, protocol 3, transform 2, hmac 1
```

continues

Example 13-26 *Debugs on the Router TED-Initiator (Continued)*

```
!The TED process below determines which address is the source address in the TED
!packet and which addresses are the proxy IDs.
01:33:56: proxy source is 13.13.13.0     /255.255.255.0   and my address (not used
  now) is 11.11.11.1
01:33:56: ISAKMP (1): ID payload
        next-payload : 5
        type         : 1
        protocol     : 17
        port         : 500
        length       : 8
01:33:56: ISAKMP (1): Total payload length: 12
!The initiator determines below that the first ID payload will be its own IP
!address, 11.11.11.1, and the second payload contains its source IPsec proxy:
!13.13.13.0/24
01:33:56: 1st ID is 11.11.11.1
01:33:56: 2nd ID is 13.13.13.0     /255.255.255.0
01:33:56: ISAKMP (0:1): beginning peer discovery exchange
!The TED probe is being sent to the destination IP address found in the original
!packet that was received on the initiator and that matched the IPsec interesting
!traffic access list.
01:33:56: ISAKMP (1): sending packet to 12.12.12.13 (I) PEER_DISCOVERY
!The peer has been discovered to be 12.12.12.13, and it responds as shown below
01:33:56: ISAKMP (1): received packet from 12.12.12.13 (I) PEER_DISCOVERY
!Upon processing the vendor ID payload, the initiator ascertains that the
!responder does indeed understand what was sent to it.
01:33:56: ISAKMP (0:1): processing vendor id payload
01:33:56: ISAKMP (0:1): speaking to another IOS box!
01:33:56: ISAKMP (0:1): processing ID payload. message ID = 0
!The responder's IP address is encoded in the ID payload. It is equal to 11.11.11.2
01:33:56: ISAKMP (0:1): processing ID payload. message ID = 1168952014
!Upon looking at the ID payload sent by the responder, the initiator finds that
!the responder's proxy ID indeed matches the proxy configured on itself.
01:33:56: ISAKMP (1): ID_IPV4_ADDR_SUBNET dst 12.12.12.0/255.255.255.0 prot 0 port 0
01:33:56: ISAKMP (1): received response to my peer discovery probe!
!Normal IKE processing starts at this point to the IP address discovered through
!TED
01:33:56  ISAKMP: initiating IKE to 11.11.11.2 in response to probe.
01:33:56: ISAKMP (2): sending packet to 11.11.11.2 (I) MM_NO_STATE
01:33:56: ISAKMP (0:1): deleting SA
01:33:56: ISAKMP (2): received packet from 11.11.11.2 (I) MM_NO_STATE
01:33:56: ISAKMP (0:2): processing SA payload. message ID = 0
01:33:56: ISAKMP (0:2): Checking ISAKMP transform 1 against priority 10 policy
01:33:56: ISAKMP:      encryption DES-CBC
01:33:56: ISAKMP:      hash SHA
01:33:56: ISAKMP:      default group 1
01:33:56: ISAKMP:      auth pre-share
01:33:56: ISAKMP (0:2): atts are acceptable. Next payload is 0
01:33:56: CryptoEngine0: generate alg parameter
01:33:56: CRYPTO_ENGINE: Dh phase 1 status: 0
01:33:56: CRYPTO_ENGINE: Dh phase 1 status: 0
01:33:56: ISAKMP (0:2): SA is doing pre-shared key authentication
```

Example 13-26 *Debugs on the Router TED-Initiator (Continued)*

```
01:33:56: ISAKMP (2): SA is doing pre-shared key authentication using id type
  ID_IPV4_ADDR
01:33:56: ISAKMP (2): sending packet to 11.11.11.2 (I) MM_SA_SETUP
01:33:56: ISAKMP (2): received packet from 11.11.11.2 (I) MM_SA_SETUP
01:33:56: ISAKMP (0:2): processing KE payload. message ID = 0
01:33:56: CryptoEngine0: generate alg parameter
01:33:57: ISAKMP (0:2): processing NONCE payload. message ID = 0
01:33:57: CryptoEngine0: create ISAKMP SKEYID for conn id 2
01:33:57: ISAKMP (0:2): SKEYID state generated
01:33:57: ISAKMP (0:2): processing vendor id payload
01:33:57: ISAKMP (0:2): speaking to another IOS box!
01:33:57: ISAKMP (2): ID payload
        next-payload : 8
        type         : 1
        protocol     : 17
        port         : 500
        length       : 8
01:33:57: ISAKMP (2): Total payload length: 12
01:33:57: CryptoEngine0: generate hmac context for conn id 2
01:33:57: ISAKMP (2): sending packet to 11.11.11.2 (I) MM_KEY_EXCH
01:33:57: ISAKMP (2): received packet from 11.11.11.2 (I) MM_KEY_EXCH
01:33:57: ISAKMP (0:2): processing ID payload. message ID = 0
01:33:57: ISAKMP (0:2): processing HASH payload. message ID = 0
01:33:57: CryptoEngine0: generate hmac context for conn id 2
01:33:57: ISAKMP (0:2): SA has been authenticated with 11.11.11.2
01:33:57: ISAKMP (0:2): beginning Quick Mode exchange, M-ID of 474637101
01:33:57: CryptoEngine0: clear dh number for conn id 1
01:33:57: IPSEC(key_engine): got a queue event...
01:33:57: IPSEC(spi_response): getting spi 348588451 for SA
        from 11.11.11.2     to 11.11.11.1     for prot 3
01:33:57: CryptoEngine0: generate hmac context for conn id 2
01:33:57: ISAKMP (2): sending packet to 11.11.11.2 (I) QM_IDLE
01:33:57: ISAKMP (2): received packet from 11.11.11.2 (I) QM_IDLE
01:33:57: CryptoEngine0: generate hmac context for conn id 2
01:33:57: ISAKMP (0:2): processing SA payload. message ID = 474637101
01:33:57: ISAKMP (0:2): Checking IPsec proposal 1
01:33:57: ISAKMP: transform 1, ESP_DES
01:33:57: ISAKMP:    attributes in transform:
01:33:57: ISAKMP:       encaps is 1
01:33:57: ISAKMP:       SA life type in seconds
01:33:57: ISAKMP:       SA life duration (basic) of 3600
01:33:57: ISAKMP:       SA life type in kilobytes
01:33:57: ISAKMP:       SA life duration (VPI) of  0x0 0x46 0x50 0x0
01:33:57: ISAKMP:       authenticator is HMAC-MD5
01:33:57: validate proposal 0
01:33:57: ISAKMP (0:2): atts are acceptable.
01:33:57: IPSEC(validate_proposal_request): proposal part #1,
  (key eng. msg.) dest= 11.11.11.2, src= 11.11.11.1,
    dest_proxy= 12.12.12.0/255.255.255.0/0/0 (type=4),
    src_proxy= 13.13.13.0/255.255.255.0/0/0 (type=4),
```

continues

Example 13-26 *Debugs on the Router TED-Initiator (Continued)*

```
            protocol= ESP, transform= esp-des esp-md5-hmac ,
            lifedur= 0s and 0kb,
            spi= 0x0(0), conn_id= 0, keysize= 0, flags= 0x4
01:33:57: validate proposal request 0
01:33:57: ISAKMP (0:2): processing NONCE payload. message ID = 474637101
01:33:57: ISAKMP (0:2): processing ID payload. message ID = 474637101
01:33:57: ISAKMP (0:2): processing ID payload. message ID = 474637101
01:33:57: CryptoEngine0: generate hmac context for conn id 2
01:33:57: ipsec allocate flow 0
01:33:57: ipsec allocate flow 0
01:33:57: ISAKMP (0:2): Creating IPsec SAs
01:33:57:          inbound SA from 11.11.11.2 to 11.11.11.1      (proxy 12.12.12.0
   to 13.13.13.0)
01:33:57:          has spi 348588451 and conn_id 2000 and flags 4
01:33:57:          lifetime of 3600 seconds
01:33:57:          lifetime of 4608000 kilobytes
01:33:57:          outbound SA from 11.11.11.1 to 11.11.11.2      (proxy 13.13.13.0
   to 12.12.12.0)
01:33:57:          has spi 132187477 and conn_id 2001 and flags 4
01:33:57:          lifetime of 3600 seconds
01:33:57:          lifetime of 4608000 kilobytes
01:33:57: ISAKMP (2): sending packet to 11.11.11.2 (I) QM_IDLE
01:33:57: ISAKMP (0:2): deleting node 474637101
01:33:57: IPSEC(key_engine): got a queue event...
01:33:57: IPSEC(initialize_sas): ,
   (key eng. msg.) dest= 11.11.11.1, src= 11.11.11.2,
     dest_proxy= 13.13.13.0/255.255.255.0/0/0 (type=4),
     src_proxy= 12.12.12.0/255.255.255.0/0/0 (type=4),
     protocol= ESP, transform= esp-des esp-md5-hmac ,
     lifedur= 3600s and 4608000kb,
     spi= 0x14C709A3(348588451), conn_id= 2000, keysize= 0, flags= 0x4
01:33:57: IPSEC(initialize_sas): ,
   (key eng. msg.) src= 11.11.11.1, dest= 11.11.11.2,
     src_proxy= 13.13.13.0/255.255.255.0/0/0 (type=4),
     dest_proxy= 12.12.12.0/255.255.255.0/0/0 (type=4),
     protocol= ESP, transform= esp-des esp-md5-hmac ,
     lifedur= 3600s and 4608000kb,
     spi= 0x7E10555(132187477), conn_id= 2001, keysize= 0, flags= 0x4
01:33:57: IPSEC(create_sa): sa created,
   (sa) sa_dest= 11.11.11.1, sa_prot= 50,
     sa_spi= 0x14C709A3(348588451),
     sa_trans= esp-des esp-md5-hmac , sa_conn_id= 2000
01:33:57: IPSEC(create_sa): sa created,
   (sa) sa_dest= 11.11.11.2, sa_prot= 50,
     sa_spi= 0x7E10555(132187477),
     sa_trans= esp-des esp-md5-hmac , sa_conn_id= 2001
```

Example 13-27 *Output of the* **show** *Commands on the Router TED-Initiator*

```
TED-Initiator#show crypto ipsec sa

interface: Ethernet0/1
    Crypto map tag: tedtag, local addr. 11.11.11.1

   local  ident (addr/mask/prot/port): (13.13.13.0/255.255.255.0/0/0)
   remote ident (addr/mask/prot/port): (12.12.12.0/255.255.255.0/0/0)
   current_peer: 11.11.11.2
     PERMIT, flags={}
    #pkts encaps: 9, #pkts encrypt: 9, #pkts digest 9
    #pkts decaps: 9, #pkts decrypt: 9, #pkts verify 9
    #pkts compressed: 0, #pkts decompressed: 0
    #pkts not compressed: 0, #pkts compr. failed: 0, #pkts decompress failed: 0
    #send errors 0, #recv errors 0

     local crypto endpt.: 11.11.11.1, remote crypto endpt.: 11.11.11.2
     path mtu 1500, media mtu 1500
     current outbound spi: 7E10555

     inbound esp sas:
      spi: 0x14C709A3(348588451)
        transform: esp-des esp-md5-hmac ,
        in use settings ={Tunnel, }
        slot: 0, conn id: 2000, flow_id: 1, crypto map: tedtag
        sa timing: remaining key lifetime (k/sec): (4607998/3557)
        IV size: 8 bytes
        replay detection support: Y

     inbound ah sas:

     inbound pcp sas:

     outbound esp sas:
      spi: 0x7E10555(132187477)
        transform: esp-des esp-md5-hmac ,
        in use settings ={Tunnel, }
        slot: 0, conn id: 2001, flow_id: 2, crypto map: tedtag
        sa timing: remaining key lifetime (k/sec): (4607998/3557)
        IV size: 8 bytes
        replay detection support: Y

     outbound ah sas:

     outbound pcp sas:
```

Example 13-28 *Debugs on the Router TED-Responder*

```
TED-Responder#show debug
Cryptographic Subsystem:
  Crypto ISAKMP debugging is on
  Crypto Engine debugging is on
  Crypto IPSEC debugging is on
TED-Responder#
!The responder has just received the TED probe and is trying to figure out if it
!is an ISAKMP initialization offer.
00:40:16: %CRYPTO-4-IKMP_NO_SA: IKE message from 1.204.0.4 has no SA and is not an
initialization offer
00:40:16: ISAKMP (0): received packet from 13.13.13.14 (N) NEW SA
00:40:16: ISAKMP (0:1): processing vendor id payload
!The responder has figured out by looking at the vendor ID payload that the other
!side is an IOS box. Now it also understands how to respond to the message.
00:40:16: ISAKMP (0:1): speaking to another IOS box!
00:40:16: ISAKMP (0:1): processing ID payload. message ID = 0
00:40:16: ISAKMP (0:1): processing ID payload. message ID = -1418395956
!By looking at the ID payload, the responder finds out that the source proxy for
!the initiator is 13.13.13.0
00:40:16: ISAKMP (1): ID_IPV4_ADDR_SUBNET src 13.13.13.0/255.255.255.0 prot 0 port 0
!The responder sends back a response to the TED probe, putting its IP address and
!its proxy in it. Below, the responder formulates the message to send to the
!initiator.
00:40:16: ISAKMP (1): responding to peer discovery probe!
00:40:16: peer's address is 11.11.11.1
00:40:16: src (him) 4, 13.13.13.0      /255.255.255.0   to dst (me) 4,
   12.12.12.0    /255.255.255.0
00:40:16: ISAKMP (1): ID payload
        next-payload : 5
        type         : 4
        protocol     : 17
        port         : 500
        length       : 12
00:40:16: ISAKMP (1): Total payload length: 16
00:40:16: ISAKMP (1): sending packet to 13.13.13.14 (R) PEER_DISCOVERY
00:40:16: ISAKMP (0:1): deleting SA
!Normal IKE processing starts on receiving a request from the initiator.
00:40:16: ISAKMP (0): received packet from 11.11.11.1 (N) NEW SA
00:40:16: ISAKMP (0:2): processing SA payload. message ID = 0
00:40:16: ISAKMP (0:2): Checking ISAKMP transform 1 against priority 10 policy
00:40:16: ISAKMP:         encryption DES-CBC
00:40:16: ISAKMP:         hash SHA
00:40:16: ISAKMP:         default group 1
00:40:16: ISAKMP:         auth pre-share
00:40:16: ISAKMP (0:2): atts are acceptable. Next payload is 0
00:40:16: CryptoEngine0: generate alg parameter
00:40:17: CRYPTO_ENGINE: Dh phase 1 status: 0
00:40:17: CRYPTO_ENGINE: Dh phase 1 status: 0
00:40:17: ISAKMP (0:2): SA is doing pre-shared key authentication
00:40:17: ISAKMP (2): SA is doing pre-shared key authentication using id
   type ID_IPV4_ADDR
```

Example 13-28 *Debugs on the Router TED-Responder (Continued)*

```
00:40:17: ISAKMP (2): sending packet to 11.11.11.1 (R) MM_SA_SETUP
00:40:17: ISAKMP (2): received packet from 11.11.11.1 (R) MM_SA_SETUP
00:40:17: ISAKMP (0:2): processing KE payload. message ID = 0
00:40:17: CryptoEngine0: generate alg parameter
00:40:17: ISAKMP (0:2): processing NONCE payload. message ID = 0
00:40:17: CryptoEngine0: create ISAKMP SKEYID for conn id 2
00:40:17: ISAKMP (0:2): SKEYID state generated
00:40:17: ISAKMP (0:2): processing vendor id payload
00:40:17: ISAKMP (0:2): speaking to another IOS box!
00:40:17: ISAKMP (2): sending packet to 11.11.11.1 (R) MM_KEY_EXCH
00:40:17: ISAKMP (2): received packet from 11.11.11.1 (R) MM_KEY_EXCH
00:40:17: ISAKMP (0:2): processing ID payload. message ID = 0
00:40:17: ISAKMP (0:2): processing HASH payload. message ID = 0
00:40:17: CryptoEngine0: generate hmac context for conn id 2
00:40:17: ISAKMP (0:2): SA has been authenticated with 11.11.11.1
00:40:17: ISAKMP (2): ID payload
        next-payload : 8
        type         : 1
        protocol     : 17
        port         : 500
        length       : 8
00:40:17: ISAKMP (2): Total payload length: 12
00:40:17: CryptoEngine0: generate hmac context for conn id 2
00:40:17: CryptoEngine0: clear dh number for conn id 1
00:40:17: ISAKMP (2): sending packet to 11.11.11.1 (R) QM_IDLE
00:40:17: ISAKMP (2): received packet from 11.11.11.1 (R) QM_IDLE
00:40:17: CryptoEngine0: generate hmac context for conn id 2
00:40:18: ISAKMP (0:2): processing SA payload. message ID = 474637101
00:40:18: ISAKMP (0:2): Checking IPsec proposal 1
00:40:18: ISAKMP: transform 1, ESP_DES
00:40:18: ISAKMP:    attributes in transform:
00:40:18: ISAKMP:        encaps is 1
00:40:18: ISAKMP:        SA life type in seconds
00:40:18: ISAKMP:        SA life duration (basic) of 3600
00:40:18: ISAKMP:        SA life type in kilobytes
00:40:18: ISAKMP:        SA life duration (VPI) of  0x0 0x46 0x50 0x0
00:40:18: ISAKMP:        authenticator is HMAC-MD5
00:40:18: validate proposal 0
00:40:18: ISAKMP (0:2): atts are acceptable.
00:40:18: IPSEC(validate_proposal_request): proposal part #1,
  (key eng. msg.) dest= 11.11.11.2, src= 11.11.11.1,
    dest_proxy= 12.12.12.0/255.255.255.0/0/0 (type=4),
    src_proxy= 13.13.13.0/255.255.255.0/0/0 (type=4),
    protocol= ESP, transform= esp-des esp-md5-hmac ,
    lifedur= 0s and 0kb,
    spi= 0x0(0), conn_id= 0, keysize= 0, flags= 0x4
00:40:18: validate proposal request 0
00:40:18: ISAKMP (0:2): processing NONCE payload. message ID = 474637101
00:40:18: ISAKMP (0:2): processing ID payload. message ID = 474637101
00:40:18: ISAKMP (2): ID_IPV4_ADDR_SUBNET src 13.13.13.0/255.255.255.0 prot 0
  port 0
```

continues

Example 13-28 *Debugs on the Router TED-Responder (Continued)*

```
00:40:18: ISAKMP (0:2): processing ID payload. message ID = 474637101
00:40:18: ISAKMP (2): ID_IPV4_ADDR_SUBNET dst 12.12.12.0/255.255.255.0 prot 0
  port 0
00:40:18: IPSEC(key_engine): got a queue event...
00:40:18: IPSEC(spi_response): getting spi 132187477 for SA
        from 11.11.11.1      to 11.11.11.2      for prot 3
00:40:18: CryptoEngine0: generate hmac context for conn id 2
00:40:18: ISAKMP (2): sending packet to 11.11.11.1 (R) QM_IDLE
00:40:18: ISAKMP (2): received packet from 11.11.11.1 (R) QM_IDLE
00:40:18: CryptoEngine0: generate hmac context for conn id 2
00:40:18: ipsec allocate flow 0
00:40:18: ipsec allocate flow 0
00:40:18: ISAKMP (0:2): Creating IPsec SAs
00:40:18:          inbound SA from 11.11.11.1  to 11.11.11.2      (proxy 13.13.13.0
  to 12.12.12.0)
00:40:18:          has spi 132187477 and conn_id 2000 and flags 4
00:40:18:          lifetime of 3600 seconds
00:40:18:          lifetime of 4608000 kilobytes
00:40:18:          outbound SA from 11.11.11.2 to 11.11.11.1      (proxy 12.12.12.0
  to 13.13.13.0)
00:40:18:          has spi 348588451 and conn_id 2001 and flags 4
00:40:18:          lifetime of 3600 seconds
00:40:18:          lifetime of 4608000 kilobytes
00:40:18: ISAKMP (0:2): deleting node 474637101
00:40:18: IPSEC(key_engine): got a queue event...
00:40:18: IPSEC(initialize_sas): ,
  (key eng. msg.) dest= 11.11.11.2, src= 11.11.11.1,
    dest_proxy= 12.12.12.0/255.255.255.0/0/0 (type=4),
    src_proxy= 13.13.13.0/255.255.255.0/0/0 (type=4),
    protocol= ESP, transform= esp-des esp-md5-hmac ,
    lifedur= 3600s and 4608000kb,
    spi= 0x7E10555(132187477), conn_id= 2000, keysize= 0, flags= 0x4
00:40:18: IPSEC(initialize_sas): ,
  (key eng. msg.) src= 11.11.11.2, dest= 11.11.11.1,
    src_proxy= 12.12.12.0/255.255.255.0/0/0 (type=4),
    dest_proxy= 13.13.13.0/255.255.255.0/0/0 (type=4),
    protocol= ESP, transform= esp-des esp-md5-hmac ,
    lifedur= 3600s and 4608000kb,
    spi= 0x14C709A3(348588451), conn_id= 2001, keysize= 0, flags= 0x4
00:40:18: IPSEC(create_sa): sa created,
  (sa) sa_dest= 11.11.11.2, sa_prot= 50,
    sa_spi= 0x7E10555(132187477),
    sa_trans= esp-des esp-md5-hmac , sa_conn_id= 2000
00:40:18: IPSEC(create_sa): sa created,
  (sa) sa_dest= 11.11.11.1, sa_prot= 50,
    sa_spi= 0x14C709A3(348588451),
    sa_trans= esp-des esp-md5-hmac , sa_conn_id= 2001
```

Example 13-29 *Output of the* **show** *Commands on the Router TED-Responder*

```
TED-Responder#show crypto ipsec sa

interface: Ethernet0/1
    Crypto map tag: tedtag, local addr. 11.11.11.2

   local  ident (addr/mask/prot/port): (12.12.12.0/255.255.255.0/0/0)
   remote ident (addr/mask/prot/port): (13.13.13.0/255.255.255.0/0/0)
   current_peer: 11.11.11.1
     PERMIT, flags={}
    #pkts encaps: 9, #pkts encrypt: 9, #pkts digest 9
    #pkts decaps: 9, #pkts decrypt: 9, #pkts verify 9
    #pkts compressed: 0, #pkts decompressed: 0
    #pkts not compressed: 0, #pkts compr. failed: 0, #pkts decompress failed: 0
    #send errors 0, #recv errors 0

     local crypto endpt.: 11.11.11.2, remote crypto endpt.: 11.11.11.1
     path mtu 1500, media mtu 1500
     current outbound spi: 14C709A3

     inbound esp sas:
      spi: 0x7E10555(132187477)
        transform: esp-des esp-md5-hmac ,
        in use settings ={Tunnel, }
        slot: 0, conn id: 2000, flow_id: 1, crypto map: tedtag
        sa timing: remaining key lifetime (k/sec): (4607998/3451)
        IV size: 8 bytes
        replay detection support: Y

     inbound ah sas:

     inbound pcp sas:

     outbound esp sas:
      spi: 0x14C709A3(348588451)
        transform: esp-des esp-md5-hmac ,
        in use settings ={Tunnel, }
        slot: 0, conn id: 2001, flow_id: 2, crypto map: tedtag
        sa timing: remaining key lifetime (k/sec): (4607998/3433)
        IV size: 8 bytes
        replay detection support: Y

     outbound ah sas:
     outbound pcp sas:
```

NAT's Interaction with IPsec

Because IPsec in tunnel mode hides private IP addresses, the need to do NAT for traffic going into an IPsec tunnel does not arise. Indeed, sometimes it is required that you *not* do NAT for traffic entering the tunnel. This is true in situations where the network administrator of two networks connected via a VPN wants to allow the users of both the networks to access all the resources on both networks using the same IP addresses. This means that if the users on Network A are accessing a server on Network A using the IP address 10.1.1.1, the users on Network B connected to Network A via a VPN should also be able to connect to this server using the IP address 10.1.1.1, despite the fact that the IPsec router in front of Network A has a static NAT translation for the server in place to allow connectivity to it from the Internet.

The configuration in Example 13-30 (which is stripped of unnecessary information) shows a method of bypassing NAT entering an IPsec tunnel. The goal of bypassing IPsec is achieved using a special policy-routing trick. It uses the rule that NAT, whether static or dynamic, kicks in only when NAT interesting traffic goes from an interface configured with the **ip nat inside** command directly to an interface set up with the **ip nat outside** command. In Example 13-30, this flow is broken by policy-routing the traffic headed for the other end of the IPsec tunnel to a loopback interface and then out the egress interface. This forces NAT not to occur for this traffic.

Example 13-30 shows the configuration needed to setup the 'NATRTR' for bypassing NAT. Figure 13-56 shows the network diagram for this case study.

Figure 13-56 *Network Diagram for This Case Study*

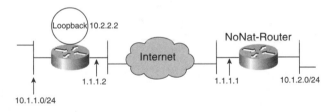

Example 13-30 *Configuration of the Router NATRTR Used in This Case Study*

```
Router#write terminal

hostname NATRTR

crypto map test 10 IPsec-isakmp
  set peer 1.1.1.1
 set transform-set transform
 match address 100
!This is the loopback the traffic will be routed to in order to change the order
!of events on the router
interface Loopback1

ip address 10.2.2.2 255.255.255.252

interface Ethernet0/0
 ip address 1.1.1.2 255.255.255.0
```

Example 13-30 *Configuration of the Router NATRTR Used in This Case Study (Continued)*

```
 ip nat outside
 crypto map test

interface Ethernet0/1
 ip address 10.1.1.1 255.255.255.0
 ip nat inside
 ip route-cache policy
!The policy route map below is used to force the IPsec interesting traffic to the
!loopback interface.
 ip policy route-map nonat
!This is the dynamic NAT configuration we are trying to bypass.
ip nat inside source access-list 1 interface Ethernet0/0 overload
!This is the static NAT entry we are trying to bypass.
ip nat inside source static 10.1.1.2 100.1.1.3
access-list 1 permit 10.0.0.0 0.255.255.255
!The access list below defines IPsec interesting traffic.
access-list 100 permit ip 10.1.1.0 0.0.0.255 10.1.2.0 0.0.0.255
!The access list below defines the traffic that is to be used by the route map
!nonat to route to the loopback interface.
access-list 120 permit ip 10.1.1.0 0.0.0.255 10.1.2.0 0.0.0.255
route-map nonat
  permit 10
!Below is the route map used to route the traffic matching access list 120 to the
!loopback interface.
route-map nonat permit 10
 match ip address 120
 set ip next-hop 10.2.2.1
```

As shown in Example 13-21, the PIX Firewall allows NAT to be bypassed using the **nat 0** command.

Interaction of Firewalls with IPsec

Two holes need to be opened to allow IPsec to work through a firewall:

- ESP or/and AH (protocols 50 and 51, respectively)
- UDP port 500 (for ISAKMP)

In addition, if UDP encapsulation is being used for NAT traversal, the UDP port being used for this purpose also needs to be allowed through the firewall. UDP encapsulation is currently not a feature supported on Cisco routers or PIX firewalls.

In case the firewall is configured on the router terminating the IPsec tunnel itself, the firewall needs to be opened for ESP/AH and ISAKMP traffic as well as the IP address pair in the decrypted IP traffic. The reason for this is that the incoming access list is processed twice for the incoming IPsec traffic. It is processed once for the encrypted traffic in the form of an ESP/AH packet, and then after the packet is decrypted, the access list is processed again. Because the packet has been decrypted, a hole in the access list needs to be opened for the IP addresses of the decrypted IP packet. This should not represent a security hole, because the IPsec routine drops any packets arriving at the incoming interface with the IP addresses in the header matching the IPsec interesting traffic access list. So, although there is a hole in the access list for these IP addresses, the IPsec routine guards it.

Summary

This chapter discussed in detail the workings and implementation of the IPsec protocol. IPsec is fast becoming the de facto VPN standard for the industry. The various ways it can be implemented to suit customer needs are aiding its popularity. We discussed in detail how the three main protocols in IPsec function. In addition, we looked at the authentication mechanism employed by IKE and how encryption and integrity checking in IPsec take place. It is important to look at the case studies presented in this chapter in light of the explanations given for the functioning of IKE and the other protocols in IPsec. You saw some of the most common scenarios in which IPsec is deployed. Because IPsec is becoming very widely deployed, its high availability, its interaction with other protocols, and its ability to seamlessly integrate with the existing network environment are constantly being tested. This is why it is important to understand the basic protocol and the workings of IPsec in addition to knowing how the configurations work. Only then can you have a complete understanding of the involved protocol that IPsec is. We will revisit IPsec in Chapter 24, "Troubleshooting Network Security Implementations," to look at some common troubleshooting techniques to use in IPsec implementations.

Review Questions

1 What does IPsec stand for?

2 What three main protocols form IPsec?

3 What is the main difference between AH and ESP's capabilities?

4 Which phase does ISAKMP go through in negotiating IPsec SAs?

5 Can an IPsec crypto map point to more than one peer?

6 What is the purpose of TED?

7 What is the purpose of the **group** command?

8 Which command defines the encryption method to be used?

9 What does IPsec use to identify L2TP as interesting traffic?

10 Does GRE encapsulate IPsec traffic, or the other way around?

Intrusion Detection

This chapter covers the following key topics:

- **The Need for Intrusion Detection**—This section discusses the motivation behind having an intrusion detection system in place.

- **Types of Network Attacks Based on Mode of Attack**—This section talks about the types of network attacks based on how they are conducted.

- **Types of Network Attacks Based on the Attack's Perpetrator**—This section talks about network attacks based on who conducts them.

- **Common Network Attacks**—This section further differentiates various types of attacks and discusses examples of some common types of attacks.

- **The Process of Detecting Intrusions**—This section discusses the various techniques used to detect network attacks and intrusions. It also looks at some common ways to do intrusion detection.

- **Case Study: Kevin Metnick's Attack on Tsutomu Shimomura's Computers and How IDS Could Have Saved the Day**—This section discusses a real-life scenario of network intrusion and shows how IDS could have prevented the hacking from taking place.

## CHAPTER 14

What Is Intrusion Detection?

Intrusion detection is the process of detecting attempts to gain unauthorized access to a network or to create network degradation. Given visibility and based on a set of rules, this unauthorized access is dealt with either automatically or through manual intervention.

Intrusion detection involves developing an understanding of how network attacks occur. Based on that understanding, you take a two-pronged approach to stopping these attacks. First, you make sure that general patterns of malicious activity are detected. Second, you ensure that specific events that don't fall into common categories of attacks are dealt with swiftly. This is why most intrusion detection systems (IDSs) rely on update mechanisms for their software that are quick enough to preempt any growing network threat. However, just detecting intrusions is insufficient. You need to trace intrusions back to the source and deal with the attacker in an effective manner. Because many attacks use spoofed IP addresses or are sourced from compromised devices, dealing with attackers is a nontrivial issue. Also, attempting to deal with attackers with or without law enforcement is complex. Industrial-strength IDSs provide some initial information as to where the attack might have originated. However, from that point onward, it is a significant law enforcement effort to track down the real source of attacks.

This chapter looks at some common types of network attacks and analyzes them to help you better understand the different types. An in-depth look at some common examples of network intrusions leads to a discussion of how intrusion detection works. This chapter concludes by examining a well-known case in which a network attack was staged. You'll see how it could have been prevented using IDS.

The Need for Intrusion Detection

The need for intrusion detection is based on the increasing number of threats faced by the computer networks in today's world. Here are some of the fundamental reasons why so many attacks are being launched on computer networks:

- Computer networks are used to carry information that is valuable not only to the intended receiver but can also be valuable to anyone else who gets his or her hands on it. Therefore, computer networks are an important source of information theft. This has led to an increase in network security breaches.

- The World Wide Web has become a very common way of delivering information to the masses. Hackers find it useful to demonstrate their beliefs and stage virtual demonstrations by attacking popular sites. In fact, simply gaining publicity in the underground community is a sufficient motivator for many hackers.

NOTE   This chapter uses the term *hacker* to describe an individual who tries to break into secure networks or disrupt legitimate services. Historically, however, a hacker is someone who expends effort to learn and build computer and security systems—generally a good guy. The technically correct term for a malicious attacker is *cracker*. However, this chapter uses the more well-known term *hacker* as an equivalent for *cracker*.

- Tools to launch network attacks are readily available. Hackers also use information to trade and barter among themselves. This means that you don't have to be a security specialist to write hacks and code tools to launch an attack. Such relatively simple-to-use tools are readily available. Also, the capabilities of "professional" hackers have increased greatly over the last few years. Figure 14-1 illustrates the rise in hacking expertise over the years.

Figure 14-1 *Rise in Hacker Capabilities*

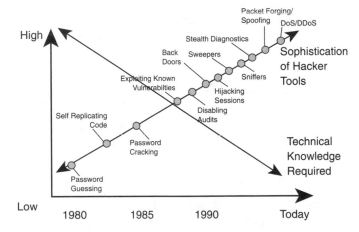

- One other potential aspect of Internet-based attacks is the relative anonymity afforded to the attacker. This sharply differs from a physical security breach, in which the attacker places himself at risk of immediate identification.

- Access to networks is easy and widespread. Anyone can gain access to the Internet. Because many networks are directly connected to the Internet in one way or another, close proximity to the targeted network can easily be achieved. Also, attacks launched internally are on the rise. They account for a major portion of the total attacks launched.

- The amount of traffic carried by networks today makes it very difficult to use traditional intrusion detection techniques, such as looking at logs, to provide a meaningful deterrent in many cases. This allows many attacks to be conducted without ever being detected.

Types of Network Attacks Based on Mode of Attack

A network intrusion is often called a network attack. Network attacks can be broken into two broad categories based on how the attack is launched. A network attack can be characterized by the goal its perpetrator is trying to achieve. These goals are generally either denial of service or unauthorized access to network resources.

Denial of Service Attacks

In denial of service (DoS) attacks, an attacker disrupts the use of services being offered by a service provider to its users. Generally, such an attack is carried out by accessing the services being offered on such a large scale that the server or the network's ability to offer services to other users is significantly impaired. One example of such an attack is a TCP SYN attack. In this kind of attack, an attacker sends a large number of TCP SYN requests to a server. After the SYN requests are sent, the handshakes are never completed. The server, in trying to maintain information about the SYN connections and waiting for the handshakes to be completed, eventually exhausts its resources and stops accepting any further TCP connection requests, thereby denying access to genuine users.

Network Access Attacks

Network access attacks are attacks in which an intruder gains unauthorized access to resources on a network and uses this access to carry out any number of unauthorized or even illegal activities. As soon as this access has been gained, it can even be used to carry out denial of service attacks against networks.

Network access can be further subdivided into two categories:

- Data access
- System access

Data Access

In a data access attack, an attacker gains unauthorized access to the data contained on devices sitting on a network. The attacker can just as easily be an internal user as an outside one. Privileged data often is available to users who have access to a certain kind of information on the network, but for whom this access is limited. These users do not have the necessary privileges to access certain confidential information. However, they gain this access by illegally increasing their privilege level. This is known as *privilege escalation*. Unauthorized data retrieval involves reading, writing, copying, or moving files that are not intended to be accessible to the intruder. Sometimes this is as easy as finding shared folders in Windows 9x or NT, or NFS exported directories in UNIX systems that have read or read and write access.

System Access

System access is a more aggravated form of network access attack in which an attacker gains access to system resources and devices. This access can include running programs on the system and using its resources to do things as commanded by the attacker. The attacker can also get access to network devices such as cameras, printers, and storage devices.

Examples of network access attacks include brute-force password attacks, Trojan horse attacks, and various attacks using tools to exploit weaknesses in the software code running on a machine.

One important type of activity that often precedes most network access and DoS attacks is *reconnaissance*. An attacker uses reconnaissance to find the vulnerabilities in a network's security posture. This can be done by using automated tools (such as SATAN) that carry out port sweeps across networks, trying to find machines that might be susceptible to a particular type of attack. This process can also be carried out manually by an experienced attacker. The general process of reconnaissance usually involves a series of steps, starting with a hacker scouting a network to find out the network's general parameters, such as the perimeter devices, IP addresses, traffic patterns, and domain names. The next step involves trying to verify which ports on various machines might be available to launch various types of attacks. Other attributes of the various machines can also be found at this point, such as the OS and software version running on the machines. All this information can divulge critical information regarding the machine's vulnerabilities that the hacker can later exploit.

Types of Network Attacks Based on the Attack's Perpetrator

In addition to classifying network attacks based on their goals, it is useful to analyze them based on who is orchestrating them. In this respect, network attacks are generally divided into four categories:

- Attacks launched by trusted (inside) users

- Attacks launched by untrusted (external) individuals
- Attacks launched by inexperienced "script-kiddy" hackers, whether internal or external
- Attacks launched by experienced "professional" hackers, whether internal or external

Attacks Launched by Trusted (Inside) Users

This is one of the most dangerous forms of network attack, because not only does the user have access to a lot of network resources, but most network policies are not very strict in defining rules and codes of behavior for users on the internal network. Everyone on the internal network is generally trusted. This can allow an inside user to launch any of the attacks just described, with devastating consequences. In fact, according to quite a few studies, the most common damage to networks is done by internal rather than external threats.

An insider attacker can be further categorized as follows:

- Unintentional inside attacker
- Deliberate inside attacker

Much damage to networks is done by inside individuals who have no real intent of causing any harm to the network, but who inadvertently manage to cause significant damage by their acts. Such acts can be as simple as letting an outside hacker learn passwords or bringing down a critical network resource due to misuse based on lack of knowledge or training. A very common example of this type of individual is one who opens a malicious e-mail attachment, exposing a whole organization to a virus attack.

The second type of attacker, the deliberate inside attacker, is more dangerous, because they have intentions that are in opposition to the rules and regulations laid down by the network security policy. This individual's intent is to launch a network attack. Special status as an insider gives the attacker a critical edge.

Attacks Launched by Untrusted (External) Individuals

This is a fairly common type of attack in which the user is not trusted on the attacked network. This type of attacker generally has a difficult time, because most network security policies have stringent measures defined against external attackers.

Attacks Launched by Inexperienced ("Script-Kiddy") Hackers

Many hacking tools are available on the Internet. You can get scripts that launch attacks with the click of a button, even if you have no real knowledge of the attack itself or the coding involved to generate it. Examples of such tools are nmap and ncat for reconnaissance. Similar tools such as Naptha (for DoS attacks) are available for launching various attacks after a vulnerability has been found. A script kiddy (what such hackers are often called) generally is not an expert in networking or operating systems. However, the use of scripts can allow the attacker to cause substantial damage to an unsuspecting network.

Attacks Launched by Experienced ("Professional") Hackers

"Professional" hackers are generally very well-versed in writing various types of code. They have substantial expertise in the TCP/IP protocol suite and a deep knowledge of the workings of various operating systems. These people generally develop the tools that the script kiddies later use. These types of hackers generally conduct attacks after doing research on the type of victim. They are often looking for high-visibility, high-profile, often well-protected victims whom they can hack to prove their hacking expertise. Professional hackers are also motivated by profit, so they often conduct corporate espionage. This is probably the most dangerous type of attacker a network can attract.

Having looked at the types of attackers, it is easy to understand that the most potent enemy a network can have is an insider with bad intentions who is also a professional hacker. Although it can be impossible to protect against all types of attacks such an individual can carry out, proper intrusion detection can expose such an individual and lead to their ouster before more damage is done.

Figure 14-2 shows types of attackers.

Figure 14-2 *Types of Attackers*

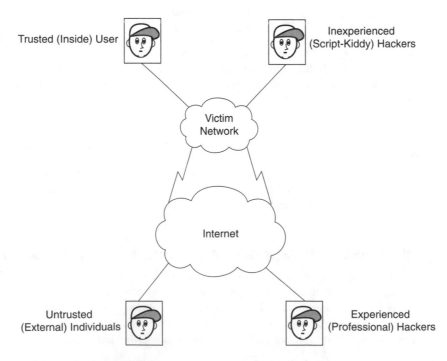

Common Network Attacks

As mentioned earlier, network attacks can be categorized into two main types of attacks:

- Denial of Service (DOS)
- Network access attacks

In order to move into a discussion of how intrusion detection works to thwart some of these attacks, it is important to look at some common examples of such attacks. Understanding these attacks helps you understand the overall concept of IDS.

Denial of Service Attacks

This section looks at DoS attacks and discusses some pertinent examples. Generally speaking, in DoS attacks, an attacker disrupts services that a service provider offers its users.

Most DoS attacks use either resource exhaustion or some vulnerability in an operating system or protocol to cause the system to stop functioning normally. We will look briefly at these two types of attacks before discussing some examples of DoS attacks.

Exploits Aimed at Resource Exhaustion

Resource exhaustion attacks are DoS attacks in which an attacker uses various mechanisms to consume the resources available on a network system. The system is unable to process legitimate users because it has run out of resources. Most of these attacks are carried out against a network's CPU resources or the bandwidth that the network offers its users in terms of connection speeds.

Exploits Aimed at Causing Immediate Cessation of Normal OS Operations

There is a large group of DoS attacks in which a vulnerability in the OS or a protocol is exploited in order to stop the OS's functioning abruptly and completely. The difference between these types of attacks and resource exhaustion attacks is that in resource exhaustion, the attacker tries to stop the system's normal functioning by consuming all its resources. With cessation of normal OS operation, the attacker simply sends data that the OS is unable to handle properly due to a bug, and the OS stops working normally. Examples of these types of attacks are ping of death attacks, UDP bomb, and land.c attacks. We will look at a couple of these attacks in the following sections to get a better understanding of them.

Types of Resource Exhaustion DoS Attacks

Resource exhaustion attacks can be divided into a large number of categories. However, to keep the discussion focused, we will look at simple DoS attacks and distributed DoS attacks.

Simple DoS Attacks

Simple DoS attacks are resource exhaustion attacks that are launched by a single attacker against one or more victims. Although the attacker may use spoofing to pretend that the attack is coming from a wide range of IP addresses, in reality the attack comes from the attacker. Examples of simple DoS attacks include TCP SYN floods, smurf attacks, and various packet storms.

TCP SYN Floods

A TCP SYN flood, as described in Figure 14-3, is a very good example of a simple DoS attack. It is carried out by sending TCP SYNs to a server. It is also known as a half-open SYN attack.

Figure 14-3 *TCP SYN Flood DoS Attack*

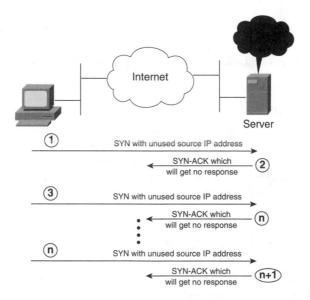

A TCP SYN flood is orchestrated by sending a large number of TCP SYN packets to a server. These packets have a source IP address that is spoofed and not in use. When the server receives these requests, it responds to them using SYN-ACK. However, because the source IP address is spoofed and unused, the TCP handshake is never completed. (It is completed only if the initiating machine sends an ACK to the server upon receiving the SYN-ACK.) The server waits for the ACK. To do so, it must allocate resources and buffer space to record the information it has received in the SYN packet and sent out in the SYN-ACK packet in response. Based on its memory and CPU resources, a server can allocate only a limited amount of such resources. How many such half-open TCP requests the server can entertain is determined by the TCP connection queue. When the queue fills up with a large number of these half-open connections, the server can no longer service new connections. Whereas some of these requests might be from the attacker, others can easily be from legitimate users. These legitimate users are thus denied access to the services that the server offered before the attack.

Generally, TCP implementations do have a timer after which a half-open connection, for which the final ACK has not been received, is dropped. Although the server can make use of this timer, a large SYN flood can make this timer meaningless. Shortening this timer to avoid SYN floods is not advisable either, because that can cause legitimate users with slow connections to have their connections dropped. Also, this can make staging a SYN flood only slightly more difficult but not improbable by any means.

How Can IDS Prevent This Attack?

Although some OSs, such as some versions of Linux, implement features such as SYN cookies that can reduce the danger from SYN floods to some extent, SYN flooding is a reality in most network environments. Most network-based IDSs can detect SYN floods and reset such connections, freeing up resources on the servers. IDSs can achieve this by looking for patterns of activity giving away SYN flooding. We will talk about how this is done in more detail in the next section.

Distributed Denial of Service Attacks

Distributed Denial of Service (DDoS) attacks are staged against victim machines by a large number of attacking machines. In reality, these machines have been compromised and forced to help launch various types of attacks—generally DoS in nature.

The DDoS attacks of the week of February 7, 2000 were a good example of DDoS attacks. These attacks brought down some major commercial Web sites on the Internet down for extended periods of time during this week.

The February 7–11, 2000 Attacks

The Feb 7–11, 2000 DDoS attacks were a combination of four types of DDoS attacks:

- Trinoo
- TFN
- TFN2K
- Stacheldraht

The next sections discuss the details of these four attacks. Although the general information is correct, the details of how these tools are implemented can easily be modified by a savvy hacker. For example, it is simple to modify the TCP ports on which Stacheldraht communicates. Also, since these attacks were originally launched, newer versions of these tools and entirely new DDoS tools (such as SubSeven) have become available.

Trinoo

Trinoo was one of the DDoS tools used to launch the aforementioned attacks. Trinoo is essentially a network of master/slave programs that coordinate with each other to launch a UDP DoS flood against a victim machine (see Figure 14-4). In a typical scenario, the following steps take place as the Trinoo DDoS network is set up:

Step 1   The attacker, using an account that is usually compromised (generally, this host is a machine with a lot of connections being made to it at any given time, making the detection of Trinoo communication unlikely), compiles a list of machines that can be compromised. Most of this process is automated and is done automatically from the compromised account. This host has a considerable amount of information stored on it, including how to find other hosts to compromise and what exploits to use to compromise other hosts.

Step 2   As soon as a list of hosts that can be compromised has been compiled, scripts are run to compromise them and convert them into the Trinoo *masters* or *daemons*. The Trinoo masters are used to control the daemons. One master can contain a number of daemons. The daemons are the compromised hosts that launch the actual UDP floods against victim machines, upon being provided with an IP address to attack by the Trinoo master. The communication between the master and the daemons uses UDP port 27444 from the master to the daemon and UDP port 31335 from the daemon to the master. The masters are controlled using TCP port 27665. Communications between the master and daemons are password-protected.

Step 3   The DDoS attack is launched when the attackers issue a command on the master hosts. This results in the masters instructing the daemons to start a DoS attack against the IP address specified in the command.

Step 4   The attack is comprised of UDP packets sent to the IP address of the victim(s) specified in the command issued on the master, with random destination ports. The attacking source IP addresses are not spoofed. The size of the packets and the duration of the attack can be specified using various commands. The contents of the packets are fairly random, and are mostly random memory contents from the physical memory of the host which has the daemon installed on it.

Figure 14-4 *Trinoo Network Attack*

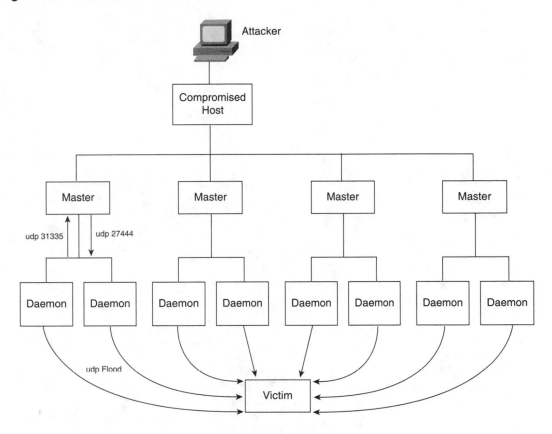

TFN and TFN2K

TFN (tribal flood network) and TFN2K are similar DDoS tools that were also used to launch the aforementioned attacks in February 2000. TFN, like Trinoo, is essentially a network of master/slave (called clients and daemons) programs that coordinate with each other to launch a SYN flood against a victim machine (see Figure 14-5). The TFN daemons, however, are capable of a larger variety of attacks, including ICMP flooding, SYN flooding, and smurf attacks. In a typical scenario, the following steps take place as the TFN DDoS network is set up. Following the steps, we will talk about the enhancements in the TFN2K version of this tool.

Figure 14-5 *TFN Network Attack*

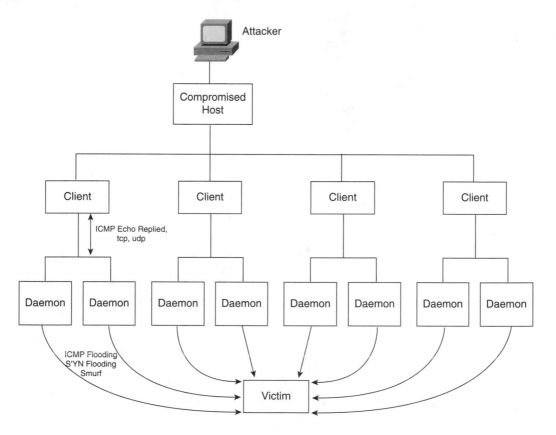

Step 1 As with Trinoo, the attacker, generally using a compromised account (usually, this host is a machine with a lot of connections being made to it at any given time, making the detection of TFN communication unlikely), compiles a list of machines that can be compromised. Most of this process is automated and is done automatically from the compromised account. This host has a considerable amount of information stored on it, including how to find other hosts to compromise and what exploits to use to compromise them.

Step 2 As soon as a list of hosts that can be compromised has been compiled, scripts are run to compromise them and convert them into TFN clients or daemons. TFN clients are used to control the daemons. One client can control a number of daemons. The daemons are the compromised hosts that launch the DoS packet flood against victim machines after being provided with an IP address to attack by the TFN client.

Communication between the client and the daemon in TFN is done using ICMP echo replies, making it difficult to detect this type of communication. The ID of the ICMP echo reply contains the command or the command reply, and the data portion contains any arguments. The clients are controlled by the attacker using CLI execution of commands on the machines with the clients installed on them. Therefore, this can be done in a number of ways, including via Telnet or ssh sessions.

Step 3   The DDoS attack is launched by the attackers issuing a command on the client host. This command has the client instruct the daemons to start a DoS attack against the IP address specified in the attack.

As stated earlier, the TFN attack is more complicated than the UDP flooding that Trinoo uses. These attacks include ICMP flooding, SYN flooding, and smurf attacks.

TFN2K introduces some enhancements to the original TFN tool. The two main enhancements concern how attacks are launched and how administration of and communication between attackers, clients, and daemons occurs. In TFN2K, attacks are launched using spoofed IP addresses, making detecting the source of the attacks more difficult than in TFN attacks. Also, TFN2K attacks are not just simple floods like those in TFN. They also include attacks exploiting OSs' vulnerabilities to malformed or invalid packets, which can cause the victim machines to crash. The TFN2K attackers no longer need to execute commands by logging into the client machines; they can execute these commands remotely. Also, communication between the clients and the daemons is no longer limited to simply ICMP echo replies. It can take place over a larger variety of mediums, such as TCP and UDP. All of these enhancements make TFN2K more dangerous and also more difficult to detect.

Stacheldraht

Stacheldraht is another tool that was used to launch the February 2000 attacks. Stacheldraht code is very similar to the Trinoo and the TFN tools, but certain key enhancements make it a greater security threat. Stacheldraht allows communication between the attacker and the masters (called *handlers*) to be encrypted. In addition, *agents* can upgrade their code automatically.

The mechanism of installation and dispersion in Stacheldraht is the same as that of Trinoo and TFN. The attacker (also known as the client in Stacheldraht nomenclature because of the presence of the encryption client on the attacker's machine) uses TCP port 16660 to communicate with the handlers. The handlers in turn use TCP 6500 or ICMP echo replies to communicate with the end machines responsible for the DoS attacks. These machines are known as the agents.

The Stacheldraht agents can launch ICMP flood attacks, SYN floods, and UDP floods. The attacks can be conducted with or without spoofing. The agents send test packets with spoofed addresses to see if the network edge routers for the network on which they are installed allow spoofed addresses. If they don't, they use only last-octet spoofing. See Chapter 21, "Using Access Control Lists Effectively," for more details on how to set up filters to prevent spoofing.

Figure 14-6 shows the architecture of the Stacheldraht network.

Figure 14-6 *Stacheldraht Attack*

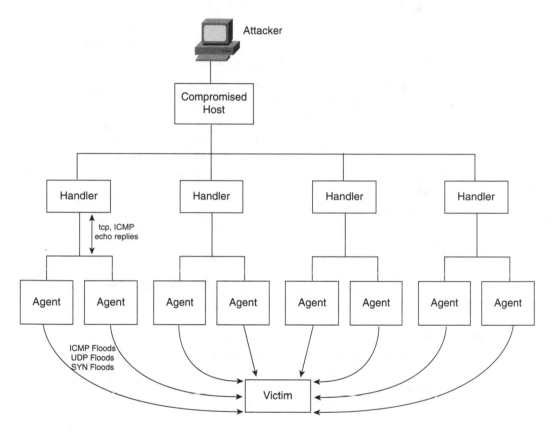

How Can IDS Prevent This Attack?

The attacks of the types conducted in February 2000 are not easy to stop, because much of the protection that the victim networks can get is based on security measures implemented on other people's networks, including intrusion detection. IDS can be used to detect the four types of tools just described after they have been set up on a network. This detection is based primarily on the telltale fingerprints of communication between the masters and slaves. IDS signatures identify the traffic between the masters and the daemons in the Trinoo network, the traffic between the clients and the daemons in the TFN2K network, and the traffic between the handlers and the agents in the Stacheldraht network. Because all these tools can use echo replies (except for Trinoo) to communicate, the signatures watch for echo replies for which they do not see an echo going out first.

Cisco IDS signatures 6505 and 6506 are used to detect Trinoo networks. 6505 looks for UDP packets containing potential commands from a Trinoo client to a server, and 6506 looks for UDP packets containing potential command replies from a Trinoo server to a client.

Cisco IDS signatures 6501 and 6502 are used to detect TFN networks. 6501 looks for ICMP echo reply packets containing potential TFN commands sent from a TFN client to a server, and 6502 looks for ICMP echo reply packets containing potential TFN commands sent from a TFN server to a client.

Cisco IDS signature 6507 detects TFN2K networks by identifying the control traffic from the hacker's client console and the clients.

Cisco IDS signatures 6503 and 6504 are used to detect the Stacheldraht networks. 6503 looks for ICMP echo reply packets containing potential commands sent from a Stacheldraht client to a server, whereas 6504 looks for ICMP echo reply packets containing potential commands sent from a Stacheldraht server to a client.

Types of Attacks Aimed at Causing Immediate Cessation of Normal OS Operations

These attacks try to exploit a bug or oversight in the code of an operating system that can cause the OS to stop functioning normally. This is different from resource exhaustion. With resource exhaustion, excessive legitimate activity is used to consume all the OS's resources. In cessation-of-operations attacks, the activity that causes the OS to crash is generally unrelated to the system's becoming overburdened with activity. The system simply malfunctions because of the malicious content of a packet sent to it.

Examples of this type of attack are the ping of death attack, land.c attack, and UDP bomb. We will look at the ping of death attack and the land.c attack to get a better understanding of how they work.

Ping of Death Attack

According to RFC 791, the largest IP packet can be 65,535 bytes in length, including the IP header, which is generally 20 bytes long unless IP options are specified. However, the actual size of a packet that goes on the wire is determined by the IP MTU, which for Ethernet segments is 1500 bytes. Packets larger than 1500 bytes are fragmented into smaller IP packets so as not to exceed the IP MTU.

Most OSs are not equipped to handle an IP packet larger than the 65,535 bytes specified in RFC 791. Generally, even if a machine receiving a packet larger than 65,535 bytes is programmed to drop such a packet, it first reassembles the packet before processing it for such illegal conditions. This is where the problem lies. A hacker can send an IP packet to a vulnerable machine such that the last fragment contains an offset where (IP offset * 8) + (IP data length) > 65535. This means that when the packet is reassembled, its total length is larger than the legal limit, causing buffer overruns in the machine's OS (because the buffer sizes are defined only to accomodate the maximum allowed size of the packet based on RFC 791). This results in hangs and crashes on many OSs.

This attack is generally carried out by sending an ICMP packet encapsulated in an IP packet. Thus, it is called a ping of death attack.

How Can IDS Prevent This Attack?

IDSs can generally recognize such attacks by looking for packet fragments that have the IP header's protocol field set to 1 (ICMP), the last fragment bit set, and (IP offset * 8) + (IP data length) > 65535. This implies a packet in which the IP offset (which represents the starting position of this fragment in the original packet, and which is in 8-byte units) plus the rest of the packet is greater than the maximum size of an IP packet.

Land.c Attack

Land.c is a DoS attack in which an attacker sends a host a TCP SYN packet with the source and destination IP address set to the host's IP address. The source and destination port numbers are the same as well. Upon receiving a SYN packet, the host responds with a SYN-ACK to itself. Having sent this packet, the TCP routine normally expects an ACK packet to complete the TCP handshake. Instead, it receives a SYN-ACK that has the same TCP sequence number it had sent rather than a different sequence number from the responder. Seeing this, the TCP routine sends out an ACK that contains the sequence number TCP was expecting to receive. This is basically a request to the sender to send the ACK with the correct sequence number again. Because the source and destination numbers for IP and TCP ports are the same, the packet gets thrown back to the same TCP routine again. The packet's sequence number is the same one that the TCP routine rejected last time. The TCP routine again rejects the packet and sends an ACK to the sender (which is itself) that contains the expected sequence number in the ACK. The packet is sent straight back to the TCP routine to again be processed in the same manner. The OS becomes trapped in this endless loop and either crashes, slows down badly, or has a kernel panic.

How Can IDS Prevent This Attack?

IDS implementations can generally detect land.c attacks by looking for IP packets that have a source IP address equal to the destination address. This is generally called an *impossible*

IP packet. Although a network-based IDS can detect this type of packet and generate an alarm, it cannot stop the packet from reaching its destination if it is in sniffing mode only. This means that an alarm might be generated, and the system administrator must take appropriate antispoofing measures to thwart additional attack attempts. But the packet will have reached its initial victim by then. IDSs that detect while sitting in the packet's path rather than just sniffing at packets, such as the PIX IDS and the Router IDS, have a better chance against such types of attacks because they can drop the malicious packets once identified.

Network Access Attacks

As mentioned earlier, in network access attacks, an intruder gains unauthorized access to resources on a network and uses this access to carry out any number of unauthorized or even illegal activities. Although data access attacks can be orchestrated without gaining system access, they often start that way. This section discusses two common examples of network access attacks—buffer overflows and privilege escalations. Although buffer overflows are often used to gain privilege escalations, they are so frequent that we will discuss them in a separate section. We will talk about privilege escalation by discussing other types of network access attacks in which a user with some rights on a system uses techniques other than buffer overflow to gain more privileges on the system.

Buffer Overflows

Buffer overflow attacks can fall into the categories of both DoS and network access attacks. The reason for this is that although buffer overflows can cause operating systems on network devices to crash and cause a denial of service, they can also be exploited by more-savvy attackers to gain access to the operating system and go beyond simply causing a DoS attack.

Buffer overflow vulnerabilities are one of the most widespread vulnerabilities on the Internet today. They account for almost half of all vulnerabilities. Consequently, it is important to understand how they work and how intrusion detection can protect against some buffer overflow attacks.

A buffer is generally defined as a contiguous block of memory used to hold data of a particular type. Buffers are used in computers to save the data while it is being processed and to move it from one place to another. Generally, programs specify the buffer size into which the data must fit. However, if a buffer somehow receives a piece of data that is larger than it can handle, a buffer overflow is said to occur.

Buffer overflows in operating systems occur when a routine writes an amount of data into a fixed-size buffer that is too small for the amount of data. This is a common occurrence in OSs based on the C language, because C's standard library of functions includes many that manipulate data without any bound checks. Java, on the other hand, has automatic bound checks that help mitigate this problem to some extent. Vulnerable routines in C include gets() and scanf(). gets() is a function that can be used to read data into a buffer without any bound checking. Routines such as these are often exploited to cause buffer overflows. It is good programming practice to build bounds checking into the code.

A buffer overflow attack is orchestrated by sending to an OS data that is too large for the relevant buffer handling the data to store. Some of the data is written into the space allocated for the buffer, and the rest of it overwrites the memory area next to the buffer memory area. An OS's buffer is co-located with other critical parts of the memory, including the memory location that contains the pointer to the next memory location that the OS is to go to after the program using the buffer is done. Therefore, important pieces of information get overwritten. An attacker can send a large piece of data that is constructed so that the memory location containing the pointer to the next memory area to go to gets overwritten by a value that refers to a memory location that contains code that the attacker wants to execute. This code can allow the hacker to get more privileges on the computer, or the access can simply be used to crash the system completely. The buffer overflow attack is illustrated in Figure 14-7.

Figure 14-7 *Buffer Overflow Attack*

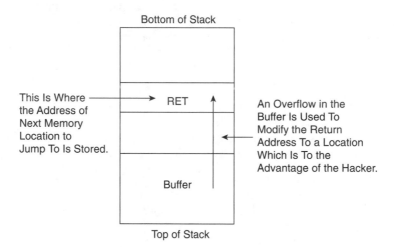

What is described here is a simple form of buffer overflow attack that is also called *smashing the stack*. More sophisticated attacks are also possible and are staged by hackers.

How Can IDS Prevent This Attack?

An IDS can ward off buffer overflow attacks by looking for data elements in packets that look suspiciously large and that can cause various types of buffer overflows. For example, Telnet daemons derived from the BSD source code contain a buffer overflow in the handling of Telnet options. This vulnerability can be exploited to stage an attack often leading to root access. The Cisco IDS detects this type of attack by looking for Telnet packets that have an abnormally long New Environment Variable Telnet option.

Privilege Escalations

Privilege escalation describes a situation in which an attacker using various means gains more access to the system resources than was intended for him or her. An example is when someone gains access to system files on a Web server where the intent was to give that person access to only the files in the published area of the Web server.

The next sections discuss two very common attacks that fall into the category of privilege escalation attacks. The first example is Unicode exploits, which are in a class of their own, with a large number of variations and attack strategies available. The second example is an exploit from Microsoft Windows NT based on a utility called getadmin.exe.

Unicode Exploits

Unicode exploits are a very common example of attacks in which a server is subjected to either a DoS or privilege escalation attack. Unicoding is basically a new encoding scheme being adopted worldwide that attempts to assign numeric codes to every symbol and character found in various languages and forms of communication.

Unicode exploits take advantage of the fact that many security routines written by OS programmers look for plain ASCII characters to guard against various security breach attempts. However, if these characters are encoded in Unicode, these routines are not sophisticated enough to be able to recognize that the Unicode characters are part of a security threat. (Many of these routines have already been patched.)

A very common example of this is the Unicode vulnerability in certain versions of the Microsoft IIS servers. In these servers, the users are allowed access to only the files that are in the WWW publishing area. Also, although the users of the IIS server are allowed to execute certain files, they can do so only if these files sit in certain predefined directories in the WWW publishing area. However, it is entirely possible for the user to execute a command such as ../../winnt/system32/cmd.exe in the specified directory in the WWW publishing area. This command should be executed, because the requirement for the user executing it from the specified directory has been met. But because it obviously tries to access areas beyond the publishing area, the IIS code watches out for commands that have the ../../ characters and denies them.

Hackers overcome this checking mechanism deployed by the IIS by encoding the offending character using Unicode. Although IIS accepts this form of coding, it does not have the necessary code to check whether the encoded text is offensive. The Unicode encoded string for ../../winnt/system32/cmd.exe is ..%c1%pc../winnt/system32/cmd.exe. Therefore, the attacker can bypass the check and gain access to executables such as cmd.exe, as well as other elements in areas outside the WWW publishing area. The attacker's privileges on the IIS server have just been significantly escalated!

How Can IDS Prevent This Attack?   IDSs can guard against these types of attacks by looking out for URLs destined for the IIS servers containing the various Unicode endings that, upon decoding, can result in privilege escalation.

Getadmin Exploit

The second example in the area of privilege escalation is a popular exploit that is generally carried out using a utility called getadmin.exe. Getadmin.exe works by manipulating a low-level kernel file in Windows NT called NTOSKRNL.EXE. By changing one of the bits here, this program turns off a checking mechanism in the OS that is critical to system security. Windows NT has a couple of routines, NtOpenProcess and NtOpenThread, that check whether a user is entitled to start a new process or thread, respectively. However, NT also has a mode that allows users who have debug privileges to execute any threads or processes. When you change that bit we talked about, the getadmin program turns off checking to see whether a user has this type of privilege. So NtOpenProcess and NtOpenThread no longer check to see whether a user has the rights to execute a process, thereby giving the hacker many more privileges than he or she originally had.

How Can IDS Prevent This Attack?   Because most getadmin attacks start with an attacker's gaining access through a guest login account, IDSs focus on detecting guest login attempts to the NT systems and providing suitable countermeasures based on the security policies. For example, Cisco IDS signature 3303 detects guest login attempts. We will talk about countermeasures in the next few sections.

Cisco's Web site lists the 25 most common vulnerabilities found in the industry based on security posture assessments. You can see this list at www.cisco.com/cgi-bin/front.x/csec/mostVul.pl.

It is very educational to go through this list and look at the various types of vulnerabilities and exploits that the Cisco IDS protects against.

The Process of Detecting Intrusions

So far, you have read a detailed discussion of the various types of attacks. We have also looked at some specific examples of attacks. Now we will look at the general theory behind how such attacks can be prevented and how network intrusions (that is how most of these attacks are classified) can be detected. This builds our path to the more specific discussion of setting up Cisco's IDS in the next chapter.

Two main ways of detecting intrusion are generally used in today's networks:

- Statistical anomaly-based IDS
- Pattern matching or signature-based IDS

Statistical anomaly-based IDS relies on establishing thresholds for various types of activity on the network, such as how many times a certain command is executed by a user in a session to a host. This type of activity can lead to detecting an intrusion taking place. However, this method is difficult to rely on solely, because many attacks do no lend themselves to easily being detected based on thresholds of this sort.

The most commonly used methods of detecting intrusions are pattern matching and signatures. A signature is a set of rules used to detect an attack in progress. A device being used to do intrusion detection is loaded with a set of signatures. Each signature contains information about the kind of activity to look for in traffic passing through the network to detect if an attack is under way. When the traffic passing through matches the pattern contained in a signature, an alarm is generated, notifying the network administrator of the intrusion in place. Often, in addition to detecting the intrusion and identifying the administrator, an IDS resets the connection established by the attacker and/or creates access control entries on a firewall device to stop further attacks by the attacker if possible. Resetting and shunning attacks come with their own set of risks, including self-imposed denial of service. These responses should be well-planned and well-implemented. The obvious drawback of such a system is where new attacks occur with no known signatures available to detect them. Regular updating of the signatures can prevent some of these issues, but the problem nevertheless is genuine.

More often than not, IDS devices implement a solution that is a combination of the two mechanisms just discussed. One example of such a solution is the Cisco IDS. It lets detection occur based on statistical anomalies where no known signature has been triggered. It also lets detection occur where attacks based on a well-known signature are taking place. Intrusion detection can be implemented either on the hosts that need to be protected or on a network device that can sniff the traffic for all the hosts on the network. Host-based IDS works by looking at the activity on the host on which it is installed, including commands being executed and logs being generated. Because host-based IDS can be used to further strengthen critical servers against attacks that slip past network-based IDS, Cisco implements a host-based IDS as well. You can get more information on Cisco's host-based intrusion detection from the following URL:

cco/univercd/cc/td/doc/product/iaabu/csids/host/index.htm

For the sake of the discussion in this chapter and the next, we will limit our discussion to how network-based intrusion detection works.

The signatures found in Cisco's IDS can be classified into two main categories based on the information they examine to detect whether an intrusion is taking place or has taken place:

- Content-based signatures
- Context-based signatures

Content-based signatures are triggered by data contained in packet payloads. Context-based signatures are triggered by data contained in packet headers.

Signatures can also be classified into two categories based on how many packets the system must examine before it can alarm on the possibility of an attack:

- Atomic signatures
- Composite signatures

Atomic signatures require only one complete packet to be examined to determine whether an attack is in progress, whereas composite signatures require more than one packet (and thus more memory to store information regarding passing packets) to detect an intrusion.

Figure 14-8 shows the types of signatures available.

Figure 14-8 *Signature Analysis*

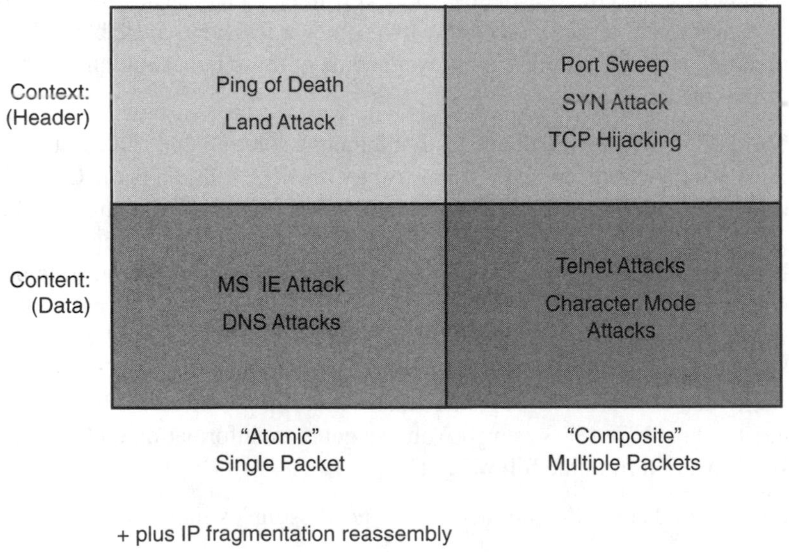

Case Study: Kevin Metnick's Attack on Tsutomu Shimomura's Computers and How IDS Could Have Saved the Day

One of the most well-known network intrusion attacks was conducted by Kevin Metnick on Christmas Day 1994. The attack resulted in a well-documented story that ended with Metnick's arrest. Tsutomu Shimomura was the computer security scientist whose computers were hacked and who finally helped bring the whole episode to a conclusion.

This case study covers the attack that Metnick launched on Shimomura's computers and analyzes how an intrusion-detection mechanism could have given a warning or even stopped the attack from occurring. Shimomura described the attack in detail in an e-mail to the newsgroups comp.security.misc, comp.protocols.tcp-ip, and alt.security sent on January 25, 1995.

Metnick's attack on Shimomura's computers was conducted in a series of steps. The following is a summary of the steps that were followed to hack the computers. You can search the archives for the string "Technical details of the attack described by Markoff in NYT" for the full description by Shimomura.

Step 1 An initial reconnaissance attack was launched against the network to gain preliminary information about it.

Step 2 The attacker launched a SYN flood against one of the servers on the network. The attack was launched on port 513 of the server, which was used to process login requests. The SYN flood packets had a spoofed address that was unused to avoid having resets sent back in response to the server's SYN-ACKs. The server's connection queue filled up very quickly.

Step 3 The attacker launched a reconnaissance attack on one of the x-terminals also connected to the same network. The purpose of this attack was to determine how the x-term generated its TCP sequence numbers. This allowed the attacker to fake packets as if they were originated by the x-term later in the attack. By sending TCP SYN packets to the x-term with a sequence number that incremented by 1 for each new SYN sent, and by analyzing the return SYN-ACKs and their sequence numbers, the attacker found out how the x-term generated its sequence numbers.

Step 4 The attacker, knowing that the x-term trusted the server that he previously disabled, spoofed a login request to pretend that it was coming from the server. The x-term replied with a SYN-ACK. The server would have responded to this SYN-ACK with a reset, but the attacker had disabled the server using the DoS attack described in Step 2. Next, the attacker forged an ACK from the server to the x-term. He could do this because, based on the sequence number attack in the preceding step, he knew the sequence number that the x-term must have sent to the server in response to the SYN the attacker sent it. The attacker then had a one-way connection established to the x-term.

Step 5   The attacker entered the following command on the x-term:

rsh x-terminal "echo + + >>/.rhosts"

This command modified the .rhosts file on the x-term so that the x-term began considering every host a trusted host. Now the attacker could connect to the x-term without having to spoof any connections.

Step 6   After gaining root access, the attacker installed a module on the x-term, allowing him to take control of the authenticated session already established on the x-term.

We will use Cisco IDS also signatures to see how the attack just described, which is really a series of attacks combined into one attack, could have been stopped.

The Cisco IDS signature 8000:51303 contains patterns that would have matched the pattern entered by the attacker to modify the .rhosts file on the x-term. Issuing this command would have triggered an alarm on the IDS, alerting the administrator of the intrusion.

Cisco's IDS also provides signatures that can detect a SYN attack being launched. However, only TCP ports 21, 23, 80, and 25 are supported. Because the attack was on TCP port 513, it would have gone undetected by this signature.

Summary

Network security attacks occur despite the protection offered by access control mechanisms such as firewalls. They can be internal or external and can involve data theft or simply a denial of service. Network intrusion detection provides a suitable mechanism for detecting and preventing these attacks. This chapter looked at some of the common types of attacks and discussed some of the more common examples. We briefly looked at how Cisco's IDS fits into the picture. Finally, we looked at the famous Kevin Metnick hacking and how the Cisco IDS could have prevented it from occurring. This chapter laid down the basic concepts and the foundation we will use to go into a more specific and targeted study of the Cisco IDS in the next chapter.

This chapter covers the following key topics:

- **Components of the Cisco Secure Intrusion Detection System (IDS)**—This section discusses the various software components of the Cisco Secure IDS.

- **Construction of the Management Console**—This section discusses the daemons that go into the making of the two management consoles: UNIX director and the CSPM IDS console.

- **Construction of the Sensor**—This section discusses the daemons that go into the making of the IDS sensors.

- **Responses to Intrusions**—This section discusses the various responses available for intrusions detected by the IDS sensors.

- **Types of Signatures**—This section talks about the various types of signatures and their default alarm levels.

- **Using a Router, PIX, or IDSM as a Sensor**—This section discusses how these devices can be used as sensors and also how they differ from each other.

- **Case Studies**—The case studies cover how to use the various types of sensors in IDS environments.

## CHAPTER 15

Cisco Secure Intrusion Detection

Cisco Secure Intrusion Detection is a complete suite of products available through Cisco that offers intrusion detection and response mechanisms. The products provide high-speed, reliable countermeasures to intrusions based on context- and content-based atomic and composite signatures (see the section "The Process of Detecting Intrusions" in Chapter 14, "What is Intrusion Defection?," for definitions of these terms). This chapter looks at the internal architecture of these products. It also discusses how to set them up to provide intrusion detection services.

Components of the Cisco Secure IDS

Cisco currently provides IDSs in two flavors—network intrusion detection and host intrusion detection. Generally, it is advisable to start by implementing IDS in a network using the network-based variety because it has less impact on the network bandwidth and also doesn't consume CPU resources on individual servers. As soon as the network IDS is operational, based on specific requirements for servers that need to be protected from attacks, host IDS can be implemented on specific machines.

This chapter concentrates on Cisco's network-based intrusion detection. You are encouraged to look at the following URL for details on the host IDS:

cco/univercd/cc/td/doc/product/iaabu/csids/host/index.htm

Cisco's intrusion detection system is composed of two primary components:

- IDS sensor
- Management console (UNIX director or Cisco Secure Policy Manager [CSPM])

The IDS sensor and the management console work together to provide a scalable, user-friendly IDS solution. The sensor is the portion of the solution that is used to sniff on the network and monitor traffic. The management console is used to manage the sensors and provide a GUI for visually observing alarms being generated on the network due to various types of activities.

The sensors and the management console can be set up in a number of ways to provide IDS functionality to a network. However, you should keep in mind a few points when placing the management console and the sensor in a network:

- The sensor should be placed in a location where it can monitor all the traffic that needs to be checked for intrusions.

- Care should be taken to make sure that the sensor's bandwidth capabilities are not exceeded.

- The management console should always be placed in a very secure location on the network due to the control it exercises over all the sensing devices on the network.

- If the traffic between the management console and the sensor must traverse an insecure portion of the network, it is highly desirable to encrypt the communication using IPsec on the devices at the edge of the secure networks.

- Multiple sensors can be used to monitor large amounts of traffic on a heavy traffic network by segmenting the network into multiple sections. All these sensors can report to the same management console.

- For increased security, a sensor can report alarms to more than one management console, so in case there is an outage on one of the management consoles (perhaps due to a denial of service [DoS] attack), the alarms can still be received at another location.

IDS sensors can be deployed in a variety of locations on a network. Following are some of the typical areas where the need to deploy IDS sensors is seen:

- **Extranet protection**—Monitors partner traffic where "trust" is implied.

- **Intranet/internal protection**—Protects data centers and critical systems from internal threats.

- **Internet protection**—Protects against threats from the untrusted public network.

- **Remote access protection**—Hardens perimeter control by monitoring remote users.

- **Server farm protection**—Protects e-business servers from attack and compromise.

Figure 15-1 shows some of the locations on a network where an IDS sensor is typically deployed.

Figure 15-1 *Locations on a Network Where an IDS Sensor Is Typically Deployed*

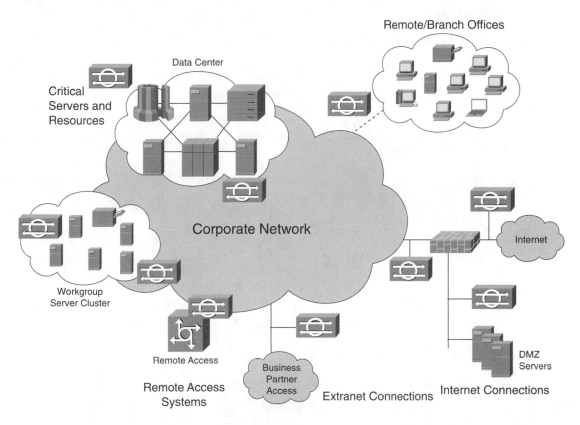

Interaction of the Sensor and the Management Console

The sensor is the device used to monitor traffic on the wire and look for patterns in traffic that might trigger alarms based on the signatures found on the sensor. Upon seeing a traffic pattern that matches one of its signatures, the sensor notifies the management console, which displays the appropriate alarm on a user interface.

Depending on the type of sensor being used, the sensor can either passively monitor the network traffic or do inline processing of the packets contained in the traffic traversing the network. Passive mode is more conducive to networks with a large amount of traffic because it does not impose any performance penalties on the network. Examples of Cisco devices that do passive monitoring are the appliance sensors and the Catalyst IDS module (IDSM). Inline processing, on the other hand, can degrade the performance of the devices that deploy this form of IDS. Examples of Cisco sensor devices that do inline processing of packets for intrusion detection are the router and the PIX with IDS functionality turned on.

Figure 15-2 shows the interaction of the sensor and the management console in the Cisco IDS solution.

Figure 15-2 *Roles of the Sensor and the Management Console in the Cisco IDS Solution*

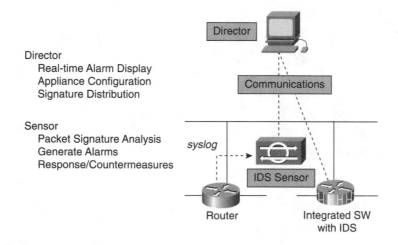

Director
    Real-time Alarm Display
    Appliance Configuration
    Signature Distribution

Sensor
    Packet Signature Analysis
    Generate Alarms
    Response/Countermeasures

Figure 15-3 shows the functionality of the appliance sensor.

Figure 15-3 *Packet Capture Using the Appliance Sensor*

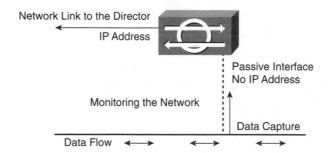

The sensor and the management console interact with each other to provide the complete IDS functionality. The following steps describe the basic IDS intrusion detection process:

Step 1   The sensor captures network packets through its monitoring interface.

Step 2   Packets are reassembled, if required, and are compared against a rule set indicating typical intrusion activity.

Step 3   The sensor logs and notifies the management console platform if an attack is detected through the command and control interface.

Step 4   If an attack is detected, the management console alarms, logs, and takes action, such as paging an administrator if it is configured to do so.

It is important to understand that a network-based intrusion detection system can alarm only on what it can see. So if the traffic that the sensor sees is encrypted, it cannot alarm on the data that is in encrypted format. Therefore, it is critical to place the sensor in a location on the network where the traffic has already been decrypted. Alternatively, for critical network resources for which encryption is occurring directly, such as SSL to web server, host-based intrusion detection systems can be set up. Host IDS can detect attacks even for encrypted traffic, because it can see the traffic after the end host has decrypted it.

Construction of the Management Console

UNIX director and CSPM are the two management consoles available for the IDS solution. The primary purpose served by the management console is to provide a central location for configuring the sensors, which can then be downloaded to the sensors themselves. The management console also provides a user interface for viewing the information collected by the sensors. A summary of the functionality provided by the management console is as follows:

- Manages and configures multiple sensors

- Provides a user interface for the configuration of signature elements

- Provides a facility for logging information collected by the sensor (the sensor itself can be used for logging as well)

- Gives the user access to the network security database, which contains information about the signatures contained in the sensors

- Sends event information to a trouble-ticketing system, pager, or e-mail to alert security personnel when security events occur

Two Types of Management Consoles

Cisco produces two separate software bundles that can provide the director functionality:

- CSPM IDS Console (Windows NT-based)

- UNIX director

Although both these software bundles provide pretty much the same functionality, some features differentiate them. Although these features can be important in certain setups, the overwhelming reason for choosing one platform over the other is mostly the availability and usability of the underlying platform (NT or UNIX). Note that the UNIX director also requires HP OpenView for its functioning.

Here are some of the more important differences between the two management console software platforms:

- CSPM does local logging to a database, whereas this logging is done to a text file in the UNIX director.

- CSPM distinguishes between alarm severities at three levels (high, medium, low), whereas the director distinguishes between them at five levels (1 through 5).

- The UNIX director can send alarms to another director, allowing the creation of a tiered hierarchy of directors. CSPM does not have this functionality built in by default.

Internal Architecture of the UNIX Director

To better understand how the director software works, it is important to understand its internal architecture. The internal architecture of the two management console types is slightly different, but there are enough similarities to see that both perform essentially the same job. Figure 15-4 shows the various daemons on the UNIX director and how they interact.

Figure 15-4 *UNIX Director Internal Architecture*

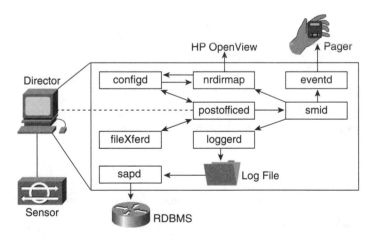

The functionality of the UNIX director is carried out by a series of processes or daemons. Figure 15-4 shows these daemons and their interrelationships. The following list describes each of the processes involved:

- **postofficed**—As the name suggests, the postofficed daemon handles communications between the director and the sensor as well as between the various services running on the director or the sensor. Like most of the other daemons described here, this daemon is present on both the management console and the sensor. When packetd (described in the Internal Architecture of the IDS Sensor section) on a sensor detects unauthorized activity, it signals postofficed on the sensor, which then communicates to the postofficed on the director using the Cisco IDS Post Office Protocol (POP). postofficed is then responsible for telling loggerd to start logging and alerting smid on the director for alarm population in HPOV. postofficed also communicates with the fileXferd daemon to communicate configuration changes between the sensor(s) and the director.

This daemon service includes the following features:

— A proprietary connection-based protocol that resends a message whenever any of its packets are lost.

— Point-to-point routes that might include intermediate post office nodes.

— Communication integrity that is maintained via alternative routes (specified in /usr/nr/etc/routes and /usr/nr/etc/destinations). When one route fails, communication is switched to an alternative route. Communication is reestablished to the preferred route as soon as it comes back online.

Routing is based on a three-part key that includes the following information:

— Organization

— Host

— Application (sensor or director or CSPM)

See the next section for details on how POP works.

- **fileXferd**—This service is responsible for pushing the configuration files created on the director to the sensors. The initial configuration, such as assigning IP addresses, the default route, and the three elements of the key, need to be done on the sensor via console login. From that point on, however, the director can use fileXferd to transfer configurations to the sensor.

- **smid**—This daemon is responsible for populating the alarm icons on the HPOV user interface on the director. HPOV is the viewing console used by the UNIX director. smid can also redirect messages to other daemon services, such as eventd and loggerd, based on DupDestination entries in the /usr/nr/etc/smid.conf file.

- **configd**—This is the daemon that takes the user input from the GUI on the director and converts it into configuration files for use on the sensors and the director.

- **loggerd**—This is the director's logging service. It is responsible for writing error, command, and alarm entries to log files.

- **sapd**—This service provides data and file management. It is responsible for moving log files to the database staging areas, offline archives, and other routine processes to prevent filesystems from filling up and overwriting saved logs. Note that Oracle or Remedy database loading is accomplished with *sapx instead of sapd*.

- **eventd**—This daemon allows the director to send out various forms of notifications based on alarms received. For example, the director can be configured to page a group of people if a level 5 alarm is reported.

These daemons interact with each other to produce the director functionality. This interaction is depicted in Figure 15-4.

postofficed, upon receiving an alarm from the sensor, interacts with the smid daemon, passing on the information about the alarm. smid takes the information, changes it so that it makes sense to the daemons it is about to pass the information to, and pushes it to the nrdirmap, eventd, and loggerd daemons. nrdirmap is the interface between the smid and the HP OpenView maps that displays the alarm data. eventd takes care of generating alerts such as pages to the administrators. loggerd takes the alarm information and populates the log files with it. This logged information can then be taken by sapd and exported to an RDBMS if it's set up to do so.

These daemons also interact when it's time to push configurations to the sensors. This is achieved by fileXferd taking the configurations done on the director and passing the information to postofficed, which uses POP to pass the information to the sensor.

Post Office Protocol

The preceding section mentioned that Post Office Protocol (POP) is used to carry out communications between the sensors and the management consoles. This section looks in detail at the construction of this protocol. Because the same protocol is used with the CSPM management console as well, we will not repeat this discussion when talking about the CSPM architecture.

The post office uses UDP port 45000 by default for its communications. It acknowledges each message exchanged through it for reliability.

It is possible to encrypt post office traffic using conventional encryption means such as IPsec. IPsec can be used to encrypt UDP port 45000 traffic to provide confidentiality and integrity of the messages exchanged.

POP uses a variety of messages for communication between the sensors and the management console. Here are the important ones:

- **Heartbeat**—Used to check the liveliness of the management console and the sensor.
- **Alarm**—Used to carry alarm data.
- **IP log**—Used to transfer IP logs from the sensor to the director.
- **Command**—Used to send configuration parameters from the management console to the sensor.
- **Error**—Used to convey problems with the functioning of the sensor or the director.

Internal Architecture of the CSPM IDS Console

While the overall functionality is the same, the internal architecture of the CSPM IDS (CIDS) console is slightly different from the UNIX director architecture. Figure 15-5 illustrates the CSPM internal architecture.

Figure 15-5 *CSPM Management Console Architecture*

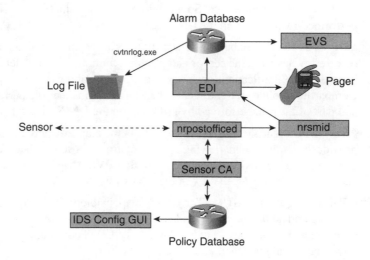

The following list describes the various elements that make up the internal architecture of the CSPM IDS (CIDS) console:

- **nr.postofficed**—This daemon handles communications between CIDS services and CIDS nodes. When nr.postofficed receives alarm information from the sensor, it passes the information to nr.smid, which handles the rest of the activity related to the alarm. This functionality is very similar to the postofficed functionality on the UNIX director.

NOTE   The preceding section discusses how the Post Office Protocol (POP) works. The functionality of the POP remains pretty much the same on the Unix director and the CIDS.

- **Sensor CA**—Sensor CA is a control agent that pushes the configuration information to a sensor. This function is similar to that achieved by fileXferd on the UNIX director. The configuration files generated and pushed to the sensor are located in the CSPM post office sensorca directory (for example, C:\Program Files\Cisco Systems\Cisco Secure Post Office\tmp\sensorca). Each sensor managed by CSPM has its own subdirectory identified by the sensor's host name and organization name (such as sensor1.pod1). A backup sensor subdirectory contains the previously generated and pushed configuration files.

- **nr.smid**—This is the security management interface daemon. This service is responsible for translating sensor data into meaningful information for EDI (discussed next). It also allows alarms to be forwarded to other services such as a secondary management console's smid service. So, nr.smid performs a function very similar to the one performed by the smid on the UNIX director.

- **EDI**—The Event Database Interface (EDI) is an nr.smid application. This program receives events from the sensor and places them in the alarm database. EDI also handles event notifications such as e-mail, paging, and custom script execution. Comparing it to the UNIX director, the EDI performs the role performed by eventd and part of the role performed by nrdirmap on the UNIX director.

- **EVS**—The Event Viewing System (EVS) is the alarm display for sensor alarms. It provides real-time event viewing and correlation in a spreadsheet format. If you compare it to the UNIX director, you see that EVS performs the functions that are taken care of by HP OpenView in the UNIX director.

- **CIDS configuration GUI**—The GUI is responsible for providing a user-friendly interface and taking user input and converting it into meaningful elements for the rest of the management console to work with. The CIDS configuration GUI is made up of three major components:

  - Sensor configuration

  - Signature templates

  - Wizards (Add and Update)

  Comparing it to the UNIX director, the GUI takes over some of the functionality offered by the director GUI and some of the functionality of configd, which is responsible for converting user input on the UNIX director into meaningful entries for the various configurations on the director.

- **cvtnrlog.exe**—This is a Windows NT CLI utility that extracts data from the alarm database to create a CIDS log file. The output of the command is sent to standard output device such as the monitor. It uses Windows **redirect** commands to create a file. The functionality is similar to that of loggerd on the UNIX director.

The CSPM IDS management console functions much like the UNIX director. When an alarm is received through POP by nr.postofficed, it passes on the information to nr.smid. nr.smid converts the data into information appropriate for the EVI and pushes it to the EVI. The EDI populates the alarm database with information it has received from smid. It also sends out any alerts that need to be sent, such as pages to administrators. The alarms are then also copied to a log file by cvtnrlog.exe.

When a sensor is configured from the CSPM management console, the sensor CA takes the configuration created using the GUI and passes it to nr.postofficed, which then conveys the information to the sensor using POP.

Construction of the Sensor

The sensor is the sniffing component of the Cisco IDS. The sensor contains signatures, which it uses to generate alarms when it sniffs suspicious traffic patterns. Apart from sending the alarm information to the director, the sensor can also log this information to log files located on itself. This way, a sensor can be used as a standalone device as well. However, this is not a very useful setup because the management console's capabilities of displaying the alarms in a user-friendly manner and generating appropriate responses (such as paging) are not used.

Cisco produces the sensor in three distinct flavors:

- **Standalone IDS 4200 series sensors**—These are standalone sensors in which a full box is dedicated to the sensor's functioning. They are often called the "appliance sensors." The discussion on the internal architecture of the sensor in the next section will focus on this type of sensor. We will leave the discussion of the workings of the other types of sensing devices to later sections of this chapter.

- **Catalyst 6000 IDSM sensor**—This is a sensor blade that fits into a Catalyst 6000 chassis. It can sniff traffic off the switch backplane.

- **Router and PIX Firewall sensors**—The IOS router software and the PIX Firewall software both can make the router and the PIX respectively act as a limited sensor device. The number of signatures supported in these softwares is limited.

Internal Architecture of the IDS Sensor

Although all three types of sensors previously listed have different hardware architectures, the software has essentially the same components. Figure 15-6 shows the components of the software that go into the making of the appliance sensor software.

| NOTE | Although the basic software architecture on the rest of the sensors is the same as the architecture for the appliance sensor shown here, the actual software implementation varies greatly, with the end result being the same. One rather major exception is the absence of the post office functionality in the PIX code, because it does not communicate with a management console. |

Figure 15-6 *Sensor Architecture*

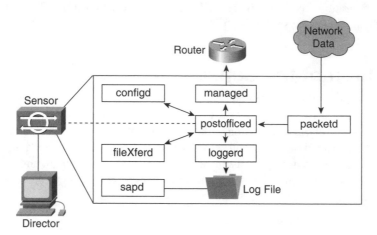

As you can see in this figure, most of the daemons that are used in the making of the UNIX director are also present in the appliance sensor software. The two new daemons present in the sensor, packetd and managed, are described in the following list:

postofficed—As in the director, this daemon handles communications between the director and sensor as well as between the various services running on the sensor. Like most of the other daemons described here, this daemon is present on both the management console and the sensor. When packetd on a sensor detects unauthorized activity, it signals postofficed on the sensor, which then communicates with the postofficed on the director using the Cisco IDS Post Office Protocol. It also communicates with the managed daemon to configure access control lists for shunning and the loggerd daemon to populate the log files with various details. The postofficed on the sensor is also responsible for communicating with configd and fileXferd, which manage configurations pushed to the sensor by the management console.

This daemon service includes the following features:

— A proprietary connection-based protocol that resends a message whenever any of its packets are lost.

— Point-to-point routes that might include intermediate post office nodes.

— Communication integrity that is maintained via alternative routes (specified in /usr/nr/etc/routes and /usr/nr/etc/destinations). When one route fails, communication is switched to an alternative route. Communication is reestablished to the preferred route as soon as it comes back online.

Routing is based on a three-part key that includes the following information:

— Organization

— Host

— Application (sensor or director or CSPM)

POP uses UDP port 45000 by default for its communications. It acknowledges each message exchanged through it for reliability.

It is possible to encrypt post office traffic using conventional encryption means such as IPsec. IPsec can be used to encrypt UDP port 45000 traffic to provide confidentiality and integrity of the messages exchanged.

- **fileXferd**—This service is responsible for receiving the configuration files, created on the director, on the sensors. The initial configuration, such as assigning IP addresses, the default route, and the three elements of the routing key, need to be done on the sensor via console login. From that point on, however, the director can use fileXferd to transfer configurations to the sensor.

- **configd**—This is the daemon that creates the configuration files and maintains them for use on the sensor.

- **loggerd**—When running on a sensor, loggerd creates two basic types of flat files: a single sensor event file, and one or more IP session logs. Data is written to flat files for reasons of performance and fault tolerance.

- **sapd**—This service provides data and file management. It is responsible for moving log files to the database staging areas, offline archives, and other routine processes to prevent file systems from filling up and overwriting saved logs.

- **packetd**—This daemon allows the sensor to capture packets directly from the network and conduct intrusion detection. Alarms based on signature matching are forwarded to postofficed for distribution.

- **managed**—This daemon is responsible for managing and monitoring routers and other devices used for shunning. (*Shunning* is the mechanism whereby access lists are created dynamically on a network device to stop an attacker from accessing the network.) When packetd identifies that a certain type of attack should be shunned, it sends a **shun** command to managed via postofficed. managed then rewrites the router's access control list to disallow access into the protected network.

The sensor's packetd monitors the wire for any pattern matches. As soon as it sees one, it alerts postofficed. postofficed communicates the alarm information to loggerd for logging (that is all it does by default for level 1 and 2 alarms), passes on the information to postofficed on the management console, and (if so configured for that alarm) talks to managed as well. managed then logs into a router and sets up an access list to do shunning for the malicious IP address.

When configurations for the sensor are being done on the management console, they are pushed to the sensor through POP and then are used by the configd daemon to set up files on the sensor appropriately.

Responses to Intrusions

This section talks about the mechanisms that the sensor has at its disposal when confronted by an attack. The sensor has the ability to react as opposed to simply logging and passing on the information to the management console. The sensor can respond to a detected signature in the following ways:

- No action
- Shun
- Log
- Shun and log
- TCP reset
- TCP reset and shun
- TCP reset and log
- TCP reset, shun, and log

The sensors can be configured to respond to various types of alarms using any one of the mechanisms listed here. For example, a sensor can be set up to respond to level 4 alarms with a TCP reset and log and to level 5 alarms with a TCP reset, shun, and log (a stricter response).

NOTE   Although IOS routers, PIX Firewalls, and the IDSM can act as a sensor, they can do only two of the three things just listed—TCP reset and log. Shunning is a capability that only the standalone appliance sensors have. However, because the IOS router and the PIX Firewall have their IDS sensing modules sitting in the packet's path through the router or the PIX Firewall, respectively, they can simply drop an offending packet. The IDSM and the appliance sensors can merely sniff passively at the traffic and therefore, can take action only after the offending packet has already reached the victim.

Let's look at each of these mechanisms.

Logging

Logging is an important feature of the Cisco IDS. Logging capabilities are available on all the sensors, but how logging is done varies from one type of sensor to another.

Logging is used for two primary purposes:

- **Event logs**—Provide information about events for which alarms were raised, as well as the errors and command executions on the sensor.
- **IP session logs**—The sensor can be configured to not only sniff for alarms but also capture the information regarding the IP packets which were part of the traffic which triggered the signature to a log file.

We will now look at how each type of sensor handles logging.

Event Logs in Appliance Sensors

The event logs in appliance sensors are ASCII files. The most important information these files contain is the IP session information for all alarmable events from levels 1 and 2. The logs for alarm levels 3 to 5 are sent to the management console to be written to the log files in the format described here. However, note that where the logs are sent is a configurable parameter. The sensor can be set up to log events for all levels of alarms. These files are written to the /usr/nr/var directory with the naming convention of log.*YYYYMMDDHHMM*. We will examine what the event log for an alarm event looks like. For alarm levels 1 and 2, the only action that the sensor takes by default is creating a log entry. It does not forward this information to the management console. Therefore, it is important to understand what the log entries on the sensor for the various alarms look like.

loggerd on the sensor is the daemon responsible for creating log files for the system.

A typical line written to a log file looks like this:

```
4,1025294,1998/04/16,16:58:36,1998/04/16,11:58:36,10008,11,100,OUT,OUT,1,20
01,0,TCP/IP,10.1.6.1,10.2.3.5,0,0,0.0.0.0,
```

Each comma-delimited field contains different data. The first field indicates what kind of record was logged. Table 15-1 shows what the first field of the log file represents.

Table 15-1 *Representation of the First Field of the Log File*

Log File Initial Field Reference ValuesFieldValue	Record Type
0	Default
1	Command
2	Error
3	Command log
4	Event
5	IP log
6	Redirect

So, in the example, 4 denotes an event record.

Table 15-2 shows what the rest of the fields in the log denote.

Table 15-2 *Representation of the Rest of the Fields in the Log File*

Log File Field Reference Values Sample Field Value	Field Type
4	Record type
1025294	Record ID
1998/04/16	GMT date stamp
16:58:36	GMT time stamp
1998/04/16	Local date stamp
11:58:36	Local time stamp
10008	Application ID
11	Host ID
100	Organization ID
OUT	Source direction
OUT	Destination direction
1	Alarm level
2001	SigID
0	SubSigID

Table 15-2   *Representation of the Rest of the Fields in the Log File (Continued)*

Log File Field Reference Values Sample Field Value	Field Type
TCP/IP	Protocol
10.1.6.1	Source IP address
10.2.3.5	Destination IP address
0	Source port
0	Destination port
0.0.0.0	Router IP address

Two other types of records, error and command log, are similar in structure to the event record. Both of these record types have the same first nine fields contained in event records (record type, record ID, GMT date stamp, GMT time stamp, local date stamp, local time stamp, application ID, host ID, and organization ID).

An error record type has a tenth field denoting the actual error string generated by a service. The command log record type also contains fields for the source application ID, host ID, and organization ID, as well as the command string. In both cases, you have a complete record of errors and commands.

IP Session Logs on Appliance Sensors

In addition to detecting attack signatures, sensord and packetd can monitor the traffic associated with a specific type of attack. For example, sensord can be configured to monitor all the packets associated with an IP spoof. sensord or packetd creates a separate log file in /usr/nr/var/iplog for each of these monitoring sessions. The name of each session log file is based on the IP address of the attacking host, such as iplog.10.145.16.152.

IP session logs capture all incoming and outgoing TCP packets associated with a specific connection and therefore contain binary data.

Event Logs on the IDSM

As in the appliance sensors, the IDSM by default logs all alarms of level 1 and 2 locally and sends only alarms of levels 3 to 5 to the management console. When logging is turned on on the IDSM, these log messages can be sent to various logging destinations, such as a syslog server, like any other syslog messages. The format of the logging messages is the same as on the appliance sensors.

IP Session Logs on the IDSM

Currently the IDSM does not support the capture of IP session logs. Various other packet-capture tools in the IDSM can be used to capture IP packet data, but parsing it without the formatting provided by the IDS remains an issue.

Event Logs on the PIX and Router-Based Sensors

Router and PIX Firewall sensors log the alarm events using normal syslog mechanisms. These logs can be displayed on the IDS management console or can be sent to a syslog. The following sections examine how the routers and PIXes function in terms of IDS event logs.

Routers

Alarm messages logged on a router follow the format shown here. Syslog messages are colon-delimited strings with the following format:

sig:sig-number:sig-name from *source-IP* to *destination-IP*

where

sig-number is the signature's number, as defined in the NetRanger Network Security Database
sig-name is the name of the signature
source-IP is the source's IP address
destination-IP is the destination's IP address

For example:

sig:1000:Bad IP Option List from %i to %i

sig:1001:IP options-Record Packet Route from %i to %i

PIX

While the router sensor supports sending alarm data to a management console, the PIX does not communicate with a management console. Therefore, the only mechanism for the PIX to display alarm data is through the logging messages, making these message even more important to understand.

IDS syslog messages on a PIX Firewall all start with %PIX-4-4000*nn* and have the following format:

%PIX-4-4000*nn* IDS:*sig_num sig_ms*g from *faddr* to *laddr* on interface *int_name*

For example:

%PIX-4-400013 IDS:2003 ICMP redirect from 10.4.1.2 to 10.2.1.1 on interface dmz

%PIX-4-400032 IDS:4051 UDP Snork attack from 10.1.1.1 to 192.168.1.1 on interface outside

The options present in the logging message for a PIX Firewall are shown in Table 15-3.

Table 15-3 *Options Found in the IDS Logging Messages for a PIX Firewall*

Option	Explanation
sig_num	The signature number.
sig_msg	The signature message. Approximately the same as the Cisco IDS signature message.
faddr	The IP address of the foreign host initiating the attack. ("Foreign" is relative; attacks can be perpetrated either from the outside to an inside host or from the inside to an outside host.)
laddr	The IP address of the local host to which the attack is directed. ("Local" is relative; attacks can be perpetrated either from the outside to an inside host or from the inside to an outside host.)
int_name	The name of the interface on which the signature originated.

IP Session Logs on the PIX and Router-Based Sensors

Because both the router and the PIX software have built-in mechanisms available for packet dump-type session logging, the IDS functionality to generate IP session logs is not available separately on these boxes. See the command references for the IOS and PIX software for the commands that can allow various levels of packet captures.

TCP Reset

TCP reset is a mechanism for responding to attacks shared by all types of sensors except the IDSM.

TCP reset, as the name implies, is a TCP reset packet sent to the source IP address of a packet that is generating a TCP-based alarm.

Note that although the reset might terminate the TCP connection, it cannot stop the TCP packets sent before the reset packet, from reaching the victim—or, for that matter, stop the offending IP address from sending future TCP packets. Inline IDSs, such as the router and PIX, can take care of this issue by dropping the offensive packets, whereas the sniffing sensors, such as the appliance sensors and the IDSM, must rely on shunning to improve their odds against attackers. Although shunning does not drop the first offensive packet, it does stop future activity. We will look at how shunning works in the next section.

Shunning

Shunning is a feature available only on the appliance sensors and the IDSM. Shunning is a feature through which the sensor can configure a network device such as the PIX Firewall, a router, or a Catalyst switch with an access control list to stop an attacker from accessing the network.

A sensor can perform shunning through a router using access control lists. The access control list can be used to prevent traffic from either a particular host or a complete subnet from passing through the router.

Catalyst 6000 MFSC, and Catalyst 5000 RSM can also be set up to do shunning at a sensor's behest. The Catalyst 6000 MFSC and the Catalyst 5000 RSM are treated as any other Cisco IOS router. However, for shunning on the Catalyst 6000 Supervisor running CatOS, the software architecture relies on security VLAN access control lists (VACLs) in the switch. These VACLs permit or deny the passage of data packets through the VLANs. Each VACL contains permit and deny conditions that apply to IP addresses.

The PIX Firewall also lends itself to being modified to do shunning through a sensor. PIX has a **shun(ip)** command that can be controlled by a sensor. So, instead of using PIX ACLs, the **shun(ip)** command takes precedence over all the ACLs or other access restriction mechanisms set up on the PIX.

Refer to the command reference for the specific type of sensor you are setting up for instructions on how to set up shunning. Setting up shunning is also known as *device management* because a device such as a router or a PIX is being managed by the sensor.

Types of Signatures

All signatures on the Cisco IDS are divided into various categories based on the types of attacks they do pattern matching for. Table 15-4 outlines the various types of signatures available on the Cisco IDS.

Table 15-4 *Various Signature Types Divided into the IDS Signature Categories*

Signature Category	Signature Types
1000 series—IP signatures	IP options
	IP fragmentation
	Bad IP packets
2000 series—ICMP signatures	ICMP traffic records
	Ping sweeps
	ICMP attacks

Table 15-4   *Various Signature Types Divided into the IDS Signature Categories (Continued)*

Signature Category	Signature Types
3000 series—TCP signatures	TCP traffic records
	TCP port scans
	TCP host sweeps
	Mail attacks
	FTP attacks
	Legacy CIDS web attacks (signature IDs 3200 through 3233)
	NetBIOS attacks
	SYN flood and TCP hijack attacks
	TCP applications
4000 series—UDP signatures	UDP traffic records
	UDP port scan
	UDP attacks
	UDP applications
5000 series—web (HTTP) signatures	Web attacks
6000 series—cross-protocol signatures	DNS attacks
	RPC services attacks
	Authentication failures
	Loki attacks
	DDoS attacks
8000 series—string match signatures	Custom string matches
	TCP applications
10000 series—ACL policy violation signatures	Defined IOS ACL violations

Signature Engines

It is also instructive to look at the various signature engines internal to the sensors that process various groups of signatures. A signature engine is a component of the Cisco IDS sensor designed to support many signatures in a certain category. An engine is composed of a parser and an inspector. Each engine has a set of legal parameters that have allowable ranges or sets of values. Table 15-5 lists the various signature engines found in Cisco IDS and their corresponding functionality.

Table 15-5 *Signature Engines Found in the Cisco IDS and Their Functionality*

Engine	Description
ATOMIC.ICMP	Simple ICMP alarms based on the following parameters:
	Type
	Code
	Sequence
	ID
ATOMIC.IPOPTIONS	Simple layer 3 alarms
ATOMIC.L3.IP	Simple layer 3 IP alarms
ATOMIC.TCP	Simple TCP packet alarms based on the following parameters:
	Port
	Destination
	Flags
ATOMIC.UDP	Simple UDP packet alarms based on the following parameters:
	Port
	Direction
	DataLength
FLOOD.HOST.ICMP	ICMP floods directed at a single host
FLOOD.HOST.UDP	UDP floods directed at a single host
FLOOD.NET	Multiprotocol floods directed at a network segment
FLOOD.TCPSYN	Connections to multiple ports using TCP SYN
SERVICE.DNS.TCP	DNS packet analyzer on TCP port 53 (includes compression handler)
SERVICE.DNS.UDP	UDP-based DNS signatures
SERVICE.PORTMAP	RPC program number sent to port mapper
SERVICE.RPC	Simple RPC alarms based on the following parameters:
	Program
	Procedure
	Length
STRING.HTTP	Specialized STRING.TCP alarms for web traffic (includes anti-evasive URL deobfuscation)
STRING.ICMP	Generic ICMP-based string search engine
STRING.TCP	Generic TCP-based string search engine
STRING.UDP	Generic UDP-based string search engine

Table 15-5   *Signature Engines Found in the Cisco IDS and Their Functionality (Continued)*

Engine	Description
SWEEP.HOST.ICMP	A single host sweeping a range of nodes using ICMP
SWEEP.HOST.TCP	A single host sweeping a range of nodes using TCP
SWEEP.PORT.TCP	TCP connections to multiple destination ports between two nodes
SWEEP.PORT.UDP	UDP connections to multiple destination ports between two nodes
SWEEP.RPC	Connections to multiple ports with RPC requests between two nodes

The IDS appliance sensors and the IDSM deploy the full range of signatures, but the router IDS and PIX IDS software deploy only 59 and 57 signatures, respectively.

PIX 6.2 supports the following single-packet IDS signature messages: 1000 to 1006, 1100, 1102, 1103, 2000 to 2012, 2150, 2151, 2154, 3040 to 3042, 40, 50 to 4052, 6050 to 6053, 6100 to 6103, 6150 to 6155, 6175, 6180, and 6190. See the complete list of signatures at the following URL:

> www.cisco.com/cgi-bin/front.x/csec/idsAllList.pl

See this URL for a list of the signatures supported on the IOS router IDS software:

> www.cisco.com/univercd/cc/td/doc/product/software/ios120/120newft/120t/120t5/io
> sfw2/ios_ids.htm#xtocid127

Default Alarm Levels

The signatures are tied to various levels of alarms that can be generated when an intrusion is detected. Although the severity of the various signature alarms is preset, it can be modified based on the variables found on a particular network. However, it is highly recommended that you not reduce the severity of the alarms generated without a thorough understanding of what the alarm does and what the consequences could be if the alarm is generated at a low level rather than a high level. Table 15-6 lists the various alarms found in the Cisco IDS. It is also educational to look at the complete database of Cisco signatures via the URL referenced in the preceding section and look at the default alarm severities for the various types of attacks discussed in there.

Table 15-6   *Severity Levels Associated with Various Signature Types and Corresponding Examples*

Severity	Description	Examples
Severities 1 and 2 (low)	These are low-severity alarms that are generated for network activity considered benign. They are generated mostly for informational purposes.	• Unknown IP protocol • FTP SITE command attempted

continues

Table 15-6   *Severity Levels Associated with Various Signature Types and Corresponding Examples (Continued)*

Severity	Description	Examples
Severity 3 (medium)	These are medium-severity alarms that are generated when abnormal activity is seen on the network that could be malicious.	• Net Sweep-echo • TCP SYN port sweep
Severities 4 and 5 (high)	These are high-severity alarms that are positive indicators of malicious activity on the network. Whether an attack is a level 4 or 5 is determined by the possible impact of the attack it is triggered for.	• BackOrifice BO2K TCP Non Stealth 1 • WWW IIS Unicode • sadmind buffer overflow

Using a Router, PIX, or IDSM as a Sensor

Both a router and a PIX Firewall can act as a sensor. However, these capabilities are somewhat limited as compared to the functionality of a standalone appliance sensor. The primary limitation in using a router or a PIX as a sensor is the number of signatures that each of them deploys in the software (59 and 57, respectively). Also, the sensor implementation on a router or a PIX cannot shun an attacker. The only attack response mechanism implemented apart from alarming is drop and reset. Another drawback in using the PIX or a router as a sensor device is throughput. The primary reason for the impact on throughput is the fact that the router and the PIX do inline intrusion detection, meaning that they inspect a packet while it is traversing them . This is significantly different from the appliance and the IDSM sensors, which passively sniff the network to do intrusion detection. Although this solution might work for smaller networks, situations with high throughput might require the deployment of higher end router or PIX hardware to take on the burden of IDS processing. Although the router IDS software can be managed through a management console, the PIX cannot be managed through a management console. It is primarily a standalone IDS device that can generate alarm logs and do drops and resets on connections.

The Catalyst 6000 IDSM is designed specifically to address switched environments by integrating the IDS functionality directly into the switch and taking traffic right off the switch backplane. The IDSM provides the same breadth of coverage as the standalone appliance IDS sensors with a full array of signatures. The use of this module in the switch does not affect the switch's performance because it does not process the actual packets through its signatures—only copies of the packets. The IDSM can provide performance at a level similar to the faster of the two appliance sensors, IDS 4230. The IDSM can shun and alarm only. It cannot, however, currently do TCP resets.

The following case studies go over the steps for setting up each of the three sensors just discussed.

Case Studies

This section looks at some common ways of deploying IDS solutions in a network. We will look at how the sensors are set up and talk about how the management console is used to communicate with them. The idea is to give you insight into the setup of common IDS configurations.

Using a Router as a Sensor Device

This case study sets up a router to act as a sensor. The director used in this case study is a UNIX director, but CSPM could have been used as effectively in this role. The router is set up to do a number of things, including excluding signatures from being processed and filtering setup so that alarms are not generated due to traffic going to and from certain hosts for certain signatures.The reason for excluding certain signatures is to decrease the number of false positives.

False positives occur when an IDS "mistakenly" reports certain benign activity as malicious, requiring human intervention to diagnose the event as benign. Obviously, false positives are undesirable because they consume valuable human resources. "False positive" is a bit of a misnomer, because the sensor is reporting on definite activity that can be malicious, such as an SNMP server doing ping sweeps of a network, but it is considered false because in that particular environment the activity is considered benign.

If many false positives are occurring on a certain signature from one or two IP addresses, it might be a good idea to filter those IP addresses from being processed against the signatures using access lists. However, if the false positives are more widespread, meaning they are being generated by a lot of different machines, it might be a good idea to exclude the signature from being processed. All these decisions need to be made having a very clear understanding of the impact they would have on the sensor's capabilities. For example, as soon as an alarm is totally disabled, it does not generate alarms, even if an outside hacker tries to exploit a vulnerability on which the signature is based. Even if the signature is disabled for the local network only, an attacker spoofing the local network's IP addressing can bypass signature triggering.

It is important to understand how the router's intrusion detection process works because the processing is somewhat different from that on the appliance sensors.

Packets going through the interface that match the audit rule are audited by a series of modules, starting with IP; then either ICMP, TCP, or UDP (as appropriate); and finally the application level. If a signature match is found in a module, the following user-configured action(s) occur:

- If the action is alarm, the module completes its audit, sends an alarm, and passes the packet to the next module.

- If the action is drop, the packet is dropped from the module, discarded, and not sent to the next module.

- If the action is reset, the packets are forwarded to the next module. Packets with the reset flag set are sent to both participants of the session if the session is TCP. It is recommended that the drop and reset actions be used together. If there are multiple signature matches in a module, only the first match fires an action. Additional matches in other modules fire additional alarms, but only one per module. This process is different on the appliance sensor, which identifies all signature matches for each packet.

The performance impact of intrusion detection on a router depends on the number of signatures enabled, the level of traffic on the router, the router platform, and other individual features enabled on the router configuration such as encryption, source route bridging, and so on. Auditing atomic signatures has no traffic-dependent memory requirement. For auditing compound signatures, CBAC allocates memory to maintain the state of each session for each connection. Memory is also allocated for the configuration database and internal caching.

Only the relevant portions of the router configuration setup to do Intrusion Detection are shown in Example 15-1. Figure 15-7 shows the network topology used for this case study.

Figure 15-7 *Using a Router as the IDS Sensor*

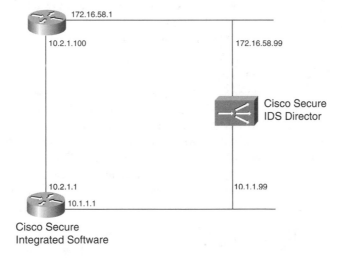

Example 15-1 *Router Configuration with the Cisco Secure Integrated Software Set Up to Do Intrusion Detection*

```
IDSRouter#show run
!The spam command below defines the maximum number of recipients
!in an e-mail after which the e-mail is considered spam.
!The number configured here is 25.
ip audit smtp spam 25
```

Example 15-1 *Router Configuration with the Cisco Secure Integrated Software Set Up to Do Intrusion Detection (Continued)*

```
!The ip audit notify command is used to specify where to send the
!alarms as they occur. Here, both the director and the log on the router
!have been specified as recipients.

ip audit notify nr-director
ip audit notify log

!The ip audit po max-events command below defines the maximum number of event
!messages that can be placed in the router's event queue. Note that each event
!consumes 32 KB of memory.

ip audit po max-events 150

!When a sensor generates an alarm, it sets a flag if the victim IP address belongs
!to what it considers to be the protected network. The command below is used to
!define what a protected network is for this router. Note that this configuration
!line makes no difference in terms of alarm generation, only that the flags
!mentioned above will be set or not set when an alarm is generated.
ip audit po protected 10.0.0.0 to 10.255.255.255

!The ip audit po commands below are used to define the parameters for the
!working of the post office daemon on the router. As you might recall
!from earlier discussions, the post office daemon is responsible for
!communication between the director and the sensor and any services
!running on them. The host IDs must be unique in a network, whereas the
!org IDs for the director and the sensor should be the same. Note
!that in this example two separate routes are specified to reach the
!same director, which is dual-homed. This has been done to achieve
!redundancy. The lower preference number specifies which route to try
!first to get to the director.

ip audit po local hostid 55 orgid 123
ip audit po remote hostid 14 orgid 123 rmtaddress 10.1.1.99 localaddress 10.1.1.1
preference 1
ip audit po remote hostid 14 orgid 123 rmtaddress 172.16.58.99 localaddress
   10.2.1.1
preference 2

!The commands below are used to disable specific signatures from being used. See
!the discussion at the start of this case study regarding disabling signatures for
!false positive alarms.

ip audit signature 2009 disable

!The audit signature commands below have been used to specify hosts
!whose traffic will be subjected to processing against specific
!signatures. Access lists are used to define the hosts.
```

continues

Example 15-1 *Router Configuration with the Cisco Secure Integrated Software Set Up to Do Intrusion Detection (Continued)*

```
ip audit signature 1100 list 91
ip audit signature 2004 list 91

!The commands below define rules to be applied to an interface of the
!router where you want intrusion detection to take place. The signatures
!on the router are broken into two categories, info and attack. The info
!signatures are mostly just informational. The attack signatures detect
!dangerous activity. Here you specify that an alarm should be generated
!when the info signatures match a traffic pattern, whereas when an
!attack signature gets triggered, an alarm as well as a drop and reset
!should take place. Drop and reset means that the latest packet is
!dropped and the TCP connection is reset. Access list 90 specifies
!which hosts to do intrusion detection for.

ip audit name AUDIT.1 info list 90 action alarm
ip audit name AUDIT.1 attack list 90 action alarm drop reset

interface e0
ip address 10.1.1.1 255.255.255.0

!Below you apply the rules defined above to an interface. Note the
!direction the rule is applied in. This direction is opposite the one
!in which a firewall rule would have been applied.

ip audit AUDIT.1 in

interface e1
ip address 10.2.1.1 255.255.0.0

!The access list below is used to make sure that the host with the IP
!address 10.1.1.55 is not subjected to intrusion detection processing.

access-list 90 deny 10.1.1.55
access-list 90 permit any

!Access list 91 below is used to make sure that the hosts 10.1.1.155
!and 10.1.1.2 and the subnet 172.16.58.0/24 do not trigger signatures
!1100 and 2004. This is done to stop false positives being generated
!on these signatures by the devices specified in this access list.

access-list 91 deny host 10.1.1.155
access-list 91 deny host 10.1.1.2
access-list 91 deny 172.16.58.0 0.0.0.255
access-list 91 permit any
```

Follow these steps to set up the UNIX director to manage the IDS router configured in Example 15-1:

Step 1   On the director, start nrConfigure by selecting **Security > Configure**.

Step 2   Double-click the name of your director machine on the displayed list.

Step 3   Double-click the currently applied configuration version (the one that is bold).

Step 4   Double-click **System Files**.

Step 5   Double-click **Hosts**. The Hosts dialog box appears.

Step 6   Click **Add** and enter the host name, host ID, and organization ID for the IDS router.

Step 7   Click **OK** to close the Hosts dialog box.

Step 8   Double-click **Routes**. The Routes dialog box appears.

Step 9   Click **Add** and enter the route to the IDS router.

Step 10   Click **OK** to close the Routes dialog box.

Step 11   Select the newly created transient version of the configuration, and click **Apply**.

The following list explains the process of configuring an IDS sensor in CSPM 2.3.1 and later instead of using a UNIX Director. These setup steps assume that the CSPM is the machine located at the 10.1.1.99 IP address. These steps show how you can set up the CSPM to manage the IDS router configured in Example 15-1:

Step 1   Launch CSPM and log in. A blank template appears (initial launch) that allows you to define your network. The following three definitions are required in the CSPM topology for IDS:

— Define the network in which the sensor's control interface resides and the network in which the CSPM host resides. If they are on the same subnet, only one network needs to be defined. Define this network first.

— Define the CSPM host in its network. Without the CSPM host definition, the sensor cannot be managed.

— Define the sensor in its network.

Next you will set up the CSPM to manage the router based on these three main steps.

Step 2   Right-click the **Internet** icon in the topology and select **New > Network** to create a new network.

Step 3   On the right side of the Network panel, add the name of the new network, the network address, and the netmask that will be used.

Step 4 Click the **IP Address** button, and enter the IP address that your network uses to reach the Internet. Normally this is the network's default gateway.

Step 5 Click **OK**. The network should be added to the topology map without any errors. In the Network topology, right-click the network you just added and select **New > Host**. CSPM should bring up a screen saying "A network Object of the specified type has been detected in the Policy Database, and the external address of the object is consistent with the parent network address. The name of the object is 'CSPM'. Is this the object you wish to insert into the network topology?"

Step 6 Click **Yes** to install the CSPM host into the topology. Verify that the information on the General screen for the CSPM host is OK.

Step 7 Click **OK** on the General screen of the CSPM host.

Step 8 Right-click the network in which your sensor resides, and select **Wizards > Add Sensor**. Enter the correct post office parameters for the sensor— hostid 55, orgid 123, sensor name IDSRouter, Organization Name Cisco, IP address 10.1.1.1, heartbeat 5.

Step 9 Click the **Check here to verify the Sensor's address** box.

Step 10 Click **Next** to define the signature versions on the sensor.

Step 11 Click the **Next** button to continue.

Step 12 Click **Finish** to complete the installation of the sensor into the topology.

Step 13 From the main CSPM menu, select **File > Save and Update** to compile the information entered in the topology into CSPM. This step is necessary to start POP on the CSPM host.

NOTE If an appliance sensor is used instead of the router, the CSPM can be used to generate some of the configuration, in this case done manually on the router, and have it pushed to the appliance sensor. Note that the CSPM or the UNIX director cannot configure a router sensor as they can configure the appliance sensors. Configurations must be done on the router sensor (such as defining which signatures to disable) manually. However, the management console can receive alarm information from the router.

Using a PIX as a Sensor Device

The PIX Firewall software can be configured to act as an IDS device as well, as shown in Example 15-2. The configuration of the PIX Firewall is similar to that of the router in many ways. The main difference between the PIX and router functionality is that the PIX does not send the alarms directly to a director. Instead, it sends the alarms to a configured syslog server. For this reason, the need to set up the post office daemon on the PIX does not arise. Also, the alarms can be buffered locally if a syslog server is unavailable.

Figure 15-8 shows the network topology used for this case study.

Figure 15-8 *Network Topology for This Case Study*

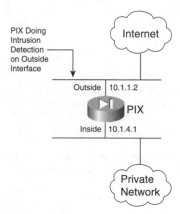

Example 15-2 *Configuration for the PIX Firewall Set Up to Do Intrusion Detection*

```
PIX-1(config)# wr t
Building configuration...
: Saved
:
PIX Version 6.0
nameif gb-ethernet0 intf2 security20
nameif gb-ethernet1 intf3 security15
nameif ethernet0 inside security100
nameif ethernet1 outside security0
enable password 8Ry2YjIyt7RRXU24 encrypted
passwd 2KFQnbNIdI.2KYOU encrypted
hostname PIX-1
fixup protocol ftp 21
fixup protocol http 80
fixup protocol h323 1720
fixup protocol rsh 514
fixup protocol smtp 25
fixup protocol sqlnet 1521
fixup protocol sip 5060
fixup protocol skinny 2000
names
access-list 1 permit tcp any host 172.16.1.1
pager lines 24
no logging console debugging
```

continues

Example 15-2 *Configuration for the PIX Firewall Set Up to Do Intrusion Detection (Continued)*

```
!Below is the syslog server to which the alarms are sent

logging host inside 10.1.4.100

interface gb-ethernet0 1000auto shutdown
interface gb-ethernet1 1000auto shutdown
interface ethernet0 auto
interface ethernet1 auto
mtu intf2 1500
mtu intf3 1500
mtu inside 1500
mtu outside 1500
ip address intf2 127.0.0.1 255.255.255.255
ip address intf3 127.0.0.1 255.255.255.255
ip address inside 10.1.4.1 255.255.255.0
ip address outside 10.1.1.2 255.255.255.0

!The command below is used to define the audit rule that will be used
!to take actions on informational signatures.

ip audit name TACaudit-1 info action alarm

!The command below is used to define the audit rule that will be used
!to take actions on attack signatures.

ip audit name TACaudit attack action alarm drop reset

!The next two commands apply the TACaudit and TACaudit-1 rules defined
!above to the outside interface. Note that up to two rules can be
!applied to an interface on the PIX. The direction in which to apply the
!rules on the PIX is immaterial.


ip audit interface outside TACaudit-1
ip audit interface outside TACaudit

!The two commands below define the default action to be taken on
!signatures in case no specific action is specified, as is done above.

ip audit info action alarm
ip audit attack action alarm

!The command below is used to disable the use of one of the signatures.
!Note that PIX, unlike the router, does not allow for creating
!exceptions for specific IP addresses from signature processing.

ip audit signature 1000 disable
```

Example 15-2 *Configuration for the PIX Firewall Set Up to Do Intrusion Detection (Continued)*

```
no failover
failover timeout 0:00:00
failover poll 15
failover ip address intf2 0.0.0.0
failover ip address intf3 0.0.0.0
failover ip address inside 0.0.0.0
failover ip address outside 0.0.0.0
pdm history enable
arp timeout 14400
static (inside,outside) 10.1.4.2 10.1.4.2 netmask 255.255.255.255 0 0
static (inside,outside) 10.1.3.2 10.1.3.2 netmask 255.255.255.255 0 0
static (inside,outside) 10.1.7.90 10.1.7.90 netmask 255.255.255.255 0 0
static (inside,outside) 10.5.91.33 10.5.91.33 netmask 255.255.255.255 0 0

conduit permit icmp host 10.1.4.2 host 10.1.1.1
conduit permit icmp host 10.1.3.2 host 10.1.2.1
conduit permit tcp host 10.1.7.90 any eq www
conduit permit tcp host 10.5.91.33 any eq www
conduit permit icmp host 10.5.91.33 any
conduit permit icmp host 10.1.7.90 any
conduit permit tcp host 10.1.7.90 any eq telnet
conduit permit tcp host 10.5.91.33 any eq telnet
route outside 0.0.0.0 0.0.0.0 10.1.1.1 1
route inside 10.0.0.0 255.0.0.0 10.1.4.2 1

timeout xlate 3:00:00
timeout conn 1:00:00 half-closed 0:10:00 udp 0:02:00 rpc 0:10:00 h323 0:05:00 s0
timeout uauth 0:05:00 absolute
aaa-server TACACS+ protocol tacacs+
aaa-server RADIUS protocol radius
no snmp-server location
no snmp-server contact
snmp-server community public
no snmp-server enable traps
floodguard enable
no sysopt route dnat
telnet timeout 5
ssh timeout 5
terminal width 80

: end
[OK]
```

The PIX Firewall cannot be managed through a management console, as is the case with most other sensors. The IDS functionality in the PIX is primarily there to improve the PIX's logging capabilities and drop/reset traffic that the PIX considers malicious. An administrator cannot see the alarms on a management console.

Using a Catalyst 6000 IDSM as a Sensor

The IDSM on a Catalyst 6000 box can provide very high IDS throughput while implementing the full range of signatures. However, because the switch backplane might be handling very high amounts of traffic (in the gigabits), the IDSM might not be able to handle the full load. However, multiple IDSMs can be placed in a chassis to scale to a larger amount of traffic. The IDSM's capacity is about 120 Mbps. Therefore, it is important that only the traffic that needs to be subjected to intrusion detection be forwarded to the IDSM in the switch. The Catalyst provides two main ways of doing this:

- **Using SPAN (Switched Port Analyzer)**—In this method, packets from specified VLANs on the backplane are copied to the IDSM for intrusion detection.

  Using SPAN to copy traffic to the IDSM is a fairly simple exercise. Commands similar to the ones shown in Example 15-3 can be used to set it up.

Example 15-3 *Using SPAN to Copy Traffic to the IDSM*

```
switch>(enable) set span 3/6 6/1 rx create

switch>(enable) set span 117 6/1 rx create
```

The two commands are being used to copy the traffic from port 3/6 and VLAN 117 to the IDSM sensing port, 6/1.

In general, it is often a good idea to use VACLs, because they allow for more granularity in terms of which traffic is passed to the IDSM for auditing. SPANs, on the other hand, are an all-or-nothing mechanism that take all the traffic on specified ports or VLANs and present it to the IDSM for monitoring. It is easy to oversubscribe the IDSM if you aren't careful to use SPAN in a heavily loaded environment.

- **Using VLAN Access Control Lists (VACLs)**—A mechanism whereby using access lists the packets to be copied over from the backplane to the IDSM are specified.

The IDSM works with any supervisor engine using SPAN, but the copy capture feature with security VACLs requires that the supervisor engine have the Policy Feature Card (PFC) option. Figure 15-9 shows how the IDSM monitors traffic passing through the Catalyst switch.

The process of setting up a VACL on the Catalyst 6000 to capture and copy traffic to the IDSM has the following three steps. We will walk through these steps in the form of a case study here:

Step 1   Creation and memory commit of a VACL to capture interesting traffic

Step 2   Mapping the VACL to a VLAN

Step 3   Assignment of a monitoring port as a VACL capture port

Figure 15-9 *Internal Architecture of the IDSM*

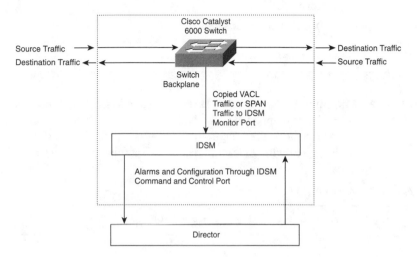

We will go through these three steps to set up a VACL called webacl to capture all web traffic headed to or from the 10.1.6.1 IP address. This happens to be the web server that the IDSM will try to protect against attacks.

Step 1   **Creation and memory commit of a VACL to capture interesting traffic**—Example 15-4 shows the configuration required to create the VACL that will be used to capture web traffic to the server at 10.1.6.1.

Example 15-4 *Configuration Required to Create the VACL That Will Be Used to Capture Web Traffic to the Server at 10.1.6.1*

```
switch>(enable) set security acl ip webacl permit tcp any host 10.1.6.1 eq 80
   capture
switch>(enable) set security acl ip webacl permit tcp host 10.1.6.1 eq 80 any
   capture
```

A **show** command for the ACLs outputs the information shown in Example 15-5 after the configuration has been done.

Example 15-5 *Output from the **show** Command for the Configuration Done in Example 15-4*

```
switch (enable) show security acl info all

set security acl ip webacl
-------------------------------------------------
permit tcp any host 10.1.6.1 eq 80 capture
permit tcp host 10.1.6.1 eq 80 any capture
```

The command shown in Example 15-6 commits the VACL just defined to memory.

Example 15-6 *Committing the Defined VACL to Memory*

```
switch>(enable) commit security acl webacl
```

Step 2   **Mapping the VACL to a VLAN**—As soon as the VACL has been defined, it is mapped to a VLAN, 250. This is done because port 1 on the IDSM monitors all traffic from all VLANs on which a security ACL has been applied with the capture feature. Example 15-7 shows how this is done.

Example 15-7 *A VACL Mapped to a VLAN*

```
switch>(enable) set security acl map webacl 250
```

Step 3   **Assignment of a monitoring port as a VACL capture port**—The command shown in Example 15-8 is used to define the port on the IDSM that will be used to monitor traffic on all VLANs that have an ACL with the **capture** keyword. Note that port 1 and port 2 on the IDSM are by default the sniffing and control ports respectively.

Example 15-8 *Defining the Port on the IDSM That Will Be Used to Monitor Traffic on All VLANs That Have an ACL with the* **capture** *Keyword*

```
switch>(enable) set security acl capture-ports 6/1
```

Another important point to remember is that the sniffing port on the IDSM, sniffing port 1, is a trunked port. By default, it gets traffic from all the VLANs on the switch with the capture ACLs applied to them. To reduce the amount of traffic going to the IDSM or to divide traffic monitoring between two IDSMs, you can use the **set trunk** and **clear trunk** commands to add or remove the VLANs for which the IDSM will monitor traffic.

Figure 15-10 shows the network topology for this case study discussing how to use ACLs to capture traffic for the IDSM.

As soon as the packet-capture mechanism on the IDSM has been set up, the rest of the configuration for the IDSM can take place. The following lines show the output captured while setting up the IDSM on a Catalyst 6000 box. Due to the nature of the Catalyst 6000 configuration, the output of **show** commands and screen captures is shown here.

Figure 15-10 *Network Topology for This Case Study*

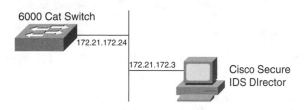

These lines show the configuration for the sensor on the IDSM:

```
Sensor
IP Address:                172.21.172.24
Netmask:                   255.255.255.0
Default Gateway:           172.21.172.1
Host Name:                 cisco_ids
Host ID:                   123
Host Port:                 45000
Organization Name:         cisco
Organization ID:           345
```

These lines show the configuration of the director to which the IDSM sends the alarms it generates:

```
Director
IP Address:                172.21.172.3
Host Name:                 director
Host ID:                   342
Host port:                 45000
Heart Beat Interval:       5
Organization Name:         cisco
Organization ID:           345
```

These lines show that the 172.21.172.0/24 subnet can Telnet to the IDSM:

```
Direct Telnet access to IDSM:   enabled
Current access list entries:
    [1] 172.21.172.0.0.0.255
```

The output from the **show** command in Example 15-9 shows that the ACL that has been created to "capture" the traffic to be copied to the IDSM to be subjected to IDS monitoring. We use an IDSM placed in slot 6 of a Catalyst 6000. Example 15-9 shows output from the **show module** and **show port** commands.

Example 15-9 *Output from the* **show module** *and* **show port** *Commands on the Catalyst*

```
Console> (enable) show module 6
Mod Slot Ports Module-Type                    Model               Status
--- ---- ----- -------------------------- ------------------- --------
6   6    2     Intrusion Detection Syste WS-X6381-IDS        ok

Mod Module-Name         Serial-Num
--- ------------------- -----------
```

continues

Example 15-9 *Output from the* **show module** *and* **show port** *Commands on the Catalyst (Continued)*

```
6                       JAB0343055J

Mod MAC-Address(es)                        Hw     Fw         Sw
--- -------------------------------- ------ ---------- ----------
6   00-e0-14-0e-f8-ee to 00-e0-14-0e-f8-ef 0.201  4.2(0.24)D version


Console> (enable) show port 6
Port  Name                Status     Vlan       Duplex Speed Type
----- ------------------- ---------- ---------- ------ ----- -----------
 6/1                      connected  trunk        ---   ---  Intrusion De
 6/2                      connected  184          full  1000 Intrusion De
```

Setting up a Router and a UNIX Director to Do Shunning

This case study shows you how a UNIX director is set up to do shunning. Shunning is the process through which an access list is automatically applied to a router by a sensor to stop an attacker from gaining access to the network.

The process for setting up shunning on a UNIX director is as follows:

Step 1   Run nrConfigure on the director.

Step 2   Open the sensor you want to manage the router.

Step 3   Open Device Management.

Step 4   Click the **Devices** tab, and click **Add**.

Step 5   Enter the router's IP address, username/password, and enable password.

Step 6   Click the **Interfaces** tab, and click **Add**.

Step 7   Enter the interface name as it appears in the router, and select the direction in which you want the access list to be applied.

Step 8   Click the **Shunning** tab, and select addresses never to shun if you want to set that up. It is recommended that you set up your local networks so that you don't accidentally block your local hosts.

Step 9   Back in nrConfigure, go to **System Files** and open the **Daemons** option. Select nr.managed, and click **OK**.

Step 10   Apply this version in nrConfigure. This sends the configuration files and restarts the netranger daemons.

Step 11 Log into the router and verify that the sensor is logged into the router and has created an access list. This is an example of what you should see:

```
router#show access-lists
Extended IP access list 199
permit ip host 10.1.1.1 any
permit ip any any
router#
```

Step 12 You can also issue the **who** command on the router. Here you see that the sensor is logged in from 172.18.124.126:

```
router#who
Line User Host(s) Idle Location
* 0 con 0 idle 00:00:00
10 vty 0 idle 00:00:11 10.1.1.1
```

Step 13 Back in nrConfigure, open Intrusion Detection.

Step 14 Under the **Profile** tab, select **Manual Configuration** and click **Modify Signatures**. Here you need to specify which signatures you want to trigger the shunning function. By default, the action taken is **None**. Change the action to **Shun** for the signatures you want to shun when that alarm gets triggered.

Step 15 Save and apply this version.

The Intrusion Detection section of nrConfigure has a General tab where you can define 'Minutes' of Automatic Shunning. The default is 15 minutes. To reset the shunning access list, stop and then restart the daemons on the sensor.

To remove the access list altogether, you need to disable shunning and then manually remove the access list by logging onto the router.

Creating Custom Signatures

It becomes necessary to create custom signatures under certain circumstances on the Cisco IDS. Generally, the following two are the main reasons that a custom signature needs to be created:

- A new threat has been introduced for which no signature is yet officially available. However, based on the information available on the web, a makeshift signature can be created to do pattern matching and detection. An example of this is the custom signatures created by some network administrators to detect the Code Red worm when it first started breaking out.

- There is activity that the normal IDS signatures do not fire on but that the network administrator considers malicious. An example could be network administrators looking for patterns in the traffic on their network containing a competitor's name. These types of alarms need to be carefully pruned to reduce false positives.

CSPM, as well as the UNIX director, allow custom signatures to be created that do pattern matching on specific types of traffic. In addition, alarm levels can be specified for the custom alarms based on their severity as assessed by the creator.

This case study looks at how the UNIX director was used to create custom signatures to detect the Code Red worm. The Code Red worm can be detected by looking for patterns such as the following in web traffic:

> GET /NULL.ida
> GET /a.ida

Although these two strings do not catch all types of malicious activity in the domain of the Code Red attack, they can capture a fair amount, leading to further detection and prevention.

Here is the process that needs to be followed on the UNIX director to create a custom signature for the first string:

Step 1 On the director interface, click a sensor icon and select **Security > Configure**.

Step 2 On nrConfigure, double-click **Intrusion Detection**.

Step 3 Click the **Profile** tab.

Step 4 Click **Manual Configuration**, and then click **Modify Sensor**.

Step 5 Scroll down to the **Matched Strings** signature and click it.

Step 6 Click **Expand** to open the String Signatures dialog box. The String Signatures dialog box consists of a grid containing the following columns: the string to search on, the SubSignature ID, the port to scan, the direction of traffic to scan, the number of string matches to allow before triggering an action, the action to trigger, and destinations for the data captured by the signature.

Step 7 Click **Add**.

Step 8 Enter **[Gg][Ee][Tt].*[.][Ii][Dd][Aa][\x00-\x7f]+[\x80-\xff]** in the **String** column. This regular expression detects instances of the strings **"GET ida {buffer}"**.

Step 9 Enter a unique number in the **ID** column.

Step 10 Enter **80** in the **Port** column. You choose port 80 because this string needs to be detected in web traffic.

Step 11 Select **To & From** in the **Direction** list because the string needs to be detected in both directions.

Step 12 Enter **1** under **Occurrences** because one occurrence of the string should be sufficient to cause an alarm.

Step 13 Select **Reset** under **Action** to reset the connection generating the GET request.

Step 14 Enter **5** in each destination column. This is the alarm level. This number is at the system administrator's discretion.

Step 15 Click **OK** to save the new signature.

Step 16 Click **OK** to close the Intrusion Detection dialog box.

Step 17 Click **Apply** to apply the new signature.

These steps create a signature that generates level 5 alarms when the matched string is found in web traffic at any time. The sensor resets the connection as a response.

Summary

Intrusion detection is fast becoming a necessary component of all network security designs. Although many security devices, such as firewalls and other security features on routing devices, can protect against a large variety of attacks, it is critical to have intrusion detection in place to protect against the ones that slip through. Cisco's IDS solution provides a comprehensive mix of devices that allow intrusion detection to take place via different means. This chapter went through Cisco's various IDS implementations. We discussed how these implementations differ from each other, as well as their similarities. We looked in detail at the various response mechanisms that are available in the IDS devices. We then looked at some implementations of the IDS on various platforms on which Cisco supports this functionality.

Review Questions

1 Why does the use of IDSM on the Catalyst switch not affect the Catalyst switch's performance?

2 What is the purpose of the post office daemon?

3 In which direction should the audit rules be applied on a router's outside interface?

4 Can two hosts with the same org ID have the same host ID as well?

5 How many audit rules can be applied to a PIX interface?

Network Access Control

This chapter covers the following key topics:

- **Definitions of the Components of AAA**—This section defines what AAA means.

- **Authentication**—We will talk about the authentication portion of AAA.

- **Authorization**—We will discuss how authorization is setup in AAA.

- **Accounting**—We will discuss the role accounting plays in AAA and how to set it up.

- **Case Studies**—We will look at a few case studies to better understand the use of AAA.

## CHAPTER 16

AAA

Authentication, authorization, and accounting (AAA) is an integral component of the security features implemented on most Cisco devices. In many cases it interacts with other features to enhance the security and scalability of secure setups. This chapter looks at the three components of AAA and discusses how they are set up to meet a network's security needs. We will discuss the topics of authentication, authorization, and accounting independently and will summarize the features available in each of these components. The chapter ends by bringing the various discussions together in a set of case studies describing how to set up AAA to meet the most common network security requirements.

Definitions of AAA Components

AAA is an architecture available to all security devices to authenticate users accessing the device or a nearby network. The authorization feature is used to restrict users' privileges after they have been authenticated. Accounting is used to keep logs of the devices' activities, as well as the activities of the users on the network or on network devices.

AAA allows its functions to be carried out on a per-user or per-service basis. In other words, it can be used to authenticate and authorize individual users as well as services such as IP and IPX. This allows AAA to be used for a variety of purposes related to its three functions.

The workings of AAA are fairly simple. AAA is set up on a router or a PIX or any other such device that needs to do AAA for users either trying to access the device itself or a network connected to the device. The specifics of how each of the three elements of AAA are to be performed are defined through *method lists*. The router can use a local database to get data to be used for AAA, such as usernames or passwords or per-user access control lists, or it can query an authentication server via a protocol such as RADIUS or TACACS+. The AAA model allows the performance of the authentication, authorization, and accounting functions independent of the protocol used (such as TACACS+, RADIUS, Kerberos, and so on).

Nomenclature

For the purpose of our discussion in this chapter and the next three chapters, the terms *access server* and *access device* imply the router, PIX, or any other such network element that is responsible for performing the AAA functions on users or other devices connecting to it. The terms *RADIUS server, TACACS+ server, security server* and *AAA server* mean the server that is set up to perform the AAA functions on the back end for the access server.

Figure 16-1 shows the basic AAA network components.

Figure 16-1 *Basic AAA Network Components*

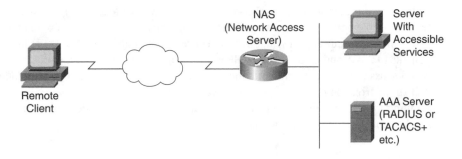

The following sections discuss the details of each of the three elements of AAA and show how to set them up on a Cisco router. We will leave the details of how to set up AAA on the PIX Firewall for Chapter 8, "PIX Firewall."

An Introduction to Authentication

Authentication is the process through which a device or a user's identity is verified before access to various types of resources can be provided.

It generally includes a mechanism by which a user or device provides a password to the authenticating device. Then the device checks the password's veracity against a database of passwords. If the password is indeed correct, the user is allowed to proceed and use the resources available based on authorization parameters, if any, that have been set up.

Authentication on a small scale can often be done using a password list maintained on a router or PIX or any other such device doing the authentication. However, for larger-scale implementations, it is often desirable to offload the burden of verifying password authenticity from the access device (such as a router or PIX) to a dedicated server such as a RADIUS or TACACS+ server. The access device passes to the server the username authentication parameters, such as the username and the password received from the user or the device trying to authenticate. The server then verifies whether the username and password match based on a database. These servers can accommodate more sophisticated methods of authentication, such as one-time passwords, changeable passwords, and authentication against external databases such as NT or UNIX databases. RADIUS and TACACS+ are the protocols that are often used by the access device to communicate with the RADIUS or TACACS+ server. We will discuss these protocols in detail in the next two chapters.

Setting up Authentication

Setting up authentication is a four-step process. We will restrict this discussion to how routers are set up to do authentication. We will leave setting up switches and PIXes for authentication for the "Case Studies" section. Most other devices can be set up for authentication following similar principles.

Enabling AAA

The first step in using authentication on a device is to enable AAA. You do this using the following command on a router:

```
Router(config)#aaa new-model
```

Setting up a Local Database of User Authentication Parameters or Setting up Access To a Configured RADIUS or TACACS+ Server

In this step, the username/devicename and password are either defined on the local router or defined on an AAA server accessible to the router via RADIUS or TACACS+. Upon being queried for the username and password, the server provides the router with the pass or fail results.

To set up authentication locally on the router, the local database can be defined as follows:

```
Router(config)#username test password result12#
```

If TACACS+ or RADIUS is to be used, the router must be set up to communicate with the TACACS+ or RADIUS server. The following command defines the IP address of the RADIUS server as well as the UDP destination port numbers to use for authentication and authorization communications with the server:

```
Router(config)#radius-server hos t 172.16.71.146 auth-port 1645 acct-port 1646
```

Setting up a Method List

Method lists are used to specify which methods of authentication are to be used to authenticate a user or device. The following is the generic form of an authentication method list:

```
Router(config)#aaa authentication <service> {default | list-name} method1
  [method2...]
```

This command requires three parameters to be provided to the router. The first is the **service** parameter. This basically defines what kind of access activity will be taking place for the users or devices subjected to this method list. The following types of services can be defined on a Cisco router:

- **ARAP**—Authentication for AppleTalk Remote Access (ARA)
- **Enable**—Authentication to determine if a user can access the privileged command level
- **Login**—Authentication for logging into the access device itself
- **PPP**—Authentication for use on serial interfaces running PPP
- **NASI**—Authentication for NetWare Asynchronous Services Interface (NASI) clients connecting through the access server

The second parameter required in the method list is the name of the list. This name is used to bind the list to a specific interface or line on the access device. However, a *default* method list can also be defined that is then applicable to all lines and interfaces unless another method list is defined and specifically applied to them. Consequently, the default list is not applied to a line or interface; it is already applied to all interfaces and lines by default.

The third parameter that needs to be defined in the method list configuration is the list of methods to be used for authentication. Up to four methods can be defined in one method list. A method is basically the mechanism the router must use to verify the authenticity of a user or device connecting to it. The authentication methods are tried in sequence one by one if the first method does not return an authentication success or failure. Note that failure to authenticate is different from an *error* in authenticating. An error occurs when the method specified is unable to verify if the user is valid, such as in the case when a RADIUS server is down and is inaccessible for this verification to occur. However, failure to authenticate means that an authentication method has verified that, for example, the password supplied by the user is incorrect. In this case, the authentication process does not go to the next method in the list. Instead, it stops there with an authentication failure.

Table 16-1 provides a complete list of authentication methods that can be defined on a router. The PIX, the switch, and other access servers generally have a smaller list of methods available on them. Refer to the documentation for each to figure out which authentication methods are available.

Table 16-1 *Router Authentication Methods*

Method	Description
enable	Uses the enable password for authentication.
krb5	Uses Kerberos 5 for authentication.
krb5-telnet	Uses the Kerberos 5 Telnet authentication protocol when using Telnet to connect to the router. If selected, this keyword must be listed as the first method in the method list.

Table 16-1   *Router Authentication Methods (Continued)*

Method	Description
line	Uses the line password for authentication.
local	Uses the local username database for authentication.
local-case	Uses case-sensitive local username authentication.
none	Uses no authentication.
group radius	Uses the list of all RADIUS servers for authentication.
group tacacs+	Uses the list of all TACACS+ servers for authentication.
group *group-name*	Uses a subset of RADIUS or TACACS+ servers for authentication, as defined by the **aaa group server radius** or **aaa group server tacacs+** command.
auth-guest	Allows guest logins only if the user has already logged in to EXEC.
guest	Allows guest logins.
if-needed	Does not authenticate if the user has already been authenticated on a TTY line.

Note that not all of these authentication methods can be associated with all five services previously outlined. For example, the **if-needed** method can be used only for PPP sessions. Table 16-2 gives a compatibility list.

Table 16-2   *Which Services Are Compatible with Which Methods*

Service	Login	NASI	Enable	ARAP	PPP
Method					
enable	√	√	√	√	
line	√	√	√	√	
group radius	√	√	√	√	
group tacacs+	√	√	√	√	
group *group_name*	√	√	√	√	√
krb5	√				√ (only for PAP)
krb5-telnet	√				
local	√	√	√	√	√
local-case		√		√	√
auth-guest				√	
guest				√	
if-needed					√
none	√	√	√		√

Here's an example of how to interpret this table: The PPP service can be authenticated using any one of the methods **group** *group_name,* **krb5**, **local**, **local-case**, **if-needed**, or **none**.

Applying the Method List

After the method list is configured, it needs to be applied to a line or an interface. The exception to this rule is when a default list is defined. A default list is automatically applicable to all the lines and interfaces unless another list is defined and specifically applied to an interface or line.

Example 16-1 shows how a method list is created and applied to an interface. Figure 16-2 shows the network topology used for this setup.

Figure 16-2 *Network Topology for the Setup in Example 16-1*

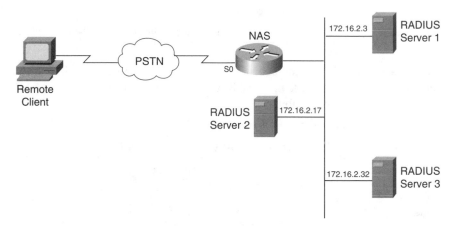

Example 16-1 *Authentication Method List Created and Applied to an Interface*

```
!The following command turns AAA on.
aaa new-model
!The username and password that follow constitute the local authentication
!database.
username Cisco password te5t12#
!The commands that follow define a group of three RADIUS servers and name it
!pppradius.
aaa group server radius pppradius
 server 172.16.2.3
 server 172.16.2 17
 server 172.16.2.32
!The command that follows defines the authentication method list for users or devices
!connecting to the router through PPP. The name of the list is PPPLIST. The two
!methods defined for authentication are group pppradius and local. If the RADIUS
```

Example 16-1 *Authentication Method List Created and Applied to an Interface (Continued)*

```
!servers fail to respond, the local database will be tried to authenticate the
!users or devices trying to do PPP to the router. The NAS will try to query each
!of the three servers before failing over to local. Note that 'pppradius' is the
!name given to the group of three RADIUS servers defined above.
aaa authentication ppp PPPLIST group pppradius local
!The command that follows defines the authentication method list to be used for
!authentication on the serial 0 interface to be PPPLIST. This is equivalent to
!applying the method list PPPLIST to the serial 0 interface.
interface serial 0
 ppp authentication PPPLIST
```

The AAA server-group feature works only when the server hosts in a group are all of the same type: RADIUS or TACACS+. Also note that the AAA group server feature is relatively new but is backward-compatible. Therefore, it also works on releases earlier than Cisco IOS Software Release 12.0(5)T.

An Introduction to Authorization

Authorization is the process through which users or devices are given controlled access to network resources. Authorization lets a network administrator control who can do what on the network. It can also be used to do such things as assign specific IP addresses to users connecting through a PPP service, to force users to use a certain type of service to connect, or to configure advanced features such as callback.

When AAA authorization is enabled, the network access server uses information retrieved from the user's profile, which is located either in the local user database or on the security server, to configure the user's session. After this is done, the user is granted access to a requested service only if the information in the user profile allows it.

Setting up Authorization

Setting up authorization is similar to setting up authentication. For authorization to function, authentication needs to be set up first and must be functional. After authentication has been set up, setting up authorization consists of setting up an authorization method list and then applying it to an interface or line (if it is not defined as the default method list). Please note that just like the default authentication method list, the default authorization method list is automatically applied to all interfaces and lines unless there is another named method list defined and specifically applied to a line or interface. In this case the named method list, applied to the line or interface, takes precedence over a default method list (if defined) as far as that particular line or interface is concerned.

Setting up a Method List

Method lists for authorization define the service that is to be authorized, along with the methods you use to do the authorization. A generic authorization method list looks like this:

```
Router(config)#aaa authorization <service> {default | list-name} method1
   [method2...]
```

In this list, three parameters need to be defined. The first one is the service. The **service** parameter defines the type of service that uses authorization. Cisco routers support the following services for authorization:

- **Auth-proxy**—Applies specific security policies on a per-user basis.

- **Commands**—Applies to the EXEC mode commands a user issues. Command authorization attempts authorization for all EXEC mode commands, including global configuration commands associated with a specific privilege level.

- **EXEC**—Applies to the attributes associated with a user EXEC terminal session. Determines whether a user can run an EXEC shell upon logging in.

- **Network**—Applies to network connections. This can include a PPP, SLIP, or ARAP connection.

- **Reverse access**—Applies to reverse Telnet sessions.

- **Configuration**—Applies to downloading configurations from the AAA server.

- **IP mobile**—Applies to authorization for IP mobile services.

The authorization method list can be made up of the following methods. Each method is tried until authorization succeeds.

- **TACACS+**—The network access server exchanges authorization information with the TACACS+ security daemon. TACACS+ authorization defines specific rights for users by associating attribute-value pairs, which are stored in a database on the TACACS+ security server, with the appropriate user.

- **If-Authenticated**—The user is allowed to access the requested function provided that authentication has occurred.

- **None**—The network access server does not request authorization information; authorization is not performed over this line/interface.

- **Local**—The router or access server consults its local database, as defined by the **username** command, for example, to authorize specific rights for users. Only a limited set of functions can be controlled via the local database.

- **RADIUS**—The network access server requests authorization information from the RADIUS security server. RADIUS authorization defines specific rights for users by associating attributes, which are stored in a database on the RADIUS server, with the appropriate user.

Applying the Method List

As soon as the method list is configured, it needs to be applied to a line or interface. The exception to this rule is when a default list is defined. A default method list is automatically applicable to all the lines and interfaces unless another list is defined and applied to an interface or line.

Example 16-2 shows an example of setting up an authorization method list, along with the corresponding authentication method list. Figure 16-3 shows the network topology for this example.

Figure 16-3 *Network Topology for the Setup in Example 16-2*

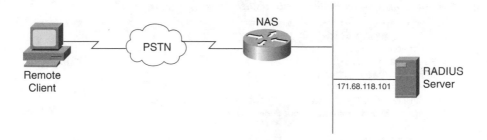

Example 16-2 *Authorization Can Be Set up in Addition to Authentication on a Router*

```
aaa new-model
aaa authentication login default group radius enable
!The following command sets up authentication to take place for PPP users/devices
!connecting to the router. The method list is named 'default', meaning it is applied
!to all lines and interfaces unless another named list is applied there. The first
!method of authentication is RADIUS, failing which the enable password is to be
!used.
aaa authentication ppp default group radius enable
!The command sequence that follows sets up authorization to take place for all
!users/devices that have been authenticated and sets up access for all types of
!network activity, including PPP. The method to be used is RADIUS.
aaa authorization network default radius

interface Async1
 ip unnumbered Ethernet0
 encapsulation ppp
 async mode dedicated
 peer default ip address pool async
 no cdp enable
 ppp authentication chap

ip local pool async 10.6.100.101 10.6.100.103
```

continues

Example 16-2 *Authorization Can Be Set up in Addition to Authentication on a Router (Continued)*

```
!The command sequence that follows defines the IP address of the RADIUS server to
!use and the key that is used by the router to authenticate to the server.

radius-server host 171.68.118.101
radius-server timeout 10
radius-server key cisco
```

This router setup uses a RADIUS AAA server at the back end to do authentication and authorization for the users. Example 16-3 shows the profiles for various users as they are set up using a RADIUS server.

Example 16-3 *RADIUS AAA Server Profiles for Users Accessing the NAS Setup in Example 16-2*

```
# User who can Telnet in to do configuratios:
username = admin
Password = "test123"
Service-Type = Administrative-User

# PPP/CHAP authentication  - password must be cleartext per chap spec
# address assigned from pool on router
username = chapuser
Password = "test345"
Service-Type = Framed-User,
Framed-Protocol = PPP

# PPP/PAP authentication
# address assigned from pool on router
# Can also have 'Password = "UNIX" which uses /etc/passwd
username = papuser
Password = "test678"
Service-Type = Framed-User,
Framed-Protocol = PPP

# PPP/CHAP authentication - password must be cleartext per chap spec
# address assigned by server
username = chapadd
Password = "test987"
Service-Type = Framed-User,
Framed-Protocol = PPP,
Framed-Address = 10.10.10.10

# PPP/PAP authentication
# address assigned by server
username = papadd
Password = "test754"
Service-Type = Framed-User,
Framed-Protocol = PPP,
Framed-Address = 10.10.10.11
```

RADIUS and TACACS+ authorization both define specific rights for users by processing attributes that are stored in a database on the security server. For both RADIUS and TACACS+, attributes are defined on the security server, associated with the user, and sent to the network access server, where they are applied to the user's connection. We will look at these attributes in the following chapters, which discuss RADIUS and TACACS+.

An Introduction to Accounting

Accounting is the last piece of the AAA puzzle. *Accounting* is the process through which the network access server reports the activities of the authenticated and/or authorized user or device to an AAA server doing accounting through RADIUS or TACACS+. Whereas authentication and authorization restrict the access of users and devices to the network resources, accounting is responsible for going one step further and keeping tabs on those who have been authenticated and/or authorized. In addition, accounting can also be used to keep track of the access device status and TACACS+/RADIUS communication.

Accounting messages are exchanged in the form of accounting records between the access device and the TACACS+ or RADIUS server. Each accounting record contains accounting attribute-value (AV) pairs and is stored on the TACACS+ or RADIUS server. This data can then be analyzed for network management, client billing, and auditing.

Setting up Accounting

Accounting is configured in a fashion similar to authorization. After a method list is set up, it needs to be applied to the interface or line on which the accounting is to take place. As before, the exception is the accounting method list named 'default'.

Setting up a Method List

A method list needs to be set up that defines the services for which accounting needs to take place and a list of methods to use.

Here is what the generic accounting method list looks like:

```
Router(config)#aaa accounting {system | network | exec | connection | commands |
   resource level} {default | list-name} {start-stop | stop-only | wait-start | none}
   [method1 [method2...]]
```

The first parameter that needs to be chosen in this method list is the service for which accounting needs to be enabled. The following list describes the options available for accounting on the routers:

- **system**—Provides information about system-level events. Examples are system reboots and reloads.

- **network**—Provides information for all PPP, SLIP, or ARAP sessions, including packet and byte counts.

- **exec**—Provides information about the network access server's user EXEC terminal sessions.

- **connection**—Provides information about all outbound connections made from the network access server, such as Telnet, local-area transport (LAT), TN3270, packet assembler/disassembler (PAD), and rlogin.

- **commands**—Provides information about the EXEC mode commands that a user issues. Command accounting generates accounting records for all EXEC mode commands, including global configuration commands associated with a specific privilege level.

- **resource**—Provides start and stop records for calls that have passed user authentication, and provides stop records for calls that fail to authenticate.

NOTE   If RADIUS is being used, the command authorization option is unavailable.

The second parameter that needs to be defined is how the accounting process is to take place. The choices are as follows:

- **start-stop**—This option is used to send more information to the RADIUS/TACACS+ server than the **stop-only** command. It sends a start accounting notice at the beginning of the requested event and a stop accounting notice at the end of the event. At the start of the session, the access server does not wait for an acknowledgment from the RADIUS or TACACS+ server. This means that the requested user process begins regardless of whether the start accounting notice was received and acknowledged by the AAA accounting server.

- **stop-only**—This option instructs the specified method (RADIUS or TACACS+) to send a stop record accounting notice at the end of the requested user process. This includes all the statistics for the session just concluded.

    wait-start—This option ensures that until the AAA accounting server has acknowledged the receipt of the accounting start notice, the user process is not allowed to begin. A stop record is sent when the session ends. It includes the session statistics.

- **none**—This command is used to stop all accounting activities on a particular line or interface.

Accounting supports only two methods. This is because accounting requires the use of a TACACS+ or RADIUS server. These methods are as follows:

— **TACACS+**—The network access server reports user activity to the TACACS+ security server in the form of accounting records. Each accounting record contains accounting AV pairs and is stored on the security server.

— **RADIUS**—The network access server reports user activity to the RADIUS security server in the form of accounting records. Each accounting record contains accounting AV pairs and is stored on the security server.

Applying the Method List to Lines and/or Interfaces

You use the following command to apply accounting to lines on a router:

```
Router(config-line)#accounting {arap | commands level | connection | exec}
    {default | list-name}
```

However, on an interface, you use the following command to turn on accounting (PPP is the only service for which accounting can be enabled on an interface):

```
Router(config-if)#ppp accounting {default | list-name}
```

Example 16-4 shows how accounting can be set up on a router. Figure 16-4 shows the network topology used for the setup done in Example 16-4.

Figure 16-4 *Network Topology for the Setup in Example 16-4*

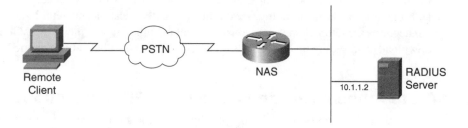

Example 16-4 *Accounting Set up on a Router*

```
aaa new-model
aaa authentication login ADMIN local
aaa authentication ppp DIALIN group radius local
aaa authorization network test group radius local
aaa accounting network ACCOUNTS start-stop group radius group tacacs+
username root password ytrymypa55w0rd
radius-server host 10.1.1.2
```

continues

Example 16-4 *Accounting Set up on a Router (Continued)*

```
radius-server key c0mpl1cat4d

interface group-async 1
 group-range 1 16
 encapsulation ppp

!The command that follows sets up CHAP authentication for PPP using the method
!list DIALIN.
 ppp authentication chap DIALIN
!The command that follows sets up authorization for PPP to occur via the method
!list test.
 ppp authorization test
!The command that follows sets up accounting for PPP to occur via the method list
!ACCOUNTS.
 ppp accounting ACCOUNTS

line 1 16
 autoselect ppp
 autoselect during-login
!Users logging into the router via PPP are authenticated as defined in the list
!ADMIN.
 login authentication ADMIN
 modem dialin
```

Case Studies

In this section we will look at some of the common ways in which AAA authentication and authorization can be utilized. It will examine how authentication and authorization for PPP connections are setup. Some more advanced uses of authorization, including ACL and route downloads and setting up of timeouts on a per user basis, will also be examined.

Using AAA to Authenticate and Authorize PPP Connections

This case study revolves around setting up PPP authentication and authorization on a router. PPP users trying to connect to this router are authenticated based on usernames and passwords stored on a RADIUS server. The RADIUS server also passes down authorization parameters for the users to the router. These parameters identify what types of services these users are entitled to use. Example 16-5 shows how AAA authentication and authorization are set up on a router for this case study. Figure 16-5 shows the network topology used for the setup done in this case study.

Figure 16-5 *Network Topology for This Case Study*

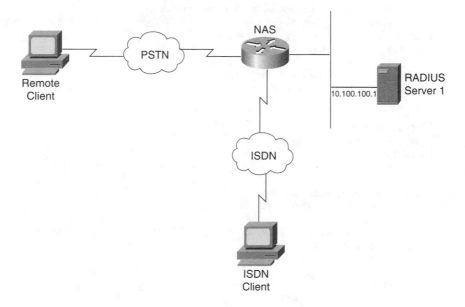

Example 16-5 *AAA Authentication and Authorization Set up on a Router for This Case Study*

```
aaa new-model
!The command below is used to set up authentication for users logging into the
!router. Since the default method list is used, any line on which another method
!list is not specifically applied uses the method defined in this list to
!authenticate users. The two methods are radius and local. If the RADIUS server(s)
!defined in the group return an error, the local database is tried for
!authentication.

aaa authentication login default group radius local
!The command below is used to disable authentication via the method NO_AUTHEN.
!This method is applied to the console port as shown below.
aaa authentication login NO_AUTHEN none
!The command below sets up PPP authentication for user/devices that have not
!already been authenticated on the TTY ports. There can be users who connect to
!the router via dialup and then, after authenticating and starting an EXEC session,
!initiate PPP. Since they are already authenticated, the if-needed keyword negates
!the need to authenticate them again. Again, if the RADIUS server returns an error,
!the local database is used for authentication.
aaa authentication ppp default if-needed group radius local
!The command below sets up authorization for users who connect through the router.
!The authorization parameters defined in the user profiles determine what type of
!services are to be allowed for the various users.
```

continues

Example 16-5 *AAA Authentication and Authorization Set up on a Router for This Case Study (Continued)*

```
aaa authorization network default group radius local
!<deleted> means that the actual encrypted password has been removed from the
!configuration as a security measure
enable secret 5 <deleted>
!
username admin password 7 <deleted>
isdn switch-type primary-ni
!
controller T1 0
 framing esf
 clock source line primary
 linecode b8zs
 pri-group timeslots 1-24
!
interface Ethernet0
 ip address 172.22.53.141 255.255.255.0
 !
!Serial 0:23 is made a member of dialer pool 23, which is defined under dialer 1.
interface Serial0:23
 no ip address
 encapsulation ppp
 dialer pool-member 23
 isdn switch-type primary-ni
 isdn incoming-voice modem
!
interface Group-Async0
 ip unnumbered Ethernet0
 no ip directed-broadcast
 encapsulation ppp
!The commands below are used to set up an interactive mode on the async interfaces,
!meaning that users can choose whether they get a shell or a PPP session when
!dialing in and connecting to this router.

 async mode interactive
 peer default ip address pool ASYNC
 ppp authentication chap
 group-range 1 48
!
!The Dialer1 interface set up below is used to terminate ISDN calls.
interface Dialer1
 ip unnumbered Ethernet0
 no ip directed-broadcast
 encapsulation ppp
 dialer pool 23
 peer default ip address pool ISDN
 no cdp enable
 ppp authentication chap
!
ip local pool ISDN 10.2.2.1 10.2.2.100
ip local pool ASYNC 10.2.1.1 10.2.1.100
ip classless
no ip http server
```

Example 16-5 *AAA Authentication and Authorization Set up on a Router for This Case Study (Continued)*

```
!
no cdp run
!
!The command below specifies the IP address of the RADIUS server, the ports to use
!for authentication and accounting, and a key to authenticate the router to the
!RADIUS server.
radius-server host 10.100.100.1 auth-port 1645 acct-port 1646 key cisco
!
line con 0
 exec-timeout 0 0
!The command below effectively disables authentication on the console port, since
!the method list NO_AUTHEN specifies none as the authentication method.

 login authentication NO_AUTHEN

line 1 48
!The command below displays the username and password prompt as soon as the user
!connects rather than have the user press Enter for the prompt to appear.
 autoselect during-login
!The command below automatically launches the PPP session when the router sees
!incoming PPP packets.
 autoselect ppp
 modem InOut
 transport preferred none
 transport input all
 transport output none
line aux 0
line vty 0 4

!
end
```

Example 16-6 shows the radius profiles defined for the async, as well as the ISDN users connecting to the router.

Example 16-6 *RADIUS Profiles Set up for Users Connecting to the Router Configured in Example 16-5*

```
user = async_client
password = "cisco"
Service-Type = Framed
Framed-Protocol = PPP


user = isdn_user
password = "cisco"
Service-Type = Framed
Framed-Protocol = PPP
```

Using AAA to Download Routes and Apply Access Lists

This case study shows a more advanced use of AAA authorization. Authorization can be used to download routes and access control lists on a per-user basis on a router to which the users are connecting. This allows routing to be set up very specifically for various users and allows access controls to be maintained on a per-user basis. Example 16-7 shows how a router can be set up to do authorization that results in routes and access control lists being downloaded to the router on a per-user basis. Figure 16-6 shows the associated network topology.

Figure 16-6 *Network Topology for This Case Study*

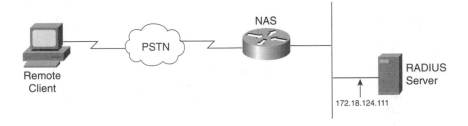

Example 16-7 *Router Set up to Do Authorization for This Case Study*

```
aaa new-model
!
!The command below is used to set up authentication for users logging into the
!router. Since the default method list is used, any line on which another method
!list is not specifically applied uses the method defined in this list to
!authenticate users. The two methods are radius and local. If the RADIUS server(s)
!defined in the group return an error, the local database is tried for
authentication.
aaa authentication login default group radius local
!The command below sets up PPP authentication for user/devices that have not
!already been authenticated on the TTY ports. There can be users who connect to the
!router via dialup and then, after authenticating and starting an EXEC session,
!initiate a PPP session. Since they are already authenticated, the if-needed
!keyword negates the need to authenticate them again. If the RADIUS server returns
!an error, the local database is used for authentication.
aaa authentication ppp default if-needed group radius local
!The command below sets up authorization for users who connect through the router
!using PPP in this case, since that is the only network service enabled on this
!router.
aaa authorization network default group radius
enable secret 5 <removed>
enable password <removed>
!
username test password <removed>
```

Example 16-7 *Router Set up to Do Authorization for This Case Study (Continued)*

```
!
ip subnet-zero
!
interface Ethernet0
 ip address 10.1.1.1 255.255.255.0
!
interface Serial0
 ip address 10.1.2.1 255.255.255.0
!
interface Serial1
 ip address 10.1.3.1 255.255.255.0
!
interface Async1
 ip unnumbered Ethernet0
 encapsulation ppp
 async mode dedicated
 peer default ip address pool test
 fair-queue 64 16 0
 no cdp enable
 ppp authentication chap
!
ip local pool test 10.1.4.1 10.1.4.100
!
ip classless
ip route 0.0.0.0 0.0.0.0 10.1.1.2
!
radius-server host 172.18.124.111 auth-port 1645 acct-port 1646
radius-server key c15c0abc
!
line con 0
 transport input all
line 1
 autoselect ppp
 modem InOut
 transport input all
 stopbits 1
 flowcontrol hardware
line 2 16
line aux 0
line vty 0 4
 password ww
```

Example 16-8 shows the profile for a user dialing in using the async interface. This is how the profile appears in RADIUS.

Example 16-8 *RADIUS Profile Set up to Download User-Specific Routes and Access Control Lists on the Router*

```
User Profile Information

User Profile Information
user = asynchuser
Password = "asynchuser"
Service-Type = Framed
Framed-Protocol = PPP
Cisco-avpair = "ip:route#1=100.1.1.0 255.255.255.0 10.1.2.2"
Cisco-avpair = "ip:route#2=110.1.1.0 255.255.255.0 10.1.3.2"
Cisco-avpair = "ip:inacl#1=permit ip 10.1.4.0 0.0.0.255 100.1.1.0 0.0.0.255"
Cisco-avpair = "ip:inacl#2=permit tcp 10.1.4.0 0.0.0.255 110.1.1.0 0.0.0.255"
```

The profile shown in Example 16-8 defines two routes to be installed on the router when the user 'asynchuser' connects to the router. Two access lists are also installed on the router at that time. This authorization results in these access lists and the routes to be installed on the router. However, these are valid only for this particular user. They affect no other user.

Using AAA to Set up PPP Timeouts

This case study demonstrates another usage of the AAA authorization feature. Authorization can also be used to set up timeout values for users who are connecting to the router using various services. In this case study, the service the users are using is PPP. Timeouts for LCP in PPP are set up using TACACS+ profiles. Example 16-9 shows how to set up the router for authorization to allow the PPP timeout values to be downloaded from the TACACS+ server. Figure 16-7 shows the network topology associated with Example 16-9.

Figure 16-7 *Network Topology for This Case Study*

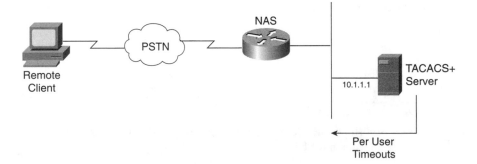

Example 16-9 *Router Set up for This Case Study*

```
aaa new-model
!The following command sets up PPP authentication using the TACACS+ server.
aaa authentication ppp default group tacacs+
!The following command is used to set up authorization for network protocols, in
!this case, PPP.
aaa authorization network default group tacacs+

tacacs-server host 10.1.1.1
tacacs-server key s1mpl15t1c
!
interface Ethernet1
 ip address 10.1.1.10 255.255.255.0

!
interface Async1
 ip unnumbered Ethernet0
 encapsulation ppp
 dialer in-band
 async dynamic routing
 async mode dedicated
 peer default ip address pool mypool
 ppp authentication chap
!
ip local pool mypool 10.1.1.100 10.1.1.200
ip classless
ip route 0.0.0.0 0.0.0.0 10.1.1.2
!
!
!
line con 0
exec-timeout 0 0
line 1
 modem InOut
 transport input all
 speed 38400
 flowcontrol hardware
line 2 16
line aux 0
line vty 0 4
!
end
```

Example 16-10 shows the user profile for userA using TACACS+.

Example 16-10 *TACACS+ Profile Set up to Allow PPP Timeouts to Be Assigned on a Per-User Basis to a User Connecting to the Router Configured in Example 16-9*

```
user = userA {
default service = permit
password = chap "userA"
service = ppp {
protocol = lcp {
set timeout=400
set idletime=100
}
protocol = ip {
}
}
```

After they are authenticated, the timeouts and idle timeouts for the user are set to the values that are shown in the profile.

Summary

This chapter discussed what AAA is and how it is used to implement security in the network. Each of the three components of AAA—authentication, authorization, and accounting—provides for increasing levels of security to a network. We looked at how authentication can be set up and looked at the various services that can be authenticated. Next, we looked at a table that summarized which services can be authenticated using the various methods. We also delved into authorization and saw how it is used to control privileges for various users on a network. Finally, we looked at accounting, which can be used to keep track of user activities through record-keeping. Although it is important to have an authentication system in place to thwart unwanted users, it is also critical to limit the accessibility of legitimate users to what is necessary. Finally, no security system is complete without a proper audit of the activities taking place on the network. Accounting provides a useful tool for such audits to take place.

Review Questions

1 What services can AAA on Cisco routers authenticate?

2 What is the purpose of authorization?

3 What does the keyword **if-authenticated** do?

4 What does the keyword **if-needed** do?

5 What risk is associated with the following command?

```
aaa authentication login default group radius none
```

This chapter covers the following key topics:

- **Introduction to TACACS+**—This section discusses the basic elements of TACACS+ functionality and how it relates to the AAA model.

- **TACACS+ Communications Architecture**—This section discusses the communications and encryption mechanisms employed by the TACACS+ protocol.

- **Authentication in TACACS+**—This section discusses the operational details of authentication taking place via TACACS+.

- **Authorization in TACACS+**—This section discusses the operational details of authorization taking place via TACACS+.

- **Accounting in TACACS+**—This section discusses the operational details of accounting taking place via TACACS+.

## CHAPTER 17

TACACS+

The preceding chapter looked at how AAA functionality is built into Cisco products, especially routers. This chapter looks at one of the protocols, TACACS+, that is used for communication between the network access server (NAS) and the AAA security server. We will start with an introduction to the TACACS+ protocol and discuss how TACACS+ implements all three features of the AAA architecture (authentication, authorization, and accounting). We will then move the discussion to an examination of the operation of TACACS+. We will go into further details of the messaging that occurs between the NAS and the AAA server for each of the three features in AAA. We will also list the attribute value (AV) pairs that are available for use with TACACS+ for authorization and accounting.

Introduction to TACACS+

TACACS+ is the name given to the protocol and the software that are used to provide AAA functionality to an access server such as a router. The TACACS+ protocol is responsible for the packet format and communications between the access server and the TACACS+ software or daemon running on a security server. The TACACS+ daemon undertakes the functions required to provide the AAA functionality.

Cisco's implementation of TACACS+ is currently commensurate with the description of the protocol in Internet draft version 1.77 and, more recently, version 1.78 of the draft. Search for the string 'draft-grant-tacacs-02.txt' using an Internet search engine to find the draft. This chapter focuses on the TACACS+ implementation based on this Internet draft.

TACACS+ Daemon Functionality

The TACACS+ daemon provides the complete AAA functionality. It allows communication between the NAS and AAA servers and facilitates the implementation of the AAA functionality on the NAS by supporting authentication, authorization, and accounting.

Here's an overview of the support provided by the TACACS+ protocol in each of these three areas:

- **Authentication**—Provides complete control over authentication through login and password dialogs, challenges and responses, and messaging support. The authentication facility lets you conduct an arbitrary dialog with the user.. In addition, the TACACS+ authentication service supports sending messages to user screens. For example, a message could notify users that their passwords must be changed because of the company's password aging policy.

- **Authorization**—Provides fine-grained control over user capabilities for the duration of the user's session, including but not limited to setting autocommands, access control, session duration, and protocol support. You can also enforce restrictions on what commands a user may execute with the TACACS+ authorization feature.

- **Accounting**—Collects and sends information used for billing, auditing, and reporting to the TACACS+ daemon. Network managers can use the accounting facility to track user activity for a security audit or to provide information for user billing. Accounting records include user identities, start and stop times, executed commands, number of packets, and number of bytes.

One of the important aspects of TACACS+ is the protocol that is responsible for the communications between the access server and daemon. This protocol not only provides for communications between the access server and the daemon but also encrypts all the exchanges between the server and the daemon, ensuring confidentiality. The next section goes into further details of the functionality of the TACACS+ protocol.

TACACS+ Communications Architecture

TACACS+ communications occur using TCP as the transport mechanism. TACACS+ uses port number 49 to communicate. TACACS+ uses the concept of a session to define the set of exchanges taking place to perform either authentication, authorization, or accounting. Typically, each session has a separate TCP connection, but multiple sessions can be multiplexed onto the same TCP connection.

In general, TCP offers quite a few advantages to TACACS+ in terms of a rugged communications architecture:

- TCP provides for a separate acknowledgment of each request that is exchanged between the NAS and the AAA server, regardless of the bandwidth.

- TCP has built-in mechanisms to adapt to congested networks and also provides much more reliable service in bursty environments.

- RADIUS protocol uses UDP for its communications. The RADIUS protocol has to include in its communication architecture various parameters such as timeouts and retransmissions to ensure delivery of its packets. In the case of TACACS+, a lot of this reliability is offered by the underlying TCP protocol.

- TCP has built-in mechanisms (TCP resets) for immediate notification of a crashed or inoperational server.

Although some of these advantages (along with certain others we will discuss later) make TACACS+ a more useful protocol than RADIUS, the fact that RADIUS is an RFC protocol makes it more attractive than TACACS+ to a lot of vendors, which is often considered Cisco-proprietary.

TACACS+ Header Format

A number of different fields can be contained in a TACACS+ packet being used for a particular purpose, but the header format is common to all packet types. The TACACS+ ID defines a 12-byte header for TACACS+. Figure 17-1 shows the TACACS+ packet header format.

Figure 17-1 *TACACS+ Packet Header Format*

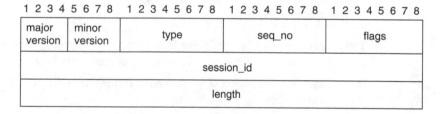

The following field descriptions are taken from the TACACS+ ID, with comments added:

- **major_version**—The major TACACS+ version number.

  TAC_PLUS_MAJOR_VER = 0xc

- **minor_version**—The minor TACACS+ version number. This is intended to allow revisions to the TACACS+ protocol while maintaining backward compatibility.

  Minor version 1 is currently defined for some commands. All other requests must use the default value.

  TAC_PLUS_MINOR_VER_DEFAULT = 0x0

  TAC_PLUS_MINOR_VER_ONE = 0x1

When a daemon receives a packet with a minor_version it does not support, it should return an ERROR status with the minor_version set to the closest supported value.

- **type**—The packet type. Legal values are

  TAC_PLUS_AUTHEN = 0x01 (authentication)

  TAC_PLUS_AUTHOR = 0x02 (authorization)

  TAC_PLUS_ACCT = 0x03 (accounting)

  As you can see, each of these values corresponds to one of the elements of AAA (authentication, authorization, accounting). Essentially, TACACS+ has three different packet types for each of the three components of AAA.

- **seq_no**—The sequence number of the current packet for the current session. The first TACACS+ packet in a session *must* have the sequence number 1, and each subsequent packet increments the sequence number by 1. Thus, clients (such as a NAS) send only packets containing odd sequence numbers, and TACACS+ daemons send only packets containing even sequence numbers.

  The sequence number must never wrap. In other words, if the sequence number 2^8-1 is ever reached, that session must terminate and be restarted with a sequence number of 1.

- **flags**—This field contains various bitmapped flags:

  — TAC_PLUS_UNENCRYPTED_FLAG

    The unencrypted flag bit specifies whether encryption is being used on the body of the TACACS+ packet (the entire portion after the header).

    If this flag is set, the packet is unencrypted. If this flag is cleared, the packet is encrypted.

    Unencrypted packets are intended for testing and are not recommended for normal use.

  — TAC_PLUS_SINGLE_CONNECT_FLAG

    If a NAS sets this flag, it supports multiplexing TACACS+ sessions over a single TCP connection. This flag needs to be examined only on the first two packets for any given connection, because after a connection's single-connect status is established, it should not be changed. The connection must instead be closed and a new connection opened if required.

    If the daemon sets this flag in the first reply packet in response to the first packet from a NAS, this indicates its willingness to support single connect over the current connection. The daemon may set this flag even if the NAS does not set it, but the NAS is under no obligation to honor it.

- **session_id**—The ID for this TACACS+ session. The session ID should be randomly chosen. This field does not change for the duration of the TACACS+ session. (If this value is not a cryptographically strong random number, it compromises the protocol's security.)

- **length**—The total length of the TACACS+ packet body (not including the header). This value is in network byte order. Packets are never padded beyond this length.

TACACS+ Packet Encryption

One of the unique features offered by TACACS+ is encryption of the entire packet beyond the header. This feature distinguishes it from RADIUS, which can encrypt only the passwords exchanged rather than the entire packet.

It is interesting to understand how TACACS+ performs encryption on the packets. The encryption that takes place is in reality a combination of hashing (which is one-way and nonreversible) and simple XOR functionality. The hash used in TACACS+ is MD5. The following steps take place in creating the cipher text in TACACS+ packets:

Step 1   A series of hashes is calculated based on some of the information contained in the TACACS+ packet header, along with a preshared secret key. This shared secret key is exchanged between the AAA server and the NAS out of band.

The first hash is calculated on a concatenation of the session_id, the key, the version number, and the sequence number used in the TACACS+ header. From the first hash, a second hash is calculated by concatenating the first hash's output with the session_id, the key, the version number, and the sequence number used in the TACACS+ header. This process continues an implementation dependent number of times.

$MD5_1$ = MD5 {session_id, preshared key, version, seq_no}

$MD5_2$ = MD5 {session_id, preshared key, version, seq_no, $MD5_1$}

.

.

.

$MD5_n$ = MD5 {session_id, preshared key, version, seq_no, $MD5_{n[nd]1}$}

Step 2   All the calculated hashes are concatenated and then truncated to the length of the data that is to be encrypted. This results in what the TACACS+ ID calls the 'pseudo_pad'.

pseudo_pad = Truncation to length of data {$MD5_1$,[$MD5_2$],...$MD5_n$}

Step 3   Cipher text is produced by doing a bytewise XOR on the pseudo_pad
with the data that is to be encrypted.

Cipher text = data XOR pseudo_pad

The recipient of the cipher text calculates the pseudo_pad on its own. It can do so correctly
because it has the preshared key. An XOR of this pseudo_pad with the cipher text results in
the clear-text data.

So far, we have looked at the general communications architecture for TACACS+. The
following sections look at the various packet types that are exchanged between the NAS
and the AAA server for the three phases of AAA.

Authentication in TACACS+

TACACS+ authentication takes place via three distinct packet exchanges between the NAS
and the TACACS+ daemon. TACACS+ authentication uses the following three types of
packets:

- START
- REPLY
- CONTINUE

Authentication starts when the NAS receives a connection request that needs to be authenticated. The NAS at this point sends a START message to the TACACS+ server. This message contains information regarding the type of authentication to be performed. It can also
contain further information, such as the username and password. In answering the START
message, the server responds with a REPLY message. If the server needs further information from the NAS to continue the authentication process, such as the password or other
parameters of an authentication process, its REPLY message indicates this. However, if the
authentication process is complete, the server responds with a REPLY message with the
authentication result. The authentication result can be any of the following three messages:

- **ACCEPT**—The user is authenticated, and service may begin. If the NAS is
  configured to require authorization, authorization begins at this time.

- **REJECT**—The user has failed to authenticate. The user might be denied further
  access or is prompted to retry the login sequence, depending on the NAS and/or the
  TACACS+ daemon.

- **ERROR**—An error occurred at some time during authentication. This can be either
  at the daemon or in the network connection between the daemon and the NAS. If an
  ERROR response is received, the NAS typically tries to use an alternative method to
  authenticate the user.

If the authentication process is to continue, the NAS responds to the REPLY request with a CONTINUE message containing the information that the TACACS+ server has requested. The AAA server responds to the last CONTINUE message with a REPLY.

Figure 17-2 shows the TACACS+ authentication process.

Figure 17-2 *TACACS+ Authentication*

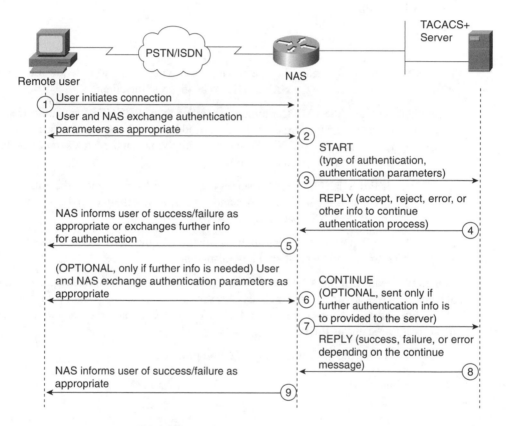

As you can see, START and CONTINUE are always sent by the NAS, and REPLY is always sent by the security/TACACS+ server.

Authorization in TACACS+

Authorization in TACACS+ takes place via two types of messages being exchanged between the NAS and the TACACS+ server.

The authorization process starts with the NAS sending an authorization REQUEST packet to the TACACS+ server. The REQUEST packet can contain information about the services or privileges that the NAS wants the AAA server to authorize the client to have. The server replies with a RESPONSE message. This RESPONSE message can specify any of the following five statuses:

- FAIL
- PASS_ADD
- PASS_REPL
- ERROR
- FOLLOW

The FAIL status simply means that the services or privileges that were requested to be authorized for the client by the NAS are not to be given to the client.

If the status is set to PASS_ADD, arguments specified in the REQUEST are authorized, and the arguments in the RESPONSE are to be used in addition to those arguments. There might not be any arguments in the RESPONSE message, implying that the AAA server has simply agreed to the attributes proposed by the NAS.

If the status is PASS_REPL, the AAA server requires the NAS to ignore the authorization parameters it sent in its REQUEST packet and simply replace them with the attribute value pairs sent in the RESPONSE packet by the AAA server.

If the status is ERROR, this implies an error situation on the AAA server. This could be a variety of issues, including preshared key mismatch.

FOLLOW means that the AAA server wants to have the authorization take place at an alternative AAA server. The alternative AAA server is listed in the packet data. Use of the alternative server is at the discretion of the NAS. If it decides not to use another server, it must treat this status as FAIL.

Figure 17-3 shows the TACACS+ authorization process.

Figure 17-3 *TACACS+ Authorization*

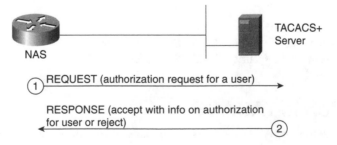

Table 17-1 lists the attribute value pairs for TACACS+ that are supported by Cisco routers for authorization.

Table 17-1   *TACACS+ Attribute Value Pairs That Are Supported by Cisco Routers for Authorization*

Attribute	Description
acl=x	ASCII number representing a connection access list. Used only when **service=shell**.
addr=x	A network address. Used with **service=slip**, **service=ppp**, and **protocol=ip**. Contains the IP address that the remote host should use when connecting via SLIP or PPP/IP—for example, **addr=10.2.3.4**.
addr-pool=x	Specifies the name of a local pool from which to get the remote host's address. Used with **service=ppp** and **protocol=ip**. Note that **addr-pool** works in conjunction with local pooling. It specifies the name of a local pool (which must be preconfigured on the NAS). Use the **ip-local pool** command to declare local pools. For example: ip address-pool local ip local pool boo 10.0.0.1 10.0.0.10 ip local pool moo 10.0.0.1 10.0.0.20 You can then use TACACS+ to return **addr-pool=boo** or **addr-pool=moo** to indicate the address pool from which you want to get this remote node's address.
autocmd=x	Specifies an autocommand to be executed at EXEC startup (for example, **autocmd=telnet example.com**). Used only with **service=shell**.
callback-dialstring	Sets the telephone number for a callback (for example, **callback-dialstring=408-555-1212**). The value is NULL, or a dial string. A NULL value indicates that the service might choose to get the dial string through other means. Used with **service=arap**, **service=slip**, **service=ppp**, **service=shell**. Not valid for ISDN.
callback-line	The number of a TTY line to use for callback (for example, **callback-line=4**). Used with **service=arap**, **service=slip**, **service=ppp**, **service=shell**. Not valid for ISDN.
callback-rotary	The number of a rotary group (between 0 and 100, inclusive) to use for callback (for example, **callback-rotary=34**). Used with **service=arap**, **service=slip**, **service=ppp**, **service=shell**. Not valid for ISDN.

continues

Table 17-1   *TACACS+ Attribute Value Pairs That Are Supported by Cisco Routers for Authorization (Continued)*

Attribute	Description
cmd-arg=x	An argument to a shell (EXEC) command. This indicates an argument for the shell command that is to be run. Multiple **cmd-arg** attributes can be specified, and they are order-dependent.
	This TACACS+ AV pair cannot be used with RADIUS attribute 26.
cmd=x	A shell (EXEC) command. This indicates the command name for a shell command that is to be run. This attribute must be specified if service equals **shell**. A NULL value indicates that the shell itself is being referred to.
	This TACACS+ AV pair cannot be used with RADIUS attribute 26.
data-service	No description available.
dial-number	Defines the number to dial.
dns-servers=x	Identifies a DNS server (primary or secondary) that can be requested by Microsoft PPP clients from the NAS during IPCP negotiation. To be used with **service=ppp** and **protocol=ip**. The IP address identifying each DNS server is entered in dotted-decimal format.
force-56	Determines whether the NAS uses only the 56 KB portion of a channel, even when all 64 KB appears to be available. To turn on this attribute, use the **true** value (**force-56=true**). Any other value is treated as false.
gw-password	Specifies the password for the home gateway during L2F tunnel authentication. Used with **service=ppp** and **protocol=vpdn**.
idletime=x	Sets a value, in minutes, after which an idle session is terminated. A value of **0** indicates no timeout.
inacl#n	ASCII access list identifier for an input access list to be installed and applied to an interface for the duration of the current connection. Used with **service=ppp** and **protocol=ip** and **service=ppp** and **protocol=ipx**. Per-user access lists do not currently work with ISDN interfaces.
inacl=x	ASCII identifier for an interface input access list. Used with **service=ppp** and **protocol=ip**. Per-user access lists do not currently work with ISDN interfaces.
interface-config#n	Specifies user-specific AAA interface configuration information with virtual profiles. The information that follows the # can be any Cisco IOS interface configuration command. Multiple instances of this attributes are allowed, but each instance must have a unique number. Used with **service=ppp** and **protocol=lcp**.
	This attribute replaces the **interface-config=** attribute.

Table 17-1   *TACACS+ Attribute Value Pairs That Are Supported by Cisco Routers for Authorization (Continued)*

Attribute	Description
ip-addresses	Space-separated list of possible IP addresses that can be used for a tunnel's endpoint. Used with **service=ppp** and **protocol=vpdn**.
l2tp-busy-disconnect	If a VPDN group on an LNS uses a virtual template that is configured to be precloned, this attribute controls the disposition of a new L2TP session that finds no precloned interface to connect to. If the attribute is true (the default), the session is disconnected by the LNS. Otherwise, a new interface is cloned from the virtual template.
l2tp-cm-local-window-size	Specifies the maximum receive window size for L2TP control messages. This value is advertised to the peer during tunnel establishment.
l2tp-drop-out-of-order	Respects sequence numbers on data packets by dropping those that are received out of order. This does not ensure that sequence numbers are sent on data packets, just how to handle them if they are received.
l2tp-hello-interval	Specifies the number of seconds for the hello keepalive interval. Hello packets are sent when no data has been sent on a tunnel for the number of seconds configured here.
l2tp-hidden-avp	When this attribute is enabled, sensitive AV pairs in L2TP control messages are scrambled or hidden.
l2tp-nosession-timeout	Specifies the number of seconds that a tunnel stays active with no sessions before timing out and shutting down.
l2tp-tos-reflect	Copies the IP ToS field from the IP header of each payload packet to the IP header of the tunnel packet for packets entering the tunnel at the LNS.
l2tp-tunnel-authen	If this attribute is set, it performs L2TP tunnel authentication.
l2tp-tunnel-password	Shared secret used for L2TP tunnel authentication and AV pair hiding.
l2tp-udp-checksum	An authorization attribute that defines whether L2TP should perform UDP checksums for data packets. Valid values are **yes** and **no**. The default is **no**.

continues

Table 17-1   *TACACS+ Attribute Value Pairs That Are Supported by Cisco Routers for Authorization (Continued)*

Attribute	Description
link-compression=x	Defines whether to turn on or turn off stac compression over a PPP link. Link compression is defined as a numeric value as follows: **0**—None **1**—Stac **2**—Stac-Draft-9 **3**—MS-Stac
load-threshold=n	Sets the load threshold for the caller at which additional links are either added to or deleted from the multilink bundle. If the load goes above the specified value, additional links are added. If the load goes below the specified value, links are deleted. Used with **service=ppp** and **protocol=multilink**. The range for n is from 1 to 255.
map-class	Allows the user profile to reference information configured in a map class of the same name on the NAS that dials out.
max-links=n	Restricts the number of links that a user can have in a multilink bundle. Used with **service=ppp** and **protocol=multilink**. The range for n is from 1 to 255.
min-links	Sets the minimum number of links for MLP.
nas-password	Specifies the password for the NAS during L2F tunnel authentication. Used with **service=ppp** and **protocol=vpdn**.
nocallback-verify	Indicates that no callback verification is required. The only valid value for this parameter is 1 (for example, **nocallback-verify=1**). Used with **service=arap**, **service=slip**, **service=ppp**, **service=shell**. There is no authentication on callback. Not valid for ISDN.
noescape=x	Prevents user from using an escape character. Used with **service=shell**. Can be either true or false (for example, **noescape=true**).
nohangup=x	Used with **service=shell**. Specifies the **nohangup** option, which means that after an EXEC shell is terminated, the user is presented with another login (username) prompt. Can be either true or false (for example, **nohangup=false**).
old-prompts	Allows providers to make the prompts in TACACS+ appear identical to those of earlier systems (TACACS and Extended TACACS). This allows administrators to upgrade from TACACS or Extended TACACS to TACACS+ transparently to users.

Table 17-1 *TACACS+ Attribute Value Pairs That Are Supported by Cisco Routers for Authorization (Continued)*

Attribute	Description
outacl#*n*	ASCII access list identifier for an interface output access list to be installed and applied to an interface for the duration of the current condition. Used with **service=ppp** and **protocol=ip** and **service=ppp** and **protocol=ipx**. Per-user access lists do not currently work with ISDN interfaces.
outacl=*x*	ASCII identifier for an interface output access list. Used with **service=ppp** and **protocol=ip** and **service=ppp** and **protocol=ipx**. Contains an IP output access list for SLIP or PPP/IP (for example, **outacl=4**). The access list itself must be preconfigured on the router. Per-user access lists do not currently work with ISDN interfaces.
pool-def#*n*	Defines IP address pools on the NAS. Used with **service=ppp** and **protocol=ip**.
pool-timeout=x	Defines (in conjunction with **pool-def**) IP address pools on the NAS. During IPCP address negotiation, if an IP pool name is specified for a user (see the **addr-pool** attribute), a check is made to see if the named pool is defined on the NAS. If it is, the pool is consulted for an IP address.
port-type	Indicates the type of physical port the NAS is using to authenticate the user.
	Physical ports are indicated by a numeric value:
	0—Asynchronous
	1—Synchronous
	2—ISDN-Synchronous
	3—ISDN-Asynchronous (V.120)
	4—ISDN-Asynchronous (V.110)
	5—Virtual
ppp-vj-slot-compression	Instructs the Cisco router not to use slot compression when sending VJ-compressed packets over a PPP link.
priv-lvl=*x*	Privilege level to be assigned for the EXEC. Used with **service=shell**. Privilege levels range from 0 to 15, with 15 being the highest.
protocol=*x*	A protocol that is a subset of a service. An example is any PPP NCP. Currently known values are **lcp**, **ip**, **ipx**, **atalk**, **vines**, **lat**, **xremote**, **tn3270**, **telnet**, **rlogin**, **pad**, **vpdn**, **osicp**, **deccp**, **ccp**, **cdp**, **bridging**, **xns**, **nbf**, **bap**, **multilink**, and **unknown**.

continues

Table 17-1 *TACACS+ Attribute Value Pairs That Are Supported by Cisco Routers for Authorization (Continued)*

Attribute	Description
proxyacl#*n*	Allows users to configure the downloadable user profiles (dynamic ACLs) by using the authentication proxy feature so that users can have the configured authorization to permit traffic going through the configured interfaces.
route	Specifies a route to be applied to an interface. Used with **service=slip**, **service=ppp**, and **protocol=ip**.
	During network authorization, the **route** attribute can be used to specify a per-user static route, to be installed by TACACS+ as follows:
	route=*dst_address mask* [*gateway*]
	This indicates a temporary static route that is to be applied. The *dst_address*, *mask*, and *gateway* are expected to be in the usual dotted-decimal notation, with the same meanings as in the familiar IP route configuration commands on a NAS.
	If *gateway* is omitted, the peer's address is the gateway. The route is expunged when the connection terminates.
route#*n*	Like the route AV pair, this specifies a route to be applied to an interface, but these routes are numbered, allowing multiple routes to be applied. Used with **service=ppp** and **protocol=ip** and **service=ppp** and **protocol=ipx**.
routing=*x*	Specifies whether routing information is to be propagated to and accepted from this interface. Used with **service=slip**, **service=ppp**, and **protocol=ip**. Equivalent in function to the **/routing** flag in SLIP and PPP commands. Can either be true or false (for example, **routing=true**).
rte-fltr-in#*n*	Specifies an input access list definition to be installed and applied to routing updates on the current interface for the duration of the current connection. Used with **service=ppp** and **protocol=ip** and **service=ppp** and **protocol=ipx**.
rte-fltr-out#*n*	Specifies an output access list definition to be installed and applied to routing updates on the current interface for the duration of the current connection. Used with **service=ppp** and **protocol=ip** and **service=ppp** and **protocol=ipx**.
sap#*n*	Specifies static Service Advertising Protocol (SAP) entries to be installed for the duration of a connection. Used with **service=ppp** and **protocol=ipx**.
sap-fltr-in#*n*	Specifies an input SAP filter access list definition to be installed and applied on the current interface for the duration of the current connection. Used with **service=ppp** and **protocol=ipx**.

Table 17-1   *TACACS+ Attribute Value Pairs That Are Supported by Cisco Routers for Authorization (Continued)*

Attribute	Description
sap-fltr-out#*n*	Specifies an output SAP filter access list definition to be installed and applied on the current interface for the duration of the current connection. Used with **service=ppp** and **protocol=ipx**.
send-auth	Defines the protocol to use (PAP or CHAP) for username-password authentication following CLID authentication.
send-secret	Specifies the password that the NAS needs to respond to a CHAP/PAP request from the remote end of a connection on an outgoing call.
service=*x*	The primary service. Specifying a **service** attribute indicates that this is a request for authorization or accounting of that service. Current values are **slip**, **ppp**, **arap**, **shell**, **tty-daemon**, **connection**, and **system**. This attribute must always be included.
source-ip=*x*	Used as the source IP address of all VPDN packets generated as part of a VPDN tunnel. This is equivalent to the Cisco **vpdn outgoing** global configuration command.
spi	Carries the authentication information needed by the home agent to authenticate a mobile node during registration. The information is in the same syntax as the **ip mobile secure host** *addr* configuration command. Basically, it contains the rest of the configuration command that follows that string, verbatim. It provides the Security Parameter Index (SPI), key, authentication algorithm, authentication mode, and replay protection time-stamp range.
timeout=*x*	The number of minutes before an EXEC or ARA session disconnects (for example, **timeout=60**). A value of **0** indicates no timeout. Used with **service=arap**.
tunnel-id	Specifies the username that is used to authenticate the tunnel over which the individual user MID is projected. This is analogous to the *remote name* in the **vpdn outgoing** command. Used with **service=ppp** and **protocol=vpdn**.
wins-servers=x	Identifies a Windows NT server that can be requested by Microsoft PPP clients from the NAS during IPCP negotiation. To be used with **service=ppp** and **protocol=ip**. The IP address identifying each Windows NT Server is entered in dotted-decimal format.
zonelist=*x*	A numeric zonelist value. Used with **service=arap**. Specifies an AppleTalk zonelist for ARA (for example, **zonelist=5**).

Accounting in TACACS+

Accounting in TACACS+ works in a fashion fairly similar to how authorization works. Accounting takes place in TACACS+ in the form of various records being sent to the TACACS+ server from the NAS. These records use all the AV pairs described in the preceding section plus many more.

TACACS+ has three main types of accounting records:

- **Start record**—Indicates that a service is about to begin. Contains information used in the authorization records as well as other account-specific information.

- **Stop record**—Indicates that a service is about to stop or has terminated. Contains information used in the authorization records as well as other account-specific information.

- **Continue record (also known as the Watchdog)**—Sent while a service is still in progress. This type of record allows the NAS to periodically provide the AAA server with updated information. Contains information used in the authorization records as well as other account-specific information.

A Record can be of both the Start and Continue types. This indicates that the update record is a duplicate of the original Start record.

Accounting in TACACS+ starts with the NAS sending a REQUEST message to the AAA server. The REQUEST contains any one of the three records just described, along with the corresponding accounting attribute value pairs. The AAA server responds to the NAS with a REPLY packet. The REPLY packet can specify the status as any one of the following:

- **SUCCESS**—If the status is set to SUCCESS, the AAA server successfully received the record sent by the NAS and has committed it to its records database.

- **ERROR**—An ERROR status implies the failure of the AAA server to commit the record to its database.

- **FOLLOW**—A FOLLOW status is sent by the AAA server to ask the NAS to send the records to another AAA server. The alternative AAA server is listed in the packet data. Use of the alternative server is at the discretion of the NAS. Figure 17-4 shows the TACACS+ accounting process.

Table 17-2 lists the TACACS+ attribute value pairs used for accounting. This list gives you an idea of the types of accounting information that TACACS+ can keep track of.

Figure 17-4 *TACACS+ Accounting*

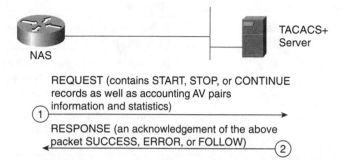

REQUEST (contains START, STOP, or CONTINUE
records as well as accounting AV pairs
information and statistics)

RESPONSE (an acknowledgement of the above
packet SUCCESS, ERROR, or FOLLOW)

Table 17-2 *TACACS+ Accounting Attribute Value Pairs*

Attribute	Description
Abort-Cause	If the fax session aborts, this attribute indicates the system component that signaled the abort. Examples of system components that can trigger an abort are FAP (Fax Application Process), TIFF (the TIFF reader or the TIFF writer), fax-mail client, fax-mail server, ESMTP client, and ESMTP server.
bytes_in	The number of input bytes transferred during this connection.
bytes_out	The number of output bytes transferred during this connection.
Call-Type	the type of fax activity: fax receive or fax send.
cmd	The command the user executed.
data-rate (also known as **nas-rx-speed**)	Specifies the average number of bits per second over the course of the connection's lifetime. This attribute is sent in accounting-stop records.
disc-cause	Specifies why a connection was taken offline. The Disconnect-Cause attribute is sent in accounting Stop records. This attribute also causes Stop records to be generated without first generating Start records if disconnection occurs before authentication is performed.
disc-cause-ext	Extends the **disc-cause** attribute to support vendor-specific reasons why a connection was taken offline.
elapsed_time	The action's elapsed time in seconds. Useful when the device does not keep real time.

continues

Table 17-2   *TACACS+ Accounting Attribute Value Pairs (Continued)*

Attribute	Description
Email-Server-Address	Indicates the IP address of the e-mail server handling the on-ramp fax-mail message.
Email-Server-Ack-Flag	Indicates that the on-ramp gateway has received a positive acknowledgment from the e-mail server accepting the fax-mail message.
event	Information included in the accounting packet that describes a state change in the router. Events described are accounting starting and accounting stopping.
Fax-Account-Id-Origin	Indicates the account ID origin as defined by the system administrator for the **mmoip aaa receive-id** or **mmoip aaa send-id** command.
Fax-Auth-Status	Indicates whether authentication for this fax session was successful. Possible values for this field are **success**, **failed**, **bypassed**, and **unknown**.
Fax-Connect-Speed	Indicates the modem speed at which this fax-mail was initially transmitted or received. Possible values are **1200**, **4800**, **9600**, and **14400**.
Fax-Coverpage-Flag	Indicates whether a cover page was generated by the off-ramp gateway for this fax session. **true** indicates that a cover page was generated; **false** means that a cover page was not generated.
Fax-Dsn-Address	Indicates the address to which DSNs are sent.
Fax-Dsn-Flag	Indicates whether DSN has been enabled. **true** indicates that DSN has been enabled; **false** means that DSN has not been enabled.
Fax-Mdn-Address	Indicates the address to which message delivery notifications (MDNs) are sent.
Fax-Mdn-Flag	Indicates whether MDN has been enabled. **true** indicates that MDN has been enabled; **false** means that MDN has not been enabled.
Fax-Modem-Time	Indicates how long in seconds the modem sent fax data (x) and the amount of time in seconds of the total fax session (y), which includes both fax-mail and PSTN time, in the form x/y. For example, 10/15 means that the transfer time took 10 seconds and the total fax session took 15 seconds.
Fax-Msg-Id=x	Indicates a unique fax message identification number assigned by Store-and-Forward Fax.

Table 17-2   *TACACS+ Accounting Attribute Value Pairs (Continued)*

Attribute	Description
Fax-Pages	Indicates the number of pages transmitted or received during this fax session. This page count includes cover pages.
Fax-Process-Abort-Flag	Indicates that the fax session was aborted or successful. **true** means that the session was aborted; **false** means that the session was successful.
Fax-Recipient-Count	Indicates the number of recipients for this fax transmission. Until e-mail servers support Session mode, this number should be 1.
Gateway-Id	Indicates the name of the gateway that processed the fax session. The name appears in the following format: *hostname.domain-name*
mlp-links-max	Gives the count of links that are known to have been in a given multilink session at the time the accounting record was generated.
mlp-sess-id	Reports the identification number of the multilink bundle when the session closes. This attribute applies to sessions that are part of a multilink bundle. This attribute is sent in authentication-response packets.
nas-rx-speed	Specifies the average number of bits per second over the course of the connection's lifetime. This attribute is sent in accounting stop records.
nas-tx-speed	Reports the transmit speed negotiated by the two modems.
paks_in	The number of input packets transferred during this connection.
paks_out	The number of output packets transferred during this connection.
port	The port the user is logged in to.
Port-Used	The slot/port number of the Cisco AS5300 used to either transmit or receive this fax-mail.
pre-bytes-in	Records the number of input bytes before authentication. This attribute is sent in accounting stop records.
pre-bytes-out	Records the number of output bytes before authentication. This attribute is sent in accounting stop records.

continues

Table 17-2 *TACACS+ Accounting Attribute Value Pairs (Continued)*

Attribute	Description
pre-paks-in	Records the number of input packets before authentication. This attribute is sent in accounting stop records.
pre-paks-out	Records the number of output packets before authentication. This attribute is sent in accounting stop records.
pre-session-time	Specifies the length of time, in seconds, from when a call first connects to when it completes authentication.
priv_level	The privilege level associated with the action.
protocol	The protocol associated with the action.
reason	Information included in the accounting packet that describes the event that caused a system change. Events described are system reload, system shutdown, or when accounting is reconfigured (turned on or off).
service	The service the user used.
start_time	The time the action started (in seconds since the epoch, 12:00 a.m. January 1, 1970). The clock must be configured to receive this information.
stop_time	The time the action stopped (in seconds since the epoch). The clock must be configured to receive this information.
task_id	Start and stop records for the same event must have matching (unique) **task_id** numbers.
timezone	The time zone abbreviation for all time stamps included in this packet.

Summary

This chapter discussed how TACACS+ performs AAA functions for the NAS. TACACS+ not only performs the back-end work for AAA, but also defines the format of how the communication between the TACACS+ server and the NAS takes place. This chapter also discussed how the TACACS+ daemon responds to the various AAA requests from the NAS.

Review Questions

1 How does the AAA server provide authorization information to the NAS?

2 What types of messages does TACACS+ use for authentication?

3 What types of messages does TACACS+ use for accounting purposes?

4 What algorithm does TACACS+ employ for encryption?

5 What is a pseudo_pad?

6 What does it mean to have the TAC_PLUS_UNENCRYPTED_FLAG value set to 01?

7 What does the PASS_ADD status in TACACS+ authorization imply?

This chapter covers the following key topics:

- **Introduction to RADIUS**— This section covers the basic architecture of RADIUS and its main functions based on RFC 2865.

- **RADIUS Communications Architecture**—This section discusses how RADIUS communications take place.

- **Authentication in RADIUS**—This section covers the operational details of authentication taking place via RADIUS.

- **Authorization in RADIUS**—This section talks about the operational details of authorization taking place via RADIUS.

- **Accounting in RADIUS**—This section discusses the operational details of accounting taking place via RADIUS.

## CHAPTER 18

RADIUS

This chapter examines the workings of the RADIUS protocol, which can be used to facilitate AAA functionality on Cisco devices. We will look at the communications architecture of RADIUS and see how it transports packets. We will also look at the mechanism RADIUS employs to ensure the confidentiality of user passwords transmitted across an unsecure link. We will then study each of the three elements of AAA as they relate to RADIUS. Finally, we will discuss what types of messages are sent back and forth between devices that use RADIUS to perform AAA.

Introduction to RADIUS

Remote Authentication Dial-In User Service (RADIUS) is a protocol used for communication between the network access server (NAS) and the AAA server. RADIUS supports all three aspects of AAA: authentication, authorization, and accounting.

RFC 2865 covers the RADIUS protocol. As described in that RFC, key features of RADIUS are as follows:

Client/Server Model—A Network Access Server (NAS) operates as a client of RADIUS. The client is responsible for passing user information to designated RADIUS servers, and then acting on the response which is returned.

RADIUS servers are responsible for receiving user connection requests, authenticating the user, and then returning all configuration information necessary for the client to deliver service to the user.

A RADIUS server can act as a proxy client to other RADIUS servers or other kinds of authentication servers.

Network Security—Transactions between the client and RADIUS server are authenticated through the use of a shared secret, which is never sent over the network. In addition, any user passwords are sent encrypted between the client and RADIUS server, to eliminate the possibility that someone snooping on an unsecure network could determine a user's password.

Flexible Authentication Mechanisms—The RADIUS server can support a variety of methods to authenticate a user. When it is provided with the user name and original password given by the user, it can support PPP PAP or CHAP, UNIX login, and other authentication mechanisms.

Extensible Protocol—All transactions are comprised of variable length Attribute-Length-Value 3-tuples. New attribute values can be added without disturbing existing implementations of the protocol.

The RADIUS protocol was originally developed by Livingston Enterprises, Inc. Essentially, RADIUS is comprised of three main components: a server, a client (NAS), and a UDP/IP-based protocol for communications between the server and the client. The RADIUS server is responsible for providing AAA functionality to the NAS, which is its client. The server might or might not be the actual repository of the user information needed to authenticate, authorize, and account for the users. It can use other databases to get that information. However, this interaction with other databases is transparent to the client (NAS). The exchange between the server and the client occurs over UDP. We will discuss using UDP versus TCP as the transport protocol in the next section. The communication between the client and the server is in the clear except for the passwords, which are encrypted. We will look at the encryption mechanism in a later section. It is interesting to note that the rest of the information exchanged between the client and the server, including the type of authentication and the authorization parameters, can be sniffed by an attacker. However, generally this risk is somewhat reduced because the client and the server usually reside on a private network with trusted users.

RADIUS Communications Architecture

RADIUS uses the UDP protocol for its communication needs. Although some early implementations of RADIUS used port 1645, the official UDP port to use for RADIUS is 1812.

The preceding chapter looked at some of the advantages of using TCP versus UDP for transmitting TACACS+ information. However, arguments based on the specific needs of the RADIUS protocol advocate the use of UDP for RADIUS communications. The following is a quote from RFC 2865, explaining the appropriateness of UDP as the transport mechanism for RADIUS:

1. If the request to a primary Authentication server fails, a secondary server must be queried. To meet this requirement, a copy of the request must be kept above the transport layer to allow for alternate transmission. This means that retransmission timers are still required.

2. The timing requirements of this particular protocol are significantly different than TCP provides. At one extreme, RADIUS does not require a "responsive" detection of lost data. The user is willing to wait several seconds for the authentication to complete. The generally aggressive TCP retransmission (based on average round trip time) is not required, nor is the acknowledgement overhead of TCP. At the other extreme, the user is not willing to wait several minutes for authentication. Therefore the reliable delivery of TCP data two minutes later is not useful. The faster use of an alternate server allows the user to gain access before giving up.

3. The stateless nature of this protocol simplifies the use of UDP. Clients and servers come and go. Systems are rebooted, or are power cycled independently. Generally this does not cause a problem and with creative timeouts and detection of lost TCP connections, code can be written to handle anomalous events. UDP however completely eliminates any of this special handling. Each client and server can open their UDP transport just once and leave it open through all types of failure events on the network.

4. UDP simplifies the server implementation. In the earliest implementations of RADIUS, the server was single threaded. This means that a single request was received, processed, and returned. This was found to be unmanageable in environments where the back-end security mechanism took real time (1 or

more seconds). The server request queue would fill and in environments where hundreds of people were being authenticated every minute, the request turn-around time increased to longer than users were willing to wait (this was especially severe when a specific lookup in a database or over DNS took 30 or more seconds). The obvious solution was to make the server multi-threaded. Achieving this was simple with UDP. Separate processes were spawned to serve each request and these processes could respond directly to the client NAS with a simple UDP packet to the original transport of the client.

Generally, the use of TCP can provide some advantages to the implementation of a security protocol such as RADIUS. However, as mentioned in the RFC, some of the functionality gained by using TCP can be offloaded to the security protocol (RADIUS) as well. In addition, some of the reliability offered by TCP might not be required in certain AAA environments where the reliability requirements require different timers than the ones offered by TCP. We discussed some of the benefits of using TCP in the preceding chapter.

RADIUS Packet Format

Although a variety of packets are used to complete the three phases of AAA in RADIUS, the packet format follows the general pattern described in this section. The following descriptions of the RADIUS packet fields are taken from RFC 2865, with some information added and deleted for clarity. Figure 18-1 shows the general packet format for RADIUS.

Figure 18-1 *General RADIUS Packet Format*

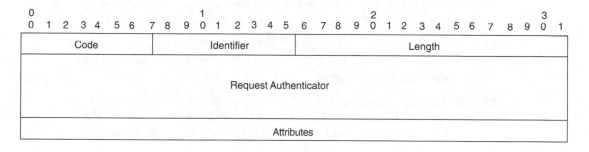

- **Code**—The Code field is one octet. It identifies the type of RADIUS packet. When a packet is received with an invalid Code field, it is silently discarded. RADIUS codes (in decimal) are assigned as follows:
    — **1**—Access-Request
    — **2**—Access-Accept
    — **3**—Access-Reject
    — **4**—Accounting-Request
    — **5**—Accounting-Response
    — **11**—Access-Challenge

- **12**—Status-Server (experimental)
- **13**—Status-Client (experimental)
- **255**—Reserved

- **Identifier**—The Identifier field is one octet. It aids in matching requests and replies. The RADIUS server can detect a duplicate request if it has the same client source IP address, source UDP port, and identifier within a short span of time.

- **Length**—The Length field is two octets. It indicates the length of the packet, including the Code, Identifier, Length, Authenticator, and Attribute fields. Octets outside the range of the Length field *must* be treated as padding and ignored on receipt. If the packet is shorter than the Length field indicates, it *must* be silently discarded. The minimum length is 20, and the maximum length is 4096.

- **Authenticator**—The Authenticator field is 16 octets. The most significant octet is transmitted first. This value is used to authenticate the reply from the RADIUS server and is used in the password-hiding algorithm. We will discuss RADIUS encryption mechanisms in the next section.

Password Encryption in RADIUS

Although RADIUS does not provide a mechanism for encrypting the entire packet like TACACS+ does, it does provide a mechanism for encrypting the password supplied by a user. The mechanism used to encrypt the user-supplied password works as follows:

Step 1   The RADIUS packet has an Authenticator field. In the packets that carry the user password, this field contains a 16-octet random number called the request authenticator.

Step 2   The request authenticator and a preshared shared secret (exchanged out of band between the NAS and the AAA server) are input into an MD5 hashing function. The result is a 16-octet hash. Let's call it Hash_A:

Hash_A = MD5 {request authenticator, preshared secret}

Step 3   The user-provided password is padded at the end with nulls so that it reaches the 16-byte octet length.

Step 4   The resultant hash, Hash A, is XORed with the padded password provided by the user to calculate the cipher text that is transmitted to the AAA server:

Cipher text = (Hash_A) XOR (padded user password)

This cipher text is then transmitted, hiding the user password from prying eyes.

Step 5   The receiving party calculates Hash_A on its own and XORs it with the cipher text to get the padded user password back in clear text.

Having looked at RADIUS's general communications architecture, the next three sections discuss how RADIUS performs each of the three AAA functions.

Authentication in RADIUS

RADIUS authentication takes place in the shape of two messages being exchanged between the NAS and the RADIUS server.

Upon being approached by a user for authentication, the NAS sends an Access-Request message to the RADIUS server. The Access-Request message contains the following information:

- The username
- The user password in an encrypted format
- The NAS IP address and the port
- The type of service the user wants

The RADIUS server responds with one of the following messages:

- Access-Accept
- Access-Reject
- Access-Challenge

The Access-Accept message is sent if the AAA server successfully authenticates the user. This message also contains authorization attribute value (AV) pairs to be applied to the user. We will discuss these in more detail in the next section.

The Access-Reject message is sent when any of the values offered by the NAS to the AAA server are unacceptable to the AAA server. This message may also include one or more Reply message attributes with a text message that the NAS may display to the user. At this point, the NAS decides whether the user gets another shot at authentication.

If the AAA server needs to challenge the user for a new password, it sends an Access-Challenge message to the NAS containing the challenge for the user. The NAS sends this information to the user and then also forwards the response to the AAA server in an Access-Request message with the user's username and challenge response. The AAA server then replies with an appropriate response based on any of the three responses shown here (accept, reject, challenge). Figure 18-2 shows this process taking place between a server, a NAS, and a user connecting to the NAS.

Figure 18-2 *RADIUS Authentication*

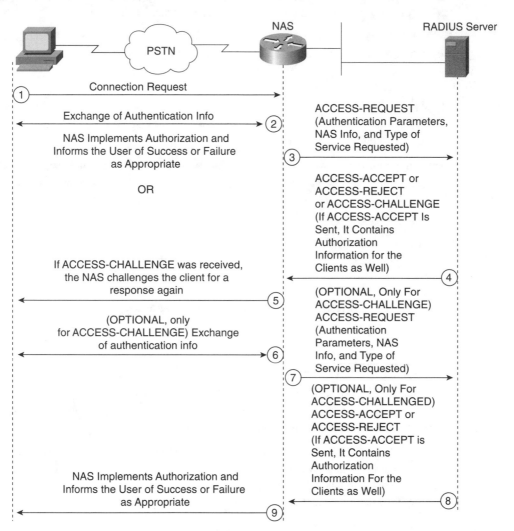

Authorization in RADIUS

RADIUS authorization takes place in conjunction with the authentication process. When
the RADIUS server returns an Access-Accept message, it also includes a list of AV pairs
describing the attributes of the session the user is entitled to. This information forms the
authorization for the NAS. Table 18-1 lists the IETF attributes that are supported on Cisco
routers for RADIUS authorization. These attributes include the vendor-specific attribute
(VSA) that is used to provide further flexibility in RADIUS implementations.

The authorization data contained in the Accept message is generally the following:

- Services that the user can access, including Telnet, rlogin, or local-area transport (LAT) connections, and PPP, Serial Line Internet Protocol (SLIP), or EXEC services
- Connection parameters, including the host or client IP address, access list, and user timeouts

Figure 18-3 shows the steps that the server and the client go through to authorize services for the user.

Figure 18-3 *RADIUS Authorization*

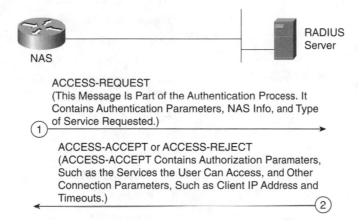

Table 18-1 *ETF Attributes Supported on Cisco Routers for RADIUS Authorization*

Number	IETF Attribute	Description
1	User-Name	Indicates the name of the user being authenticated by the RADIUS server.
2	User-Password	Indicates the user's password or the user's input following an Access-Challenge. Passwords longer than 16 characters are encrypted using RFC 2865 specifications.
3	CHAP-Password	Indicates the response value provided by a PPP Challenge Handshake Authentication Protocol (CHAP) user in response to an Access-Challenge.
4	NAS-IP Address	Specifies the IP address of the NAS that is requesting authentication. The default value is 0.0.0.0/0.
5	NAS-Port	Indicates the physical port number of the NAS that is authenticating the user.

continues

Table 18-1   *ETF Attributes Supported on Cisco Routers for RADIUS Authorization (Continued)*

Number	IETF Attribute	Description
6	Service-Type	Indicates the type of service requested or the type of service to be provided.
		In a request:
		Framed for known PPP or SLIP connection.
		Administrative User for **enable** command.
		In response:
		Login—Make a connection.
		Framed—Start SLIP or PPP.
		Administrative User—Start an EXEC or **enable ok**.
		Exec User—Start an EXEC session.
		Service type is indicated by a particular numeric value, as follows:
		1—Login
		2—Framed
		3—Callback-Login
		4—Callback-Framed
		5—Outbound
		6—Administrative
		7—NAS-Prompt
		8—Authenticate Only
		9—Callback-NAS-Prompt
7	Framed-Protocol	Indicates the framing to be used for framed access. No other framing is allowed.
		Framing is indicated by a numeric value, as follows:
		1—PPP
		2—SLIP
		3—ARA
		4—Gandalf-proprietary single-link/multilink protocol
		5—Xylogics-proprietary IPX/SLIP
8	Framed-IP-Address	Indicates the IP address to be configured for the user by sending the user's IP address to the RADIUS server in the Access-Request.

Table 18-1   *ETF Attributes Supported on Cisco Routers for RADIUS Authorization (Continued)*

Number	IETF Attribute	Description
9	Framed-IP-Netmask	Indicates the IP netmask to be configured for the user when the user is a router to a network. This attribute value causes a static route to be added for Framed-IP-Address with the mask specified.
10	Framed-Routing	Indicates the routing method for the user when the user is a router to a network. Only the None and Send and Listen values are supported for this attribute.
		The Routing method is indicated by a numeric value, as follows:
		0—None
		1—Send routing packets
		2—Listen for routing packets
		3—Send routing packets and listen for routing packets
11	Filter-Id	Indicates the name of the filter list for the user. Is formatted as follows: %d, %d.in, or %d.out. This attribute is associated with the most recent **service-type** command.
12	Framed-MTU	Indicates the maximum transmission unit (MTU) that can be configured for the user when the MTU is not negotiated by PPP or some other means.
13	Framed-Compression	Indicates a compression protocol used for the link. This attribute results in a "/compress" being added to the PPP or SLIP autocommand generated during EXEC authorization. Not currently implemented for non-EXEC authorization.
		The compression protocol is indicated by a numeric value, as follows:
		0—None
		1—VJ-TCP/IP header compression
		2—IPX header compression
14	Login-IP-Host	Indicates the host to which the user connects when the Login-Service attribute is included. (This begins immediately after login.)

continues

Table 18-1   *ETF Attributes Supported on Cisco Routers for RADIUS Authorization (Continued)*

Number	IETF Attribute	Description
15	Login-Service	Indicates the service that should be used to connect the user to the login host.
		The service is indicated by a numeric value, as follows:
		0—Telnet
		1—rlogin
		2—TCP-Clear
		3—PortMaster
		4—LAT
16	Login-TCP-Port	Defines the TCP port to which the user is to be connected when the Login-Service attribute is also present.
18	Reply-Message	Indicates text that might be displayed to the user via the RADIUS server.
19	Callback-Number	Defines a dialing string to be used for callback.
20	Callback-ID	Defines the name (consisting of one or more octets) of a place to be called, to be interpreted by the NAS.
22	Framed-Route	Provides routing information to be configured for the user on this NAS.
23	Framed-IPX-Network	Defines the IPX network number configured for the user.
24	State	Allows state information to be maintained between the NAS and the RADIUS server. This attribute is applicable only to CHAP challenges.
26	Vendor-Specific	Allows vendors to support their own extended attributes that are unsuitable for general use. The Cisco RADIUS implementation supports one vendor-specific option using the format recommended in the specification. Cisco's vendor-ID is 9, and the supported option has vendor-type 1, which is named cisco-avpair. The value is a string of this format:
		protocol : *attribute sep value*

Table 18-1 *ETF Attributes Supported on Cisco Routers for RADIUS Authorization (Continued)*

Number	IETF Attribute	Description
26 (cont.)	Vendor-Specific	*protocol* is a value of the Cisco *protocol* attribute for a particular type of authorization. *attribute* and *value* are an appropriate AV pair defined in the Cisco TACACS+ specification, and *sep* is = for mandatory attributes and * for optional attributes. This allows the full set of features available for TACACS+ authorization to also be used for RADIUS. See Table 17-1 for TACACS+ AV pairs that can be used in conjunction with RADIUS vendor-specific AV pair 26.
27	Session-Timeout	Sets the maximum number of seconds of service to be provided to the user before the session terminates. This attribute value becomes the per-user "absolute timeout."
28	Idle-Timeout	Sets the maximum number of consecutive seconds of idle connection allowed to the user before the session terminates. This attribute value becomes the per-user Session-Timeout.
29	Termination-Action	Termination is indicated by a numeric value, as follows: 0—Default 1—RADIUS request
32	NAS-Identifier	String identifying the NAS originating the Access-Request.
33	Proxy-State	An attribute that can be sent by a proxy server to another server when forwarding Access-Requests. This must be returned unmodified in the Access-Accept, Access-Reject, or Access-Challenge and removed by the proxy server before the response is sent to the NAS.
34	Login-LAT-Service	Indicates the system to which the user is to be connected by LAT. This attribute is available only in EXEC mode.
35	Login-LAT-Node	Indicates the node to which the user is to be automatically connected by LAT.
36	Login-LAT-Group	Identifies the LAT group codes that this user is authorized to use.

continues

Table 18-1   *ETF Attributes Supported on Cisco Routers for RADIUS Authorization (Continued)*

Number	IETF Attribute	Description
37	Framed-AppleTalk-Link	Indicates the AppleTalk network number that should be used for serial links to the user, which is another AppleTalk router.
38	Framed-AppleTalk-Network	Indicates the AppleTalk network number that the NAS uses to allocate an AppleTalk node for the user.
39	Framed-AppleTalk-Zone	Indicates the AppleTalk default zone to be used for this user.
52	Acct-Input-Gigawords	Indicates how many times the Acct-Input-Octets counter has wrapped around 2^{32} over the course of the provided service.
53	Acct-Output-Gigawords	Indicates how many times the Acct-Output-Octets counter has wrapped around 2^{32} while delivering service.
55	Event-Timestamp	Records the time, in seconds, when the event occurred on the NAS.
60	CHAP-Challenge	Contains the CHAP challenge sent by the NAS to a PPP CHAP user.
61	NAS-Port-Type	Indicates the type of physical port the NAS is using to authenticate the user. Physical ports are indicated by a numeric value, as follows: 0—Asynchronous 1—Synchronous 2—ISDN-Synchronous 3—ISDN-Asynchronous (V.120) 4—ISDN-Asynchronous (V.110) 5—Virtual
62	Port-Limit	Sets the maximum number of ports provided to the user by the NAS.
63	Login-LAT-Port	Defines the port to which the user is to be connected by LAT.
64	Tunnel-Type	Indicates the tunneling protocol(s) used. Cisco IOS Software supports two possible values for this attribute: L2TP and L2F. If this attribute is not set, L2F is used as a default.

Table 18-1 *ETF Attributes Supported on Cisco Routers for RADIUS Authorization (Continued)*

Number	IETF Attribute	Description
65	Tunnel-Medium-Type	Indicates the transport medium type to use to create a tunnel. This attribute has only one available value for this release: IP. If no value is set for this attribute, IP is used as the default.
66	Tunnel-Client-Endpoint	Contains the address of the initiator end of the tunnel.
67	Tunnel-Server-Endpoint	Indicates the address of the server end of the tunnel. The format of this attribute varies depending on the value of Tunnel-Medium-Type. Because this release supports only IP as a tunnel medium type, the IP address or the host name of LNS is valid for this attribute.
68	Acct-Tunnel-Connection-ID	Indicates the identifier assigned to the tunnel session. This attribute, along with the Tunnel-Client-Endpoint and Tunnel-Server-Endpoint attributes, may be used to provide a means to uniquely identify a tunnel session for auditing purposes.
69	Tunnel-Password	Defines the password to be used to authenticate to a remote server. This attribute is converted into different AAA attributes based on the value of Tunnel-Type: AAA_ATTR_l2tp_tunnel_pw (L2TP) AAA_ATTR_nas_password (L2F) AAA_ATTR_gw_password (L2F)
70	ARAP-Password	Identifies an Access-Request packet containing a Framed-Protocol of ARAP.
71	ARAP-Features	Includes password information that the NAS should send to the user in an ARAP "feature flags" packet.
72	ARAP-Zone-Access	Indicates how the ARAP zone list for the user should be used.
73	ARAP-Security	Identifies the ARAP security module to be used in an Access-Challenge packet.
74	ARAP-Security-Data	Contains the actual security module challenge or response. It can be found in Access-Challenge and Access-Request packets.
75	Password-Retry	Indicates how many times a user may attempt authentication before being disconnected.

continues

Table 18-1 *ETF Attributes Supported on Cisco Routers for RADIUS Authorization (Continued)*

Number	IETF Attribute	Description
76	Prompt	Indicates to the NAS whether it should echo the user's response as it is entered (0 = no echo, 1 = echo).
77	Connect-Info	Provides additional call information for modem calls. This attribute is generated in start and stop accounting records.
78	Configuration-Token	Indicates the type of user profile to be used. This attribute should be used in large distributed authentication networks based on proxy. It is sent from a RADIUS proxy server to a RADIUS proxy client in an Access-Accept; it should not be sent to a NAS.
79	EAP-Message	Encapsulates Extended Access Protocol (EAP) packets that allow the NAS to authenticate dial-in users via EAP without having to understand the EAP protocol.
80	Message-Authenticator	Prevents spoofing Access-Requests using CHAP, ARAP, or EAP authentication methods.
81	Tunnel-Private-Group-ID	Indicates the group ID for a particular tunneled session.
82	Tunnel-Assignment-ID	Indicates to the tunnel initiator the particular tunnel to which a session is assigned.
83	Tunnel-Preference	Indicates the relative preference assigned to each tunnel. This attribute should be included if the RADIUS server returns more than one set of tunneling attributes to the tunnel initiator.
84	ARAP-Challenge-Response	Contains the response to the challenge of the dial-in client.
85	Acct-Interim-Interval	Indicates the number of seconds between each interim update for this specific session. This value can appear only in the Access-Accept message.
86	Acct-Tunnel-Packets-Lost	Indicates the number of packets lost on a given link. This attribute should be included in Accounting-Request packets that contain an Acct-Status-Type attribute having the value Tunnel-Link-Stop.
87	NAS-Port-ID	Contains a text string that identifies the NAS port that is authenticating the user.
88	Framed-Pool	Contains the name of an assigned address pool that should be used to assign an address for the user. If the NAS does not support multiple address pools, it should ignore this attribute.

Table 18-1   *ETF Attributes Supported on Cisco Routers for RADIUS Authorization (Continued)*

Number	IETF Attribute	Description
90	Tunnel-Client-Auth-ID	Specifies the name used by the tunnel initiator (also known as the NAS) when authenticating tunnel setup with the tunnel terminator. Supports the L2F and L2TP protocols.
91	Tunnel-Server-Auth-ID	Specifies the name used by the tunnel terminator (also known as the home gateway) when authenticating tunnel setup with the tunnel initiator. Supports the L2F and L2TP protocols.
200	IETF-Token-Immediate	Determines how RADIUS treats passwords received from login users when their file entry specifies a handheld security card server. The value for this attribute is indicated by a numeric value, as follows: 0—No, meaning that the password is ignored 1—Yes, meaning that the password is used for authentication

In addition to the IETF AV pairs listed in Table 18-1, Cisco's implementations of RADIUS on routers also support the vendor-specific attributes. Table 18-2 contains a partial list of these attributes. Search for "Vendor-Proprietary RADIUS Attributes" on the CCO to reach the URL containing the complete list.

Table 18-2   *Vendor-Specific Attributes Supported on Cisco Routers for RADIUS Authorization*

Number	Vendor-Proprietary Attribute	Description
17	Change-Password	Specifies a request to change a user's password.
21	Password-Expiration	Specifies an expiration date for a user's password in the user's file entry.
194	Maximum-Time	Specifies the maximum length of time (in seconds) allowed for any session. After the session reaches the time limit, its connection is dropped.
195	Terminate-Cause	Reports details on why the connection was terminated.
208	PW-Lifetime	Lets you specify on a per-user basis the number of days a password is valid.

continues

Table 18-2 *Vendor-Specific Attributes Supported on Cisco Routers for RADIUS Authorization (Continued)*

Number	Vendor-Proprietary Attribute	Description
209	IP-Direct	Specifies in a user's file entry the IP address to which the Cisco router redirects packets from the user. When you include this attribute in a user's file entry, the Cisco router bypasses all internal routing and bridging tables and sends all packets received on this connection's WAN interface to the specified IP address.
210	PPP-VJ-Slot-Comp	Instructs the Cisco router not to use slot compression when sending VJ-compressed packets over a PPP link.
212	PPP-Async-Map	Gives the Cisco router the asynchronous control character map for the PPP session. The specified control characters are passed through the PPP link as data and used by applications running over the link.
217	IP-Pool-Definition	Defines a pool of addresses using the following format: $X\ a.b.c\ Z$ where X is the pool index number, $a.b.c$ is the pool's starting IP address, and Z is the number of IP addresses in the pool. For example, 3 10.0.0.1 5 allocates 10.0.0.1 through 10.0.0.5 for dynamic assignment.
218	Assign-IP-Pool	Tells the router to assign the user and IP address from the IP pool.
228	Route-IP	Indicates whether IP routing is allowed for the user's file entry.
233	Link-Compression	Defines whether to turn "stac" compression on or off over a PPP link.
234	Target-Util	Specifies the load-threshold percentage value for bringing up an additional channel when PPP multilink is defined.
235	Maximum-Channels	Specifies the allowed/allocatable maximum number of channels.
242	Data-Filter	Defines per-user IP data filters. These filters are retrieved only when a call is placed using a RADIUS outgoing profile or is answered using a RADIUS incoming profile. Filter entries are applied on a first-match basis; therefore, the order in which filter entries are entered is important.

Table 18-2 *Vendor-Specific Attributes Supported on Cisco Routers for RADIUS Authorization (Continued)*

Number	Vendor-Proprietary Attribute	Description
243	Call-Filter	Defines per-user IP data filters. On a Cisco router, this attribute is identical to the Data-Filter attribute.
244	Idle-Limit	Specifies the maximum time (in seconds) that any session can be idle. When the session reaches the idle time limit, its connection is dropped.

Accounting in RADIUS

RADIUS accounting works by sending messages at the start and end of sessions that contain information about the session. The RADIUS accounting functions allow data to be sent at the start and end of services, indicating the amount of resources (such as time, packets, bytes, and so on) among other things used during the session. The messages are sent using UDP port 1813.

RFC 2866 describes the accounting process for RADIUS as follows:

> When a client is configured to use RADIUS Accounting, at the start of service delivery it will generate an Accounting Start packet describing the type of service being delivered and the user it is being delivered to, and will send that to the RADIUS Accounting server, which will send back an acknowledgement that the packet has been received. At the end of service delivery the client will generate an Accounting Stop packet describing the type of service that was delivered and optionally statistics such as elapsed time, input and output octets, or input and output packets. It will send that to the RADIUS Accounting server, which will send back an acknowledgement that the packet has been received.
>
> The Accounting-Request (whether for Start or Stop) is submitted to the RADIUS accounting server via the network. It is recommended that the client continue attempting to send the Accounting-Request packet until it receives an acknowledgement, using some form of backoff. If no response is returned within a length of time, the request is re-sent a number of times. The client can also forward requests to an alternate server or servers in the event that the primary server is down or unreachable. An alternate server can be used either after a number of tries to the primary server fail, or in a round-robin fashion. Retry and fallback algorithms are the topic of current research and are not specified in detail in this document.
>
> The RADIUS accounting server MAY make requests of other servers in order to satisfy the request, in which case it acts as a client.
>
> If the RADIUS accounting server is unable to successfully record the accounting packet it MUST NOT send an Accounting-Response acknowledgment to the client.

The RADIUS accounting process works through the exchange of Accounting-Request and Accounting-Response messages between the RADIUS server and the NAS. The NAS, if configured to do so, sends the RADIUS server an Accounting-Request message at the start and end of a user session, as configured. The Start message contains information about the identity of the user and the type of service that is being offered to it. When the user session ends, the NAS sends a Stop message using the Accounting-Request packet to the server, informing the server of the type of service that was delivered to the user. This message can also contain further information about the user session. This information can be related to the amount of time the user was connected, the amount of data transmitted by the user, and so on.

The server responds to the Accounting-Request messages with an Accounting-Response message. This message informs the NAS that the information it sent in the Accounting-Request message has been recorded. Figure 18-4 shows the exchange of messages taking place for RADIUS accounting.

Figure 18-4 *RADIUS Accounting*

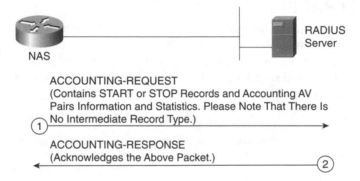

The Accounting information sent by the NAS to the server is sent using accounting AV pairs. These pairs work in a fashion very similar to how the RADIUS IETF authorization AV pairs work. Table 18-3 lists the RADIUS Accounting AV pairs that are supported on Cisco routers for various services offered through Cisco routers being used as NASs.

Table 18-3 *RADIUS IETF Accounting AV Pairs Supported on Cisco Routers*

Number	Attribute	Description
25	Class	An arbitrary value that the NAS includes in all accounting packets for this user if supplied by the RADIUS server.
30	Called-Station-Id	Allows the NAS to send the telephone number the user called as part of the Access-Request packet (using Dialed Number Identification [DNIS] or a similar technology). This attribute is supported only on ISDN and on modem calls on the Cisco AS5200 if used with PRI.
31	Calling-Station-Id	Allows the NAS to send the telephone number the call came from as part of the Access-Request packet (using Automatic Number Identification or a similar technology). This attribute has the same value as remote-addr from TACACS+. This attribute is supported only on ISDN and on modem calls on the Cisco AS5200 if used with PRI.

Table 18-3 *RADIUS IETF Accounting AV Pairs Supported on Cisco Routers (Continued)*

Number	Attribute	Description
40	Acct-Status-Type	Indicates whether this Accounting-Request marks the beginning (start) or end (stop) of the user service.
41	Acct-Delay-Time	Indicates how long, in seconds, the client has been trying to send a particular record.
42	Acct-Input-Octets	Indicates how many octets have been received from the port over the course of providing this service.
43	Acct-Output-Octets	Indicates how many octets have been sent to the port over the course of delivering this service.
44	Acct-Session-Id	A unique accounting identifier that makes it easy to match start and stop records in a log file. Acct-Session-Id numbers restart at 1 each time the router is power-cycled or the software is reloaded.
45	Acct-Authentic	Indicates how the user was authenticated, whether by RADIUS, the NAS itself, or another remote authentication protocol. This attribute is set to radius for users authenticated by RADIUS; to remote for TACACS+ and Kerberos; or to local for local, enable, line, and if-needed methods. For all other methods, this attribute is omitted.
46	Acct-Session-Time	Indicates how long, in seconds, the user has received service.
47	Acct-Input-Packets	Indicates how many packets have been received from the port over the course of providing this service to a framed user.
48	Acct-Output-Packets	Indicates how many packets have been sent to the port over the course of delivering this service to a framed user.
49	Acct-Terminate-Cause	Reports details on why the connection was terminated.
50	Acct-Multi-Session-Id	A unique accounting identifier used to link multiple related sessions in a log file. Each linked session in a multilink session has a unique Acct-Session-Id value but shares the same Acct-Multi-Session-Id.
51	Acct-Link-Count	Indicates the number of links known in a given multilink session at the time an accounting record is generated. The NAS can include this attribute in any accounting request that might have multiple links.
61	NAS-Port-Type	Indicates the type of physical port the NAS is using to authenticate the user.

In addition to these AV pairs, Cisco has its own vendor-specific accounting AV pairs. Most of these AV pairs are related to voice accounting.

Summary

RADIUS is a standardized protocol that can help you implement AAA functionality on Cisco devices. This chapter discussed how RADIUS is used to help perform AAA functions for a NAS. The RADIUS packet format was discussed, along with how it encrypts the user passwords for secrecy. We looked at the three aspects of AAA as they correspond to RADIUS. This chapter concludes the two chapters devoted to the discussion of the security server (AAA server) protocols that are supported on Cisco devices. The usefulness of these protocols, however, remains evident throughout the book.

Review Questions

1   What are VSAs?

2   What types of messages does the RADIUS protocol use in the authentication process?

3   What types of information are relayed from the RADIUS server during RADIUS authorization?

4   Which hashing algorithm is used to encrypt user passwords?

5   What is the Authenticator Request field?

6   What types of attributes can the Access-Reject packet carry?

This chapter covers the following key topics:

- **Using AAA to Provide Preshared Keys for IPsec**—This section talks about how AAA can be used to store preshared authentication keys for use by a router to do ISAKMP authentication.

- **Using AAA for X-Auth in ISAKMP**—This section covers how per-user authentication can be set up in ISAKMP using a AAA server.

- **Using AAA for Authentication Proxy (Auth-Proxy)**—This section discusses the role AAA plays in the authentication proxy feature.

- **Using AAA for VPDN**—This section talks about how AAA can be used to provide information to routers, allowing them to set up a VPDN tunnel.

- **Using AAA for Lock and Key**—This section discusses how the lock and key feature can be implemented using AAA.

- **Using AAA for Command Authorization**—This section talks about the use of AAA for limiting the privileges of various users to execute various commands on a router.

## CHAPTER 19

Special Cases of Using AAA for Implementing Security Features

This chapter looks at some specific case studies that use AAA. Chapter 16, "AAA," looked at a few common ways of using AAA, primarily associated with simple dialup scenarios. This chapter covers some unique scenarios in which the AAA functionality has been adapted to fulfill some very specific security needs.

Using AAA to Provide Preshared Keys for IPsec

AAA can be used to provide the preshared keys for authenticating ISAKMP in IPsec implementations. IPsec is covered in more detail in Chapter 13, "IPsec." This section concentrates on the authentication and authorization portion of this particular setup. This mechanism works only when using aggressive mode in ISAKMP. The ID (see Chapter 13) of the peer is used to query the AAA server for the tunnel attributes, i.e. the pre-shared secret. Please note that main mode cannot be used with this method because it does not allow the ID to be available in time for the AAA lookup to occur.

It is useful to have AAA provide the preshared key for two primary reasons:

- **Scalability**—Instead of maintaining a large number of keys for a large number of peers on a router itself, a RADIUS or TACACS+ server can be setup to maintain the keys.

- **Security**—Because the keys are stored on a server in a secure location, they are more protected than if they were to be stored on the router itself.

Example 19-1 shows the configuration needed to set up a router to use preshared keys stored on a RADIUS server for authentication. Example 19-2 shows the significant information from the RADIUS profile on the AAA server used for this setup. Figure 19-1 shows the network diagram for Example 19-1.

Figure 19-1 *Network Diagram for Example 19-1*

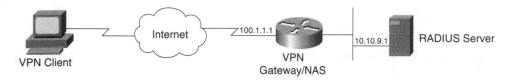

Example 19-1 *Setting Up a Router to Use Preshared Keys Stored on a RADIUS Server for Authentication*

```
Router#write terminal

aaa new-model
aaa authentication login default group radius

!The command below is used to turn on authorization for ISAKMP. This will allow the
!password on the RADIUS server to be used.
aaa authorization network ISAKMPauthorization group radius
!
crypto isakmp policy 10
 hash md5
 authentication pre-share
crypto isakmp client configuration address-pool local mypool
!
crypto ipsec transform-set myset esp-des esp-md5-hmac
!
crypto dynamic-map dynmap 10
 set transform-set myset
!
!The commands below bind the crypto map, intmap, to the method list,
!ISAKMPauthorization, meaning that authentications taking place for this crypto
!map need to use this method list.

crypto map intmap isakmp authorization list ISAKMPauthorization
crypto map intmap client configuration address initiate
crypto map intmap client configuration address respond
crypto map intmap 10 ipsec-isakmp dynamic dynmap
!
interface Serial0
 ip address 100.1.1.1 255.255.255.0
 crypto map intmap
!
ip local pool mypool 10.1.2.1 10.1.2.254

ip route 0.0.0.0 0.0.0.0 100.1.1.2
!
radius-server host 10.10.9.1 auth-port 1645 acct-port 1646 key cisco123
radius-server retransmit 3
radius-server timeout 10
!
```

Example 19-2 *Significant Information Needed in the RADIUS Profile on the AAA Server to Be Used by the Router Setup*

```
! The password 'cisco' is a special keyword for Cisco IOS, indicating a group profile
!must be referenced. This value should always be set to 'cisco'.
User = test
Password = "cisco"

Service Type = Outbound
Tunnel-type = IP Encapsulating Security Payload in the Tunnel-mode (ESP)
Tunnel-Medium-Type = IPv4

!The preshared key for ISAKMP authentication is defined below for the user test

Cisco-avpair = "ipsec:tunnel-password=pa55w0rd123"
Cisco-avpair = "ipsec:key-exchange=ike"
```

Examples 19-1 and 19-2 use scenarios in which a remote-access client connects to a router using aggressive mode. However, preshared keys stored on a AAA server can also be used in conjunction with site-to-site setups that don't involve remote-access clients. However, the version of IOS in these cases must support the use of aggressive mode.

Using AAA for X-Auth in ISAKMP

The PIX configuration in this section shows you how AAA is used to provide extended authentication (x-auth) for VPN users connecting to the PIX using IPsec.

A case of two users is shown in Example 19-3. Example 19-4 shows the TACACS+ profiles for these two users. In the case of UserA, the only thing that AAA provides is a username and password for authentication. But for UserB, AAA provides not only a username and password for authentication but also provides for authorization. Authorization comes in the form of deploying access list 110 for UserB after it has connected to the PIX.

See Part IV, "Virtual Private Networks," and Chapter 8, "PIX Firewall," for details on the non-AAA commands in this configuration.

Figure 19-2 shows the network topology for Example 19-3.

Figure 19-2 *Network Topology for Example 19-3*

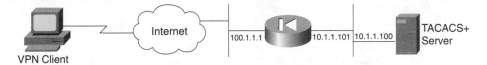

Example 19-3 *Setting Up a PIX to Use Keys Stored on a RADIUS Server for Extended Authentication for Remote-Access Clients*

```
pix#write terminal

PIX Version 5.2
nameif ethernet0 outside security0
nameif ethernet1 inside security100
enable password <removed> encrypted
passwd <removed> encrypted
hostname pix
<fixup commands removed to save space>
access-list 101 permit ip 10.1.1.0 255.255.255.0 192.168.1.0 255.255.255.0
!Access list 110 is used to deny access to the machine using  the IP address
!10.1.1.100 (the AAA server) for UserB. See the user profile of UserB to see how
!this access list is deployed.
access-list 110 deny ip any host 10.1.1.100

<logging commands removed to save space>
interface ethernet0 10baset
interface ethernet1 10baset

mtu outside 1500
mtu inside 1500
ip address outside 100.1.1.1 255.255.255.0
ip address inside 10.1.1.101 255.255.255.0
ip local pool test 192.168.1.1-192.168.1.254
<failover commands removed to save space>

arp timeout 14400
global (outside) 1 100.1.1.2
nat (inside) 0 access-list 101

Nat (inside) 1 10.1.1.0 255.255.255.0 0 0
timeout xlate 3:00:00
timeout conn 1:00:00 half-closed 0:10:00 udp 0:02:00 rpc 0:10:00 h323 0:05:00
sip 0:30:00 sip_media 0:02:00
timeout uauth 0:05:00 absolute
AAA-server TACACS+ protocol tacacs+
AAA-server RADIUS protocol radius
!The two commands below define the method list AuthInbound, which uses TACACS+ and
!the server sitting at 10.1.1.100 for AAA purposes.
AAA-server AuthInbound protocol tacacs+
AAA-server AuthInbound (inside) host 10.1.1.100 s1mpl15t1c timeout 5
<SNMP server commands removed to save space>
floodguard enable
sysopt connection permit-ipsec
no sysopt route dnat
crypto ipsec transform-set myset esp-des esp-md5-hmac
crypto dynamic-map dynmap 10 set transform-set myset
crypto map mymap 10 ipsec-isakmp dynamic dynmap
crypto map mymap client configuration address initiate
crypto map mymap client configuration address respond
```

Example 19-3 *Setting Up a PIX to Use Keys Stored on a RADIUS Server for Extended Authentication for Remote-Access Clients (Continued)*

```
!The command below ties the AAA method list AuthInbound to the crypto map mymap.
crypto map mymap client authentication AuthInbound
crypto map mymap interface outside
isakmp enable outside
isakmp key ******** address 0.0.0.0 netmask 0.0.0.0
isakmp identity address
isakmp client configuration address-pool local test outside

!The ISAKMP policy below works for Cisco VPN client 2.5 or CS-VPN client 1.1
isakmp policy 10 authentication pre-share
isakmp policy 10 encryption des
isakmp policy 10 hash md5
isakmp policy 10 group 1
isakmp policy 10 lifetime 86400
telnet timeout 5
ssh timeout 5
terminal width 80
: end
[OK]
```

Example 19-4 *Significant Information Needed in the TACACS+ Profile on the AAA Server to Be Used by the PIX Setup*

```
!The profile for User A simply provides a password for authentication.

user = userA
Password = clear "********"
!The profile for User B has an ACL defined in it, which is applied for User B
!when it successfully authenticates. Please see PIX configuration for ACL 110.

user = userB
password = clear "********"

Cisco-avpair = "acl=110"
```

Extended authentication using AAA generally needs to be set up for remote-access VPN clients that are not using digital certificates for authentication. Extended authentication provides additional security on top of the minimal security offered by the use of a wildcard preshared key, which is shared by all the VPN clients connecting to the IPsec gateway.

Using AAA for Auth-Proxy

Auth-proxy is a technique in which users passing through a router are authenticated using AAA mechanisms. Generally speaking, the router is set up with an access list that normally block the passage of users through the router to a private network behind it. However, with auth-proxy deployed, the users can get access to the network behind the router after they authenticate using AAA. Auth-proxy provides the mechanism through which the authentication takes place. After the authentication has occurred, the access list blocking access is modified to allow the authenticated user to go through. Example 19-5 shows the configuration needed to set up a router to do proxy authentication. Example 19-6 shows the accompanying RADIUS configuration on the AAA server. Figure 19-3 shows the network topology for Example 19-5.

Figure 19-3 *Network Topology for Example 19-5*

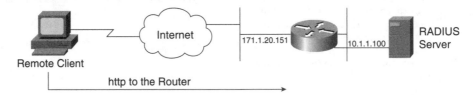

Example 19-5 *Setting Up a Router to Do Proxy Authentication*

```
router#write terminal

hostname router
!
aaa new-model
aaa group server radius PROXY
 server 10.1.1.100
!
aaa authentication login default group PROXY local

!The command below sets up auth-proxy authorization to take place. A special keyword
!'auth-proxy' is used to signify the type of authentication this method list is being
!setup for.
aaa authorization auth-proxy default group PROXY

enable secret 5 <removed>
enable password <removed>
!
ip subnet-zero
!
ip inspect name myfw ftp timeout 3600
ip inspect name myfw http timeout 3600
ip inspect name myfw udp timeout 15
ip inspect name myfw tcp timeout 3600
!The following command displays the name of the firewall router in the
!authentication proxy login page.
ip auth-proxy auth-proxy-banner
!This command sets the global authentication proxy idle timeout value in minutes.
!If the timeout expires, user authentication entries are removed, along with any
!associated dynamic access lists.
```

Example 19-5 *Setting Up a Router to Do Proxy Authentication (Continued)*

```
ip auth-proxy auth-cache-time 10
!The following command creates authentication proxy rules. This command associates
!connections initiating HTTP protocol traffic with an authentication proxy name--
!AUTHPROXY in this case.
ip auth-proxy name AUTHPROXY http

interface FastEthernet0/0
 ip address 171.1.20.151 255.255.255.0
 ip access-group 112 in
 ip nat outside
!The command below applies the auth-proxy rule created above to the FastEthernet0/0
!interface--the router's egress interface.

 ip auth-proxy AUTHPROXY
!
interface FastEthernet1/0
 ip address 10.1.1.1 255.255.255.0
 no ip directed-broadcast
 ip nat inside
 ip inspect myfw in
!
ip nat pool natpool 171.1.20.160 171.1.20.170 netmask 255.255.255.0
ip nat inside source list 1 pool natpool
ip nat inside source static 10.1.1.110 171.1.20.171

ip classless
ip route 0.0.0.0 0.0.0.0 171.1.20.150

no ip http server
!
access-list 1 permit 10.1.1.0 0.0.0.255
access-list 112 permit icmp any 171.1.20.0 0.0.0.255 unreachable
access-list 112 permit icmp any 171.1.20.0 0.0.0.255 echo-reply
access-list 112 permit icmp any 171.1.20.0 0.0.0.255 packet-too-big
access-list 112 permit icmp any 171.1.20.0 0.0.0.255 time-exceeded
access-list 112 permit icmp any 171.1.20.0 0.0.0.255 traceroute
access-list 112 permit icmp any 171.1.20.0 0.0.0.255 administratively-prohibited
access-list 112 permit icmp any 171.1.20.0 0.0.0.255 echo
access-list 112 deny ip any any

radius-server host 10.1.1.100
!
line con 0
 transport input none
line aux 0
line vty 0 4
 password <removed>
!
end
```

Example 19-6 uses RADIUS to set up a profile for UserA. After authentication, User A can access the network behind the router set up in Example 19-5 using TCP or UDP traffic.

The **proxyacl** entries define the user access privileges. After the user has successfully used the authentication proxy to log in, these entries are transferred to the firewall router. Each entry in the profile must specify permit access for a service or application.

The source address in each entry is set to **any**, which is replaced with the IP address of the authenticating host when the profile is downloaded to the firewall. The privilege level must be set to 15 for all AAA users.

Example 19-6 *Configuration Needed on the AAA Server to Work with the Auth-Proxy Configuration in Example 19-5*

```
user = userA
Password = "Cisco"

Cisco-avpair = "auth-proxy:priv-lvl=15"
!Based on the following ACLs, the user, userA, is set up to pass all TCP and UDP
!traffic after he or she has successfully authenticated
Cisco-avpair = "auth-proxy:proxyacl#1=permit tcp any any"
Cisco-avpair = "auth-proxy:proxyacl#2=permit udp any any"
```

The authentication proxy feature on Cisco routers monitors the level (number) of incoming HTTP requests. For each request, the authentication proxy prompts for the user's login credentials. A high number of open requests could indicate that the router is being subjected to a denial of service (DoS) attack. The authentication proxy limits the level of open requests and drops additional requests until the number of open requests has dropped below 40.

Using AAA for VPDN

Virtual Private Dialup Networking (VPDN) is a mechanism for allowing a private dialup network to be expanded so that users can dial up to a number of participating ISPs and have their sessions connected to their home gateways as if they were dialing directly into their home gateways rather than dialing into an ISP's network access server (NAS).

Participating ISPs' NASs are configured such that when a user who is identified as belonging to a particular private dialup network tries to connect to them using PPP, a connection with the user's home gateway is initiated. The NAS and the home gateway first authenticate each other as configured, and then the NAS passes the traffic from the user to the home gateway. The home gateway authenticates the user and proceeds to negotiate PPP with it. All this negotiation is done by passing the traffic back and forth between the home gateway and the NAS, with the NAS forwarding the messages from the home gateway to the user.

In Example 19-7, **NAS** is the ISP NAS that the user initially dials into. The router named **homegw** is the user's home gateway. Example 19-8 shows the profile set up on the TACACS+ server that the NAS is using. Example 19-9 shows the configuration needed to allow the home gateway for the user test@cisco.com to accept forwarded connections from the NAS set up in Example 19-7. Example 19-10 shows the profile saved on the AAA server for the home gateway. Figure 19-4 shows the network topology for Examples 19-7 through 19-10. Please see Chapter 12, "L2TP," for details on L2TP commands not explained in this case study.

Figure 19-4 *Network Topology for Examples 19-7 Through 19-10*

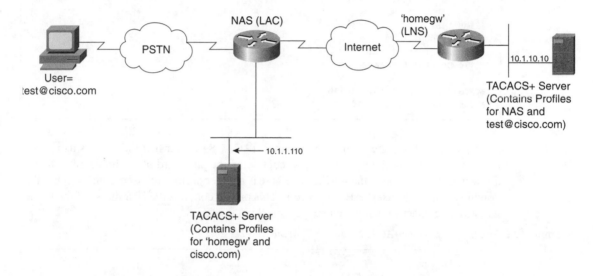

Example 19-7 *Setting Up a Router, NAS, to Forward Connections to a User's Home Gateway*

```
NAS#write terminal
  hostname NAS
  !
  aaa new-model

  aaa authentication ppp default group tacacs+ local
  aaa authorization network group tacacs+

  enable password <removed>
  !
!The following command turns on VPDN on the router.

  vpdn enable
  !
```

continues

Example 19-7 *Setting Up a Router, NAS, to Forward Connections to a User's Home Gateway (Continued)*

```
  interface Ethernet0
   ip address 10.1.1.2 255.255.255.0
   !
  interface Async7
   ip unnumbered Ethernet0

   encapsulation ppp
   async mode dedicated
   no peer default ip address
   no cdp enable
   ppp authentication chap
   !
  line 1 8
   modem InOut
   transport input all
   flowcontrol hardware
   !
tacacs-server host 10.1.1.110
tacacs-server key s1mpl15t1c
```

Example 19-8 shows the profile set up on the TACACS+ server that the NAS is using. It contains a profile for the user 'homegw' containing the password of the home gateway to allow it to authenticate to the NAS. Also, there is another profile for cisco.com, which is the domain name of the user test@cisco.com. This profile contains the IP address of the home gateway to contact for users that supply this domain name.

Example 19-8 *Profile Set Up on the TACACS+ Server That the NAS Is Using*

```
user = homegw {
        chap  = cleartext "foo"
        }

user = cisco.com {
                service = ppp protocol = vpdn {
                        tunnel-type = l2tp
                        tunnel-id = NAS
                        ip-addresses = 10.1.10.1
                        }
   }
```

Example 19-9 *Configuration That Allows the Home Gateway for the User test@cisco.com to Accept Forwarded Connections from the NAS Set Up in Example 19-7*

```
homegw#write terminal
  hostname homegw
  !
  aaa new-model
```

Example 19-9 *Configuration That Allows the Home Gateway for the User test@cisco.com to Accept Forwarded Connections from the NAS Set Up in Example 19-7 (Continued)*

```
  aaa authentication ppp default group tacacs+ local

  enable password <removed>
  !
  vpdn enable
!The command below sets up the home gateway to use virtual template 1 to clone an
!interface for the user connecting via the VPDN connection.
  vpdn incoming NAS homegw virtual-template 1
  !
  interface Ethernet0
   ip address 10.1.10.1 255.255.255.0
   !
  interface Virtual-Template1
   ip unnumbered Ethernet0
   peer default ip address pool test
   ppp authentication chap
   !
  tacacs-server host 10.1.10.10
  tacacs-server key c15c0123

ip local pool test 150.1.1.1 150.1.1.254
```

Example 19-10 shows the profile saved on the AAA server for the home gateway. It contains the username and the NAS's password to authenticate it, as well as a profile to authenticate the user test@cisco.com.

Example 19-10 *Profile Saved on the AAA Server for the Home Gateway*

```
user = NAS {
        chap = cleartext "foo"
        }


user = test@cisco.com {
        chap = cleartext "cisco"

        service = ppp protocol = lcp { }
        service = ppp protocol = ip { }
}
```

Some of the previous configurations on the AAA server can also be done locally on the router. However, in order for an ISP to support a large number of customers and their end users, it is often necessary to use AAA servers to store profiles.

Using AAA for Lock and Key

Lock and key is a feature similar to auth-proxy. When this feature is configured, a user trying to gain access to the network behind the router is normally blocked due to an access list on the router's egress interface (access list 102 in this case). However, with lock and key configured, the user can first Telnet to the router, which prompts the user for authentication. If the authentication succeeds, the router reconfigures the incoming access list to temporarily allow the user to gain access to the network behind it. Example 19-11 shows the configuration needed on a router to setup Lock and Key. Figure 19-5 shows the network diagram for Example 19-11.

Figure 19-5 *Network Diagram for Example 19-11*

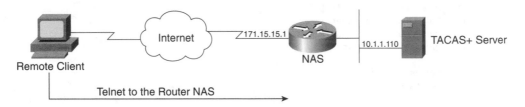

Example 19-11 *Setting Up a Router to Enable Lock and Key*

```
Router#write terminal

aaa new-model
!The command below sets up TACACS+ authentication for users trying to log in to the
!router.
!This allows users who Telnet into a router to be authenticated via the lock and
!key feature, enabling the user to initiate connections into the network to which
!access is normally blocked due to ACL 102.
aaa authentication login default group tacacs+ local

enable password <removed>
!
isdn switch-type basic-dms100
!
interface ethernet0
ip address 10.1.1.1 255.255.255.0
!
interface BRI0
 ip address 171.15.15.1 255.255.255.0
 encapsulation ppp
 dialer idle-timeout 3600
 dialer wait-for-carrier-time 100
 dialer map ip 171.15.15.2 name userA
```

Example 19-11 *Setting Up a Router to Enable Lock and Key (Continued)*

```
 dialer-group 1
 isdn spid1 <removed>
  ppp authentication chap
 ip access-group 102 in
 !
 access-list 102 permit tcp any host 171.15.15.1 eq telnet
 !The dynamic access list set up below allows the authenticated user to have
 !complete IP access after he or she has authenticated via TACACS+.
 access-list 102 dynamic LIST timeout 5 permit ip any any
 !
 ip route 0.0.0.0 0.0.0.0 171.15.15.2

 tacacs-server host 10.1.1.110
 tacacs-server key s1mpl15t1c
 !
 dialer-list 1 protocol ip permit
 !
 line con 0
 line aux 0
 line VTY 0 4
 !The access-enable command configured below is used to turn on lock and key when
 !the users Telnet to the router. Please note that the access-enable command can be
 !set up as part of the user profile on the TACACS+ server as well, limiting the
 !users who will have the lock and key feature offered to them.
  autocommand access-enable host timeout 5

 password C15c01231nc
```

In general, authentication proxy is taking over the functionality of the lock and key feature set in most new network implementations. Nevertheless, the lock and key example is a standard AAA-based configuration that you need to understand.

Using AAA for Command Authorization

Command authorization is a Cisco IOS feature that allows privilege levels to be established for various users who need to have shell access to a router for administrative purposes. Based on the users' AAA profiles, a router can allow users to execute only the set of commands for which they are authorized while stopping them from executing all other commands. This is a very important feature in environments where there is a need to allow various users to access the routers but where control needs to be exercised to prevent intentional or unintentional abuses to the router setup. Example 19-12 shows how to set up command authorization on a router.

Example 19-12 *Setting Up Command Authorization on a Router*

```
Router#write terminal

aaa new-model

aaa authentication login default group tacacs+ enable

!The following command sets the authentication for enable (privileged mode) on a
!per-user basis, to first the TACACS+ and then to the enable password in case the
!TACACS+ server is unavailable.

aaa authentication enable default group tacacs+ enable

!The following command sets up authorization for the EXEC shell. An EXEC shell
!authorization decides whether the user is permitted to even start an EXEC shell.
!This is needed to do command authorization.

aaa authorization exec default group tacacs+

!The following two commands set up command authorization for commands at level 1
!and level 15. Note that you simply define two levels and not more because you can
!define in the AAA server profile what each level means for each user. For example,
!a level 15 for Jack might mean that Jack can do only show run, whereas for Jane
!the same level 15 might mean that she can do anything she wants to on the router.

aaa authorization commands 1 default group tacacs+
aaa authorization commands 15 default group tacacs+

!The following command sets up accounting for the EXEC sessions to the router for
!start and stop records.

aaa accounting exec default start-stop group tacacs+

!The following command sets up accounting for the EXEC sessions to the router such
!that for each command belonging to privilege level 1 or 15, an accounting record
!is sent to the AAA server. This allows for the complete activity of a user on
!the router to be logged. Note that this functionality, known as command
!accounting, is available only via TACACS+ and is fairly CPU-intensive. (It should
!be turned on only after you thoroughly understand its impact on a router's
!performance.)

aaa accounting command 1 default start-stop group tacacs+
aaa accounting command 15 default start-stop group tacacs+
```

By default, the router has three command levels:

- Privilege level 0 includes the **disable**, **enable**, **exit**, **help**, and **logout** commands.
- Privilege level 1 includes all user-level commands at the router> prompt.
- Privilege level 15 includes all enable-level commands at the router# prompt.

Using the AAA server, you can modify the default meanings of these privilege levels for specific users to be more or less restrictive than their defaults. Example 19-13 shows what the user profiles on a TACACS+ AAA server look like.

Example 19-13 *Setting Privilege Levels on the AAA Server for Users Needing Varying Degrees of Control Over the Router Setup*

```
!UserA is assigned level 15. Level 15 for him/her means that he/she can perform all
!commands permitted by default for level 15.

User Profile Information
user = userA{
password = clear "********"

service=shell {
set priv-lvl=15
default cmd=permit
default attribute=permit
}
}
!UserB can perform only the default level 0 commands (disable, enable, exit, help,
!and logout)

User Profile Information
user = userB{
password = clear "********"

service=shell {
set priv-lvl=0
}
}
!While UserC, like User A, also gets privilege level 15, his/her level 15 privilege
!is limited to only the show run command

User Profile Information
user = userC{
password = clear "********"

service=shell {
set priv-lvl=15
cmd=show {
permit "run"
}
}
}
```

With simple EXEC authorization, you have to define the various command levels (from 1 to 15) on the router. These are global. So you can give a certain level of command authorization to someone, such as John, so that he can perform commands at privilege level 7. You also can define what level 7 means. But if there are 50 people to whom you want to give different levels of access, you can define only 15 different levels. So the level of granularity is not as much as you would want. With command authorization, you can define per-user commands that a user is authorized to carry out. For example, you can set up a profile that says that John can do only pings to 150.1.1.1 and nothing more. This allows for much more granularity and control over who can do what on a router.

Summary

This chapter looked at some examples of how AAA can be used in various situations in cohesion with various other Cisco IOS features to allow enhanced security. We discussed how AAA can help the authentication processes involved in IKE negotiating IPsec-based tunnels, as well as how AAA can be used in VPDN and auth-proxy scenarios. We also looked at an example of how command authorization can be set up to control administrative access to a router. AAA is becoming more and more pervasive in the various features that are being implemented in Cisco OSs. Therefore, it is important to get a feel for how it is implemented in conjunction with the various features discussed in this chapter. Similar setups are used to bridge other features with the AAA functionality.

Review Questions

1 What functionality does auth-proxy provide?

2 Which command enables the lock and key feature on a router?

3 How does a NAS participating in a VPDN setup find out the IP address of the home gateway?

4 What is the purpose of command authorization?

5 What commands are allowed by default for a user authorized at privilege level 1?

# PART V

Service Provider Security

This chapter covers the following key topics:

- **Motivation for Having Service Provider Security**—This section discusses the motivation behind having security at the service provider level.

- **Key Components of Service Provider Security**—This section defines some of the main components that go into building a secure service provider network.

## CHAPTER 20

Benefits and Challenges of Service Provider Security

Service providers can often help supplement their customers' security infrastructure. Various ways and means available to the service providers can be used for this purpose. This chapter looks at some of the reasons why it is important for service providers to be part of the security process in place for their customers. We will look at the benefits such an arrangement provides, as well as look at some of the challenges that such a setup presents to the service providers. We will use the motivation built from the discussion in this chapter and move in the next three chapters to a more specific discussion of some of the tools service providers can use to implement security. The discussion of routing protocol security in Chapter 4, "Secure Routing," covered some of the facets of service provider security by covering how to securely set up various routing protocols, including BGP.

Motivation for Having Service Provider Security

For the purpose of this discussion, a *service provider* is defined as a large network entity that is responsible for providing network services to smaller network entities. Service providers of various sizes peer with each other to form what is known as the Internet. The reason for having this discussion is that although much security is implemented on edge networks, such as small to medium-sized corporate networks, there is a need to enhance the amount of security provided by the service provider, allowing these corporate networks to connect to each other via larger networks (the Internet) in a more secure manner. The reasons for enabling this kind of security on service provider networks are manifold. Many of these reasons are addressed in the following sections.

The Ability to Stop and Deflect Attacks

It is sometimes easier to stop attacks on the service provider level than at the edge network level. This is evident in the case of attacks that gather strength as they pass through networks (the snowball effect). It is far easier to stop these attacks at their earlier stages than at the later stages, when they have gained more strength. One example of this is a smurf attack. The best place to stop a smurf attack is from the network where the attack is being launched. If the service provider has made sure that spoofed addresses are not allowed to pass through its network devices, the possibility of a smurf attack's being launched becomes very small.

Chapter 21, "Using Access Control Lists Effectively," has more details on how to implement this type of security. Another type of attack in which service providers can restrict the spread of an attack is the distributed denial of service (DDoS) attack. Mechanisms can be set up to control the spread of networks, such TFN and Trinoo, that are set up to launch such attacks.. By setting up these types of mechanisms, the service provider can stop these kinds of DDOS networks from becoming more widespread by spreading to other networks and customers connected by the service provider. Chapter 22, "Using NBAR to Identify and Control Attacks," and Chapter 23, "Using CAR to Control Attacks," have more details on mechanisms service providers can use to control these types of setups.

Another role that service providers are sometimes asked to play is to deflect an attack from the intended victim. This is often done in the case of denial of service (DoS) attacks. When a DoS attack threatens to overwhelm the victim's capabilities or starts dramatically exhausting the bandwidth that the victim shares with other hosts, the service provider can sometimes be called upon to set up a *sinkhole*. A sinkhole (also known as a *Honey Pot*) is simply a router with much bandwidth and significant resources that starts advertising the victim host's IP address into the network as its own. The result is that the attack's traffic is sent to the sinkhole router rather than to the intended victim. Although this means that the legitimate traffic intended for the victim host is also sent to the sinkhole, this technique allows the bandwidth on the link to the victim host to be made available to other hosts sharing that bandwidth. The service provider can then also analyze the information collected by the sinkhole router. This information can be used to block the attack traffic close to the attack's point of origin (if possible). Figure 20-1 shows how a sinkhole router is used to deflect an attack from the intended victim and its network.

Here is a description of the steps shown in Figure 20-1:

Step 1   The attacker sends traffic destined for the victim IP address, 150.1.1.1.

Step 2   The service provider edge router receives the traffic. Based on routing information for the 150.1.1.1/24 subnet, it forwards the traffic to the router on the edge of the customer network.

Step 3   The edge router forwards the traffic to the victim, overwhelming the victim and possibly the link from the customer network to the service provider network.

Step 4   Upon being notified of the attack, the service provider sets up the honey pot to advertise the 150.1.1.1 host route to the rest of the network.

Step 5   The edge router starts forwarding traffic intended for the 150.1.1.1 address to the sink hole instead of the victim.

Service providers generally also have more technical know-how and networking skills to thwart an attack than the end users. This is another reason to use service providers to stop network attacks rather than relying on end users to have the knowledge of how to do so. Of course, this is not possible in all cases.

Figure 20-1 *A Sinkhole Router in a Service Provider Network Deflecting an Attack from the Intended Victim*

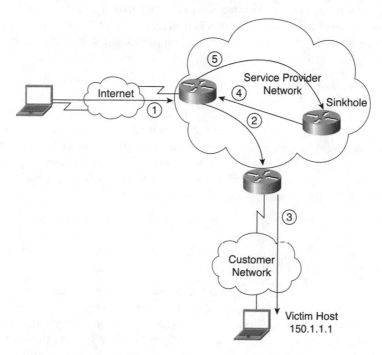

The Ability to Track Traffic Patterns

Due to the large volume of traffic that service providers handle, it is sometimes possible for them to identify patterns that can indicate an attack at an early stage, especially in cases when attacks get started on a disparate range of end networks. Malicious traffic at the early stages of these attacks, might not be sufficiently large on these individual networks for them to diagnose themselves the start of an attack. The IDS on a customer's network, set up at many different places, might see only small quantities of the malicious traffic, which might not trigger an alarm. However, the ISP can see the accumulation of all this malicious traffic and thus might be in a better position to detect this type of attack.

The Ability to Track Down the Source of the Attack

Service providers' large networks make it easier for them to track the source of an attack. Of course, many network attacks do not lend themselves to this kind of detective work. They might also have footprints across quite a few service provider networks.

Tracing attacks is often not easy. Many attacks are sourced from spoofed addresses. Even when it is not spoofed, the source address is often that of a host that has been compromised by the attacker to use for the attack. However, in both of these cases, it can help greatly to be able to get as close as possible to the source of the attack. After this is done, you can investigate further to discover the real source of the attack.

Service providers can use various techniques to try to track the source of network attacks, especially DoS attacks. An attack that is launched from a compromised host where the attacker has not tried to spoof the source address is somewhat easier to track. Often the cooperation of multiple service providers must be sought because the compromised machine might sit across quite a few service provider networks. Often, issues concerning the legality of tracking attackers across networks in certain countries can also arise in such situations. The process of tracking the source address is often done hop by hop, tracing the source address back to the often-compromised host.

When the attacker uses spoofed IP addresses, tracking is much more difficult. However, certain techniques have been developed that help a service provider point out where malicious traffic is entering its network, irrespective of what source address it is coming from. One such technique is known as *backscatter traceback*.

Backscatter traceback is done through a series of steps on the routers in the service provider network. The first step is setting up a static route on all routers, sending all the traffic destined for the 'test' network to Null 0. The test network is any address range that is not being used anywhere in the service provider network. Whenever these routers receive a packet they need to route to the test network, they drop the packet, because it is to be routed to the Null interface, and send an ICMP unreachable message to the source IP address.

The next requirement is to set up a sinkhole router that advertises the IANA unallocated network range to the service provider network. This is a range that IANA has not allocated to anyone. It is often used by attackers as a spoofed source address. Note that once the actual attack has started, this range may need to be modified based on the actual spoofed address range the attacker is using. Care is taken at this juncture not to leak this advertisement outside the service provider network (because this range cannot legally be used to route traffic).

When the attacker launches an attack on the victim and the service provider is notified of the attack, the service provider sets up the sinkhole router to advertise the victim's host IP address to the service provider network, with the next hop set to the 'test' network. The edge router serves as the ingress point into the service provider network for the attacker's traffic. Based on this routing information, the edge router starts dropping the traffic destined for the victim IP address, because it thinks that its next hop is the test network. The test network, as previously stated, is routed to Null 0.

In addition, if the attacker is using the IANA unallocated range of addresses as the spoofed source address, the edge router generates ICMP unreachable messages and sends them to the source IP addresses. Because the sinkhole router has already advertised these unallocated addresses as belonging to it, these ICMP unreachables are sent to the sinkhole router. These ICMP unreachables contain the IP address of the edge router that originated them. In this way, the network administrator on the sinkhole router can figure out which edge router is the entry point for the attack traffic. By repeating this process on the service provider to which the edge router connects, the attacker can be traced even if it is using spoofed IP addresses.

Figure 20-2 shows how backscatter traceback works.

Figure 20-2 *Using Backscatter Traceback to Trace Attacks Carried Out Using Spoofed IP Addresses*

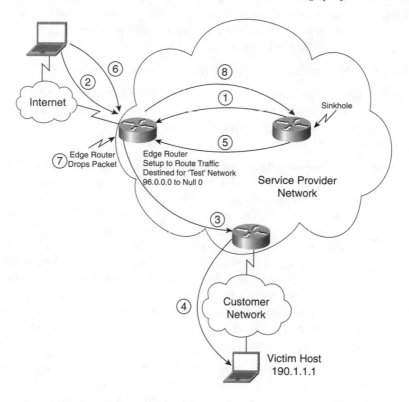

Here is a description of the steps shown in Figure 20-2:

Step 1   The sinkhole advertises the IANA unallocated network range to the service provider network as belonging to itself. Note that once the actual attack has started the network administrator may need to modify this address range to reflect the actual IP address range the attacker is using to spoof its packets. Also, the Edge Routers are setup to route traffic destined for the 'Test' Network 96.0.0.0 to the Null 0 interface.

Step 2   The attacker sends packets to the victim host at 190.1.1.1 with the source IP address spoofed as one of the IANA unallocated addresses.

Step 3   The service provider edge router receives the traffic. Based on routing information for the 190.1.1.0/24 subnet, it forwards the traffic to the router on the edge of the customer network.

Step 4   The edge router forwards the traffic to the victim, overwhelming the victim and possibly the link from the customer network to the service provider network.

Step 5   Upon being notified of the attack, the service provider sets up the sinkhole to advertise 190.1.1.1 to the rest of the network, with the 'test' network, 96.0.0.0, set as the next hop.

Step 6   The attacker continues sending traffic to the victim host.

Step 7   The edge router, upon seeing a packet from the attacker destined for 190.1.1.1, tries to route it to the test network. Upon doing a lookup for the test network, it finds that the next hop is set to Null 0. Therefore, it drops the packet.

Step 8   Upon dropping the packet, the edge router prepares to send an ICMP unreachable message to the dropped packet's source IP address. The source IP address has been spoofed and, as described earlier, is an address from the IANA unallocated range. Because the sinkhole router has been advertising this address range as belonging to itself, the edge router, looking at its routing table, sends the ICMP unreachable message to the sinkhole router. By looking at the sinkhole router's logs and seeing where the ICMP unreachable message is coming from, the network administrator can tell exactly where the entry point is for the attacker in his network. This process can be repeated for the other service provider that connects the attacker entry point router to the rest of the Internet until the source of the attack can be discovered.

It is interesting to note that this method and its variations need the service provider to be ready to implement the method before an attack occurs. In addition, the service provider might need to adjust the range of addresses that the sinkhole router advertises as belonging to it. This change is done by looking at the source address space the attacker is using as spoofed addresses. Both these factors require that the service provider have a written plan in place that its network administrators can execute efficiently and quickly with a fair amount of flexibility to counter attacks on their customers' networks.

Challenges of Implementing Security at the Service Provider Level

Despite the reasons for having security at the service provider level, it is not always easy or meaningful to attempt to do so. There are often difficulties and challenges in implementing security at the service provider level.

Due to the diverse nature of traffic passing through a service provider's network, it is difficult to implement policies to look for certain kinds of traffic to block or identify as an attack. What might be good traffic for one user of the service provider might be a network attack for another set of users. Although some types of attacks are generic enough to be malicious to all kind of networks, it is difficult to classify traffic in all cases for all kinds of end users.

Other types of challenges surround performance as well. For example, since one of primary goals a service provider has is to pass traffic as fast and accurately as possible, security implementations on service provider routers and other network devices can become a potential bottleneck and can affect performance. There often needs to be a trade-off between performance and the need to have service provider security.

It is interesting to note that typical ISPs do not filter traffic or carry out other security-related operations for a customer unless the customer asks them to do so. Therefore, it is important for the customers to be aware of the service provider's capabilities and use them proactively as well as in reactive situations.

For service providers, security implementations can also mean an added source of revenue. In addition, some of the techniques and implementations that are necessary for a service provider to provide various types of security to its customers (such as NBAR and CAR), can also be used for traffic monitoring and traffic engineering. These types of implementations can allow the service provider to further customize its services and enhance its revenues. In essence, the process of enabling security in a service provider's networks can have a beneficial cumulative effect on the constituent parts of the ISP's entire operation.

To summarize, although providing security to its customers might be challenging for a service provider in some respects, in the emerging networking environment, which places greater emphasis on security, service providers often are expected to treat security as a necessary service they provide.

Key Components of Service Provider Security

Service provider security implementations can be broken down into the following main components:

- Securing the routing decisions made on the service provider routers.
- Device security of the service provider's network components.

- Auditing of the logs on service provider routers for prosecution and attack-detection purposes. When collected using some of the traceback mechanisms discussed in this chapter, these logs can be used to trace the source of an attack.

- Use of access-control mechanisms to block certain types of DoS attacks.

- Use of pattern-detection techniques to identify malicious content in the traffic traversing the service provider network. The traffic can be dropped, or rate-limiting techniques can be used to control its amount.

Securing routing decisions and device security were discussed in detail in Chapters 3 and 4. The chapters following this look at the mechanisms available to implement some of the service provider security components described in this chapter.

Summary

Service provider security is increasingly becoming an important service offered by service providers. Indeed, some elements of security are better implemented by the service provider then by the end customers on edge networks. In general, it is important for service providers to be prepared with techniques such as using a sinkhole router to help customers who are under attack. The more security capability a service provider has, the more likely that its other services will not be disrupted in the event of an attack.

This chapter described what service provider security means and why it is needed. We covered a general overview of some of the benefits of service provider security and also looked at the difficulties associated with such implementations. We have laid the groundwork for a more detailed discussion of some of the more specific elements of service provider security. The next three chapters look at three important features available on Cisco routers that service providers can use to provide various types of services to their customers.

Review Questions

1 What is a sinkhole router?

2 What is backscatter traceback?

3 Why are unallocated IP addresses often used in DoS attacks?

4 Where is the best place to stop a smurf attack?

5 What is the purpose of logging on service provider devices?

This chapter covers the following key topics:

- **Overview of Access Control Lists**—This section gives a brief overview of how access control lists work.

- **Using Access Control Lists to Stop Unauthorized Access**—This section discusses how access control lists can be used to stop unauthorized access to a network.

- **Using Access Control Lists to Recognize Denial of Service Attacks**—This section discusses how access control lists can be used to identify and track network attacks.

- **Using Access Control Lists to Stop Denial of Service Attacks**—This section discusses how access control lists can be used to stop attacks.

- **IP Fragment Handling by Access Control Lists**—This section discusses how ACLs handle IP fragments. We will also discuss the network attacks associated with IP fragments and how ACLs deal with them.

- **Performance Impact of Access Control Lists**—This section looks at how ACL processing can affect a router's performance. We'll also look at some ways to improve the processing speed of ACLs.

- **Turbo Access Control Lists**—This section discusses the turbo ACL feature, which can be used to greatly enhance the performance of large ACLs under a heavy load.

- **NetFlow Switching and Access Control Lists**—This section looks at how NetFlow switching is used to enhance the performance of access control lists.

## CHAPTER 21

Using Access Control Lists Effectively

Access control lists (ACLs) are a basic access control mechanism available on Cisco routers to allow traffic filtering. Although this chapter is in Part VII, "Service Provider Security," the information here is useful for the usage of access control lists in any environment. ACLs are often used in conjunction with a variety of features. This chapter looks at their most important functions—recognizing various types of traffic passing through a router and filtering traffic entering or leaving a router. We will also look specifically at how ACL traffic characterization capabilities can be used to recognize and thwart certain types of network attacks. Although ACLs give service providers some useful functionality to offer to their customers, they often have a performance impact on the router they are deployed on, especially when they contain a large number of entries. The last two sections of this chapter discuss two mechanisms available to improve the performance of ACLs on routers.

Overview of Access Control Lists

Access control lists are essentially traffic filters that are used on routers to identify specific kinds of packets based on a packet attribute, such as the IP address. Access control lists can then be used to take specific actions after the packets have been identified, such as stopping them from passing through a specific interface.

Access control lists are comprised of a series of Access Control Elements (ACEs), each of which is a single rule designed to match a particular type of packet. An access list is a set of ACEs grouped and identified via a number or a name. An ACE defines the protocol it watches out for, any protocol options that are associated with that protocol, and whether the matching traffic is permitted or denied. A permit or a deny by the ACE does not necessarily mean that the traffic is stopped from passing through the router. That decision is based on how the ACL is applied to the router.

Access control lists work by identifying traffic that is passing through the router based on the ACEs. The ACL functionality is turned on by applying the access list to an interface using an access group, turning on debugs based on the access list, or referencing the ACL in some other fashion, such as through a route map or Network Address Translation (NAT) configuration. When the traffic passing through a router matches one of the ACEs of an

ACL that has been referenced in this manner, the action defined in the referencing configuration takes place based on whether the ACE has a permit or a deny in it. Generally, if the traffic matches an ACE and the ACE specifies permitting the traffic, the action associated with the configuration referencing the ACE takes place. For example, if the ACL is referenced by a **debug** command, the debugs for the traffic matching the ACL as defined by the **debug** command are displayed. Or if the ACL is referenced by an access group, traffic is forwarded or dropped based on whether it is permitted or denied by the ACE it matches.

This section discusses ACLs from the perspective of using them on a Cisco router. However, note that the PIX Firewall also uses ACLs in a similar fashion as the routers. In addition, switches use ACLs such as VLAN ACLs. Also, there are types of ACLs other than the IP ACLs we discuss in this chapter. We will focus our discussion on IP ACLs, because these ACLs can be used most beneficially by service providers to provide some level of protection to their customers.

Types of ACLs

IP ACLs fall into two main categories based on their functionality:

- Standard access
- Extended access

Standard IP ACLs use source addresses for matching operations. Extended IP ACLs use source and destination addresses for matching operations and optional protocol type information for finer granularity of control.

An example of a standard access list is shown in Example 21-1.

Example 21-1 *Standard ACL*

```
access-list 10 deny 150.1.1.0 0.0.0.255
```

This access control list denies traffic with a source IP address contained in the subnet 150.1.1.0/24. The mask specified at the end of this **access-list** command is a wildcard mask, meaning that it is the opposite of the normal mask used for IP addressing. 0s in a wildcard mask specify the corresponding relevant bits in the IP address, and 1s in a wildcard mask specify the corresponding bits in the IP address that are unimportant for getting a match against this access list.

Figure 21-1 shows how standard ACLs are processed on a router's interface. As you can see, for the purpose of restricting traffic passing through an interface, the application of an access group to an interface in a specific direction is the toggle switch for turning ACL processing on or off in this manner. No more than one ACL can be applied to an interface in a given direction.

Figure 21-1 *Using Standard ACLs to Restrict Traffic from Passing Through a Router Interface*

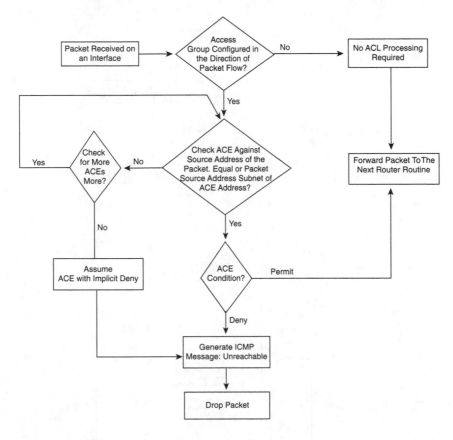

Example 21-2 shows an extended access control list. In this example, the host 100.1.1.1 is allowed to access the web server at 200.1.1.1 on port 80 (HTTP). However, all other traffic is denied. Masks are used in extended access lists the same way they are used in standard access lists.

Example 21-2 *Extended ACL*

```
access-list 100 permit tcp host 100.1.1.1 host 200.1.1.1 eq 80
access-list 100 deny ip host 100.1.1.1  host 200.1.1.1
```

The **host** keyword is typically used in place of a wildcard mask of 0.0.0.0.

Extended access lists use the numbers 100 to 199, whereas standard access lists use the numbers 1 to 99.

Figure 21-2 shows how extended ACLs are processed on a router's interface.

Figure 21-2 *Using Extended ACLs to Restrict Traffic from Passing Through a Router Interface*

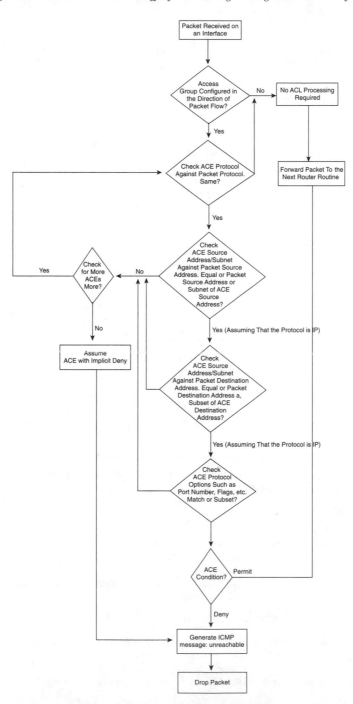

See the Cisco IOS command reference for more details on how to configure ACLs.

Features and Characteristics of ACLs

Some of the main features and characteristics of ACLs on Cisco routers are described in this section. ACEs and ACLs constitute the bulk of these characteristics.

ACE Order Based on the Necessity of a Match

ACLs are processed in a top-down fashion. The processing stops when a match is found. (Also see the section "IP Fragment Handling by ACLs.") Therefore, it is important to set up the ACEs in such a manner that host-specific entries occur first, subnet matches occur next, then classful network matches, and at the very end ACEs for "any" matches. This is important. If the intent of an ACL is to allow a specific host from a subnet and to disallow the rest of the subnet and the ACEs have been configured with the subnet entry before the specific host entry, the subnet entry gets matched first and no more ACEs are processed. The subnet ACE is applied for the specific host that was to be allowed based on the next ACE (which never got processed).

ACE Order Based on the Likelihood of a Match

ACLs are processed in a top-down manner, meaning that the entries listed on the top of the access list as shown in the router configuration are processed first. Then the rest of the entries are processed one by one if the first entry does not match the type of traffic being examined. The processing of the access list(s) stops when a match is made. Due to this characteristic of ACLs, it is useful to configure the entries that are more likely to be matched toward the top an access list. However, this must be done keeping in mind the principle described in the section "ACE Order Based on the Necessity of a Match". This can save some CPU consumption. As a rule of thumb, the performance impact of an extended access list increases linearly with an increasing number of entries in the access list.

Implicit Deny ACE

Any defined access list has an implied **deny all** at the end of all the ACL's configured entries. This means that if none of the criteria in the access list are matched, the packet being examined is considered to be denied. The exception to this rule is an access list that is being referenced but for which no entry has been configured. In this case, the access list is considered to contain a single entry of **permit all**.

ACL Processing in a Distributed Environment

In the case of a router with an RSP and a VIP card, the VIP can do the ACL processing provided that dCEF is configured on the router. However, if logging is configured for the hits made to an access list using the **log** keyword at the end of the access list, the RSP still needs to process the logging functionality.

ACL ACE Addition Order

ACLs are not the easiest-to-maintain entities on a router. To remove an ACE entry from an access list, you need to remove the whole access list. However, you can make additions to an access list without taking such measures. In the case of a large access control list, it is often a good idea to modify the list in a text editor and then cut/copy/paste the changes after carefully removing the to-be-changed access list.

permit all ACE for an Undefined ACL

If an access control list is applied to an interface using the **access-group** command, but it is never created in the configuration, Cisco IOS assumes that the access list contains the single ACE specifying **permit ip any any**.

Using ACLs to Stop Unauthorized Access

One of the primary purposes of having ACLs is to stop unauthorized access to a network. ACLs can be used in two primary ways to control access:

- They can be configured to stop unauthorized access to the router on which the lists are configured.
- They can be configured to stop unauthorized access to devices sitting upstream or downstream from the box.

Chapter 3, "Device Security," discussed how you can use ACLs to block access to routers. This section discusses how ACLs can be used to stop unauthorized access to devices sitting upstream or downstream from a router.

ACLs can also be used as mechanisms for collecting log information on the traffic that matches the various ACEs. This is generally done using the **log** or **log-input** keywords at the end of an ACE. Often these keywords are used at the end of the ACEs that are being used to deny some form of traffic. This is important, because one of the important elements in stopping unauthorized access to a network is to have an accounting method in place to verify which traffic was denied access. This can be achieved using the **log** keyword at the end of an ACE. This causes an informational logging message about the packet that matches the entry to be sent to the console. (The level of messages logged to the console is controlled by the **logging console** command.)This message includes the access list number;

whether the packet was permitted or denied; the protocol, whether it was TCP, UDP, ICMP, or a number; and, if appropriate, the source and destination addresses and source and destination port numbers. The message is generated for the first packet that matches, and then at 5-minute intervals, including the number of packets permitted or denied in the preceding 5-minute interval.

The logging facility might drop some logging message packets if there are too many to be handled or if more than one logging message needs to be handled in 1 second. This behavior prevents the router from crashing due to too many logging packets. Therefore, the logging facility should not be used as a billing tool or as an accurate source of the number of matches to an access list.

Using the **log-input** keyword at the end of an ACE ensures that the input interface and source MAC address or VC are included in the logging output.

In the following sections we will look at some of the ways in which ACLs are used to control various types of traffic from passing through a network.

Basic Access Control Function of ACLs

The basic function of an access list in a network is to restrict access to network resources to a limited set of IP addresses accessing a limited set of services.

Generally speaking, it is a better idea to create ACLs allowing only traffic that is considered legitimate for the network and to block everything else. It is often futile to design an ACL the other way around.

However, based on my experience with network attacks, certain types of traffic should be given special consideration for blocking from entering a network. The following sections define and describe the types of traffic that should be stopped from entering any given network. Obviously, these types are not appropriate for all networks. Based on the requirements of various networks, certain types of traffic might need to be allowed in, whereas others need to be blocked.

Using ACLs to Block ICMP Packets

ICMP packets play an important role in managing an IP network. However, they can also be used as part of network attacks and as reconnaissance tools. Therefore, it is often appropriate to drop a large variety of ICMP packets at the edge of a network rather than allow them through. However, because some ICMP messages are very critical to the proper functioning of the network, they should be allowed through even when other types of ICMPs are being dropped. The following sections discuss the types of ICMPs that need to be allowed to pass through the ACLs set up to block most other types of ICMP messages.

ICMP Echo and Echo Reply

Although ICMP echo and echo reply are important administrative tools, they can easily be used in denial of service (DoS) attacks. Therefore, although it is important to allow them through, it is also necessary to make sure that only restricted amounts of these messages be allowed through the access control mechanisms. In most networks, an administrator can determine that there is little need to allow echo messages to enter the private network from the public network and that access is needed only to allow echo replies sent in response to echoes originated on the private network to come back in. In this case, ACLs can be set up to drop echo messages and allow echo replies to only a restricted set of IP addresses. In addition, it is often important that the amount of traffic due to ICMP echoes and echo replies through a router on the network edge be controlled using a mechanism such as CAR. This is important in situations where a DoS attack is launched using ICMP echo and echo reply messages and, due to administrative reasons, the ACLs allow such packets to go through. We will discuss the use of Committed Access Rate (CAR) to control the amount of ICMP traffic in Chapter 23, "Using CAR to Control Attacks."

ICMP Destination Unreachable

ICMP unreachables play an important part in identifying routing issues as well as in path MTU discovery on a network. If, based on its routing tables, a router determines that a packet's destination is unreachable, it sends back a message saying so to the packet's source. In addition, if a host sets a packet's "do not fragment" bit to 1 and the packet is too large to be sent across a link on which a router needs to send the packet, the router again sends an ICMP unreachable message to the host, notifying it to either reduce its MTU or unset the DF bit in the future packets. If this message is dropped before it can reach the host that is setting by the DF bit, by an access list configured on an intermediate router, an MTU black hole is said to have been created. Because the host sending the large packets has no idea that its packets are getting dropped as far as Layer 3 of the OSI model is concerned, it continues sending large packets that now start getting dropped silently by the router, which has a smaller MTU available on a link on which it must forward the packet. As far as the host is concerned, it is now sending all its packets into a black hole. This situation is a direct result of unnecessary filtering of ICMP unreachable messages. Blocking them is one of the major causes of MTU black holes on networks today. Therefore, this is one type of ICMP message that should generally be allowed to pass through all routers set up with ACLs.

ICMP Source Quench

ICMP source quench messages are used to control TCP and UDP traffic flows. According to RFC 792:

> A gateway may discard internet datagrams if it does not have the buffer space needed to queue the datagrams for output to the next network on the route to the destination network. If a gateway discards a datagram, it may send a source quench message to the internet source host of the datagram. The source

quench message is a request to the host to cut back the rate at which it is sending traffic to the internet destination. The gateway may send a source quench message for every message that it discards. On receipt of a source quench message, the source host should cut back the rate at which it is sending traffic to the specified destination until it no longer receives source quench messages from the gateway. The source host can then gradually increase the rate at which it sends traffic to the destination until it again receives source quench messages.

Therefore, ICMP source quench messages are important. If blocked, they can cause TCP and UDP protocols to lose some of their ability to regulate traffic without suffering too much traffic drop.

ICMP Time Exceed

IP packets are sent with a Time to Live (TTL) field set to a certain value. The purpose of this field is to have the packet dropped in case the packet gets stuck in a routing loop. At each hop, the router forwarding the IP packet decrements the field by 1. If the packet reaches a router with its TTL field equal to 0, that router must drop the packet and send back a notification to that effect to the host sending the packet. This helps network administrators determine if there are routing loops on their networks. Therefore, ICMP time exceed messages should be allowed to pass through most access control list filtering setups.

Using ACLs to Block Backets with Spoofed IP Addresses

Another important use of ACLs is filtering spoofed packets. We will discuss this in detail in the section "Using ACLs to Stop Traffic from Invalid IP Addresses."

Using ACLs to Block Traffic Destined for Services Not in Use on the Network

One important purpose of ACLs is to allow traffic for only those services that are configured as accessible on a network based on a network security policy. For example, if the only service being offered by a network to the outside world is HTTP, the gateway router should implement an access list to allow only HTTP TCP packets to go through.

Using ACLs to Block Known Offenders

ACLs can be implemented as an interim solution to block certain IP addresses from accessing a network after it has been identified that these IP addresses are involved in malicious activities. Offenders can be identified through the use of an intrusion detection system (IDS) or other means of monitoring system activity. The Cisco IDS has a mechanism called *shunning,* which allows an access list to be automatically configured on a network edge device, stopping access from IP addresses considered to be the source of network attacks. Chapter 15, "Cisco Secure Intrusion Detection," has more details on this feature. It is important to understand that most professional hackers use spoofed IP addresses to launch attacks rather than using their real IP addresses. So although blocking one of the these IP addresses might slow down an attack, it is not a long-term fix. It's easy for an attacker to start launching the attack using another compromised machine with a different IP address or simply start spoofing another source IP address. The real mechanism for mitigating the threat of such attacks is having a proper IDS in place.

Using ACLs to Block Bogus and Unnecessary Routes

ACLs play an important role in conjunction with routing protocols to filter unnecessary and bogus routes. These routes can cause routing issues on a network and also can be used to cause DoS by instigating network outages. However, nowadays IP prefix lists are being adopted in many large networks instead of ACLs to filter such routes. IP prefix lists tend to be faster than the normal ACLs. Chapter 4, "Secure Routing," discusses how to set up IP prefix lists and the advantages they offer. Chapter 4 also provides more details on how to do filtering for specific routing protocols running in a network.

Using ACLs to Recognize Denial of Service Attacks

ACLs on routers can serve the important purpose of recognizing attacks. This is a critical functionality that can allow a service provider to set up mechanisms to thwart an attack soon after it starts.

One of the most common ways of using an access list in this manner is to use it to recognize a packet flood in the form of a smurf attack. The following sections describe using a set of ACLs to achieve this goal.

Using an Access List to Recognize a Smurf Attack

A smurf attack, shown in Figure 21-3, is a DoS attack. An attacker sends a ping echo request to a broadcast address on a network. The source address of the echo request is the IP address of the attack's intended victim. Because the destination IP address is a broadcast address, the echo request is received by all the machines sitting on the IP address segment in that broadcast domain. This way, all these machines send echo replies to the victim's IP address. By sending a large number of such requests, the attacker can generate a proportionately larger-sized packet flood toward the victim. Because the number of hosts replying to a single echo request can be in the hundreds, the amount of traffic received by the victim can become very significant, very fast.

Figure 21-3 *How a Smurf Attack Is Orchestrated*

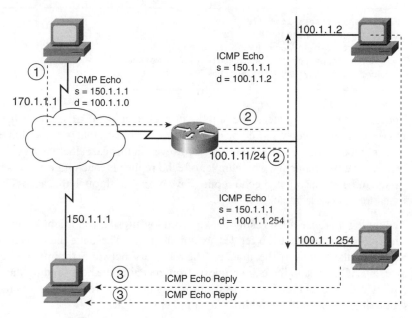

To recognize that such an attack is occurring, you can set up the access list shown in Example 21-3 on one of the service provider's edge routers.

Example 21-3 *ACL Used to Recognize a Smurf Attack*

```
access-list 170 permit icmp any any echo
access-list 170 permit icmp any any echo-reply
access-list 170 permit ip any any

interface serial 0
 ip access-group 170 in
```

As you can see, this access list does not deny any traffic. All it does is look at traffic entering the router through the serial interface coming from the outside public network. However, if you look at the statistics of the packets matching this access list on the serial interface, you can get a very clear idea of whether a smurf attack is in progress. Example 21-4 shows output from the **show access-list** command for the configuration shown in Example 21-3.

Example 21-4 *Output of the* **show access-list** *Command for the Access List Used to Recognize a Smurf Attack*

```
2503-1#show access-list 170
    Extended IP access list 170
    permit icmp any any echo (13 matches)
    permit icmp any any echo-reply (15001 matches)
    permit ip any any (101 matches)
```

Under normal circumstances, the number of packets matching the access list's echo entry and the echo-reply entry should be quite close. This means that you should get roughly the same number of echoes as echo replies. However, in this case, there is a great dissimilarity between the two numbers. The number of echo replies is much higher. This means that a large number of unsolicited echo replies have been sent through this access list. This is the signature of a smurf attack.

By logging this access list (using the keyword **log-input**), you might be able to find out which IP addresses the echo replies are coming from. These are the *reflectors,* which are being sent the echoes by the attacker. The reflectors' network administrator can then help by using ACLs to stop the echo requests from reaching the host sending the replies or by turning off directed broadcast on various routes in the network. An access list can also be set up to drop the traffic in addition to simply logging it.

It is interesting to note that, although smurf attacks can best be stopped by checking for spoofing on all networks, this is not something that network administrators can depend on to secure their own networks. It is always a bad practice to depend on other network administrators' security consciousness and ability for your own security. This is why it is necessary to have mechanisms in place to thwart smurf attacks as and when they arise without hoping that they will be stopped by a conscientious administrator at their source.

Using an Access List to Recognize a Fraggle Attack

A fraggle attack is a variation of a smurf attack. Instead of using ICMP echoes, the fraggle attacker uses UDP echoes and the resulting UDP echo replies to stage an attack. The technique used is the same: exploiting the network's broadcast facility. You can use ACLs to identify a fraggle attack, as shown in Example 21-5.

Example 21-5 *Using an Access List to Recognize a Fraggle Attack*

```
access-list 180 permit udp any any eq echo
access-list 180 permit udp any eq echo any
access-list 180 permit ip any any

interface serial 0
 ip access-group 180 in
```

A high number of hits on the second ACE as compared to the first one suggests that a fraggle attack might be in progress on a host behind the router with the access list. The replies to a UDP echo have their source port set to port 7, and the echo requests have their destination ports set to this value. This characteristic is used to differentiate between the two types of packets in the access list shown in Example 21-6.

Example 21-6 *Output of the* **show access-list** *Command for the Access List Used to Recognize a Fraggle Attack*

```
2503-1#show access-list 180

        permit udp any any eq echo (100 matches)
        permit udp any eq echo any (13398 matches)
        permit ip any any (101 matches)
```

Using an Access List to Recognize a SYN Flood

SYN floods are DoS attacks caused by sending a large number of TCP synchronization requests to a server without completing the handshake. Upon receiving the SYN packet, the serve responds with a SYN-ACK. However, the source of the original packet is often an unused IP address, resulting in the SYN-ACK's getting lost. A server can handle only a certain number of such SYN requests in a given amount of time. After that, its buffers fill up, and it can no longer service any more SYN requests—not even legitimate ones.

Again, ACLs can be used to find out if indeed a SYN DoS attack is being orchestrated on hosts behind a router. This can be done using an access list similar to the one shown in Example 21-7.

Example 21-7 *Access List Set Up to Detect SYN Floods*

```
access-list 190 permit tcp any any established
access-list 190 permit tcp any any
access-list 190 permit ip any any

interface serial 0
 ip access-group 190 in
```

The first instance of this ACLs gets matched every time a packet that is not a SYN request but that is another type of TCP packet comes across this access list. The second instance of the access list, however, matches only on SYN requests. This is a technique to separate all TCP traffic into two categories: SYNs and everything else. The first element gets matched on every packet with the ACK bit set, and the second element gets matched on everything else, which legitimately should only be SYNs.

Under normal circumstances, the SYN packets passing through a router on their way to a server behind it are less than half the number of packets that are something other than SYN requests. The actual number might vary, depending on the services being run. Services needing small bursty TCP sessions might have a lower ratio than others, but generally the non-SYNs outnumber the SYNs by a factor of 3 or 4.

However, in the event that a SYN flood is being orchestrated, this ratio can easily shift the other way around. This means that the number of SYN packets can easily outnumber the number of non-SYN packets. The actual numbers vary depending on the attack's severity. Example 21-8 shows an access list and its statistics captured during a SYN flood.

We will discuss the use of CAR to control these types of attacks in Chapter 23, "Using CAR to Control Attacks."

Example 21-8 *Output of the* **show access-list** *Command for the Access List Set Up to Detect SYN Flooding*

```
2503-1#show access-list 190

permit tcp any any established (1345 matches)
permit tcp any any (4220 matches)
         permit ip any any (110 matches)
```

Using ACLs to Stop Denial of Service Attacks

DoS attacks are network attacks in which an attacker tries to reduce the amount of legitimate access to a network by using up that network's resources. These resources could be the bandwidth on the link connecting the target network to the rest of the world or the amount of memory available on a router or server to process incoming connections or other similar resources. Chapter 14, "What Is Intrusion Detection?," has more details on DoS attacks and some examples.

The following sections present some of the most basic strategies for using ACLs to prevent DoS attacks.

Using ACLs to Stop Traffic from Invalid IP Addresses

There can be quite a few reasons why an attacker forges a source address while staging a DoS attack, but here are the two main reasons:

- To avoid detection upon staging the attack. This is because of the difficulty in tracing the source of an IP packet that has a spoofed IP address as its source IP address.

- To stage a twofold attack. One example of such an attack is a smurf attack. In a smurf attack, the attacker attacks in two places at the same time. Not only is the end target affected by the large number of echo replies received, but the network that acts as the reflector is also affected by the large amount of traffic.

ACLs can be used to ensure that traffic destined for a specific network is coming from valid addresses. Two main qualifiers for the traffic to be valid are as follows:

- The traffic originating from a network should have source IP addresses allocated to that network.

- The source IP addresses should not be spoofed to be the addresses on the destination network's IP address range.

These two criteria, although often difficult to implement, are the most effective measures an ISP can take to protect its customers. The reason for having the first requirement is to ensure that an attacker is unable to use a forged IP address to attack a network. The second requirement protects against attackers changing the source addresses of their packets to be the addresses on a network belonging to one of the ISP's customers. This kind of spoofing can fool systems into thinking that the traffic is coming from a trusted site, whereas it is not in reality.

RFC 2827 provides a good set of rules for applying such ACLs. Figure 21-4 is taken from this RFC.

Figure 21-4 *Spoofing Scenario Described in RFC 2827*

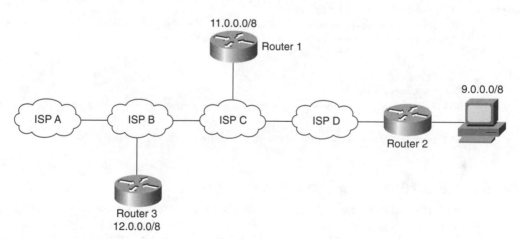

In Example 21-9, Router 2 contains an access list on its ingress interface network (the one connected to 9.0.0.0/8—serial 0 in this case).

Example 21-9 *Access List Set Up for Anti-Spoofing*

```
access-list 101 permit ip 9.0.0.0 0.255.255.255 any
access-list 101 deny ip any any

int serial 0
 ip access-group 101 in
```

This access list allows only packets from the 9.0.0.0/8 subnet range to enter the router on their way to the ISP B router. So if an attacker living on the 9.0.0.0/8 network wants to stage an attack on the 12.0.0.0/8 network using a forged source IP address (such as 100.1.1.1), the packets sent from this source address are dropped on Router 2 because they do not match the access list. You can further enhance this implementation's security by adding the keyword **log** at the end of the deny ACE, thereby keeping a record of forgery attempts.

To achieve the goal of filtering traffic that is invalid because the source IP address is spoofed, you need to use an access list on a router close to the network that needs to be protected from the attack. This access list should block packets arriving at the interface of the router headed toward the to-be-attacked network with a source IP address belonging to the address range from the to-be-attacked network. Generally this means that enterprises should implement this type of filtering on their gateway routers and that their service providers should implement this filtering on their customer- (enterprise) facing routers.

To understand this scenario, refer to Figure 21-4. To protect the 12.0.0.0/8 network from being attacked with packets having source addresses in the range 12.0.0.0/8, an access list, shown in Example 21-10, is applied to Router 3. This blocks access to the 12.0.0.0/8 network from the source subnet 12.0.0.0/8.

Example 21-10 *Access List Set Up for Anti-Spoofing*

```
accesss-list 131 deny ip 12.0.0.0 0.255.255.255 any
access-list 131 permit ip any any

int serial1
 ip access-group 131 out
```

In this case, serial1 is the interface connected toward the 12.0.0.0/8 network.

Filtering RFC 1918 Address Space

RFC 1918 address space addresses can also be used by attackers as forged source addresses while staging network attacks. Because these are nonroutable addresses, the return packets are dropped. Example 21-11 shows an ACL set up to filter the RFC 1918 address space. Interface serial0 is the interface of the router connected toward the public network.

Example 21-11 *ACL Set Up to Filter the RFC 1918 Address Space*

```
access-list 111 deny ip 172.16.0.0 0.15.255.255 any
access-list 111 deny ip 192.168.0.0 0.0.255.255 any
access-list 111 deny ip 10.0.0.0 0.255.255.255 any

int serial0
 ip access-group 111 in
```

Denying Other Unnecessary Traffic

Although it is difficult to give a comprehensive access list to use for the purpose of denying unnecessary traffic, the following list helps you get started. As stated earlier, a best practice is to identify what traffic needs to be allowed to enter and leave a network and then deny all other traffic.

- Deny IP packets with source addresses set to multicast or broadcast addresses or the reserved loopback addresses. The access list in Example 21-12 shows some of the addresses that need to be filtered.

Example 21-12 *ACL Set Up to Filter Traffic Sourced from IP Addresses That Might Be IlLegitimate Source Addresses*

```
access-list number deny ip 127.0.0.0 0.255.255.255 any
access-list number deny ip 224.0.0.0 31.255.255.255 any
access-list number deny ip host 0.0.0.0 any
```

- Deny unnecessary ICMP packets. See the earlier section "ICMP Packets" for details on what to allow for ICMPs.
- Deny traffic for all ports not being serviced by the network.
- Deny traffic from known offending IP addresses.

IP Fragment Handling by ACLs

IP fragments pose a special challenge to ACL processing on routers. IP fragments contain limited information, making it difficult for ACLs to process them properly. In addition, they can be used to stage certain types of attacks. This section looks at how Cisco's implementation of ACLs deals with IP fragmentation-based issues.

Filtering IP Fragments

Noninitial fragments do not contain Layer 4 and above information. For most legitimate packets, this information is contained in the packet's initial fragment (fragment offset [FO] = 0 for the initial fragment). Therefore, it is impossible for access lists set up to do filtering on Layer 4 information, such as TCP port numbers, to figure out whether a fragment that contains no Layer 4 information is to be allowed through.

Noninitial fragments are traditionally allowed to pass through ACLs because, if evaluated based on on the layer 3 info, they could be incorrectly blocked based on Layer 3 information in them. However, because these packets do not contain Layer 4 information, they do not match the Layer 4 information in the ACL entry, if it exists. Allowing the noninitial fragments of an IP datagram through is acceptable, because the host receiving the fragments cannot reassemble the original IP datagram without the initial fragment.

As we discussed in Chapters 8, "PIX Firewall" and 9, "IOS Firewall," firewalls have an advantage over simple ACLs when it comes to fragment handling. Because firewalls maintain state information for packets passing through them, they can filter fragments based on a table of packet fragments indexed by source and destination IP address, protocol, and IP ID. In addition, PIX firewall can also do virtual re-assembly or completed reassembly of packets before forwarding them on. Because routers set up with ACLs do not maintain such information, they follow the traditional methodology of allowing the fragments to pass through if the Layer 3 information matches, irrespective of the Layer 4 information.

It is important to note that, as of Cisco IOS Software Releases 12.1(2) and 12.0(11), the new ACL code drops fragments that do not match any Layer 3 information contained on any of the permit ACEs in an access control list. Earlier releases allow noninitial fragments through if they do not match Layer 3 information on any of the permit ACEs in an access control list. This means that as of Cisco IOS Software Releases 12.1(2) and 12.0(11), if a noninitial fragment is sent to a router with an ACL containing permit ACEs with Layer 4 information in them, the fragment must match at least one of these ACEs as far as the Layer 3 information is concerned to be let through. The checking was more lenient in the earlier releases, where a fragment was allowed through even if it did not match any of the permit ACEs in the ACL based on the Layer 3 information.

However, in certain situations, a network administrator might decide that no fragments are to allowed to reach a certain host sitting behind a router configured with an access control list. In this case, the keyword **fragment** at the end of an ACE can be used to identify fragments and process them according to the rule defined in the ACE.

As shown in Table 21-1, there are six different types of ACL lines, and each has a consequence if a packet does or does not match. In the table, FO = 0 indicates a nonfragment or an initial fragment in a TCP flow, FO > 0 indicates that the packet is a noninitial fragment, L3 means Layer 3, and L4 means Layer 4.

NOTE	When there is both Layer 3 and Layer 4 information in the ACL line and the **fragments** keyword is present, the ACL action is conservative for both permit and deny actions. The actions are conservative because you do not want to accidentally deny a fragmented portion of a flow, because the fragments do not contain sufficient information to match all the filter attributes. In the deny case, instead of denying a noninitial fragment, the next ACL entry is processed. In the permit case, it is assumed that the Layer 4 information in the packet, if available, matches the Layer 4 information in the ACL line. Table 21-1 shows how a router processes various types of traffic based on the information contained in the packets.

Table 21-1   *How a Router Processes Various Types of Traffic Based on the Information Contained in the Packets*

Type of Access Control List	Action Taken Based on Information Contained in the Packet
Permit ACL line with L3 information only	If a packet's L3 information matches the L3 information in the ACL line, it is permitted.
	If a packet's L3 information does not match the L3 information in the ACL line, the next ACL entry is processed.
Deny ACL line with L3 information only	If a packet's L3 information matches the L3 information in the ACL line, it is denied.
	If a packet's L3 information does not match the L3 information in the ACL line, the next ACL entry is processed.
Permit ACL line with L3 information only and the **fragments** keyword present	If a packet's L3 information matches the L3 information in the ACL line, the packet's fragment offset is checked.
	If a packet's FO > 0, the packet is permitted.
	If a packet's FO = 0 , the next ACL entry is processed.
Deny ACL line with L3 information only and the **fragments** keyword present	If a packet's L3 information matches the L3 information in the ACL line, the packet's fragment offset is checked.
	If a packet's FO > 0, the packet is denied.
	If a packet's FO = 0, the next ACL line is processed.
Permit ACL line with L3 and L4 information	If a packet's L3 and L4 information matches the ACL line and FO = 0, the packet is permitted.
	If a packet's L3 information matches the ACL line and FO > 0, the packet is permitted.
Deny ACL line with L3 and L4 information	If a packet's L3 and L4 information matches the ACL entry and FO = 0, the packet is denied.
	If a packet's L3 information matches the ACL line and FO > 0, the next ACL entry is processed.

The flow chart in Figure 21-5 shows the information in Table 21-1 in a graphical format.

Let's look at an example of how the **fragment** keyword is used in a real-world application to better understand its implementation.

Figure 21-5 *How ACLs Process Packets (Fragments as Well as Nonfragments) Based on Layer 3 and Layer 4 Information in the Packets and the ACEs*

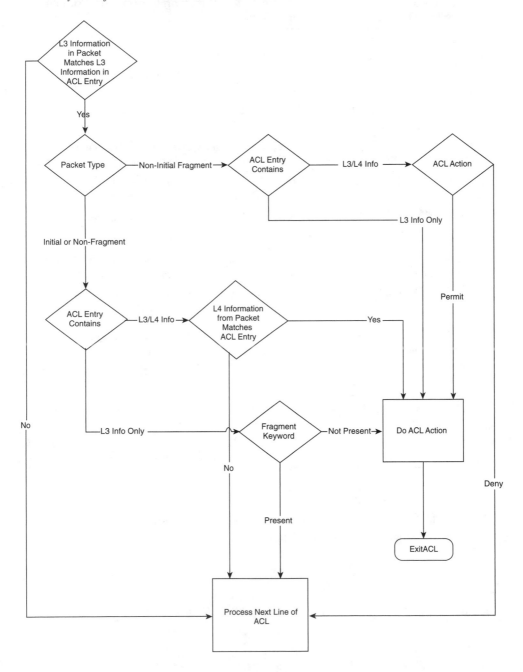

Router B connects to a web server, and the network administrator does not want to allow any fragments to reach the server. This scenario shows what happens if the network administrator implements ACL 100 versus ACL 101. Example 21-13 shows ACL 100, and Example 21-14 shows ACL 101. The ACL is applied inbound on Router A's Ethernet0 (e0) and should allow only nonfragmented packets to reach the web server. Figure 21-6 shows the use of the **fragment** keyword.

Example 21-13 *Access List 100 Set Up Without the* **fragment** *Keyword*

```
access-list 100 permit tcp any host 171.16.23.1 eq 80

access-list 100 deny ip any any
```

The first line of ACL 100 allows only HTTP to the server, but it also permits noninitial fragments to any TCP port on the server. It permits these packets because noninitial fragments do not contain Layer 4 information and the ACL logic assumes that if the Layer 3 information matches, the Layer 4 information also matches, if it is available. The second line is implicit and denies all other traffic.

It is important to note that, as of Cisco IOS Software Releases 12.1(2) and 12.0(11), the new ACL code drops fragments that do not match any other line in the ACL. Earlier releases allow noninitial fragments through if they do not match any other line of the ACL.

Example 21-14 *Access List 101 Set Up with the* **fragment** *Keyword*

```
access-list 101 deny ip any host 171.16.23.1 fragments

access-list 101 permit tcp any host 171.16.23.1 eq 80

access-list 101 deny ip any any
```

Figure 21-6 *Scenario in the Example of Using the* **fragment** *Keyword*

Internet   www Server
                                                        171.16.23.1

ACL 101, in Example 21-6, does not allow noninitial fragments through to the server because of the first line. A noninitial fragment to the server is denied when it encounters the first ACL line, because the Layer 3 information in the packet matches the Layer 3 information in the ACL line.

Initial or nonfragments to port 80 on the server also match the first line of the ACL for Layer 3 information, but because the **fragments** keyword is present, the next ACL entry (the second line) is processed. The second line of the ACL permits the initial or nonfragments because they match the ACL line for Layer 3 and Layer 4 information.

This ACL blocks noninitial fragments destined for the TCP ports of other hosts on the 171.16.23.0 network. The Layer 3 information in these packets does not match the Layer 3 information in the first ACL line, so the next ACL line is processed. The Layer 3 information in these packets does not match the Layer 3 information in the second ACL line either, so the third ACL line is processed. The third line is implicit and denies all traffic.

The network administrator in this scenario decides to implement ACL 101 because it permits only nonfragmented HTTP flows to the server.

Protecting Against IP Fragment Attacks

ACLs also provide protection against two main types of network attacks based on IP fragmentation. These two types of fragment attacks, described in RFC 1858, can be significant threats to a network:

- Tiny fragment attack
- Overlapping fragment attack

These are described in the following sections.

Tiny Fragment Attack

A tiny fragment attack is staged by sending an IP packet with the first (initial) fragment so small that it contains only the source and destination port information for TCP, not the TCP flags. These are sent in the next fragment. If the ACLs are set up to drop or allow packets based on TCP flags such as SYN = 0 or 1 or ACK = 0 or 1, they cannot test the first fragment for this information and do not check the rest of the fragments and let them pass through. These fragments, when coalesced by the end host, result in a packet that has flags set in a manner that the ACL was not supposed to let through. This way, an attacker can get an illegitimate packet through to an end host sitting behind the router set up with ACLs.

You protect against this type of attack on the routers by using the following algorithm to test packets:

IF FO = 1 and PROTOCOL = TCP then
DROP PACKET

FO is 1 only if the first (initial) fragment is so small that the second fragment has an offset of only eight octets, or FO = 1. This forces the router to drop this fragment, thereby stopping any reassembly at the end host, because now one of the IP packet's fragments is missing. The "interesting" fields (meaning the fields containing the port information and the flags of the common transport protocols, except TCP) lie in the first eight octets of the transport header, so it isn't possible to push them into a nonzero-offset fragment. So the threat of this attack does not exist for these protocols.

Overlapping Fragment Attack

An overlapping fragment attack uses the conditions set in RFC 791 to reassemble IP fragments for end hosts. It describes a reassembly algorithm that results in new fragments overwriting any overlapped portions of previously-received fragments. This behavior allows an attacker to send the TCP flags in two fragments of the IP packet. The first fragment contains flags that are allowed to pass through the configured access list (SYN = 0). However, the same flags are repeated in the second fragment, and this time they are set to a different value (SYN = 1). The access list allows the first fragment to go through because it matches the requirements. As usual, the access list does not run any tests on the remaining fragments. Therefore, when an end host receives the two fragments, it overwrites the first fragment's flags with the ones in the second fragment, defeating the purpose of the access list. This type of attack can be stopped using the same algorithm used for the tiny fragment attack. For all the relevant TCP header information to be contained in the first fragment and to not overlap with another fragment, the minimum offset that the second fragment must have is 2 (meaning that the first fragment contains at least 16 octets). Therefore, dropping fragments with FO = 1, routers eliminate the possibility of this type of attack as well.

Performance Impact of ACLs

ACLs can degrade a router's performance. The effect of processing ACLs on a busy router can be significant.

Here are some of the rules you should keep in mind while implementing ACLs on a router so as to minimize their impact on performance:

- ACLs are processed in a top-down manner. The packets are inspected first against the topmost entry in the access list, and then the access list is worked downward until a hit is made. (If no hit is made on an ACE in the access list, the implicit deny ACE at the end gets hit.) The ACL processing stops as soon as this occurs. Therefore, whenever possible, it is advisable to keep the entries most likely to be hit near the top of the access list.

- As a general rule, a router's performance decreases linearly as the depth of an access list increases. Figure 21-7 shows the performance of a non-turbo ACL versus a turbo ACL. Note that this figure is based on a very simple test. Results vary greatly based on the platform in question and the type of traffic, among other things.

Figure 21-7   *Non-Turbo ACL Versus Turbo ACL*

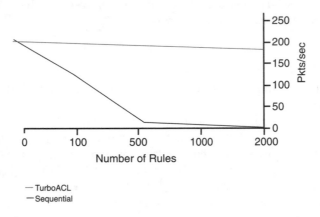

- Wherever possible, it is a good idea to summarize the address ranges identified through multiple instances of an access list into a single instance of the access list. The fewer the instances or access control elements in an access list, the faster the access list processing will be.

Turbo ACLs

Turbo ACLs are a feature implemented in the Cisco 7200 and 7500 series routers and Cisco 12000 series gigabit switch routers. They evaluate ACLs for more expedient packet classification and access checks. PIX Firewall also supports turbo ACLs starting in version 6.2. Turbo ACLs are a mechanism to get around the performance problems caused by normal ACLs, which are searched sequentially until a match is found. This kind of processing not only can create excessive overhead for the CPU, but also introduces an element of uncertainty in the router's performance, because the depth at which an access list element gets hit is uncertain.

The turbo ACL feature compiles the ACL ACEs into a set of special lookup tables while maintaining the first-match requirements. These tables allow for lookups on a consistently fast basis. Packet header information is used to access these tables in a small, fixed number of lookups, independent of the existing number of ACEs. Here are some benefits of this feature:

- For ACLs larger than five ACE entries, the CPU load required to match the packet to the predetermined turbo ACL compiled packet-matching rule is lessened. The CPU load is fixed, regardless of the ACL's size, allowing for larger ACLs without incurring any CPU overhead penalties. The larger the ACL, the greater the benefit.

- The time taken to match the packet is fixed, so the latency for the packets to be processed is smaller (significantly, in the case of large ACLs) and, more importantly, consistent, allowing better network stability and more accurate transit times.

For fewer than five entries, a standard or extended ACL can outperform a turbo ACL.

Configuring turbo ACLs is fairly easy. ACLs are set up as normal, but an additional command, **access-list compiled**, is added to the configuration. This causes the router to look through its configuration for ACLs that can be compiled into tables and creates tables for these. Each time a change is made to an access list, a recompilation needs to take place. Normal processing mechanisms (top-down search) are used while the compilation is occurring.

Example 21-15 shows how turbo ACLs can be set up on a router. It is interesting to note that the turbo ACL feature works not only for ACLs being used for access control but also for ACLs being used for any other purposes. For example, in the configuration shown in Example 21-15, compiled ACL 101 is used to define interesting IPsec traffic. (See Chapter 13, "IPsec," for more details on how IPsec works.)

Example 21-15 *How Turbo ACLs Can Be Set Up on a Router, and the Corresponding Outputs for Some of the* **show** *Commands*

```
7204#wr t
Building configuration...

Current configuration : 1478 bytes
!
version 12.2
service timestamps debug uptime
service timestamps log uptime
no service password-encryption
!
hostname 7204
!
ip cef
!
!
crypto isakmp policy 1
 authentication pre-share
crypto isakmp key <removed> address 200.1.1.2
!
!
crypto ipsec transform-set myset esp-des esp-md5-hmac
!
crypto map vpn 10 ipsec-isakmp
 set peer 200.1.1.2
 set transform-set myset
 match address 101
!
controller ISA 2/1
```

continues

Example 21-15 *How Turbo ACLs Can Be Set Up on a Router, and the Corresponding Outputs for Some of the* **show** *Commands (Continued)*

```
!
interface Ethernet3/3
 ip address 20.1.1.1 255.255.255.0
 ip access-group 3 out
 duplex half
!
interface Hssi4/0
 ip address 200.1.1.2 255.255.255.0
 fair-queue 64 16 0
 serial restart_delay 0
 crypto map vpn
!
ip classless
ip route 0.0.0.0 0.0.0.0 172.16.186.1
!
!The following command compiles the ACLs set up on the router into turbo ACL
!tables.
access-list compiled

!Below are the ACLs shown in their normal format. They get compiled into tables
!when the command shown above is configured. Note that the configuration still
!shows them in their normal format rather than in table format.
access-list 1 deny    any
access-list 2 deny    192.168.0.0 0.0.0.255
access-list 2 permit any
access-list 3 permit 192.168.1.0 0.0.0.255
access-list 3 permit any
access-list 4 permit 192.168.2.0 0.0.0.255
access-list 4 deny    any
access-list 101 permit ip 20.1.1.0 0.0.0.255 10.1.1.0 0.0.0.255
!
line con 0
line aux 0
line vty 0 4
!
end
```

```
7204#sh access-lists
Standard IP access list 1 (Compiled)
    deny    any
Standard IP access list 2 (Compiled)
    deny    192.168.0.0, wildcard bits 0.0.0.255
    permit any
Standard IP access list 3 (Compiled)
    permit 192.168.1.0, wildcard bits 0.0.0.255
    permit any
Standard IP access list 4 (Compiled)
    permit 192.168.2.0, wildcard bits 0.0.0.255
    deny    any
```

Example 21-15 *How Turbo ACLs Can Be Set Up on a Router, and the Corresponding Outputs for Some of the* **show** *Commands (Continued)*

```
Extended IP access list 101 (Compiled)
    permit ip 20.1.1.0 0.0.0.255 10.1.1.0 0.0.0.255 (14161 matches)
```

```
7204#sh access-lists compiled
Compiled ACL statistics:
5 ACLs loaded, 5 compiled tables
 ACL          State     Tables  Entries  Config  Fragment  Redundant  Memory
 1         Operational    1        2        1        0          0       1Kb
 2         Operational    1        3        2        0          0       1Kb
 3         Operational    1        3        2        0          0       1Kb
 4         Operational    1        3        2        0          0       1Kb
 101       Operational    1        2        1        0          0       1Kb
 199       Deleted
First level lookup tables:
 Block    Use              Rows      Columns   Memory used
   0    TOS/Protocol       1/16       5/8       262656
   1    IP Source (MS)     3/16       5/8       262656
   2    IP Source (LS)     4/16       5/8       262656
   3    IP Dest (MS)       2/16       5/8       262656
   4    IP Dest (LS)       2/16       5/8       262656
   5    TCP/UDP Src Port   1/16       5/8       262656
   6    TCP/UDP Dest Port  1/16       5/8       262656
   7    TCP Flags/Fragment 1/16       5/8       262656
```

Turbo access lists are an important means of improving the performance of high-end routers that have considerable processing load routing and forwarding traffic.

NetFlow Switching and ACLs

NetFlow is a switching mechanism in Cisco IOS that has certain characteristics that allow for faster processing of ACLs. NetFlow switching works by creating network flows for the traffic passing through a router. A network flow is defined as a unidirectional sequence of packets between a given source and destination endpoints. Network flows are highly granular; flow endpoints are identified by both IP address and transport layer application port numbers. NetFlow also uses the IP Protocol type, type of service (ToS), and input interface identifier to uniquely identify flows. Figure 21-8 shows how NetFlow uses various parameters for switching.

Figure 21-8 *How NetFlow Uses Various Parameters for Switching*

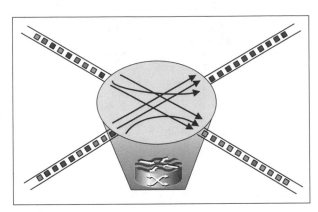

Seven Keys
Define a Flow:
1. Source Address
2. Destination Address
3. Source Port
4. Destination Port
5. Layer 3 Protocol
6. TOS Byte (DSCP)
7. Input Interface

NetFlow Switching Functionality

NetFlow monitors TCP traffic based on IP addresses as well as Layer 4 information such as port numbers and flags. Each time a packet is received on the router, NetFlow looks for an entry for it in its flow table. If it finds a matching entry, it forwards the packet based on that entry. If no entry exists, a new entry is created. These entries are regularly cleaned up when a packet matching a certain flow with its FIN bit set is received. These entries can also simply time out.

NetFlow also tracks UDP connections in a manner similar to the way it tracks TCP. However, in the case of UDP, it clears up flow entries from its tables based on timeouts, because UDP does not have connection-oriented sessions.

Access Control List Performance Enhancements Due to NetFlow Switching

NetFlow switching manages traffic in terms of flows between network layer source-destination address pairs. Unlike conventional destination prefix-based forwarding, it also provides visibility to the Layer 4 information. By caching this level of information on a per-session basis, NetFlow switching is designed to support complex packet filtering security without incurring any per-packet overhead.

With NetFlow enabled, only the first packet in any given flow undergoes ACL checking. Because the NetFlow cache maintains information that determines flow uniqueness, it can identify packets belonging to existing (active) flows and packets belonging to nonexistent (new) flows. Packets in the former category bypass all ACL checks and are switched according to the first packet in the flow, without needing to be matched against the complete set of ACLs. Packets in the latter category create a new flow cache entry, undergo ACL checks, and are switched accordingly. This significant simplification lets NetFlow maintain high performance when ACLs are used for packet filtering.

Specific performance varies based on the number and complexity of the ACLs. Generally, the benefit for longer ACLs is greater than the benefit for shorter ACLs. In addition, if a larger number of packets match a small number of flows, this can further enhance the effect of NetFlow switching on ACL performance.

Using NetFlow

NetFlow switching is turned on a per-interface basis. Example 21-16 shows how NetFlow switching is turned on on an interface.

Example 21-16 *Turning on NetFlow Switching on an Interface*

```
interface serial 3/0/0
 ip route-cache flow
```

NetFlow can be resource-consumptive on a highly loaded box. Therefore, a full understanding of its requirements is needed before it is turned on as the switching mode.

Summary

ACLs are a very basic mechanism available on routers to prevent traffic not permitted through the network security policy from traversing the network. They are an important resource available to service providers that do not want to implement full-fledged firewalls but that still want to provide their customers with some level of protection against malicious traffic. Although ACLs provide a good level of control, they are no match for a context-based access control mechanism such as a firewall. This chapter discussed various situations in which ACLs can be used to provide security to a network. We also looked at some of the important limitations of ACLs and how ACL performance can be improved. The following chapters look at other mechanisms that are available to give service providers some level of security to their customers. You will see that ACLs play an integral part in the implementation of these mechanisms.

Review Questions

1   In what order are regular ACLs processed on a Cisco router?

2   What can be an advantage of having a VIP card on a router in terms of access list processing?

3 What set of ACLs can be used to detect a SYN flood?

4 What is a smurf attack?

5 How do turbo ACLs increase the speed of access list processing?

6 Why is it important to stop traffic from spoofed addresses from entering a network?

This chapter covers the following key topics:

- **Overview of NBAR**—This section gives a brief overview of how NBAR works.

- **Using NBAR to Classify Packets**—This section discusses ways that packets can be marked using NBAR. This marking is then used for security purposes.

- **Using NBAR to Counter Network Attacks**—This section discusses how NBAR can be used to deter attacks as soon as the offensive traffic has been classified.

- **Using PDLM in Conjunction with NBAR to Classify Network Attacks**—This section discusses how PDLM can be used to help classify custom protocols.

- **Performance Impact of Using NBAR-Based Access Control Techniques**—This section touches on NBAR's performance impact on a router.

- **Case Study: The Code Red Worm and NBAR**—This section discusses how NBAR was used to stop the Code Red worm.

## CHAPTER 22

Using NBAR to Identify and Control Attacks

Network-Based Application Recognition (NBAR) is a mechanism available in the Cisco IOS Software to identify various types of traffic based on the characteristics of the traffic pertaining to Layers 4 through 7. This ability can be used to identify certain types of traffic that might be part of a network attack. This chapter looks at how NBAR is used to identify attacks and how, after the traffic has been identified as malicious, it can be dropped using various mechanisms. We will first look at mechanisms that identify various types of traffic using NBAR, and then we will discuss what to do after the traffic has been identified as malicious. Because attacks can come in a wide variety of forms and may use any number of protocols as transport mechanisms, we will also discuss the use of PDLM, which can enhance NBAR's identification capabilities. We will complete our discussion of the use of NBAR as a security tool by talking about how NBAR was used to stop the spread of the Code Red virus.

Overview of NBAR

NBAR is an intelligent classification engine implemented in Cisco IOS Software. NBAR's primary function is related to QoS (quality of service). The goal of QoS implementations in Cisco IOS Software is to ensure higher QoS to certain types of traffic in terms of bandwidth allocation, priority queuing, delay, jitter, and packet loss. This means that because Cisco IOS Software has mechanisms built in, it can give certain types of traffic precedence over others in terms of the elements just described. However, in order to achieve this goal, the packets passing through a router need to be classified or tagged first. After this has been done, QoS features can be applied to these differentiated classes, and priority can be given to certain classes over others. NBAR is one of the tools available to do this classification.

NBAR provides intelligent network classification for traffic entering a router. NBAR is a classification engine that can recognize a wide variety of applications, including web-based applications and client/server applications that dynamically assign TCP or UDP port numbers. After NBAR has recognized and put into various classes the traffic entering a router, these classes can be dealt with by the QoS features implemented in Cisco IOS Software.

NBAR is available on the Cisco 7100 and 7200 platforms starting with the 12.0(5)XE2 release and the Cisco 2600 and 3600 starting with the 12.1.(4)T release.

In effect, NBAR can identify applications and protocols from Layer 4 all the way up to Layer 7 in the traffic passing through its engines. Following is a list of applications, protocols, and protocol components that NBAR can recognize and classify:

- Statically assigned TCP and UDP port numbers

- Non-UDP and non-TCP IP protocols

- Dynamically assigned TCP and UDP port numbers during connection establishment. Classification of such applications and protocols requires stateful inspection—the ability to discover the data connections to be classified by parsing the control connections over which the data connection port assignments are made.

- Subport classification, which is based on HTTP URLs, Multipurpose Internet Mail Extension (MIME), or host names

- Heuristic/holistic classification. NBAR classifies an application based on information from the whole packet and makes a determination based on the behavior of the whole packet.

Tables 22-1 through 22-3 list applications and protocols that can be classified using NBAR.

Table 22-1   *TCP- and UDP-Based Protocols That Use Dynamic Port Assignment and That NBAR Can Recognize*

TCP- or UDP-Based Protocol with Dynamic Port Assignment	Type	Description
FTP	TCP	File Transfer Protocol
Exchange	TCP	MS-RPC for Exchange
HTTP	TCP	HTTP with URL or MIME classification
Netshow	TCP/UDP	Microsoft Netshow
RealAudio	TCP/UDP	RealAudio streaming protocol
r commands	TCP	rsh, rlogin, rexec
StreamWorks	UDP	Xing Technology StreamWorks audio/video
SQL*NET	TCP/UDP	SQL*NET for Oracle
SunRPC	TCP/UDP	Sun Remote Procedure Call
TFTP	UDP	Trivial File Transfer Protocol
VDOLive	TCP/UDP	VDOLive streaming video

Table 22-2 *TCP- and UDP-Based Protocols That Use Static Port Assignment and That NBAR Can Recognize*

TCP- or UDP-Based Protocol with Static Port Assignment	Type	Well-Known Port Number	Description
BGP	TCP/UDP	179	Border Gateway Protocol
CU-SeeMe	TCP/UDP	7648, 7649	Desktop videoconferencing
CU-SeeMe	UDP	24032	Desktop videoconferencing
DHCP/Bootp	UDP	67, 68	Dynamic Host Configuration Protocol/Bootstrap Protocol
DNS	TCP/UDP	53	Domain Name System
Finger	TCP	79	Finger user information protocol
Gopher	TCP/UDP	70	Internet Gopher protocol
HTTP	TCP	80	Hypertext Transfer Protocol
HTTPS	TCP	443	Secured HTTP
IMAP	TCP/UDP	143, 220	Internet Message Access Protocol
IRC	TCP/UDP	194	Internet Relay Chat
Kerberos	TCP/UDP	88, 749	Kerberos Network Authentication Service
L2TP	UDP	1701	L2TP tunnel
LDAP	TCP/UDP	389	Lightweight Directory Access Protocol
MS-SQLServe	TCP	1433	Microsoft SQL Server desktop videoconferencing
NetBIOS	TCP	137, 139	NetBIOS over IP (Microsoft Windows)
NFS	TCP/UDP	2049	Network File System
NNTP	TCP/UDP	119	Network News Transfer Protocol
Notes	TCP/UDP	352	Lotus Notes
NTP	TCP/UDP	123	Network Time Protocol
PCAnywhere	TCP	5631, 65301	Symantec PCAnywhere
PCAnywhere	UDP	22, 5632	Symantec PCAnywhere
POP3	TCP/UDP	10	Post Office Protocol
PPTP	TCP	1723	Point-to-Point Tunneling Protocol
RIP	UDP	520	Routing Information Protocol

continues

Table 22-2 *TCP- and UDP-Based Protocols That Use Static Port Assignment and That NBAR*
Can Recognize (Continued)

TCP- or UDP-Based Protocol with Static Port Assignment	Type	Well-Known Port Number	Description
RSVP	UDP	1698,1699	Resource Reservation Protocol
SFTP	TCP	990	Secure FTP
SHTTP	TCP	443	Secure HTTP
SIMAP	TCP/UDP	585, 993	Secure IMAP
SIRC	TCP/UDP	994	Secure IRC
SLDAP	TCP/UDP	636	Secure LDAP
SNTP	TCP/UDP	563	Secure NNTP
SMTP	TCP	25	Simple Mail Transfer Protocol
SNMP	TCP/UDP	61, 162	Simple Network Management Protocol
SOCKS	TCP	080	Firewall security protocol
SPOP3	TCP/UDP	995	Secure POP3
SSH	TCP	22	Secure shell
STELNET	TCP	992	Secure Telnet
Syslog	UDP	514	System logging utility
Telnet	TCP	23	Telnet protocol
X Window System	TCP	6000-6003	X11, X Window System Telnet protocol

Table 22-3 *Non-TCP- and Non-UDP-Based Protocols That NBAR Can Recognize*

Non-UDP or Non-TCP Protocol	Type	Well-Known Port Number	Description
EGP	IP	8	Exterior Gateway Protocol
GRE	IP	47	Generic Routing Encapsulation
ICMP	IP	1	Internet Control Message Protocol
IP/IP	IP	4	IP in IP
IPsec	IP	50, 51	IP encapsulating security payload/authentication header
EIGRP	IP	88	Enhanced Interior Gateway Routing Protocol

NBAR can also classify Citrix Independent Computing Architecture (ICA) traffic and perform subport classification of Citrix traffic based on Citrix published applications. NBAR classifies Citrix traffic by looking for TCP port 1494. NBAR can classify the various applications being requested by the clients from a publishing server by looking at the client request messages containing the name of the published application. However, in situations where the whole desktop is published together by the Citrix server using the same TCP session, NBAR cannot distinguish between the various applications contained therein, because it no longer sees any traffic for requests containing application names. In Citrix's seamless session sharing mode, all the applications use the same TCP session mode, thereby making it impossible for NBAR to detect individual sessions.

Although NBAR essentially is a QoS classification tool, the insight it gives Cisco IOS Software into the types of packets that traverse it makes it a very important security tool as well. For example, as soon as NBAR can classify certain types of traffic as malicious, other mechanisms such as rate limiting and access lists can be used to drop such traffic. The case study near the end of this chapter discusses one such scenario in detail.

Service providers and administrators of large networks can use NBAR to analyze and control traffic entering their networks.

This chapter discusses how to set up NBAR, as well as how to use it for security purposes.

Using NBAR to Classify Packets

NBAR classification is set up by defining a *class map* on a router. Before NBAR can be set up on a router, Cisco Express Forwarding (CEF) needs to be enabled on the router. The **class-map** command is used to define one or more traffic classes by specifying the criteria that the NBAR engine uses to identify the traffic.

The following example shows snippets from a router configuration in which the **class-map** command is used to define various types of traffic. This class map is used to classify all HTTP traffic intended for the URL containing the directory /test/. The * is a wildcard, meaning that it matches any characters that appear before or after the /.

```
class-map match-all http_test
    match protocol http url "*/test/*"
```

The next class map classifies into a category all traffic that uses secure HTTP (SHTTP). SHTTP traffic flows using TCP port 443.

```
class-map match-all http_secure
    match protocol secure-http
```

The next class map binds the two class maps just defined into a single class map so that similar QoS or other attributes can be assigned to both class maps at the same time. The **match-any** keyword means that traffic matching any of the parameters defined in the class map is categorized into a class. **match-all** is a more stringent requirement. It means that in order for a match to occur and for traffic to be categorized into a class, all the parameters defined in the class map must match.

```
class-map match-any ecommerce
    match class-map http_test
    match class-map http_secure
```

The next class map classifies all Citrix traffic carrying the application CARE into a single class. NBAR can classify only Citrix applications published individually. It cannot distinguish between applications published as part of an entire desktop.

```
class-map match-all citrix-A
    match protocol citrix application CARE
```

The next class map classifies all Citrix traffic carrying the application EXCEL into a single class:

```
class-map match-any citrix-B
    match protocol citrix application EXCEL
```

The next class map uses an access list to classify traffic into a single class:

```
class-map match-all privatenetwork
    match access-group 101
access-list 101 permit ip 10.1.1.0 0.0.0.255 10.2.2.0 0.0.0.255
```

The next class map classifies HTTP URLs based on MIME type matching. The MIME type can contain any user-specified text string.

```
class-map match-any audio_video
    match protocol http mime "audio/*"
    match protocol http mime "video/*"
```

The next class map is used to classify the URL that contains the image type extensions .gif, .jpg, or .jpeg:

```
class-map match-any web_images
    match protocol http url "*.gif"
    match protocol http url "*.jpg¦*.jpeg"
```

The | (OR) function plays the same role as setting up two separate **match protocol** lines, one for *.jpg and another for *.jpeg.

This discussion shows how **class-map** uses NBAR to categorize traffic into various compartments. The next section shows how the classes of traffic that have been created can be used in terms of security applications.

As you can see from the examples in this section, NBAR allows a great deal of flexibility in defining various types of protocols based on their content. This property of NBAR makes NBAR very useful for detecting malicious content contained in the payload of various protocols. Especially significant among the protocols where NBAR is used in a security context is HTTP. As you have seen in this section, NBAR can parse the URLs contained in HTTP traffic and thus can, for example, identify "get" requests, which might indicate some types of malicious activity. The following sections show how various techniques can be used in conjunction with NBAR to "mark" the traffic that NBAR has classified based on certain parameters. You will also see how this marking can be used to control the amount of traffic or simply drop it.

Using NBAR to Counter Network Attacks

You have seen how to use NBAR to classify traffic. As soon as traffic has been classified, the **policy-map** commands are used to match the various classes with either QoS or security rules. We will concentrate on the various security rules that can be applied using the policy maps.

There are a few ways that NBAR-classified packets can be dealt with using policy maps:

- Using DSCP or ToS with simple access lists to mark and drop packets
- Using DSCP or ToS with policy routing to mark and drop NBAR classified traffic
- Using traffic policing to manage NBAR classified traffic

We will look at each of these in the following sections.

Using DSCP or ToS with Simple Access Lists to Mark and Drop Packets

Packets classified using NBAR can be marked using Differentiated Services Code Point (DSCP) or type of service (ToS) fields. We will discuss how these fields can be used to mark packets that have been identified and classified using NBAR. As soon as these packets have been branded using values in these fields, they can be dropped by access control lists that match on values contained in these fields.

In the following configuration, any packets belonging to the response for an HTTP GET request sent to an URL containing default.ida are matched on by NBAR. The class map is used to group specific URLs, as described in the previous sections:

```
class-map match-any http-hacks
    match protocol http url "*default.ida*"
```

The following policy map binds the class just defined with the rule **set ip dscp 1**, meaning that all packets belonging to the traffic for the URL have their DSCP field set to 1:

```
policy-map mark-inbound-http-hacks
    class http-hacks
    set ip dscp 1
```

The service policy command configured next binds the policy map just defined to an interface. In this case, ATM4/0 is the interface connected to the public network, such as the Internet. Any traffic entering it, bound for the internal interfaces (such as the FE2/0), is marked based on the policy map just configured.

```
interface ATM 4/0
    service-policy input mark-inbound-http-hacks
```

On the interface connected to the private network, access list 105 is applied. This access list, based on the DSCP field, filters any packets containing the undesirable URL:

```
interface FastEthernet 2/0
    ip access-group 105 out
access-list 105 deny ip any any dscp 1 log
access-list 105 permit ip any any
```

This example uses the DSCP field. However, the ToS field can be used in a manner similar to how the DSCP field is used. The idea is that as long as traffic of a certain type can be marked, it can be handled by various means available on Cisco routers such as ACLs.

Using DSCP or ToS with Policy Routing to Mark and Drop NBAR Classified Traffic

Policy routing can also be used to drop NBAR classified traffic. This section looks at how policy routing can be set up in conjunction with NBAR to drop traffic that NBAR classifies as malicious.

Most of the configuration is the same as the one shown in the preceding section. However, instead of using an access group to drop packets at the interface, policy routing is used to route the traffic to a NULL interface, where the traffic is dropped. This technique has its advantages when there are a large number of egress ports. If you used the access list method described in the preceding section, the access group would have to be applied to all the egress interfaces. However, using the policy routing method described here, you can avoid this, and the traffic is dropped immediately after hitting the ingress interface (ATM in this case). In addition, using a Null route instead of ACLs has performance benefits.

```
class-map match-any http-hacks
    match protocol http url "*default.ida*"
policy-map mark-inbound-http-hacks
    class http-hacks
    set ip dscp 1
access-list 106 permit ip any any dscp 1
```

The route map defined next sets the next-hop interface for all the traffic matched on access list 106 to the NULL interface:

```
route-map test 10
    match ip address 106
    set interface Null 0
```

The policy route map defined next applies the route map just defined to the ATM interface on the router:

```
interface ATM 4/0
    ip policy route-map test
    service-policy input mark-inbound-http-hacks
```

An additional advantage of using NULL 0 routing is the savings in terms of CPU usage. The packet is dropped using the routing routines and is never sent to an access control list, which can be resource-consumptive.

Using Traffic Policing to Manage NBAR Classified Traffic

Another method of controlling traffic classified by NBAR is by using traffic policing. Traffic policing allows the amount of bandwidth allocated to a class of traffic to be limited based on a number of parameters. We will discuss the following configuration snippet to begin describing how this technique works. This class map classifies **http get** traffic contains the word 'bad' in it.

```
class-map match-any http-hack
    match protocol http url "*/bad*"
```

In the following policy map, the **police** command is used to define the maximum amount of bandwidth to allocate to the traffic defined by the class just shown. Any traffic above the limit (10 KB) is dropped. This is an example of a situation in which it is not possible to clearly segregate the packets belonging to an attack. Therefore, instead of blocking all traffic for suspected packets, the maximum bandwidth allocated to them is limited.

```
policy-map drop-inbound-http-hack
    class http-hack
    police 10000 conform transmit exceed drop
interface ATM 4/0
    service-policy input drop-inbound-http-hack
```

The use of policing to control traffic classified using NBAR is an important implementation of security through NBAR. Policing often needs to be done from a security perspective when it is not possible to very clearly define whether the traffic that is being classified through NBAR is all malicious. In such a situation, policing can be done to drop any classified traffic that is in excess of the normal traffic amounts seen on the network under normal working conditions.

Using PDLM in Conjunction with NBAR to Classify Network Attacks

Protocol Description Language Module (PDLM) is used to allow support for new protocols that are not supported natively by the Cisco IOS Software NBAR code that a router is running. There are three main reasons for having PDLMs available:

- They allow the capabilities of the native Cisco IOS Software NBAR to be enhanced without the need for a complete reimaging or reload of the router.

- Support for new protocols becomes available more quickly to Cisco customers through PDLMs, without their having to wait for a new Cisco IOS Software release incorporating the new protocols in its NBAR code.

- Custom PDLMs allow network administrators to define their own protocol and port number pairs. NBAR can then identify these pairs in the course of its operations, just as it can identify the protocols listed in Tables 22-1 through 22-3.

From a security point of view, custom PDLMs are an important enhancement available to a network administrator. The reason for this is that in case the network administrator is running custom services on his or her network, he or she can use the custom PDLM to set up the router to perform normal NBAR functions on these services as well.

Search for "Determining the Traffic Not Recognized by NBAR" on the CCO for more information on how to download and install PDLMs on a router.

Performance Impact of Using NBAR-Based Access Control Techniques

Using NBAR can incur some performance penalties on a router. Based on testing done using typical traffic originated to and from an enterprise network, the increase in CPU utilization can be from 12 to 15%. This is based on testing done for classification of protocols that have their ports dynamically assigned or negotiated with 300-byte packets with average flow lengths of 90 Mbps. This range of performance degradation is similar for the 2600, 3600, and 7200 series routers.

Although NBAR can be used to classify traffic for protocols that have statically assigned port numbers, this can also be done using ACLs. The performance impact of both methods is similar in this case.

NBAR uses 150 bytes of DRAM to track each stateful protocol flow. By default, NBAR allocates 1 MB of memory for flow resources, allowing NBAR to track about 5000 stateful flows without allocating more memory. NBAR automatically allocates additional memory if needed.

Case Study: The Code Red Worm and NBAR

Code Red is a worm that spreads by attacking Microsoft IIS WWW servers and installing a Trojan in the compromised systems. After a system has become infected, it tries to infect other systems by trying to install Trojans on those systems as well. Although an attacker can use the back door to get access to a compromised system, the compromised systems themselves carry a program that stages attacks on certain web sites (such as whitehouse.org) by all infected hosts at the same time. The details of the attacks can vary from version to version of the virus.

The URL www.caida.org/analysis/security/code-red/ has a detailed analysis of the Code Red worm and its functionality.

The Code Red worm is spread and exploited by sending HTTP requests to various Microsoft servers. Some of the files these URLs might try to access include cmd.exe, root.exe, and default.ida. NBAR can be used to detect these GET requests and block such traffic from reaching the target servers.

A new version of the Code Red worm known as Code Red II spreads the GET requests over multiple packets; thus, NBAR can't detect it. The following is an extract from the CCO web site on how NBAR deals with HTTP:

NBAR can classify application traffic by looking beyond the TCP/UDP port numbers of a packet. This is subport classification. NBAR looks into the TCP/UDP payload itself and classifies packets on content within the payload such as transaction identifier, message type, or other similar data.

Classification of HTTP by URL, HOST, or MIME type is an example of subport classification. NBAR classifies HTTP traffic by text within the URL or HOST fields of a GET request using regular expression matching. NBAR uses the UNIX filename specification as the basis for the URL or HOST specification format. The NBAR engine then converts the specified match string into a regular expression.

NBAR recognizes HTTP GET packets containing the URL and classifies all packets that are sent to the destination of the HTTP GET request (which is the HTTP server in this case). Figure 22-1 illustrates a network topology with NBAR in which Router Y is the NBAR-enabled router.

Figure 22-1 *An NBAR-Enabled Router Classifying HTTP GET Requests Sent to an HTTP Server Behind It*

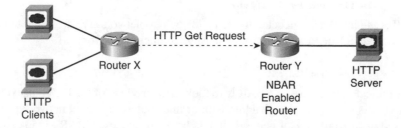

When you specify an URL for classification, only the portion of the URL following www.*hostname*.*domain* in the **match** statement needs to be included. For example, for the URL www.cisco.com/latest/whatsnew.html, only /latest/whatsnew.html is included.

HOST specification is identical to URL specification. NBAR performs a regular expression match on the HOST field contents inside an HTTP GET packet and classifies all packets from that host. For example, for the URL www.cisco.com/latest/whatsnew.html, include only www.cisco.com.

For MIME type matching, the MIME type can contain any user-specified text string. A list of Internet Assigned Numbers Authority (IANA)-supported MIME types can be found at ftp://ftp.isi.edu/in-notes/iana/assignments/media-types/media-types.

In MIME type matching, NBAR classifies the packet containing the MIME type and all subsequent packets, which are sent to the source of the HTTP GET request.

NBAR supports URL and HOST classification in the presence of persistent HTTP. NBAR does not classify packets that are part of a pipelined request. With pipelined requests, multiple requests are pipelined to the server before previous requests are serviced. Pipelined requests are a less commonly used type of persistent HTTP request.

The following commands can be configured to detect Code Red packets based on the files discussed earlier in this section:

```
class-map match-any codered
 match protocol http url "*default.ida*"
 match protocol http url "*cmd.exe*"
 match protocol http url "*root.exe*"
```

The policy map sets the DSCP field of the traffic marked by NBAR to 1:

```
policy-map mark-codered
 class codered
 set ip dscp 1
```

Here, the policy map is applied to the router's ingress interface:

```
int s 0
 service-policy input mark-codered

access-list 100 deny ip any any dscp 1
access-list 100 permit ip any any
```

e0 is the interface connected to the inside private network. We are using the access list to block any Code Red traffic from entering the internal network.

```
int e 0
ip access-group 100 out
```

A typical security use of NBAR is to look at the payload of the HTTP packets and classify them. As soon as a network administrator finds out what type of network protocol is being used in a certain type of network attack, he or she can use NBAR to look for specific elements in the payloads for the protocol and classify and control malicious traffic based on this classification.

Summary

NBAR can be a critical component of the tools a service provider can have at his or her disposal. NBAR's ability to classify packets based on content in the packets' payloads allows the service provider to stop the spread of certain types of attacks from one customer to another. This is critically important in the case of fast-spreading worms. This chapter discussed what NBAR is and how it operates. Based on how NBAR works, we discussed how NBAR can provide elements of security to the network. We also discussed how NBAR interacts with other Cisco IOS Software features to provide security. Although NBAR is an important tool that service providers can deploy on their end to protect their customers, it is equally important for customers to have strong and up-to-date intrusion detection mechanisms in place to detect and stop attacks. NBAR can by no means be the substitute for a strong IDS strategically placed in a network.

Review Questions

1. What does NBAR stand for?

2. Why is NBAR useful in security implementations?

3. What is the purpose of the policy map in NBAR configurations?

4. How can NBAR protect against Code Red attacks?

This chapter covers the following key topics:

- **Overview of Committed Access Rate**—This section gives a brief overview of how CAR works.

- **Using CAR to Drop Excessive Malicious Traffic**—This section discusses how CAR is used to drop traffic which is in the form of a flood.

- **Case Study: Using CAR to Limit DDoS Attacks**—This case study will look at how CAR can be utilized to limit traffic which may constitute a denial of service attack.

## CHAPTER 23

Using CAR to Control Attacks

Committed Access Rate (CAR), like NBAR, is basically a quality of service (QoS) feature borrowed for use in security implementations. However, it can be a very effective tool in controlling denial of service (DoS) attacks where it is not possible to completely segregate malicious traffic from nonmalicious traffic and therefore the only way out is to limit the amount of, rather than completely stop, certain types of traffic. SYN floods are a good example of such an attack. A SYN packet on its own is not malicious but is an integral component of the TCP handshake; however, a flood of SYN packets can bring any network to its knees. CAR can help limit the number of SYN packets being sent through a router based on the various factors we will discuss in this chapter. We will look at how CAR can be used to either drop traffic that has been clearly identified as malicious or reduce the amount of traffic that is suspected of containing malicious elements. This chapter concludes with a case study showing how CAR can be used in a real-life situation to control attacks.

Overview of CAR

CAR is a QoS mechanism that also lends itself to use in security implementations. CAR's primary function is to control the amount of traffic flowing through an interface based on various configured parameters. CAR can perform two basic functions:

- Bandwidth management
- Traffic classification for use by other QoS mechanisms

This chapter concentrates on CAR's first function—bandwidth management on a router.

CAR uses rate limit definitions to control the traffic flowing through an interface. CAR uses three main criteria to perform bandwidth management:

- **Average rate**—Determines the long-term average transmission rate.
- **Normal burst size**—Determines how large traffic bursts can be before some traffic exceeds the rate limit.
- **Excess burst size**—Determines how large traffic bursts can be before all traffic exceeds the rate limit.

In order to correctly use CAR for security purposes, it is important to understand how the rate limits just defined work. The average rate is simply the rate that is committed to be available on an interface for a long period of time. It does not mean that this is the maximum rate that can be allowed at any given time. The maximum rate that can be used is determined by the normal burst rate and the excess burst rate. It is important to understand why burst parameters are needed. The burst parameters are there in order to have a slow lead into a situation in which packets need to be dropped or other actions need to be taken because the maximum allowed rate of transmission has been exceeded. If you only had the average rate as the limiting parameter, the drop or similar actions would simply take place on the last packets to arrive on an interface after the average rate has been achieved. The presence of the two burst rates allows the router to have a mechanism to "borrow" bandwidth it can use to keep bursty traffic flowing. The router keeps tabs on the excess bandwidth used so that over a long period of time the average rate of traffic remains under the configured average rate. The average rate is important in terms of the long-term rate at which the traffic passes through the interface. However, TCP and other protocols (as well as normal human activity) on networks are generally bursty in nature. Putting a definite limit on the maximum bandwidth to be allocated would jeopardize many applications that would conform to the average rate over the long term. This is why burst parameters are available in CAR to take care of these situations.

CAR uses the concept of a *token bucket* (see Figure 23-1) to measure how much traffic can be allowed based on the configured rate parameters. Tokens are put into the bucket at the rate defined by the average rate. The bucket's size is defined by the normal burst size. As traffic arrives at the interface on which CAR is configured, tokens corresponding to the amount of traffic are taken from the bucket, and the traffic is allowed to pass. While this is happening, new tokens are continuously being added to the bucket based on the average rate defined for CAR. Traffic continues to flow normally until a point at which, due to excessive traffic during a given period of time, all the tokens in the bucket are exhausted. At this point, CAR borrows tokens from future time periods up to the limit defined by the excess burst rate parameter. These tokens are then used to allow the traffic to continue flowing. However, during the next time period, the new tokens being put into the bucket are first used to pay off the "loan" CAR has taken from the future time periods, before any of the tokens can be used to transmit traffic. This way, the CAR can keep the rate of traffic flowing through it within the average rate. The idea behind borrowing tokens from future periods is that because the traffic arriving at the interface is bursty, as soon as the current burst has been taken care of using the loan, there will be less traffic to transmit during the next time periods. This allows the loan to be paid back. If this is not the case, based on the parameters defined, traffic can be dropped even though new tokens are arriving in the bucket, because they would be used to pay off the loan first.

Figure 23-1 *Token Bucket Concept Used in CAR*

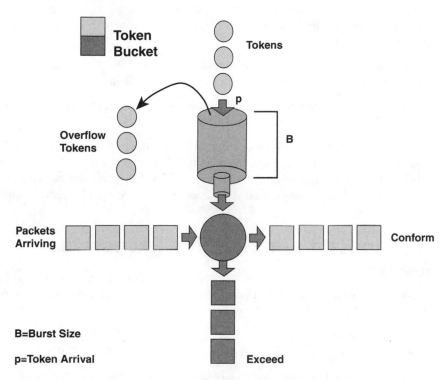

CAR uses a concept known as *compound interest measurement* to police and detect excessive traffic and drop packets. In this way, CAR can avoid tail-drop behavior and instead engage in behavior like Random Early Detection (RED). If a packet arrives and needs to borrow *n* tokens because the token bucket contains fewer tokens than its packet size requires, CAR compares the following two values:

- **Extended burst parameter value**
- **Compounded debt**—This is computed as the sum over all a_i, where *a* indicates the actual debt value of the flow after packet *i* is sent.

Compound Debt = $a_1 + a_2 + a_3 + a_4 + .. + a_n$

Actual debt is simply a count of how many tokens the flow has borrowed. *i* indicates the *i*th packet that has attempted to borrow tokens since the last time a packet was dropped.

If the compounded debt is greater than the extended burst value, CAR's exceed action takes effect. After a packet is dropped, the compounded debt is effectively set to 0. CAR then computes a new compounded debt value equal to the actual debt for the next packet that needs to borrow tokens.

If the actual debt is greater than the extended limit, all packets are dropped until the actual debt is reduced through accumulation of tokens in the token bucket.

Dropped packets do not count against any rate or burst limit. That is, when a packet is dropped, no tokens are removed from the token bucket.

CAR is a very effective tool for service providers to use to protect their clients' networks. Due to the large amount of traffic passing through their networks, it is somewhat easier to classify traffic rates and act on them accordingly. The following sections look at how CAR can be used to either drop or control the amount of malicious or suspected traffic.

Using CAR to Rate-Limit or Drop Excessive Malicious Traffic

CAR can be used to rate-limit suspected malicious traffic. There are two main scenarios in which it can be used:

- Rate-limiting DoS attacks
- Rate-limiting suspected malicious content

DoS attacks are often conducted using traffic that would have been legitimate if not sent in such excessive quantities so as to overwhelm the intended host and also consume significant amounts of network bandwidth. Often it is very difficult to differentiate the malicious from the non-malicious traffic during these types of attacks. CAR is an ideal mechanism for controlling these types of traffic, where it is difficult to differentiate legal from illegal traffic.

CAR can also be used to drop or limit traffic that has been positively identified as malicious using a tagging mechanism that uses a technique such as NBAR.

Rate-Limiting Denial of Service Attacks

The best use of the CAR technique in terms of security is rate-limiting DoS attacks. Two of the most common types of attacks that CAR can help with are ICMP-based attacks such as smurf attacks and SYN floods.

Using CAR to Rate-Limit ICMP Floods

In the following example, the serial interface is the router's outside interface. The rate limit has been configured for the traffic matched on access list 102. Access list 102 matches on ICMP echoes and echo replies that might be used in the DoS attack. The average rate allowed for the ICMPs is 256 Kbps. However, a normal burst rate of 8000 bytes is allowed. In this case, no additional excess burst rate is configured. This means that as soon as the normal burst rate is consumed in addition to the average rate, all additional traffic is dropped. No borrowing from future time periods is allowed.

```
interface serial 0
        rate-limit input access-group 110 256000 8000 8000 conform-action
        transmit exceed-action drop
access-list 110 permit icmp any any echo
access-list 110 permit icmp any any echo-reply
```

The first ACE is useful in identifying and thereby limiting ICMP echoes that can be part of a DoS attack. These can either be the echoes that are being used as the primary mechanism of a DoS attack or the echoes that are being sent to a network behind this router, which is being exploited as a reflector in a smurf attack. The second ACE is useful in identifying echo replies that are being sent as part of a smurf attack from a reflector network.

The actual values for these paramenters depend on the type of interface and the total bandwidth available to it.

Using CAR to Rate-Limit SYN Floods

Another important use of CAR is helping mitigate SYN floods.

As discussed in Chapter 21, "Using Access Control Lists Effectively," the second instance of access list 110 is designed to match SYN requests, whereas the first instance matches all other TCP traffic. This access list is referenced by the rate limit configuration shown here to limit the number of SYN requests allowed to pass through the serial interface. The average rate allowed for the SYNs is 64 Kbps. However, a normal burst rate of 8000 bytes is allowed. In this case, no additional excess burst rate is configured. This means that as soon as the normal burst rate is consumed in addition to the average rate, all additional traffic is dropped. No borrowing from future time periods is allowed.

```
access-list 110 deny tcp any any established
access-list 110 permit tcp any any

interface serial0
        rate-limit input access-group 110 64000 8000 8000 conform-action transmit
        exceed- action drop
```

Although it isn't hard to come up with a number to use for configuring the rate limit in the case of ICMP echo and echo reply packets (because there aren't very many of them in normal networks, and making some mistakes in guessing the correct amount is forgivable), it is more challenging to find the right number for SYN requests. Keep in mind the following two rules when determining these numbers:

- The actual number of SYN packets varies from network to network based on applications, usage, and time of usage. Therefore, you must have a historical record of the number of SYNs during times when no attacks are under way. You can use these numbers to configure CAR properly.

- It is often prudent to check the number of connections established before and after CAR is applied (with no attack under way) to ensure that no changes in the rate and number of such connections have taken place.

- You can also use some of the rules of thumb for the number of SYN packets in a normal TCP conversation described in Chapter 21. However, the preceding two points are often the only sure test of a good number.

As a preparatory action before an actual attack occurs, you can use an access list such as 110, that permits all traffic to determine how many TCP packets are "established" and how many aren't (SYNs) under normal circumstances in a given network. This information can be very useful in defining CAR's average and burst parameters.

Rate-Limiting Suspected Malicious Content

Another role that CAR can play is in conjunction with traffic classification engines such as NBAR. We discussed NBAR in detail in the preceding chapter. In the following example, suspected malicious traffic contains the word "test" in the URL. However, because not all traffic destined for this URL is malicious, simple drop mechanisms don't work. You must set up a mechanism whereby drops occur only when the requests to this URL exceed a certain limit. This can be done by first marking the suspect packets. You set the DSCP field to decimal 1 and then rate-limit on the Ethernet interface such that only a limited amount of the marked traffic makes it to the Web server sitting on the Ethernet 0 segment. Chapter 22, "Using NBAR to Identify and Control Attacks," has more details on how you can use NBAR to classify traffic that can then be subjected to the CAR mechanism.

```
class-map match-any http-hacks
    match protocol http url "*/test/*"
policy-map mark-inbound-http-hacks
    class http-hacks
    set ip dscp 1
access-list 106 permit ip any any dscp 1
int e0
rate-limit output access-group 106 256000 8000 8000 conform-action transmit
  exceed-action drop
```

It is important to note that CAR drops both legitimate and illegitimate traffic after the configured rate is reached. Therefore, it is important to have good data to identify legitimate and illegitimate amounts of traffic.

Case Study: Using CAR to Limit DDoS Attacks

A distributed denial of service (DDoS) attack is launched when attackers install hidden programs on compromised hosts (in some cases called handlers, see Chapter 14, "What is Intrusion Detection," for more details). These hosts in turn compromise more hosts (in some cases called agents, see Chapter 14 for more details) and install special programs to run on them. This way, a multiplicative effect is achieved, whereby each compromised host compromises more hosts. The endgame is for all the agents to launch an attack together, usually a DoS attack, on a victim host. Due to the large number of agents launching the attack from a variety of places, this kind of attack can be difficult to control after it is launched. In this case, as in any other, prevention is the best medicine.

In association with other packet-filtering mechanisms, you can use CAR to reduce the effects of distributed DoS attacks.

In the most common DDoS attacks, communication between the attacker, the handlers, and the agents uses forged ICMP echo and echo reply messages (this, however, is not universally true; see Chapter 14 for more details). This important characteristic can be used not only to detect the presence of compromised hosts, but also to block such traffic when it exceeds normal traffic patterns. Figure 23-2 shows how a typical DDoS network is set up. Chapter 14 has more details on how these types of networks operate.

Figure 23-2 *Typical DDoS Network*

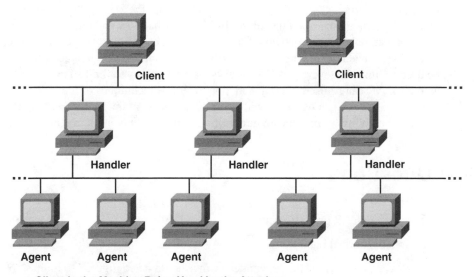

- Client Is the Machine Being Used by the Attacker.
- Handler Is a Compromised Host with Trojans and Special Programs to Infect Other Hosts Installed On It.
- Agents Are the End Machines Compromised by the Handlers. These Are the Machines Which Generally Are Responsible for Actually Launching DoS.

One kind of DDoS network that has been used in the past to launch DDoS attacks is TFN. The communication between the handler and the agent, as shown in Figure 23-2, in TFN is done using ICMP echo replies, making this type of communication difficult to detect. The ID of the ICMP echo reply contains the command or the command reply, and the data portion contains any arguments. You can detect and control this type of traffic using CAR. Example 23-1 shows the configuration needed to set up CAR to drop excessive echo reply traffic on the network.

Example 23-1 *Setting Up CAR to Drop Excessive Echo Reply Traffic on the Network*

```
interface serial 0
        rate-limit input access-group 110 256000 8000 8000 conform-action
        transmit exceed-action drop

access-list 110 permit icmp any any echo-reply
```

As discussed earlier, the actual CAR parameters that need to be set up depend on the network's normal traffic patterns.

Summary

CAR is an important IOS feature that can be used to control the amount of traffic passing through an interface. This ability, when combined with the knowledge of what type the malicious traffic is and good data describing the normal flow and amount of traffic on a network, can help control network attacks, such as DoS attacks. This chapter discussed what CAR is and how it is used for security implementation. We looked at how CAR can be used to limit the severity of DoS attacks, as well as how to limit suspected malicious activity. CAR can be used in conjunction with simple techniques of identifying various types of traffic, such as ACLs, or with more advanced techniques, such as NBAR. The end result is the ability to limit the amount of traffic that might contain malicious content.

Review Questions

1 What is CAR?

2 How can CAR provide security?

3 What is normal burst rate?

4 How can you figure out how much traffic should be configured to limit SYN attacks?

5 How can CAR be used to control DDoS attacks?

Troubleshooting

This chapter covers the following key topics:

- **Troubleshooting NAT**—This section examines some of the common tools available to troubleshoot NAT operations. It also looks at about some of the common issues faced by network administrators implementing NAT and these can be resolved.

- **Troubleshooting PIX Firewalls**—This section discusses the methodology to root cause PIX issues. It looks at the common troubleshooting tools available on PIX firewall as well as solutions to commonly seen PIX problems. In addition, a couple of case studies are included to aid the understanding of the reader.

- **Troubleshooting IOS Firewalls**—This section examines the tools available to troubleshoot IOS firewall implementations as well as some common IOS firewall issues and their resolutions.

- **Troubleshooting IPsec VPNs**—This section contains a detailed examination of how issues in IPsec VPN setups can be diagnosed and resolved. It discusses the debugs available in IPsec and what these debugs mean. The section concludes with discussion into some of the common IPsec problems and their resolution.

- **Troubleshooting Intrusion Detection**—This section discusses some of the common problems administrators run into while using the Unix based director as well as the CSPM director tool. It also addresses some ways to resolve some of these problems.

- **Troubleshooting AAA**—This section describes some of the common AAA issues and ways to diagnose and fix them. The emphasis is kept on router implementations of AAA however the techniques are also equally valid when applied to other platforms such as the PIX. It also looks at techniques which can be used to troubleshoot Auth-proxy implementations.

## CHAPTER 24

Troubleshooting Network Security Implementations

Troubleshooting is an important part of any security implementation. It is important to understand the techniques as well as the methodology used to troubleshoot the various technologies discussed in this book. This chapter discusses the troubleshooting techniques you can use to narrow down various problems encountered in implementing security technologies on the network. We will look at the various tools that are available, as well as discuss the more common mistakes and issues seen in implementations. We will also summarize the most common operation verification commands used for each of these technologies.

Troubleshooting NAT

Network Address Translation (NAT) is fairly easy to implement but because it is intricately integrated into so many security implementations, it can be tricky to troubleshoot. We will focus on NAT's implementation on Cisco routers in this section. We will talk about NAT issues on the PIX in a later section.

NAT Order of Operations

The first thing to be aware of when troubleshooting NAT is the order in which NAT takes place. Understanding this can eliminate many problems. Table 24-1 lists the order of operations of various features vis-á-vis NAT. "Inside" is generally the private network behind the router, and "outside" is the network on the public side of the router.

Table 24-1 *Order in Which Various Operations Are Performed for Packets Passing Through a Router*

Inside to Outside		Outside to Inside	
1	If IPsec, check input access list	1	If IPsec, check input access list
2	Decryption for CET (Cisco Encryption Technology) or IPsec	2	Decryption for CET or IPsec
		3	Check input access list
3	Check input access list	4	Check input rate limits
4	Check input rate limits	5	Input accounting
5	Input accounting	6	Inspect
6	Inspect	7	NAT outside to inside (global-to-local translation)
7	Policy routing		
8	Routing	8	Policy routing
9	Redirect to web cache	9	Routing
10	NAT inside to outside (local-to-global translation)	10	Redirect to web cache
11	Crypto (check map and mark for encryption)	11	Crypto (check map and mark for encryption)
12	Check output access list	12	Check output access list
13	Inspect	13	Inspect
14	TCP intercept	14	TCP intercept
15	Encryption	15	Encryption

Make special note of the order of access control list processing and crypto map checks. Also, it is interesting to note how the order of operations is reversed going from inside to outside to outside to inside.

NAT Debugs

The most useful command that can be used to troubleshoot NAT is **debug ip packet** [*access-list* | **detail**]. This debug command essentially shows all the packets that hit the access list for which this command is used. With a properly configured access list, it is often very easy to figure out what is happening to packets as they get routed through the router and where they are headed.

Another useful NAT debugging command is **debug ip nat**. This command shows the translations being created on the router as well as packets that are being translated using the NAT translations.

So the two most important NAT debugs are

- **debug ip packet** [*access-list* | **detail**]
- **debug ip nat** or **debug ip nat** [*access-list* | **detail**]

Example 24-1 shows sample output from the **debug ip nat** command turned on in conjunction with the **debug ip packet** [*access-list* | **detail**] command.

Example 24-1 *NAT Configuration and Sample Output for* **debug ip nat** *Turned on in Conjunction with* **debug ip packet** [*access-list* | **detail**]

```
Router#write terminal

interface Ethernet0
      ip address 10.10.3.4 255.255.255.0
      ip nat inside
interface Ethernet1
      ip address 172.16.4.4 255.255.255.0
      ip nat outside

ip nat pool letmeout 200.200.200.1 200.200.200.4 pre 24
ip nat inside source list 7 pool letmeout

ip route 172.16.6.0 255.255.255.0 172.16.4.6
access-list 7 permit 10.10.3.0 0.0.0.255

!The output shown below is from turning on the debug commands listed earlier.

IP: NAT enab = 1 trans = 0 flags = 80

!The NAT debug output below shows a translation for 10.10.3.3 to 200.200.200.1
!taking place for the traffic headed for the outside local/global address
!172.16.6.6. The traffic as can be seen from the IP debugs is ICMPs.
NAT: s=10.10.3.3->200.200.200.1, d=172.16.6.6 [30]
IP: s=200.200.200.1 (Ethernet0), d=172.16.6.6 (Ethernet1), g=172.16.4.6, len 100,
   forward ICMP type=8, code=0
```

NAT show **Commands**

The command most often used to troubleshoot NAT is **show ip nat translations**. Example 24-2 shows sample output from this command.

Example 24-2 *Sample Output for the* **show ip nat translations** *Command*

```
Router#show ip nat translations

Pro   Inside global        Inside local         Outside local        Outside global
udp   171.69.233.209:1220  192.168.1.95:1220    171.69.2.132:53      171.69.2.132:53
tcp   171.69.233.209:11012 192.168.1.89:11012   171.69.1.220:23      171.69.1.220:23
```

Another useful command is **show ip nat translations verbose** (see Example 24-3), which gives more information than shown in Example 24-2.

Example 24-3 *Sample Output for the* **show ip nat translations verbose** *Command*

```
Router#show ip nat translations verbose

Pro Inside global          Inside local      Outside local    Outside global
udp 171.69.233.209:1220    192.168.1.95:1220   171.69.2.132:53  171.69.2.132:53
          create 00:00:02,      use 00:00:00,  flags:  extended
tcp   171.69.233.209:11012 192.168.1.89:11012 171.69.1.220:23  171.69.1.220:23
          create 00:01:13,      use 00:00:50,  flags:  extended
```

Here is an explanation of the additional fields in this command:

- **create**—How long ago the entry was created (in hours:minutes:seconds).
- **use**—How long ago the entry was last used (in hours:minutes:seconds).
- **flags**—Indicates the type of translation. Possible flags are
  - **extended**—Extended translation
  - **static**—Static translation
  - **destination**—Rotary translation
  - **outside**—Outside translation
  - **timing out**—Translation is no longer used due to a TCP FIN or RST

In general, the following is the terminology used in the **show** commands to display various addresses:

- **Inside local address**—The IP address that is assigned to a host on the inside network. The address is probably not a legitimate IP address assigned by the Network Information Center (NIC) or service provider. This is typically an RFC 1918 address.
- **Inside global address**—A legitimate IP address (assigned by the NIC or service provider) that represents (after translation) one or more inside local IP addresses to the outside world.
- **Outside local address**—The IP address of an outside host as it appears to the inside network. Not necessarily a legitimate address, it can be allocated from address space routable on the inside.
- **Outside global address**—The IP address assigned to a host on the outside network by the host's owner. The address was allocated from a globally routable address or network space.

show ip nat statistics is another useful command that gives the administrator information about NAT statistics. Example 24-4 is sample output from this command.

Example 24-4 *Sample Output for the* **show ip nat statistics** *Command*

```
Router#show ip nat statistics

Total translations: 2 (0 static, 2 dynamic; 0 extended)
Outside interfaces: Serial0
Inside interfaces: Ethernet1
Hits: 135  Misses: 5
Expired translations: 2
Dynamic mappings:
-- Inside Source
access-list 1 pool net-208 refcount 2
 pool net-208: netmask 255.255.255.240
        start 171.69.233.208 end 171.69.233.221
        type generic, total addresses 14, allocated 2 (14%), misses 0
```

To summarize, the two relevant NAT **show** commands are

- **show ip nat translations** or **show ip nat translations verbose**
- **show ip nat statistics**

Common NAT Problems and Resolutions

Some of the most common issues when implementing NAT in the field are described next. Most of these are common configuration mistakes, but some of them are due to a lack of understanding of how NAT is supposed to work.

The symptoms of most of these problems are similar, meaning that the devices, whose IP addresses are NATed, are unable to access the public network as they are supposed to.

Most of these issues can be diagnosed by understanding what goal NAT is being implemented to achieve and then looking at the configuration to see if one of the following mistakes is the source of the problem:

- **Access lists blocking NATed or non-NATed traffic**—It is important to keep in mind NAT's operation in relation to the access control lists. Opening an access list for non-NATed traffic, when in reality the traffic hitting it is NATed traffic, causes traffic to be dropped. For instance, ACLs on the interface that has **ip nat inside** configured on it should use the non-NATed addressing for traffic entering it from the private netwok, and ACLs on the interface that has **ip nat outside** configured on it should use NATed addressing for traffic entering it from the public side. Table 24-1 describes the order in which NAT and ACL processing take place on a router.

- **NAT access list is missing networks to be NATed**—The access list that is used to define interesting traffic for the NAT operation must define all the network ranges that need to be NATed. Missing an address or a number of addresses from this access list keeps NAT from occurring for the traffic coming from these addresses.

- **Missing the overload keyword in the NAT statement**—If only a limited number of globally routable addresses are available to do NAT, Port Address Translation (PAT) or Overload NAT must be used to allow all the hosts on the RFC 1918 addressed network to reach the public network. To set up PAT, the keyword **overload** must be used at the end of the NAT configuration command. Omitting this command causes PAT not to be turned on, resulting in only a limited number of hosts being able to access the public network or the Internet. Here is an example of using the **overload** keyword:

ip nat inside source access list 1 interface Ethernet0/0 overload

- **Asymmetric routing causes NAT to fail**—NAT occurs when a packet enters an interface configured with the **ip nat inside** command and leaves via an interface configured with the **ip nat outside** command. On a router with multiple interfaces, you must make sure that all interfaces on which traffic, that needs to be NATed, enters the router, and all interfaces from which this traffic exits, are configured with the **ip nat inside** and **ip nat outside** commands, respectively. Failure to do so causes NAT not to occur for traffic passing through the interface that does not have the appropriate NAT command configured on it.

- **Overlapping addresses in the NAT pool and static NAT entries**—It is important to make sure that the IP addresses in the NAT pool are not also being used for a static NAT translation. This can cause NAT to fail intermittently.

- **Using extended access lists to define interesting traffic for NAT**—By default, the translations that NAT creates contain only entries for the inside global and inside local address unless PAT is being used. This is done because this is all the information that is needed for simple NAT of inside local addresses to inside global addresses and to de-NAT the return traffic. However, this remains true even when extended access lists are used to define the interesting traffic, as shown in Example 24-5.

Example 24-5 *Using Extended ACLs to Define Interesting Traffic for NAT Processing*

```
ip nat inside source list 110 pool NAT1
ip nat inside source list 111 pool NAT2

access-list 110 permit ip 10.1.1.0 0.0.0.255 100.1.1.0 0.0.0.255
access-list 111 permit ip 10.1.1.0 0.0.0.255 200.1.1.0 0.0.0.255
```

This is not good, because the intent of the extended access lists here is to allow a different pool to be used when the hosts on the 10.1.1.0/24 network are trying to access 100.1.1.0/24 as compared to when they are trying to access 200.1.1.0/24.

However, with only the inside local and inside global entries being saved in the NAT table, as soon as an entry in the table is created for a host, it continues using it without consideration as to which outside global/local address it is trying to access.

The resolution to this problem, other than using PAT only, is to use route maps to define the interesting traffic. Route maps force NAT to create complete translation tables, including the outside local and outside global entries, forcing the router to create new translations for each separate outside global/local address that each inside host tries to access. Example 24-6 shows how this can be done for the setup described in Example 24-5.

Example 24-6 *Using Route Maps to Create Extended NAT Translation Tables*

```
ip nat inside source route-map MAPA pool NAT1
ip nat inside source route-map MAPB pool NAT2

access-list 110 permit ip 10.1.1.0 0.0.0.255 100.1.1.0 0.0.0.255
access-list 111 permit ip 10.1.1.0 0.0.0.255 200.1.1.0 0.0.0.255

route-map MAPA permit 10
    match ip address 110

route-map MAPB permit 10
    match ip address 111
```

- **NAT occurs for traffic that is to be encapsulated using IPsec**—It is not desirable to have NAT occur for traffic that is entering an IPsec tunnel setup between two sites. IPsec encapsulation (if tunnel mode is being used) hides the private addresses from the Internet, so NAT does not need to perform this function. To connect two networks transparently, it is necessary to ensure that NAT does not kick in when traffic goes from one local network to the other through the IPsec tunnel.

  The goal of bypassing IPsec is achieved by using a special policy routing trick. Note that simple route maps, as shown in Example 24-6, can take care of only dynamic NAT, not static NAT entries, which still kick in for packets matching those entries. It is also important to note that NAT is still needed for traffic headed for the rest of the Internet.

  The trick uses the rule that NAT, whether static or dynamic, kicks in only when interesting NAT traffic goes from an interface configured with the **ip nat inside** command directly to an interface set up with an **ip nat outside** command. In Example 24-7, this flow is broken by policy-routing the traffic headed for the other end of the IPsec tunnel to a loopback interface and then, through the use of the normal routing set up on the router, out the egress interface. This keeps NAT from occurring for this traffic. Example 24-7 shows how this setup can be done on a router.

Example 24-7 *Using Policy Routing to Bypass Static and Dynamic NAT for Traffic Going into the VPN Tunnel*

```
Router#write terminal

crypto map test 10 IPsec-isakmp

 set peer 1.1.1.1
 set transform-set transform
 match address 100

!This is the loopback interface traffic is policy-routed to.


interface Loopback1
ip address 10.2.2.2 255.255.255.252

interface Ethernet0/0

!This is the egress interface.

 ip address 1.1.1.2 255.255.255.0
 ip nat outside
 crypto map test

interface Ethernet0/1

!This is the ingress interface.

 ip address 10.1.1.1 255.255.255.0
 ip nat inside
 ip route-cache policy

!The policy route map below is used to force the interesting IPsec traffic to the
!loopback interface.

 ip policy route-map nonat

ip nat inside source access list 1 interface Ethernet0/0 overload
ip nat inside source static 10.1.1.2 100.1.1.3
access list 1 permit 10.0.0.0 0.255.255.255

!The access list below defines interesting IPsec traffic.

access list 100 permit ip 10.1.1.0 0.0.0.255 10.1.2.0 0.0.0.255

!The access list below defines the traffic that is to be used by the route map
!nonat to route to the loopback interface.

access list 120 permit ip 10.1.1.0 0.0.0.255 10.1.2.0 0.0.0.255
```

Example 24-7 *Using Policy Routing to Bypass Static and Dynamic NAT for Traffic Going into the*
VPN Tunnel (Continued)

```
!Below is the route map used to route the traffic matching access list 120 to the
!loopback interface.

route-map nonat permit 10
 match ip address 120
 set ip next-hop 10.2.2.2
```

Troubleshooting PIX Firewalls

Because PIX Firewalls are often placed at a network's periphery, their malfunctioning can have a detrimental effect on the whole network. Therefore, it is very important to have a good understanding of the PIX troubleshooting tools available and how they can be used. Various tools and techniques can be used to troubleshoot PIX functionality. We will go through some of them in this section. In addition, we will discuss some of the common PIX issues and see what their resolutions are.

Root Causing PIX-Related Problems

Because PIX often is the gateway to the Internet for the network, it is normally blamed for problems that occur when a user cannot access the Internet. Although the PIX might be the problem in these situations, there are many other elements involved that might be causing the problem. The following is a list of questions that a PIX administrator needs to ask to ascertain that the problem is not somewhere else on the network:

- User's host machine
  - Can the host ping devices on the external network by either name or IP address?
  - Can the host machine ping to anything else on the inside network?
  - Is the proper default gateway assigned?
  - Can the host machine ping the PIX's inside interface if it is allowed on the PIX?
- Protected inside router
  - Can the router ping the PIX's inside interface?
  - Can the router ping the user's host?
  - Can the router ping anything on the external network by either name or IP address?

- PIX

  — Can the PIX ping the outside router?

  — Can the PIX get to an external site past the outside router?

  — Is the user's host address defined in the **nat** command? (The **nat** command on the PIX defines interesting traffic to be processed by NAT, similar to the NAT interesting traffic ACL on a router.)

  — Are there enough addresses defined in the global pool for all the internal hosts?

- Unprotected outside router

  — Can the outside router get to the Internet?

  — Does the outside router see packets coming from the PIX?

  — Can the outside router ping the inside PIX network if this is allowed through the PIX?

After you have answered all these questions, it is possible to say with some certainty that there might be a problem with how PIX is set up. Without doing this troubleshooting, troubleshooting an extensive PIX configuration can be both time-consuming and unfruitful.

PIX NAT Order of Operations

Because NAT plays a very important role in the functioning of the PIX Firewall, it is important to have a good look at how NAT works in the PIX Firewall and what the order of operations is. Figure 24-1 shows the order of operations that NAT goes through in the PIX. This diagram can be a useful tool to have when you're troubleshooting PIX functionality.

Figure 24-1 *PIX NAT Order of Operations*

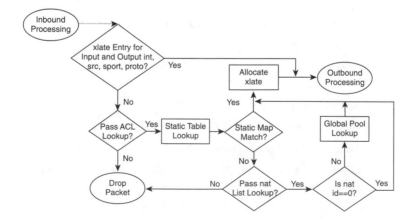

PIX Debugs

PIX debugs can be useful in some situations to troubleshoot connectivity issues through the PIX. However, they are completely effective only when used in conjunction with the **show** command.

The following commands are helpful when debugging the PIX Firewall:

- **debug icmp trace**—When a host is pinged through the PIX Firewall from any interface, the trace output appears on the console. Example 24-8 shows a successful ping from an external host (209.165.201.2) to the PIX Firewall unit's outside interface (209.165.201.1).

Example 24-8 *Sample Output for the* **debug icmp trace** *Command*

```
PIX#debug icmp trace
Inbound ICMP echo reply (len 32 id 1 seq 256) 209.165.201.1 > 209.165.201.2

Outbound ICMP echo request (len 32 id 1 seq 512) 209.165.201.2 > 209.165.201.1

Inbound ICMP echo reply (len 32 id 1 seq 512) 209.165.201.1 > 209.165.201.2

Outbound ICMP echo request (len 32 id 1 seq 768) 209.165.201.2 > 209.165.201.1

Inbound ICMP echo reply (len 32 id 1 seq 768) 209.165.201.1 > 209.165.201.2

Outbound ICMP echo request (len 32 id 1 seq 1024) 209.165.201.2 > 209.165.201.1

Inbound ICMP echo reply (len 32 id 1 seq 1024) 209.165.201.1 > 209.165.201.2
```

- **debug packet** *if_name*—Used to debug a packet. Example 24-9 lists the information as it appears in a packet.

Example 24-9 *Sample Output for the* **debug packet inside** *Command*

```
PIX#debug packet inside
-------- PACKET ---------
-- IP --
4.3.2.1 ==>     255.3.2.1
      ver = 0x4       hlen = 0x5      tos = 0x0       tlen =
0x60
      id = 0x3902     flags = 0x0     frag off=0x0
      ttl = 0x20      proto=0x11      chksum = 0x5885
      -- UDP --
            source port = 0x89      dest port = 0x89
            len = 0x4c      checksum = 0xa6a0
      -- DATA --
            00000014:                                 00 01 00 00|
      ....
            00000024: 00 00 00 01 20 45 49 45 50 45 47 45 47 45 46 46| ..
```

continues

Example 24-9 *Sample Output for the* **debug packet inside** *Command (Continued)*

```
.. EIEPEGEGEFF
                   00000034: 43 43 4e 46 41 45 44 43 41 43 41 43 41 43 41 43| CC
NFAEDCACACACAC
                   00000044: 41 43 41 41 41 00 00 20 00 01 c0 0c 00 20 00 01| AC
AAA.. ...... ..
                   00000054: 00 04 93 e0 00 06 60 00 01 02 03 04 00| ..
....\Q......
-------- END OF PACKET --------
```

- **debug packet** *if_name* **[src source_ip [netmask mask]] [dst dest_ip [netmask mask]] [[proto icmp] | [proto tcp [sport src_port] [dport dest_port]] | [proto udp [sport src_port] [dport dest_port]] [rx | tx | both]**—Used to see the contents of a packet as it travels between two destinations.

  Syntax description:

  — *if_name*—Interface name from which the packets are arriving. For example, to monitor packets coming into the PIX Firewall from the outside, set *if_name* to **outside**.

  — **src** *source_ip*—Source IP address.

  — **netmask** *mask*—Network mask.

  — **dst** *dest_ip*—Destination IP address.

  — **proto icmp**—Displays ICMP packets only.

  — **proto tcp**—Displays TCP packets only.

  — **sport** *src_port*—Source port.

  — **dport** *dest_port*—Destination port.

  — **proto udp**—Displays UDP packets only.

  — **rx**—Displays only packets received at the PIX Firewall.

  — **tx**—Displays only packets that were transmitted from the PIX Firewall.

  — **both**—Displays both received and transmitted packets.

  Using the following command displays the contents of the TCP packets on port 25 with a source address of 200.200.200.20 and a destination address of 100.100.100.10:

  debug packet outside src 200.200.200.20 dst 100.100.100.10 proto tcp dport 25 both

  To allow the ping packet to go through, the PIX **conduit permit icmp any** command or the equivalent access list command needs to be added to the configuration. This lets pings go outbound and inbound.

Please note that the **conduit** command affects only pings through the firewall, not to the firewall itself. The **icmp** command controls ICMP traffic that terminates on the

PIX Firewall. If no ICMP control list is configured, the PIX Firewall accepts all ICMP traffic that terminates at the interface. The syntax for this command is

```
icmp permit | deny [host] src_addr [src_mask] [type] interface_name
```

- In PIX 6.2 code and later, the **capture** command has been introduced. The **capture** command offers more options to the firewall administrator, who can now use this command to store the sniffed output to a file and then view it using software such as Ethereal. The **capture** command, unlike the **debug packet** command, allows an access list to be configured for defining the traffic that needs to be captured. Here is the syntax of the **capture** command:

```
capture capture_name [access-list acl_id][buffer bytes] [ethernet-type type]
    [interface name] [packet-length bytes]
```

Refer to the PIX 6.2 command reference for more detailed information on the workings of the **capture** command.

Recommended PIX Timeout Values

One problem that is often encountered in PIX setups is the use of overly aggressive or too-relaxed timeouts for the basic PIX functions. The following is a list of recommended timeout values. Actual implementation is, of course, dependent on specific applications running through the PIX. However, in most cases, the following default timeouts are appropriate:

```
timeout xlate 3:00:00
timeout conn 1:00:00 half-closed 0:10:00 udp 0:02:00 rpc 0:10:00 h323 0:05:00
    sip 0:30:00 sip_media 0:02:00
timeout uauth 0:05:00 absolute
```

Please see the command reference or the case studies in Chapter 8, "PIX Firewall," for a more detailed explanation of these commands.

PIX show Commands

The two most commonly used **show** commands on the PIX are **show xlate** and **show connections**.

The **show xlate detail** command (introduced in PIX version 6.2) displays the contents of the NAT translation slots, as demonstrated in Example 24-10.

Example 24-10 *Sample Output for the* **show xlate detail** *Command*

```
pixfirewall(config)#show xlate detail

3 in use, 3 most used
```

continues

Example 24-10 *Sample Output for the* **show xlate detail** *Command (Continued)*

```
Flags: D - DNS, d - dump, I - identity, i - inside, n - no random,
  o - outside, r - portmap, s - static
TCP PAT from inside:10.1.1.15/1026 to outside:192.150.49.1/1024 flags ri
UDP PAT from inside:10.1.1.15/1028 to outside:192.150.49.1/1024 flags ri
ICMP PAT from inside:10.1.1.15/21505 to outside:192.150.49.1/0 flags ri
```

The three PATs shown at the end of Example 24-10 are described as follows:

- The first entry is a TCP portmap (PAT) translation for host-port (10.1.1.15, 1026) on the inside network to host-port (192.150.49.1, 1024) on the outside network. The flag **r** denotes that the translation is a portmap (PAT) translation. The **i** flag denotes that the translation applies to the inside address-port.

- The second entry is a UDP portmap (PAT) translation for host-port (10.1.1.15, 1028) on the inside network to host-port (192.150.49.1, 1024) on the outside network. The flag **r** denotes that the translation is a portmap (PAT) translation. The **i** flag denotes that the translation applies to the inside address-port.

- The third entry is an ICMP portmap (PAT) translation for host-ICMP-id (10.1.1.15, 21505) on the inside network to host-ICMP-id (192.150.49.1, 0) on the outside network. The flag **r** denotes that the translation is a portmap (PAT) translation. The **i** flag denotes that the translation applies to the inside address-ICMP-id.

Table 24-2 lists the flags that can be seen using the **show xlate detail** command.

Table 24-2 *Flags Displayed by the* **show xlate detail** *Command*

Flag	Description
s	Static translation slot
d	Dump translation slot on next cleaning cycle
r	Portmap translation
n	No randomization of TCP sequence number
o	Outside address translation
i	Inside address translation
D	DNS A RR rewrite
I	Identity translation from nat 0

The **show connection detail** command (introduced in PIX version 6.2) displays the number of and information about the active TCP connections, as demonstrated in Example 24-11.

Example 24-11 *Sample Output for the* **show conn detail** *Command*

```
pix515#show connection detail

6 in use, 16378 remain, 6 most used

TCP out 204.31.17.41:80 in 10.3.3.4:1404 idle 0:00:00 Bytes 11391 flags UHrIO

TCP out 204.31.17.41:80 in 10.3.3.4:1405 idle 0:00:00 Bytes 3709 flags UHrIO

TCP out 204.31.17.41:80 in 10.3.3.4:1406 idle 0:00:01 Bytes 2685 flags UHrIO

TCP out 204.31.17.41:80 in 10.3.3.4:1407 idle 0:00:01 Bytes 2683 flags UHrIO

TCP out 204.31.17.41:80 in 10.3.3.4:1403 idle 0:00:00 Bytes 15199 flags UHrIO

TCP out 204.31.17.41:80 in 10.3.3.4:1408 idle 0:00:00 Bytes 2688 flags UHrIO

UDP out 192.150.50.70:24 in 10.3.3.4:1402 idle 0:01:30 flags d

UDP out 192.150.50.70:23 in 10.3.3.4:1397 idle 0:01:30 flags d

UDP out 192.150.50.70:22 in 10.3.3.4:1395 idle 0:01:30 flags d
```

It is useful to understand what the flags listed at the end of each output line mean. In this example, host 10.3.3.4 on the inside has accessed a website at 204.31.17.41. The global address on the outside interface is 192.150.50.70. The flags indicate that the first five TCP connections are up (U), for HTTP (H), in use (r), and that data has gone in (I) and out (O). The last three UDP connections are in dump (d—clean-up) state.

Table 24-3 lists these flags.

Table 24-3 *Flags Displayed by the* **show conn detail** *Command*

Connection Slot Flag	Description
U	Up
f	Inside FIN
F	Outside FIN
r	Inside acknowledged FIN
R	Outside acknowledged FIN
s	Awaiting outside SYN
S	Awaiting inside SYN

continues

Table 24-3 *Flags Displayed by the* **show conn detail** *Command (Continued)*

Connection Slot Flag	Description
M	SMTP data
H	HTTP get
T	TCP SIP connection
I	Inbound data
O	Outbound data
q	SQL*Net data
d	Dump
P	Inside back connection
E	Outside back connection
G	Group
p	Replicated (unused)
a	Awaiting outside ACK to SYN
A	Awaiting inside ACK to SYN
B	Initial SYN from outside
R	RPC
H	H.323
T	UDP SIP connection
m	SIP media connection
t	SIP transient connection
D	DNS

Another command that can be useful in troubleshooting traffic passing through the PIX or PIX hardware connectivity issues is the **show interface** command. The output in Example 24-12 serves to explain the various elements in this command.

Example 24-12 *Sample Output for the* **show interface** *Command*

```
PIX-1#show interface
interface ethernet0 "inside" is up, line protocol is up
  Hardware is i82559 ethernet, address is 0002.b326.1521
  IP address 10.11.1.82, subnet mask 255.255.255.0
  MTU 1500 bytes, BW 10000 Kbit half duplex
        3111608 packets input, 236206960 bytes, 0 no buffer
        Received 17203 broadcasts, 0 runts, 0 giants
        0 input errors, 0 CRC, 0 frame, 0 overrun, 0 ignored, 0 abort
        8608 packets output, 550912 bytes, 0 underruns
```

Example 24-12 *Sample Output for the* **show interface** *Command (Continued)*

```
      0 output errors, 0 collisions, 0 interface resets
      0 babbles, 0 late collisions, 0 deferred
      0 lost carrier, 0 no carrier
      input queue (curr/max blocks): hardware (128/128) software (0/1)
      output queue (curr/max blocks): hardware (0/2) software (0/1)
```

Table 24-4 describes the various fields shown in this command. An understanding of these fields is useful in troubleshooting hardware issues that can result in connectivity and/or performance concerns.

Table 24-4 *Fields Displayed by the* **show interface** *Command*

Field	Description
Ethernet string	Indicates that you have used the **interface** command to configure the interface. This field indicates either **outside** or **inside** and whether the interface is available (**up**) or unavailable (**down**).
line protocol is up	Means a working cable is plugged into the network interface. If the message is **line protocol is down**, the cable is either incorrect or not plugged into the interface connector.
Network interface type	In Example 24-12, the interface type is **Hardware**.
Interrupt vector	It is acceptable for interface cards to have the same interrupts. Intel cards start with i, and 3Com cards start with 3c. In Example 24-12, the interrupt vector is i82559.
MAC address	In Example 24-12, the MAC address is 0002.b326.1521.
IP address, subnet mask	In Example 24-12, the IP address and subnet mask are 10.11.1.82 and 255.255.255.0, respectively.
MTU (maximum transmission unit)	The size in bytes at which data can best be sent over the network.
Line speed	10BASE-T is listed as **10000 Kbit**; 100BASE-TX is listed as **100000 Kbit**.
Line duplex status	**half duplex** indicates that the network interface switches back and forth between sending and receiving information. **full duplex** indicates that the network interface can send or receive information.
nn **packets input**	Indicates that packets are being received in the PIX Firewall.
xx **bytes**	Indicates the number of bytes that have been received on the PIX Firewall.

continues

Table 24-4   *Fields Displayed by the* **show interface** *Command (Continued)*

Field	Description
no buffer	The number of times PIX Firewall was out of memory or slowed down due to heavy traffic and could not keep up with the received data.
runts	Packets with less information than expected.
giants	Packets with more information than expected.
CRC (cyclic redundancy check)	Packets that contain corrupted data (checksum error).
frame	Framing errors.
overrun	Overruns occur when the network interface card is overwhelmed and cannot buffer received information before more needs to be sent.
ignored and **abort** errors	Provided for future use; are not currently checked. The PIX Firewall does not ignore or abort frames.
underruns	Underruns occur when the PIX Firewall is overwhelmed and cannot get data to the network interface card fast enough.
nn **packets output**	Indicates that packets are being sent from the PIX Firewall.
collisions (single and multiple collisions)	The number of messages retransmitted due to an Ethernet collision. This usually occurs on an overextended LAN (the Ethernet or transceiver cable is too long, there are more than two repeaters between stations, or there are too many cascaded multiport transceivers). A packet that collides is counted only once by the output packets.
interface resets	The number of times an interface has been reset. If an interface is unable to transmit for 3 seconds, PIX Firewall resets the interface to restart transmission. During this interval, connection state is maintained. An interface reset can also happen when an interface is looped back or shut down.
babbles	Currently unused. ("Babble" means that the transmitter has been on the interface longer than the time taken to transmit the largest frame.)
late collisions	The number of frames that were not transmitted because a collision occurred outside the normal collision window. A late collision is a collision that is detected late in the packet's transmission. Normally, these should never happen. When two Ethernet hosts try to talk at once, they should collide early in the packet and both back off, or the second host should see that the first one is talking and wait.
deferred	The number of frames that were deferred before transmission due to activity on the link.

Table 24-4   *Fields Displayed by the* **show interface** *Command (Continued)*

Field	Description
lost carrier	The number of times the carrier signal was lost during transmission.
input queue	The input (receive) hardware and software queue.
hardware (curr/max blocks)	The number of blocks currently present on the input hardware queue, and the maximum number of blocks previously present on that queue. In Example 24-12, there are currently 128 blocks on the input hardware queue, and the maximum number of blocks ever present on this queue is 128.
software (curr/max blocks)	The number of blocks currently present on the input software queue, and the maximum number of blocks previously present on that queue. In Example 24-12, there are currently 0 blocks on the input software queue, and the maximum number of blocks ever present on this queue is 1.
output queue	The output (transmit) hardware and software queue.
hardware (curr/max blocks)	The number of blocks currently present on the output hardware queue, and the maximum number of blocks previously present on that queue. In Example 24-12, there are currently 0 blocks on the output hardware queue, and the maximum number of blocks ever present on this queue is 2.
software (curr/max blocks)	The number of blocks currently present on the output software queue, and the maximum number of blocks previously present on that queue. In Example 24-12, there are currently 0 blocks on the output software queue, and the maximum number of blocks ever present on this queue is 1.

Common PIX Problems and Resolutions

This section looks at some of the more common problems in PIX implementations. Most of these problems show up as users on the inside not being able to access the public network across the PIX or the inability of users on the public network to access the servers sitting behind the PIX.

Generally, most of these issues can be diagnosed simply by understanding what PIX is set up to do and then looking at the configuration to see if one of the mistakes, described in the following sections, is the source of the problem.

nat Statement Missing Networks to be NATed

PIX, in order to NAT traffic going from a high-security interface to a low-security interface, needs NAT done on the packets. It is common to see PIX configurations where this does not happen because the administrator failed to define all the subnets that need to be NATed on a high-security interface in the command **nat** [(*if_name*)] *id address* [*netmask* [**outside**] [**dns**] [**norandomseq**] [**timeout** *hh*:*mm*:*ss*] [*conn_limit* [*em_limit*]]]. This generally happens in situations where the high-security interface network has a large number of discontiguous subnets.

Overlapping Addresses in the NAT Pool and Static NAT Entries

The NAT pool (and PAT address, with the exception of interface PAT) must use IP addresses that are not used by any other device on the network. This includes static addresses (for translations) or addresses used on the interfaces. Overlapping addresses can keep users from being able to gain access through the PIX. This can also lead to orphaned connections and corrupted xlate databases.

Missing Statics or Conduits/ACLs for Servers

For users on low-security interface networks to access servers and machines on high-security interface networks, static NAT translations need to be set up for each IP address that needs to be so accessed. Failure to do so results in the server's being inaccessible from the lower-security networks.

A missing access list or conduit to allow traffic to reach the servers and machines on the high-security interface networks causes similar problems.

Missing **alias** Command

If the DNS server is on the outside of the PIX, and internal users want to access the internal servers with their DNS name, the **alias** command must be used to doctor the DNS response from the DNS server. See the detailed discussion of the **alias** command in Chapter 8 for more details.

Missing **route** Statements

PIX uses the **route** statements to route a connection's initial packet before an xlate and a connection entry are built that are used for subsequent routing. It is important for the PIX to have routes to all the networks to which it needs to send packets. In the newer versions of PIX, 5.0 and higher, only one default route can be defined on a PIX.

Incorrect ARP Entries on the Default Outside Router

If a change is made to the global pool of addresses on the PIX, the ARP cache on the router sitting on the outside interface of the PIX should be cleared. Similarly, if IP address schemes are changed on the PIX, it is a good precaution to clear ARP tables on the routers directly connected to the PIX.

IPsec Issues on the PIX

You can troubleshoot PIX IPsec issues using techniques similar to the ones used for router IPsec. Please see the section, "Troubleshooting IPsec VPNs" for details on how to trouble-shoot IPsec.

PIX Troubleshooting Case Studies

In this section looks at a few case studies involving troubleshooting PIX Firewall. The purpose of the case studies is to give you an idea of what is involved in figuring out connectivity problems related to the PIX. Although the techniques described here are fairly general, each situation demands its own set of tools and innovative thinking to narrow down the cause of problems.

An Internal User Cannot Access the Internet

The following steps provide a practical approach to troubleshooting common problems associated with internal users having difficulty accessing resources on the public network/Internet.

Step 1 Go to the end user's machine and have the user ping the PIX's internal interface. If you get a response, go to the next step. If you do not get a response, check the following for possible solutions:

— If the user cannot ping any internal address, check the interface card on the user's system.

— If the user can ping other systems on the same network but cannot ping the PIX (assuming that there is a router between the user's system and the PIX), check the following:

— The default route on the user's system.

— The default route or static route on the inside router. Make sure that the inside router is configured to route traffic both ways.

— If PIX cannot ping the user's system (assuming that the user's system is not on the same network), check the internal router. If the PIX can ping the internal router but not beyond that, make sure that the PIX knows how to get to that subnet. Check the following:

— Check the inside route on the PIX. The following example has a default route configured toward the inside network:

```
route inside 0.0.0.0 0.0.0.0 100.100.100.2 1
```

— Check the routing table on the inside router to make sure that the inside router knows how to properly route the packets.

Step 2   On the PIX, turn on **debug icmp trace**.

— Allow ICMP traffic through the PIX by entering the following command:

```
conduit permit icmp any any
```

— Next, find out if the user's system has a translated address by using the following command:

```
show xlate local ip_address
```

— If there is a translated address, you need to clear it. Use the following command:

```
clear xlate local ip_address
```

Step 3   Try to access a website from the user's system.

Step 4   Check the translation table to make sure that a translation was built for the user's system. Refer to the commands in Step 2.

Step 5   If no translation was built, have the user's system try to ping an outside system, and then watch the output from the **debug** command. If you do not see any output, the packet is not making it to the PIX. If the packet is making it to the PIX, check the syslog output and make sure that there are enough addresses in the global command. Verify that the user's address is included in the **nat** command addresses. Check other items between the PIX and the user's system. Confirm that there is a valid default route.

Step 6   If a translation was built, turn on debugging for the packet using **debug packet** *interface_name,* and see if the packet is traveling through the PIX.

Step 7   If the packet goes out but you do not get a return, the outside router might not know how to return the traffic. Check the routing table on the outside router.

External Users Cannot Access an Internal System (Web Server or Mail Server)

The following steps provide a practical approach to troubleshooting common problems associated with external users having difficulty accessing a company's Internet/mail servers.

Step 1   The first step in this type of debugging is to allow pings from the external source for testing purposes. Use these commands or the equivalent **access-list** commands:

```
conduit permit icmp any any echo
conduit permit icmp any any echo-reply
```

Step 2   Turn on **debug icmp trace**.

Step 3   Have an external site try to ping the internal system via the translated address. For example, if your web server has an internal address of 10.10.10.1 and a translated address of 200.200.200.1, have the external site ping the 200.200.200.1 address.

Step 4   If you do not see the packets on the PIX, check the external router to ensure that they are making it there. If they are, check the routing table on the external router to make sure that the router knows how to route the packet. If the routing tables are correct, check the ARP table on the router to make sure that it has the proper MAC address for the packet. It should be the same as the PIX's external MAC address.

Step 5   Check the **static** and **conduit** statements in the PIX configuration for the server in question, and ensure that they are correct. You can also check using the following commands:

— **show static**—Shows all the static addresses that are currently assigned.

— **show conduit**—Shows all the conduits that are currently applied.

If the packet goes through, have the external site try to get to the server again. This time, use port 80 (web browsing). Also try by DNS name as well as IP address to rule out any DNS issues. If the external user cannot get to the server, check the log for his or her address. Check to see if the address is getting denied due to some reason.

Troubleshooting IOS Firewalls

IOS Firewalls require relatively few steps to set up. Therefore, misconfigurations are few and far between. This section looks at some of the issues that can cause the IOS Firewall to behave unexpectedly.

IOS Firewall Order of Operations

As with NAT, understanding at what point in a packet's path CBAC kicks in and how the access lists are processed can make implementing a firewall much easier and more trouble-free. Table 24-5 shows the order in which various packets pass through the router. "Inside" is generally the private network behind the router, and "outside" is the network on the public side of the router.

Table 24-5 *Order in Which Various Operations Are Performed for Packets Passing Through a Router*

	Inside to Outside		Outside to Inside
1	If IPsec, check input access list	1	If IPsec, check input access list
2	Decryption for CET or IPsec	2	Decryption for CET or IPsec
3	Check input access list	3	Check input access list
4	Check input rate limits	4	Check input rate limits
5	Input accounting	5	Input accounting
6	Inspect	6	Inspect
7	Policy routing	7	NAT outside to inside (global-to-local translation)
8	Routing		
9	Redirect to web cache	8	Policy routing
10	NAT inside to outside (local-to-global translation)	9	Routing
		10	Redirect to web cache
11	Crypto (check map and mark for encryption)	11	Crypto (check map and mark for encryption)
12	Check output access list	12	Check output access list
13	Inspect	13	Inspect
14	TCP intercept	14	TCP intercept
15	Encryption for CET or IPsec	15	Encryption for CET or IPsec

Especially important to note in this table is the order in which NAT and inspect are performed, because these two often interact in most implementations.

IOS Firewall show Commands

The most commonly used **show** command in IOS Firewalls is **show ip inspect {name** *inspection-name* | **config** | **interfaces** | **session [detail]** | **all}**. This command is used to get information about what the IOS Firewall has been set up to do and to get information on the sessions that are currently active through the IOS Firewall. Example 24-13 shows sample output from this command.

Example 24-13 *Sample Output for the* **show ip inspect all** *Command*

```
router#show ip inspect all
Session audit trail is disabled
one-minute (sampling period) thresholds are [400:500] connections
max-incomplete sessions thresholds are [400:500]
max-incomplete tcp connections per host is 50. Block-time 0 minute.
tcp synwait-time is 30 sec -- tcp finwait-time is 5 sec
tcp idle-time is 3600 sec -- udp idle-time is 30 sec
dns-timeout is 5 sec
Inspection Rule Configuration
 Inspection name all
     tcp timeout 3600
     udp timeout 30
     ftp timeout 3600
Interface Configuration
 Interface Ethernet0
  Inbound inspection rule is all
     tcp timeout 3600
     udp timeout 30
     ftp timeout 3600
  Outgoing inspection rule is not set
  Inbound access list is not set
  Outgoing access list is not set
 Established Sessions
  Session 25A6E1C (30.0.0.1:46065)=>(40.0.0.1:21) ftp SIS_OPEN
  Session 25A34A0 (40.0.0.1:20)=>(30.0.0.1:46072) ftp-data SIS_OPEN
```

This output shows some of the parameters we discussed in Chapter 9, "IOS Firewall." It also shows a session (for FTP) that is currently open through the IOS Firewall (shown as two sessions in the output).

Another useful command is **show ip inspect sessions detail**, as shown in Example 24-14. This command provides detailed output on the sessions that are currently live through the firewall.

Example 24-14 *Sample Output for the* **show ip inspect sessions detail** *Command*

```
router#show ip inspect sessions detail
Established Sessions
 Session 25A335C (40.0.0.1:20)=>(30.0.0.1:46069) ftp-data SIS_OPEN
   Created 00:00:07, Last heard 00:00:00
   Bytes sent (initiator:responder) [0:3416064] acl created 1
   Inbound access-list 111 applied to interface Ethernet1
 Session 25A6E1C (30.0.0.1:46065)=>(40.0.0.1:21) ftp SIS_OPEN
   Created 00:01:34, Last heard 00:00:07
   Bytes sent (initiator:responder) [196:616] acl created 1
   Inbound access-list 111 applied to interface Ethernet1
```

This output includes times, the number of bytes sent, and which access list was applied.

The **show access-list** command can also be useful in troubleshooting the IOS Firewall because it displays the dynamic access list entries created for the sessions originating from behind the firewall. These dynamic entries and their hit count are seen at the top of the access list that is used to filter ingress traffic coming to the public/outside network and going to the inside/private network.

IOS Firewall debug **Commands**

The most commonly used CBAC debugs are

- **debug ip inspect tcp**
- **debug ip inspect object-creation**
- **debug ip inspect object-deletion**
- **debug ip inspect events**

Example 24-15 shows sample output for **debug ip inspect object-creation**, **debug ip inspect object-deletion**, and **debug ip inspect events**.

Example 24-15 *Sample Output for the* **debug ip inspect object-creation**, **debug ip inspect object-deletion**, *and* **debug ip inspect events** *Commands*

```
!The debug line below shows preparation for a SIS to be created for outgoing
!traffic.
*Mar  2 01:18:51: CBAC OBJ_CREATE: create pre-gen sis 25A3574

!The line below refers to the dynamic access control list being created to allow
!traffic to return.

*Mar  2 01:18:51: CBAC OBJ_CREATE: create acl wrapper 25A36FC -- acl item 25A3634

!The two lines below show the source and destination addresses and the source and
!destination port numbers that are being used to set up the SIS.

*Mar  2 01:18:51: CBAC Src 10.1.0.1 Port [1:65535]
*Mar  2 01:18:51: CBAC Dst 30.0.0.1 Port [46406:46406]

!The line below shows a SIS that has been created for the traffic shown above.

*Mar  2 01:18:51: CBAC Pre-gen sis 25A3574 created: 10.1.0.1[1:65535]
30.0.0.1[46406:46406]
*Mar  2 01:18:51: CBAC OBJ_CREATE: create sis 25C1CC4
*Mar  2 01:18:51: CBAC sis 25C1CC4 initiator_addr (10.1.0.1:20) responder_addr
(30.0.0.1:46406)
```

The **debug ip inspect tcp** output shown in Example 24-16 shows the communication between two hosts, 10.0.0.1 and 10.1.0.1, using FTP. Note that CBAC uses Layer 7 inspection to process FTP transactions.

Example 24-16 *Sample Output for the* **debug ip inspect tcp** *Command*

```
router#debug ip inspect tcp
*Mar  2 01:20:43: CBAC* sis 25A3604 pak 2541C58 TCP P ack 4223720032
  seq 4200176225(22)
(10.0.0.1:46409) => (10.1.0.1:21)
*Mar  2 01:20:43: CBAC* sis 25A3604 ftp L7 inspect result: PROCESS-SWITCH packet
*Mar  2 01:20:43: CBAC sis 25A3604 pak 2541C58 TCP P ack 4223720032
  seq 4200176225(22)
(10.0.0.1:46409) => (10.1.0.1:21)
*Mar  2 01:20:43: CBAC sis 25A3604 ftp L7 inspect result: PASS packet
*Mar  2 01:20:43: CBAC* sis 25A3604 pak 2544374 TCP P ack 4200176247
  seq 4223720032(30)
(10.0.0. 1:46409) <= (10.1.0.1:21)
*Mar  2 01:20:43: CBAC* sis 25A3604 ftp L7 inspect result: PASS packet
*Mar  2 01:20:43: CBAC* sis 25A3604 pak 25412F8 TCP P ack 4223720062
  seq 4200176247(15)
(10.0.0. 1:46409) => (10.1.0.1:21)
*Mar  2 01:20:43: CBAC* sis 25A3604 ftp L7 inspect result: PASS packet
*Mar  2 01:20:43: CBAC sis 25C1CC4 pak 2544734 TCP S seq 4226992037(0)
  (10.1.0.1:20) =>
(10.0.0.1:46411)
*Mar  2 01:20:43: CBAC* sis 25C1CC4 pak 2541E38 TCP S ack 4226992038
  seq 4203405054(0)
(10.1.0.1:20) <= (10.0.0.1:46411)
```

This output shows TCP packets being processed and lists the corresponding acknowledge (ACK) packet numbers and sequence (SEQ) numbers. The number of data bytes in the TCP packet is shown in parentheses—for example, (22). For each packet shown, the addresses and port numbers are separated by a colon. For example, (10.1.0.1:21) indicates an IP address of 10.1.0.1 and a TCP port number of 21.

Entries with an asterisk (*) after the word CBAC are entries where the fast switching path is used; otherwise, the process switching path is used.

Common IOS Firewall Problems and Resolutions

This section looks at some common IOS Firewall issues and examines their causes.

Inspect Statement Is Applied in the Wrong Direction

One of the most common issues with CBAC's not inspecting traffic and consequently not opening dynamic entries in the access list for return traffic is that the inspect rules are applied in the wrong direction. Inspection must take place on the router for the traffic going from the protected/inside network to the outside/public/unprotected network. In addition, if denial of service (DoS) protection is sought, the traffic entering the router from the public network must also be inspected. Figure 24-2 explains the inspection rule logic.

Figure 24-2 *IP Inspect and ACL Direction*

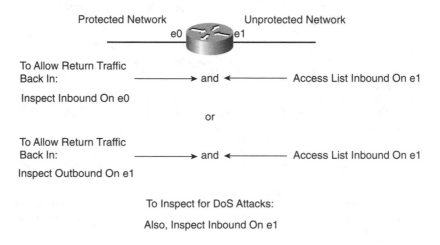

Relevant Application-Level Protocol Is Not Being Inspected

For the PIX to perform firewall services for special application-level protocols such as FTP, RealAudio, and other multimedia applications, the router must be configured to do so. Generic TCP and UDP inspection does not allow application-specific CBAC functionality to take place. Chapter 9 contains a more detailed discussion of how IOS Firewall deals with application-level protocols.

Inspection Does Not Take Place on the Correct Interface

For the inspection to occur, all the router's ingress interfaces should have the **ip inspect** *name of firewall* command configured. An alternative is to inspect the egress interfaces (if there are fewer of them) in the outbound direction.

CBAC Does Not Inspect ICMP Packets and Router Self-Generated Packets

ICMP messages do not contain state information. Therefore, you shouldn't use them to test CBAC functionality, because CBAC does not inspect them. Similarly, packets generated with one of the router interfaces as the source are not inspected either.

Troubleshooting IPsec VPNs

IPsec VPNs are discussed in significant detail in Chapter 13, "IPsec." Because IPsec is a combination of multiple protocols, it is important to have a very strong understanding of how these protocols work together to troubleshoot IPsec. A thorough understanding of ISAKMP is also very useful in identifying negotiation problems in IPsec. This section looks at some of the tools available to troubleshoot IPsec, as well as some of the common issues surrounding its implementation.

IPsec's Order of Events

IPsec's order of events is important to know because IPsec interacts with a wide variety of protocols running on a router. Because IPsec adds an additional header on top of the original header with a changed IP address in the case of ESP tunnel mode, it is important to understand how the various other routines affect this new header. Table 24-6 outlines the sequence of events. "Inside" is generally the private network behind the router, and "outside" is the network on the public side of the router.

Table 24-6 *Order in Which Various Operations Are Performed for Packets Passing Through a Router*

Inside to Outside		Outside to Inside	
1	If IPsec, check input access list	1	If IPsec, check input access list
2	Decryption for CET or IPsec	2	Decryption for CET or IPsec
3	Check input access list	3	Check input access list
4	Check input rate limits	4	Check input rate limits
5	Input accounting	5	Input accounting
6	Inspect	6	Inspect
7	Policy routing	7	NAT outside to inside (global-to-local translation)
8	Routing		
9	Redirect to web cache	8	Policy routing
10	NAT inside to outside (local-to-global translation)	9	Routing
		10	Redirect to web cache
11	Crypto (check map and mark for encryption)	11	Crypto (check map and mark for encryption)
12	Check output access list	12	Check output access list
13	Inspect	13	Inspect
14	TCP intercept	14	TCP intercept
15	Encryption for CET or IPsec	15	Encryption for CET or IPsec

It is interesting to note that for IPsec traffic, the incoming access list is processed twice—once before decryption and once after decryption. Therefore, not only does ESP traffic need to be allowed through the incoming access list, but a hole needs to be opened for the subnets that are considered interesting traffic for IPsec and are being tunneled. However, because the router drops any packets arriving on its outside interface that match the IPsec interesting traffic access list and are not IPsec-encapsulated, the risk of an attacker's using this hole to gain access to the network behind the router is minimized.

IPsec Debugs

IPsec debug messages are a very important source for understanding any issues that might creep into the implementation of IPsec VPNs. The three most commonly used **debug** commands to troubleshoot IPsec are

- **debug crypto isakmp**
- **debug crypto ipsec**
- **debug crypto engine**

The first two **debug** commands are valid for the PIX Firewall as well. PIX has similar debugs as the ones shown for a router.

Example 24-17 shows the configuration of the router on one end of the IPsec tunnel. The router on the other end has a corresponding configuration (see Chapter 13 for more details). This configuration is used to generate the debugs shown here.

Example 24-17 *IPsec Configuration on a Router Used to Generate Sample Debugs*

```
Router#write terminal

crypto isakmp policy 1
 encr 3des
 authentication pre-share
crypto isakmp key jw4ep9846804ijl address 172.16.172.20
!
crypto ipsec transform-set myset esp-3des esp-md5-hmac
!
crypto map vpn 10 ipsec-isakmp
 set peer 172.16.172.20
 set transform-set myset
 match address 101

interface Ethernet0/0
 ip address 10.1.1.1 255.255.255.0
!
interface Ethernet1/0
 ip address 172.16.172.10 255.255.255.240
 crypto map vpn
!

access-list 101 permit ip 10.1.1.0 0.0.0.255 10.1.2.0 0.0.0.255
```

Example 24-18 shows the debug messages generated by turning on the three debugs just mentioned.

NOTE   In the sample debugs shown in Example 24-18, the explanation of the debug is followed by the actual debugs for that explanation.

Example 24-18 *IPsec Debugs Generated by Issuing the Commands* **debug crypto isakmp**, **debug crypto ipsec**, *and* **debug crypto engine**

```
Router#debug crypto ISAKMP
Router#debug crypto engine
Router#debug crypto ipsec

!Ping source and destination addresses matched the address access list for the
!crypto map VPN

   00:04:10: IPSEC(sa_request): ,
   (key eng. msg.) OUTBOUND local= 172.16.172.10, remote= 172.16.172.20,
   local_proxy = 10.1.1.0/255.255.255.0/0/0 (type=4),
   remote_proxy = 10.1.2.0/255.255.255.0/0/0 (type=4),

!The 'local' is the local tunnel endpoint, and the 'remote' is the remote crypto
!endpoint as configured in the map. The local proxy is the src interesting traffic
!as defined by the match address access list. The remote proxy is the destination
!interesting traffic as defined by the match address access list.

          protocol= ESP, transform= esp-3des esp-md5-hmac ,
      lifedur= 3600s and 4608000kb,
      spi= 0x4A10F22E(1242624558), conn_id= 0, keysize= 0, flags= 0x400C

!The protocol and the transforms are specified by the crypto map that has been
!hit, as are the lifetimes
!negotiate phase I SA parameters.

   ISAKMP: received ke message (1/1)
   ISAKMP: local port 500, remote port 500
   ISAKMP (0:1): Input = IKE_MESG_FROM_IPSEC, IKE_SA_REQ_MM Old State =
        IKE_READY  New State = IKE_I_MM1
   ISAKMP (0:1): beginning Main Mode exchange
   00:04:10: ISAKMP (0:1): sending packet to 172.16.172.20 (I) MM_NO_STATE
   00:04:10: ISAKMP (0:1): received packet from 172.16.172.20 (I) MM_NO_STATE
   00:04:10: ISAKMP (0:1): Input = IKE_MESG_FROM_PEER, IKE_MM_EXCH
   Old State = IKE_I_MM1  New State = IKE_I_MM2
```

continues

Example 24-18 *IPsec Debugs Generated by Issuing the Commands* **debug crypto isakmp**, **debug crypto ipsec**, *and* **debug crypto engine** *(Continued)*

```
00:04:10: ISAKMP (0:1): processing SA payload. message ID = 0
00:04:10: ISAKMP (0:1): found peer pre-shared key matching 172.16.172.20
00:04:10: ISAKMP (0:1): Checking ISAKMP transform 1 against priority 1 policy
00:04:10: ISAKMP:        encryption 3DES-CBC
00:04:10: ISAKMP:        hash SHA
00:04:10: ISAKMP:        default group 1
00:04:10: ISAKMP:        auth pre-share
00:04:10: ISAKMP:        life type in seconds
00:04:10: ISAKMP:        life duration (VPI) of  0x0 0x1 0x51 0x80
00:04:10: ISAKMP (0:1): atts are acceptable. Next payload is 0
00:04:10: ISAKMP (0:1): Input = IKE_MESG_INTERNAL, IKE_PROCESS_MAIN_MODE
Old State = IKE_I_MM2  New State = IKE_I_MM2
```

```
!Policy 1 on this router and the atts offered by the other side matched.
!The third and fourth packets complete the  Diffie-Hellman Exchange.
```

```
ISAKMP (0:1): sending packet to
172.16.172.20 (I) MM_SA_SETUP
ISAKMP (0:1): Input = IKE_MESG_INTERNAL,
  IKE_PROCESS_COMPLETE Old State = IKE_I_MM2  New State = IKE_I_MM3
ISAKMP (0:1): received packet from 172.16.172.20 (I) MM_SA_SETUP
ISAKMP (0:1): Input = IKE_MESG_FROM_PEER, IKE_MM_EXCH
Old State = IKE_I_MM3  New State = IKE_I_MM4

ISAKMP (0:1): processing KE payload. message ID = 0
ISAKMP (0:1): processing NONCE payload. message ID = 0
ISAKMP (0:1): found peer pre-shared key matching 172.16.172.20
ISAKMP (0:1): SKEYID state generated
ISAKMP (0:1): processing vendor id payload
```

```
!The fifth and sixth packets complete IKE authentication. Phase I SA established.
```

```
ISAKMP (0:1): SA is doing pre-shared key
authentication using id type ID_IPV4_ADDR
...
ISAKMP (0:1): sending packet to 172.16.172.20
(I) MM_KEY_EXCH
ISAKMP (0:1): Input = IKE_MESG_INTERNAL,
IKE_PROCESS_COMPLETEOld State = IKE_I_MM4  New State = IKE_I_MM5

ISAKMP (0:1): received packet from 172.16.172.20 (I) MM_KEY_EXCH
ISAKMP (0:1): Input = IKE_MESG_FROM_PEER, IKE_MM_EXCH
Old State = IKE_I_MM5  New State = IKE_I_MM6
ISAKMP (0:1): processing ID payload. message ID = 0
ISAKMP (0:1): processing HASH payload. message ID = 0
ISAKMP (0:1): SA has been authenticated with 172.16.172.20
ISAKMP (0:1): Input = IKE_MESG_INTERNAL, IKE_PROCESS_COMPLETE
Old State = IKE_I_MM6  New State = IKE_P1_COMPLETE
```

Example 24-18 *IPsec Debugs Generated by Issuing the Commands* **debug crypto isakmp**, **debug crypto ipsec**, *and* **debug crypto engine** *(Continued)*

```
!Begin Quick Mode exchange. IPsec SA is negotiated in QM.

ISAKMP (0:1): beginning Quick Mode exchange, M-ID of 965273472
ISAKMP (0:1): sending packet to 172.16.172.20 (I) QM_IDLE
ISAKMP (0:1): Node 965273472, Input = IKE_MESG_INTERNAL, IKE_INIT_QM Old State =
  IKE_QM_READY  New State = IKE_QM_I_QM1
ISAKMP (0:1): received packet from 172.16.172.20 (I) QM_IDLE

!The IPsec SA proposal offered by the far end is checked against the local crypto
!map configuration

ISAKMP (0:1): processing HASH payload. message ID = 965273472
ISAKMP (0:1): processing SA payload. message ID = 965273472

ISAKMP (0:1): Checking IPsec proposal 1
ISAKMP: transform 1, ESP_3DES
ISAKMP:    attributes in transform:
ISAKMP:        encaps is 1
ISAKMP:        SA life type in seconds
ISAKMP:        SA life duration (basic) of 3600
ISAKMP:        SA life type in kilobytes
ISAKMP:        SA life duration (VPI) of  0x0 0x46 0x50 0x0
ISAKMP:        authenticator is HMAC-MD5
ISAKMP (0:1): atts are acceptable.
IPSEC(validate_proposal_request): proposal part #1,
  (key eng. msg.) INBOUND local= 172.16.172.10, remote= 172.16.172.20,
  local_proxy= 10.1.1.0/255.255.255.0/0/0 (type=4),
  remote_proxy= 10.1.2.0/255.255.255.0/0/0 (type=4),
  protocol= ESP, transform= esp-3des esp-md5-hmac ,
  lifedur= 0s and 0kb,
  spi= 0x0(0), conn_id= 0, keysize= 0, flags= 0x4

!Two IPsec SAs have been negotiated--an incoming SA with the SPI generated by the
!local machine and an outbound SA with the SPIs proposed by the remote end.


ISAKMP (0:1): Creating IPsec SAs
inbound SA from 172.16.172.20 to 172.16.172.10(proxy 10.1.2.0 to 10.1.1.0)
has spi 0x8EAB0B22 and conn_id 2029 and flags 4
 lifetime of 3600 seconds lifetime of 4608000 kilobytes
outbound SA from 172.16.172.10   to 172.16.172.20 (proxy 10.1.1.0 to 10.1.2.0)
has spi -343614331 and conn_id 2030 and flags C
  lifetime of 3600 seconds lifetime of 4608000 kilobytes

!The IPsec SA info negotiated by IKE will be populated into the router's SADB.

00:04:10: IPSEC(key_engine): got a queue event...
00:04:10: IPSEC(initialize_sas): ,
  (key eng. msg.) INBOUND local= 172.16.172.10, remote= 172.16.172.20,
```

continues

Example 24-18 *IPsec Debugs Generated by Issuing the Commands* **debug crypto isakmp***,* **debug crypto ipsec***, and* **debug crypto engine** *(Continued)*

```
    local_proxy= 10.1.1.0/255.255.255.0/0/0 (type=4),
    remote_proxy= 10.1.2.0/255.255.255.0/0/0 (type=4),
    protocol= ESP, transform= esp-3des esp-md5-hmac ,
    lifedur= 3600s and 4608000kb,
     spi= 0x8EAB0B22(2393574178), conn_id= 2029, keysize= 0, flags= 0x4
  00:04:10: IPSEC(initialize_sas): ,
    (key eng. msg.) OUTBOUND local= 172.16.172.10, remote= 172.16.172.20,
    local_proxy= 10.1.1.0/255.255.255.0/0/0 (type=4),
    remote_proxy= 10.1.2.0/255.255.255.0/0/0 (type=4),
    protocol= ESP, transform= esp-3des esp-md5-hmac ,
    lifedur= 3600s and 4608000kb,
    spi= 0xEB84DC85(3951352965), conn_id= 2030, keysize= 0, flags= 0xC
  !IPsec SA created in SADB, sent out last packet with commit bit set. IPsec
  !tunnel established.
  IPSEC(create_sa): sa created,
   (sa) sa_dest= 172.16.172.10,
    sa_prot= 50,
    sa_spi= 0x8EAB0B22(2393574178),
    sa_trans= esp-3des esp-md5-hmac ,
    sa_conn_id= 2029
  IPSEC(create_sa): sa created,
    (sa) sa_dest= 172.16.172.20, sa_prot= 50, sa_spi= 0xEB84DC85(3951352965),
    sa_trans= esp-3des esp-md5-hmac , sa_conn_id= 2030
  ISAKMP (0:1): sending packet to 172.16.172.20 (I) QM_IDLE
  ISAKMP (0:1): Node 965273472, Input = IKE_MESG_FROM_PEER, IKE_QM_EXCH
  Old State = IKE_QM_I_QM1  New State = IKE_QM_PHASE2_COMPLETE
```

The debugs shown in Example 24-18 can be even more instructive if you read them in conjunction with the description of IKE protocol functionality in Chapter 13.

IPsec show **Commands**

IPsec **show** commands are particularly useful in debugging IPsec. Having established basic connectivity, the network administrator can use **show** commands to see the issues related to the operation of IPsec on top of the basic network connectivity. Three **show** commands are most commonly used to view the status of an IPsec connection:

- **show crypto isakmp sa**
- **show crypto ipsec sa**
- **show crypto engine connection active**

The **show** command output in Example 24-19 shows one ISAKMP SA and two IPsec SAs established. The packet count for each of the IPsec SAs, along with the negotiated parameters, are also shown.

Example 24-19 *Sample Output for the* **show crypto engine connection active** *Command*

```
Router#show crypto engine connection active
ID    Interface        IP-Address       State  Algorithm                  Encrypt    Decrypt
1     <none>           <none>           set    HMAC_SHA+3DES_56_C              0          0
!Shown above is the ISAKMP SA. It shows the hashing algorithm, SHA-HMAC, which is
!being used for authentication, as well as the encryption algorithm, 3DES, used to
!encrypt the IKE negotiation messages. The encrypt and decrypt counts are 0
!because the ISAKMP SA is not used to encrypt and decrypt data.
2029  Ethernet1/0      172.16.172.10    set    HMAC_MD5+3DES_56_C              0          4
2030  Ethernet1/0      172.16.172.10    set    HMAC_MD5+3DES_56_C              4          0
!Shown above are the two IPsec SAs. They show the hashing algorithm, SHA-HMAC,
!which is used for message integrity checking, as well as the encryption
!algorithm, 3DES, used to encrypt the ESP packets. The first SA is the incoming
!SA, because the packet count shows decrypts in it. The other one is the outgoing
!SA, showing only encrypts.
```

The **show** command in Example 24-20 shows the ISAKMP SA. It is in QM_IDLE state, meaning that quick mode has been successfully completed.

Example 24-20 *Sample Output for the* **show crypto isakmp sa** *Command*

```
Router#show crypto isakmp sa
dst             src            state         conn-id    slot
172.16.172.20   172.16.172.10  QM_IDLE             1       0
```

The ISAKMP SA can be in a number of states, depending on which state the negotiation is in. The following tables list these states. They are an excellent reference if you are trying to use **show** command output to find out the point at which a negotiation is. Table 24-7 shows the states displayed in the **show crypto isakmp sa** command when main mode is being negotiated. Table 24-8 shows the states displayed in the **show crypto isakmp sa** command when aggressive mode is being negotiated. Table 24-9 shows the state displayed in the **show crypto isakmp sa** command when quick mode is being negotiated or has been negotiated. In general, the states shown in these tables are the most commonly seen states. Some other states might also be seen, but these shown here are by far the most important.

Table 24-7 *States Displayed in the* **show crypto isakmp sa** *Command When Main Mode Is Being Negotiated*

State	Description
OAK_MM_NO_STATE	The ISAKMP SA has been created, but nothing else has happened yet. It is "larval" at this stage—there is no state.
OAK_MM_SA_SETUP	The peers have agreed on parameters for the ISAKMP SA.
OAK_MM_KEY_EXCH	The peers have exchanged Diffie-Hellman public keys and have generated a shared secret. The ISAKMP SA remains unauthenticated.
OAK_MM_KEY_AUTH	The ISAKMP SA has been authenticated. If the router initiated this exchange, this state transitions immediately to OAK_QM_IDLE, and a quick mode exchange begins.

Table 24-8 *States Displayed in the* **show crypto isakmp sa** *Command When Aggressive Mode Is Being Negotiated*

State	Description
OAK_AG_NO_STATE	The ISAKMP SA has been created, but nothing else has happened yet. It is "larval" at this stage—there is no state.
OAK_AG_INIT_EXCH	The peers have done the first exchange in aggressive mode, but the SA is not authenticated.
OAK_AG_AUTH	The ISAKMP SA has been authenticated. If the router initiated this exchange, this state transitions immediately to OAK_QM_IDLE, and a quick mode exchange begins.

Table 24-9 *State Displayed in the* **show crypto isakmp sa** *Command When Quick Mode Is Being Negotiated or Has Been Negotiated*

State	Description
OAK_QM_IDLE	The ISAKMP SA is idle. It remains authenticated with its peer and may be used for subsequent quick mode exchanges. It is in a quiescent state.

The **show** commands in Example 24-21 show the packets, counts, SPI, and various other parameters for both of the IPsec SAs in place between the two routers.

Example 24-21 *Sample Output for the* **show crypto IPsec sa** *Command*

```
Router#show crypto IPsec sa
interface: Ethernet1/0
    Crypto map tag: vpn, local addr. 172.16.172.10

   local  ident (addr/mask/prot/port): (10.1.1.0/255.255.255.0/0/0)
   remote ident (addr/mask/prot/port): (10.1.2.0/255.255.255.0/0/0)
   current_peer: 172.16.172.20
     PERMIT, flags={origin_is_acl,}
    #pkts encaps: 4, #pkts encrypt: 4, #pkts digest 4
    #pkts decaps: 4, #pkts decrypt: 4, #pkts verify 4
    #pkts compressed: 0, #pkts decompressed: 0
    #pkts not compressed: 0, #pkts compr. failed: 0, #pkts decompress failed: 0
    #send errors 6, #recv errors 0

     local crypto endpt.: 172.16.172.10, remote crypto endpt.: 172.16.172.20
     path mtu 1500, media mtu 1500
     current outbound spi: EB84DC85


   inbound esp sas:
       spi: 0x8EAB0B22(2393574178)
         transform: esp-3des esp-md5-hmac ,
         in use settings ={Tunnel, }
```

Example 24-21 *Sample Output for the* **show crypto IPsec sa** *Command (Continued)*

```
               slot: 0, conn id: 2029, flow_id: 1, crypto map: vpn
               sa timing: remaining key lifetime (k/sec): (4607998/3347)
               IV size: 8 bytes
               replay detection support: Y

      outbound esp sas:
           spi: 0xEB84DC85(3951352965)
             transform: esp-3des esp-md5-hmac ,
             in use settings ={Tunnel, }
             slot: 0, conn id: 2030, flow_id: 2, crypto map: vpn
             sa timing: remaining key lifetime (k/sec): (4607999/3347)
             IV size: 8 bytes
             replay detection support: Y
```

Commonly Seen IPsec Problems and Resolutions

IPsec issues can arise from a wide variety of reasons. This section discusses some of the more common problems with setting up IPsec tunnels and their functioning.

Incompatible ISAKMP Policy or Preshared Key

It is important for the ISAKMP preshared key, if that is the method of authentication being used, to match on the two IPsec peers. If this doesn't happen, the tunnel won't come up. The failure occurs in phase one of ISAKMP.

Example 24-22 shows the debugs seen on a Cisco IOS router when the preshared keys do not match.

Example 24-22 *Sample Debug Output Seen on a Cisco IOS Router When the Preshared Keys Configured on It and Its Peer Do Not Match*

```
Router#debug crypto ISAKMP
Router#debug crypto engine
Router#debug crypto ipsec

ISAKMP: reserved no zero on payload 5!
%CRYPTO-4-IKMP_BAD_MESSAGE: IKE message from 155.0.0.1   failed its
sanity check or is malformed
```

It is also important for at least one ISAKMP policy on the two peers to match. If this does not happen, phase 1 of ISAKMP fails.

Example 24-23 contains sample debugs seen on a router when ISAKMP policies fail to match.

Example 24-23 *Sample Debug Output Seen on a Router When ISAKMP Policies Fail to Match*

```
Router#debug crypto ISAKMP
Router#debug crypto engine
Router#debug crypto ipsec

ISAKMP (0:1): Encryption algorithm offered does not match policy!
ISAKMP (0:1): atts are not acceptable. Next payload is 0
ISAKMP (0:1): no offers accepted!
ISAKMP (0:1): phase 1 SA not acceptable!
```

Incorrect Access Lists for Interesting Traffic

For IPsec to work correctly, the access control lists on the two peers must define interesting traffic such that the two peers can agree that they want to encrypt the same traffic. In most cases, the access lists configured on the two peers are exact reflections of each other. However, it is permissible for the traffic specified by an access list defined on one peer to be a subset of the traffic specified by the access list configured on the other peer. In the case of VPN clients, dynamic crypto maps need to be used to get over the problem of the VPN clients coming from an unknown IP address.

Example 24-24 shows the debugs that appear on the routers when the access lists configured on two peers negotiating IPsec are neither the same nor the subsets of each other.

Example 24-24 *Sample Debug Output When the Access Lists Configured on Two Peers Negotiating IPsec Are Not the Same or Are Subsets of Each Other*

```
Router#debug crypto ISAKMP
Router#debug crypto engine
Router#debug crypto ipsec

3d00h: IPsec(validate_transform_proposal): proxy identities not supported
3d00h: ISAKMP (0:3): IPsec policy invalidated proposal
3d00h: ISAKMP (0:3): phase 2 SA not acceptable!
```

Crypto Map Is on the Wrong Interface

Generally, the crypto map needs to be applied to the outgoing interface of the router or the PIX. Not applying the map to the egress interface stops IPsec from kicking in at all, and no ISAKMP debugs are generated. The crypto map needs to be applied to tunnel interfaces as well if you are using GRE with IPsec. In general, if a logical interface is used in conjunction with a physical interface to pass IPsec traffic, the crypto map needs to be applied to both of them.

Routing Issues

Routing can play an important role in bringing up an IPsec tunnel successfully. Keep in mind the following points when examining routing issues in IPsec implementations:

- A packet needs to be routed to the interface that has the crypto map configured on it before IPsec kicks in.

- Routes need to be there not only for the router to reach its peer's address but also for the IP subnet addresses in the IP packets' heads after they have been decrypted.

- Use the **debug ip packet** *acl* **detailed** command to see if the routing is occurring correctly.

Bypassing NAT

We have already discussed how NAT can be bypassed on a router for traffic that is to be encapsulated in an IPsec tunnel.

On the PIX Firewall, the **nat (inside) 0 access-list** command can be used to bypass NAT in a fashion similar to the routers.

Time Settings for Certificates

Digital certificates are issued for a time frame. They become invalid after that and are invalid before the time frame starts. The clock and calendar of the machine on which the certificates are installed are used to determine the certificates' validity. It is important to have the correct time and date configured on the router or the PIX using certificates so that they can function properly.

Firewall or Access List Is Blocking IPsec Negotiations or Traffic

A firewall in the middle of an IPsec tunnel must allow the following protocols to go through it for IPsec to function properly:

- ESP and/or AH
- UDP port 500

The IPsec router, if it has an access list configured on the egress interface, must have holes in that access list not only for these two protocols but also to accommodate the fact that the incoming access list is applied twice to the IPsec traffic. See the discussion at the start of this section for details.

IPsec MTU Issues

IPsec adds significant overhead to the original IP packet being encapsulated. Therefore, it is possible that the new encapsulated packet's size might be more than the MTU on certain segments over which the IPsec packets must pass. Normal Path MTU mechanisms using ICMP packets can take care of fixing the MTU size, but when such ICMPs are blocked by a firewall or an access list somewhere along the path that the IPsec packet takes, issues can arise. The symptoms of these issues are often the inability of users to run applications such as e-mail and large file FTPs across the IPsec tunnel. Figure 24-3 shows how Path MTU discovery with IPsec works. If a router in the path of the packet being sent by the end host is unable to transmit the frame using the size of the frame it has received, it sends back an ICMP packet to the end host, asking for the packet size to be reduced to the maximum size the router can support. The end host then transmits the packets in frames of reduced size, which the router can transmit. This process is repeated as necessary by all the routers in the path of the packets transmitted by the end host.

Figure 24-3 *IPsec Path MTU*

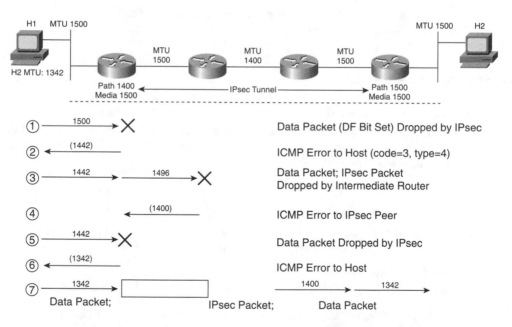

However, there are situations in which the ICMP packets generated in the fashion previously described are blocked (perhaps by a firewall) from reaching the end host. Therefore, the end host never finds out that there is a problem with the MTU of the packets it is sending and continues sending frames with the large MTU size resulting in these large packets being dropped by the device which does have an MTU size large enough to accommodate these packets. Another situation arises when the end host does receive the ICMP packets but due to a bug or faulty implementation of the TCP/IP stack does not reduce its MTU size. The result is the same as described for ICMPs being blocked from reaching the end host.

In both of these cases, two options remain for the network administrator to fix the problem:

- Setting up the TCP MSS on an edge router, forcing a small TCP MSS to be negotiated
- Manually reducing the MTU on the end hosts that are not receiving the ICMP packets or are choosing to ignore them

To use either of these methods, you must know how to calculate the size of the packet after the IPsec header has been added. The following formula is used to calculate the size to which the original IP packet must be restricted to remain within the smallest MTU available on the path that is traversed by the IPsec tunnel:

maximum original packet size allowed = floor((IPsec packet size allowed),8) – (IPsec header+SPI+sequence number+HMAC) – (IV+pad+pad length+next header)

where

IPsec header = 20 bytes in ESP tunnel mode
SPI (Security Parameter Index) = 4 bytes
Sequence number = 4 bytes
ESP-HMAC MD5/SHA 96 digest = 12 bytes
IV (Initialization Vector) = 8 bytes
Pad = 1 byte
Pad length = 1 byte
Next header = 1 byte

The floor function here is calculated by finding the largest whole number (a number such as 1200.0 or 1300.0, not 1200.345 or 1300.897) that is fully divisible by 8 *and* that is less than "IPsec packet size allowed." For example, if the IPsec packet size allowed is 876, the floor to 8 would be 872, because 872 is fully divisible by 8 (872 / 8 = 109.0) and 872 is the largest such number that is less than 876.

See Chapter 13 for more details on some of the elements in the previous equation.

A sample calculation is shown next. In this case, the network administrator has found out that the smallest MTU on the IPsec tunnel path is 1330 bytes:

maximum original packet size allowed = floor((1330),8) – (20+4+4+12) – (8–1–1–1) = 1328 – 40 – 11 = 1277

Therefore, the network administrator can manually configure the end host not to send a packet larger than 1277 bytes.

If the network administrator does not want to change the MTU on the end host, such as when there are too many of them, he or she can use the **tcp mss** command on the router's ingress interface. The router for the default gateway for the end hosts is:

```
ip tcp adjust-mss number
```

This command forces the router to sniff on the incoming TCP SYN packets and tweak the TCP MSS field to the number configured in this command. With the MSS value tweaked, the two end hosts sitting behind the two IPsec peers must agree to this tweaked, negotiated TCP MSS value.

The number is calculated by taking into account the size of the TCP header in the packet. The calculation is as follows:

Maximum TCP MSS value allowed = maximum original packet size allowed – 40

So, in the case of our example, the TCP MSS number would be 1277 – 40 = 1237 bytes.

Troubleshooting Intrusion Detection

Troubleshooting the Cisco IDS solution is somewhat different from troubleshooting some of the other technologies and products you have seen so far. Instead of having a central set of debugs and **show** commands, the administrator more so needs to understand the functioning of the various daemons on the IDS boxes, as well as how the underlying UNIX OS works, to troubleshoot the issues arising in these implementations.

The following sections discuss the various commonly seen problems in the IDS and their solutions. You will become familiar with some of the common techniques used to diagnose and rectify these problems.

Commonly Seen IDS Problems and Resolutions

This section discusses the most common IDS problems and shows you how to resolve them. Each section lists the set of tools used to diagnose the problem. Some of these tools are operating system-specific, others are for OpenView or other interactive devices, and others are for the IDS system itself.

UNIX Director smid Is Not Functioning Properly

The smid daemon on the UNIX director populates the alarm icons on the HPOV maps. If it is not working properly, the most common symptom is the error message "Cannot write message to Director."

In this situation, you should check and fix the following items:

- Make sure smid and all the daemons it interacts with are running (use **nrstatus**). If not, do an **nrstart**.

- smid writes to a socket created in /usr/nr/tmp. Make sure that the socket is created as socket.dircomm=. If it isn't, (stop and) start OpenView (**ovw**).

- The socket smid writes to can overflow. This means that the messages are not getting removed fast enough to OpenView. Check to see if OpenView is running (**ovstatus-c**). If it isn't, start it (**ovw &**).

- smid and nrdirmap need to have adequate permissions to communicate. Make sure that smid is owned by netrangr and that nrdirmap is SUID netrangr. If they aren't, log out and log back in as netrangr, and restart all processes.

Alarms Aren't Being Reported on UNIX Director

Alarms are reported based on the severity level and destination. If alarms are not being reported despite smid's functioning properly, try and test the following things:

- Alarms on the director are reported only if they are above the configured minimum limit. Confirm that the sensor is generating alarms higher than the lower limits. If it isn't, adjust the director's minimum critical level and/or minimum marginal level for the sensor in question.

- Alarm data is pushed to the director log files by either the smid or the sensor itself. If no logs are being created, make sure that either an entry for **loggerd** exists in the sensor destinations file or that a **DupDestination** entry exists in the smid.conf file. If they don't, make either of the two changes. A sample entry in the destinations file is

  DupDestination director.training loggerd 1 EVENTS,ERRORS,COMMANDS

- The sensor postofficed communicates to the director smid only the alarms that are specified in the destinations file. Make sure that the destinations file contains the correct level of alarms. If it doesn't, adjust the destinations file entry. For example, to propagate level 2 and above alarms to director.training, use

  1 director.training smid 2 EVENTS,ERRORS,COMMANDS

UNIX Sensor Is Not Sniffing

The sensor sniffs the network on one of its interfaces—generally spwr0 or iprb0 in the new sensors. If the sensor is not sniffing, investigate the following issues:

- The sensor sniffs the network only when its sniffing daemon, packetd, is running, so make sure that packetd is running (using **nrstatus**). If it isn't, restart the daemon (using **nrstart**). If the daemon still does not come up, check the daemons file to make sure it is one of the listed daemons. If it isn't, **vi** the daemons file to include it.

- The sensor sniffs the network on the interface that is considered to be in the path of interesting traffic. Check packetd.conf to see if the sniffing interface is indeed configured:

  grep NameOfPacketDevice /usr/nr/etc/packetd.conf

NameOfPacketDevice /dev/spwr0

NameOfPacketDevice /dev/iprb0

If it isn't, on the director, change the Data Sources tab in intrusion detection and download the configurations to the sensor again.

Sensor and UNIX Director Are Unable to Communicate

The sensor communicates with the director to feed it information for alarms. It also needs to send resets to offensive devices.

- The sensor uses the information in the routes (/usr/nr/etc) file to reach the director. Confirm that the routes file has the correct entry for the director. Sample output is shown here:

  sensor.cisco 1 10.1.9.201 45000 1

  director.cisco 1 10.1.9.200 45000 1

  If the entry is incorrect, modify the director's sensor configuration, and download files to the sensor again.

- A firewall sitting between the sensor and the director can disrupt the communications between them. Make sure that the firewall allows the two to communicate. If it doesn't, open a hole for port 45000, and also create any necessary network address translation.

Sensor Is Unable to Reset Connections

A sensor uses TCP resets to drop particularly offensive connections. If the sensor is hanging off a switch, the switch can stop these resets from going through. Make sure that the switch is configured to allow the resets through.

If it isn't, make sure that the switch can receive packets from the sensor (**inpkts** on Catalyst 5000) and that the switch does not learn the sensor's MAC address and use it to discard spoofed MAC addresses (**learning** on Catalyst 5000).

CSPM Director Is Not Communicating with the Sensor

The inability of the CSPM director to communicate with the sensing device is a common reason for alarms not being reported on the director. The CSPM director needs to have the correct configuration for the IDS network architecture for it to communicate with the sensing device.

Check the hosts file in Program Files\Cisco Secure Policy Manager\PostOffice\.

Make sure that the device names and IDs are correct. An example is shown here:

137.100   localhost
137.100   test.cisco
22.100   sensord.cisco
23.100   sensor1.cisco

CSPM Director Is Not Displaying Alarms

If the CSPM and the sensor are communicating, but the CSPM is not receiving alarms, there could be a variety of reasons why. However, two of the most important things to verify are if the sensor is logging the alarms and if the CSPM is generating the event logs.

Step 1   Do an **nrstatus** on the sensor to see if loggerd is running.

Step 2   In CSPM, click the sensor icon and select the Logging tab.

Step 3   Check 'Generate audit event log' and then Update and Approve.

Catalyst IDSM (Catalyst 6000 Module) Sensor Cannot Come Online

Many of the issues with the Catalyst IDSM are related to the module's not coming online. The following are some of the things to test and try to resolve this issue:

- Execute **show module** *mod #* to see if the module is powered up. Example 24-25 shows some sample results.

Example 24-25 *Sample Output for the* **show module** *Command*

```
Console> (enable) show module
Mod Slot Ports Module-Type                Model             Status
--- ---- ----- -------------------------- ----------------- ------
1   1    2     1000BaseX Supervisor       WS-X6K-SUP1A-2GE  ok
6   6    2     Intrusion Detection Syste  WS-X6381-IDS      ok
```

- Use **set module power up** *mod #* to turn on the module's power.

- Verify if the module is enabled using **show module** *mod #*. If it is disabled, use **set module enable** *mod #* to enable it. If the module still fails to come online, use **reset** *mod #* and wait for 5 minutes for the module to come up.

- Execute **show test** *mod #* and check if the hardware and operating system are OK. If the PORT status is Fail, you need to replace the card. If the hdd status is Fail, you need to reimage the application portion.

- Verify if the maintenance operating system is OK. Execute **reset** *mod #* **hdd:2**. This resets the IDSM to the maintenance partition. Verify if the cached image is the correct version, and then install the application partition:

```
cisco_ids(diag)# ids-installer system /cache /show
cisco_ids(diag)# ids-installer system /cache /install
Console> (enable) reset 4 hdd:1
```

Troubleshooting AAA

AAA debugs are by far the easiest and most common mechanism for troubleshooting AAA issues. Although you can use **show** commands to check the various stages a negotiation is in, debugs are by far the best sources of information for failing AAA setups.

AAA show **Commands**

AAA **show** commands are often used in conjunction with **debug** commands and play a supporting role to the **debug** commands. However, they can often be used to gather summary information about the status of the AAA features and the TACACS+ and RADIUS feature sets. This can come in handy when you troubleshoot AAA-related issues. Some of the commonly used **show** commands for TACACS+ and RADIUS are

- **show tacacs+**
- **show radius statistics**
- **show caller user** *userid* **detail**

AAA debug **Commands**

This section focuses on the use of **debug** commands to troubleshoot AAA issues. Here are some commands you can use to debug AAA functionality:

- **debug aaa authentication**—Enabling this **debug** command displays authentication information with TACACS+ and RADIUS client/server interaction.
- **debug aaa authorization**—Enabling this **debug** command displays authorization information with TACACS+ and RADIUS client/server interaction.
- **debug aaa accounting**—Enabling this **debug** command displays accounting information with TACACS+ and RADIUS client/server interaction.
- **debug aaa per-user**—Enabling this **debug** command displays AAA information on a per-user basis.
- **debug tacacs**—Enabling this **debug** command displays TACACS+ interaction between the Cisco IOS client and the AAA server.
- **debug radius**—Enabling this **debug** command displays RADIUS interaction between the Cisco IOS client and the AAA server.

Common AAA Issues and Resolutions

This section looks at some common AAA issues. The primary strategy is using the **debug** commands to isolate the problem and then using the logs on the AAA server (Cisco Secure UNIX in this case) to diagnose the source of the issue.

AAA Server Key Is Incorrect in the NAS or AAA Server

The main purpose of the AAA server key is to authenticate the NAS to the AAA server and to secure the communication between the two machines.

The output shown in Example 24-26 is from a **debug aaa authentication** command executed on a NAS. As you can see, the authentication attempt failed, but no more information is given.

Example 24-26 *Sample Output for the* **debug aaa authentication** *and* **debug TACACS+** *Commands Where the AAA Server Key Is Incorrect in the NAS or AAA Server*

```
Router#debug aaa authentication
Router#debug TACACS+

TAC+: received bad AUTHEN packet: length = 68, expected 67857
TAC+: Invalid AUTHEN/START packet (check keys)
AAA/AUTHEN (1771887965): status = ERROR

!Upon accessing warnings and errors reported in the AAA server log file:
<CSUserver>$tail -f /var/log/csuslog

!The AAA server log file reports the following warning when no key is specified
!(indicating that there is no encryption key):

Jan 27 18:35:17 coachella CiscoSecure: WARNING - Insecure configuration: No
  encryption key for NAS <default>
```

Invalid User Password

If the user enters an invalid password, you see output similar to Example 24-27. This output is from a **debug aaa authentication** command executed on a NAS. The last line in Example 24-27 shows the AAA authentication request sent to the AAA server for user dial_tac.

Example 24-27 *Sample Output for the* **debug aaa authentication** *Command Where the User Password Is Invalid*

```
Router#debug aaa authentication

092852: Jan 27 22:19:06.713 CST: AAA/AUTHEN (543609479): status = GETPASS
092853: Jan 27 22:19:07.985 CST: AAA/AUTHEN/CONT (543609479): continue_login
```

continues

Example 24-27 *Sample Output for the* **debug aaa authentication** *Command Where the User Password Is Invalid (Continued)*

```
(user='dial_tac')
!The NAS receives FAIL from the AAA server for the user.
092854: Jan 27 22:19:07.985 CST: AAA/AUTHEN (543609479): status = GETPASS
092855: Jan 27 22:19:07.985 CST: AAA/AUTHEN (543609479): Method=ADMIN (tacacs+)
092856: Jan 27 22:19:07.985 CST: TAC+: send AUTHEN/CONT packet id=543609479
092857: Jan 27 22:19:08.185 CST: TAC+: ver=192 id=543609479 received AUTHEN
   status = FAIL
092858: Jan 27 22:19:08.185 CST: AAA/AUTHEN (543609479): status = FAIL
!The user session is torn down, and the AAA process is freed.
092859: Jan 27 22:19:10.185 CST: AAA/MEMORY: free_user (0x61D87A70) user='dial_tac'
ruser='' port='tty51' rem_addr='172.22.2.3' authen_type=ASCII service=LOGIN
priv=1

!Entering the tail command to assess warnings and errors reported in the AAA server
!log file displays the following information:
<CSUserver>$tail -f /var/log/csuslog

!In this case, the AAA server log reports an incorrect password for user dial_tac

Jan 27 22:19:08 coachella CiscoSecure: NOTICE - Authentication - Incorrect password;
[NAS
= 172.22.63.1, Port = tty51, User = dial_tac, Service = 1, Priv = 1]
Jan 27 22:19:08 coachella CiscoSecure: INFO - Profile: user = dial_tac {
Jan 27 22:19:08 coachella set server current-failed-logins = 1
```

Nonexistent User

This is similar to the issue discussed in the preceding section, but here the username entered by the user is incorrect. The following output is from a **debug aaa authentication** command executed on a NAS.

Example 24-28 shows the AAA process starting on NAS.

Example 24-28 *Sample Output for the* **debug aaa authentication** *Command Where the User Does Not Exist in the AAA Server Database*

```
Router#debug aaa authentication

092794: Jan 27 22:15:39.132 CST: AAA/MEMORY: create_user (0x61D87A70) user=''
   ruser=''
port='tty51' rem_addr='172.22.2.3' authen_type=ASCII service=LOGIN priv=1
092795: Jan 27 22:15:39.132 CST: AAA/AUTHEN/START (3576082779): port='tty51'
list='INSIDE' action=LOGIN service=LOGIN

!GETPASS is sent to the AAA server for verification for user dial_test:
092806: Jan 27 22:15:41.132 CST: AAA/AUTHEN/START (3285027777): Method=ADMIN
   (tacacs+)
092807: Jan 27 22:15:41.132 CST: TAC+: send AUTHEN/START packet ver=192
   id=32850=27777
```

Example 24-28 *Sample Output for the* **debug aaa authentication** *Command Where the User Does Not Exist in the AAA Server Database (Continued)*

```
092808: Jan 27 22:15:41.936 CST: TAC+: ver=192 id=3285027777 received AUTHEN
  status = GETPASS
092809: Jan 27 22:15:41.936 CST: AAA/AUTHEN (3285027777): status = GETPASS
092810: Jan 27 22:15:43.340 CST: AAA/AUTHEN/CONT (3285027777): continue_login
(user='dial_test')
092811: Jan 27 22:15:43.340 CST: AAA/AUTHEN (3285027777): status = GETPASS
092812: Jan 27 22:15:43.340 CST: AAA/AUTHEN (3285027777): Method=ADMIN (tacacs+)

!The NAS then receives the authentication FAIL message from the AAA server:
092813: Jan 27 22:15:43.340 CST: TAC+: send AUTHEN/CONT packet id=3285027777
092814: Jan 27 22:15:43.540 CST: TAC+: ver=192 id=3285027777 received AUTHEN
  status = FAIL
092815: Jan 27 22:15:43.540 CST: AAA/AUTHEN (3285027777): status = FAIL

!The session is torn down, and the AAA process is freed:
092816: Jan 27 22:15:45.540 CST: AAA/MEMORY: free_user (0x61D87A70) user=
  'dial_test'
ruser='' port='tty51' rem_addr='172.22.2.3' authen_type=ASCII service=LOGIN priv=1
092817: Jan 27 22:15:45.540 CST: AAA: parse name=tty51 idb type=-1 tty=-1
092818: Jan 27 22:15:45.540 CST: AAA: name=tty51 flags=0x11 type=5 shelf=0 slot

!Enter the following command to assess warnings and errors reported in the AAA
!server log file:
<CSUserver>$tail -f /var/log/csuslog

!The AAA server log file shows that the AAA server did not find user dial_test in
!the cache (profile caching is enabled):
Jan 27 22:15:41 coachella CiscoSecure: DEBUG - Profile USER = dial_test not found in
cache.

!The AAA server log file also shows that the AAA server did not find the user in
!the database. Next, the AAA server conducts a search for the unknown_user account:
Jan 27 22:15:41 coachella CiscoSecure: WARNING - User dial_test not found, using
unknown_user

!The AAA server finally again reports user not found after exhausting its search:
Jan 27 22:15:41 coachella CiscoSecure: DEBUG - Password:
Jan 27 22:15:43 coachella CiscoSecure: DEBUG - AUTHENTICATION CONTINUE request
  (c3cd8bc1)
Jan 27 22:15:43 coachella CiscoSecure: DEBUG - Authentication - User not found;
[NAS = 172.22.63.1, Port = tty51, User = dial_test, Service = 1]

!Enter the following command to view a user profile in the database:
<CSUserver>$/opt/ciscosecure/CLI/ViewProfile -p 9900 -u dial_test

Error: Unable to find profile
RC = 3
```

Missing Service

For users being authorized via a AAA server to gain access to services such as PPP, their profiles must be set up correctly with the parameters for the specific service. Example 24-29 shows a user trying to connect without the PPP service authorized in it's profile. This output is from a **debug aaa authentication** command executed on a NAS. The output shows the PPP service authorization request being initiated for user dial_tac and then being denied by the AAA server.

Example 24-29 *Sample Output for the* **debug aaa authentication** *and* **debug aaa authorization** *Commands Where the PPP Service Is Not Enabled in a User's Profile*

```
Router#debug aaa authentication
Router#debug aaa authorization

111802: Feb  3 20:48:53.015 CST: As2 AAA/AUTHOR/LCP (153050196): send AV service=
  ppp
111803: Feb  3 20:48:53.015 CST: As2 AAA/AUTHOR/LCP (153050196): send AV protocol=
  lcp
111804: Feb  3 20:48:53.015 CST: As2 AAA/AUTHOR/LCP (153050196): found list
  "default"
111805: Feb  3 20:48:53.015 CST: As2 AAA/AUTHOR/LCP (153050196): Method=tacacs+
  (tacacs+)
111806: Feb  3 20:48:53.015 CST: AAA/AUTHOR/TAC+: (153050196): user=dial_tac
111807: Feb  3 20:48:53.015 CST: AAA/AUTHOR/TAC+: (153050196): send AV service=ppp
111808: Feb  3 20:48:53.015 CST: AAA/AUTHOR/TAC+: (153050196): send AV protocol=
  lcp
111809: Feb  3 20:48:53.219 CST: As2 AAA/AUTHOR (153050196): Post authorization
  status =
FAIL
111810: Feb  3 20:48:53.219 CST: As2 AAA/AUTHOR/LCP: Denied

!Enter the following command to assess warnings and errors reported in the AAA
!server log file:
<CSUserver>$tail -f /var/log/csuslog

!The AAA server log file shows that the AAA server successfully authenticated the
!user, but the PPP service request was denied due to an authorization failure:

Feb  3 20:48:58 coachella CiscoSecure: DEBUG - Authentication - LOGIN successful;
  [NAS = 172.22.63.1, Port = Async2, User = dial_tac, Priv = 1]
Feb  3 20:48:58 coachella CiscoSecure: DEBUG - AUTHORIZATION request (468d69de)
Feb  3 20:48:58 coachella CiscoSecure: DEBUG - Authorization - Failed service;
  [NAS = 172.22.63.1, user = dial_tac, port = Async2, input: service=ppp
  protocol=lcp output: ]
```

Adding **service=ppp** and related AVPs, **protocol=ip** and **protocol=lcp,** can take care of this problem.

AVP Is Not Assigned Due to a Missing Authorization Command

For the appropriate AVPs to be assigned to users, authorization needs to be turned on for the services that users are trying to access. A missing authorization command keeps the AVPs from being assigned.

In reviewing the group profile shown in Example 24-30, you can see that **inacl=110** is assigned to the aaa_test_group profile.

Example 24-30 *Group Profile with AVPs Configured to Be Assigned to the Users Belonging to This Group Connecting to the NAS*

```
<CSUserver>$/opt/ciscosecure/CLI/ViewProfile -p 9900 -g aaa_test_group

Group Profile Information
group = aaa_test_group{
profile_id = 64
profile_cycle = 7
service=ppp {
protocol=ip {
inacl=110
}
protocol=lcp {
}
}

}
```

The output shown in Example 24-31 is from a **debug aaa authentication** command executed on a NAS. It shows that no AAA authorization for **service=net** is taking place.

Example 24-31 *Sample Output for the **debug aaa** Command and the Logs on the AAA Server Showing No Authorization Done for the Authenticated User*

```
Router#debug aaa authentication

112037: Feb  3 21:18:04.994 CST: AAA/MEMORY: create_user (0x61DF0AE8) user=
  'dial_tac' ruser='' port='Async5' rem_addr='async/81560' authen_type=PAP
  service=PPP priv=1

!Enter the following command to assess warnings and errors reported in the AAA
!server log file:
<CSUserver>$tail -f /var/log/csuslog

!The following log file fragment confirms that access is permitted, with no AAA
!authorization attributes pushed to the client
Feb  3 21:18:05 coachella CiscoSecure: DEBUG - Authentication - LOGIN successful;
  [NAS = 172.22.63.1, Port = Async5, User = dial_tac, Priv = 1]
Feb  3 21:18:05 coachella CiscoSecure: INFO - Profile: user = dial_tac {
Feb  3 21:18:05 coachella        set server current-failed-logins = 0
Feb  3 21:18:05 coachella profile_cycle = 12
Feb  3 21:18:05 coachella }
```

Adding the **aaa authorization network default group tacacs+** global command to the NAS configuration can resolve this issue.

Troubleshooting Auth-Proxy

The debugs just shown, along with the following two debugs, can be also be used to troubleshoot auth-proxy implementations:

- **debug ip auth-proxy {function - trace}**—Displays the authentication proxy functions.

- **debug ip auth-proxy {http}**—Displays HTTP events related to the authentication proxy.

The following sections describe some of the common issues seen with auth-proxy and their resolutions.

AAA Server Is Unreachable

For auth-proxy to be able to download the relevant access lists from the AAA server, the server has to be reachable from the router. If the server is not reachable, the user sees the error "500 Internal Server Error." On the router, you see debugs similar to the ones shown in Example 24-32 if RADIUS is being used as the security protocol.

Example 24-32 *Sample Output for the* **debug radius** *and* **debug aaa authentication** *Commands Where the AAA Server Is Unreachable*

```
Router#debug aaa authentication
Router#debug radius

01:30:39: RADIUS: Initial Transmit  id 6 171.68.118.115:1645, Access-Request,
  Len 67
01:30:39:          Attribute 4 6 0A1F0196
01:30:39:          Attribute 61 6 00000000
01:30:39:          Attribute 1 11 70726F78
01:30:39:          Attribute 2 18 E552A3E5
01:30:39:          Attribute 6 6 00000005
01:30:44: RADIUS: Retransmit id 6
01:30:49: RADIUS: Retransmit id 6
01:30:59: RADIUS: Marking server 171.68.118.115 dead
01:30:59: RADIUS: Tried all servers.
01:30:59: RADIUS: No valid server found. Trying any viable server
01:30:59: RADIUS: Tried all servers.
01:30:59: RADIUS: No response for id 6
01:30:59: RADIUS: No response from server
01:30:59: AAA/AUTHEN (1597176845): status = ERROR
```

Incorrect Username and/or Password

If the user enters an incorrect username and/or password upon being prompted by the router, debugs similar to the ones shown in Example 24-33 show up, and the user sees the "Authentication Failed!" message.

Example 24-33 *Sample Output for the* **debug radius** *and* **debug aaa authentication** *Commands Where the Username and Password Are Incorrect*

```
Router#debug aaa authentication
Router#debug radius

01:37:42: RADIUS: Received from id 10 171.68.118.115:1645, Access-Reject, Len 20
01:37:42: AAA/AUTHEN (3558550985): status = FAIL
01:37:42: AAA/MEMORY: free_user (0x61C549F0) user='junk' ruser='' port=''
  rem_addr='' authen_type=ASCII service=LOGIN priv=0
```

Incorrect Privilege Level for Auth-Proxy

For the auth-proxy access lists to be applied correctly to the router, the privilege level for auth-proxy should be set to 15. If this is not the case, the user sees a message saying "Authentication Failed!", and the access lists are not applied to the router. The debugs shown in Example 24-34 are an example of such a situation.

Example 24-34 *Sample Output for the* **debug radius***,* **debug aaa authorization***, and* **debug aaa authentication** *Commands Where the Privilege Level for Auth-Proxy Is Not Set to 15*

```
Router#debug aaa authentication
Router#debug aaa authorization
Router#debug radius

02:00:54: RADIUS: saved authorization data for user 61CA670C at 61C5585C
02:00:54: AAA/AUTHEN (706562375): status = PASS
02:00:54:  AAA/AUTHOR/HTTP (4224202114): Port='' list='default' service=AUTH-PROXY
02:00:54: AAA/AUTHOR/HTTP:  (4224202114) user='baduser'
02:00:54:  AAA/AUTHOR/HTTP (4224202114): send AV service=auth-proxy
02:00:54:  AAA/AUTHOR/HTTP (4224202114): send AV cmd*
02:00:54:  AAA/AUTHOR/HTTP (4224202114): found list "default"
02:00:54:  AAA/AUTHOR/HTTP (4224202114): Method=RTP (radius)
02:00:54: RADIUS: cisco AVPair "auth-proxy:priv-lvl=1"
```

Summary

Troubleshooting any networking issue requires a thorough understanding of how the implementation has been done. However, even more important to understand in a security implementation is the implementation's ultimate goal. As soon as this goal has been clearly identified, you can use various tools to verify if the implementation is doing what it is supposed to be doing. **debug** and **show** commands are the most commonly used tools for troubleshooting. Various **debug** and **show** commands are often used in succession in an effort to understand the nature of the problem and narrow it down.

The aim of this chapter is to leave you with an understanding of some of the troubleshooting aspects of the principles and practices discussed in this book. The two complement each other. It is impossible to be good at troubleshooting without thoroughly understanding the underlying principles, just as it is difficult to do a successful implementation of any reasonable complexity without having well-honed troubleshooting skills.

Review Questions

1   How can asymmetric routing cause NAT to fail on a router?

2   How does using route maps to define interesting traffic affect NAT on a router?

3   For a packet being sent from the inside network to the outside network on a router, what occurs first, routing or NAT?

4   How does the **conduit** command affect ICMP traffic destined for the PIX Firewall?

5   What is the purpose of the **ip tcp adjust-mss** *number* command?

6   Why is it not a good idea to use pings to test the functionality of the IOS Firewall?

7   What type of error message is seen on the NAS if the keys configured on the NAS and the AAA server do not match?

8   At which stage of IKE negotiation does the **show crypto isakmp sa** command show the ISAKMP SA to be in the OAK_MM_KEY_EXCH state?

9   Where does the crypto map need to be applied when you set up IPsec over GRE?

10   What do a large number of late collisions on an Ethernet interface indicate?

PART IX

Appendixes

Answers to Review Questions

Chapter 1

1 What is the first step when you're starting to think about network security?

Answer: The first step is to define the assets you're trying to protect. This leads to identifying the types of threats that are likely.

2 What are some of a modern network's assets?

Answer: Networking equipment, databases, and network bandwidth constitute modern network assets.

3 What is risk assessment?

Answer: Risk assessment is a measurement of the cost associated with fulfilling a threat against an asset.

4 What is the difference between risk assessment and threat assessment?

Answer: Threat assessment analyzes what threats to a network are likely, whereas risk assessment measures the cost if such an attack materializes. The cost of an attack takes into account the likelihood of an attack and the amount of damage that would be caused if such an attack were successful. Threat assessment is the first step toward risk assessment.

5 What is the difference between a permissive security policy and a restrictive security policy?

Answer: Permissive means that everything not expressly prohibited is allowed. Restrictive means that everything not expressly permitted is prohibited. Generally speaking, a security policy falls somewhere in between these two. However, it's best to lean toward being restrictive, because that is the only way to build a secure network with the plethora of access means available in today's networks.

6 What is a privacy policy?

Answer: A privacy policy defines reasonable expectations of privacy regarding such issues as monitoring e-mail, logging keystrokes, and accessing users' files. (See RFC 2196.)

 7 What is an access policy?

 Answer: An access policy defines access rights and privileges to protect assets from loss or disclosure by specifying acceptable-use guidelines for users, operations staff, and management. (See RFC 2196.)

 8 What is an accountability policy?

 Answer: An accountability policy defines the responsibilities of users, operations staff, and management. (See RFC 2196.)

 9 What is an availability statement?

 Answer: An availability statement sets users' expectations for the availability of resources. It should address redundancy and recovery issues, as well as specify operating hours and maintenance downtime periods. (See RFC 2196.)

 10 What is an information technology system and network maintenance policy?

 Answer: An information technology system and network maintenance policy describes how both internal and external maintenance people are allowed to handle and access technology. (See RFC 2196.)

Chapter 2

 1 What is a DMZ?

 Answer: A DMZ is the zone in the network that is segregated from the rest of the network due to the nature of the devices contained on it. A DMZ is often a subnet that typically resides between the private network and the public network. Connections from the public network terminate on DMZ devices, which can then be accessed relatively securely by private network devices.

 2 What is a dirty DMZ?

 Answer: A dirty DMZ is one in which the DMZ is located off a separate interface of the edge router connecting the firewall to the public network. This type of setup provides very little security to the devices sitting on the DMZ network.

 3 What is a bastion host?

 Answer: A bastion host is a host exposed to a public network and strengthened to face network attacks.

 4 Why is logging important on a bastion host?

 Answer: Logging allows the network administrator to track attempts to compromise these vulnerable machines, as well as provide insights into further improving the security of the bastion host.

5 Why are dirty DMZs often created?

Answer: Dirty DMZs are often set up because the firewall is unable to handle the traffic load put on it as it tries to cater to all the traffic that is intended for the internal network, as well as the traffic that is intended for the servers on the DMZ. Because the traffic to the servers on the DMZ (which are often public servers) can be considerable, the network administrators are forced to locate the servers outside the firewall on a DMZ so that the firewall does not have to process this traffic.

6 How does the PIX Firewall support zoning?

Answer: PIX Firewall uses the concept of security levels for its interfaces to place them in various zones based on the security requirements of the devices sitting off these interfaces.

Chapter 3

1 What are floating static routes?

Answer: Generally speaking, floating static routes are routes that do not come into play under normal circumstances. They are installed in the routing table when the routes derived from the routing protocols become unavailable. Floating statics are used when the preferred route to the same destination becomes unusable.

2 What is HSRP?

Answer: HSRP stands for Hot Standby Router Protocol. It provides redundancy between two routers. The redundancy is configured on an interface basis.

3 Which encryption algorithm is recommended to save passwords on a router?

Answer: MD5.

4 What is a core file?

Answer: A core file is an image of the router memory when a router crashes.

5 What is the purpose of the nagle protocol service?

Answer: The nagle protocol improves the performance of certain TCP applications, such as Telnet.

6 Which version of SSH is supported on Cisco devices?

Answer: v1.x only.

7 Is SSH the recommended method of secure administrative access on Cisco routers?

Answer: No. IPsec is the recommended method of access. However, SSH is a more preferred method than Telnet.

8 What are examples of TTY ports on a router?

Answer: Console and auxiliary ports.

9 How does CEF improve router security?

Answer: CEF maintains a complete table of all the routing entries rather than putting new destinations in the routing cache. Therefore, its performance is unaffected by a DoS attack with packets distributed to a wide variety of destinations, much as other router switching paths could be.

10 What are the methods of accessing a switch?

Answer: SSH, Telnet, console, and HTTP.

Chapter 4

1 What is a net police filter?

Answer: It is a filter that does not allow any routes with prefixes more specific than /20 (or perhaps up to /24) to come in.

2 Why is fast convergence important for security?

Answer: A fast-converging routing architecture is quicker to recover from network-disruptive attacks, thereby reducing the impact of such attacks.

3 What is a null interface?

Answer: A null interface is a Cisco IOS interface that is used to drop traffic routed to it. It is sometimes used as an alternative to access lists.

4 What is prefix filtering?

Answer: Prefix filtering is a technique used to filter routes wherein instead of using specific subnets such as the ones in an access list, filtering is done based on prefix lengths.

5 Which algorithm is used for BGP peer authentication?

Answer: MD5 is used as the hashing algorithm for BGP peer authentication.

6 Turning off directed broadcasts can protect against what types of attacks?

Answer: It protects against some types of packet floods, such as smurf attacks.

7 Why is it important to set up good route dampening values in BGP?

Answer: Proper route dampening gives more leeway to route flapping for more-established Internet routes (the ones with generally shorter prefix lengths) as compared to less-established routes (the ones with generally longer prefix lengths). This decreases the routers' CPU load and makes the network more stable.

8 What is the danger of having BGP multihop enabled?

Answer: Attackers several hops away can attempt BGP peering with BGP routers.

9 What is an advantage of using loopback interfaces as the router ID in OSPF?

Answer: This method provides more stability in the OSPF network, because loopback interfaces never go down.

10 What is IP source routing?

Answer: IP source routing is an IP option that allows a user to set a field in the IP packet specifying the path he or she wants the packet to take.

Chapter 5

1 Why is it imprudent to rely on VLANs to provide isolation and security?

Answer: VLAN protocols are not written with security in mind. Additional measures need to be in place to ensure security.

2 What does port security do?

Answer: Port security is a mechanism available on the Catalyst switches to restrict the MAC address that can connect via a particular port of the switch.

3 Which protocols are covered under IP permit lists?

Answer: Telnet, SSH, HTTP, and SNMP.

4 What is an isolated VLAN port?

Answer: An isolated port has complete Layer 2 separation from other ports within the same private VLAN, with the exception of the promiscuous port.

5 What is a promiscuous VLAN port?

Answer: A promiscuous port is one that can communicate with all other private VLANs.

6   What is the purpose of the 802.1x standard?

Answer: The primary idea behind this standard is that devices that need to access the LAN need to be authenticated and authorized before they can connect to the physical or logical port of the switch that is responsible for creating the LAN environment.

7   What is EAP?

Answer: EAP is a fairly flexible protocol that was designed to carry PPP authentication parameters only. However, it can be used by other protocols such as 802.1x for their authentication needs. EAP can carry authentication data between two entities that want to set up authenticated communications between themselves. It supports a variety of authentication mechanisms.

8   What is the purpose of the EAPOL standard?

Answer: The communication between the supplicant and the authenticator is done using an encapsulation technique known as Extensible Authentication Protocol (EAP). The 802.1x standard uses the version of EAP known as EAP Over LANs (EAPOL) for LAN environments.

9   What is the purpose of EAP-Request Identity type messages?

Answer: The identity message is generally sent by the authenticator to the supplicant in the 802.1x scheme of things. The purpose of the message is to ask the supplicant to send its identity information (such as the username) to the authenticator. The supplicant responds with an EAP-Response message of the same type containing the requested information.

10   What is the EAP-Response NAK message used for?

Answer: The NAK message is generally sent by the supplicant to the authenticator when the authentication mechanism offered by the authenticator is unacceptable to the supplicant.

Chapter 6

1   What is port address translation?

Answer: In PAT, the RFC 1918 addresses are translated into a small number of routable IP addresses (often just one routable IP address). The device doing PAT distinguishes between the traffic destined for the various RFC 1918 addresses by tracking the source TCP or UDP ports used when the connection is initiated.

2   What is the primary difference between NAT and proxy?

Answer: NAT is transparent to the end hosts, but proxy is not.

3 What is PAT's security advantage?

Answer: PAT disallows connections to devices sitting behind the PAT device that have not initiated connections to the outside world themselves.

4 What is the difference between connection table maintenance for PAT and that of a firewall?

Answer: A firewall maintains TCP and UDP state information and information on various other flags. PAT tracks only IP addresses and port numbers.

Chapter 8

1 How does ASA keep track of UDP connections?

Answer: It uses timers.

2 What does ASA do to the TCP sequence number of packets passing through it?

Answer: It randomizes the TCP sequence number and keeps track of the change in the new and old sequence numbers.

3 What does the PIX's mail guard feature do?

Answer: It allows only the seven well-known SMTP commands to go through and returns an OK while discarding any other commands.

4 What is the purpose of the ARP test in PIX's failover mechanism?

Answer: The ARP test consists of reading the unit's ARP cache for the 10 most recently acquired entries. The unit sends ARP requests one at a time to these machines, attempting to stimulate network traffic. After each request, the unit counts all received traffic for up to 5 seconds. If traffic is received, the interface is considered operational. If no traffic is received, an ARP request is sent to the next machine. If at the end of the list no traffic has been received, the ping test begins.

5 What is the purpose of the **sysopt connection tcpmss** command?

Answer: It forces proxy TCP connections to have a maximum segment size no greater than *a configurable number of bytes.*

6 What is the purpose of PIX's **telnet** command?

Answer: The telnet command specifies the host IP addresses from which the PIX can accept telnet connections.

7 What is the purpose of the **alias** command?

Answer: The alias command is used to doctor the IP address resolved and returned in a DNS response to a different address.

8 What is the purpose of the failover Ethernet cable?

Answer: It is used to carry the state information from the primary PIX to the standby PIX in case of a failover.

9 How is the PAT address specified in the PIX configuration?

global interface name tag <PAT IP address>.

Chapter 9

1 What is meant by Java blocking in the IOS Firewall world?

Answer: IOS Firewall can stop Java applets from being downloaded from Web sites that are not explicitly permitted to send Java applets to the machines behind the firewall.

2 How does the IOS Firewall protect against TCP SYN floods?

Answer: IOS Firewall protects against SYN floods by monitoring the total number of half-open TCP connections as well as new TCP connections being opened each minute. If these numbers reach a configurable threshold, it starts tearing down the half-open connections.

3 How does FTP work through the IOS Firewall?

Answer: CBAC monitors the FTP connections being established from behind the firewall. When CBAC detects a new FTP session, it watches the negotiation to find out the port on which the server will connect to the client for the data connection. It then opens a hole in the access lists to allow that traffic to go through.

4 How does IOS Firewall keep track of UDP sessions?

Answer: It uses timers.

5 Are TCP and UDP payload inspected if you are inspecting only for TCP and UDP on the IOS Firewall?

Answer: No. The payloads are inspected only if specific application-layer protocols are being inspected for.

Chapter 11

1 What does GRE stand for?

Answer: Generic Routing Encapsulation

2   Is it possible to use a private IP address as the "tunnel destination" IP address when using GRE to carry traffic over the public Internet?

Answer: No. The tunnel destination address is used to populate the destination IP address field in GRE's delivery header. This IP address needs to be routable.

3   How many pairs of routers can one GRE tunnel connect?

Answer: One

4   What is the most common reason for using loopback interfaces as the source of a GRE tunnel?

Answer: Loopbacks don't go down like normal interfaces.

5   How do you identify a GRE packet on a sniffer trace?

Answer: By looking for IP protocol 47, which is the protocol number used for GRE.

6   What does recursive routing mean in the context of a GRE tunnel?

Answer: It means that the GRE tunnel is down because the routing protocol is sending the packets destined for the tunnel destination through the GRE tunnel itself.

Chapter 12

1   What do LAC and LNS stand for?

Answer: L2TP Access Concentrator and L2TP Network Server.

2   What is the purpose of the ZLB ACK message?

Answer: It is sent to indicate that there are no more messages in the queue.

3   What is the purpose of tunnel authentication in the router configuration?

Answer: It is used to authenticate the control session between the LAC and the LNS.

4   Which port number does L2TP use?

Answer: UDP 1701.

5   How can L2TP reduce dial setup costs?

Answer: It allows a PPP connection to be established to the LNS over IP connectivity provided by a local ISP.

Chapter 13

1 What does IPsec stand for?

Answer: IP Security.

2 What three main protocols form IPsec?

Answer: ESP, AH, and IKE.

3 What is the main difference between AH and ESP's capabilities?

Answer: ESP provides data encryption and data integrity, whereas AH provides only data integrity for the whole packet.

4 Which phase does ISAKMP go through in negotiating IPsec SAs?

Answer: Quick mode.

5 Can an IPsec crypto map point to more than one peer?

Answer: Yes. If the first peer configured is unresponsive, the next one is tried, and so on, until a responsive peer is found.

6 What is the purpose of TED?

Answer: To dynamically discover peer IP addresses without needing to configure them.

7 What is the purpose of the **group** command?

Answer: It defines the Diffie-Hellman group that is used to choose one of the parameters in the DH calculation.

8 Which command defines the encryption method to be used?

Answer: crypto ipsec transform-set.

9 What does IPsec use to identify L2TP as interesting traffic?

Answer: L2TP uses UDP port 1701. IPsec is set up to treat traffic on UDP 1701 as interesting.

10 Does GRE encapsulate IPsec traffic, or the other way around?

Answer: In general, IPsec encapsulates and (optionally if using ESP) encrypts GRE packets. Although it is conceivable that the reverse can also be set up, the usefulness of such a setup would be limited.

Chapter 15

1 Why does the use of IDSM on the Catalyst switch not affect the Catalyst switch's performance?

Answer: Because the IDS module works on copies of the packets, not the actual packet flow.

2 What is the purpose of the post office daemon?

Answer: The post office daemon is used for communications between the director and the sensor and any services running on them.

3 In which direction should the audit rules be applied on a router's outside interface?

Answer: In the direction of the traffic entering the router from the outside network (inbound).

4 Can two hosts with the same org ID have the same host ID as well?

Answer: No, because host IDs are unique identifiers of systems in a single org.

5 How many audit rules can be applied to a PIX interface?

Answer: Two. Only one of the rules can be for info signatures, and only one can be for attack signatures.

Chapter 16

1 What services can AAA on Cisco routers authenticate?

Answer: ARAP, NASI, Enable, Login, and PPP.

2 What is the purpose of authorization?

Answer: Authorization is the process by which users or devices are given controlled access to network resources. Authorization lets a network administrator control who can do what on the network.

3 What does the keyword **if-authenticated** do?

Answer: The user can access the requested function if he or she has been authenticated successfully.

4 What does the keyword **if-needed** do?

Answer: The NAS does not authenticate again if the user has already been authenticated on a TTY line.

5 What risk is associated with the following command?

```
aaa authentication login default group radius none
```

Answer: If the authentication attempt with RADIUS returns an error, the user is not subjected to another authentication attempt and is allowed to log in.

Chapter 17

1 How does the AAA server provide authorization information to the NAS?

Answer: It uses the authorization response message containing the attributes for authorization.

2 What types of messages does TACACS+ use for authentication?

Answer: It uses four types of messages for authentication: Accept, Reject, Fail, and Continue.

3 What types of messages does TACACS+ use for accounting purposes?

Answer: It uses start record, stop record, and continue record for accounting.

4 What algorithm does TACACS+ employ for encryption?

It uses a combination of XOR and MD5 to calculate cipher texts.

5 What is a pseudo_pad?

All the hashes calculated using MD5 are concatenated and then are truncated to the length of the data that is to be encrypted. This results in what the TACACS+ ID calls the pseudo_pad.

6 What does it mean to have the TAC_PLUS_UNENCRYPTED_FLAG value set to 01?

If this flag is set, the packet is unencrypted. If this flag is cleared, the packet is encrypted.

7 What does the PASS_ADD status in TACACS+ authorization imply?

If the status is set to PASS_ADD, the arguments specified in the REQUEST are authorized, and the arguments in the RESPONSE are to be used in addition to those arguments. If there are no arguments in the RESPONSE message, the AAA server has simply agreed to the attributes proposed by the NAS.

Chapter 18

1   What are VSAs?

   Answer: Vendor-specific attributes are derived from attribute 26 of RADIUS, which allows various vendors to define their customized RADIUS attributes.

2   What types of messages does the RADIUS protocol use in the authentication process?

   Answer: RADIUS uses four types of messages during authentication: request, accept, reject, and challenge.

3   What types of information are relayed from the RADIUS server during RADIUS authorization?

   Answer: Two types of information are exchanged during RADIUS authorization: services that the user can access, and parameters regarding these services.

4   Which hashing algorithm is used to encrypt user passwords?

   Answer: The user password is XORed with an MD5-generated hash to produce the encrypted form of the password.

5   What is the Authenticator Request field?

   Answer: The RADIUS packet has an Authenticator field. In the packets that carry the user password, this field contains a 16-octet random number called the request authenticator.

6   What types of attributes can the Access-Reject packet carry?

   Answer: This message may include one or more Reply message attributes with a text message that the NAS may display to the user.

Chapter 19

1   What functionality does auth-proxy provide?

   Answer: Auth-proxy provides a mechanism for authenticating users and allowing access through a router set up with an access list to block access.

2   Which command enables the lock and key feature on a router?

   Answer: access-enable configured under a VTY port.

3   How does a NAS participating in a VPDN setup find out the IP address of the home gateway?

   Answer: The NAS finds this information by querying a AAA server configured with a profile for the domain that the client is coming in with. (This information can be set up locally on the router as well.)

4   What is the purpose of command authorization?

Answer: Command authorization is a feature in Cisco IOS that allows privilege levels to be established for various users who need to have shell access to a router for administrative purposes.

5   What commands are allowed by default for a user authorized at privilege level 1?

Answer: Privilege level 1 includes all user-level commands at the router> prompt.

Chapter 20

1   What is a sinkhole router?

Answer: A sinkhole is a router that has much bandwidth and significant resources. It starts advertising the victim's host IP address into the network as its own. The result is that the attack's traffic is sent to the sinkhole router rather than to the intended victim.

2   What is backscatter traceback?

Answer: Backscatter traceback is a technique used to trace the origins of a spoofed network attack.

3   Why are unallocated IP addresses often used in DoS attacks?

Answer: Unallocated IP address spaces are often used in DoS attacks because they are not routed to any specific network on the Internet. Therefore, the responses from the victim simply get dropped. This is necessary in some DoS attacks, such as SYN floods, where the response from the victim must be dropped for the attack to be effective.

4   Where is the best place to stop a smurf attack?

Answer: Then best place to stop a smurf attack is close to its origin.

5   What is the purpose of logging on service provider devices?

Answer: Logs on service provider routers can be used for prosecution and attack-detection purposes. When collected using traceback mechanisms, these logs can be used to trace an attack's source.

Chapter 21

1   In what order are regular access control lists processed on a Cisco router?

Answer: Access control lists are scanned top-down sequentially to find a match.

2 What can be an advantage of having a VIP card on a router in terms of access list processing?

Answer: A VIP card with dCEF enabled can process access control lists rather than burdening the main CPU.

3 What set of access control lists can be used to detect a SYN flood?

Answer:

access-list 190 permit tcp any any established

access-list 190 permit tcp any any

access-list 190 permit ip any any

4 What is a smurf attack?

Answer: A smurf attack is an ICMP flood created using IP directed broadcasts.

5 How do turbo access control lists increase the speed of access list processing?

Answer: Turbo access control lists increase the speed of ACL processing by precompiling ACLs and then allowing almost uniform time of access to all the entries in the access list.

6 Why is it important to stop traffic from spoofed addresses from entering a network?

Answer: Spoofed source addresses not only make tracking an attacker more difficult but also can trick secure systems into thinking that the traffic is coming from a trusted source.

Chapter 22

1 What does NBAR stand for?

Answer: Network-Based Application Recognition.

2 Why is NBAR useful in security implementations?

Answer: NBAR allows traffic to be categorized based on the content in the application packets contained in the traffic. After such packets have been recognized, appropriate action can be taken on them.

3 What is the purpose of the policy map in NBAR configurations?

Answer: A policy map matches the traffic classified by NBAR to an action to be taken on it.

4 How can NBAR protect against Code Red attacks?

Answer: NBAR allows detection of some of the packets being used in a Code Red attack by the infected machines as well as the attackers themselves, allowing this traffic to be blocked or reduced.

Chapter 23

1 What is CAR?

Answer: Committed access rate is a feature that allows the amount of bandwidth to be committed to a particular class of traffic. CAR is the underlying software base for both packet classification and access rate limiting functionality.

2 How can CAR provide security?

Answer: CAR can be used to stem packet floods as well as keep the total amount of traffic suspected of being malicious under control.

3 What is normal burst rate?

Answer: Normal burst rate in CAR is the value that determines the excess traffic beyond the normal average rate of traffic that is allowed through an interface.

4 How can you figure out how much traffic should be configured to limit SYN attacks?

Answer: The best way to figure out how much traffic needs to be configured for SYN attacks is to use data collected during normal times and after applying CAR to do checks on the total number of connections being made to the servers. This ensures that no connection reduction is taking place.

5 How can CAR be used to control DDoS attacks?

Answer: DDoS attack agents and handlers use ICMPs and other such traffic to communicate with each other. CAR can be used to limit this traffic. Also, as soon as the attack has been launched, CAR can be used to limit the amount of traffic being put into the attack.

Chapter 24

1 How can asymmetric routing cause NAT to fail on a router?

Answer: NAT occurs when a packet enters an interface configured with the ip nat inside **command and leaves via an interface configured with the** ip nat outside **command. On a router with multiple interfaces, you must make sure that all interfaces on which traffic that needs to be NATed enters the router, and all interfaces from which the traffic exits, are configured with the** ip nat inside **and** ip nat outside **commands, respectively. Failure to do so causes NAT not to occur for the traffic passing through the interface that does not have the** nat **command configured on it.**

2 How does using route maps to define interesting traffic affect NAT on a router?

Answer: Route maps force NAT to create complete translation tables, including the outside local and outside global entries, forcing the router to create new translations for each separate outside global/local address that each inside host tries to access.

3 For a packet being sent from the inside network to the outside network on a router, what occurs first, routing or NAT?

Answer: Routing occurs first. As soon as the egress interface has been identified, the NAT translation is built provided that all the other requirements for doing NAT are fulfilled.

4 How does the **conduit** command affect ICMP traffic destined for the PIX Firewall?

Answer: The conduit **command affects only pings through the firewall, not to the firewall itself. The icmp command controls ICMP traffic that terminates on the PIX Firewall.**

5 What is the purpose of the **ip tcp adjust-mss** *number* command?

Answer: This command forces the router to sniff on the incoming TCP SYN packets and tweak the TCP MSS field to the number configured in the command. With the MSS value tweaked, the two end hosts sitting behind the two IPsec peers must agree to this tweaked, negotiated TCP MSS value. This is helpful in forcing the end hosts to use a smaller MTU value when sending out packets.

6 Why is it not a good idea to use pings to test the functionality of the IOS Firewall?

Answer: ICMP packets are not inspected by the IOS Firewall, so their passage through the router or lack thereof does not indicate the health of the IOS Firewall configuration.

7 What type of error message is seen on the NAS if the keys configured on the NAS and the AAA server do not match?

Answer: An error message with "check keys" is seen on the NAS.

8 At which stage of IKE negotiation does the **show crypto isakmp sa** command show the ISAKMP SA to be in the OAK_MM_KEY_EXCH state?

Answer: This state occurs right after Diffie-Hellman exchange has been completed and authentication is about to take place.

9   Where does the crypto map need to be applied when you set up IPsec over GRE?

Answer: The crypto map needs to be applied to both the tunnel and the physical interfaces.

10   What do a large number of late collisions on an Ethernet interface indicate?

Answer: A late collision is a collision that is detected late in the packet's transmission. Normally, this should never happen. When two Ethernet hosts try to talk at once, they should collide early in the packet and both back off, or the second host should see that the first one is talking and wait. The common causes are large repeated networks and Ethernet networks running beyond the specification.

APPENDIX B

SAFE: A Security Blueprint for Enterprise Networks White Paper

by Sean Convery and Bernie Trudel
URL:www.cisco.com/warp/public/cc/so/cuso/epso/sqfr/safe_wp.htm
Copyright, Cisco Systems, Inc.

All material excerpted from this white paper is "as is." Cisco Press has not modified the content of this white paper in any way other than formatting to fit the design constraints of the book.

Authors

Sean Convery (CCIE #4232) and Bernie Trudel (CCIE #1884) are the authors of this White Paper. Sean is the lead architect for the reference implementation of this architecture at Cisco's headquarters in San Jose, CA USA. Sean and Bernie are both members of the VPN and Security Architecture Technical Marketing team in Cisco's Enterprise Line of Business.

Abstract

The principle goal of Cisco's secure blueprint for enterprise networks (SAFE) is to provide best practice information to interested parties on designing and implementing secure networks. SAFE serves as a guide to network designers considering the security requirements of their network. SAFE takes a defense-in-depth approach to network security design. This type of design focuses on the expected threats and their methods of mitigation, rather than on "Put the firewall here, put the intrusion detection system there." This strategy results in a layered approach to security where the failure of one security system is not likely to lead to the compromise of network resources. SAFE is based on Cisco products and those of its partners.

This document begins with an overview of the architecture, then details the specific modules that make up the actual network design. The first three sections of each module describe the traffic flows, key devices, and expected threats with basic mitigation diagrams. Detailed technical analysis of the design follows, along with more detailed threat mitigation techniques and migration strategies. Appendix A details the validation lab for SAFE and includes configuration snapshots. Appendix B is a primer on network security. Readers who are unfamiliar with basic network security concepts are encouraged to read this section before the rest of the document. Appendix C contains glossary definitions of the technical terms used in this document and a legend for the included figures.

This document focuses heavily on threats encountered in enterprise environments. Network designers who understand these threats can better decide where and how to deploy mitigation technologies. Without a full understanding of the threats involved in network security, deployments tend to be incorrectly configured, are too focused on security devices, or lack threat response options. By taking the threat-mitigation approach, this document should provide network designers with information for making sound network security choices.

Audience

Though this document is technical in nature, it can be read at different levels of detail, depending on the reader. A network manager, for example, can read the introductory sections in each area to obtain a good overview of network security design strategies and considerations. A network engineer or designer can read this document in its entirety and gain design information and threat analysis details, which are supported by configuration snapshots for the devices involved.

Caveats

This document presumes that you already have a security policy in place. Cisco Systems does not recommend deploying security technologies without an associated policy. This document directly addresses the needs of large enterprise customers. While most of the principles discussed here also apply directly to small and medium businesses, and even home offices, they do so on a different scale. A detailed analysis of these business types is outside the scope of this document. However, in order to address the issue of smaller-scale networks in a limited manner, the "Alternatives" and "Enterprise Options" sections outline devices that you can eliminate if you want to reduce the cost of the architecture.

Following the guidelines in this document does not guarantee a secure environment, or that you will prevent all intrusions. True absolute security can only be achieved by disconnecting a system from the network, encasing it in concrete, and putting it in the bottom floor of Fort Knox. Your data will be very safe, though inaccessible. However, you can achieve reasonable security by establishing a good security policy, following the guidelines in this document, staying up to date on the latest developments in the hacker and security communities, and maintaining and monitoring all systems with sound system administration practices. This includes awareness of application security issues that are not comprehensively addressed in this paper.

Though virtual private networks (VPNs) are included in this architecture, they are not described in great detail. Information such as scaling details, resilience strategies, and other topics related to VPNs are not included. Like VPNs, identity strategies (including certificate authorities [CAs]) are not discussed at any level of detail in this paper. Similarly, CAs require a level of focus that this document could not provide and still adequately address all the other relevant areas of network security. Also, because most enterprise networks have yet to deploy fully functional CA environments, it is important to discuss how to securely deploy networks without them. Finally, certain advanced networked applications and technologies (such as content networking, caching, and server load balancing) are not included in this document. Although their use within SAFE is to be expected, this paper does not cover their specific security needs.

SAFE uses the products of Cisco Systems and its partners. However, this document does not specifically refer to products by name. Instead, components are referred to by functional purpose rather than model number or name. During the validation of SAFE, real products were configured in the exact network implementation described in this document. Specific configuration snapshots from the lab are included in Appendix A, "Validation Lab."

Throughout this document the term "hacker" denotes an individual who attempts to gain unauthorized access to network resources with malicious intent. While the term "cracker" is generally regarded as the more accurate word for this type of individual, hacker is used here for readability.

Architecture Overview

Design Fundamentals

SAFE emulates as closely as possible the functional requirements of today's enterprise networks. Implementation decisions varied depending on the network functionality required. However, the following design objectives, listed in order of priority, guided the decision-making process.

- Security and attack mitigation based on policy
- Security implementation throughout the infrastructure (not just on specialized security devices)
- Secure management and reporting
- Authentication and authorization of users and administrators to critical network resources
- Intrusion detection for critical resources and subnets
- Support for emerging networked applications

First and foremost, SAFE is a security architecture. It must prevent most attacks from successfully affecting valuable network resources. The attacks that succeed in penetrating the first line of defense, or originate from inside the network, must be accurately detected and quickly contained to minimize their effect on the rest of the network. However, in being secure, the network must continue to provide critical services that users expect. Proper network security and good network functionality can be provided at the same time. The SAFE architecture is not a revolutionary way of designing networks, but merely a blueprint for making networks secure.

SAFE is also resilient and scalable. Resilience in networks includes physical redundancy to protect against a device failure whether through misconfiguration, physical failure, or network attack. Although simpler designs are possible, particularly if a network's performance needs are not great, this document uses a complex design as an example because designing security in a complex environment is more involved than in simpler environments. Options to limit the complexity of the design are discussed throughout this document.

At many points in the network design process, you need to choose between using integrated functionality in a network device versus using a specialized functional appliance. The integrated functionality is often attractive because you can implement it on existing equipment, or because the features can interoperate with the rest of the device to provide a better functional solution. Appliances are often used when the depth of functionality required is very advanced or when performance needs require using specialized hardware. Make your decisions based on the capacity and functionality of the appliance versus the integration advantage of the device. For example, sometimes you can chose an integrated higher-capacity Cisco IOS™ router with IOS firewall software as opposed to a smaller IOS router with a separate firewall. Throughout this architecture, both types of systems are used. Most critical security functions migrate to dedicated appliances because of the performance requirements of large enterprise networks.

Module Concept

Although most enterprise networks evolve with the growing IT requirements of the enterprise, the SAFE architecture uses a green-field modular approach. A modular approach has two main advantages. First, it allows the architecture to address the security relationship between the various functional blocks of the network. Second, it permits designers to evaluate and implement security on a module by module basis, instead of attempting the complete architecture in a single phase.

Figure B-1 illustrates the first layer of modularity in SAFE. Each block represents a functional area. The Internet service provider (ISP) module is not implemented by the enterprise, but is included to the extent that specific security features should be requested of an ISP in order to mitigate against certain attacks.

Figure B-1 *Enterprise Composite Module*

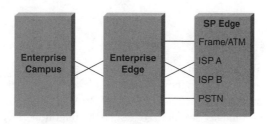

The second layer of modularity, which is illustrated in Figure B-2, represents a view of the modules within each functional area. These modules perform specific roles in the network and have specific security requirements, but their sizes are not meant to reflect their scale in a real network. For example, the building module, which represents the end-user devices, may include 80 percent of the network devices. The security design of each module is described separately, but is validated as part of the complete enterprise design.

Figure B-2 *Enterprise SAFE Block Diagram*

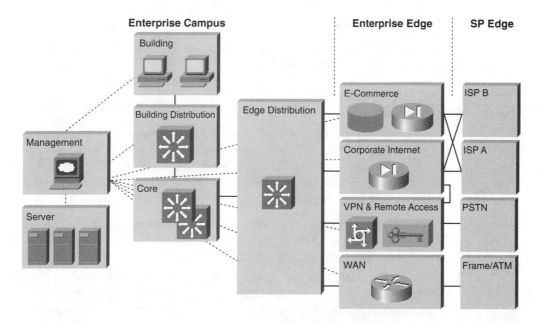

While it is true that most existing enterprise networks cannot be easily dissected into clear-cut modules, this approach provides a guide for implementing different security functions throughout the network. The authors do not expect network engineers to design their networks identical to the SAFE implementation, but rather use a combination of the modules described and integrate them into the existing network.

SAFE Axioms

Routers Are Targets

Routers control access from every network to every network. They advertise networks and filter who can use them, and they are potentially a hacker's best friend. Router security is a critical element in any security deployment. By their nature, routers provide access and, therefore, you should secure them to reduce the likelihood that they are directly compromised. You can refer to other documents that have been written about router security. These documents provide more detail on the following subjects:

- Locking down telnet access to a router
- Locking down Simple Network Management Protocol (SNMP) access to a router
- Controlling access to a router through the use of Terminal Access Controller Access Control System Plus (TACACS+)
- Turning off unneeded services
- Logging at appropriate levels
- Authentication of routing updates

The most current document on router security is available at the following URL: www.cisco.com/warp/customer/707/21.html

Switches Are Targets

Like routers, switches (both Layer 2 and Layer 3) have their own set of security considerations. Unlike routers, not as much public information is available about the security risks in switches and what can be done to mitigate those risks. Most of the security techniques detailed in the preceding section, "Routers Are Targets," apply to switches. In addition, you should take the following precautions:

- Ports without any need to trunk, should have any trunk settings set to off, as opposed to auto. This prevents a host from becoming a trunk port and receiving all traffic that would normally reside on a trunk port.
- Make sure that trunk ports use a virtual LAN (VLAN) number not used anywhere else in the switch. This prevents packets tagged with the same VLAN as the trunk port from reaching another VLAN without crossing a Layer 3 device. For more information, refer to the following URL: www.sans.org/newlook/resources/IDFAQ/vlan.htm
- Set all unused ports on a switch to a VLAN that has no Layer 3 connectivity. Better yet, disable any port that is not needed. This prevents hackers from plugging in to unused ports and communicating with the rest of the network.

- Avoid using VLANs as the sole method of securing access between two subnets. The capability for human error, combined with understanding that VLANs and VLAN tagging protocols were not designed with security in mind, makes their use in sensitive environments inadvisable. When VLANs are needed in security deployments, be sure to pay close attention to the configurations and guidelines mentioned above.

Within an existing VLAN, private VLANs provide some added security to specific network applications. Private VLANs work by limiting which ports within a VLAN can communicate with other ports in the same VLAN. Isolated ports within a VLAN can communicate only with promiscuous ports. Community ports can communicate only with other members of the same community and promiscuous ports. Promiscuous ports can communicate with any port. This is an effective way to mitigate the effects of a single compromised host. Consider a standard public services segment with a Web, FTP, and Domain Name System (DNS) server. If the DNS server is compromised, a hacker can pursue the other two hosts without passing back through the firewall. If private VLANs are deployed, once one system is compromised, it cannot communicate with the other systems. The only targets a hacker can pursue are hosts on the other side of the firewall.

Hosts Are Targets

A host is the most likely target during an attack and presents some of the most difficult challenges from a security perspective. There are numerous hardware platforms, operating systems, and applications, all of which have updates, patches, and fixes available at different times. Because hosts provide the application services to other hosts that request them, they are extremely visible within the network. For example, many people have visited www.whitehouse.gov, which is a host, but few have attempted to access s2-0.whitehouseisp.net, which is a router. Because of this visibility, hosts are the most frequently attacked devices in any network intrusion attempt.

In part because of the security challenges mentioned above, hosts are also the most successfully compromised devices. For example, a given Web server on the Internet might run a hardware platform from one vendor, a network card from another, an operating system from still another vendor, and a Web server that is either open source or from yet another vendor. Additionally, the same Web server might run applications that are freely distributed via the Internet, and might communicate with a database server that starts the variations all over again. That is not to say that the security vulnerabilities are specifically caused by the multi-source nature of all of this, but rather that as the complexity of a system increases, so does the likelihood of a failure.

To secure hosts, pay careful attention to each of the components within the systems. Keep any systems up to date with the latest patches, fixes, and so forth. In particular, pay attention to how these patches affect the operation of other system components. Evaluate all updates on test systems before you implement them in a production environment. Failure to do so might result in the patch itself causing a denial of service (DoS).

Networks Are Targets

The worst attack is the one that you cannot stop. When performed properly, distributed denial of service (DDoS) is just such an attack. As outlined in Appendix B, "Network Security Primer," DDoS works by causing tens or hundreds of machines to simultaneously send spurious data to an IP address. The goal of such an attack is generally not to shut down a particular host, but rather to make the entire network unresponsive. For example, consider an organization with a DS3 (45 Mbps) connection to the Internet that provides e-commerce services to its Web site users. Such a site is very security conscious and has intrusion detection, firewalls, logging, and active monitoring. Unfortunately, all these security devices do not help when a hacker launches a successful DDoS attack.

Consider 100 devices around the world, each with DS1 (1.5 Mbps) connections to the Internet. If these systems are remotely told to flood the serial interface of the e-commerce organization's Internet router, they can easily flood the DS3 with erroneous data. Even if each host is only able to generate 1 Mbps of traffic, (lab tests indicate that a stock Unix workstation can easily generate 50 Mbps with a popular DDoS tool), that amount is still more than twice the amount of traffic that the e-commerce site can handle. As a result, legitimate Web requests are lost, and the site appears to be down for most users. The local firewall drops all the erroneous data, but by then, the damage is done. The traffic has crossed the WAN connection and filled up the link.

Only through cooperation with their ISP can this fictitious e-commerce company hope to thwart such an attack. An ISP can configure rate limiting on the outbound interface to the company's site. This rate limiting can drop most undesired traffic when it exceeds a pre-specified amount of the available bandwidth. The key is to correctly flag traffic as undesired.

Common forms of DDoS attacks are ICMP floods, TCP SYN floods, or UDP floods. In an e-commerce environment, this type of traffic is fairly easy to categorize. Only when limiting a TCP SYN attack on port 80 (http) does an administrator run the risk of locking out legit-imate users during an attack. Even then, it is better to temporarily lock out new legitimate users and retain routing and management connections, than to have the router overrun and lose all connectivity.

More sophisticated attacks use port 80 traffic with the ACK bit set so that the traffic appears to be legitimate Web transactions. It is unlikely that an administrator could properly cate-gorize such an attack because acknowledged TCP communications are exactly the sort that you want to allow into your network.

One approach to limiting this sort of attack is to follow the guidelines outlined in RFC 1918 and RFC 2827. RFC 1918 specifies the networks that are reserved for private use and should never be seen across the public Internet. RFC 2827 filtering is discussed in the "IP Spoofing" section of Appendix B, "Network Security Primer." For inbound traffic on a router that is connected to the Internet, you could employ RFC 1918 and 2827 filtering to prevent unauthorized traffic from reaching the corporate network. When implemented at the ISP, this filtering prevents DDoS attack packets that use these addresses as sources from traversing the WAN link, potentially saving bandwidth during the attack. Collectively, if ISPs worldwide were to implement the guidelines in RFC 2827, source address spoofing would be greatly diminished. While this strategy does not directly prevent DDoS attacks, it does prevent such attacks from masking their source, which makes traceback to the attacking networks much easier.

Applications Are Targets

Applications are coded by human beings (mostly) and, as such, are subject to numerous errors. These errors can be benign—for example, an error that causes your document to print incorrectly—or malignant—for example, an error that makes the credit card numbers on your database server available via anonymous FTP. It is the malignant problems, as well as other more general security vulnerabilities, that intrusion detection systems (IDSs) aim to detect. Intrusion detection acts like an alarm system in the physical world. When an IDS detects something that it considers an attack, it can either take corrective action itself or notify a management system for actions by the administrator. Some systems are more or less equipped to respond and prevent such an attack. Host-based intrusion detection can work by intercepting OS and application calls on an individual host. It can also operate by after-the-fact analysis of local log files. The former approach allows better attack prevention, while the latter approach dictates a more passive attack response role. Because of the specificity of their role, host-based IDS (HIDS) systems are often better at preventing specific attacks than Network IDS (NIDS), which usually only issue an alert upon discovery of an attack. However, that specificity causes a loss of perspective to the overall network. This is where NIDS excels. Cisco recommends a combination of the two systems—HIDS on critical hosts and NIDS looking over the whole network—for a complete intrusion detection system.

Once deployed, you must tune an IDS implementation to increase its effectiveness and remove "false-positives."

False-positives are defined as alarms caused by legitimate traffic or activity. False-negatives are attacks that the IDS system fails to see. Once the IDS is tuned, you can configure it more specifically as to its threat mitigation role. As was mentioned above, you should configure HIDS to stop most valid threats at the host level because it is well prepared to determine that certain activity is indeed a threat.

When deciding on mitigation roles for NIDS there are two primary options:

The first option, and potentially the most damaging if improperly deployed, is to "shun" traffic through the addition of access control filters on routers. When a NIDS detects an attack from a particular host over a particular protocol, it can block that host from coming into the network for a predetermined amount of time. While on the surface this might seem like a great aid to a security administrator, in reality it must be very carefully implemented, if at all. The first problem is that of spoofed addresses. If traffic that matches an attack is seen by the NIDS, and that particular alarm triggers a shun response, the NIDS will deploy the access list to the device. However, if the attack that caused the alarm used a spoofed address, the NIDS has now locked out an address that never initiated an attack. If the IP address that the hacker used happens to be the IP address of a major ISP's outbound HTTP proxy server, a huge number of users could be locked out. This by itself could be an interesting DoS threat in the hands of a creative hacker.

To mitigate the risks of shunning, you should generally use it only on TCP traffic, which is much more difficult to successfully spoof than UDP. Use it only in cases where the threat is real and the chance of the attack being a false positive is very low. However, in the interior of a network, many more options exist. With effectively deployed RFC 2827 filtering, spoofed traffic should be very limited. Also, because customers are not generally on the internal network, you can take a more restrictive stance against internally originated attack attempts. Another reason for this is that internal networks do not often have the same level of stateful filtering that edge connections possess. As such, IDS needs to be more heavily relied upon than in the external environment.

The second option for NIDS threat mitigation is the use of TCP resets. As the name implies, TCP resets operate only on TCP traffic and terminate an active attack by sending TCP reset messages to the attacking and attacked host. Because TCP traffic is more difficult to spoof, you should consider using TCP resets more often than shunning.

From a performance standpoint, NIDS observes packets on the wire. If packets are sent faster than the NIDS can process them, there is no degradation to the network because the NIDS does not sit directly in the flows of data. However, the NIDS will lose effectiveness and packets could be missed causing both false-negatives and false-positives. Be sure to avoid exceeding the capabilities of IDS so that you can get their benefit. From a routing standpoint, IDS, like many state-aware engines, does not operate properly in an asymmetrically routed environment. Packets sent out from one set of routers and switches and returning through another will cause the IDS systems to see only half of the traffic, causing false-positives and negatives.

Secure Management and Reporting

"If you're going to log it, read it." So simple a proposition, that almost everyone familiar with network security has said it at least once. Yet logging and reading information from over 100 devices can prove to be a challenging proposition. Which logs are most important? How do I separate important messages from mere notifications? How do I ensure that logs are not tampered with in transit? How do I ensure my time-stamps match each other when multiple devices report the same alarm? What information is needed if log data is required for a criminal investigation? How do I deal with the volume of messages that can be generated by a large network? You must address all these questions when considering managing log files effectively. From a management standpoint, a different set of questions needs to be asked: How do I securely manage a device? How can I push content out to public servers and ensure that it is not tampered with in transit? How can I track changes on devices to troubleshoot when attacks or network failures occur?

From an architectural point of view, providing out-of-band management of network systems is the best first step in any management and reporting strategy. Out-of-band (OOB), as its name implies, refers to a network on which no production traffic resides. Devices should have a direct local connection to such a network where possible, and where impossible, (due to geographic, or system-related issues) the device should connect via a private encrypted tunnel over the production network. Such a tunnel should be preconfigured to communicate only across the specific ports required for management and reporting. The tunnel should also be locked down so that only appropriate hosts can initiate and terminate tunnels. Be sure that the out-of-band network does not itself create security issues. See the "Management Module" section of this document for more details.

After implementing an OOB management network, dealing with logging and reporting becomes more straightforward. Most networking devices can send syslog data, which can be invaluable when troubleshooting network problems or security threats. Send this data to one or more syslog analysis hosts on the management network. Depending on the device involved, you can choose various logging levels to ensure that the correct amount of data is sent to the logging devices. You also need to flag device log data within the analysis software to permit granular viewing and reporting. For example, during an attack the log data provided by Layer 2 switches might not be as interesting as the data provided by the intrusion detection system. Specialized applications, such as IDS, often use their own logging protocols to transmit alarm information. Usually this data should be logged to separate management hosts that are better equipped to deal with attack alarms. When combined, alarm data from many different sources can provide information about the overall health of the network. To ensure that log messages are time-synchronized to one another, clocks on hosts and network devices must be in sync. For devices that support it, network time protocol (NTP) provides a way to ensure that accurate time is kept on all devices. When dealing with attacks, seconds matter because it is important to identify the order in which a specified attack took place.

From a management standpoint, which for the purposes of this document refers to any function performed on a device by an administrator other than logging and reporting, there are other issues and solutions. As with logging and reporting, the OOB network allows the transport of information to remain in a controlled environment where it is not subject to tampering. Still, when secure configuration is possible, such as through the use of secure socket layer (SSL) or secure shell (SSH), it should be preferred. SNMP should be treated with the utmost care because the underlying protocol has its own set of security vulnerabilities. Consider providing read-only access to devices via SNMP and treat the SNMP community string with the same care you might treat a root password on a critical Unix host.

Configuration change management is another issue related to secure management. When a network is under attack, it is important to know the state of critical network devices and when the last known modifications took place. Creating a plan for change management should be a part of your comprehensive security policy, but, at a minimum, record changes using authentication systems on the devices, and archive configurations via FTP or TFTP.

Enterprise Module

The enterprise comprises two functional areas: the campus and the edge. These two areas are further divided into modules that define the various functions of each area in detail. Following the detailed discussion of the modules in the "Enterprise Campus" and "Enterprise Edge" sections, the "Enterprise Options" section of this document describes various options for the design.

Expected Threats

From a threat perspective, the Enterprise network is like most networks connected to the Internet. There are internal users who need access out and external users who need access in. There are several common threats that can generate the initial compromise that a hacker needs to further penetrate the network with secondary exploits.

First is the threat from internal users. Though statistics vary on the percentage, it is an established fact that the majority of all attacks come from the internal network. Disgruntled employees, corporate spies, visiting guests, and inadvertent bumbling users are all potential sources of such attacks. When designing security, it is important to be aware of the potential for internal threats.

Second is the threat to the publicly addressable hosts that are connected to the Internet. These systems will likely be attacked with application layer vulnerabilities and DoS attacks.

The final threat is that a hacker might try to determine your data phone numbers by using a "war-dialer" and try to gain access to the network. War-dialers are software and/or hardware that are designed to dial many phone numbers and determine the type of system on the other end of the connection. Personal systems with remote-control software installed by the user are the most vulnerable, because they typically are not very secure. Because these devices are behind the firewall, once hackers have access via the host they dialed in to, they can impersonate users on the network.

For a complete discussion of threat details, refer to Appendix B, "Network Security Primer."

Enterprise Campus

The following is a detailed analysis of all the modules contained within the Enterprise Campus.

Figure B-3 *Enterprise Campus Detail*

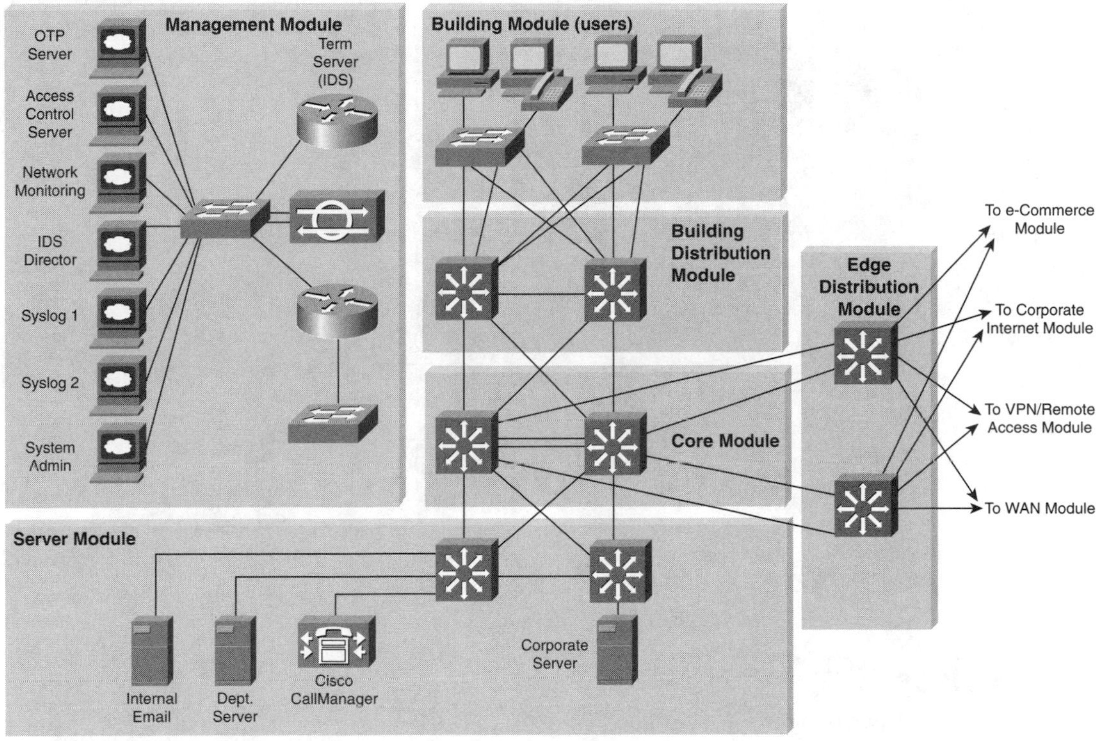

Management Module

The primary goal of the management module is to facilitate the secure management of all devices and hosts within the enterprise SAFE architecture. Logging and reporting information flow from the devices through to the management hosts, while content, configurations, and new software flow to the devices from the management hosts.

Figure B-4 *Management Traffic Flow*

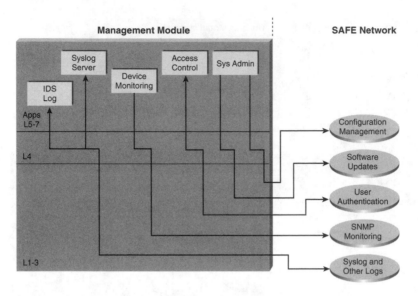

Key Devices

- **SNMP Management host**—provides SNMP management for devices
- **NIDS host**—provides alarm aggregation for all NIDS devices in the network
- **Syslog host(s)**—aggregates log information for Firewall and NIDS hosts
- **Access Control Server**—delivers one-time, two-factor authentication services to the network devices
- **One-Time Password (OTP) Server**—authorizes one-time password information relayed from the access control server
- **System Admin host**—provides configuration, software, and content changes on devices
- **NIDS appliance**—provides Layer 4 to Layer 7 monitoring of key network segments in the module
- **Cisco IOS Firewall**—allows granular control for traffic flows between the management hosts and the managed devices
- **Layer 2 switch (with private VLAN support)**—ensures data from managed devices can only cross directly to the IOS firewall

Figure B-5 *Management Module: Detail*

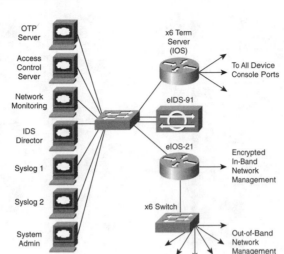

Threats Mitigated

- **Unauthorized Access**—filtering at the IOS firewall stops most unauthorized traffic in both directions

- **Man-in-the-Middle Attacks**—management data is crossing a private network making man-in-the-middle attacks difficult

- **Network Reconnaissance**—because all management traffic crosses this network, it does not cross the production network where it could be intercepted

- **Password Attacks**—the access control server allows for strong two-factor authentication at each device

- **IP Spoofing**—spoofed traffic is stopped in both directions at the IOS firewall

- **Packet Sniffers**—a switched infrastructure limits the effectiveness of sniffing

- **Trust Exploitation**—private VLANs prevent a compromised device from masquerading as a management host

Figure B-6 *Attack Mitigation Roles for Management Module*

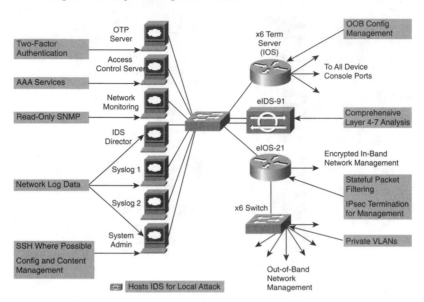

Design Guidelines

As can be seen in the above diagram, the SAFE enterprise management network has two network segments that are separated by an IOS router that acts as a firewall and a VPN termination device. The segment outside the firewall connects to all the devices that require management. The segment inside the firewall contains the management hosts themselves and the IOS routers that act as terminal servers. The remaining interface connects to the production network but only for IPsec-protected management traffic from predetermined hosts. This allows for management of a Cisco device that did not physically have enough interfaces to support the normal management connection. The IOS firewall is configured to allow syslog information into the management segment, as well as telnet, SSH, and SNMP if these are first initiated by the inside network.

Both management subnets operate under an address space that is completely separate from the rest of the production network. This ensures that the management network will not be advertised by any routing protocols. This also enables the production network devices to block any traffic from the management subnets that appears on the production network links.

The management module provides configuration management for nearly all devices in the network through the use of two primary technologies: Cisco IOS routers acting as terminal servers and a dedicated management network segment. The routers provide a reverse-telnet function to the console ports on the Cisco devices throughout the enterprise. More extensive management features (software changes, content updates, log and alarm aggregation, and SNMP management) are provided through the dedicated management network segment. The few other unmanaged devices and hosts are managed through IPsec tunnels that originate from the management router.

Because the management network has administrative access to nearly every area of the network, it can be a very attractive target to hackers. The management module has been built with several technologies designed to mitigate those risks. The first primary threat is a hacker attempting to gain access to the management network itself. This threat can only be mitigated through the effective deployment of security features in the remaining modules in the enterprise. All the remaining threats assume that the primary line of defense has been breached. To mitigate the threat of a compromised device, access control is implemented at the firewall, and at every other possible device, to prevent exploitation of the management channel. A compromised device cannot even communicate with other hosts on the same subnet because private VLANs on the management segment switches force all traffic from the managed devices directly to the IOS firewall where filtering takes place. Password sniffing only reveals useless information because of the one-time password environment. Host and Network IDS are also implemented on the management subnet and are configured in a very restrictive stance. Because the types of traffic on this network should be very limited, any signature match on this segment should be met with an immediate response.

SNMP management has its own set of security needs. Keeping SNMP traffic on the management segment allows it to traverse an isolated segment when pulling management information from devices. With SAFE, SNMP management pulls information only from devices rather than allowing it to push changes. To ensure this, each device is only configured with a "read-only" string.

Proper aggregation and analysis of the syslog information is critical to the proper management of a network. From a security perspective, syslog provides important information regarding security violations and configuration changes. Depending on the device in question, different levels of syslog information might be required. Having full logging with all messages sent might provide too much information for an individual or syslog analysis algorithm to sort. Logging for the sake of logging does not improve security.

For the SAFE validation lab, all configurations were done using standalone management applications and the command-line interface (CLI). Nothing in SAFE, however, precludes using policy management systems for configuration. Establishing this management module makes deployments of such technology completely viable. CLI and standalone management applications were chosen because the majority of current network deployments use this configuration method.

Alternatives

Complete out-of-band management is not always possible because some devices might not support it or there might be geographic differences that dictate in-band management. When in-band management is required, more emphasis needs to be placed on securing the transport of the management protocols. This can be through the use of IPsec, SSH, SSL, or any other encrypted and authenticated transport that allows management information to traverse it. When management happens on the same interface that a device uses for user data, importance needs to be placed on passwords, community strings, cryptographic keys, and the access-lists that control communications to the management services.

Future Near-Term Architecture Goals

The current reporting and alarming implementation is split across multiple hosts. Some hosts have intelligence for analyzing firewall and IDS data, while others are better-suited to analyze router and switch data. In the future, all data will aggregate to the same set of redundant hosts so that event correlation between all the devices can occur.

Core Module

The core module in the SAFE architecture is nearly identical to the core module of any other network architecture. It merely routes and switches traffic as fast as possible from one network to another.

Key Devices

- **Layer 3 switching**—route and switch production network data from one module to another

Figure B-7 *Core Module: Detail*

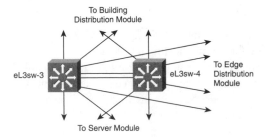

Threats Mitigated

- **Packet sniffers**—a switched infrastructure limits the effectiveness of sniffing

Design Guidelines

Standard implementation guidelines were followed in accordance with the "core, distribution, and access layer" deployments commonly seen in well-designed Cisco-based networks.

Though no unique requirements are defined by the SAFE architecture for the core of enterprise networks, the core switches follow the switch security axiom in the "Switches Are Targets" section, to ensure that they are well protected against direct attacks.

Building Distribution Module

The goal of this module is to provide distribution layer services to the building switches; these include routing, quality of service (QoS), and access control. Requests for data flow into these switches and onto the core, and responses follow the identical path in reverse.

Key Devices

- **Layer 3 switches**—aggregate Layer 2 switches in building module and provide advanced services

Figure B-8   *Building Distribution Module: Detail*

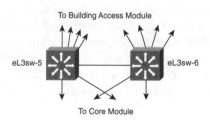

Threats Mitigated

- **Unauthorized access**—attacks against server module resources are limited by Layer 3 filtering of specific subnets
- **IP spoofing**—RFC 2827 filtering stops most spoofing attempts
- **Packet sniffers**—a switched infrastructure limits the effectiveness of sniffing

Figure B-9   *Attack Mitigation Roles for Building Distribution Module*

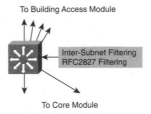

Design Guidelines

In addition to standard network design fundamentals, the optimizations described in the "Switches Are Targets" section were implemented to provide added security within the enterprise user community. Intrusion detection is not implemented at the building distribution module because it is implemented in the modules that contains the resources that are likely to be attacked for their content (server, remote access, Internet, and so forth). The building distribution module provides the first line of defense and prevention against internally originated attacks. It can mitigate the chance of a department accessing confidential information on another department's server through the use of access control. For example, a network that contains marketing and research and development might segment off the R&D server to a specific VLAN and filter access to it ensuring that only R&D staff have access to it. For performance reasons, it is important that this access control be implemented on a hardware platform that can deliver filtered traffic at near wire rates. This generally dictates the use of Layer 3 switching as opposed to more traditional dedicated routing devices. This same access control can also prevent local source-address spoofing through the use of RFC 2827 filtering. Finally, subnet isolation is used to route voice-over-IP (VoIP) traffic to the call manager and any associated gateways. This prevents VoIP traffic from crossing the same segments that all other data traffic crosses, reducing the likelihood of sniffing voice communications, and allows a smoother implementation of QoS.

Alternatives

Depending on the size and performance requirements of the network, the distribution layer can be combined with the core layer to reduce the number of devices required in the environment.

Building Module

SAFE defines the building module as the extensive network portion that contains end-user workstations, phones, and their associated Layer 2 access points. Its primary goal is to provide services to end users.

Key Devices

- **Layer 2 switch**—provides Layer 2 services to phones and user workstations
- **User workstation**—provides data services to authorized users on the network
- **IP phone**—provides IP telephony services to users on the network

Figure B-10 *Building Access Module: Detail*

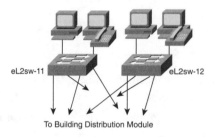

Threats Mitigated

- **Packet sniffers**—a switched infrastructure and default VLAN services limit the effectiveness of sniffing
- **Virus and Trojan horse applications**—host-based virus scanning prevents most viruses and many Trojan horses

Figure B-11 *Attack Mitigation Roles for Building Access Module*

Design Guidelines

Because user devices are generally the largest single element of the network, implementing security in a concise and effective manner is challenging. From a security perspective, the building distribution module, rather than anything in the building module, provides most of the access control that is enforced at the end-user level. This is because the Layer 2 switch that the workstations and phones connect to has no capability for Layer 3 access control. In addition to the network security guidelines described in the switch security axiom, host-based virus scanning is implemented at the workstation level.

Server Module

The server module's primary goal is to provide application services to end users and devices. Traffic flows on the server module are inspected by on-board intrusion detection within the Layer 3 switches.

Key Devices

- **Layer 3 switch**—provides layer three services to the servers and inspects data crossing the server module with NIDS
- **Call Manager**—performs call routing functions for IP telephony devices in the enterprise
- **Corporate and department servers**—delivers file, print, and DNS services to workstations in the building module
- **E-Mail server**—provide SMTP and POP3 services to internal users

Figure B-12 *Server Module: Detail*

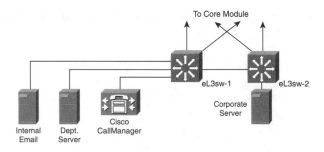

Threats Mitigated

- **Unauthorized access**—mitigated through the use of host-based intrusion detection and access control

- **Application layer attacks**—operating systems, devices, and applications are kept up to date with the latest security fixes and protected by host-based IDS

- **IP spoofing**—RFC 2827 filtering prevents source address spoofing

- **Packet sniffers**—a switched infrastructure limits the effectiveness of sniffing

- **Trust exploitation**—trust arrangements are very explicit, private VLANs prevent hosts on the same subnet from communicating unless necessary

- **Port redirection**—host-based IDS prevents port redirection agents from being installed

Figure B-13 *Attack Mitigation Roles for Server Module*

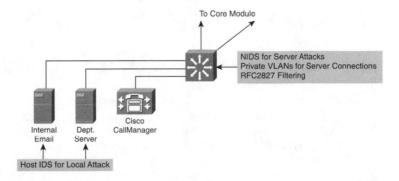

Design Guidelines

The server module is often overlooked from a security perspective. When examining the levels of access most employees have to the servers to which they attach, the servers can often become the primary goal of internally originated attacks. Simply relying on effective passwords does not provide for a comprehensive attack mitigation strategy. Using host and network-based IDS, private VLANs, access control, and good system administration practices (such as keeping systems up to date with the latest patches), provides a much more comprehensive response to attacks.

Because the NIDS system is limited in the amount of traffic it can analyze, it is important to send it attack-sensitive traffic only. This varies from network to network, but should likely include SMTP, Telnet, FTP, and WWW. The switch-based NIDS was chosen because of its ability to look only at interesting traffic across all VLANs as defined by the security policy. Once properly tuned, this IDS can be set up in a restrictive manner, because required traffic streams should be well known.

Alternatives

Like the building distribution module, the server module can be combined with the core module if performance needs do not dictate separation. For very sensitive high-performance server environments, the NIDS capability in the Layer 3 switch can be scaled by installing more than one NIDS blade and directing policy-matched traffic to specific blades.

Edge Distribution Module

This module's goal is to aggregate the connectivity from the various elements at the edge. Traffic is filtered and routed from the edge modules and routed into the core.

Key Devices

- **Layer 3 switches**—aggregate edge connectivity and provide advanced services

Figure B-14 *Edge Distribution Module: Detail*

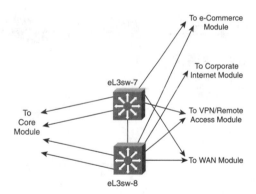

Threats Mitigated

- **Unauthorized access**—filtering provides granular control over specific edge subnets and their ability to reach areas within the campus
- **IP spoofing**—RFC 2827 filtering limits locally initiated spoof attacks
- **Network reconnaissance**—filtering limits nonessential traffic from entering the campus limiting a hackers ability to perform network recon
- **Packet sniffers**—a switched infrastructure limits the effectiveness of sniffing

Figure B-15 *Attack Mitigation Roles for Edge Distribution Module*

Design Guidelines

The edge distribution module is similar in some respects to the building distribution module in terms of overall function. Both modules employ access control to filter traffic, although the edge distribution module can rely somewhat on the entire edge functional area to perform additional security functions. Both modules use Layer 3 switching to achieve high performance, but the edge distribution module can add additional security functions because the performance requirements are not as great. The edge distribution module provides the last line of defense for all traffic destined to the campus module from the edge module. This includes mitigation of spoofed packets, erroneous routing updates, and provisions for network layer access control.

Alternatives

Like the server and building distribution modules, the edge distribution module can be combined with the core module if performance requirements are not as stringent as the SAFE reference implementation. NIDS is not present in this module, but could be placed here through the use of IDS line cards in the Layer 3 switches. It would then reduce the need for NIDS appliances at the exit from the critical edge modules as they connect to the campus. However, performance reasons may dictate, as they did in SAFE's reference design, that dedicated intrusion detection be placed in the various edge modules as opposed to the edge distribution module.

Figure B-16 *Enterprise Edge—Part 1*

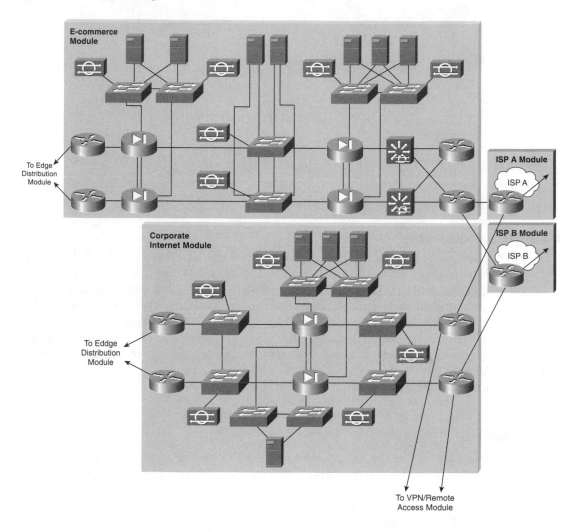

Figure B-17 *Enterprise Edge Detail—Part 2*

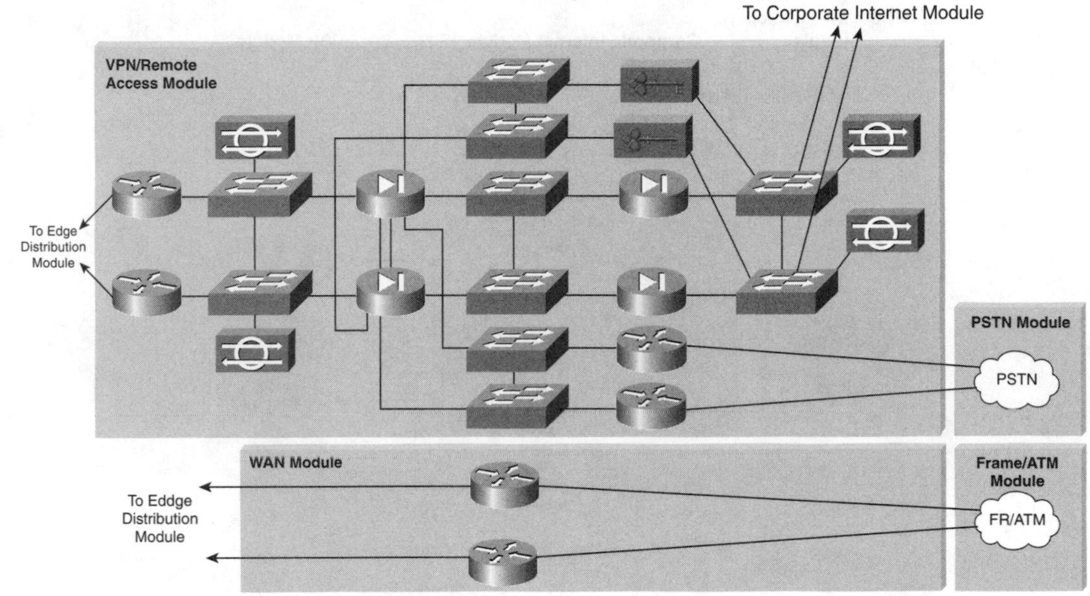

Corporate Internet Module

The Corporate Internet module provides internal users with connectivity to Internet services and Internet users access to information on public servers. Traffic also flows from this module to the VPN and remote access module where VPN termination takes place. This module is not designed to serve e-commerce type applications. Refer to the "E-Commerce Module" section later in this document for more details on providing Internet commerce.

Figure B-18 *Corporate Internet Traffic Flow*

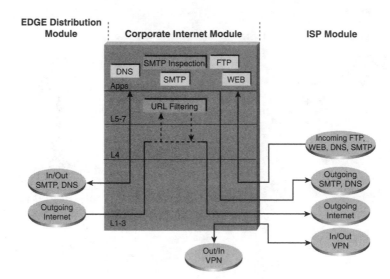

Key Devices

- **SMTP server**—acts as a relay between the Internet and the Internet mail servers—inspects content

- **DNS server**—serves as authoritative external DNS server for the enterprise, relays internal requests to the Internet

- **FTP/HTTP server**—provides public information about the organization

- **Firewall**—provides network-level protection of resources and stateful filtering of traffic

- **NIDS appliance**—provides Layer 4 to Layer 7 monitoring of key network segments in the module

- **URL filtering server**—filters unauthorized URL requests from the enterprise

Figure B-19 *Corporate Internet Module: Detail*

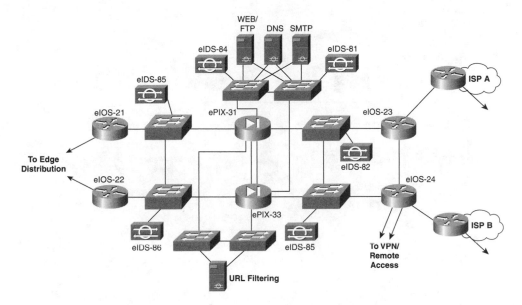

Threats Mitigated

- **Unauthorized Access**—mitigated through filtering at the ISP, edge router, and corporate firewall

- **Application layer attacks**—mitigated through IDS at the host and network levels

- **Virus and trojan horse**—mitigated through e-mail content filtering and host IDS

- **Password attacks**—limited services available to brute force, OS and IDS can detect the threat

- **Denial of service**—CAR at ISP edge and TCP setup controls at firewall

- **IP spoofing**—RFC 2827 and 1918 filtering at ISP edge and enterprise edge router

- **Packet sniffers**—switched infrastructure and host IDS limits exposure

- **Network Reconnaissance**—IDS detects recon, protocols filtered to limit effectiveness

- **Trust Exploitation**—restrictive trust model and private VLANs limit trust-based attacks

- **Port Redirection**—restrictive filtering and host IDS limit attack

Figure B-20 *Attack Mitigation Roles for Corporate Internet Module*

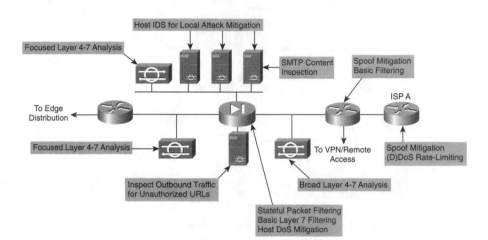

Design Guidelines

The heart of the module is a pair of resilient firewalls, which provide protection for the Internet public services and internal users. Stateful inspection examines traffic in all directions ensuring only legitimate traffic crosses the firewall. Aside from the Layer 2 and Layer 3 resilience built into the module and the stateful failover capability of the firewall, all other design considerations center around security and attack mitigation.

Starting at the customer-edge router in the ISP, the egress out of the ISP rate-limits non-essential traffic that exceeds prespecified thresholds in order to mitigate against DoS attacks. Also at the egress of the ISP router, RFC 1918 and RFC 2827 filtering mitigate against source-address spoofing of local networks and private address ranges.

At the ingress of the first router on the Enterprise network, basic filtering limits the traffic to the expected (addresses and IP services) traffic, providing a coarse filter for the most basic attacks. RFC 1918 and 2827 filtering is also provided here as a verification of the ISP's filtering. In addition, because of the enormous security threat that they create, the router is configured to drop most fragmented packets that should not generally be seen for standard traffic types on the Internet. Any legitimate traffic lost because of this filtering is considered acceptable when compared to the risk of allowing such traffic. Finally, any IPsec traffic destined for the VPN and remote access module is routed appropriately. Filtering on the interface connected to the VPN module is configured to allow only IPsec traffic to cross, and only when originated from and sent to authorized peers. With remote access VPNs you generally do not know the IP address of the system coming in so filtering can be specific only to the head-end peers with which the remote users are communicating.

The NIDS appliance at the public side of the firewall is monitoring for attacks based on Layer 4 to Layer 7 analysis and comparisons against known signatures. Because the ISP and enterprise edge router are filtering certain address ranges and ports, this allows the NIDS appliance to focus on some of the more complex attacks. Still, this NIDS should have alarms set to a lower level than appliances on the inside of the firewall because alarms seen here do not represent actual breaches, but merely attempts.

The firewall provides connection state enforcement and detailed filtering for sessions initiated through the firewall. Publicly addressable servers have some protection against TCP SYN floods through the use of half-open connection limits on the firewall. From a filtering standpoint, in addition to limiting traffic on the public services segment to relevant addresses and ports, filtering in the opposite direction also takes place. If an attack compromises one of the public servers (by circumventing the firewall, host-based IDS, and network-based IDS) that server should not be able to further attack the network. To mitigate against this type of attack, specific filtering prevents any unauthorized requests from being generated by the public servers to any other location. As an example, the Web server should be filtered so that it cannot originate requests of its own, but merely respond to requests from clients. This helps prevent a hacker from downloading additional utilities to the compromised box after the initial attack. It also helps stop unwanted sessions from being triggered by the hacker during the primary attack. An attack that generates an xterm from the Web server through the firewall to the hacker's machine is an example of such an attack. In addition, private VLANs prevent a compromised public server from attacking other servers on the same segment. This traffic is not even detected by the firewall, which is why private VLANs are critical.

Traffic on the content inspection segment is limited to URL filtering requests from the firewall to the URL filtering device. In addition, authenticated requests are allowed from the enterprise URL filtering device out to a master server for database updates. The URL filtering device inspects outbound traffic for unauthorized WWW requests. It communicates directly with the firewall and approves or rejects URL requests sent to its URL inspection engine by the firewall. Its decision is based on a policy managed by the enterprise using classification information of the WWW provided by a third-party service. URL inspection was preferred over standard access filtering because IP addresses often change for unauthorized Web sites, and such filters can grow to be very large. Host-based IDS software on this server protects against possible attacks that somehow circumvent the firewall.

The public services segment includes an NIDS appliance in order to detect attacks on ports that the firewall is configured to permit. These most often are application layer attacks against a specific service or a password attack against a protected service. You need to set this NIDS in a more restrictive stance than the NIDS on the outside of the firewall because signatures matched here have successfully passed through the firewall. Each of the servers have host intrusion detection software on them to monitor against any rogue activity at the OS level, as well as activity in common server applications (HTTP, FTP, SMTP, and so forth). The DNS host should be locked down to respond only to desired commands and eliminate any unnecessary responses that might assist hackers in network reconnaissance.

This includes preventing zone-transfers from anywhere but the internal DNS servers. The SMTP server includes mail content inspection services that mitigate against virus and Trojan-type attacks generated against the internal network that are usually introduced through the mail system. The firewall itself filters SMTP messages at Layer 7 to allow only necessary commands to the mail server.

The NIDS appliance on the inside interface of the firewall provides a final analysis of attacks. Very few attacks should be detected on this segment because only responses to initiated requests, and a few select ports from the public services segment, are allowed to the inside. Only sophisticated attacks should be seen on this segment because they generally mean a system on the public services segment has been compromised and the hacker is attempting to leverage this foot-hold to attack the internal network. For example, if the public SMTP server were compromised, a hacker might try to attack the internal mail server over TCP port 25, which is permitted to allow mail transfer between the two hosts. If attacks are seen on this segment, the responses to those attacks should be more severe than those on other segments because they probably indicate that a compromise has already occurred. The use of TCP resets to thwart, for example, the SMTP attack mentioned above, should be seriously considered.

Alternatives

There are several alternative designs for this module. For example, depending on your attitude towards attack awareness, the NIDS appliances might not be required in front of the firewall. In fact, without basic filtering on the access router, this type of monitoring is not recommended. With the appropriate basic filters, which exist in this design, the IDS outside the firewall can provide important alarm information that would otherwise be dropped by the firewall. Because the amount of alarms generated on this segment is probably large, alarms generated here should have a lower severity than alarms generated behind a firewall. Also, consider logging alarms from this segment to a separate management station to ensure that legitimate alarms from other segments get the appropriate attention. With the visibility that NIDS outside the firewall provides, evaluation of the attack types your organization is attracting can be better seen. In addition, evaluation of the effectiveness of ISP and enterprise edge filters can be performed.

Another possible alternative to the proposed design is the elimination of the router between the firewall and the edge distribution module. Though its functions can be integrated into the edge distribution module, the functional separation between modules would be lost because the edge distribution switches would need to be aware of the entire topology of the corporate Internet module to ensure proper routing. In addition, this limits your ability to deploy this architecture in a modular fashion. If an enterprise's current core is Layer 2, for example, the routing provided in the corporate Internet module would be required.

Near-Term Architecture Goals

Developing Cisco firewall technology that can communicate directly with other content inspection devices is needed (for example, network-based virus scanning). Currently, URL filtering is the only supported content filtering function that is directly integrated with Cisco firewall technology. Nonintegrated products rely on users operating in a proxy mode that does not properly scale.

VPN and Remote Access Module

As the name implies, the primary objective of this module is three-fold: terminate the VPN traffic from remote users, provide a hub for terminating VPN traffic from remote sites, and terminate traditional dial-in users. All the traffic forwarded to the edge distribution is from remote corporate users that are authenticated in some fashion before being allowed through the firewall.

Figure B-21 *Remote Access VPN Module Traffic Flow*

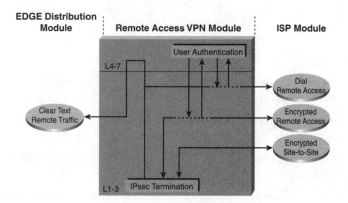

Key Devices

- **VPN Concentrator**—authenticate individual remote users using Extended Authentication (XAUTH) and terminate their IPsec tunnels

- **VPN router**—authenticate trusted remote sites and provide connectivity using GRE/IPsec tunnels

- **Dial-in server**—authenticate individual remote users using TACACS+ and terminate their analog connections

- **Firewall**—provide differentiated security for the three different types of remote access

- **NIDS appliance**—provide Layer 4 to Layer 7 monitoring of key network segments in the module

Figure B-22 *Remote Access VPN Module: Detail*

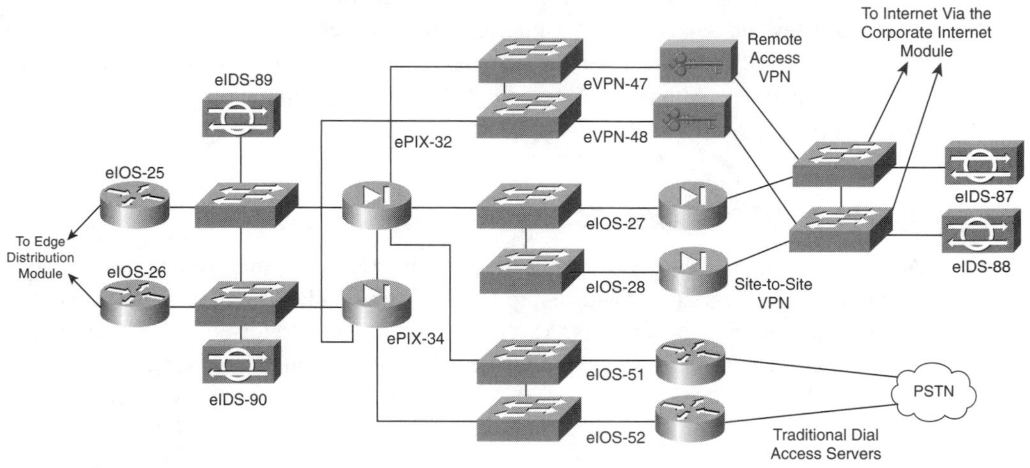

Threats Mitigated

- **Network topology discovery**—only Internet Key Exchange (IKE) and Encapsulating Security Payload (ESP) are allowed into this segment from the Internet

- **Password attack**—OTP authentication reduces the likelyhood of a successful password attack

- **Unauthorized access**—firewall services after packet decryption prevent traffic on unauthorized ports

- **Man-in-the-middle**—mitigated through encrypted remote traffic

- **Packet sniffers**—a switched infrastructure limits the effectiveness of sniffing

Design Guidelines

Resilience aside, the core requirement of this module is to have three separate external user services authenticate and terminate. Because the traffic comes from different sources outside of the Enterprise network, the decision was made to provide a separate interface on the firewall for each of these three services. The design consideration for each of these services are addressed next.

Figure B-23 *Attack Mitigation Roles for Remote Access VPN Module*

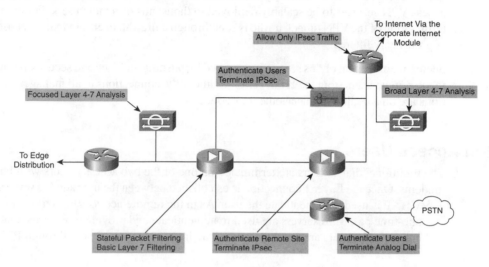

Remote-Access VPN

The VPN traffic is forwarded from the corporate Internet module access routers, where it is first filtered at the egress point to the specific IP addresses and protocols that are part of the VPN services. Today's remote-access VPNs can use several different tunneling and security protocols. Although IPsec is the tunneling protocol of choice, many organizations choose Point-to-Point Tunneling Protocol (PPTP) and Layer 2 Tunneling Protocol (L2TP) because they are natively supported by popular desktop operating systems. In SAFE, IPsec was chosen because the clients require minimal configuration and at the same time provide good security.

The remote-access VPN traffic will be addressed to one specific public address using the IKE (UDP 500) protocol. Because the IKE connection is not completed until the correct authentication information is provided, this provides a level of deterrence for the potential hacker. As part of the extensions (draft RFCs) of IKE, XAUTH provides an additional user authentication mechanism before the remote user is assigned any IP parameters. The VPN concentrator is "connected" to the access control server on the management subnet via its management interface. Strong passwords are provided via the one-time password server.

Once authenticated, the remote user is provided with access by receiving IP parameters using another extension of IKE, MODCFG. Aside from an IP address and the location of name servers (DNS and WINS), MODCFG also provides authorization services to control the access of the remote user. For example in SAFE, users are prevented from enabling split tunneling, thereby forcing the user to access the Internet via the corporate connection. The IPsec parameters that are being used are Triple DES for encryption and SHA-HMAC for data integrity. The hardware encryption modules in the VPN concentrator allow remote access VPN services to be scalably deployed to thousands of remote users. Following termination of the VPN tunnel, traffic is sent through a firewall to ensure that VPN users are appropriately filtered.

Secure management of this service is achieved by pushing all IPsec and security parameters to the remote users from the central site. Additionally, connections to all management functions are on a dedicated management interface.

Dial-in Access Users

The traditional dial-in users are terminated on one of the two access routers with built-in modems. Once the Layer 1 connection is established between the user and the server, three-way CHAP is used to authenticate the user. As in the remote-access VPN service the AAA and one-time password servers are used to authenticate and provide passwords. Once authenticated the users are provided with IP addresses from an IP pool through PPP.

Site-to-site VPN

The VPN traffic associated with site-to-site connections consists of GRE tunnels protected by an IPsec protocol in transport mode using Encapsulated Security Payload (ESP). As in the remote-access case, the traffic that is forwarded from the corporate Internet module can be limited to the specific destination addresses on the two VPN routers and the source addresses expected from the remote sites. The ESP protocol (IP 50) and the IKE protocol will be the only two expected on this link.

GRE is used to provide a full-service routed link which will carry multiprotocol, routing protocol, and multicast traffic. Because routing protocols (Enhanced Interior Gateway Routing Protocol [EIGRP] is being used between remote sites) can detect link failure, the GRE tunnel provides a resilience mechanism for the remote sites if they build two generic routing encapsulation (GRE) connections one to each of the central VPN routers.

As in remote-access VPN, 3DES and SHA-HMAC are used for IKE and IPsec parameters to provide the maximum security with little effect on performance. IPsec hardware accelerators are used in the VPN routers.

Rest of the Module

The traffic from the three services is aggregated by the firewall onto one private interface before being sent to the edge distribution module via a pair of routers. The firewall must be configured with the right type of constraining access control to allow only the appropriate traffic through to the inside interface of the firewall from each of the services. A pair of NIDS appliances are positioned at the public side of the module to detect any network "reconnaissance" activity targeted at the VPN termination devices. On this segment, only

IPsec (IKE/ESP) traffic should be seen. Because the NIDS system can not see inside the IPsec packets, any alarm on this network indicates a failure or compromise of the surrounding devices. As such, these alarms should be set to high severity levels. A second pair of NIDS are positioned after the firewall to detect any attacks that made it through the rest of the module. This NIDS device also has a restrictive policy in place. All users crossing this segment should be bound to, or coming from an remote location so any shunning or TCP resets will only affect those users.

Alternatives

In VPN and authentication technology, there are many alternatives available depending on the requirements of the network. These alternatives are listed below for reference, but the details are not addressed in this document.

- Smart-card and/or Bio-metric authentication
- L2TP and/or PPTP remote-access VPN tunnels
- Certificate Authorities (CAs)
- IKE keep-alive resilience mechanism
- Multiprotocol Label Switching (MPLS) VPNs

WAN Module

Rather than being all-inclusive of potential WAN designs, this module shows resilience and security for WAN termination. Using Frame Relay encapsulation, traffic is routed between remote sites and the central site.

Key Devices

- **IOS router**—using routing, access-control, QoS mechanisms

Figure B-24 *WAN Module: Detail*

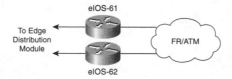

Threats Mitigated

- **IP spoofing**—mitigated through L3 filtering
- **Unauthorized access**—simple access control on the router can limit the types of protocols to which branches have access

Figure B-25 *Attack Mitigation Roles for WAN Module*

Design Guidelines

The resilience is provided by the dual connection from the service provider, through the routers, and to the edge distribution module. Security is provided by using IOS security features. Input access-lists are used to block all unwanted traffic from the remote branch.

Alternatives

Some organizations that are very concerned about information privacy encrypt highly confidential traffic on their WAN links. Similarly to site-to-site VPNs, you can use IPsec to achieve this information privacy.

E-Commerce Module

Because e-commerce is the primary objective of this module, the balance between access and security must be carefully weighed. Splitting the e-commerce transaction into three components allows the architecture to provide various levels of security without impeding access.

Figure B-26 *E-Commerce Traffic Flow*

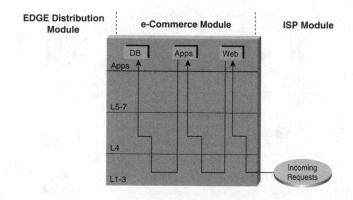

Key Devices

- **Web server**—acts as the primary user interface for the navigation of the e-commerce store

- **Application server**—is the platform for the various applications required by the Web server

- **Database server**—is the critical information that is the heart of the e-commerce business implementation

- **Firewall**—governs communication between the various levels of security and trust in the system

- **NIDS appliance**—provides monitoring of key network segments in the module

- **Layer 3 switch with IDS module**—is the scalable e-commerce input device with integrated security monitoring

Figure B-27 *E-Commerce Module: Detail*

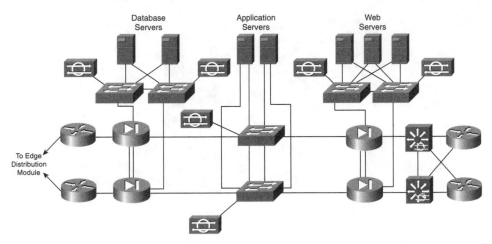

Threats Mitigated

- **Unauthorized access**—stateful firewalling and ACLs limit exposure to specific protocols

- **Application layer attacks**—attacks are mitigated through the use of IDS

- **Denial of service**—ISP filtering and rate-limiting reduce DoS potential

- **IP spoofing**—RFC 2827 and 1918 prevent locally originated spoofed packets and limit remote spoof attempts

- **Packet sniffers**—a switched infrastructure and HIDS limits the effectiveness of sniffing

- **Network reconnaissance**—ports are limited to only what is necessary, ICMP is restricted

- **Trust exploitation**—firewalls ensure communication flows only in the proper direction on the proper service

- **Port redirection**—HIDS and firewall filtering limit exposure to these attacks

Figure B-28 *Attack Mitigation Roles for E-Commerce Module*

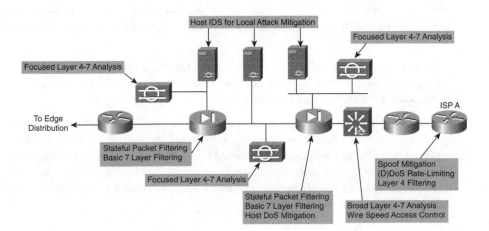

Design Implementation Description

The heart of the module is two pairs of resilient firewalls that provide protection for the three levels of servers: Web, application, and database. Some added protection is provided by the ISP edge routers at the ISP and the Enterprise. The design is best understood by considering the traffic flow sequence and direction for a typical e-commerce transaction.

The e-commerce customer initiates an HTTP connection to the Web server after receiving the IP address from a DNS server hosted at the ISP network. The DNS is hosted on a different network to reduce the amount of protocols required by the e-commerce application. The first set of firewalls must be configured to allow this protocol through to that particular address. The return traffic for this connection is allowed back, but there is no need for any communication initiated by the Web server back out the Internet. The firewall should block this path in order to limit the options of hackers if they had control of one of the Web servers.

As the user navigates the Web site, certain link selections cause the Web server to initiate a request to the application server on the inside interface. This connection must be permitted by the first firewall, as well as the associated return traffic. As in the case with the Web server, there is no reason for the application server to initiate a connection to the Web server or even out to the Internet. Likewise, the user's entire session runs over HTTP and SSL with no ability to communicate directly with the application server or the database server.

At one point, the user will want to perform a transaction. The Web server will want to protect this transaction and the SSL protocol will be required from the Internet to the Web server. At the same time, the application server might want to query or pass information on to the database server. These are typically SQL queries that are initiated by the application server to the database server and not vice versa. These queries run through the second firewall to the database server. Depending on the specific applications in use, the database server might need to communicate with back-end systems located in the server module of the enterprise.

In summary, the firewalls must allow only three specific communication paths, each with its own protocol, and block all other communication unless it is the return path packets that are associated with the three original paths.

The servers themselves must be fully protected—especially the Web server—which is a publicly-addressable host. The operating system and Web server application must be patched to the latest versions and monitored by the host intrusion detection software. This should mitigate against most application layer primary and secondary attacks such as port redirection and root kits. The other servers should have similar security in case the first server or firewall is compromised.

Beyond the Firewall

The e-commerce firewalls are initially protected by the customer edge router at the ISP. At the router egress point, towards the enterprise, the ISP can limit the traffic to the small number of protocols required for e-commerce with a destination address of the Web servers only. Routing protocol updates (generally Border Gateway Protocol [BGP]) are required by the edge routers, and all other traffic should be blocked. The ISP should implement rate limiting as specified in the "SAFE Axioms" section in order to mitigate (D)DoS attacks. In addition, filtering according to RFC1918 and RFC2827 should also be implemented by the ISP.

On the enterprise premises, the initial router serves only as an interface to the ISP. The Layer 3 switch does all the network processing because it has features off-loaded to hardware processors. The Layer 3 switches participate in the full BGP routing decision in order to decide which ISP has the better route to the particular user. The Layer 3 switches also provide verification filtering in keeping with the ISP filtering described above; this provides overlapping security. Thirdly, the Layer 3 switches provide built-in IDS monitoring. If the connection to the Internet exceeds the capacity of the IDS line card, you might need to look only at inbound Web requests from the Internet on the IDS line card. While this will miss some http alarm signatures (approximately 10 percent), it is better than looking at the entire stream in both directions, where many misses would occur. The other NIDS appliances behind the various interfaces of the firewall monitor the segments for any attacks that might have penetrated the first line of defense. For example, if the Web server is out of date, hackers could compromise it over an application layer attack assuming they were able to circumvent the HIDS. As in the corporate Internet module, the false-positives must be removed so that all true attack detections are treated with the correct level of priority. In fact, because only certain types of traffic exist on certain segments, you can tune NIDS very tightly.

From an application standpoint, the communications paths between the various layers (web, apps, dbase) should be encrypted, transactional, and highly authenticated. For example, if the apps server were to get data from the database over some type of scripted interactive session (SSH, FTP, Telnet, and so forth) a hacker could leverage that interactive session to initiate an application layer attack. By employing secure communications, you can limit potential threats.

The Layer 2 switches that supporting the various firewall segments provide the ability to implement private VLANs, thereby implementing a trust model that matches the desired traffic communication on a particular segment and eliminates all others. For example, there is usually no reason for one Web server to communicate with another Web server.

The management of the entire module is done completely out of band as in the rest of the architecture.

Alternatives

The principle alternative to this deployment is co-locating the entire system at an ISP. Though the design remains the same, there are two primary differences. The first is that bandwidth is generally larger to the ISP and uses a LAN connection. Though not recommended, this potentially eliminates the need for the edge routers in the proposed design. The additional bandwidth also creates different requirements for (D)DoS mitigation. The second is the connection back to the enterprise, which needs to be managed in a different way. Alternatives include encryption and private lines. Using these technologies creates additional security considerations depending on the location of the connections and their intended use.

There are several variations on the primary design for this module. Aside from listing the alternatives, further discussion is beyond the scope of this paper.

- The use of additional firewalls is one alternative. Sample communications would be edge routing → firewall → web server firewall → applications server → firewall → database server. This allows each firewall to only control communications for one primary system.

- Load-balancing and caching technologies are not specifically discussed in this paper, but can be overlaid onto this architecture without major modifications. A future paper will address these needs.

- For very high security requirements, the use of multiple firewall types may be considered. Note that this creates additional management overhead in duplicating policy on disparate systems. The goal of these designs is to avoid a vulnerability in one firewall from circumventing the security of the entire system. These types of designs tend to be very firewall centric and do not adequately take advantage of IDS and other security technologies to mitigate the risk of a single firewall vulnerability.

Enterprise Options

The design process is often a series of trade-offs. This short subsection of the document highlights some of the high-level options that a network designer could implement if faced with tighter budget constraints. Some of these trade-offs are done at the module level, while others are done at the component level.

A first option is to collapse the distribution modules into the core module. This reduces the number of Layer 3 switches by 50 percent. The cost savings would be traded-off against performance requirements in the core of the network and flexibility to implement all the distribution security filtering.

A second option is to merge the functionality of the VPN and Remote Access module with the corporate Internet module. Their structure is very similar, with a pair of firewalls at the heart of the module, surrounded by NIDS appliances. This may be possible without loss of functionality if the performance of the components matches the combined traffic requirements of the modules and if the firewall has enough interfaces to accommodate the different services. Keep in mind that as functions are aggregated to single devices the potential for human error increases. Some organizations go even further and include the e-commerce functions in the corporate Internet/VPN module. The authors feel that the risk of doing this far outweighs any cost savings unless the e-commerce needs are minimal. Separation of the e-commerce traffic from general Internet traffic allows the e-commerce bandwidth to be better optimized by allowing the ISP to place more restrictive filtering and rate-limiting technology to mitigate against DDoS attacks.

A third option is to eliminate some of the NIDS appliances. Depending on your operational threat response strategy, you might need fewer NIDS appliances. This number is also affected by the amount of Host IDS deployed because this might reduce the need for NIDS in certain locations. This is discussed, where appropriate, in the specific modules.

Clearly, network design is not an exact science. Choices must always be made depending on the specific requirements facing the designer. The authors are not proposing that any designer would implement this architecture verbatim, but would encourage designers to make educated choices about network security grounded in this proven implementation.

Migration Strategies

SAFE is a guide for implementing security on the enterprise network. It is not meant to serve as a security policy for any enterprise networks, nor is it meant to serve as the all-encompassing design for providing full security for all existing networks. Rather, SAFE is a template that enables network designers to consider how they design and implement their enterprise network in order to meet their security requirements.

Establishing a security policy should be the first activity in migrating the network to a secure infrastructure. Basic recommendations for a security policy can be found at the end of the document in Appendix B, "Network Security Primer." After the policy is established, the network designer should consider the security axioms described in the first section of this document and see how they provide more detail to map the policy on the existing network infrastructure.

There is enough flexibility in the architecture and detail about the design considerations to enable the SAFE architecture elements to be adapted to most enterprise networks. For example, in the VPN and Remote Access module, the various flows of traffic from public networks are each given a separate pair of terminating devices and a separate interface on the firewall. The VPN traffic could be combined in one pair of devices, if the load requirements permitted it and the security policy was the same for both types of traffic. On another network, the traditional dial-in and remote-access VPN users might be allowed directly into the network because the security policy puts enough trust in the authentication mechanisms that permit the connection to the network in the first place.

SAFE allows the designer to address the security requirements of each network function almost independently of each other. Each module is generally self-contained and assumes that any interconnected module is only at a basic security level. This allows network designers to use a phased approach to securing the enterprise network. They can address securing the most critical network functions as determined by the policy without redesigning the entire network. The exception to this is the management module. During the initial SAFE implementation, the management module should be implemented in parallel with the first module. As the rest of the network is migrated, the management module can be connected to the remaining locations.

This first version of the SAFE architecture is meant to address the security implementation of a generic enterprise network. The authors know that there are many areas that need further detailed research, exploration, and improvement. Some of these areas include, but are not limited to, the following:

- In-depth security management analysis and implementation
- Specialized design information for smaller networks
- In-depth identity, directory services, AAA technologies, and certificate authority analysis and implementation
- Scaled versions of VPN head-end and WAN design

Overall Guidelines

The configurations presented here correspond in part to the SAFE Axioms presented earlier in this document.

Bibliography

RFC Reference

INDEX

Numerics

3DES encryption, 311
802.1x port authentication, 114
    communications, 115–121
    configuring on Catalyst 6000 switches, 123–125
    functionality, 122

A

AAA (authentication, authorization and accounting)
    accounting, 469, 479
        method lists, applying, 481–482
        method lists, configuring, 479–481
    applying access lists, 486–488
    authentication, 470
        configuring, 471
        local database, configuring, 471
        method list, configuring, 471–474
    authorization, 469, 475
        method lists, applying, 477–479
        method lists, configuring, 475–476
    auth-proxy, 541–542, 544
    command authorization, configuring, 549–552
    debug commands, 670
    downloading routes, 486–488
    lock and key, configuring, 548–549
    method lists, 469
    network components, 470
    PPP
        authentication and authorization, 482–485
        timeouts, configuring, 488–489
    providing preshared keys for IPsec, 537, 539
    RADIUS, 515, 519–520, 522–530
        accounting, 531–533
        communications architecture, 516
        packet format, 517–518
        password encryption, 518–519
        router support, 521–531
    resolving common problems, 671–677
    show commands, 670

TACACS+
    accounting, 508–512
    authentication, 498
    authorization, 499–507
    communications architecture, 494
    daemon functionality, 493–494
    header architecture, 495–497
    packet encryption, 497
VPDN, 544, 546–547
x-auth in ISAKMP, 539–541
acceptable usage policies, defining, 16
access control. *See also* CBAC
    PIX, 72
    switches, 75
access lists. *See* ACLs
access policies, defining, 16–17
Access-Accept messages (RADIUS), 519
accessing firewalls, vulnerabilities, 140
Access-Reject messages (RADIUS), 519
accountability policies, defining, 16
accounting, 479
    method lists
        applying, 481–482
        configuring, 479–481
    RADIUS, 515, 531–532
        IETF Accounting AV pairs, 532–533
    TACACS+, 508–512
ACEs (Access Control Elements), 567
ACKs, ZL ACKs, 248
ACLs (access control lists), 153. *See also* turbo ACLs
    applying to IP fragments, 583–584, 587–588
        overlapping fragment attacks, 589
        tiny fragment attacks, 588
    applying with AAA, 486–488
    blocking ICMP packets, 573–575
    blocking known offenders, 575
    blocking spoofed IP addresses, 575
    extended, 569, 571
    functionality, 567–568, 573
    impact on performance, 590
    implicit deny all entry, 571
    logging facility, 573
    NetFlow switching, 594–595
    restricting traffic, 572–573
    standard, 568

B

G

Garfinkel, S., 8
getadmin exploits, 417–418
goal of network security, 5
gratuitous ARP, 113
GRE (Generic Routing Encapsulation), 223
    connecting IPX sites, 235–239
    connecting multiple sites, 230–235
    implementations, 224
    non-IP traffic encapsulation, 227
    RFC 1701 implementation, 224–226
    RFC 2784 implementation, 226–227
    tunneling between private networks, 227–230
Group field (HSRP), 46
guard feature (PIX Firewall)
    DNS guards, 165
    flood guards, 162
    frag guards, 163–164
    mail guards, 164

H

hackers, 400
    experienced, 404
    Metnick, Kevin, 421–422
    professional, 404
    script kiddies, 403
    versus crackers, 400
half-open SYN attacks, 405, 407
hard coding BGP version information, 94
hash payload (IKE main mode message), 290
hashing, 312–313
    MD5-HMAC, 84–87
headers
    L2TP, format, 248–250
    TACACS+, 495–497
Heartbeat messages (POP), 432
Hellotime field (HSRP), 45
heuristic/holistic classification, NBAR, 600
high-availability IPsec over GRE, 360–365
high-severity alarms, 448
HMAC (Message Authentication Codes using
   Hashing), integrity checking, 312–313
holdtime (HSRP active routers), 43
Holdtime field (HSRP), 45

home gateways, VPDN configuration, 544–547
Honey Pots, 558
host intrusion detection, 425
HSRP (Hot Standby Router Protocol), 42
    active routers, 43
    Failover protocol, 49
    failure detection, 43
    functionality, 47–49
    implementations, 46–47
    packet format, 44–46
    versus VRRP, 49

I

ICMP (Internet Control Message Protocol)
    floods, rate limiting with CAR, 617
    maintaining path integrity, 91
    packet filtering, 573–575
identifying resources to protect, 6
identity payload
    EAP messages, 117
    IKE main mode message, 290
IDSM
    event logging, 441–442
    IP session logging, 442
    sensor implementation, 448
IDSs
    Catalyst 6000 IDSM
        configuring as sensors, 458–461
    Cisco Secure IDS
        categories of signatures, 444–445
        management console, 426–433
        sensors, 426–428, 435–444
        signature engines, 446–447
    PIX Firewall, configuring as sensors, 454–457
    resolving common problems, 666–670
    routers, configuring as sensors, 449–454
    signature-based, 419
    statistical anomaly-based, 419
IEEE 802.1x port authentication, 114
    communications, 115–21
    configuring on Catalyst 6000 switches,
       123–125
    functionality, 122
IETF Accounting AV pairs (RADIUS), 532–533
IETF attributes supported on Cisco routers, 521–531

J-K

L

S

X-Y-Z